United States
Department
of Agriculture

Forest Service

Rocky Mountain
Research Station

General Technical Report
RMRS-GTR-30WWW

October 1999

Ecology and Conservation of Lynx in the United States

Leonard F. Ruggiero
Keith B. Aubry
Steven W. Buskirk
Gary M. Koehler
Charles J. Krebs
Kevin S. McKelvey
John R. Squires

D1608850

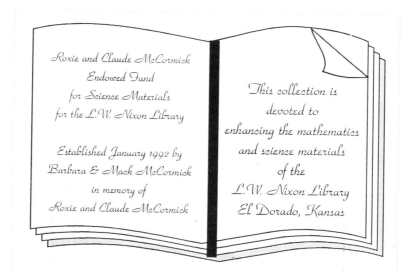

The Authors

Leonard F. Ruggiero is a scientist at the Rocky Mountain Research Station's Forestry Sciences Lab in Missoula, MT.

Keith B. Aubry is a scientist at the Pacific Northwest Research Station in Olympia, WA.

Steven W. Buskirk is professor of zoology and physiology at University of Wyoming in Laramie.

Gary M. Koehler is research biologist with the Washington Department of Fish & Wildlife in Olympia, WA.

Charles J. Krebs is professor of zoology at the University of British Columbia.

Kevin S. McKelvey is a scientist at the Rocky Mountain Research Station's Forestry Sciences Lab in Missoula, MT.

John R. Squires is a research associate at the University of Montana in Missoula.

Copyright © 2000

Published by the University Press of Colorado and the USDA, Rocky Mountain Research Station

All rights reserved.
Printed in the United States of America.

The University Press of Colorado is a cooperative publishing enterprise supported, in part, by Adams State College, Colorado State University, Fort Lewis College, Mesa State College, Metropolitan State College of Denver, University of Colorado, University of Northern Colorado, University of Southern Colorado, and Western State College of Colorado.

The paper used in this publication meets the minimum requirements of the American National Standard for Information Sciences—Permanence of Paper for Printed Library Materials. ANSI Z39.48-1984

Library of Congress Cataloging-in-Publication Data

Ecology and conservation of lynx in the United States / Leonard F. Ruggiero ... [et al].
      p.   cm. — (General technical report RMRS ; GTR-30WWW)
   Includes bibliographical references.
   ISBN 0-87081-577-6 (alk. paper). — 0-87081-580-6 (pbk. : alk. paper).
   1. Lynx—Ecology—United States. 2. Wildlife conservation—United States. I. Ruggiero, Leonard F. II. Series.

   QL737.C23 E36 2000
   599.75'317—dc21   99-059214

09 08 07 06 05 04 03 02 01 00   10 9 8 7 6 5 4 3 2 1

Contents

Ecology and Conservation of Lynx in the United States

When we began the task of elucidating the scientific basis for lynx conservation in June 1998, I had little idea how constrained our time would be. The request to do this job came from a consortium of federal land management agencies in response to the U.S. Fish and Wildlife Service's "proposed rule" to list the Canada lynx as a threatened or endangered species throughout its range in the contiguous United States. I underestimated the extent to which legal mandates and the expectations of information-hungry biologists and decision-makers would push us. By late February 1999 we had provided nearly 800 pages of "working drafts" to agency personnel who were responsible for various products associated with the potential listing. But the situation grew even more urgent later in the spring when the USFWS decided to delay its final listing decision by six months, from July 1999 to January 2000, so they could consider the entirety of our final product. Although unknown to me at the time, this decision necessitated that our work be made available for public comment *in final form* far sooner than we had planned. We were told that if we failed to meet this timeline, legal constraints would ensure that agency officials and the general public would not be able to use our findings in decision-making and public involvement attendant to the listing process. Moreover, we were told that in order for all this to happen, our work would have to be disseminated via the *Internet*! To say the least, it was disconcerting that our "rush job" would be available all over the globe, and that the prospects for publishing our work in book form might be compromised. But as scientists interested in the application of our work, we had little choice.

Two fortunate circumstances helped to mitigate this dilemma. First, the Rocky Mountain Research Station has a first-class Publishing Services staff under the direction of Louise Kingsbury. It was the professional capability and dedication of this group that made it possible for us to get camera-ready copies of Chapters 1-16 onto the Internet within the allotted time. Published electronically as USDA Forest Service, General Technical Report RMRS–GTR-30WWW, this version of our work was made available to agency personnel as well as to the general public. Thus, all of the most pertinent information in this book was available for use in the sociopolitical process defined pursuant to the Endangered Species Act.

The second fortuitous circumstance was that our work caught the attention of Darrin Pratt, Acquisitions Editor of the University of Colorado Press. Mr. Pratt's interest and the ultimate acceptance of our book for publication by the University of Colorado Press has been extremely gratifying. Accordingly, we are deeply grateful to Louise Kingsbury, Darrin Pratt, and to all those who have been instrumental in the editing, production, and publication of both the electronic and hard copy editions of this book.

In this book, and in our related activities, we have drawn a clear line between science and policy. Our job as scientists was to summarize the state of knowledge, articulate meaningful understandings when possible, and identify important knowledge gaps relative to the information needed for conservation plans and policy. Perhaps a more difficult job was left to our land-management colleagues who must use this information as the basis for complex and controversial judgments about land management actions. In this regard, we appreciate the efforts of Bill Ruediger and members of his "Lynx Biology Team" for their efforts to apply the information in this volume on behalf of the resource. We also offer a special thanks to Kathy McAllister, Deputy Regional Forester for the Northern Region of the National Forest System and Leader of the Interagency Lynx Steering Committee. Although beset by great pressure to meet procedural deadlines requiring our information, Kathy was patient and understanding, even though from her perspective the pace of our work was ponderous. Her support, and the support of Steering Committee "Chief of Staff," Dr. Martin Prather, has done much to ensure the incorporation of science into policy and to facilitate effective working relationships between scientists and managers.

My deepest gratitude is reserved for my colleagues and friends on the Lynx Science Team. Dr. Keith Aubry's writing skill, even temperament, and tireless work was key to our success. Keith was absolutely selfless in his efforts, and his ability to synthesize and communicate complex material was central to much of our work. Professor Steven Buskirk lent his well-deserved credentials as an internationally respected mammalogist and carnivore ecologist to our team. In addition to his full-time teaching responsibilities, Steve contributed innumerable hours to this effort; his scientific acumen, broad expertise, and high standard of scholarship were tremendous assets. Professor Charles Krebs is one of the most respected ecologists in the world, as well as one of the premier authorities on lynx and snowshoe hare ecology in Canada. I am indebted to him for his participation on this committee, for his dependable good humor, and for his representation of the cadre of outstanding Canadian researchers of lynx and snowshoe hares. Dr. Gary Koehler is the most experienced lynx researcher in the United States, and his work has formed the basis for most of what is known about lynx in this country. Gary's open-mindedness, commitment to the resource, first-hand knowledge of lynx ecology, and impeccable professionalism made him a great asset to the Team. Dr. Kevin McKelvey contributed expertise as a modeler, forest ecologist, and experienced analyst of population patterns and viability. Kevin is an enviably well-rounded and thoughtful scientist whose analytical skills and keen intellect played a critical role in our work. Dr. John Squires is currently managing the most ambitious lynx study undertaken to date. His first-hand knowledge and insights gained from this work along with his command of the scientific literature and his extensive field experience with lynx and other wide-ranging carnivores was of great value to the group. It was an honor for me to lead this team, and I deeply respect the professional competence and dedication of each of these men.

Although Lynx Science Team members are officially listed as technical editors of this volume, this group wrote over two-thirds of the text and authored 13 of the 18 chapters. In addition, each Team Member served as editor on multiple chapters for which they were not authors. In this capacity, they managed the peer review process, presided over chapter revisions, and worked with me in making final decisions about acceptance of chapters for publication. As anyone who has served in this capacity knows, peer review is often a demanding, lengthy, iterative process requiring time and patience on the part of both authors and editors. This book was no exception, and it is only through the tremendous efforts of the above mentioned Science Team members that we were able to complete this process so quickly.

In this context, we extend our gratitude to a cadre of peer reviewers, most of whom were asked to provide detailed technical reviews in ridiculously short times. Included here we thank: Fred Allendorf, Clayton Apps, Theodore Bailey, Christina Hargis, Greg Hayward, Doug Houston, John McKay, Chuck Meslow, Francois Messier, Scott Mills, Garth Mowat, Erin O'Doherty, Mark O'Donoghue, Dan Pletscher, Roger Powell, Martin Raphael, Kermit Ritland, Mike Wisdom, Bill Zielinski, and numerous anonymous reviewers.

We extend a special thanks to Tina Mainey for her invaluable administrative and moral support and for her attention to endless details throughout this project. For additional administrative support we also thank Lori Moffatt, Deanna Crawford, Stacey Clark, and Sarah Day. Our special thanks also goes to Lane Eskew, Lead Editor for this project, who did an amazing job of correcting countless errors and of bringing consistency to our presentations. We also thank Madelyn Dillon and Louise Kingsbury for additional editorial work; Joyce Stoddard and Nancy Chadwick for their lead production work; Loa Collins and Karen Eason for additional production work; and to Suzy Stephens for getting all this on the Web. All of these people sacrificed nights and weekends to get this job done on schedule, and we are grateful.

Leonard F. Ruggiero
Lynx Science Team Leader

Toward a Defensible Lynx Conservation Strategy: A Framework for Planning in the Face of Uncertainty

Leonard F. Ruggiero, USDA Forest Service,
  Rocky Mountain Research Station, 800 E. Beckwith, Missoula, MT 59801

Kevin S. McKelvey, USDA Forest Service,
  Rocky Mountain Research Station, 800 E. Beckwith, Missoula, MT 59801

Background

On April 2, 1993, the incumbent U.S. President traveled to Portland, Oregon, to intervene in a national political crisis engendered by public concern over the conservation of native wildlife on public lands. Environmentalists had successfully used existing statutes, most notably the National Forest Management Act and pursuant regulations, to shut down timber industry operations on commercially important federal lands in the Pacific Northwest. Widespread economic dislocations were expected, and the federal courts showed no signs of reversing the decision to suspend timber-harvesting activities. At the core of this enormously divisive legal controversy was the effect of timber management on the viability of northern spotted owl populations—an issue that arguably defined one of the most significant conservation conflicts of this century.

5

The spotted owl controversy catalyzed heightened concern over the conservation of "sensitive" species on public lands, especially those species thought to be negatively affected by land management practices such as timber harvesting. In 1993, the National Forest System (the land management branch of the USDA Forest Service) responded to this concern by identifying a number of species and species groups with the potential to become conservation issues. Included were a group of Pacific salmon, the marbled murrelet, Mexican spotted owl, northern goshawk, two species of trout, several forest owls, and four forest carnivores—notably including the lynx. The basis for concern over most of these species was their putative association with late-successional forests—the stage of forest development most frequently removed from managed forest landscapes (Thomas et al. 1993). Land managers decided to assess the state of ecological knowledge for each of these species relative to the information needed for defensible conservation planning. In late 1993, scientists in the research branch of the Forest Service were asked to lead these assessments.

The findings of the forest carnivore conservation assessment were published in a report entitled, *The Scientific Basis for Conserving Forest Carnivores: American Marten, Fisher, Lynx and Wolverine in the Western United States* (Ruggiero et al. 1994b). One of the major conclusions of this assessment was that, "Major information gaps exist for these forest carnivores. A sustained commitment to research is needed for developing scientifically sound conservation strategies to ensure the persistence of forest carnivore populations" (Lyon et al. 1994, p. 137). Regarding lynx in the western United States, the Assessment read, "...there is a need for the most basic information on habitat relationships, at any spatial or temporal scale and at any level of measurement. Virtually any new data on habitat relationships involving lynx in the western conterminous 48 states would be a substantive increase in knowledge" (Ruggiero et al. 1994a, p. 142). The state of knowledge was found to be equally inadequate for all other aspects of lynx ecology in the western United States. Although a considerable amount is known about lynx ecology in northwestern Canada, the Assessment concluded that (1) the applicability of this information to ecosystems in the western United States is unknown, and (2) potential ecotypic variation in lynx populations warns against the application of this information in the western United States (southern) portion of the lynx's range (Ruggiero et al. 1994a).

Knowledge of lynx ecology in the United States has not improved substantially since publication of the Forest Carnivore Conservation Assessment in 1994: there have been no new research findings published on lynx ecology in the United States. Management agencies were thus poorly prepared to deal with the July 8, 1998, "proposed rule" by the U.S. Fish and Wildlife Service (USFWS) to list the lynx as a threatened or endangered species throughout its range in the contiguous United States. This action by the USFWS followed a long history of public concern, petitions to list the lynx, and lawsuits against the USFWS based on societal responses to perceived declines in lynx populations (see Table 1.1 for an overview of these events). The listing process dictates that unless compelling new evidence emerges to the contrary, the lynx will be designated threatened or endangered in January 2000, 1.5 years from the publication of the proposed rule in the Federal Register (U. S. Fish and Wildlife Service 1998).

In response to this situation, representatives of the USFWS, Bureau of Land Management (BLM), and USDA Forest Service (USFS) met in Salt Lake City, Utah, several weeks before the proposed rule was published. There they discussed how land management agencies could best prepare for the potential listing, particularly the consultation provisions of the Endangered Species Act. If the lynx became a threatened or endangered species, how could management agencies demonstrate to the USFWS that their actions did not jeopardize the continued existence of lynx populations? A decision was made to produce a *conservation strategy* of sufficient detail to direct the actions of land managers such that a "jeopardy opinion" by the USFWS could be avoided. The dilemma, of course, was how to produce a strategy that could reliably evaluate the effects of various management actions on the viability of lynx populations given the paucity of existing information on lynx ecology in the southern portion of its range.

Scientists from the Research Branch of the USFS, including authors of the 1994 Forest Carnivore Conservation Assessment, were asked to address this dilemma. The course of action these scientists recommended was predicated on the lack of crucial scientific information and included a provisional (interim) reassessment of our understanding of lynx ecology. This process (Fig. 1.1) would build on the 1994 Assessment by: (1) conducting new analyses of lynx distribution (based on new and old information), (2) examining all published and unpublished information that may contribute to our understanding of lynx distribution and ecology in the contiguous United States, (3) reanalyzing existing data using the latest technology, (4) reviewing relevant ecological theory, and (5) attempting to elucidate new insights about lynx ecology based on steps 1-4.

A Lynx Science Team was assembled to implement this process and attempt a useful interpretation of limited information. Through this process, the scientific basis for conserving lynx would be documented and, to the extent possible, resulting insights about lynx ecology would be elucidated for use by land managers. Management biologists and decision-makers would then use the Science Team's report to produce an *Interim Conservation Strategy*, which would establish and detail management policy. Integral to this strategy would be an explicit program of studies (Chapter 17), which, if

Table 1.1—Overview of events leading to the U.S. Fish and Wildlife Service's proposed rule to list the lynx as a threatened or endangered species throughout its range in the contiguous United States (McMaster, personal communication).

August 22, 1991	A petition to list the "North American" (Canada) lynx in the North Cascades ecosystem of Washington as an endangered species and to designate critical habitat was received by the Fish and Wildlife Service (Service) from the National Audubon Society and 11 other organizations.
October 6, 1992	The Service published a notice of a 90-day finding (57 FR 46007) indicating that the petition to list the "North American" (Canada) lynx in the North Cascades did not provide substantial information. Region 1 (Portland Regional Office) had the lead on the petition because the petitioned area was confined to that Region. Region 6 (Denver Regional Office) had the national lead for the lynx.
Late 1992 or 1993	The Greater Ecosystem Alliance and other organizations sued the Service over the negative 90-day finding announced on October 6, 1992.
April 28, 1993	A settlement agreement was reached whereby the Service agreed to reevaluate the negative 90-day finding announced on October 6, 1992, in light of new information that was submitted by the petitioners.
July 9, 1993	The Service published a notice (58 FR 36924) indicating that the negative 90-day finding had been revisited by Region 1, but that there still was not substantial information to support the petitioned action. However, the Service announced in the notice that it believed that sufficient evidence existed to indicate that an in-depth rangewide status review for the lynx should be conducted and that the Service intended to commence this status review.
November 30, 1993	A second settlement agreement was reached. The Service agreed to complete and publish the results of a status review throughout the lower 48 States by November 14, 1994.
February 2, 1994	The Service published a notice (59 FR 4887) indicating that it was soliciting information for a rangewide status review. The Service indicated that it would complete and publish its finding no later than November 15, 1994. Region 6 was given the
April 27, 1994	A petition to list the "North American" (Canada) lynx in the contiguous U.S. and to emergency list the southern Rocky Mountain population was received from the Biodiversity Legal Foundation and four individuals.
August 26, 1994	The Service published a notice (59 FR 44123) indicating that the Service's administrative 90-day finding found that the petition received April 27, 1994, presented substantial information indicating the requested action for the contiguous U.S population may be warranted, but there was not substantial information to indicate that an emergency listing of a southern Rocky Mountain population was warranted.
December 27, 1994	The Service published a notice (59 FR 66507) indicating that the Service's 12-month finding was listing the Canada lynx in the contiguous U.S. was not warranted. The finding represented the Service's administrative finding as a result of the status review agreed to in the April 28, 1993, lawsuit settlement and the administrative 12-month finding for the petition received April 27, 1994.
January 30, 1996	The Defenders of Wildlife and 14 other organizations and individuals sued the Service in the U.S. District Court, District of Columbia, over the not-warranted petition finding announced in the Federal Register on Dec. 27, 1994.
March 27, 1997	The court issued an opinion and order setting aside the not-warranted finding and remanded it back to the Service for further consideration. The Service was ordered to publish a 12-month finding on the status of the lynx within 60 days.
May 27, 1997	The Service published a 12-month petition finding (62 FR 28643) that the Canada lynx population in the contiguous U.S. was warranted for listing under the Endangered Species Act but precluded by actions on other species of higher taxonomic status. This warranted but precluded finding automatically elevated the Canada lynx to candidate species status.
September 15, 1997	Defenders of Wildlife, et al., filed suit against the Service in the U.S. District Court, District of Columbia, arguing that the Service violated the Endangered Species Act in finding that listing the Canada lynx population in the contiguous U.S. was warranted but precluded (published in the Federal Register, May 27, 1997).
December 22, 1997	The court denied the plaintiffs' Motion to Enforce Judgment against the Service's May 1997 finding that listing the Canada lynx population in the contiguous U.S. was warranted but precluded. At the same time, the court set an expedited schedule and hearing date (March 18, 1998) for the lawsuit filed in September, 1997.
February 11, 1998	The Service and the Plaintiffs reached a settlement that calls for the Service to publish a proposed rule to list the Canada lynx in the contiguous U.S. by June 30, 1998. The settlement was submitted to the U.S. District Court, District of Columbia, for
July 08, 1998	Proposed rule to list the lynx was published (63 FR 36994).

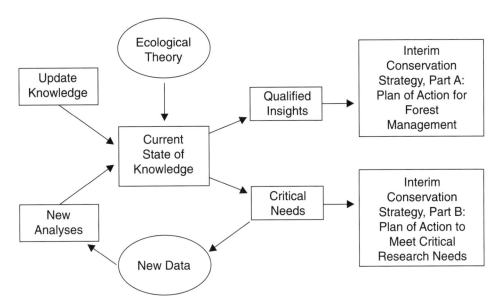

Figure 1.1—Process for developing an interim conservation strategy given that current understandings are extremely limited.

implemented, would provide the information needed for more substantive and defensible conservation planning. This book is the formal report of the Lynx Science Team.

Scientific Context

We face the dilemma of conserving lynx without adequate knowledge of lynx ecology. We do not yet understand many of the factors that determine lynx distribution and abundance; hence, we do not have a very sophisticated understanding of how human activities affect the persistence of lynx populations. Indeed, the entirety of published research on lynx in the United States comes from only seven studies (Chapters 10 and 13). Similarly, there are few published studies on the ecology of the snowshoe hare, the lynx's primary prey, in the contiguous United States (Chapter 7). A substantial amount of research has been conducted on both species in Canada and Alaska (Chapters 6 and 9) but, as discussed above, the applicability of these studies to lynx conservation in the southern portions of its range is unknown.

This situation has three important ramifications for any attempt to elucidate the scientific basis for lynx conservation. First, this book is not a substitute for reliable knowledge gained through a sustained commitment to scientific research. Hence, Chapter 17, "An Action Plan to Fill Critical Knowledge Gaps," must be viewed as a critical part of any conservation strategy based on information contained herein. The second and corollary ramification is that any management strategy based all or in part on the information contained in this volume must be clearly identified as *interim*. A more enduring strategy is contingent upon the acquisition of additional knowledge about lynx ecology and greater understanding of factors influencing the persistence of lynx populations. Finally, because the insights offered here embody a poorly developed "state of the art," we use the term *qualified insight* to remind the reader of this limitation and to stress the need for cautious, conservative decision-making.

We know some basic things about lynx ecology. For example, we know lynx are well adapted to living in cold climates with deep snow, they are closely associated with coniferous forests, and they rely on the snowshoe hare as a primary source of food. However, we don't understand why lynx are not very abundant in some places where these requirements appear to be met (e.g., southwestern Colorado and western Wyoming). This lack of understanding underscores the inadequacy of our knowledge about the factors controlling lynx abundance and distribution.

Similarly, conventional wisdom holds that a landscape dominated by coniferous forest will support lynx if it: (1) produces adequate numbers of snowshoe hares, (2) includes a small amount of old forest needed for den sites, and (3) includes a mixture of forest age classes dominated by early successional stands. The key ingredient here appears to be snowshoe hares, and prime hare habitat is described as regenerating, dense young forest. This paradigm enjoys such broad acceptance that many acres of public land will be modified to fit this description in the name of lynx conservation (e.g., Envriodata Systems Inc. 1993; Washington Department of Natural Resources 1996). Based on this concept of lynx habitat, most timber harvest activities would be considered beneficial and, given that trapping no longer occurs in the United States outside Montana, we might expect lynx populations to be stable or increasing throughout their range. It is hard to reconcile this with the perception that lynx numbers and distribution in the United States are so sparse as to warrant listing under the Endangered Species Act (U. S. Fish and Wildlife Service 1998).

We believe it is critically important to recognize the risks associated with management decisions made in the face of this kind of uncertainty. Management-induced landscape changes, when based on untested hypotheses, can result in conditions antithetical to their stated purpose. An interim strategy has special properties in this regard. Interim direction will be altered within a specified time period, and actions taken during the interim period must not foreclose options for future management. Interim management actions must also be conservative in order to reflect the poorly developed knowledge base upon which they were developed. Unfortunately, the sociopolitical pressure to "do something" usually precludes this conservative approach. Rather, in natural resource management, decisions based upon the best available knowledge tend to treat that knowledge as if it were complete, even when it is woefully inadequate. It is within this context that this book seeks to reexamine existing knowledge, search for new information, and generate qualified insights that can be used to build an interim conservation strategy for the lynx.

The need for action in the face of uncertainty is not unique to the lynx. Our knowledge concerning many organisms is even more limited, and the processes of habitat destruction continue. The ongoing alteration of the natural world ensures a large queue of threatened organisms for the legal machinery of the Endangered Species Act to process. We hope that the approach embodied in this book will be of value in other conservation planning efforts.

Conservation Planning and Uncertainty

Our inability to completely understand ecological processes will always result in varying degrees of uncertainty when planning for species conservation. We are often uncertain about the details of a species' status even when conservation action is clearly appropriate. Comparative census data are usually lacking and, even when such data are present, we are often uncertain about how to interpret population changes relative to natural fluctuations. If we decide that a population is in decline, there will often be uncertainty about the causes of the decline and perhaps additional uncertainty about appropriate restoration efforts. For species with broad historical ranges such as the lynx, these uncertainties increase, as do the consequences of poor decisions. The potential listing of the lynx under the Endangered Species Act, for instance, could impact 16 States.

In conservation planning there is often a fundamental mismatch between the state of knowledge, the feasibility of obtaining specific knowledge, and the actions that society would have land managers take towards species conservation. Land management agencies are asked difficult and very specific questions, such as how the construction of a road or a timber sale will affect the viability of a lynx population. In asking these questions, society (1) presupposes highly sophisticated ecological knowledge, (2) assumes these questions have unequivocal answers, and (3) believes that land managers can develop plans that will solve the problem. Unfortunately, these suppositions are rarely true, and conservation planning always occurs in the face of varying degrees of uncertainty.

There is much society can do to reduce uncertainty and thus improve conservation planning. We have the tools to improve our understanding of ecological systems in almost all cases—it is the political will to do so that is often lacking. Nonetheless, the reality of uncertainty has given rise to several approaches to conservation planning. If uncertainty is limited and quantifiable, a number of stochastic simulation (Noon and McKelvey 1996; Akçakaya and Raphael 1998; Marshall et al. 1998) or formal fuzzy logic (Todd and Burgman 1998) approaches can be used. In most cases, however, uncertainty is addressed less quantitatively. Here, we briefly discuss two widely accepted approaches, then present the alternative approach embodied in this book.

Burden of Proof Approach to Conservation

Conservation disputes are often resolved in the judicial system, where legal constraints require that an action must be proved harmful to a species before the action is precluded; i.e., the "burden of proof" rests with conservationists (Murphy and Noon 1991; Dayton 1998). This results in reactive conservation, whereby proposed actions become the issue, rather than species' conservation. In addition, when little is known about species of concern, e.g., those that are rare and/or difficult to study, substantial harm may occur before such proof is possible. It has therefore been suggested that the burden of proof be shifted so that uncertainty favors, or at least is not destructive to, conservation (Dayton 1998).

However, shifting the burden of proof in the judicial process is unlikely to provide sociopolitical solutions to conservation problems. The process is still flawed, the burden has simply been shifted from one side to the other. Proving harm or lack of harm in a conservation context is costly, time-consuming, and often impractical, regardless of where the burden lies. Because the burden-of-proof approach creates an environment in which one side or the other benefits from a lack of information, this approach also devalues the acquisition of new information. Moreover, because decisions are binary (i.e., an action is either allowed or precluded) knowledge gained through this process (or the identification of significant knowledge gaps), may be lost once a decision is made.

The Delphi Approach to Conservation

A second approach for dealing with conservation in the face of uncertainty has been to seek consensus rather than knowledge. Commonly called the "Delphi method" (Ziglio 1996), this approach evolved out of the need to confront the uncertainties associated with multi-species management (Cleaves 1994). The formalized Delphi process adopted by the Forest Ecosystem Management Assessment Team (FEMAT 1993), involved more than 70 experts having special knowledge of individual species or species groups. These experts participated on panels wherein they were given 100 "likelihood points" that were distributed across four outcomes (Meslow et al. 1994). For each species and management plan, the possible outcomes were that the plan would (1) produce a stable, well distributed population, (2) produce a stable but restricted distribution, (3) only produce widely spaced refugia, or (4) lead to extirpation from federal lands (Meslow et al. 1994). The votes from the panel were then summed to represent the group's collective opinion regarding the quality of each management option.

The Delphi method, in various forms, has become very popular as a means of incorporating scientific input into management decisions (Marcot et al. 1997). This method is popular because it is quick, has proven to be robust in court, and requires no new knowledge. Furthermore, it generally limits decision-making by scientific experts to evaluation of a pre-established set of management alternatives rather than incorporating their input directly into the process of plan development. In short, the value of the Delphi process as applied to conservation planning lies mostly in its expedience.

From a scientific perspective, Delphi processes are inappropriate as a basis for conservation decisions. In the FEMAT example, the only data integral to the Delphi process relates to the opinions of the panel. These data are not reproducible and, perhaps more importantly, the relationship of these data to the ecology of the organisms in question is unknown. The subtle fact that this process results in an assessment of opinion, rather than an assessment of what is known about species' ecologies, is inevitably lost. For example, in the absence of definitive information, if a panel believes strongly that an organism needs a specific habitat type, conservation planning will likely proceed based on this belief, and management actions or general management policy will be set accordingly. The collective opinion of the group therefore becomes a surrogate for a science-based understanding even though no new information has been brought to bear on the problem. This process might be reasonably benign if the expert opinions reflected the state of knowledge—that is, if uncertainty in information lead to uncertainty in conclusions. However, this is seldom the case, and the illusion of knowledge-based understanding is created. For instance in evaluating the results of the FEMAT process, Meslow et al. (1994) state: "Some species did not respond to habitat protection on federal lands, i.e., did not fare well under any option." (p. 26). In truth, the response of these species to protection is unknown. There was no species response. A correct statement would be that in the opinion of the panel, none of the options afforded adequate protection for some species.

To a certain extent, the Delphi process can be altered so that the judgments and opinions are more specific and limited. Marcot et al. (1997), for instance, asked the experts to provide their opinions concerning the basic ecology and species-environment interactions for those species where they had expertise, rather than to evaluate species viability associated with various management scenarios. We believe that this is an improvement because the opinions of the experts will be much closer to their areas of expertise and can, to the extent that these opinions are based on unpublished findings, represent new information. In the final analysis, however, there is no way to determine which inferences are based on data and which on opinion, and the distinction will be lost.

History is replete with scientific conventional wisdom, strongly held at the time, but found by subsequent investigation to be false. Holding strong beliefs based on minimal data is a human propensity, but one that is antithetical to the scientific method. Delphi encourages this propensity and, in the process, suppresses the acknowledgment of uncertainty needed to qualify all scientific discourse and to inform sociopolitical processes. Additionally, Delphi methods fail to sufficiently elucidate knowledge gaps and identify the importance and necessity of obtaining new information.

The Inductive Approach: A Science-Based Method

We have chosen an alternative approach that is based on the assumption that knowledge is never complete and never universal. Some research findings are strong enough that they can be assumed to be true. Even in such cases, however, a strict scientific interpretation limits the scope of inference to the specific study site, the specific population of organisms studied, and the time of the investigation. We must also acknowledge that sometimes, in spite of our best sampling efforts, the individuals we study may not be representative of the population inhabiting the study area, thus further limiting the utility of our findings. Peer-reviewed scientific publications generally provide strong local information, but there are limitations to using such knowledge. Statistical inferences apply only to the populations, places, and times actually studied, and neither the most sophisticated mathematical models nor the most impressive computer-mapping technology can change this.

This scientific reality does not diminish the importance of the information derived through this process. Indeed, this is the nature of scientific investigation; through a gradual accumulation of limited pieces of knowledge, more generalizable interpretations emerge and scientific paradigms are formed. In the interim, if we wish to apply limited knowledge to the solution of large-scale problems, we do so using subjective methods. However, such methods rely on a series of untested assumptions concerning the generalizability of existing knowledge.

These subjective interpretations are an important part of the scientific process. Indeed, the most difficult and often the most important part of the scientific process is the interpretation of research findings within the broader context of "what is known." This aspect of science is similar to the creative process that gives rise to insights about appropriate and meaningful research questions. The critical component of both processes is to limit one's interpretations to scientifically defensible inferences based on empirical data. This aspect of the scientific process is evident in thorough research proposals and in the discussion sections of published manuscripts. In both cases, limited knowledge is aggregated and synthesized to derive insights that have scientific merit as judged by the peer-review process.

The qualified insights we are attempting to produce embrace this scientific tradition. What we seek here is a middle ground between demanding certainty and embracing opinion. This middle ground is the result of interpretation, a fundamentally subjective process based on scientific judgment. In taking this approach we acknowledge that judgments are an essential part of the scientific process, but they must be based on empirical data and theory, and they must be specific. It is the specificity of the linkage between data and inference that separates even the most highly qualified of insights from the opinion-based approaches described above. We can, for instance, make qualified insights concerning the probable dietary dependence of lynx on snowshoe hares at the southern periphery of their range. In doing so, we rely on specific data concerning lynx, hares, and the prey communities in areas such as the Great Lakes States or the Rocky Mountains. The inference is qualified: we know a great deal about these relationships in certain areas and we are inferring the degree to which these understandings are transferrable to areas where we lack local knowledge. We cannot, however, make qualified insights concerning how well the lynx would respond to protection on federal lands in the contiguous United States unless we can find a similar body of information from which valid inferences concerning lynx viability can be drawn.

Organization of the Book

Chapters 2 through 5 of this book provide a context for scientific judgments. We review pertinent ecological theory and examine fundamentally important information about relevant ecological systems. Viewed within this context, even scant information about lynx ecology may acquire meaning that would otherwise remain obscure. Moreover, placing data into the context of ecological theory diminishes the data-dependency of the qualified insights. For instance, an important issue in conservation biology is the impact of adult mortality, which is often influenced by human behavior, on population dynamics. Ecological theory tells us that long-lived organisms with low fecundity are more sensitive to adult mortality than are short-lived organisms with high fecundity. By knowing something about the life history of an organism and applying this theoretical understanding, it is possible to infer that increasing adult survival will have a positive effect on the population.

For reasons discussed above, the process we have chosen incorporates all the empirical information we could locate. We critically evaluate all such data; thus, we are free to incorporate data from published as well as unpublished sources. Data may be weak for a variety of reasons, but even weak data will contribute to understanding when viewed in a rigorous analytical framework. We discriminate between weak data and opinions based on weak data. For instance, a picture of a lynx shot in low-elevation rangeland would be considered weak in one sense because it is not part of a representative sample. However, to the extent that we know that a lynx occurred in that time and place, we have a small but legitimate datum to add to our knowledge base. Opinions about why the lynx was there, what it was doing, and whether it may be representative of a population are not based on additional data and, therefore, are not pertinent. Accordingly, Chapters 6 through 13 are dedicated to the review and assessment of existing information and to the presentation of new data about the ecology of lynx and snowshoe hares.

Building on the integration of existing information and relevant ecological theory, Chapters 14 and 15 synthesize existing information and begin to make interpretations relative to lynx conservation. It is here that we attempt to place lynx conservation into the larger context of ecosystem management by considering the needs of diverse vertebrate communities. This synthesis leads directly to a discussion of qualified insights in Chapter 16, and that, in turn, to the use of qualified insights to frame an action plan, as outlined in Chapter 17.

An Ecological Framework

The questions we address through qualified insights must be pertinent to lynx conservation. The science of conservation biology provides a conceptual framework that informs us about the kind of information most critical to this task; these include:

1. Present and historical patterns of lynx distribution.
2. Factors limiting the geographic distribution of lynx.
3. Principal habitat features affecting lynx.
4. Food habits of lynx.
5. Habitat requirements of key prey species.
6. Population dynamics of key prey species.
7. Principal community factors affecting lynx.
8. Principal factors affecting lynx movements and dispersal.
9. Key demographic properties and dynamics of lynx populations.
10. Geographic variation among lynx populations.
11. Direct human influences on lynx.

Our discussion of qualified insights in Chapter 16 is organized according to this framework, although many of these key areas are not mutually exclusive. The ecological relationships implicit in this framework are illustrated in Figure 1.2. We know from the outset that much of this information is unavailable for the lynx, but our task primarily involves developing qualified insights about lynx ecology in those areas where critical information is lacking. In addition, the process of developing insights in these data-poor areas will serve to highlight important knowledge gaps. Thus, Chapter 16 is both a compilation of knowledge-based inferences and a compendium of critical information needs for future research.

Because we cannot depend upon the slow accumulation of independent research findings to provide a foundation for the conservation of lynx, we need to identify a plan of action that will, if followed, close important knowledge gaps in a timely manner. The last and probably the most critical part of our approach to dealing with uncertainty is to use our qualified insights to frame this action plan, as presented in Chapter 17.

Present and historical distribution
    Limiting factors
        Physical (too hot, too cold, etc.)
        Barriers (simply couldn't get there)
            Lynx movement capability
        Competitors
            Effects on survival, fecundity, also exclusion
        Prey
            Lynx diet and variation in diet
                Ecological requirements of key prey species
                Factors limiting the population
                dynamics of prey
Lynx biology
    Habitat relationships
        Use patterns
        Movement patterns
    Demographics
        Influence of competitors (fecundity, survival)
        Influence of prey (fecundity, survival)
        Influence of habitat structure (fecundity, survival)—includes snow

Figure 1.2—Hierarchical representation of key areas of understanding needed for conservation planning.

Literature Cited

Akçakaya, H. R. and M. G. Raphael. 1998. Assessing human impact despite uncertainty: viability of the northern spotted owl metapopulation in the western USA. Biodiversity and Conservation 7:875-894.

Cleaves, D. A. 1994. Assessing uncertainty in expert judgment: a rationale and guidelines for application in ecosystem management. U.S. Department of Agriculture, Forest Service, General Technical Report SO-110.

Dayton, P. K. 1998. Ecology - reversal of the burden of proof in fisheries management. Science 279:821-822.

Enviadata Systems, Inc. 1993. Meadows integrated resource analysis: a technical report addressing lynx habitat. *in* Okanogan National Forest. 1993. Meadows area integrated resource analysis. Tonasket and Winthrop Ranger Districts, Okanogan National Forest, WA.

FEMAT. 1993. Forest ecosystem management: and ecological, economic, and social assessment. Report of the Forest Ecosystem Management Assessment Team. USDA Forest Service; USDC National Oceanographic and Atmospheric Administration and National Marine Fisheries Service; USDI Bureau of Land Management, Fish and Wildlife Service, and National Park Service; and U. S. Environmental Protection Agency, Washington, DC.

Lyon, L. J., K. B. Aubry, W. J. Zielinski, S. W. Buskirk, and L. F. Ruggiero. 1994. The scientific basis for conserving carnivores: considerations for management. Pages 128-137 *in* L. F. Ruggiero, K. B. Aubry, S. W. Buskirk, L. J. Lyon, and W. J. Zielinski, technical editors. The scientific basis for conserving forest carnivores: American marten, fisher, lynx, and wolverine in the Western United States. U.S. Department of Agriculture, Forest Service, General Technical Report RM-254.

Marcot, B. G, M. A. Castellano, J. A. Christy, L. K. Croft, J. F. Lehmkuhl, R. H. Naney, R. E. Rosentreter, R. E. Sandquist, E. Zieroth, K. Nelson, C. G. Niwa, and B. C. Wales. 1997. Pages 1497-1673 *in* T. M. Quigley and S. J. Arbelbide, technical editors. An assessment of ecosystem components in the Interior Columbia Basin and portions of the Klamath and Great Basins: Volume III. U.S. Department of Agriculture, Forest Service, General Technical Report PNW-GTR-405.

Marshall, E., R. Haight and F. R. Homans. 1998. Incorporating environmental uncertainty into species management decisions: Kirtland's warbler habitat management as a case study. Conservation Biology 12:975-985.

Meslow, E. C., R. S. Holthausen, and D. A. Cleaves. 1994. Assessment of terrestrial species and ecosystems. Journal of Forestry 92(4):24-27.

Murphy, D. D. and B. R. Noon. 1991. Coping with uncertainty in wildlife biology. Journal of Wildlife Management 55:773-782.

Noon, B. R. and K. S. McKelvey. 1996. Management of the spotted owl: a case history in conservation. Annual Review of Ecology and Systematics 27:135-162.

Ruggiero, L. F., K. B. Aubry, S. W. Buskirk, L. J. Lyon, and W. J. Zielinski. 1994a. Information needs and a research strategy for conserving forest carnivores. Pages 138-152 *in* L. F. Ruggiero, K. B. Aubry, S. W. Buskirk, L. J. Lyon, and W. J. Zielinski, technical editors. The scientific basis for conserving forest carnivores: American marten, fisher, lynx, and wolverine in the Western United States. U.S. Department of Agriculture, Forest Service, General Technical Report RM-254.

Ruggiero, L. F., K. B. Aubry, S. W. Buskirk, L. J. Lyon, and W. J. Zielinski, technical editors. 1994b. The scientific basis for conserving forest carnivores: American marten, fisher, lynx, and wolverine in the Western United States. U.S. Department of Agriculture, Forest Service, General Technical Report RM-254.

Thomas J. W., et al. 1993. Viability assessments and management considerations for species associated with late-successional and old-growth forests in the Pacific Northwest. U.S. Department of Agriculture, Forest Service, Washington, DC.

Todd, C. R. and M. A. Burgman. 1998. Assessment of threat and conservation priorities under realistic levels of uncertainty and reliability. Conservation Biology 12:966-974.

U.S. Fish and Wildlife Service. 1998. Proposal to list the contiguous United States distinct population segment of the Canada lynx: proposed rule. Federal Register 63(130):36994-37013.

Washington Department of Natural Resources. 1996. Lynx habitat management plan for DNR managed lands. Washington State Department of Natural Resources, Olympia, WA.

Ziglio, E. 1996. The Delphi method and its contribution to decision-making. Pages 4-33 *in* M. Adler and E. Ziglio, Editors. Gazing into the Oracle: the Delphi method and its application to social policy and public health. Jessica Kingsley Publishers, Bristol, PA.

Chapter 2

Theoretical Insights into the Population Viability of Lynx

Kevin S. McKelvey, USDA Forest Service, Rocky Mountain Research Station, 800 E. Beckwith, Missoula, MT 59801

Steven W. Buskirk, Department of Zoology and Physiology, Box 3166, University of Wyoming, Laramie, WY 82071

Charles J. Krebs, Department of Zoology, University of British Columbia, Vancouver, BC V6T 1Z4 Canada

Abstract—We discuss ecological theory and population models pertinent to the population biology of southern lynx. Fragmented forest cover types, high vagility of lynx, and linkages in population dynamics suggest that lynx in the contiguous United States are arranged as metapopulations. Metapopulation stability depends on not only habitat quality but also dispersal rates between habitat islands. Models indicate that dispersal rates between habitat islands should sharply decrease as the islands become smaller and more distant and the risks associated with crossing between islands increase. Southern lynx populations may fluctuate, which affects both rates of extinction and colonization of habitat islands. Synchronous population fluctuations can decrease the viability of metapopulations. Southern habitat islands probably are source-sink mosaics that shift with disturbance and succession. Models indicate that temporally transient habitat may be underutilized by organisms. Lagged synchronous patterns observed in both northern and southern populations suggest broad connectivity between subpopulations, but empirical data are lacking and some subpopulations may be isolated. Models that combine dispersal into spatial predator-prey models generate similar patterns, and dispersal can provide a synchronizing mechanism. We emphasize the dangers associated with ignoring either local habitat quality or regional connectivity.

Introduction

To conserve lynx we must rely on both applicable ecological theory and specific information about lynx ecology like that presented in the middle section of this book. The purpose of this chapter is to review the ecological concepts and parameters used in evaluating population viability. We identify some of the specific problems associated with applying these concepts to lynx.

Population Viability

The population, not the species, is the appropriate taxonomic level of focus for most conservation efforts (Chapter 5, Ruggiero et al. 1994). The National Forest Management Act of 1976 requires the U.S. Forest Service to maintain viable populations of all native vertebrate species, and the Endangered Species Act of 1973 recognizes distinct population segments as appropriate levels of statutory protection. Biologically, the importance of maintaining viable populations is based on the idea of ecological dependency (Ruggiero et al. 1988), which implies a dynamic relationship between a population and the environment that supports it.

Population viability refers to the probability that a population will persist for a specified time into the future (Boyce 1992). Formal Population Viability Analysis (PVA), however, requires information on many variables that are difficult to estimate for low-density populations (Beissinger and Westphal 1998) like the lynx. For even the simplest deterministic models, information on age structure, breeding schedule, and survival rates are needed. These models assume that demographic rates are constant, which certainly is not true for lynx. Given even this minimal list of parameters, we cannot build these models for southern populations of lynx given the scarcity and uncertainty of data on lynx vital rates (Chapter 13). We can, however, evaluate ecological theory as it pertains to lynx at the southern periphery of their range and evaluate potential risks to population persistence.

Stochastic Factors That Affect Viability

Small populations are usually thought to have low viability because of their vulnerability to chance events. The elements of chance that affect viability are demographic stochasticity, environmental stochasticity, genetic stochasticity, and catastrophe (Shaffer 1981). Demographic and environmental stochasticity are terms generally associated with birth and death rates. Demographic stochasticity refers to chance events that work at the level of the individual; environmental stochasticity to chance events that affect the vital rates of the population such as low reproductive rates during a drought.

Catastrophes differ substantially from either demographic or environmental stochasticity. Both demographic and environmental stochasticity affect expected times to extinction and are sensitive to population size. Catastrophes can eliminate an entire population at a single moment in time regardless of its size. Many catastrophes are associated with disturbance processes such as fire, flood, or volcanic eruption and have limited geographic scope. Such processes may kill all of the organisms within the disturbed area, but populations outside will be unaffected. In species like the lynx with a broad geographic distribution, catastrophe is not likely to play a major role in species persistence. However, small southern populations of lynx could be affected by catastrophic events, with consequences for viability in the contiguous United States.

Genetic stochasticity is similar to demographic stochasticity but operates at the genetic level and is expressed indirectly through demographic processes (Saccheri et al. 1998). For example, genes associated with disease-resistance may be lost by chance in matings among closely related individuals, and the resulting progeny would experience increased mortality rates. In small populations, this can produce a positive feedback between genetic and demographic processes: genetic losses reduce fitness, which leads to smaller populations, increased rates of genetic loss, and further fitness reductions. This process has been called an extinction vortex (Gilpin and Soulé 1986).

The genetic properties of populations are vital to both short and long term population persistence and these issues are discussed more fully in Chapter 5. In this chapter, the models and theory deal strictly with demographic processes and do not address the genetic processes described above. While ignoring genetic factors is clearly artificial, genetic and demographic processes tend to happen at very different rates. For instance, demographic population rescue requires that enough immigrants enter a population on average to make up the difference between population losses (emigration and mortality) and birth rates. This rate of immigration is generally several orders of magnitude greater than is necessary to accomplish genetic rescue, which entails offsetting the loss of alleles through genetic drift (See Gilpin 1991 for a discussion of genetic drift in small, fragmented populations).

Population Viability Concerns for Southern Lynx Populations

Southern lynx occur at relatively low densities, are found almost exclusively in cool, moist, coniferous forest types (Chapter 8), eat a winter diet dominated by two species (snowshoe hare and red squirrel; Chapters 9 and 13), and, at least in Canada and Alaska, exhibit strongly cyclic population dynamics (Chapter 9). In the contiguous United States, forest cover types in which lynx have occurred are either peninsular extensions of larger habitat areas in Canada or discrete islands (Chapter 8, Figs. 8.19-8.23, Map Insert). Given the low densities of lynx in these southern habitats (Chapter 13), many of these habitat islands will contain relatively few individuals and may collectively function as metapopulations. Alternatively, many of these habitat islands may function as separate, isolated populations unto themselves, rendering each isolated population highly vulnerable to extirpation.

In southern boreal forests, hares appear to exist in many areas at densities close to the lower limits required for lynx reproduction (Chapter 7) and lynx densities are correspondingly low (Chapter 13). Prey densities vary with forest type and stand age. For a population at equilibrium (birth rates = death rates), small changes in habitat quality can produce a sink (birth rates < death rates). Because southern lynx populations appear to exist close to this threshold, southern lynx habitat probably is a shifting mosaic of source and sink areas.

Lynx populations in the taiga exhibit cyclic dynamics with high-amplitude fluctuations (Elton and Nicholson 1942; Stenseth et al. 1997; Chapters 8, 9). There is some evidence that hares (Chapter 7) and lynx (Chapter 8) fluctuate in the south as well. Population fluctuations potentially change the dynamics of local extinction and colonization, and can produce a number of unique spatio-temporal patterns such as travelling waves (Okubo 1980). These are population fluctuations that move, like waves, across broad geographic areas (See Moss et al. in press for a well-documented example). Adjacent geographic areas experience peaks and troughs that are lagged behind those at the origin of the wave, producing the "lagged synchrony" referred to in later chapters.

Based on these understandings, we believe that three areas of ecological theory are particularly pertinent to southern lynx populations: metapopulation dynamics, source-sink habitat relationships, and special properties of cyclic systems.

Metapopulation Dynamics

Metapopulation models view a population as a number of discrete sub-populations within habitat patches or "islands" connected by dispersal. Through time, subpopulations may go extinct and be recolonized, but the larger metapopulation persists. The original metapopulation model described a population of equal-sized habitat islands separated by areas that contained no resident organisms, but which allowed dispersal (Levins 1969, 1970). According to the model, subpopulations were in one of two states: either populated or extinct. The dynamics of Levins' model are described by the differential equation:

$$\frac{dp}{dt} = mp(1-p) - ep \tag{1}$$

where p is the proportion of habitat islands occupied, m is the colonization rate, and e is the extinction rate of the subpopulations. The expected equilibrium proportion of occupied islands is:

$$\hat{p} = 1 - \frac{e}{m} \tag{2}$$

Hence, if the extinction rate is less than the colonization rate, the metapopulation will persist on at least some of the islands. If the subpopulations are completely isolated, ($m = 0$), then the metapopulation cannot persist.

An important inference from this model is that when the rate of local extinction equals that of colonization, all islands are unoccupied and the entire metapopulation goes extinct. For most of the islands in a metapopulation to be occupied at a given time, the colonization rate must greatly exceed that of local extinction. If subpopulations on islands are extinction-prone, then a stable metapopulation requires a high rate of dispersal between the islands.

Recently it has been argued that classical metapopulations, consisting of equal-sized, equidistant islands, are a theoretical construct that rarely exists in nature; mainland-island systems in which one island is much larger than the others are more common (Hanski 1982; Harrison 1993). These systems are not prone to the same kinds of instabilities as classical metapopulations, because the mainland is large enough that its population is not prone to extinction. However, Harrison's (1993) criticism of applying metapopulation theory to conservation is pertinent only if one is concerned just with the persistence of the mainland population. For lynx in the contiguous United States, we are interested in the dynamics of the islands, where population persistence will be determined by colonization and extinction rates among habitat islands.

Colonization

The effect of distance—Assuming a habitat island is unoccupied, its colonization will occur through the dispersal of organisms from either other islands or the mainland. The probability of colonization will be a function of the number of dispersers, and the distance to and difficulty of reaching the islands. Lamberson et al. (1994) modeled dispersal between same-sized habitat islands by partitioning the probability into two components: the time it takes to travel to the island (and hence the probability that the organism will live long enough to reach it), and the likelihood that a dispersing individual will encounter the island. For an organism to successfully disperse, it needs to survive long enough to reach the island and it needs to travel in the right direction. Thus, the probability of successful dispersal rapidly declines with distance. For a single distant island, only a small proportion of dispersers will travel in the right direction and, if dispersal is risky, many will die in transit. We illustrate this using the algorithms presented by Lamberson et al. (1994). If an organism travels in a straight-line 1 km per day and has a 1% chance of mortality per day while dispersing, 13.5% of the dispersers will find a 10-km wide island at a distance of 10 km. Only 0.7% would find that same island at a distance of 100 km. This estimate of the decline in probability of successful colonization with distance probably is conservative. Lamberson et al. (1994) assumed a constant probability of mortality for each time-unit spent dispersing, but it is likely that death rates increase as dispersals get longer. During dispersal, organisms are thought not to forage as efficiently as in a home range, and the disperser's body condition likely will decline with time. Thus, dispersal across long distances is risky, and successful colonization will be rare. If a disperser stops at the first suitable site, this behavior leads to a geometric decline in dispersals with distance, a pattern observed in a variety of organisms (Waser 1985; Buechner 1987).

Dispersal in spatially heterogeneous, cyclic populations—Levins' (1969,1970) metapopulation model assumes equal habitat conditions in all islands and constant rates of dispersal over time. Lynx, at least in the taiga, display strongly cyclic population dynamics. In non-cyclic populations, dispersal is thought to be a relatively passive process; a proportion of the population disperses, and that proportion is determined by the evolutionary consequences to fitness of dispersing and its opposite, philopatry (Hamilton and May 1977). In temporally stable habitats, dispersal should generally lead to decreased fitness and therefore should not be favored (Hastings 1983; Holt 1985). In a temporally unstable environment, however, dispersal can be favored even if fitness costs are high (Levin et al. 1984; Frank 1986; Cohen and Levin 1991).

Dispersal may be particularly important for regulating cyclic populations, but the mechanisms are poorly understood. Krebs (1992) described a phenomenon, the "fence effect," in voles: if a vole population is physically enclosed ("fenced"), the population will rise to high densities and subsequently crash, a dynamic not seen in adjacent unfenced populations. Here, dispersal is a pre-saturation phenomenon with a population-regulatory function. Krebs (1992) speculated that cyclic populations are characterized by pre-saturation dispersal, whereas non-cyclic populations exhibit saturation dispersal. In general, dispersal is thought to be more critical for cyclic populations and may help generate or propagate the cycles. In Canada, lynx are strongly cyclic, but long-range movements are more frequent during those periods when hares are rapidly declining (Chapter 9), indicating post-saturation dispersal. The extent to which these movements result in successful dispersal is, however, unknown.

Successful dispersal—Colonization of islands in a metapopulation differs fundamentally from within-island or within-mainland dispersal, in that the latter does not require crossing extensive unsuitable habitats. Dispersal, by definition, describes movement from site of origin to site of next mating, and successful dispersal to the entire process of movement, subsequent mating, and production of young (Shields 1987). If dispersal to distant habitat islands is rare, successful dispersal must be even more so. Early models (e.g. MacArthur and Wilson 1967; Richter-Dyn and Goel 1972), concerned only females, and males were assumed to either automatically follow along or to have impregnated females before dispersal. For most mammals that do not exhibit embryonic diapause, these assumptions are unrealistic; successful dispersal requires, at the very least, a male and a female to arrive at the destination at about the same time. In the example above, if the source island produced 10 dispersers per year, then about one animal per year would successfully disperse 10 km. If the organism were fairly long-lived, this would provide a reasonable probability of a mating pair co-occurring in the destination island and dispersing successfully. At 100 km, however, a dispersing animal would find the island only once every 14 years, greatly reducing the probability of successful dispersal.

These problems are exacerbated if long-range dispersal is sex-biased. It is widely believed, for example, that dispersal in many mammals is male-dominated (Greenwood 1980; Cockburn et al. 1985; Clark et al. 1988), although for many species the evidence is weak (see Gaines and McClenaghan 1980) and based on questionable methods (Porter and Dueser 1989). Still, if most long-range dispersal were by males, then simultaneous male-female occurrences at destinations would be rarer than overall dispersal rates suggest. Data on lynx in southern Yukon concerning sex-bias in emigration are equivocal. In general, rates of emigration showed no sex bias, but 14 of 17 detected movements >100 km were males (Chapter 9). Data on rates of dispersal, successful and otherwise, are few. Dickman and Doncaster (1989) found that in urban environments wood mice and bank voles recolonized distant sites (200-400 m) more slowly than close sites (50-140 m).

The previous discussions concerning dispersal only consider animals that move independently and disperse in random directions. These assumptions may be inappropriate. Animals may have knowledge acquired through exploratory movements or may have direct visual clues that allow them to move directly from one habitat island to the next. Similarly, if an organism leaves a scent trail during dispersal, then other dispersers can follow it thereby increasing the number of dispersers that reach a specific location. We do not know if lynx have dispersal mechanisms that allow them to more efficiently colonize islands, but exploratory movements appear to be fairly common in southern populations (Chapters 11, 13).

Introductions and reintroductions of organisms, which are human-facilitated dispersals, are better documented than natural dispersal events. Introductions allow us to look at the likelihood of success, given dispersal. Although introductions and dispersal differ in important ways, some of the factors that lead to failure (animals arriving in poor condition, behaviors poorly adapted to the destination, importance of stochasticity in small populations) will be similar. Importantly, introductions are intended to succeed and designed to that end. Even so, introductions often fail. In desert bighorn sheep, all introductions in which the initial population was less than 50 individuals failed within 50 years (Berger 1990). Of 353 insect introductions to control exotic weeds, 70% failed, and success was insensitive to initial population size: 66% of the introductions in which the initial population was ≤20 failed compared with 70% of those with initial populations >100 (Simberloff 1989). It is reasonable to conclude that even with large numbers of dispersers, colonization will frequently be unsuccessful.

Pulsed dispersal and colonization—The role of cyclic dispersal in colonization has been little studied. As we have shown, colonization of distant areas is very unlikely if animals disperse at constant rates over time. If, however, dispersers are pulsed so that at some times many dispersers are searching simultaneously, then the probability of distant colonization increases significantly. Assume, as in our earlier example, that each disperser has a 0.07% chance of successful arrival at a habitat island, that 90% of those that arrive survive for a year, and that at least two animals co-occurring at the destination will result in colonization. If the source population produces 10 dispersers every year then, on average, the island will have ≥2 organisms about 3% of the time. If, however, 100 dispersers are produced once every 10 years, this increases to about 10%. Of course, not all sets of two organisms will mate; they will be of the same sex about half the time. If we assume that at least four organisms are needed for colonization, producing 10 dispersers per year will virtually never achieve this (0.05%), whereas a 10-year pulse of immigrants will put ≥ 4 organisms on the island about 8% of the time.

Extinction after successful dispersal—After a habitat island is colonized by successful dispersal, the risk of extinction should decrease as the population gets larger. But the relation between extinction risk and population size is critically dependent on the kind of extinction risk. Early models (MacArthur and Wilson 1967; Richter-Dyn and Goel 1972) considered only demographic stochasticity. Demographic stochasticity in a very small population can be viewed as being similar to a series of coin flips: if heads the population decreases by one, if tails, it increases by one. If population size = 3, then HHH would cause extinction, as would HHTHH. In very small populations, random events leading to extinction are likely and extinction rates are high. As population size increases, even to as few as 20 reproducing females, the probability of this type of random event leading to extinction becomes vanishingly small (MacArthur and Wilson 1967; Richter-Dyn and Goel 1972).

If demographic stochasticity were the only extinction risk, then except for tiny, isolated populations metapopulation dynamics would be unimportant. However, environmental stochasticity, including weather, affects the demography of the metapopulation. Harrison and Quinn (1989) included correlated environmental stochasticity in a model of metapopulation dynamics and found that if the means and variances of subpopulation extinction rates were high, temporal correlation of subpopulation events greatly reduced the average time to metapopulation extinction. However, if the extinction rate of subpopulations was low or moderate and consistent among subpopulations, high environmental correlation among subpopulations did not predispose the metapopulation to go extinct. The largest differences between correlated and non-correlated systems were seen in metapopulations with many islands. So, number of islands in a metapopulation, rate of subpopulation extinction, and environmental correlation among subpopulations are all related to the persistence of metapopulations.

Source-Sink Dynamics

Southern lynx populations appear to exist at lower densities and to have lower reproductive rates than northern populations (Chapter 13). Habitat heterogeneity is also much higher than in the taiga (Chapter 3); therefore, southern populations likely occur partly in areas which act as "sinks" and are dependent on immigration from "sources." Source environments produce surplus animals, which must disperse to have a chance of surviving. Sink environments do not produce enough animals to sustain themselves and, in the absence of immigration from source areas, populations living in sink areas go extinct (Pulliam 1988). To determine whether a particular area is a source or a sink, we need to know the birth and death rates of the population (Krebs 1994). We cannot use the surrogate measure of population density to determine source or sink environments; ecologists have repeatedly pointed out that sink areas may contain high population densities (Van Horne 1983; Hobbs and Hanley 1990).

In source-sink models (Pulliam 1988; Pulliam and Danielson 1991; Howe et al. 1991) equilibrium dynamics depend on specific rules concerning habitat selection, as well as the vital rates associated with the source and sink areas. If, for instance, a few areas were very productive, but in the rest of the landscape birth and death rates were nearly in balance, a very large population could be supported by a few source areas. Conversely, the loss of a few important areas could destabilize a very large population that depended on sources to maintain population viability.

Source-sink dynamics tend to be modeled as spatial rather than temporal; a given area is assumed to be either a source or a sink environment permanently (Pulliam 1988; Pulliam and Danielson 1991). Source-sink concepts as they relate to lynx, however, are complicated by strong temporal components. In the North, the same areas that produce excess animals at one phase in the cycle are strong sinks a few years later. Similarly, because the densities of prey change as stands undergo succession (Chapters 6, 7, and 14), areas that are sinks today may be sources in a few decades, or vice-versa. When evaluating landscape-level changes and their impacts on source-sink dynamics, it is therefore necessary to determine both current and long-term productivity of a particular area.

Fahrig (1992) modeled habitat change using a simple model in which habitat was either suitable or not and found that the model was far more sensitive to turnover rates of habitat than it was to the distance between habitat islands. While not a source-sink model in a formal sense, it indicated that temporal changes in habitat quality could have a profound impact on population stability. To address this question using a source-sink model, Pulliam et al. (1991) built a more complex simulation model for the Bachman's sparrow (BACHMAP; Pulliam et al. 1991) that allowed habitat areas to change quality over time so as to simulate active forest management. Bachman's sparrow, which historically was found in old pine forests, has declined over much of its range (Pulliam et al. 1991). An interesting aspect in this decline is that Bachman's sparrows breed in newly planted pine fields as well as old-growth areas, but seldom in intermediate-aged stands (Pulliam et al. 1991). Young stands areas are plentiful in the short-rotation southern pine plantations, and reproductive rates in these areas are no different from those in old forests (Haggerty 1988). Source-sink dynamics were therefore allowed to vary; the highest recruitment rates were in very old and very young forests. Surprisingly, Pulliam's (1991) model consistently showed that population sizes were maximized when the largest amount of old forest was retained. As with Fahrig's (1992) model, the rapid turnover of the source habitat after cutting precluded its effective utilization.

Cyclic and Spatial Dynamics: Synchronizing Elements and Traveling Waves

Predator-Prey Dynamics

In mathematical models, populations of specialist predators can exhibit stable, cyclic, or chaotic behavior. These dynamics reflect interactions between the predator and the prey; the predator affects prey densities and is, in turn, affected by the prey (May 1973; Hanski et al. 1993). The inclusion of generalist predators, which can switch prey, tends to dampen cyclic behavior and produce more stable systems (Hanski et al. 1991). Because of prey-switching behavior, predator populations tend to become decoupled from dynamics of a specific prey (Erlinge et al. 1991; Hanski et al. 1991). For instance, in northern Canada coyotes depend entirely on snowshoe hares (O'Donoghue 1997, Chapter 4), and their populations cycle much like those of lynx in response to hare densities. Because they are hare specialists, their addition to northern ecosystems in the early 20th century would not necessarily change the cyclic behavior of hares or other hare predators. However, in areas farther south where coyotes switch to ungulate prey when hares are scarce (Chapter 4), we would expect them to have a very different influence. This is consistent with the generally stronger appearance of cyclic dynamics in northern, less species-rich ecological systems. Similarly, microtine rodent populations in northern Scandinavia are more cyclic than those farther south, likely because there are more generalist predators in southern areas (Erlinge et al. 1991; Hanski et al. 1991).

Diffusion-Reaction Models

Simple predator-prey models assume homogeneity in vital rates and the interactions between predators to prey. These models therefore apply only to small geographic areas. For larger areas, predator-prey dynamics are linked through movement. The inclusion of movement into population models generally changes their dynamics. In many cases, dispersal acts to stabilize (Doebeli 1995) or synchronize (Blasius et al. 1999) intrinsically unstable or chaotic systems. These dynamics have been conceptualized as diffusion-reaction models (Okubo 1980), in which the diffusion is movement and the reaction is predator-prey dynamics defined in space and time.

Diffusion-reaction models tend to generate traveling waves (Skellam 1951; Okubo 1980), that resemble the cyclic behavior of lynx populations over broad geographic areas (Blasius et al. 1999). For instance, in the simple case where a population originates at a particular point in space and time, population growth will spread outward from that point in the form of a wave. The wave travels at a rate defined by the intrinsic growth rate of the population and the rate of movement (Okubo 1980; Shigesada and Kawasaki 1997). Unless the predator population is zero behind the frontal wave, the system is characterized by a "wake" of smaller following waves, the magnitude, duration, and character of which depend on characteristics of the system being modeled (Gurney et al. 1998). The degree to which actual dispersal behavior is correctly modeled by diffusion is unknown for most species. Skellam (1951), however, demonstrated that dispersal of muskrats in Europe closely followed model expectations.

Large-scale synchrony can be achieved through the coupling of cyclic or chaotic systems through dispersal (Blasius et al. 1999). Of particular interest to lynx dynamics is "phase synchronization," characterized by synchronization of periodicity but not of amplitude (Blasius et al. 1999). This pattern, which appears to describe lynx dynamics in Canada during the 20th century (Chapter 9 Fig. 9.4, Blasius et al. 1999), occurs at intermediate levels of diffusive coupling.

Discussion

If a landscape provides small habitat islands, then the system will only be stable if it functions as a metapopulation. Very small isolated populations are subject to a variety of risks and are prone to extinction. For a metapopulation to persist, rates of colonization must greatly exceed rates of extinction. Colonization rates, in turn, are driven by the number of colonizers produced by the islands and the probability of successful dispersal between islands. Because metapopulations depend both on population size within and dispersals between islands, they can easily be destabilized. If, for instance, adult mortality were increased so that populations on the islands were generally below carrying capacity, even if these populations appeared stable, dispersal would be greatly reduced: there would be fewer potential dispersers and more of these would likely remain on their natal islands. Similarly, maintaining populations on the islands at carrying capacity, but reducing between-island dispersal, would also potentially destabilize the metapopulation.

For lynx, it is likely that rates of dispersal between both the large mainland population in the North and between other islands in the contiguous United States are highly variable. Lynx populations therefore may exist as several smaller but effectively isolated metapopulations. Arguably, the lynx in the northeastern United States are effectively isolated from the main Canadian populations by the St. Lawrence Seaway (Chapter 8) and from the Great Lake States by agricultural conversion and urban development. Similarly, boreal forests in Colorado and Utah are separated from the larger areas of boreal forest in Wyoming by at least 100 km (Chapter 8). If these areas have become effectively isolated, then they represent special areas of concern and, if they still contain native populations, these populations are particularly endangered.

We know very little about lynx biology in the southern portions of its range, but the population dynamics we observe are complex and appear to be spatially interconnected (Chapter 8). We do not know the degree of connectivity or its role in the viability of the species, but we assume that connectivity per se is important. We do not know, for example, how population dynamics in Saskatchewan affect those in Montana. In later chapters, however, we demonstrate lagged synchronous fluctuations that resemble the traveling waves produced in predator-prey models that include movement. Thus, we have support for the importance of the connectivity of lynx populations from metapopulation theory, spatial models and, limited empirical data.

We know very little about the densities of snowshoe hares or red squirrels in the contiguous United States, but recognize tremendous variability in these densities among forest types and successional stages. Given this variability, source-sink modeling suggests that landscape proportions, spatial arrangement, and turnover rates of these successional stages may be critically important to the stability of lynx subpopulations.

We suspect that competition from other carnivores could mediate lynx-prey interactions (Chapter 4), and we know that generalist predators can alter the cyclic dynamics of prey populations. But we do not know how these variables are affected by forest fragmentation, nor how they affect lynx demography; we cannot parameterize the simplest model that we might construct of a lynx population. Without better empirical knowledge of the biology of the lynx-prey-vegetation system, these concepts and models can only guide us in the most general sense. Even so, they provide us with useful, and in some cases the only, guideposts on the path to scientific management of lynx.

Our uncertainty about the ecology of lynx, combined with the obviously complex interactions of cycling populations over an expansive assumed metapopulation structure, make the lynx-prey-vegetation system a complex ecological problem. Several recent conceptual developments, like source-sink and metapopulation theories, clearly have major implications for lynx populations in the contiguous United States; but without more empirical data and modeling efforts, we can only guess at what those are. We know remarkably little about the current status and numbers of lynx in the contiguous United States (Chapter 8). However, what little we know indicates that the subpopulations are not large. Until we better determine the current location and sizes of lynx sub-populations, it is unwise to assume that these populations can be reduced or further isolated without sharply increasing the risk of their individual and collective extinction.

Literature Cited

Beissinger, S. R. and M. I. Westphal. 1998. On the use of demographic models of population viability in endangered species management. Journal of Wildlife Management 62: 821-841.

Berger, J. 1990. Persistence of different-sized populations: an empirical assessment of rapid extinctions in bighorn sheep. Conservation Biology 4:91-98.

Blasius, B., A. Huppert, and L. Stone. 1999. Complex dynamics and phase synchronization in spatially extended ecological systems. Nature 399:354-359.

Boyce, M. S. 1992. Population viability analysis. Annual Review of Ecology and Systematics 23:481-506.

Buechner, M. 1987. A geometric model of vertebrate dispersal: tests and implications. Ecology 68:310-318.

Clark, B. K., D. W. Kaufman, G. A. Kaufman, E. J. Finck, and S. S. Hand. 1988. Long-distance movements by *Reithrodontomys megalotis* in tallgrass prairie. American Midland Naturalist 120:276-281.

Cockburn, A. M., P. Scott, and D. J. Scotts. 1985. Inbreeding avoidance and male-biased natal dispersal in *Antechinus* spp. (Marsupialia: Dasyuridae). Animal Behavior 33:908-915.

Cohen, D. and S. A. Levin. 1991. Dispersal in patchy environments: effects of temporal and spatial structure. Theoretical Population Biology 39:63-99.

Dickman, C. R. and C. P. Doncaster. 1989. The ecology of small mammals in urban habitats. II. Demography and dispersal. Journal of Animal Ecology 58:119-127.

Doebeli, M. 1995. Dispersal and dynamics. Theoretical population biology 47:82-106.

Elton, C. and M. Nicholson. 1942. The ten-year cycle in numbers of the lynx in Canada. Journal of Animal Ecology 11: 215-244.

Erlinge S., J. Agrell, J. Nelson, and M. Sandell. 1991. Why are some microtine rodent population cycles cyclic while others are not? Acta Theriologica 36:63-71.

Fahrig, L. 1992. Relative importance of spatial and temporal scales in a patchy environment. Theoretical Population Biology 41:300-314.

Frank, A. S. 1986. Dispersal polymorphisms in subdivided populations. Journal of Theoretical Biology 122:303-309.

Gaines, M. S. and L. R. McClenaghan, Jr. 1980. Dispersal in small mammals. Annual Reviews of Ecology and Systematics 11:163-196.

Gilpin, M. 1991. The genetic effective size of a metapopulation. Biological Journal of the Linnean Society 42:165-175.

Gilpin, M. E. and M. E. Soulé. 1986. Minimum viable populations: processes of species extinction. Pages 19-34 *in* M. E. Soulé, editor. Conservation biology. Sinauer Associates, Sunderland, MA.

Greenwood, P. J. 1980. Mating systems, philopatry and dispersal in birds and mammals. Animal Behavior 28: 1140-1162.

Gurney, W. S. C., A. R. Veitch, I. Cruickshank, and G. McGeachin. 1998. Circles and spirals: population persistence in a spatially explicit predator-prey model. Ecology 71: 2516-2530.

Haggerty, T. M. 1988. Aspects of the breeding biology and productivity of Bachman's sparrow in central Arkansas. Wilson Bulletin 100:247-255.

Hamilton, W. D. and R. M. May. 1977. Dispersal in stable habitats. Nature 269:578-581.

Hanski, I. 1982. Dynamics of regional distribution: the core and satellite species hypothesis. Oikos 38:210-221.

Hanski, I., L. Hansson, and H. Henttonen. 1991. Specialist predators, generalist predators, and the microtine rodent cycle. Journal of Animal Ecology 60:353-367.

Hanski, I., P. Turchin, E. Korpomaki, and H. Henttonen. 1993. Population oscillations of boreal rodents: regulation by mustelid predators leads to chaos. Nature 364:232-235.

Harrison, S. 1993. Metapopulations and conservation. Pages 111-128 *in* P. J. Edwards, R. M. May, and N. R. Webb, editors. Large scale ecology and conservation biology. Blackwell Scientific Publications, Boston.

Harrison S. and J. F. Quinn. 1989. Correlated environments and the persistence of metapopulations. Oikos 56:293-298.

Hastings, A. 1983. Can spatial variation alone lead to selection dispersal? Theoretical Population Biology 24:244-251.

Hobbs, N. T. and T. A. Hanley 1990. Habitat evaluation: do use/availability data reflect carrying capacity? Journal of Wildlife Management 54:515-521.

Holt, R. D. 1985. Population dynamics in two-patch environments: some anomalous consequences of an optimal habitat distribution. Theoretical Population Biology 28:181-208.

Howe, R. W., G. J. Davis, and V. Mosca. 1991. The demographic significance of 'sink' populations. Biological Conservation 57:239-255.

Krebs, C. J. 1994. Ecology: the experimental analysis of distribution and abundance. Harper Collins, New York.

Krebs, C. J. 1992. The role of dispersal in cyclic rodent populations. Pages 160-173 *in* N. C. Stenseth and W. Z. Lidicker, Jr., editors. Animal dispersal. Chapman & Hall, London.

Lamberson, R. H., B. R. Noon, C. Voss, and K. S. McKelvey. 1994. Reserve design for territorial species: the effects of patch size and spacing on the viability of the northern spotted owl. Conservation Biology 8:185-195.

Levin, S., D. Cohen, and A. Hastings. 1984. Dispersal strategies in patchy environments. Theoretical Population Biology 26: 165-191.

Levins, R. 1969. The effects of random variation of different types on population growth. Proceedings of the National Academy of Science 62:1061-1065.

Levins, R. 1970. Extinction. Lectures on Mathematics in the Life Sciences 2:75-107.

MacArthur, R. H. and E. O. Wilson. 1967. The theory of island biogeography. Volume 1. Monographs in population biology. Princeton Univ. Press, Princeton, NJ.

May, R. M. 1973. Stability in randomly fluctuating versus deterministic environments. American Naturalist 107:621-650.

Moss, R, D. A. Elston, and A. Watson. In press. Spatial asynchrony and demographic travelling waves during red grouse population cycles. Ecology.

O'Donoghue, M. 1997. Responses of coyotes and lynx to the snowshoe hare cycle. Ph. D. Dissertation, University of British Columbia, Canada.

Okubo, A. 1980. Diffusion and ecological problems: mathematical models. Springer-Verlag, New York.

Porter, J. H. and R. D. Dueser. 1989. A comparison of methods for measuring small-mammal dispersal by use of a Monte-Carlo simulation model. Journal of Mammalogy 70:783-793.

Pulliam, H. R. 1988. Sources, sinks, and population regulation. American Naturalist 132:652-661.

Pulliam, H. R. and B. J. Danielson 1991. Sources, sinks, and habitat selection: a landscape perspective on population dynamics. American Naturalist 137:S50-S66.

Pulliam, H. R., J. B. Dunning, and J. Liu. 1991. Population dynamics in complex landscapes: a case study. Ecological Applications 2:165-177.

Richter-Dyn N. and N. S. Goel. 1972. On the extinction of colonizing species. Theoretical Population Biology 3:406-33.

Ruggiero, L. F., G. D. Hayward, and J. R. Squires. 1994. Viability analysis in biological evaluations: concepts of population viability analysis, biological population, and ecological scale. Conservation Biology 8: 364-372.

Ruggiero, L. F., R. S. Holthausen, B. G. Marcot, K. B. Aubry, J. W. Thomas, and E. C. Meslow. 1988. Ecological dependency: the concept and its implications for research and management. Transactions of the Fifty-third North American Wildlife and Natural Resources Conference 53:115-126.

Saccheri, I., M. Kuussaari, M. Kankare, P. Vikman, W. Fortelius, and I. Hanski. 1998. Inbreeding and extinction in a butterfly metapopulation. Nature 392:491-494.

Shaffer, M. L. 1981. Minimum population sizes for species conservation. BioScience 31:131-134.

Shields, W. M. 1987. Dispersal and mating systems: investigating their causal connections. Pages 3-24 *in* B. D. Chepko-Sade and Z. T. Halpin, editors. Mammalian dispersal patterns. University of Chicago Press, Chicago, IL.

Shigesada, N. and K. Kawasaki. 1997. Biological invasions: theory and practice. Oxford University Press, New York.

Skellam, J. G. 1951. Random dispersal in theoretical populations. Biometrika 38:196-218.

Simberloff, D. 1989. Which insect introductions succeed and which fail? Pages 61-75 *in* J. A. Drake et al., editors. Biological Invasions: a Global Perspective. John Wiley and Sons.

Stenseth, N. C., W.,Falck, O. N. Bjornstad, and C. J. Krebs. 1997. Population regulation in snowshoe hare and Canadian lynx: asymmetric food web configurations between hare and lynx. Proceedings of the National Academy of Sciences of the USA 94: 5147-5152.

Van Horne, B. 1983. Density as a misleading indicator of habitat quality. Journal of Wildlife Management 47: 893-901.

Waser, P. M. 1985. Does competition drive dispersal? Ecology 66:1170-1175.

Chapter 3

Disturbance Ecology of North American Boreal Forests and Associated Northern Mixed/ Subalpine Forests

James K. Agee, College of Forest Resources
Box 352100, University of Washington, Seattle, WA 98195

Abstract—Disturbance dynamics differ in the three subregions of the North American boreal forest (taiga, western United States, and eastern United States) where lynx are found, resulting in a range of potential effects on lynx populations. Fire severity tends to be high in most of the forest types where lynx habitat occurs, although subsequent succession will differ among the subregions. Other disturbance dynamics involve insects, disease, wind, and human ownership and use, such as logging, mining, agriculture, and fire suppression. The author addresses three general lynx management implications based on disturbance dynamics.

Introduction

The distribution of the lynx in North America is closely associated with the distribution of the North American boreal forest. The range of the lynx extends south from the classic boreal forest zone, called the taiga, into the subalpine forests of the western United States, and the boreal/hardwood forest ecotone in the eastern United States (Chapter 8). This chapter summarizes the forest ecology of lynx habitat within the boreal zone of North America, including the effects of a variety of disturbance agents.

Divisions of the North American Boreal Forest

There are few, if any, forest classification schemes that have directly comparable boundaries for forest biomes. Criteria for classification often differ, and scientists often apply subjective rules. Even the acceptance of a zonal versus gradient classification spurs debate: Larsen (1980), in his classic treatment of the boreal ecosystem, describes the major types but favors a gradient approach so does not map his types. Yet of all the forest biomes, the boreal forest probably comes closest to a broadly accepted definition. The circumpolar boreal forest is commonly perceived as a set of homogeneous arboreal stands, dominated by conifers during later stages of succession, and by arboreal members of the birch and willow families in early succession. Many of the shrub species are circumpolar in distribution, but none of the tree species are (Solomon 1992). The northern border of the boreal forest is defined by tundra. While authors disagree slightly on where the boundary should be drawn along the gradient from closed-canopy forest to treeless tundra (Solomon 1992), this boundary is from one easily recognized type to another (Fig. 3.1). In North America, the southern boundary of the boreal forest is much more contentious, as the boreal forest changes to subalpine forest in the western continent, to prairie in mid-continent, and to a mixed coniferous/deciduous temperate forest in the east. These southern transitions are recognized in three broad groups, for the purposes of describing lynx habitat south of Canada, across an east-west gradient (map insert): Northeastern and the Great Lakes boreal forests that include eastern hardwoods and temperate conifers, as well as boreal conifers, and Western boreal forest, that includes subalpine forests similar to boreal forests.

Consistent and broadly recognized terminology is essential to effective presentation. I have chosen here to refer to the boreal forest as any forest with boreal features. This includes not only the taiga, but forests to the south such as the higher elevation portions of the Cascades, Sierra Nevada, and Rocky Mountains. Tree species are referred to by common name, with an appendix at the end of the chapter that includes Latin names; shrubs are mentioned by common and Latin name in the text. I have chosen here to refer to the northern boreal forest in general as taiga (e.g., Viereck 1983), with closed forest and the more open lichen-woodland as constituents. Other authors would disagree: taiga is variously defined as the "boreal forest" (Oechel and Lawrence 1985; Van Cleve et al. 1983) and "the great northern coniferous

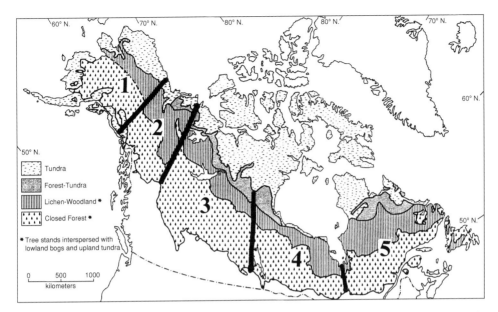

Figure 3.1—Major divisions of the taiga, patterned after Larsen (1980). Descriptions of each zone are in Table 3.1. 1 = Alaska; 2 = The Cordillera; 3 = Interior Forest; 4 = Canadian Shield; 5 = Eastern Canada.

biome" (Larsen 1980) but is also defined as only the northern part of the boreal forest representing that portion from closed forest canopy to the forest-tundra treeless boundary (Sirois 1992). The closed-canopy boreal forest has been called the "main boreal forest" (Hare 1969). To delineate boreal forest to the north from the transitional boreal zones to the south, the northern zone will be referred to as taiga, with closed and open subdivisions. The transitional boreal regions will be called, in the west, Western boreal forests, and in the east, either Great Lakes or Northeastern boreal forests, recognizing each has elements of boreal character.

The Physical Environment

The physical environment of the boreal forest is similar around the world. Unlike most other forest biomes, the boreal forest can be defined on the basis of structure as much as species composition (Hare and Ritchie 1972; Solomon 1992), and these structural characteristics are closely associated with climatic and edaphic factors (particularly permafrost). Climatic gradients across the type include decreasing radiation to the north, differing air mass trajectories that influence cloud cover and precipitation, topography, and maritime/continental location (Elliott-Fisk 1988). Long, bitterly cold winters, short and cool summers, and brief springs and autumns are characteristic of the boreal climate (Trewartha 1968). Although the growing season is short, unusually long summer days compensate to some extent for the brief and cool summers. These summer periods include times with low fuel moisture and strong winds, associated with severe fire behavior (Schroeder and Buck 1970).

The northern limit of treeline in the Arctic generally occurs along the 13° July isotherm. Boreal forest is bounded on the north by 30 or fewer days with mean temperature above 10°C, and to the south by 120 days with mean temperature above 10°C. Mean yearly temperatures increase from a minimum of –6.2°C near the forest tundra ecotone to 2.5°C near the southern closed boreal forest boundary. Precipitation is concentrated in the summer months, and snow cover lasts more than half the year. Although North American boreal winters are not as severe as those of Siberia (due to a smaller land mass), large parts of the region are permanently frozen, and the depth of thaw of the permafrost layer during the summer has a great effect on rooting depth and nutrient availability (Trewartha 1968; Van Cleve et al. 1983).

Western boreal forest is primarily subalpine rather than a classically boreal climate. Most of these areas border temperate forest at lower elevation and alpine communities at higher elevation. This is analogous to the much wider borders of the taiga with tundra to the north and temperate forest to the south. Western boreal forests are found at elevations above 1,400 m in Washington (Agee and Kertis 1987), but the rainshadow effect of the coastal mountains raises the elevations of all the forest zones to the east, so that boreal forest is found at 2,700 m elevation in the Colorado Front Range (Peet 1981). The elevation of the Western boreal zone may shift with climatic change or disturbance (Agee and Smith 1984; Rochefort et al. 1994). Western boreal forests generally receive more solar radiation and have higher diurnal temperature fluctuations and warmer temperatures, as well as shorter growing season day lengths, than classic boreal environments of the taiga (Oechel and Lawrence 1985). Local topographic variation makes climatic information difficult to generalize for Western boreal environments. Water stress may affect photosynthesis at some locations, and severe winter winds, carrying snow and soil particles, have a significant detrimental effect on plants that emerge above the snow line in timberline environments.

The Great Lakes and Northeastern boreal forests tend to be warmer than the taiga, with mean annual temperatures from 1.6 to 7.2°C (Rowe 1972). They tend to have more available moisture than either the taiga or the Western boreal forests (Rowe 1972).

Composition of the Major Boreal Forest Types

The Taiga

Within the broad structural classes of closed boreal forest and lichen woodland that comprise the taiga are geographic variants. As one travels east or west, continuous change is present although not obvious over short distances (Larsen 1980). Larsen classified the taiga into various regions from west to east (Table 3.1), with each region having a south-north gradient from the closed boreal forest on the south to lichen woodland to forest tundra (Fig. 3.1).

Rowe (1972) defined eight major forest regions in Canada: the taiga is by far the largest. He subdivides the taiga into three parts: a "predominately forest" type, equivalent to closed boreal forest, a "forest-grass" type which fringes the plains in southern Alberta, Saskatchewan, and Manitoba, and a "forest-barren" type, that borders the "predominately forest" type to the north and is transitional to tundra. He defines roughly 33 geographically based "forest sections" within the taiga, with white and black spruce common across the spectrum. Eastern larch, balsam fir, and jack pine are common in the eastern portions, and subalpine fir and lodgepole pine are more common in the west, particularly in the transition to subalpine forest. Although primarily coniferous, the taiga does include white birch and its

Table 3.1–Major forest regions of the taiga, adapted from Larsen (1980) and Elliott-Fisk (1988).

Region and description

1. Alaska
Upland and lowland forests dominated by white spruce, black spruce. Paper birch and quaking aspen are common pioneer species, with balsam poplar along streams and floodplains. Fire and permafrost important environmental factors.

2. The Cordillera
Mesophytic uplands dominated by white spruce and white birch. North aspects dominated by black spruce, with a different shrub understory. Southward, into the subalpine forest type, forest dominants are Engelmann spruce, subalpine fir, subalpine larch, and balsam poplar.

3. Interior Forest
This forest is composed of black spruce, white spruce, lodgepole pine, quaking aspen, and balsam poplar, extending from the Cordilleran foothills to the Canadian Shield. Black spruce is again common on north aspects, with white spruce typically dominant in the floodplains. The eastern portion of this zone also includes jack and/or lodgepole pine (ridges and sandy soils), and some eastern larch and balsam fir.

4. Canadian Shield
Both east and west of Hudson Bay, this forest is relatively uniform, with richer forests (more species) to the south. In the southerly regions, balsam fir/white spruce is dominant in valleys, with jack pine on uplands and black spruce in lowlands. To the north, black spruce, white spruce, and jack pine are common, with black spruce dominant near the northern forest border.

5. Eastern Canada
The Gaspe-Maritime forests are closely related to those of the Great Lakes—St.Lawrence region. Forests are primarily coniferous with balsam fir playing a prominent role; associated dominants are black spruce, white spruce, and paper birch. In Labrador-Ungava, black spruce and white spruce are often dominants, but balsam fir, eastern larch, paper birch, and balsam poplar are also found. Quaking aspen, jack pine, and white cedar are found to the south. Complex topography and geology has produced a complex mosaic of plant communities. Black spruce becomes more important to the north.

varieties, as well as quaking aspen and balsam poplar. The proportion of black spruce and eastern larch increases to the north. The eastern portion of the taiga includes an intermix of species that are summarized below under Great Lakes and Northeastern boreal forest. Viereck and Dyrness (1980) extend the taiga forest classification into Alaska and create a wide number of potential vegetation types aggregated into bottomland, lowland, and upland forests.

Great Lakes and Northeastern Boreal Forest

The boreal forests of the Great Lakes and Northeast are southern extensions of boreal forest. These forests, as transitional types from boreal to temperate forest, are not well described in either the boreal forest (Elliott-Fisk 1988) or the deciduous forest (Greller 1988) descriptions of the North American terrestrial vegetation (Barbour and Billings 1988). While having the boreal species, this heterogeneous type also has many elements of the forests to the south (Pastor and Mladenoff 1992). Balsam fir is an important species, and appears to replace white spruce in an ecological sense. White pine, white cedar, and white birch are all more "important" than white spruce. Three species of *Populus* and three maples are also important members of the community. Black spruce and eastern larch are found in lowlands and nutrient poor sites (Larsen 1980). The distribution of both the Great Lakes and Northeastern boreal forest (map insert) closely resembles the range maps for balsam fir and black spruce (Fig. 3.2).

Balsam fir and northern white cedar are more important as soil moisture increases, with white pine and white spruce decreasing in importance. Sugar maple is important on mesic sites and jack pine, black spruce, and eastern hemlock distributions are bimodal, peaking at the extremes of the moisture gradient (Maycock and Curtis 1960; Pastor and Mladenoff 1992). Many of the understory species are circumpolar, but for trees, only genera are circumpolar, with significant species differences between the northern and southern parts of the mixed forest type.

In Wisconsin, the boreal forest can be divided into three somewhat distinct types: first, old stands of pure conifers with balsam fir and white spruce as major dominants, along with eastern white pine, red pine, or white cedar; associated hardwoods are paper birch, mountain ash, red maple, and mountain maple. Second, in mixed conifer-hardwood stands, found on inland mesic sites, shade tolerant hardwoods slowly replace the conifers; and third, dense stands of balsam fir or white spruce replacing a decadent canopy of white birch or aspen, with occasional balsam poplar (Curtis 1959). Some of these divisions represent successional sequences more than environmental heterogeneity.

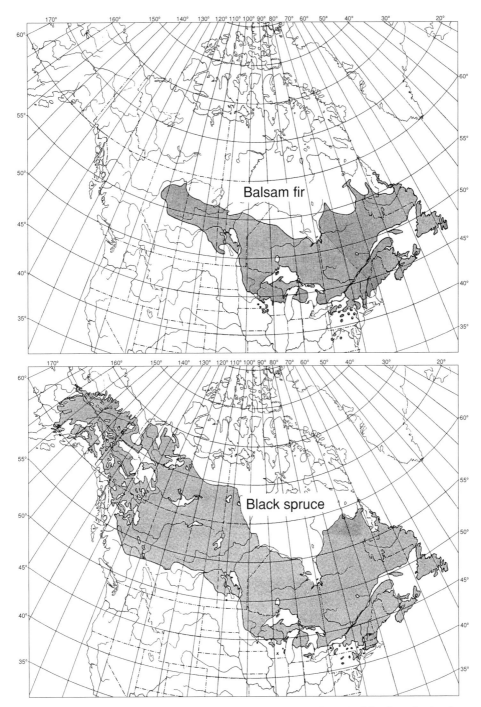

Figure 3.2—The ranges of balsam fir and black spruce (Little 1971) south of the Canadian border closely parallel the distribution of boreal forest in the Great Lakes and Northeast.

Western Boreal Forests

The extension of boreal features into the subalpine forests of the western United States where lynx are found is a southern modification of the boreal conifer forests, which are similar floristically and structurally (Peet 1988). Engelmann spruce, subalpine fir, and lodgepole pine, the primary dominants across the Western boreal forest, are genetically similar to, and sometimes hybridize with, the northern boreal species white spruce, balsam fir, and jack pine. Each species of the first group (Peet 1988) is genetically heterogeneous, and it is thought that the more genetically homogeneous boreal species of each pair may be derived from the more heterogeneous one (Taylor 1959; Parker et al. 1981; Critchfield 1985). North of about 54°N latitude, white spruce replaces Engelmann spruce. As one moves south, white spruce occurs at lower elevations than Engelmann spruce and hybridizes with it (Peet 1988). Boreal habitat becomes more fragmented to the south, with the Colorado Rockies separated from similar habitat in Utah and northwestern Wyoming (Findley and Anderson 1956).

The Western boreal forests where lynx habitat has historically occurred (map insert) are surprisingly uniform in their tree species composition: Engelmann spruce, subalpine fir, and lodgepole pine are found across the range. At the western edge of these relatively cold and dry forests, maritime influences allow mountain hemlock to be found on protected sites (Arno and Hammerly 1984; Agee and Kertis 1987). At timberline in the west, whitebark pine and subalpine larch replace spruce and fir (Arno and Habeck 1972). In Colorado, limber pine is a timberline species on xeric sites (Peet 1981; Veblen 1986), but across these subalpine forests, both Engelmann spruce and subalpine fir can be found to the margin of alpine tundra.

Other western boreal forests apparently do not support lynx. The boreal zones of the western Cascades of Washington and the Olympic Peninsula contain subalpine fir, but are dominated by Pacific silver fir and mountain hemlock. Winter snow often exceeds 3 m depth (Franklin and Dyrness 1973). The Oregon Cascades boreal zone has mountain hemlock and lodgepole pine mixed with noble fir, and noble fir is replaced by red fir in the southern Oregon Cascades. In the California Sierra Nevada, lodgepole pine and red fir constitute the primary boreal forest species. The winter snow accumulation can be quite deep in these areas, too (Barbour and Woodward 1985). In the southern Rocky Mountains, the boreal zone becomes a series of disjunct and isolated "islands" of mountaintops separated by wide areas of woodland or nonforest vegetation.

Boreal Forest Disturbance Dynamics

Disturbance is common in boreal forests. In fact, the taiga has been referred to as a "disturbance forest" because of the ubiquitous nature of fire (Rowe 1961). Fires and insect epidemics are both major disturbance processes. Fire frequencies can range from 50 to 250 years (Viereck 1973; Heinselman 1981). Fire return intervals are longer (up to 500 years) in the Northeastern boreal forest (Foster 1983) and in some of the Western boreal forests (Romme and Knight 1981). Spruce beetles have killed white spruce across wide areas of south-central Alaska (Werner and Holsten 1983) and Engelmann spruce in the subalpine forests of the lower 48 states. Spruce budworm has been a major defoliating disturbance in eastern Canada and the northeastern United States (Blais 1968).

Forests are dynamic systems, and within a forest ecosystem, the only constant is change. For forest trees, change occurs through tree growth and death, and for boreal forest trees, natural disturbance has been a major factor in terminating the life of trees. There are a number of natural disturbance factors, including insects, wind, disease, and fire, but it is generally recognized that fire and insects were the most important disturbances across the boreal landscape. The *process* of disturbance creates variability in forest *pattern*, and it clearly varies in frequency by forest type. Landscape pattern over time will depend on whether the processes are *cyclic* or *stochastic*, and whether *equilibrium* or *non-equilibrium* systems result.

Cyclic and Stochastic Properties of Disturbance

Editor's note: Elements of the following disussion were drawn from a fire training lesson plan written by Kevin McKelvey, USDA Forest Service, Missoula, MT.

Any forest stand has a probability that a disturbance will enter and kill the trees in the stand. The nature of the probabilistic process can either be *cyclic* or *stochastic*, independent of the actual probability of disturbance. Consider a coin with heads (H) and tails (T) as the only possible outcomes. If it is turned alternatively from side to side, it will create a pattern of HTHTHT, etc. The probability, p, is 0.5 for a head or a tail. This is a cyclic process, as it is very regular and predictable. If the coin is flipped in the air, the probability for a head or tail remains 0.5, but the pattern might be HHTTTH, so that subsequent tosses might produce runs of heads or tails. This is a stochastic process, even though the probability of head or tail is exactly the same as the cyclic process.

Now consider the distribution of forest stand ages as a cyclic or deterministic process (Fig. 3.3). The even-aged, area-regulated managed forest is a

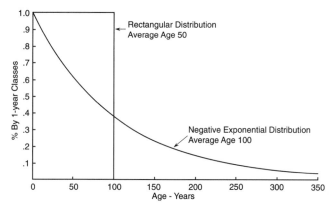

Figure 3.3—Comparison of a cyclic age class distribution (the regulated forest) with a stochastic age class distribution (the negative exponential) (from Van Wagner 1978).

prime example of a cyclic system (assuming that natural disturbances are eliminated). The probability of age class x moving to age class $x + 1$ is one ($p = 1.0$), and the probability of being "recycled" to age 0 is zero ($p = 0$, assuming that all disturbances are controlled), until the rotation age is reached, at which time the stand is cut and it moves to age class 0 with $p = 1$. Forest stands operating under a cyclic process will have a rectangular age class distribution, truncated at the rotation age (R). The average stand age is $R/2$, and there are no stands older than R.

Forests can also be "regulated" by stochastic processes. Boreal forests are the classic example of a natural forest regulated by fire acting in a stochastic manner (Van Wagner 1978; Johnson and Van Wagner 1985). The probability of any stand being burned in a given year is low, described by p. The probability of a stand of age x moving to age $x + 1$ is then $(1 - p)$. If this process is carried out for a long time, then a negative exponential distribution like that shown in Figure 3.3 will result. The frequency of any age class x is

$$f(x) = pe^{-px}$$

This distribution assumes that the ignition pattern is random, that the area burned per year is roughly constant, and that stands of all ages are equally likely to burn (constant flammability). The average stand age is $1/p$, or C, and this is commonly called the fire cycle. Roughly one-third of the stands are older than the average stand age, and there is no maximum age for a stand, in contrast to the distribution created by cyclic processes. Of course, the number of older stands is small, and they are likely to be affected by disease or insects if protected from fire, but this disturbance is usually at a finer grain than the landscape effects of fire. Another useful feature of this distribution is that if the proportion of the landscape above or below a certain age x is known, the entire age-class distribution can be defined:

$$\sum f(x) = 1 - e^{-px}$$

where $\sum f(x)$ is the proportion of all age classes up to age x. The negative exponential model is simple and has a number of appealing characteristics (Rowe 1983). For example, about one-third of the stands are older than the mean age, or fire cycle, so that if structural characters by stand age are known, then habitat character can be inferred, although non-spatially, just by knowing the fire cycle.

The major criticism of the negative exponential model is its assumption of equal flammability of stands over time. Johnson and Van Wagner (1985) show that the negative exponential model is a simple case of the Weibull distribution where flammability, the shape parameter of the model, c, is constant at $c = 1$. Other options for flammability in the Weibull model are monotonic increases ($c > 1$) or decreases ($c < 1$) of flammability with stand age.

Stochastic models have become popular for describing fire history in a variety of forest types (Table 3.2; also, Lesica 1996). There is an implicit assumption that the fire regime is constant over time such that the age class data represent an ecosystem in equilibrium. Attempts have been made to disaggregate the age class data to analyze changes in fire frequency over time, and these are discussed below. The notions of stochasticity and equilibrium are relevant to the stability of adequate habitat over time for both lynx and its prey.

Landscape Equilibria

If a given cyclic or stochastic process remains constant over time, then an equilibrium landscape is eventually produced, and the shape of the age-class distribution will remain constant over time, although quite different between the cyclic and stochastic models. However, if the probabilities of disturbance change over time, then a non-equilibrium state is introduced which may "ripple" through the age class distribution as a "blip," or if the probabilities of disturbance are continually changing, there may be no predictable range of variability for any age class or the age class distribution as a whole. Assumptions about disturbance probabilities will have major implications for the management of lynx habitat.

Equilibrium is in part a function of scale, that in a cartographic sense decreases as the considered area increases. As scale decreases, the total area becomes larger, more fires will occur, and the average fire size as a proportion of the total landscape declines. As this occurs, the assumptions necessary to

Table 3.2–Fire frequency in the boreal forest. Each set is arranged west to east.

Biome and forest type	Fire return interval	Location[a]	Type of record[b]
	Yrs	- - - Citation - - -	
Taiga (closed forest only)			
Black spruce	49	Porcupine River, AK (1) (Yarie 1979)	Stand ages - NE, W
Black spruce	200	Alaska (1) (Viereck 1983)	Fire records
Black spruce	100	N. British Columbia (2) (Smith and Henderson 1970)	Stand ages
Subboreal black/white spruce	125	N. British Columbia (2)	BC Forest Service
Subboreal pine-spruce	150	(Bunnell 1995)	estimates
Subboreal spruce	125		
Spruce willow-birch	175		
Jack pine	30-70	Mackenzie River (2-3)	Stand ages
Black spruce	80-90	(Rowe et al. 1974)	
White spruce	300+		
Black spruce and others	130	S. Quebec (5) (Cogbill 1985)	
Black spruce	500	SE Labrador (5) (Foster 1983)	Fire scars, reports, air photos
Western boreal forest			
Subalpine fir	109-137	North Cascades (Agee et al. 1990)	Stand ages - NFR
Subalpine fir	250	Pasayten, WA (Fahnestock 1976)	Stand ages
Spruce-fir	250	British Columbia (Bunnell 1995)	Stand ages
Whitebark pine	30-300	N. Rocky Mtns. (Arno 1980, 1986) (Arno and Peterson 1983) (Morgan and Bunting 1990)	Fire scars
Spruce-fir	300-350	Yellowstone (Romme 1982)	Stand ages
Spruce-fir/upland	300	Medicine Bow, WY	Stand ages
Spruce-fir/drainages	300+	(Romme and Knight 1981)	
Spruce-fir	202	Colorado (Veblen et al. 1994)	Stand ages-NFR
Great Lakes boreal forest			
Northern pines	22	Itasca State Park, MN Frissell (1973)	Fire scars
Northern pines	100	BWCA Minnesota (Heinselman 1973)	Stand ages-NFR
Northern pines	50	BWCA, Minnesota[c] (Van Wagner 1978)	Stand ages - NE
Mixed forest	50-100	S. Ontario (Alexander and Euler 1981)	Stand ages
Northeastern boreal forest			
Red spruce/hemlock/pine	230	New Brunswick (Wein and Moore 1977)	–
Mixed Forest	200	Nova Scotia (Wein and Moore 1979)	–
Mixed forest	800	NE Maine (Lorimer 1977)	Land survey records

[a] Numbers 1-5 at taiga locations refer to Larsen's (1980) general subdivisions of the taiga summarized in Table 3.1 and Figure 3.1.
[b] NFR = natural fire rotation method; NE = negative exponential; W = Weibull; blank = estimate that may or may not be quantitative.
[c] The Heinselman and Van Wagner estimates use the same data but different techniques.

apply a model such as the negative exponential become more reasonable, and equilibrium landscape conditions are therefore more plausible. What is an appropriate scale? The scale must be such that fire is not "episodic" and individual fires do not burn "large" proportions of the landscape. Because individual fires can burn thousands of hectares, the total area necessary to consider can be quite large. The minimum equilibrium landscape size, called the "minimum dynamic area" (Pickett and Thompson 1978), contains representative age classes of the major stages of succession and will depend on the historic fire size distribution. The Yellowstone National Park, USA, landscape (2+ million acres) is a good example of a non-equilibrium landscape. It is a broad subalpine plateau that rarely burns, but much of it burned in the early 1700s (Romme 1982). The forest age classes created by those early fires created a very large age class that moved as a "wave" through the age class distribution over time, so that much of the park's forest became old growth by the late 20th century, with lodgepole pine being replaced by subalpine fir on many sites. In 1988, the large fires that burned the national park killed much of the old growth age class, as well as stands of younger ages, too, and much of the park forest is now (1999) in the 10-year-old age class, which may move as a similar age class "wave" in the future or be broken up by other non-equilibrium fires. Obviously, for the past 300 years, and now for centuries to come, the Yellowstone forests have not and will not possess any equilibrium age class structure. If larger subalpine areas of the Rockies are considered, fire may well be more an equilibrium-maintaining process at that scale, particularly if topography is broken so that individual fires cannot burn large proportions of the landscape in any year.

Attempts to quantify changes in fire regimes using stochastic models is a work in progress. Johnson and Larsen (1991) developed a graphical technique to evaluate changes in slope of cumulative age class distributions over time. It has been criticized on three grounds: (1) different analysts would draw the subjectively placed "breaks in slope" of the lines in different places; (2) the use of empirical, sampled age class data effectively "censors" the oldest age classes and this "missing tail" of the distribution imparts a false trend to the graphical technique (Finney 1995); and (3) the actual standing age distribution, rather than the cumulative age class distributions, should be used to estimate the time-since-fire (survivorship) distribution (Huggard and Arnesault, in review). Most studies have incorrectly used the former rather than the latter distribution. The use of stochastic models remains a technique in development yet will remain important in analyzing disturbance in the boreal forest. For example, Ratz (1995) built a spatial simulation model and tested the flammability assumptions of the Weibull model. He found that an increasing flammability with time ($c > 1$) fit real data sets from

Alberta (Eberhart and Woodard 1987) better than a constant flammability assumption.

Equilibrium models have been criticized on the basis that past climate change, in the presence of long-lived conifers, results in no single "natural" cycle expressed by age-class distributions on a landscape. The landscape mosaic is a reflection of a dynamic fire cycle and carries the memory of different past fire cycles (Johnson et al. 1998). Yet time-since-fire distributions necessary to draw such inference are rare, and the influence of climate change on disturbance frequency is difficult to estimate. These criticisms apply to setting the parameters, or form, of the models over time, more than a rejection of the models. Although climate change is likely to affect fire activity, the direction of the change is uncertain. Flannigan and Van Wagner (1991) projected an increase in fire activity across boreal landscapes with future global warming, while Flannigan et al. (1998) now suggest less fire activity in these landscapes with global warming.

The application of a concept such as landscape equilibrium implies that within limits, the forest landscape does possess equilibrium properties at some scale, yet we should be using such models to consider alternative states that might be more realistic. Such models might be best thought of as operational than actual, a way to conceptualize approaches to managing a landscape more than prescribing a precise equilibrium landscape as a desired future condition.

Forest Fire Regimes

A fire regime is a generalized picture of the role fire plays in an ecosystem (Agee 1993). It is often simpler to describe the fire regime than to infer its effects on stand or landscape attributes, but the fire regime is clearly the starting point. Most of what we know about the fire regime of the boreal forest has been published in the last 25 years.

Fire Frequency and Variability—The fire frequency in forests where lynx habitat occurs varies by over an order of magnitude. Average fire return intervals using a variety of methods have been estimated for the taiga, as well as the Western, Great Lakes, and Northeastern boreal forests (Table 3.2). Variation is partly due to the method employed; for example, in the Great Lakes boreal forest, the Boundary Water Canoe Area estimates of 50 and 100 years use the same data but different analysis techniques. Nevertheless, useful trends emerge from these studies.

In the taiga, there is a trend of increasing fire return intervals (FRI) from west to east. The drier, continental portions of the closed forests have shorter FRIs than the more mesic eastern maritime boreal forests. Within local areas, ridgetops or sandy soil areas tend to have shorter FRI than bottomlands. The

Western boreal forests, with FRI ranging from 150-300 years, have generally longer FRI than the taiga, where FRIs tend to range from 50-150 years. Western boreal timberline variants such as whitebark pine, or isolated boreal "islands" surrounded by lower elevation types (Agee et al. 1990), may have shorter FRI. The Great Lakes boreal forest FRIs appear to be similar to the boreal forest to the north. The Northeastern boreal forest, with a greater maritime influence, tends to have longer FRIs, with fire becoming less important than wind and insects in coastal areas (Heinselman 1981) and to the north (Payette et al. 1989).

Fire Spread and Intensity—Fire intensity tends to be high in most of the forest types where lynx habitat is found. This creates conditions for extensive even-aged patches of regenerating conifer forest to occur. In boreal forest, fast-spreading, high-intensity fires are the ones that burn most of the area (Van Wagner 1983). Sustained fire spread rates over a day of 100 m/min with intensities of 50,000-100,000 kW/m (flame lengths of 13-18 m) have been measured (Kiil and Grigel 1969). Van Wagner (1983) summarizes the fire behavior in northern mixed and boreal forests. These fires spread during unusual weather conditions (e.g., Johnson and Wowchuck 1993) and under those conditions are essentially unmanageable. In the Great Lakes and Northeastern boreal forest, and portions of the Western boreal forests, fire behavior also tends to be intense (Lorimer 1977; Romme 1982; Agee 1993). The portions of southern boreal forests where lynx have not historically been found tend to have a more mixed fire intensity and a moderate-severity fire regime (Agee 1993). These may be more open timberline environments, such as the western boreal forest with whitebark pine, or lower elevation forest with more fire-tolerant conifers.

Although crown fires are common, fires of lower intensity do occur in boreal forests where lynx historically occurred, although they typically are a small proportion of the total fire area. Where trees with tall crowns or sufficiently thick bark occur (such as red, white, or jack pine), some residual trees may be expected (Johnson 1992). In areas where fuels are limited due to site conditions, moderate intensity fires may occur and multi-aged stands may result (Heinselman 1981; Gauthier et al. 1993; Roberts and Mallik 1994). Some isolated stands on poor soils may have non-serotinous forms of jack pine and all-aged pine structure (Conkey et al. 1995). Generally, fires in the taiga, Great Lakes and Northeastern boreal forests and the Western boreal forests are stand replacement events, either because of typically severe fire behavior or the inability of the trees to survive even moderate intensity events; these fires set the stage for open-grown regeneration. The succesional dynamics of post-fire seres are discussed in this chapter in section "Successional Patterns After Disturbance."

Different forest types have differing propensities to burn (Van Wagner 1983): jack and lodgepole pines have high flammability throughout the season; black spruce forest is less prone to surface fire but supports crown fire when weather conditions are severe; aspen and birch are highly flammable in spring when their litter layers are exposed and can dry quickly, but all hardwood stands are less flammable in summer because their shaded litter layers are compact and their crowns do not support crown fire; and lowland forests require a longer drought to become flammable than upland forests of pine or spruce.

Fire Extent and Patchiness—Fires in the taiga, as with most high-severity fire regimes (Agee 1998b), can become quite large. A typical pattern is to have the frequency of fire sizes skewed to the smaller fires while area burned is skewed to the larger fires (Fig. 3.4) (Foster 1983; Payette et al. 1989; Hunter 1993). A small number of fires is associated with the majority of the area burned; therefore, while average patch size created by fires is small, the landscape area is dominated by the less frequent but much larger patches. Topographic barriers in the taiga are often absent and severe weather conditions may drive the fires for days or weeks. Many fires may reach 50,000 ha, and fires of >200,000 ha are possible (Viereck 1983). In the maritime region of Northeastern boreal forests, fires of 80,000 ha have been recorded (Lorimer 1977). Where terrain is more heterogeneous, either because of mountains or lakes, fire spread may be interrupted (Bergeron 1991; Dansereau and Bergeron 1993; Bergeron et al. 1997). Average fire size in the Great Lakes boreal forest is about 360 ha (Baker 1994), but the average is a poor descriptor of the distribution. Heinselman's (1973) fire maps of the Boundary Waters Canoe Area in Minnesota show many fires that appear to have been stopped at lake edges. In Western boreal forests, fires may be quite large where few fire barriers are present (e.g., the Yellowstone Plateau) but in many areas the boreal zone abuts rock, alpine vegetation, ridgetops, or other barriers to limit fire size (Agee 1993).

Most fire studies have concentrated on disturbed areas, so that little is known about residual vegetation around and within the fires that may contribute substantial patchiness to the burn. Eberhart and Woodard's (1987) study of large fires in Alberta evaluated fires more than 20 ha in size and found that the unburned island area, shape index, and edge index increased with fire size (Table 3.3). Although the number of islands per 100 ha declined for the largest fires (E3), the unburned island area of this fire size class was much larger than for the other fire size classes. These islands covered less than 5% of the interior area of the fire. In interior Alaska, a 1985 fire had about 6% of its area in unburned islands (Paragi et al. 1997). Unburned area may occur because of higher foliar moisture, terrain, or

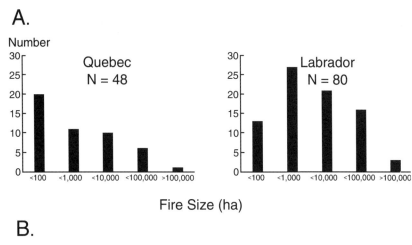

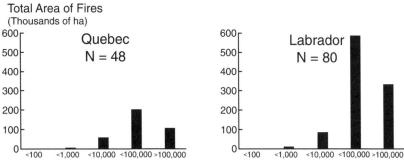

Figure 3.4—Typical patterns of frequencies of boreal fire sizes and area burned by fire size. A. Size-frequency distributions of fires in Quebec and Labrador. B. Total area of fires in each size class shown in A (from Hunter 1993).

Table 3.3–Mean values of percent disturbed area, median island area, number of islands per 100 ha, fire shape index, and edge index by fire size class for large fires in northern Alberta, 1970-83 (Eberhart and Woodard 1987). No similar data are available south of the Canadian border.

	Fire size class[a]				
Variable	C	D	E_1	E_2	E_3
% disturbed area	100.0	99.3	96.3	96.6	94.8
No. of islands/100 ha	0.0	0.38	0.96	0.87	0.39
Median island area (ha)	–	2.29	2.50	2.59	9.39
Fire shape index[b]	1.79	2.40	2.36	2.96	3.78
Edge index[b]	2.17	3.29	3.48	5.11	7.47

[a] Fire size class: C = 20-40 ha; D = 41-200 ha; E_1 = 201-400 ha; E_2 = 401-2,000 ha; E_3 = 2,001-20,000 ha.
[b] Shape index is calculated as total exterior fire perimeter divided by the perimeter of a circle of equal area to the fire. Edge index is similarly calculated but perimeters of all islands are added to the exterior fire perimeter.

changes in fire weather such as a major wind shift. These unburned areas are also known as stringers (Quirk and Sykes 1971) or fire skips (Hunter 1993). In the boreal forests south of the Canadian border, little is known of the distribution of residual patches. Because lynx may be able to den in small patches of old growth, the presence of small fire skips may be critical for lynx habitat. In British Columbia, DeLong (1998) showed for the "dry cool boreal" and "moist very cold subalpine" forest types, transitional between taiga and Western boreal forest, that 40-60% of the area burned is in patches greater than 1,000 ha, and 60-85% in patches greater than 250 ha in size.

Fire Seasonality and Synergistic Effects—The major fire seasons vary across the boreal forest. In Alaska taiga, May, June, and July are the major fire months (Viereck 1983), with the latter part of June and early July the critical time (Barney 1971). Throughout much of the rest of the boreal forest, including the Western boreal forest, July and August are the months with the largest area burned (Johnson and Wowchuck 1993). Some fires that begin early in the season have the potential to burn into September, although most do not (Johnson 1992; Despain 1990).

Synergistic disturbance effects are defined as increased probability of one disturbance given the occurrence of another. A number of authors have suggested that spruce budworm-killed balsam fir may increase fire hazard, and refer to the Miramachi fire of 1825 in New Brunswick (Furyaev et al. 1983). Although most hurricanes lose strength before reaching the Northeastern boreal forest, these eastern seaboard hurricanes clearly create excessive fuel hazards from the creation of dead fuel from the windblown trees. Lorimer (1977) suggests a large fire in 1803 in northern Maine was fueled by a large blowdown that occurred within the previous decade. Surface fuels, and therefore fire hazard, will accumulate any time there is canopy mortality, but the hazard may exist for a short window of time. In Western boreal forest, Veblen et al. (1994) suggest that fires essentially "block out" spruce beetles for many decades until the trees in the recovering stands reach a size suitable for the beetles to attack. Conversely, Bergeron and Leduc (1998) suggested that when fire return intervals lengthen, basal area loss due to spruce budworm will increase because of the proportional increase in budworm-susceptible balsam fir in these stands.

Other Natural Forest Disturbances

Forest Insects—The history of major insect outbreaks in the boreal forest is more difficult to track than the history of forest fire. Insects may kill only one species in a mixed stand, and they may remove either early successional (pine beetle on pines) or late successional (budworms on firs) species. While fires usually thin a stand from below (kill smallest trees first, with the largest, thickest barked trees left), insects often take the largest trees and thin the stand from above. There are clearly some boreal forest areas where insects have a significant history as a disturbance agent, primarily where fire return intervals either are very long on average or an unusually long fire-free period has occurred. In Alaska taiga, spruce beetles have killed substantial white spruce (Werner and Holsten 1983). Spruce budworm appears to have a major effect on white spruce in the southern taiga, reducing the importance of spruce in late successional forests (Bergeron and Dubuc 1989). During the 1910-1920s outbreak, it is estimated that 40-50% of the total balsam fir volume in eastern Canada was killed (Furyaev et al. 1983).

In the Northeastern boreal forest, spruce budworm has defoliated balsam fir in outbreaks that have traced back over previous centuries (Blais 1968; Lorimer 1977). The most recent outbreak has occurred from 1970 to the early 1980s (Kettela 1983). Once a local outbreak exceeds a certain size, it can become self-propagating and spread much like a wildfire but more slowly (Holling 1992). Occasional spruce beetle epidemics have caused considerable mortality in red spruce stands (Hopkins 1901). In 1985, the boreal forest types of the northeastern United States had about 45% of the area in "light" damage (less than 10% dead trees), 28% of the area in "moderate" damage (11-30% dead trees), and 27% of the area in "heavy" (more than 30% dead trees) damage classes (Miller-Weeks and Smoronk 1993).

Significant insects of Western boreal forests are those that attack lodgepole pine (mountain pine beetle), Engelmann spruce (spruce beetle), and subalpine fir. While spruce budworm can become epidemic on lower elevation firs (Douglas-fir, grand fir) in the West (Swetnam and Lynch 1993; Despain 1990), it is less important in the subalpine zone, although it does attack subalpine fir and white spruce in the boreal zone (Van Sickle 1995). Lodgepole pine becomes more susceptible to mountain pine beetle as it ages, and a beetle attack will allow understory spruce and fir to release ingrowth (Agee 1993; Veblen et al. 1994). Where recent beetle attack has occurred, surface fuels will increase, but a fire is not necessarily guaranteed. Despain (1990) suggests that the loss of crown fuels reduces crown fire risk at the same time that surface fuels increase.

The spruce beetle attacks Engelmann spruce, and the additional surface fuels from this mortality have been implicated in severe fires in riparian zones (Agee 1998b). In Colorado, the return interval for spruce beetle is estimated at 116 years (Veblen et al. 1994). Attacks were dated by analyzing growth releases on firs and spruces too small to be attacked, indicating that beetle attacks in mixed species stands are usually not stand-destroying events like intense wildfires.

The dynamics of insect outbreaks are very complex. Although we may predict that older stands with target species of minimum size are more at risk than younger stands, the triggers for outbreaks are not well understood. Pine beetles often become epidemic during drought periods (Despain 1990), but western spruce budworm often irrupts during periods of above-normal precipitation (Swetnam and Lynch 1993).

Disease and Wind—Forest ecosystems are affected by a wide variety of natural disturbances. We typically concentrate on the most important ones for a given forest type, such as fire or insects. Diseases are often ignored because they generally operate at long timeframes, and mortality may be gradual or associated with crown dieback (Hawksworth and Shigo 1980). Agents such as wind often remove the trees before they break or fall over from stem or root rot. Windsnap and windthrow can be important disturbances (Coutts and Grace 1995), but severe events are often widely spaced in time and not easily reconstructed. In boreal forests, wind as a disturbance event is poorly understood. There is little evidence that windthrow is a significant disturbance in the mature taiga.

In the Northeastern and Great Lakes boreal forest, wind can be a significant disturbance, especially for those types that burn infrequently (Canham and Loucks 1984; Seymour and Hunter 1992). Most frequently, small gaps are created in the Great Lakes boreal forest, with an annual gap creation rate of 1% of the forest area per year (Runkle 1982; Mladenoff 1987). Although catastrophic events may occur only once a millennium, these extreme events can alter forest dynamics over wide areas. In July 1977, about 15,000 ha of forest in eastern Minnesota and northern Wisconsin were devastated by a windstorm (Loucks 1983). The historic (1834-1873 era) forest patch blowdown size distribution in hemlock-hardwood forest of Wisconsin (excluding the southern, mature forests of the state) ranged from 1 to 6,000 ha with a mean size of 160 ha and median size of 30 ha (Loucks 1983). In these mature hemlock-hardwood forests, wind may be a more significant disturbance factor than fire (Canham and Loucks 1984). At least one large windthrow event occurred in northern Maine early in the 19th century (Lorimer 1977), but its effects were variable and localized. In New England, high-elevation balsam fir forests have a wave-like pattern largely due to persistent effects of wind on the forest (Sprugel 1976).

In the Western boreal forest, however, wind has profound physiological effects across open areas. Severe winter winds can retard succession above the winter snow line by abrading and desiccating foliage that emerges (Hadley and Smith 1983). In contrast to this annual disturbance, less frequent but powerful windstorms can result in large blowdown patches in western boreal forests, occasionally greater than 5,000 ha (Knight 1994).

Land Ownership and Land Use History

Land ownership patterns and the history of land use vary considerably over the boreal forest, and particularly in the three areas of potential lynx habitat south of the Canadian border. This affects not only the condition of the land today but a variety of challenges in terms of future habitat management.

The Taiga—Much of the northern boreal forest habitat has been less affected by modern human influence than boreal forests to the south (Johnson et al. 1998). Low timber productivity, difficult access, and distance from markets has kept much of the boreal forest from being logged in the past, except around settlements. Fire suppression has been of limited effectiveness for the same reasons: values protected have been low, access for firefighters and equipment is poor, and even fire-detection capability is limited. The southern taiga has likely been affected more than the northerly parts, but in general, less modern human influence is detectable in the taiga than in the boreal forest types of the contiguous United States.

The Northeast Boreal Forest—European settlement in the Northeastern forest began in the early 1600s, and white pine was selectively harvested soon thereafter (Ferguson and Longwood 1960). Eastern hemlock was cut, its bark stripped for tanning purposes, and the logs left behind. Spruce was also selectively removed, and the pine and spruce harvest peaked in the 1850-1900 period (Ferguson and Longwood 1960). Pulp markets for hardwoods developed after 1900. The history of selective harvest for favored species (Barrett 1962) to some extent mirrored the pattern of natural disturbances by insects (particularly spruce budworm and spruce beetle) and wind. Stand-replacing harvests, like stand-replacing natural disturbances, were not the most common event (Seymour and Hunter 1992).

Forest lands were also cleared for agriculture. Land clearing and farming reached a peak in the mid-1800s. By 1880, forest covered only 27% of Connecticut, 74% of Maine, 40% of Massachusetts, 50% of New Hampshire, 34% of Rhode Island, and 35% of Vermont (Barrett 1962). Since that time, there has been a gradual increase in forest land in all of these states. Maine is now 87% forested (Ferguson and Longwood 1960) and Vermont is now 70% forested (Klyza and Trombulak 1994), in various stages of succession.

The forest today is somewhat different in character than it once was. Seymour and Hunter (1992) suggest at least three major differences. First, there appears to be less old growth, and in this boreal forest type old growth was more common than to the north because of extended natural disturbance intervals. Once-favored species such as eastern white pine and red spruce are less common, and recent land-use practices such as clearcutting are imprinting a new landscape pattern. These land use practices are symptomatic of concerns about the future of what is locally called the "Northern Forest."

The Northeastern forest area has the least amount of publicly owned forest of the three boreal forest areas south of the Canadian border. In Maine, for example, only 1-2% of the forest land is publicly owned, with 38% in forest industry ownership and about 60% in non-industrial ownership (Ferguson and Longwood 1960). The percentage of industrial forest ownership in Maine is the highest of the Northeastern states. In the Northeast, timberland area has continued to increase (about 9% since 1952), but ownership patterns suggest that fragmentation is also occurring. In 1958, about 25% of the land base of Maine was in ownerships less than 40 ha, 25% in ownerships of 40-20,000 ha, and 50% in ownerships greater than 20,000 ha. None of these were necessarily contiguous blocks of land. Changes over the past 25 years have resulted in further fragmentation of the ownership pattern (NRC 1998). Today, almost 32% of forestland area nationally, and 36% in the New England states exclusive of Maine (Brooks and Birch 1988), are in owner-ships of less than 40 ha.

Recent concern has centered on changing forest industry ownership and management (Reidel 1994; Seymour and Hunter 1992). Industrial forest land began to be marketed for its development value in the 1980s, and the northern states affected were concerned enough to form a Northern Forest Lands Council (NFLC 1994). The intent was to stabilize the land ownership and management patterns that had characterized the region for decades, rather than to replace them with public ownership. Industrial forest man-agement, particularly in Maine, was evolving to greater reliance on clear-cuts, with a first pass providing landscape diversity and second one within several years liquidating the remaining mature forest (Seymour and Hunter 1992).

The Great Lakes Forest—The Great Lakes area was the second major area of the boreal forest south of Canada to be settled by Europeans. Land clearing there relieved the pressure to farm the marginal lands of the Northeast forest, and as deforestation occurred in the Great Lakes, it was coincident with the process of reforestation in the Northeastern forest. Land settlement first began in the southern portions of Michigan, Wisconsin, and Minnesota and gradually moved northward (Barlowe 1983). Widespread, unregulated cutting and indiscriminate slash burning and clearing was rampant during the mid- to late-1800s. Some of the largest and most destructive forest fires in the lower 48 states occurred during this time, including the Peshtigo (Michigan, 1871) and Hinckley (Minnesota, 1884) fires.

Early logging was focused on pine, with large quantities of northern white-cedar also harvested (Sandberg 1983). By 1920, other species became dominant in the timber economy, and many of the hardwood species began to be utilized to produce charcoal. The charcoal industry was largely gone by 1930 and was replaced by a pulp industry with less exacting standards for size. Much of the new forest that replaced the early logged forest was aspen, and it remains a staple of the pulpwood industry. Jack pine and balsam fir are also used for pulp. Much of the Great Lakes forest is in an early successional state because of timber harvesting and farming over the past century (Curtis 1959).

Substantial public ownership exists for the Great Lakes boreal forest. National forests began to be reserved in 1908 (later than in the West), and new national forests were created in the 1920s and 1930s. Lands added between then and 1948 almost tripled the size of national forest ownership, from about 800,000 ha to 2,500,000 ha (Barlowe 1983). National Park system lands were added (Pictured Rocks and Sleeping Dunes National Lakeshores), among the over 400,000 ha that has been added to public ownership since World War II. The north-central region of the United States has the largest absolute area, and greatest percentage, of State and County/Municipal timberland in the country. This is primarily due to reversion of tax-delinquent land, almost 7,000,000 ha by 1950 (Barlowe 1951). In the eastern area of the Great Lakes boreal forest, in northern Michigan, about 20-40% of the land base is now publicly owned, and this percentage increases to about 40-60% in northern Wisconsin and more than 60% in northern Minnesota (Barlowe 1983).

Continued fire suppression has allowed development of more complex forest structure in previously farmed/logged areas but has also disrupted the fire regime in unlogged areas. Baker (1989, 1994) suggests that restoration of the natural fire regime, where desired, will restore natural pattern without additional restoration measures. Continuation of current suppression policies has significant implications for the boreal forest, discussed in section "Successional Patterns After Disturbance" (Frelich and Reich 1995).

The Western Boreal Forest—The western boreal forest region has never had the human-created forestland impact experienced by the other two boreal forest regions south of the Canadian border. This region was the last settled by Europeans in the expansion to the Pacific Coast, and development and exploitation occurred around the fringe of these areas or along narrow corridors passing through them. These areas were the focus of the first land reservations for forest reserves, and today much of the National Park System and National Wilderness System is centered on these western boreal forests. The distribution of these boreal forests is patchier than in the other two boreal regions described in this chapter, so that land use in the intervening lands can affect lynx migration, but the human history of land use that changed area of forestland, disturbance patterns, and dominant tree species is much less prevalent in the West than in the Great Lakes or the Northeast boreal forest.

Mining was the first large-scale land use practice to affect the western boreal forest, and it had significant impacts on a local scale. Where mining occurred, not only was there surface soil disruption, but extensive human-caused forest fires were set to provide easier access to local timber for firewood, mining timbers, etc. Larger scale timber harvest practices did not begin until after World War II, and the boreal forest areas were cut only when the more accessible lands were cutover. The carving of national parks from the forest reserves, and later from national forests, preserved much of this land from cutting, and the creation of the Wilderness Act in 1964 further preserved much of the western boreal forest. Of all the western forest types, it has the highest proportion of reserved land, largely because it is primarily in public ownership and is the least productive timberland, making the land-use tradeoffs between preservation and extraction less controversial than for other public lands. In the Western boreal forest zone, fire suppression has been in effect for much of this century, but the long natural fire return intervals (Table 3.2) suggest that removal of fire has not been as significant as in the lower severity fire regimes of the West (Agee 1998b).

Successional Patterns After Disturbance

Across much of the range of the lynx in North America, a high severity fire regime occurs, and succession follows a series of paths from early- to late-successional communities. Within a given forest type, many potential sequences may be possible: a function of fire duration and soil heating, species composition at the time of the fire, post-fire climate, biotic interactions, and other factors. The rate of succession will also vary depending on site conditions. In this section, the common successional sequences in each of the four major boreal forest divisions (taiga, Northeast, Great Lakes, and Western) are summarized.

After a stand replacement event, the post-fire sere will include a herbaceous stage, a shrub/sapling stage, a dense, small tree stage, a transition stage (in many cases a hardwood to conifer transition, but in others just a shift in conifer species), and a mature/old growth stage. Depending on the fire return interval, the mature stage may never develop far before it is disturbed. The timing of these stages will depend on the adaptations of the species that will possibly grow on the site (Table 3.4). Where a tree or shrub

Table 3.4–Responses of common tree species of the boreal forests to disturbance. The "Rowe Class" is a set of life history characters associated with response to disturbance (Rowe 1983), and the specific adaptations are listed for each of the species.

Tree species	Rowe class[a]	Thick bark	Cone serotiny	Sprouter	Light seeds
Black spruce	Evader		X		
White spruce	Avoider				
Aspen	Endurer, Invader			X	X
Paper birch	Endurer, Invader			X	X
Balsam poplar	Endurer, Invader			X	X
Jack pine	Evader, Resister		X		
Red pine	Resister	X			
Eastern white pine	Resister	X			
Balsam fir	Avoider				
Red spruce	Avoider				
Lodgepole pine	Evader		X		
Engelmann spruce	Avoider				
Subalpine fir	Avoider				

[a]Invaders = highly dispersive pioneering species with short-lived disseminules
Evaders = species with long-lived propagules stored in soil or canopy
Resisters = shade-intolerant species whose adult stages can survive low-severity fires
Endurers = sprouting species with shallow or deep buried perennating buds
Avoiders = shade tolerant, late successional species that slowly reinvade burned areas

species is able to sprout or develop new plants from a soil or canopy seed bank, succession is likely to progress more rapidly. Most of the species listed in Table 3.4 are well-adapted to disturbance. A simple collation of the life-history strategies of the common species of a site will give an indication of the likely rate of recovery. Where evaders and endurers are common, the post-fire sere will likely begin with those same species. Where avoiders are the norm, transformation to non-forest vegetation is likely until tree reestablishment is eventually successful, a function of seed source and post-fire climate (Agee and Smith 1984).

Where the disturbance removes the overstory but leaves the understory relatively intact, as in a typical blowdown, the successional sequence will be similar but the species composition will be heavily weighted to the shade-tolerant understory trees, either conifers or hardwoods, that were able to persist in the shade of the overstory trees. Because of the high-severity fire regime, the live trees on the site become snags and eventually logs as the snags fall. In a typical post-fire sequence of this nature, there will be (1) a large post-fire increase in coarse woody debris, (2) a mid-seral decline as the initial input is over, existing coarse woody debris decays, and the new stand is not yet large enough to produce more coarse woody debris, and then (3) a slow increase in late succession as large trees occasionally die or are killed by insect outbreaks (Harmon et al. 1986).

The Taiga

The taiga has two major environmental gradients that affect species composition and successional patterns. The first is a set of local gradients from dry/warm to wet/cold, and the second is an east/west continental gradient that affects both climate and the biogeography of species mixes. In the Alaskan taiga, the local gradients create a complex mix of successional pathways (Fig. 3.5A) (Viereck 1973; Lutz 1956; Rowe and Scotter 1973). One of the common themes in taiga forest ecology is that the species mixes are relatively stable, replacing themselves after disturbance, so the major successional stages are structural in nature. In most cases the disturbance intervals by fire are short enough that the later successional sequences, shown at the top of the diagram, are rarely reached. Tree colonization occurs rapidly, but tree dominance may take 50+ yrs due to early dominance by shrubs and generally low productivity.

In Alaska, Foote (1983) summarized the major stages on closed-forest white spruce and black spruce sites. Many of the species are common to both white and black spruce sites, although relative dominance will differ. On white spruce sites, the newly burned stage lasts only a few weeks, and sprouts of rose, highbush cranberry, and willow emerge, along with fireweed. Sprouts of aspen emerge as well, with seedlings of both aspen and paper birch. White spruce is rarely present immediately after the fire. Within one to five years post-fire, these plants expand cover and several species of mosses dominate the ground layer at the site (up to 30% cover). Tall shrubs and tree saplings dominate the tall shrub-sapling stage (three to 30 years post-fire). The dense tree stage (26-45 years post-fire) is dominated by the young trees that initially established, rose, highbush cranberry, mountain-cranberry, and Labrador-tea. Lichens are best developed at this time, and feathermosses are now established. Willows, herbs, and the seral mosses are no longer important. The hardwood stage is a further development of the hardwood tree layer, with similar understory shrubs to the dense tree stage and *Hylocomium splendens* on the forest floor. As the hardwood trees die (150+ years), white spruce, which has persisted (but rarely as a dominant), becomes the dominant overstory species. It will persist until the next disturbance.

On mesic black spruce sites, the initial patterns are similar (Foote 1983) but bog blueberry and Labrador-tea are dominant shrubs in early succession, and black spruce is present rather than white spruce. Black spruce may average 18,000 stems ha^{-1}, and quaking aspen 11,000 stems ha^{-1}. Hardwood dominance is usually less than on white spruce sites. In the tall shrub-sapling stage, willows dominate at densities up to 15,000 stems ha^{-1}, herbaceous

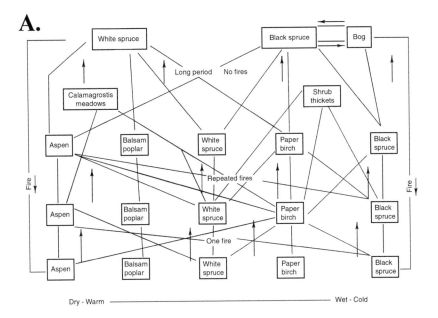

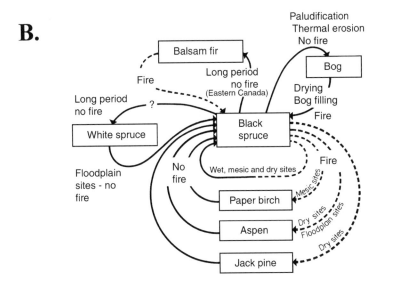

Figure 3.5—Successional sequences in the (A) Alaska taiga and (B) eastern taiga (Viereck 1973, 1983).

species decline, and the tree layer continues to expand. The dense tree stage (30-55 years post-fire) is dominated by trees, with low shrubs, feathermosses, and lichens below. Black spruce density averages 2,500 stems ha^{-1}. A mixed hardwood-spruce stage occurs 56-90 years post-fire, but hardwoods usually are not dominant. In the spruce stage (90 years post-fire +), a thick feathermoss-Spaghnum ground cover allows permafrost to increase from 80+ cm depth to about 60 cm. Fire usually burns these sites before they reach 200 years old.

The first three successional stages (newly-burned, moss-herb, and tall shrub-sapling) last about 20-25 years on white spruce sites and 30-35 years on black spruce sites. The hardwood stage is better defined and lasts longer on white spruce sites. Vegetative and *in situ* seed (such as serotinous cones) is greater on black spruce sites (Black and Bliss 1978; Foote 1983). Succession on lichen-woodland sites is similar to the closed-forest black spruce, except that crown closure rarely occurs and the sequence of stages is usually prolonged (130+ years for mature woodland [Maikawa and Kershaw 1976]).

In the central and eastern taiga, a similar set of successional sequences is postulated (Fig. 3.5B) (Viereck 1983). Balsam poplar, although present, is less a component of the sere, jack pine is added, and balsam fir appears where fire return intervals are longer. To the north, jack pine is the first species to disappear, followed by balsam poplar, eastern larch, and black spruce (Payette et al. 1989), a pattern supported by the rooting depth of the species and shallower permafrost (Larsen 1980). Balsam fir and white spruce are the late successional species on mesic sites, while succession toward black spruce is the trend on more xeric sites (Bergeron and Dubuc 1989). A majority of the post-fire seedlings become established in a three- to 10-year period (Lavoie and Sirois 1998). On the xeric sites, low productivity and the presence of species like red pine, jack pine, or white pine can result in multi-aged stands, although this appears to be most common in the transitional mixed northern forest (Heinselman 1981). On more mesic sites without these pines, quaking aspen and paper birch are common early successional species (Bergeron and Dubuc 1989) after stand-replacing disturbances, particularly if the fire exposes substantial areas of bare ground (Payette 1992). The succession of black spruce stands to balsam fir occurs in some stands (Dammon 1964) but does not appear to happen on other sites (Carleton and Maycock 1978).

Coarse woody debris trends differ between white and black spruce stands. Black spruce sites are poor, and large stems will never be found on these sites. In Alaska, the average diameter at breast height for 51-year-old upland and lowland stands was 2-3 cm, and there were no logs greater than 5 cm diameter on the forest floor (Barney and Van Cleve 1973). If these stands burned, there would be almost no snags or logs created that would be more than 5 cm. More productive black spruce sites of greater age (130 years old) had five to 10 times the mass of live stem wood (Van Cleve 1981) that would become coarse woody debris if the site burned. By 25 years post-fire, all snags had been converted to logs in a black spruce stand (Paragi et al. 1997). In white spruce stands, the same post-fire increase will be seen, but generally more significant. Coarse woody debris cover in black spruce sites ranged from 2 to 6% compared to 5 to 16% for a white spruce sere (Foote 1983). Because more of the coarse woody debris in white spruce stands will be hardwoods, decay rates are more rapid for coarse woody debris in white spruce stands (Harmon et al. 1986).

Northeastern and Great Lakes Boreal Forests

Successional sequences after disturbance in the Northeastern and Great Lakes boreal forests represent a mix of species common to the deciduous forest and boreal biomes and a mix of disturbances common to both. Therefore, the successional dynamics are covered together here. As noted earlier, fire tends to be more important in the Great Lakes boreal forest than the Northeastern boreal forest. In the Great Lakes, windthrow and insects may become locally as important as fire, creating a complex series of successional pathways (Fig. 3.6) (Pastor and Mladenoff 1992). In the Northeastern boreal forest, longer fire return intervals (Lorimer 1977) and higher frequencies of insect outbreak (spruce budworm) and wind (Seymour 1992) resulted in many disturbances that were less than stand-replacing in severity. The Northeastern forest, also called the Acadian forest, had greater potential diversity and age structure as a result (Seymour and Hunter 1992).

Boreal conifers are more frequent on cooler sites or at the extremes of the moisture gradient (Larsen 1980), while northern hardwoods follow the early successional species on more mesic and warmer sites (Maycock and Curtis 1960). Like the more northerly boreal forest, tree establishment on stand replacement burns is rapid. The hardwoods sprout, some like paper birch have light seeds that disperse widely, and jack pine reproduces from a seed bank in serotinous cones. On poorly drained sites, black spruce reproduces from semi-serotinous cones that retain at least part of the seed production.

Jack pine is a common dominant on drier sites where morainal, coarse-textured soils predominate (Conkey et al. 1995). After fire, jack pine and quaking aspen form dense stands. In the 5-15 year period, jack pine may reach 10,000-30,000 stems ha^{-1}, with 500-13,000 stems ha^{-1} of aspen (Roe and Stoeckler 1950; Cayford and McRae 1983; Agee 1998a). At 40+ years, the pine-aspen overstory has a black spruce, balsam fir, and shade tolerant hardwood understory (sugar maple and paper birch). By age 75, the overstory begins a decline, with subsequent release of the understory species,

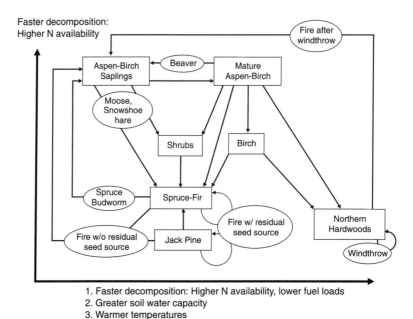

Faster decomposition:
Higher N availability

Fire after windthrow

Aspen-Birch Saplings

Beaver

Mature Aspen-Birch

Moose, Snowshoe hare

Shrubs

Birch

Spruce Budworm

Spruce-Fir

Fire w/ residual seed source

Northern Hardwoods

Fire w/o residual seed source

Jack Pine

Windthrow

1. Faster decomposition: Higher N availability, lower fuel loads
2. Greater soil water capacity
3. Warmer temperatures

Figure 3.6—Multiple successional sequences in the Great Lakes boreal forest (Pastor and Mladenoff 1992).

and by age 165, the jack pine and aspen are largely replaced by a multi-storied black spruce-balsam fir-hardwood forest, unless an intervening fire creates another even-aged pine-aspen stand. Heinselman (1973) projected that spruce would become more dominant over time but found remnant jack pines to live more than 200 yrs. Mixed pine stands (red pine, eastern white pine, jack pine) are often indicative of the limited boreal forest area in a moderate-severity fire regime. These sites will commonly have fire-scarred pines and represent a succession of multi-aged stands on poor sites. Where the fire thins few trees, more shade-tolerant species will regenerate, while hotter fires that kill more trees may create another age class of shade-intolerant pines.

Fire suppression in the Great Lakes area has changed the dominant successional pathways (Frelich and Reich 1995). Many stands are undergoing a transition from even-aged stands of catastrophic origin to uneven-aged stands due to small scale openings. Jack or red pine or aspen stands are moving toward an old-growth mix of black spruce, balsam fir, paper birch, and white cedar, in patches of 10-30 m created by wind, insects, and disease (Frelich and Reich 1995). At scales of 1-16 ha, succession leads to a convergence on a mixture of species. It is not clear whether reintroduction of catastrophic disturbance will lead back to the original landscape character of this region. In the heavily altered landscapes at the southern edge of the boreal forest, the historic landscape character is probably permanently altered. Second-growth forest landscapes caused by harvest have generally smaller forest patches and are significantly simpler in shape; important ecosystem juxtapositions (such as old-growth hemlock adjacent to lowland conifers) have been largely eliminated (Mladenoff et al. 1993).

While the jack pine type is of interest to fire ecologists, many of the forests of the Great Lakes and Northeastern boreal forest burn less frequently. On mesic sites, with longer fire intervals (Table 3.2), hardwoods typically occupy a more important niche, and as the conifer component decreases, so does the flammability of the forest (Van Wagner 1983). Other disturbances such as wind (Pastor and Mladenoff 1992) or insects (Baskerville 1975) become more important disturbance agents. Replacement of resinous, multi-year evergreen foliage with deciduous foliage that maintains a higher average foliar moisture content reduces the probability of intense fire. Seed source for jack pine may be gone by the time a site burns. In Maine, a search of old records showed pine to be a minor component of the forest in most areas (Lorimer 1977). In these areas, aspen and birch tend to be the dominant early successional species. White and gray birch composed >70% of early successional (younger than 25-year-old) stands, at densities of 1,500-7,600 stems ha^{-1} (Lorimer 1977). Wet sites tend to be dominated by black spruce and eastern larch boreal species. Successional trends tend to follow those of the more classical boreal forest (Damman 1964).

Coarse woody debris loads are significantly greater in the Great Lakes and Northeastern boreal forest than the taiga, due to higher productivity, longer disturbance intervals, and minor disturbances such as gap-creating wind events that periodically replenish the log supply. Unburned stands up to 250 years old had bole mass of 190 to 344 t ha^{-1} (Gordon 1981), while young jack pine stands (younger than 60 years old) had less than 20 t ha^{-1} of stem biomass (Green and Grigal 1979). Young balsam fir stands from 12 to 52 years old had coarse woody debris mass decreasing from 35 to 13 t ha^{-1} (Lambert et al. 1980). Snag biomass decreased from 27 to 0.25 t ha^{-1} over the same sequence.

Western Boreal Forests

The Western boreal forests within the range of the lynx are dominated by three tree species: lodgepole pine, Engelmann spruce, and subalpine fir. Like the remainder of the forests with boreal features, these ecosystems are subjected to disturbance by fire on a periodic basis. Yet there are numerous characteristics of the subalpine forests that distinguish them from their more northerly boreal neighbors: longer intervals between major disturbances (Table 3.2); species that are less fire-adapted (Table 3.4), implying a longer post-fire recovery period; absence of a tall shrub component following disturbance, except where aspen is present; and more post-fire coarse woody debris.

Many of the forest types below the boreal zone in western forests have more frequent disturbance by fire than the boreal zone (Agee 1993) and contain the serotinous-coned lodgepole pine allowing dense, young lodgepole stands to develop after severe fire. However, these stands have occasional lower intensity fires or more representation of fire-tolerant species more typical of lower elevations (western larch and Douglas-fir). These species may be representative of a moderate-severity fire regime (Agee 1993), and multiple age classes may occur in these stands (Arno 1976; Arno 1980; Arno et al. 1993). Where residual density is high, post-fire regeneration is likely to be sparse and dominated by shade-tolerant species. Where residuals are absent, the dense lodgepole pine stands common to higher elevations will be found in a mosaic with the residual-dominated stands.

Across the range of western boreal forests, many fire return intervals are long enough that relatively short-lived lodgepole pine may be removed from the stands by mountain pine beetles before another fire event occurs. In such cases, the old-growth dominants Engelmann spruce and subalpine fir may compose the dominant tree component, but when burned, the spruce and fir are killed and the species do not quickly re-establish. The seeds of both species are large, so they are not easily dispersed by wind, and they do not easily establish on freshly burned sites. Tree colonization may take decades to centuries (Stahelin 1943, Agee 1993), although occasionally spruce or fir will immediately regenerate (Loope and Gruell 1973; Habeck and Mutch 1973; Doyle et al. 1998). During the interim period, vegetation cover is a herbaceous-low shrub meadow (Stahelin 1943). Near timberline the trees may return in a "ribbon forest" pattern (Billings 1969), where linear strips of forest are interspersed with meadow as a result of snow accumulation patterns.

Seventeen years after the Waterfalls Canyon fire in Wyoming, sedges provided the most vegetative cover, with total shrub cover at 4-6% and a seedling-sapling density of 2,000-5,000 ha^{-1}, dominated by Engelmann spruce (Doyle et al. 1998). On the Yellowstone Plateau, on the less productive end of the western subalpine forest productivity gradient, Romme (1982) simulated forest succession after fire in two plant associations (Table 3.5) and estimated the longevity of each stage as a function of plant association, restocking rate, and lodgepole pine mortality from bark beetles. The immature pine stage (closed canopy) in all cases began at a minimum age of 40 years post-fire.

Table 3.5–Postfire successional stages (years) in the Yellowstone Plateau area of northwestern Wyoming (adapted from Romme 1982).

	Lodgepole pine/sedge				Subalpine fir/huckleberry		
Successional stage	"Typical" stands	Slow restocking	Early pine canopy mortality	Late pine canopy mortality	"Typical" stands	Early pine canopy mortality	Late Pine canopy mortality
Herbaceous	0-20	0-40	0-20	0-20	0-20	0-20	0-20
Seedling-sapling	20-40	40-80	20-40	20-40	20-40	20-40	20-40
Immature pine	40-150	80-200	40-150	40-150	40-150	40-150	40-150
Mature pine	150-200	200-250	150-170	150-300	150-300	150-180	150-350
Transitional	200-300	250-350	170-240	300-400	300-400	180-280	350-450
Climax forest[a]	300+	350+	240+	400+	400+	280+	450+

[a]Climax forest is defined as the potential vegetation on the sites. For the lodgepole pine/sedge plant association (infertile sites) it is lodgepole pine, and for the subalpine fir/huckleberry plant association it is subalpine fir and Engelmann spruce.

Where wind is the disturbance agent, or bark beetles remove an overstory of lodgepole pine or whitebark pine, Engelmann spruce and/or subalpine fir, released from the understory, are likely to be the post-disturbance dominants (Morgan and Bunting 1990; Agee 1993). They may or may not develop as dense stands of small (and usually not young) conifers.

Coarse woody debris in western subalpine forests follows a U-shaped trend after stand-replacing disturbances, with snags and logs most common in the young stands, declining to a low in mid-succession (Clark et al. 1998). Not all the pre-fire log biomass is consumed, and post-fire log biomass is fed by the fall of snags created by the fire. Unburned spruce-fir forests in Colorado had 120-135 t ha^{-1} of stem mass (Landis and Mogren 1975) that would become coarse woody debris if the stand burned. On old-growth spruce-fir sites, where lodgepole pine mortality adds a new cohort of coarse woody debris, log biomass may exceed 100 t ha^{-1} (Brown and See 1981), and much of that will remain after fire passes through the stand. In these environments, decay is slow, so that 50-100 years after the fire, some snags and many logs still reflect the fire evidence (Agee and Smith 1984). During the successional stages, there is clearly a substantial mass of coarse woody debris on site (Huff et al. 1989).

Landscape Management Implications

The natural landscapes of the boreal forest within which the lynx has successfully existed have been profoundly affected by disturbance, primarily by fire. Although most of the lynx range is included in the high-severity fire regime, there is considerable range in the frequency with which fire occurred on these landscapes, and because of that a wide variation in successional stages present. Further variation has occurred due to local site conditions, intensity and duration of the fire, forest age at the time of fire, and post-fire climate. Mimicking this pattern of natural disturbance has been suggested as a way to maintain biodiversity in managed forests (Hunter 1990; Bunnell 1995).

For the boreal forest, there are several general principles that must be addressed in landscape management plans if harvesting or fire disturbance is to be incorporated:

1. The habitat will be a product of the cumulative effect of all disturbances. The substitution of logging for fire, for example, is only meaningful if fire can be successfully removed from the environment, and even then, logging will not totally mimic fire as a disturbance process because of roading and coarse woody debris differences.

2. Typical models used for fire history studies suggest that fire selected a range of stand ages to burn. Harvesting only the oldest ages will decrease the average stand age of the landscape and will remove the complex boreal stand structure that may be critical for lynx denning. Young and old stands need to be part of any landscape disturbance plan.

3. Size and juxtaposition of stands is critical. Most fires are small. Most of the landscape, however, is affected by larger fire patches, with unburned areas inside the fire perimeter (stringers, islands, fire skips).

There are a range of prescriptions for lynx or lynx habitat that have quite different implications for management. Koehler and Aubry (1994), addressing the "southern latitude" habitat (equivalent to Western boreal forest), suggest that although approximating the natural disturbance frequency and spatial patterns will provide the best habitat for lynx, large openings (greater than 100 m across) may create barriers to lynx movement and travel corridors are needed for cover for lynx. Typical spatial patterns of historic fires in this type suggest much larger patches were the norm in boreal forests and that there are no guaranteed "travel corridors" or connectivity between fire patches or among unburned islands within fires. The discrepancies within Koehler and Aubry's (1994) recommendations probably represent the difference between what is "natural" and what may be optimum for one species that occupies this natural environment. An example of problems caused by openings smaller than the natural scale is discussed by Hunter (1993). Small openings by cutting in boreal forest were ideal for moose but less so for caribou; wolf populations increased and thereby depressed caribou populations, a result of creating openings smaller than what historic fires had done.

Summary

It is clear that boreal forests, in addition to covering a wide geographic area, contain many unusual combinations of species and disturbance regimes. Few generalizations beyond broad climatic conditions apply over the large geographic range of boreal forests. Fire has been the primary natural disturbance in boreal forests, although its influence decreases in the eastern boreal region. Stand replacement disturbances are common and are often large with few islands. Across much of the boreal forest, insects and other disturbances generate small scale heterogeneity, although spruce budworm can create widespread epidemic mortality in the eastern boreal forest region. Fire disturbances tend to fit stochastic models well, although the specific parameters of the models may be difficult to fit. These models suggest that large proportions of young forest were characteristic of the boreal region but that fair amounts of quite old forest were part of the mosaic as well. These natural landscapes diverged significantly from even-aged silvicultural systems: fewer roads, more coarse woody debris, older age structures, and complex juxtaposition of different-aged stands. Post-fire successional sequences are very different in the taiga, eastern, midwest, and western forest types, particularly in the proportion of deciduous vegetation.

Ecology is a science of place, and scientific recommendations for lynx will have to take the natural and cultural features and history of each boreal subregion into account.

Literature Cited

Agee, J. K. 1993. Fire ecology of Pacific Northwest forests. Island Press, Washington, DC.

Agee, J. K. 1998a. The ecological role of fire in pine forests. Pages 193-218 *in* Richardson, D. M. ,ed. The genus *Pinus*. Cambridge University Press, Cambridge.

Agee, J. K. 1998b. The landscape ecology of western forest fire regimes. Northwest Science 72 (special issue): 24-34.

Agee, J. K., M. Finney, and R. deGouvenain. 1990. Forest fire history of Desolation Peak, Washington. Canadian Journal of Forest Research 20: 350-56.

Agee, J. K. and J. Kertis. 1987. Forest types of the North Cascades National Park Service Complex. Canadian Journal of Botany 65: 1520-1530.

Agee, J. K. and L. Smith 1984. Subalpine tree reestablishment after fire in the Olympic Mountains, Washington. Ecology 65: 810-19.

Alexander, M. E., and D. L. Euler. 1981. Ecological role of fire in the uncut boreal mixedwood forest. Pages 42-64 *in* Proceedings of the boreal mixedwood symposium. Canadian Forest Service Pub. COFRC Symp. Proc. O-P-9.

Arno, S. F. 1976. The historical role of fire on the Bitterroot National Forest. Res. Pap. INT-187. Ogden, UT: U.S. Department of Agriculture, Forest Service, Intermountain Research Station.

Arno, S. F. 1980. Forest fire history of the northern Rockies. Journal of Forestry 78: 460-65.

Arno, S. F. 1986. Whitebark pine cone crops: A diminishing source of wildlife food. Western Journal of Applied Forestry 1: 92-94.

Arno, S. F. and J. R. Habeck. 1972. Ecology of alpine larch (*Larix lyallii* Parl.) in the Pacific Northwest. Ecological Monographs 42: 417-450.

Arno, S. F. and R. P. Hammerly. 1984. Timberline: mountain and Arctic forest frontiers. The Mountaineers. Seattle, WA.

Arno, S. F. and T. D. Peterson. 1983. Variation in estimates of fire intervals: a closer look at fire history on the Bitterroot National Forest. Res. Pap. INT-301. Ogden, UT: U.S. Department of Agriculture, Forest Service, Intermountain Research Station.

Arno, S. F., E. D. Reinhardt, and J. H. Scott. 1993. Forest structure and landscape patterns in the subalpine lodgepole pine type: a procedure for quantifying past and present conditions. Gen. Tech. Rep. INT-294. Ogden, UT: U.S. Department of Agriculture, Forest Service, Intermountain Research Station.

Baker, W. L. 1989. Landscape ecology and nature reserve design in the Boundary Waters Canoe Area, Minnesota. Ecology 70 (1) 23-35.

Baker, W. L. 1994. Restoration of landscape structure altered by fire suppression. Conservation Biology 8: 763-769.

Barbour, M. G. and W. D. Billings, eds. 1988. North American terrestrial vegetation. Cambridge University Press, Cambridge.

Barbour, M. G. and R.A. Woodward. 1985. The red fir forest of California. Canadian Journal of Forest Research 15: 570-576.

Barlowe, R. 1951. Administration of tax-reverted lands in the Lake States. Michigan Agricultural Experiment Station Tech. Bull. 225.

Barlowe 1983. Changing land use and policies: The Lake States. Chapter 10 *in* Flader, S. L., ed. The Great Lakes Forest: an environmental and social history. University of Minnesota Press, Minneapolis, MN.

Barney, R. J. 1971. Selected 1966-69 interior Alaska wildfire statistics with long-term comparisons. Res. Note PNW-154. Portland, OR: U.S. Department of Agriculture, Forest Service, Pacific Northwest Research Station.

Barney, R. J. and K. Van Cleve. 1973. Black spruce fuel weights and biomass in two interior Alaska stands. Canadian Journal of Forest Research 3: 304-11.

Barrett, J. W. 1962. The Northeast Region. Chapter 2 *in* Barrett, J. W. ed. Regional silviculture of the United States. John Wiley and Sons, New York.

Baskerville, G. L. 1975. Spruce budworm: super silviculturist. Forestry Chronicle 51: 138-140.

Bergeron, Y. 1991. The influence of island and mainland lakeshore landscapes on boreal forest fire regimes. Ecology 72: 1980-92.

Bergeron, Y. and M. Dubuc. 1989. Succession in the southern part of the Canadian boreal forest. Vegetatio 79: 51-63.

Bergeron, Y. and A. Leduc. 1998. Relationships between changes in fire frequency and mortality due to spruce budworm outbreaks in the southeastern Canadian boreal forest. Journal of Vegetation Science 9: 492-500.

Bergeron, Y., A. Leduc, and L. Ting-xian. 1997. Explaining the distribution of *Pinus* spp. in a Canadian boreal insular landscape. Journal of Vegetation Science 8: 37-44.

Billings, W. D. 1969. Vegetational patterns near alpine timberline as affected by fire-snowdrift interactions. Vegetatio 19: 192-207.

Black, R. A. and L. C. Bliss 1978. Recovery sequence of *Picea mariana-Vaccinium uliginosum* forests after burning near Inuvik, Northwest Territories, Canada. Canadian Journal of Botany 56: 2020-30.

Blais, J. R. 1968. Regional variation in susceptibility of eastern North American forests to budworm attack based on history of outbreaks. Forestry Chronicle 44: 17-23.

Brooks, R. T. and T. W. Birch. 1988. Changes in New England forests and forest owners: implications for wildlife habitat resources and management. Transactions of the 53rd North American Wildlife and Natural Resources Conference: 78-87.

Brown, J. K. and T. E. See. 1981. Downed dead woody fuel and biomass in the northern Rocky Mountains. Gen. Tech. Rep. INT-117. Ogden, UT: U.S. Department of Agriculture, Forest Service, Intermountain Forest and Range Experiment Station.

Bunnell, F. 1995. Forest-dwelling vertebrate faunas and natural fire regimes in British Columbia: patterns and implications for conservation. Conservation Biology 9: 636-644.

Canham, C. D. and O. L. Loucks. 1984. Catastrophic windthrow in the presettlement forests of Wisconsin. Ecology 65: 803-09.

Carleton, T. J. and P. F. Maycock. 1978. Dynamics of the boreal forest south of James Bay, Canada. Canadian Journal of Botany 56: 1157-1173.

Cayford, J. H. and D. H. McRae. 1983. The ecological role of fire in jack pine forests. Pages 183-199 *in* Wein, R. W. and D. A. MacLean. The role of fire in northern circumpolar ecosystems. John Wiley and Sons, New York.

Clark, D. F., D. D. Kneeshaw, P. J. Burton, and J. A. Antos. 1998. Coarse woody debris in sub-boreal spruce forests of west-central British Columbia. Canadian Journal of Forest Research 28: 284-90.

Cogbill, C. V. 1985. Dynamics of the boreal forests of the Laurentian Highlands, Canada. Canadian Journal of Forest Research 15: 252-61.

Conkey, L. E., M. Keifer, and A. H. Lloyd. 1995. Disjunct jack pine (*Pinus banksiana* Lamb.) structure and dynamics, Acadia National Park, Maine. Ecoscience 2: 168-176.

Coutts, M. P. and J. Grace. 1995. Wind and trees. Cambridge University Press. Cambridge, England.

Critchfield, W. B. 1985. The late Quaternary history of lodgepole and jack pines. Canadian Journal of Forest Research 15: 749-772.

Curtis, J. T. 1959. The vegetation of Wisconsin. University of Wisconsin Press, Madison.

Dammon, A. W. H. 1964. Some forest types of central Newfoundland and their relations to environmental factors. Forest Science Monographs 8.

Dansereau, P.-R. and Y. Bergeron. 1993. Fire history in the southern boreal forest of northwestern Quebec. Canadian Journal of Forest Research 23: 25-32.

DeLong, S. C. 1998. Natural disturbance rates and patch size distribution of forests in northern British Columbia: implications for forest management. Northwest Science 72 (special issue): 35-48.

Despain, D. G. 1990. Yellowstone vegetation. Roberts Rinehart. Boulder, CO.

Doyle, K. M., D. H. Knight, D. L. Taylor, W. J. Barmore, Jr., and J. M. Benedict. 1998. Seventeen years of forest succession following the Waterfall Canyon fire. International Journal of Wildland Fire 8: 45-55.

Eberhart, K. E., and P. M. Woodard. 1987. Distribution of residual vegetation associated with large fires in Alberta. Canadian Journal of Forest Research 17: 1207-12.

Elliott-Fisk, D. L. 1988. The boreal forest. Pages 33-62 in Barbour, M. G. and W. D. Billings, eds. North American terrestrial vegetation. Cambridge University Press, Cambridge.

Fahnestock, G. R. 1976. Fires, fuel, and flora as factors in wilderness management: The Pasayten case. Tall Timbers Fire Ecology Conf. 15: 33-70.

Ferguson, R. H. and F. R. Longwood. 1960. The timber resources of Maine. USDA Forest Service, Northeastern Forest Experiment Station, Upper Darby, PA.

Findley, J. S. and S. Anderson. 1956. Zoogeography of the montane mammals of Colorado. Journal of Mammalogy 37: 80-82.

Finney, M. A. 1995. The missing tail and other considerations for the use of fire history models. International Journal of Wildland Fire 5: 197-202.

Flannigan, M. D. and C. E. Van Wagner. 1991. Climate change and wildfire in Canada. Canadian Journal of Forest Research 21: 66-72.

Flannigan, M. D., Y. Bergeron, O. Engelmark, and B. M. Wotton. 1998. Future wildfire in circumboreal forests in relation to global warming. Journal of Vegetation Science 9: 469-476.

Foote, M. J. 1983. Classification, description, and dynamics of plant communities after fire in the taiga of interior Alaska. Res. Pap. PNW-307. Portland, OR: U.S. Department of Agriculture, Forest Service, Pacific Northwest Research Station.

Foster, D. R. 1983. The history and pattern of fire in the boreal forest of southeastern Labrador. Canadian Journal of Botany 61: 2459-71.

Franklin, J. F. and C. T. Dyrness. 1973. Natural vegetation of Oregon and Washington. Gen. Tech. Rep. PNW-8. Portland, OR: U.S. Department of Agriculture, Forest Service, Pacific Northwest Research Station.

Frelich, L. E. and P. B. Reich. 1995. Spatial patterns and succession in a Minnesota southern-boreal forest. Ecological Monographs 65: 325-346.

Frissell, S. S. 1973. The importance of fire as a natural ecological factor in Itasca State Park, Minnesota. Quaternary Research 3: 397-407.

Furyaev, V. V., R. W. Wein, and D. A. MacLean. 1983. Fire influences in *Abies*-dominated forests. Pages 221-234 *in* Wein, R. W. and D. A. MacLean. The role of fire in northern circumpolar ecosystems. John Wiley and Sons, New York.

Gauthier, S., J. Gagnon, and Y. Bergeron. 1993. Population age structure of *Pinus banksiana* at the southern edge of the Canadian boreal forest. Journal of Vegetation Science 4: 783-790.

Gordon, A. G. 1981. Woodlands data set: Ontario site Region 5 sites 1-4. Pages 576-79 *in* Reichle, D. E., ed. Dynamic properties of forest ecosystems. International Biological Programme 23. Cambridge University Press, Cambridge.

Green, D. C. and D. F. Grigal. 1979. Jack pine biomass accretion on shallow and deep soils in Minnesota. Soil Science Society of America Proceedings 43: 1233-37.

Greller A. M. 1988. Deciduous forest. Pages 288-316 *in* Barbour, M. G. and W. D. Billings, eds. North American terrestrial vegetation. Cambridge University Press. Cambridge.

Habeck, J. R. and R. W. Mutch. 1973. Fire-dependent forests in the northern Rocky Mountains. Quaternary Research 3: 408-424.

Hadley, J. L. and W. K. Smith. 1983. Influence of wind exposure on needle desiccation and mortality for timberline conifers in Wyoming. Arctic and Alpine Research 15: 127-35.

Hare, F. K. 1969. Climate and zonal divisions of the boreal forest formation in eastern Canada. Pages 7-23 *in* Nelson, J. G., and M. J. Chambers eds. Vegetation, soils, and wildlife. Methuen Publications, Toronto.

Hare, F. K. and J. C. Ritchie. 1972. The boreal bioclimates. Geographical Review 62: 333-65.

Harmon, M. E., J. F. Franklin, F. J. Swanson, P. Sollins, S. V. Gregory, J. D. Lattin, N. H. Anderson, S. P. Cline, N. G. Aumen, J. R. Sedell, G. W. Liemkaemper, K. Cromack, Jr., and K. W. Cummins. 1986. Ecology of coarse woody debris in temperate ecosystems. Advances in Ecological Research 15: 133- 302.

Hawksworth, F. G. and A. L. Shigo. 1980. Dwarf mistletoe on red spruce in the White Mountains of New Hampshire. Plant Disease Reporter 64: 880-992.

Heinselman, M. L. 1973. Fire in the virgin forests of the Boundary Waters Canoe Area, Minnesota. Quaternary Research 3: 329-82.

Heinselman, M. L. 1981. Fire intensity and frequency as factors in the distribution and structure of northern ecosystems. Pages 7-57 *in* Mooney, H. and others, eds. Fire Regimes and Ecosystem Properties. Gen. Tech. Rep. WO-26. Washington, DC: U.S. Department of Agriculture, Forest Service.

Holling, C. S. 1992. The role of forest insects in structuring the boreal landscape. Pages 170-91 *in* Shugart, H. H., R. Leemans, and G. B. Bonan, eds. A systems analysis of the global boreal forest. Cambridge University Press, Cambridge.

Hopkins, A. D. 1901. Insect enemies of spruce in the Northeast. USDA Forest Service, Bureau of Entomology Bull. 28.

Huff, M. H., J. K. Agee, M. Gracz, and M. Finney. 1989. Fuel and fire behavior predictions in subalpine forests of Pacific Northwest National Parks. USDI National Park Service Rep. CPSU/UW 89-4. College of Forest Resources, University of Washington. Seattle.

Huggard, D. and A. Arsenault. In review. Mistakes in fire frequency analysis.

Hunter, M. L. 1990. Wildlife, forests, and forestry, principles of managing forests for biological diversity. Prentice Hall, Englewood Cliffs, NJ.

Hunter, M. L. 1993. Natural fire regimes as spatial models for managing boreal forests. Biological Conservation 65: 115-120.

Johnson, E. A. 1992. Fire and vegetation dynamics: Studies from the North American boreal forest. Cambridge University Press, Cambridge.

Johnson, E. A. and C. P. S. Larsen. 1991. Climatically-induced change in fire frequency in the southern Canadian Rockies. Ecology 72: 194-201.

Johnson, E. A., K. Miyanishi, and J. M. H. Weir. 1998. Wildfires in the western Canadian boreal forest: landscape patterns and ecosystem management. Journal of Vegetation Science 9: 603-610.

Johnson, E. A. and C. E. Van Wagner. 1985. The theory and use of two fire history models. Canadian Journal of Forest Research 15 (1): 214-220.

Johnson, E. A. and D. R. Wowchuck. 1993. Wildfires in the southern Canadian Rocky Mountains and their relationship to mid-tropospheric anomalies. Canadian Journal of Forest Research 23: 1213-22.

Kettela, E. G. 1983. A cartographic history of spruce budworm defoliation 1967-81 in Eastern North America. Canadian Forest Service Information Report DPC-X-14. Ottawa, Ontario.

Kiil, A. D. and J. E. Grigel. 1969. The May 1968 forest conflagrations in central Alberta. Canadian Forest Service Information Rep. A-X-24.

Klyza, C. M. and S. C. Trombulak. 1994. The future of the Northern Forest. Middlebury College Press. Hanover, NH.

Knight, D. H. 1994. Mountains and plains: the ecology of Wyoming landscapes. Yale University Press, New Haven, CN.

Koehler, G. M. and K. B. Aubry. 1994. Lynx. Pages 74-98 in Ruggiero, L. F., K. B. Aubry, S. W. Buskirk, L. J. Lyon, and W. J. Zielinski, eds. The scientific basis for conserving forest carnivores: American marten, fisher, lynx, and wolverine in the Western United States. USDA Forest Service Gen. Tech. Rep. RM-254.

Lambert, R. C., G. E. Lang, and W. A. Reiners. 1980. Loss of mass and chemical change in decaying boles of a subalpine balsam fir forest. Ecology 61: 1460-73.

Landis, T. D. and E. W. Mogren. 1975. Tree strata biomass of subalpine spruce-fir stands in southwestern Colorado. Forest Science 21: 9-12.

Larsen, J. A. 1980. The boreal ecosystem. Academic Press, New York.

Lavoie, L. and L. Sirois. 1998. Vegetation changes caused by recent fires in the northern boreal forest of eastern Canada. Journal of Vegetation Science 9: 483-492.

Lesica, P. 1996. Using fire history models to estimate proportions of old growth forest in northwest Montana, USA. Biological Conservation 77: 33-39.

Little, E. L. 1971. Atlas of United States trees. Volume 1. Conifers and important hardwoods. USDA Forest Service Miscellaneous Publication 1146.

Loope, L. L. and G. E. Gruell. 1973. The ecological role of fire in the Jackson Hole area, northwestern Wyoming. Quaternary Research 3: 425-443.

Lorimer, C. G. 1977. The presettlement forest and natural disturbance cycles of northeast Maine. Ecology 58: 139-148.

Loucks, O. L. 1983. New light on the changing forest. Chapter 2 *in* Flader, S. L., ed. The Great Lakes Forest: an environmental and social history. University of Minnesota Press, Minneapolis, MN.

Lutz, H. J. 1956. Ecological effects of forest fires in the interior of Alaska. USDA Technical Bulletin 1133.

Maikawa, E. and K. A. Kershaw. 1976. Studies on lichen-dominated systems. XIX. The post-fire recovery sequence of black spruce-lichen woodland in the Abitau Lake region, N.W.T. Canadian Journal of Botany 54: 2679-2687.

Maycock, P. F. and J. T. Curtis. 1960. The phytosociology of boreal conifer-hardwood forests of the Great Lakes region. Ecological Monographs 30: 1-35.

Miller-Weeks, M. and D. Smoronk. 1993. Aerial assessment of red spruce and balsam fir condition in the Adirondack Region of New York, the Green Mountains of Vermont, the White Mountains of New Hampshire, and the mountains of western Maine, 1985-86. USDA Forest Service, Northeastern Area Report NA-TP-16-93, Durham, NH.

Mladenoff, D. J. 1987. Dynamics of nitrogen mineralization and nitrification in hemlock and hardwood treefall gaps. Ecology 68: 1171-80.

Mladenoff, D. J., M. A. White, J. Pastor, and T .R. Crow. 1993. Comparing spatial patterns in unaltered old-growth and disturbed forest landscapes. Ecological Applications 3: 294-306.

Morgan, P. and S. Bunting. 1990. Fire effects in whitebark pine forests. Pages 166-170 *in* Schmidt, W. C. and K. J. McDonald, comps. Proceedings: Symposium on whitebark pine ecosystems: Ecology and management of a high-mountain resource. Gen. Tech. Rep. INT-270. Ogden, UT: U.S. Department of Agriculture, Forest Service, Intermountain Research Station.

National Research Council. 1998. Forested landscapes in perspective: prospects and opportunities for sustainable management of America's nonfederal forests. National Academy Press, Washington, DC.

Northern Forest Lands Council (NFLC). 1994. Finding common ground: conserving the Northern Forest. Northern Forest Lands Council. Concord, NH.

Oechel, W. C. and W. T. Lawrence. 1985. Taiga. *in* Chabot, B. F. and H. A. Mooney, eds. Physiological ecology of North American plant communities. Chapman and Hall, New York.

Paragi, T. F., W. N. Johnson, D. D. Katnik, and A. J. Magoun. 1997. Selection of post-fire seres by lynx and snowshoe hares in the Alaskan taiga. Northwestern Naturalist 78: 77-86.

Parker, W. H., J. Maze, and G. E. Bradfield. 1981. Implications of morphological and anatomical variation in *Abies balsamea* and *A. lasiocarpa* (Pinaceae) from Western Canada. American Journal of Botany 68: 843-854.

Pastor, J. and D. J. Mladenoff. 1992. The southern boreal-northern hardwood forest border. Pages 216-240 *in* Shugart, H. H., R. Leemans, and G. B. Bonan, eds. A systems analysis of the global boreal forest. Cambridge University Press, Cambridge.

Payette, S. 1992. Fire as a controlling process in the North American boreal forest. Pages 144-169 *in* Shugart, H. H., R. Leemans, and G. B. Bonan, eds. A systems analysis of the global boreal forest. Cambridge University Press Cambridge.

Payette, S., C. Morneau, L. Sirois, and M. Desponts. 1989. Recent fire history of the northern Quebec biomes. Ecology 70: 656-73.

Peet, R. K. 1981. Forest vegetation of the Colorado Front Range. Vegetatio 45: 3-75.

Peet, R. K. 1988. Forests of the Rocky Mountains. Pages 63-102 *in* Barbour, M. G. and W. D. Billings, eds. North American terrestrial vegetation. Cambridge University Press, Cambridge.

Pickett, S. T. A. and Thompson, J. N. 1978. Patch dynamics and the design of nature reserves. Biological Conservation 13: 27-37.

Quirk, W. A. and D. J. Sykes. 1971. White spruce stringers in a fire-patterned landscape in interior Alaska. Pages 179-197 *in* Proceedings of the symposium, fire in the environment. Portland, OR: U.S. Department of Agriculture, Forest Service.

Ratz, A. 1995. Long-term spatial patterns created by fire: a model oriented towards boreal forests. International Journal of Wildland Fire 5: 25-34.

Reidel, C. 1994. The political process of the Northern Forest lands study. Chapter 6 *in* Klyza, C. M. and S. C. Trombulak. 1994. The future of the Northern Forest. Middlebury College Press. Hanover, NH.

Roberts, B. A. and A. V. Mallik. 1994. Response of *Pinus resinosa* in Newfoundland to wildfire. Journal of Vegetation Science 5: 187-196.

Rochefort, R. M., R. L. Little, A. Woodward, and D. L. Peterson. 1994. Changes in sub-alpine tree distribution in western North America: a review of climatic and other factors. The Holocene 4(1): 89-100.

Romme, W. H. 1982. Fire and landscape diversity in subalpine forests of Yellowstone National Park. Ecological Monographs 52: 199-221.

Romme, W. H. and D. H. Knight. 1981. Fire frequency and subalpine forest succession along a topographic gradient in Wyoming. Ecology 62: 319-326.

Roe, E. I. and J. H. Stoeckler. 1950. Thinning over-dense jack pine seedling stands in the Lake States. Journal of Forestry 48: 861-865.

Rowe, J. S. 1961. Critique of some vegetational concepts as applied to forests of northwestern Alberta. Canadian Journal of Botany 39: 1007-17.

Rowe, J. S. 1972. Forest regions of Canada. Canadian Department of Environment. Canadian Forestry Service Publication 1300. Ottawa.

Rowe, J. S. 1983. Concepts of fire effects on plant individuals and species. Pages 135-154 *in* Wein, R. W. and D. A. MacLean. The role of fire in northern circumpolar ecosystems. John Wiley and Sons, New York.

Rowe, J. S., J. L. Bergsteinsson, G. A. Padbury, and R. Hermesh. 1974. Fire studies in the Mackenzie Valley. Canadian Department of Indian Affairs and Northern Development. ALUR Rep. 73-74-61. 123 p.

Rowe, J. S. and G. W. Scotter. 1973. Fire in the boreal forest. Quaternary Research 3: 444-64.

Runkle, J. R. 1982. Patterns of disturbance in some old-growth mesic forests of Eastern North America. Ecology 63: 1533-46.

Sandberg, L. 1983. The response of forest industries to a changing environment. Chapter 12 *in* Flader, S. L. ed. The Great Lakes Forest: an environmental and social history. University of Minnesota Press, Minneapolis, MN.

Schroeder, M. and C. Buck. 1970. Fire weather. USDA Agricultural Handbook 360.

Seymour, R. S. 1992. The red spruce-balsam fir forest of Maine: evolution of silvicultural practice in response to stand development patterns and disturbances. Pages 217-244 *in* Kelty, M. J. et al., eds. The ecology and silviculture of mixed-species forests: A festschrift for David M. Smith. Kluwer Publishers, Norwell, MA.

Seymour, R. S. and M. L. Hunter, Jr. 1992. New forestry in eastern spruce-fir forests: Applications to Maine. Maine Agricultural Experiment Station Misc. Pub. 716.

Sirois, L. 1992. The transition between boreal forest and tundra. Pages 196-215 *in* Shugart, H. H., R. Leemans, and G. B. Bonan, eds. A systems analysis of the global boreal forest. Cambridge University Press, Cambridge.

Smith, J. H. G. and R. C. Henderson. 1970. Impact of fire control practices on ecosystem development. pp 86-98 *in* Role of fire in the Intermountain West. University of Montana, Missoula.

Solomon, A. M. 1992. The nature and distribution of past, present, and future boreal forests: lessons for a research and modeling agenda. Pages 291-307 *in* Shugart, H. H., R. Leemans, and G. B. Bonan, eds. A systems analysis of the global boreal forest. Cambridge University Press, Cambridge.

Sprugel, D. G. 1976. Dynamic structure of wave-regenerated *Abies balsamea* forests in the Northeastern United States. Journal of Ecology 64: 889-91.

Stahelin, R. 1943. Factors influencing the natural restocking of high altitude burns by coniferous trees in the central Rocky Mountains. Ecology 24: 19-30.

Swetnam, T. W. and A. M. Lynch. 1993. Multicentury, regional-scale patterns of western spruce budworm outbreaks. Ecological Monographs 63: 399-424.

Taylor, T. M. C. 1959. The taxonomic relationship between *Picea glauca* (Moench) Voss and *Picea engelmannii* Parry. Madrono 15: 111-115.

Trewartha, G. T. 1968. An introduction to climate. 4th Edition. McGraw-Hill, New York.

Van Cleve, K. 1981. Woodlands data set: black spruce feathermoss and muskeg sites 1-2. Pages 648-650 In Reichle, D. E., ed. Dynamic properties of forest ecosystems. International Biological Programme 23. Cambridge University Press, Cambridge.

Van Cleve, K., C. T. Dyrness, L. A. Viereck, J. Fox, F. S. Chapin, III, and W. Oechel. 1983. Taiga ecosystems in interior Alaska. Bioscience 33, 1: 39-44.

Van Sickle, G. A. 1995. Forest insect pests in the Pacific and Yukon region. Pages 74-89 *in* Armstrong, J. A. and W. G. H. Ives, eds. Forest insect pests in Canada. Natural Resources Canada, Canadian Forest Service, Science and Sustainable Development Directorate.

Van Wagner, C. E. 1978. Age-class distribution and the forest fire cycle. Canadian Journal of Forest Research 8: 220-7

Van Wagner, C. E. 1983. Fire behavior in northern conifer forests and shrublands. Pages 65-80 *in* Wein, R. W. and D. A. MacLean. The role of fire in northern circumpolar ecosystems. John Wiley and Sons, New York.

Veblen, T. T. 1986. Age and size structure of subalpine forests in the Colorado Front Range. Bulletin of the Torrey Botanical Club 113: 225-40.

Veblen, T. T., K. S. Hadley, E. M. Nel, T. Kitzberger, M. Reid, and R. Villalba. 1994. Disturbance regime and disturbance interactions in a Rocky Mountain subalpine forest. Journal of Ecology 82: 125-135.

Viereck, L. A. 1973. Wildfire in the taiga of Alaska. Quaternary Research 3: 465-95.

Viereck, L. A. 1983. The effects of fire on black spruce ecosystems of Alaska and Northern Canada. Pages 201-220 *in* Wein, R. W. and D. A. MacLean. The role of fire in northern circumpolar ecosystems. John Wiley and Sons, New York.

Viereck, L. A. and C. T. Dyrness 1980. A preliminary classification system for vegetation of Alaska. Gen. Tech. Rep. PNW-106. Portland, OR: U.S. Department of Agriculture, Forest Service, Pacific Northwest Station.

Wein, R. W. and J. M. Moore. 1977. Fire history and rotations in the New Brunswick Acadian Forest. Canadian Journal of Forest Research 7: 285-294.

Wein, R. W. and J. M. Moore. 1979. Fire history and recent fire rotation periods in the Nova Scotia Acadian Forest. Canadian Journal of Forest Research 9: 166-178.

Werner, R. A. and E. H. Holsten. 1983. Mortality of white spruce during a spruce beetle outbreak on the Kenai Peninsula in Alaska. Canadian Journal of Forest Research 13: 96-101.

Yarie, J. 1979. A preliminary analysis of stand age distribution in the porcupine inventory unit (abstract). Page 12 *in* Proceedings 30th Alaska Science Conference, Fairbanks, Alaska.

Chapter 4

Habitat Fragmentation and Interspecific Competition: Implications for Lynx Conservation

Steven W. Buskirk, Department of Zoology and Physiology, University of Wyoming, P.O. Box 3166, Laramie, WY 82071

Leonard F. Ruggiero, Rocky Mountain Research Station, 800 E. Beckwith, P.O. Box 8089, Missoula, MT 59807

Charles J. Krebs, Department of Zoology, University of British Columbia, 6270 University Blvd., Vancouver, BC V6T 1Z4 Canada

Abstract—Habitat fragmentation and interspecific competition are two important forces that potentially affect lynx populations. Fragmentation operates by various mechanisms, including direct habitat loss, vehicle collisions and behavioral disturbance from roads, and changes in landscape features such as edges. Competition takes two forms: Exploitation competition involves potential competitors, such as coyotes and raptors, for food with lynx. Interference competition involves aggressive acts, almost always by a larger animal, that can include attacking and killing. Habitat fragmentation tends to facilitate competition by generalist predators, of which the most likely beneficiary is the coyote. Other potential interference competitors with lynx include cougars and bobcats. Of these three carnivores, all are more widespread and more abundant within the southern distribution of the lynx than 50 years ago.

Introduction

Fragmentation (Dayan et al. 1989) and competition (Rosenzweig 1966) are major forces shaping the evolution, composition, and function of carnivore communities ("carnivorans" is a more precise term referring to members of the Order Carnivora; we use "carnivoran" and "carnivore" synonymously). In human-dominated landscapes, fragmentation and competition are strongly linked because vegetation mosaics in landscapes provide high quality environments for generalist species such as the coyote and great-horned owl (Goodrich and Buskirk 1995). Under such conditions, generalist predators are favored over habitat specialists such as the spotted owl and American marten. As humans change the patterns of natural landscapes through timber harvest, construction of roads and buildings, and conversion of land to other uses, ecological processes such as competition, dispersal, and predation are affected in various ways (Wilcove 1985). Although many of these effects are poorly understood, it is clear that the structure and function of animal communities can be dramatically altered (Wilcove et al. 1986; Yahner 1988; Oehler and Litvaitis 1996). Here, we discuss how interspecific competition affects carnivores in general, how habitat fragmentation may mediate this process, and how lynx populations in particular may be affected.

Habitat Fragmentation

The term "fragmentation" is used widely to describe human alterations of natural landscapes (Knight et al., in press). Lord and Norton (1990) defined this process as the disruption of continuity, especially as it relates to ecosystem processes. Forman (1995) discussed how fragmentation affects the area, size, shape, and configuration of landscape elements, in an overall process of land transformation that has major implications for conservation (Lord and Norton 1990; Wilcove et al. 1986). Fragmentation has been variously defined to describe a reduction of total area, increased isolation of patches, and reduced connectedness among patches of natural vegetation (Rolstad 1991). Fragmentation tends to reduce habitat area and to isolate patches of native vegetation (especially in late seral stages) from each other, both of which can lead to local species extirpations (Wilcox 1980; Wilcox and Murphy 1985). Moreover, the loss of some species in this way can lead to multiple extinctions through community-level secondary effects (Wilcox and Murphy 1985).

Fragmentation has been applied to both natural (Andrén 1994) and human-caused alterations of landscape patterns. Here, we use the term "patchiness" when referring to natural processes (Buskirk et al., in press) and "fragmentation" to anthropogenic disruption of natural patterns and the secondary effects of such disruption (e.g., behavioral disturbance to wildlife), and the effects of cars, pets, garbage, and other human accoutrements (Buskirk et al., in press).

Although appropriate to any landscape, fragmentation has been preferentially applied to forests (Simberloff 1994; Lehmkuhl and Ruggiero 1991; Harris 1984). In this context, some have argued that the negative effects of forest fragmentation are ameliorated in areas like the Rocky Mountains because of naturally patchy landscapes. This contention is unlikely to be true given that, by definition, fragmentation disrupts the natural landscape pattern regardless of the scale of the undisturbed pattern. That is, fragmentation is not scale-limited (Lord and Norton 1990). Moreover, natural landscape pattern is a complex function of topography with its associated (e.g., edaphic, microclimatic) gradients and natural disturbance processes, the most important of which is fire. Clearly, the kinds, amounts, and arrangements of forested environments differ markedly between natural and anthropogenic disturbances (Harris 1984; Ruggiero et al. 1991).

Fragmentation has been shown to affect a fairly wide range of birds and mammals (reviewed by Harris 1984, Bright 1993, Andrén 1994, and Oehler and Litvaitis 1996). This is not surprising, considering the wide range of mechanisms whereby vertebrates can be impacted—for example, loss of area, isolation of patches, vehicle collisions, increased predation by edge-preferring predators, changes in boundary conditions including altered moisture regimes near stand edges, and changes in the habitat matrix or context within which undisturbed habitats exist. Several of these mechanisms can mediate competitive relationships by permitting generalist predators such as coyotes access to landscapes occupied by specialist species that are ecologically separated in natural landscapes (Hunter 1990). Moreover, our considerable understanding of ecological systems and mechanisms of competition provides a plausible basis for believing habitat-mediated competition is an important factor in population persistence. Finally, as clearly stated by Wilcox and Murphy (1985:884), "That current ecological theory is inadequate for resolving many of the details should not detract from what is obvious and accepted by most ecologists: habitat fragmentation is the most serious threat to biological diversity and is the primary cause of the present extinction crisis."

Direct habitat effects of fragmentation of most concern in lynx conservation are (1) reduction of area and patch size of late-successional forest and of optimal snowshoe hare habitat; (2) creation of openings that facilitate access by potentially competing carnivores; (3) increased densities of edges between early successional and other forest types; and (4) changes in the amounts and structural complexity of seral forest stands within landscapes. Although landscape-level studies have not determined how fragmentation affects lynx ecology and population persistence (Koehler and Aubry 1994), rare species associated with wilderness, such as the lynx, generally are considered most susceptible to fragmentation (Bright 1993). Likewise, habitat specialists with large individual spatial needs, including the lynx (Quinn and Parker 1987; O'Donoghue et al. 1998), are likely to be impacted by habitat fragmentation (Andrén 1994). This is so because generalist predators tend to dominate the predator guild in fragmented landscapes (Oehler and Litvaitis 1996).

Competition

Keddy (1989:2) defined competition as "the negative effects which one organism has upon another by consuming, or controlling access to, a resource that is limited in availability." Two qualitatively different kinds of interspecific competition can be illustrated by examples involving the lynx (Fig. 4.1).

Exploitation (resource) competition (Litvaitis 1992) occurs when other species, such as the northern goshawk, bobcat, or coyote, use resources that limit the fitness of a lynx. Thus, if northern goshawks exploit snowshoe hares in an area so thoroughly that lynx die sooner (from starvation or while dispersing to a new place), breed less (from females failing to mate or give birth), or produce smaller litters of kittens than they would otherwise, we say that northern goshawks competed (exploitatively) with lynx. Although the competition might have been reciprocal, that issue is academic from our perspective here.

Interference competition (Case and Gilpin 1974) occurs when one species acts aggressively toward another, denying it access to a resource (Fig. 4.1). For example, if a cougar were to chase a lynx away from a hare carcass, or kill one of its kittens, or scent mark an area so that lynx were deterred from foraging there, this would constitute interference competition. Exploitation competition is not particularly affected by the relative body sizes of the participants, as in the hypothetical example of the smaller goshawk and the larger-bodied lynx. Interference competition, by contrast, is almost invariably inflicted by a larger carnivore on a smaller one (Fig. 4.2). Further, the likelihood of interference competition among carnivores seems to be greatest when two species are similar in body form and size (Buskirk in press); for example, wolves are more likely to exert interference competition on coyotes than on red foxes (similar shape but different size: Johnson and Sargeant 1977) or on badgers (different shape).

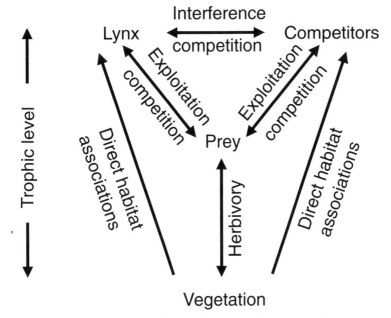

Figure 4.1—Competitive, trophic, and habitat relationships involving lynx. Interference competition, when it involves killing, can include ingestion. Direct habitat associations refer to needs of animals and constraints imposed by physical structure such as live vegetation, coarse woody debris, and snow.

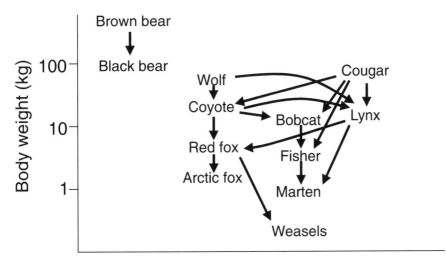

Figure 4.2—Interference competitive interactions among North American carnivores. Arrows point from dominant to subordinate participant and in all cases point downward on the body-weight axis. Interactions are documented in Litvaitis (1992), Buskirk (1999), and this chapter.

Interference competition appears to be capable of influencing carnivore populations to remarkable degrees. Although exploitation competition can reduce prey abundance and thus cause predators to become rare (the numerical response: Taylor 1984), interference competition can drive them to local or regional extinction. For example, Ashbrook and Walker (1925) described how one red fox eradicated all (at least six) of the arctic foxes on Chowiet Island, Alaska (56° 2' N., 156° 40' W., 0.8 km^2 in area) in less than three years. Similarly, wolves on Isle Royale, Michigan (Krefting 1969) and the Kenai Peninsula, Alaska (Thurber et al. 1992) have been credited with eradicating coyotes upon arrival in the former area and with preventing their sympatry before the extinction of wolves of the latter area. The potentially high importance of interference competition, compared with exploitation competition, is surprising unless one considers the prey-switching ability that is a common adaptation of carnivores (Taylor 1984). Alternate prey can allow carnivores to persist when preferred prey are scarce, but an effective interference competitor can pursue its enemy to scarcity or extinction. Thus, interference competition and prey availability are both critically important issues in the distribution and abundance of mesocarnivores, including the lynx.

The effects of fragmentation on predator-prey interactions (and thus perhaps interference competition) depend on the specific behaviors of the species in question (Kareiva 1987) and its environment. Thus, predation and competition are highly context-specific phenomena. Various biotic and abiotic factors can mediate competitive interactions (direct habitat associations, Fig. 4.1), so that a dominant competitor in one setting coexists or is subordinate in another (Sargeant et al. 1987). Many such mediated relationships have been reported. In carnivores, for example, Paquet (1991) reported that coyotes did not avoid wolves during winter, and Gese et al. (1996) concluded that coyotes tolerated red foxes in Yellowstone National Park during a high prey year, but not at other times. A strong abiotic affect on interactions between another pair of forest-dwelling carnivores, the marten and fisher, has been described by Krohn et al. (1995). Martens, with their proportionally larger feet, can travel in deeper, softer snow than can fishers, and martens predominate in parts of Maine with deep soft snow. But, fishers are competitively (interference) dominant over martens, and therefore are the more common species where snow is shallow or crusted.

We summarize possible relationships between lynx and potential competitors in Table 4.1 and Figure 4.2. As discussed earlier, direct evidence of competition is very difficult to collect and therefore scarce. The fact that there have been very few intensive studies of lynx in the United States contributes to the lack of empirical information. In some cases, exploitation of a common

Table 4.1–Possible competitive impacts to lynx, mediating factors, and our evaluation of the likely importance of the causes in the decline of lynx in the contiguous United States.

Possible impact	Potential competitors	Likely importance
Exploitation (food)	Birds of prey (goshawk and great-horned owl)	Minimal impact
	Coyote	Locally or regionally important
	Wolf	Minimal impact
	Cougar	Minimal impact
Interference	Coyote	Possible
	Bobcat	Possible where bobcats occupy high-elevation habitats
	Wolverine	Documented, but likely rare
	Cougar	Likely in summer or where lynx venture out of deep snow areas

prey species (e.g., snowshoe hares) and numerical (great-horned owl - Rohner and Krebs 1996, 1998) or functional (red-tailed hawk - Adamcik et al. 1979) responses to increasing hare abundance serves to indicate potentially important competitive relationships. For predators such as the great-horned owl, a functional response to hare abundance could lead to owl predation on lynx kittens, although this has not been reported (C. Rohner, personal communication). Thus, functional responses to increased prey abundance may have the primary effect of increased exploitation competition and a secondary or indirect effect of increased interference competition.

Competition With Cougars

Interference competition between cougars and bobcats was reported by Koehler and Hornocker (1991), who found that cougars killed bobcats when both species were forced to lower elevations in winter. Squires and Lorean (Chapter 11) document two lynx killed by cougars in western Montana during fall and early winter. Based on these observations and because cougars are larger than lynx and have become more abundant in the western United States in recent years (Green 1991), cougars may be significant interference competitors with lynx. Deep snow, however, is a hindrance to cougar movements (Fig. 4.3), and should spatially separate lynx and cougars under normal winter conditions. Strong demographic consequences of interference have been reported for another pair of felids, the cheetah and African lion. Caro and Laurenson (1994) reported that lions killed entire cheetah litters, contributing to a survival rate at age two months of 29%. Such killing of litters has not been reported for lynx. Other carnivores,

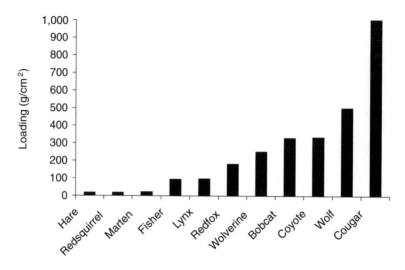

Figure 4.3—Foot loadings of North American mammals important as prey and community associates of Canada lynx. Weights were taken from Chapman and Feldhamer (1982) and Silva and Downing (1995). Foot surface areas were estimated for the larger foot of each species by first enlarging the drawings of tracks in snow depicted in Forrest (1988) so that their length was the mid-range reported by Forrest (1988). The area of the track (cm²) was then measured by digital planimetry (Tamaya Digital Planimeter). Foot loading is an approximation of the pressure exerted by the animal walking on snow, and therefore its sinking depth. High sinking depth suggests that, other factors being equal, an animal exerts more energy to traverse snow while walking. The snowshoe hare has the lowest foot loading of any mammal considered, the cougar the highest.

including wolverines and feral dogs (reviewed by McCord and Cordoza 1982 and Quinn and Parker 1987), occasionally kill or take food from lynx.

Competition With Bobcats

Bobcats attain larger body size than lynx (Hall 1981) and may be larger than sympatric lynx in some areas. Among a small sample of sympatric bobcats and lynx in western Wyoming, the largest male bobcat was 2-4 kg larger than the largest male lynx (T. Lorean, personal communication). Such a body-size difference would set the stage for interference competition dominated by bobcats. Further, the diets of both species (reviewed by Rolley 1987 and Quinn and Parker 1987) tend to be dominated by leporids, creating the potential for exploitation competition. Where bobcats attain high densities and body sizes larger than those of sympatric lynx, competitive impacts upon lynx should be suspected. Although bobcats and lynx are generally thought to be ecologically separated by deep snow, interactions between these two species under other conditions are poorly understood. For example, in Montana, Smith (1984) reported that bobcat home ranges during winter were located at significantly lower elevations than were lynx home ranges, but that this difference disappeared during spring and autumn. Similarly, in western Maine, Major (1983) found that snowshoe hares ranked first or second in frequency of occurrence in bobcat diets during all seasons over a three-year period. Toweill (1986) found that bobcats in the western Oregon Cascades ate snowshoe hares regularly. These findings indicate that bobcats may be significant competitors with lynx under some conditions. That lynx can be excluded by bobcats is suggested by Parker et al. (1983), who believed that bobcats, recent immigrants to Cape Breton Island, caused the displacement of lynx from low areas. These accounts suggest the potentially important influence of bobcats on lynx.

Competition With Coyotes and Wolves

The coyote, because of its wide habitat niche, heavy predation on snowshoe hares (O'Donoghue et al. 1998), high reproductive rate (Quinn and Parker 1987), great behavioral plasticity (Murray and Boutin 1991), and high tolerance of humans (Litvaitis 1992), must be considered a potentially formidable competitor with mesocarnivores, including the lynx. Indeed, coyotes are suspected in various declines of mesocarnivores, as evidenced by documented cases of coyotes competing with or preying on sensitive and endangered species (reviewed by Litvaitis 1992 and Goodrich and Buskirk 1995).

The distribution of coyotes has expanded dramatically during the past few decades, especially to the northeast (Fuller and Kittredge 1996), but also to the northwest. Coyote numbers have increased dramatically in New England, as indexed by numbers of coyotes caught by trappers in New Hampshire (Fig. 4.4). Virtually no coyotes were trapped in New Hampshire before 1970, but coyotes were common by the mid-1970s and continued to increase through the mid-1990s. Pelt price, a strong predictor of harvest of many furbearers, explains little of the increase in coyote harvests in New Hampshire over this period (Fig. 4.4). Similarly, coyote harvests from Washington increased from the five-year period ending 1964-1965 (mean = 362/year) to the five years ending 1983-1984 (mean = 16,250/year; Novak et al. 1987). Consistent with this, coyotes were rare or nonexistent in coniferous forests of the Oregon and Washington Cascades until timber wolves were extirpated around 1930 (Ozoga and Harger 1966).

The ecology of coyotes suggests further that they should be potent competitors. Coyotes at times kill lynx (O'Donoghue et al. 1995), probably most often when lynx are young or in poor condition. O'Donoghue (1997) also

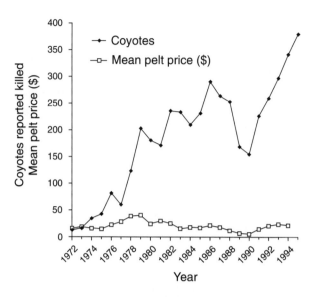

Figure 4.4—Abundance of coyotes in New Hampshire, as indexed by numbers killed in the State and sealed by the State of New Hampshire Game and Fish Department (unpublished data) and mean price paid per pelt to trappers for coyote pelts, as indexed by the same agency (unpublished data). Price is plotted because of the strong influence of price on harvest effort. The year - coyote correlation was r (Pearson) = 0.77, whereas the price - coyote correlation was r = 0.03. Therefore, we conclude that the strong upward linear trend in coyotes killed is the result of their increased abundance.

showed that, comparing densities of lynx, hares, and coyotes between his Yukon study area and that of Keith et al. (1977) in central Alberta, lynx were more abundant where coyotes were less dense, rather than where hares were more dense. Thus, interactions with coyotes appear to influence lynx more than availability of snowshoe hares, generally considered to be the limiting factor for lynx numbers. Similarly, coyotes compete with bobcats in various settings (Nunley 1978; Litvaitis and Harrison 1989). Interference competition (direct killing) of bobcats by coyotes has been documented by Anderson (1986), Jackson (1986), and Toweill (1986), and coyotes have been implicated in bobcat declines in some areas. Considering that bobcats can be larger and are more aggressive than lynx, coyote predation on bobcats suggests the potential for strong interference competition between coyotes and lynx. As with cougars and lynx, this potential likely is the greatest during low-snow periods—the season for which our understanding of lynx ecology is the weakest. Further, coyotes prey primarily on leporids (Voigt and Berg 1987);

within the range of the lynx, coyotes prey heavily on snowshoe hares (Todd et al. 1981; Todd and Keith 1983; Parker 1986; O'Donoghue et al. 1998), and attain high densities (up to $0.44/km^2$; Todd et al. 1981) when snowshoe hare populations are high. O'Donoghue et al. (1998) found that in Yukon Territory coyotes preyed on snowshoe hares during snowshoe hare highs at a higher rate than the lynx predation, suggesting potentially important exploitation competition with lynx. Further, coyote abundance tracked that of snowshoe hares through the cycle much as did lynx, enough that coyotes contributed to the cyclic dynamics of snowshoe hare populations (O'Donoghue et al. 1997). In a similar way, coyote densities have tracked those of snowshoe hares in forest habitats in the contiguous United States during the 1990s (Montana Department of Fish, Wildlife and Parks, unpublished data; Fig. 4.5), which probably is attributable to switching of habitats and prey by coyotes, corresponding with hare population changes. This illustrates the strong prey- and habitat-switching abilities of the coyote (reviewed by Patterson et al., in press), which contribute to its success as a competitor.

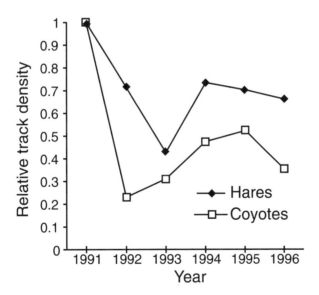

Figure 4.5—Relative abundance of coyotes and snowshoe hares on transects in Montana, 1991 to 1996. The correlation between hare and coyote track densities, without any time lag, is significant ($r = 0.81$, $df = 4$, $P = 0.05$). The absence of a lag in the correlation suggests that the relationship is at least partially due to habitat and prey switching by coyotes in response to fluctuating hare densities.

Numerous reports describe coyotes accessing high-elevation, deep snow areas by moving along paths, roads, and snowshoe hare trails (Bider 1962; Ozoga and Harger 1966; Murray et al. 1995). Unpublished data from Oregon (USDA Forest Service, unpublished report) and Colorado (Byrne 1998, unpublished) also suggest that coyotes use high elevation areas, although their means of access is not known. Byrne (1998, unpublished) conducted track surveys for snowshoe hares and recorded other species' tracks on 1,160 km of snow transects within presumed snowshoe hare habitat (7,500-11,800 feet elevation) in winter. Coyotes were the second most common carnivore taxon (after weasels) encountered, with 628 tracks recorded. The elevation zone with the highest frequency of coyote tracks was 8,000-9,000 feet but coyote tracks were fairly common (about 0.45/km of transect) in the 9,000-10,000 and 10,000-11,000 foot elevation zones. These results indicate that coyotes are much more common in high elevation, deep snow areas of western mountains than generally has been believed to be the case.

Nevertheless, some basis exists to believe that coyotes and lynx are spatially segregated in winter by deep snow. In central Alberta, Todd et al. (1981) found that coyote use of open habitats increased from November to March, which they attributed to snow accumulation in forest and the greater compactness and load-bearing strength of snow in openings. This intolerance of deep snow resulted in a diet shift from snowshoe hares to ungulate carrion in winter. Also in Alberta, Murray et al. (1994) found that coyotes were more selective of hard or shallow snow conditions than were lynx. In the western (Murray and Boutin 1991) and northeastern United States (Litvaitis 1992), this morphological difference causes coyotes and lynx to be spatially segregated by snow conditions. In the West, this occurs along an elevational gradient. Such separation should minimize competition between the two species. However, this separation may break down where human modifications to the environment increase access by coyotes to deep snow areas. Such modifications include expanded forest openings throughout the range of the lynx in which snow may be drifted, and increased snowmobile use in deep snow areas of western mountains. Recreational snowmobile use has expanded dramatically in the contiguous United States in the past 25 years, with hundreds of thousands of km of trails (>19,000 km of groomed trails in Maine alone) within the pre-settlement range of the lynx (Maine Snowmobile Association, World Wide Web site, Zesiger 1997). Various unpublished accounts describe snowmobile and snowshoe trails facilitating access by coyotes to areas used by hares and lynx. In the Yukon, coyotes use both snowshoe and snowmobile trails (O'Donoghue, personal communication). This facilitation of travel, in general, could help explain possible lynx reductions in the West via human-facilitated competition from coyotes and other generalist predators. Better understanding of this postulated relationship is critical.

Although wolves have been reported to kill lynx, only for Fennoscandia is there evidence that wolves exert population-level interference competition with lynx (Pulliainen 1965). We suspect that a more likely effect of wolves on lynx is by reducing numbers of coyotes, one of the strongest examples of fierce interference competition among carnivores (Buskirk 1999). In a few areas of the contiguous United States, wolves are becoming more common and coyotes more scarce. Lynx should fare better with sympatric wolves than with sympatric coyotes, because wolves prey little on leporids (Mech 1970) and are marginally too large to be interference competitors with lynx (Fig. 4.2). We predict that the Greater Yellowstone Area and northern Montana, with expanding wolf and shrinking coyote populations, will increase their suitability for occupancy by lynx in coming years.

Conclusions

Fragmentation of habitats occupied by lynx (including increased openings, higher road densities, exurban residential development, and wider use of snowmobiles and devices that compact snow in areas with deep, soft snow) is a plausible mechanism for the questionable conservation status of the lynx in the contiguous United States. Competition could take the form of exploitation by other predators of snowshoe hares, particularly the coyote, or involve interference competition, with larger-bodied carnivores acting aggressively toward lynx, even killing them. The coyote, because of its broad niche tolerances, high reproductive rate, and expanding range in the contiguous United States, is particularly suspect in competition. In spite of this evidence suggesting that coyotes may exploitatively compete with lynx, we suspect that, at least where hare populations cycle, exploitative competition impacting lynx is unlikely. Competitive systems involving cycling snowshoe hares never come to equilibrium and the primary impact of the competition should be overwhelmed by the large changes in prey availability. Even so, in the southern part of the range of lynx, if hares fluctuate less dramatically than they do in the North, exploitation competition inflicted by coyotes may reduce lynx numbers. Overall, we suspect that interference competition is more likely to be the critical form of competition that needs to be evaluated for lynx in the contiguous United States. Cougars, in particular, appear to be effective interference competitors with lynx.

Literature Cited

Adamcik, R. S., A. W. Todd, and L. B. Keith. 1979. Demographic and dietary responses of red-tailed hawks during a snowshoe hare fluctuation. Can. Field-Nat. 93:16-27.

Anderson, E. M. 1986. Bobcat behavioral ecology in relation to resource use in southeastern Colorado. Ph.D. Diss., Colorado State University, Fort Collins.

Andrén, H. 1994. Effects of habitat fragmentation on birds and mammals in landscapes with different proportions of suitable habitat: a review. Oikos 71:355-366.

Ashbrook, F. G. and E. P. Walker. 1925. Blue fox farming in Alaska. USDA Bulletin No. 1350.

Bider, J. R. 1962. Dynamics and the temporo-spatial relations of a vertebrate community. Ecology 43:634-646.

Bright, P. W. 1993. Habitat fragmentation - problems and predictions for British mammals. Mammal Review 23: 101-111.

Buskirk, S. W. 1999. Mesocarnivores of Yellowstone. Pages 165-187 in Clark, T. W., S. C. Minta, P. M. Kareiva, and P. M. Curlee, editors. Carnivores in ecosystems. Yale University Press, New Haven, CT.

Buskirk, S. W., W. H. Romme, F. W. Smith, and R. L. Knight. In press. An overview of forest fragmentation in the southern Rocky Mountains. in R. L. Knight, F. W. Smith, S. W. Buskirk, W. H. Romme, and W. L. Baker, editors. Forest fragmentation in the southern Rocky Mountains. University Press of Colorado, Boulder.

Byrne, G. 1998. A Colorado winter track survey for snowshoe hares and other species. Unpublished report, Colorado Division of Wildlife, Glenwood Springs, CO.

Caro, T. M. and M. K. Laurenson. 1994. Ecological and genetic factors in conservation: a cautionary tale. Science 263:485-486.

Case, T. J. and M. R. Gilpin. 1974. Interference competition and niche theory. Proceedings of the National Academy of Sciences 71:3073-3077.

Chapman, J. A. and G. A. Feldhamer. 1982. Wild mammals of North America. Johns Hopkins University Press, Baltimore, MD. 1147.

Dayan, T., D. S. Simberloff, E. T. Chernov, and Y. Yom-Tov. 1989. Inter- and intra-specific character displacement in mustelids. Ecology 70:1526-1539.

Forman, R. T. T. 1995. Land mosaics: the ecology of landscapes and regions. Cambridge University Press, Cambridge, UK.

Forrest, L. R. 1988. Field guide to tracking animals in snow. Stackpole Books, Harrisburg, PA.

Fuller, T. K. and D. B. Kittredge, Jr. 1996. Conservation of large forest carnivores. Pages 137-164 in R. M. DeGraaf and R. I. Miller, editors. Conservation of faunal diversity in forested landscapes. Chapman and Hall, London, UK.

Gese, E. M., T. E. Stotts, and S. Grothe. 1996. Interactions between coyotes and red foxes in Yellowstone National Park, Wyoming. Journal of Mammalogy 77:377-382.

Goodrich, J. M. and S. W. Buskirk. 1995. Control of abundant native vertebrates for conservation of endangered species. Conservation Biology 9:1357-1364.

Green, K. A. 1991. Summary: mountain lion - human interaction questionnaires, 1991. Unpublished abstract, Mountain lion - human interaction workshop. Colorado Division of Wildlife, Denver, CO.

Hall, E. R. 1981. The mammals of North America. John Wiley and Sons, New York, NY.

Harris, L. D. 1984. The fragmented forest: island biogeography theory and the preservation of biotic diversity. University of Chicago Press, Chicago, IL.

Hunter, M. L., Jr. 1990. Wildlife, forests and forestry. Prentice Hall, Englewood Cliffs, NJ.

Jackson, D. H. 1986. Ecology of bobcats in east-central Colorado. Ph.D. Dissertation, Colorado State University, Fort Collins, CO.

Johnson, D. H. and A. B. Sargeant. 1977. Impact of red fox predation on the sex ratio of prairie mallards. U.S. Fish and Wildlife Service, Wildlife Research Report 6.

Kareiva, P. 1987. Habitat fragmentation and the stability of predator-prey interactions. Nature 326:388-390.

Keddy, P. A. 1989. Competition. Chapman and Hall, New York, NY.

Keith, L. B., A. W. Todd, C. J. Brand, R. S. Adamcik, and D. H. Rusch. 1977. An analysis of predation during a cyclic fluctuation of snowshoe hares. Proceedings of the International Congress of Game Biologists 13:151-175.

Knight, R. L., F. W. Smith, S. W. Buskirk, W. H. Romme, and W. L. Baker. In press. Forest fragmentation in the southern Rocky Mountains. University Press of Colorado.

Koehler, G. M. and K. B. Aubry. 1994. Lynx. Pages 74-98 in L. F. Ruggiero, K. B. Aubry, S. W. Buskirk, L. J. Lyon, and W. J. Zielinski, editors. The scientific basis for conserving forest carnivores: American marten, fisher, lynx, and wolverine in the western United States. USDA Forest Service, General Technical Report RM-254.

Koehler, G. M. and M. G. Hornocker. 1991. Seasonal resource use among mountain lions, bobcats and coyotes. Journal of Mammalogy 72-391-396.

Krefting, L. W. 1969. The rise and fall of the coyote on Isle Royale. Naturalist 20(3):24-31.

Krohn, W. B., K. D. Elowe, and R. B. Boone. 1995. Relations among fishers, snow and martens: development and evaluation of two hypotheses. Forestry Chronicle 71:97-105.

Lehmkuhl, J. F. and L. F. Ruggiero. 1991. Forest fragmentation in the Pacific Northwest and its potential effects on wildlife. Pages 35-46 in L. F. Ruggiero, K. B. Aubry, A. B. Carey, and M. H. Huff, editors. Wildlife and vegetation of unmanaged Douglas-fir forests. USDA Forest Service General Technical Report PNW-285.

Litvaitis, J. A. 1992. Niche relations between coyotes and sympatric Carnivora. Pages 73-85 in A. H. Boer, editor. Ecology and management of the eastern coyote. University of New Brunswick Wildlife Research Unit, Fredericton, NB.

Litvaitis, J. A. and D. J. Harrison. 1989. Bobcat-coyote niche relationships during a period of coyote population increase. Canadian Journal of Zoology 67:1180-1188.

Lord, J. M. and D. A. Norton. 1990. Scale and the spatial concept of fragmentation. Conservation Biology 4(2):197-202.

Major, J. T. 1983. Ecology and interspecific relationships of coyotes, bobcats, and red foxes in western Maine. Ph.D. Dissertation, University of Maine.

McCord, C. M. and J. E. Cardoza. 1982. Bobcat and lynx. Pages 728-766 *in* J. A. Chapman and G. A. Feldhamer, editors. Wild mammals of North America. Johns Hopkins University Press, Baltimore, MD.

Mech, L. D. 1970. The wolf: the ecology and behavior of an endangered species. Natural History Press, Garden City, NY.

Murray, D. L. and S. Boutin. 1991. The influence of snow on lynx and coyote movements: does morphology affect behavior? Oecologia 88:463-469.

Murray, D. L., S. Boutin, and M. O'Donoghue. 1994. Winter habitat selection by lynx and coyotes in relation to snowshoe hare abundance. Canadian Journal of Zoology 72:1444-1451.

Murray, D. L., S. Boutin, M. O'Donoghue, and V. O. Nams. 1995. Hunting behavior of a sympatric felid and canid in relation to vegetative cover. Animal Behavior 50:1203-1210.

Novak, M., M. E. Obbard, J. G. Jones, R. Newman, A. Booth, A. J. Satterthwaite, and G. Linscombe. 1987. Furbearer harvests in North America, 1600-1984. Ontario Trappers Association, Ontario, Canada.

Nunley, G. L. 1978. Present and historical bobcat trends in New Mexico and the West. Proceedings of the Vertebrate Pest Conference 8:77-84.

O'Donoghue, M. 1997. Responses of coyotes and lynx to the snowshoe hare cycle. Ph.D. Dissertation, University of British Columbia, Vancouver.

O'Donoghue, M., S. Boutin, C. J. Krebs, and E. J. Hofer. 1997. Numerical responses of coyotes and lynx to the snowshoe hare cycle. Oikos 80:150-162.

O'Donoghue, M., S. Boutin, C. J. Krebs, G. Zuleta, D. L. Murray, and E. J. Hofer. 1998. Functional response of coyotes and lynx to the snowshoe hare cycle. Ecology 79:1193-1208.

O'Donoghue, M., E. Hofer, and F. I. Doyle. 1995. Predator versus predator. Natural History 104:6-9.

Oehler, J. D. and J. A. Litvaitis. 1996. The role of spatial scale in understanding responses of medium-sized carnivores to forest fragmentation. Canadian Journal of Zoology 74:2070-2079.

Ozoga, J. J. and E. M. Harger. 1966. Winter activities and feeding habits of northern Michigan coyotes. Journal of Wildlife Management 30(4):809-818.

Paquet, P. 1991. Winter spatial relationships of wolves and coyotes in Riding Mountain National Park, Manitoba. Journal of Mammalogy 72:397-401.

Parker, G. R. 1986. The seasonal diet of coyotes, *Canis latrans*, in northern New Brunswick. Canadian Field-Naturalist 100:74-77.

Parker, G. R., J. W. Maxell, and L. D. Morton. 1983. The ecology of the lynx (*Lynx canadensis*) on Cape Breton Island. Canadian Journal of Zoology 61:770-786.

Patterson, B. R., L. K. Benjamin, and F. Messier. In press. Prey switching and the feeding habits of eastern coyotes in relation to the densities of snowshoe hare and white-tailed deer. Canadian Journal of Zoology.

Pulliainen, E. 1965. Studies of the wolf in Finland. Ann. Zool. Fenn. 2:215-259.

Quinn, N. W. S. and G. Parker. 1987. Lynx. Pages 683-694 *in* M. Novak, J. A. Baker, M. E. Obbard, and B. Malloch, editors. Wild furbearer management and conservation in North America. Ontario Ministry of Natural Resources, Ontario.

Rohner, C. and C. J. Krebs. 1996. Owl predation on snowshoe hares: consequences of antipredator behaviour. Oecologia 108:303-310.

Rohner, C. and C. J. Krebs. 1998. Responses of great-horned owls to experimental "hot spots" of snowshoe hare density. Auk 115:694-705.

Rolstad, J. 1991. Consequences of forest fragmentation for the dynamics of bird populations: conceptual issues and the evidence. Biological Journal of the Linnean Society 42:149-163.

Rolley, R. E. 1987. Bobcat. Pages 671-681 *in* M. Novak, J. A. Baker, M. E. Obbard, and B. Malloch, editors. Wild furbearer management and conservation in North America. Ontario Ministry of Natural Resources, Ontario.

Rosenzweig, M. L. 1966. Community structure in sympatric Carnivora. Journal of Mammalogy 47:602-612.

Ruggiero, L. F., K. B. Aubry, A. B. Carey, and M. H. Huff. 1991. Wildlife and vegetation of unmanaged Douglas-fir forests. USDA Forest Service General Technical Report PNW-285.

Sargeant, A. B., S. H. Allen, and J. O. Hastings. 1987. Spatial relations between sympatric coyotes and red foxes in North Dakota. Journal of Wildlife Management 51:285-293.

Silva, M. and J. A. Downing. 1995. CRC handbook of mammalian body masses. CRC Press, Boca Raton, FL.

Simberloff, D. 1994. How forest fragmentation hurts species and what to do about it. Pages 85-90 *in* W. W. Covington and L. F. Debano, editors. Sustainable ecological systems: implementing an ecological approach to land management. USDA Forest Service General Technical Report RM-247.

Smith, D. S. 1984. Habitat use, home range, and movements of bobcats in western Montana. M.S. Thesis, University of Montana, Missoula.

Taylor, R. J. 1984. Predation. Chapman and Hall, New York, NY.

Thurber, J. M., R. O. Peterson, J. D. Wollington, and J. A. Vucetich. 1992. Coyote coexistence with wolves on the Kenai Peninsula, Alaska. Canadian Journal of Zoology 70:2494-2498.

Todd, A. W., L. B. Keith, and C. A. Fischer. 1981. Population ecology of coyotes during a fluctuation of snowshoe hares. Journal of Wildlife Management 45:629-640.

Todd, A. W. and L. B. Keith. 1983. Coyote demography during a snowshoe hare decline in Alberta. Journal of Wildlife Management 47:394-404.

Toweill, D. E. 1986. Resource partitioning by bobcats and coyotes in a coniferous forest. M.S. Thesis, Oregon State University, Corvallis.

Voigt, D. R. and W. E. Berg. 1987. Coyote. Pages 344-357 *in* M. Novak, J. A. Baker, M. E. Obbard, and B. Malloch, editors. Wild furbearer management and conservation in North America. Ministry of Natural Resources, Toronto, Ontario.

Wilcove, D. S. 1985. Nest predation in forest tracts and the decline of migratory songbirds. Ecology 66:1211-1214.

Wilcove, D. S., C. H. McLellan, and A. P. Dobson. 1986. Habitat fragmentation in the Temperate Zone. Pages 237-256 *in* M. E. Soulé, editor. Conservation biology: the science of scarcity and diversity. Sinauer Associates, Sunderland, MA.

Wilcox, B. A. 1980. Insular ecology and conservation. Pages 95-118 *in* M. E. Soulé and B. A. Wilcox, eds. Conservation biology: an evolutionary-ecological perspective. Sinauer, Sunderland, MA.

Wilcox, B. A. and D. D. Murphy. 1985. Conservation strategy: the effects of fragmentation on extinction. American Naturalist 125:879-887.

Yahner, R. H. 1988. Changes in wildlife communities near edges. Conservation Biology 2:333-339.

Zesiger, S. 1997. Zero to sixty in three seconds (cold). Fortune 135(6):178.

Chapter 5

Species Conservation and Natural Variation Among Populations

Leonard F. Ruggiero, USDA Forest Service, Rocky Mountain Research Station, 815 E. Beckwith, Missoula, MT 59801

Michael K. Schwartz, Wildlife Biology Program, University of Montana, Missoula, MT 59812

Keith B. Aubry, USDA Forest Service, Pacific Northwest Research Station, 3625 93rd Ave. SW, Olympia, WA 98512

Charles J. Krebs, Department of Zoology, University of British Columbia, Vancouver, BC V6T 1Z4, Canada

Amanda Stanley, Department of Zoology, University of Washington, Seattle, WA 98195

Steven W. Buskirk, Department of Zoology and Physiology, University of Wyoming, P.O. Box 3166, Laramie, WY 82071

*Modifications of the phenotype that do not involve genetic changes
have long been considered...to lack evolutionary significance.
This view is not correct.*

- Ernst Mayr

Introduction

In conservation planning, the importance of natural variation is often
given inadequate consideration. However, ignoring the implications of
variation within species may result in conservation strategies that jeopardize, rather than conserve, target species (see Grieg 1979; Turcek 1951;
Storfer 1999). Natural variation in the traits of individuals and populations
is the product of the genetic composition of the individual and the environment to which the individual is exposed. Inherited traits are those that are
largely genetically determined, whereas non-inherited traits result primarily from environmental influences and are not under *direct* genetic control.
Inherited and non-inherited traits are an oversimplification of a complex
phenomenon and represent two ends of a gradient of variation.

Natural variation exists within and among populations. It is unwise to
assume that behavioral or genetic attributes exhibited by one population are
within the range of behavioral or genetic potential of another (Ruggiero et al.
1988). When this assumption is false, it can result in failed reintroduction
efforts or a net loss of genetic or behavioral variability (e.g., Halloran and Glass
1959 and examples provided in Storfer 1999). Similarly, problems can also
result from applying ecological knowledge from one population to the conservation needs of other populations inhabiting substantially different habitats.

In this chapter, we review fundamental concepts related to patterns of
natural variation in populations and discuss their relevance to the process of
species conservation. First, we define some of the terms used in this chapter
and discuss how geographic variation in environmental conditions may
lead to variation among populations. We then discuss differences between
inherited and non-inherited variation and the role each may play in structuring populations within species. Lastly, we discuss the implications of natural
variation among populations to lynx conservation.

We use the following terms and concepts: *genotype* refers to a particular set
of genes possessed by an individual, and *phenotype* is the outward appearance and behavior of the individual (Ricklefs 1990), which is determined by
interactions between the genotype and the environment. *Phenotypic plasticity* is the capacity for a single genotype to produce multiple phenotypes,

often as the result of varying environmental influences (Falconer and Mackay 1996). *Adaptation* is a trait that permits an organism to function well in its environment and endows it with capabilities especially appropriate for its particular environment (Roughgarden 1979).

Within- and Among-Population Variation

Populations and Species

Natural variation exists between individuals in a population and between populations of a species. A *population* is a group of conspecific organisms living near enough to one another that both ecological and reproductive interactions occur more frequently within the group than with members of other populations (Futuyma 1986). Populations are composed of unique individuals possessing varying behavioral and physical traits, and can only be characterized by the range of variation in these traits. Variation also exists among populations within a species (Endler 1986; Lott 1991). Differences among populations generally increase with distance and/or isolation.

In general, the aggregation of these populations comprises a species (for more specific definitions of the species see reviews in Futuyma 1998; Mallet 1995). Therefore, a species encompasses variation occurring both within and among populations. Species are not composed of uniform, interchangeable populations; they are more like jigsaw puzzles with many unique pieces.

Species Range and Dispersal Capability

Diversity among populations can be reduced when a species' dispersal capability is great relative to the spatial extent of its range, and when barriers do not impede dispersal or gene flow (Mills and Allendorf 1996; Wright 1969). However, in widely distributed species, such as the lynx, distance alone can function as a barrier to genetic exchange among populations, even when individuals are capable of long-distance movements. This is known as *isolation by distance* (see Britten et al. 1995; Hartl and Clark 1989; Wright 1943). Physical features of geography and habitat may also act as both absolute and psychological barriers to movements and dispersal (e.g., Buskirk and Ruggiero 1994; Diamond 1975; Mayr 1970) and impede gene flow. Thus, dispersal and gene flow are not simply mechanical processes governed by a species' movement capabilities, they are also affected by geographic influences on the movements of individuals, behavioral responses to perceived barriers, and the probability of successful reproduction in new environments.

Central vs. Peripheral Populations

Central populations are usually large, continuous, and occupy favorable habitats. Peripheral populations, by contrast, can be more or less isolated, fragmented, and subject to a more variable physical environment (Carson 1959; Lesica and Allendorf 1995). Accordingly, peripheral populations will often experience different selection pressures than central populations, which may lead to genetic divergence (but see Kirkpatrick and Barton 1997).

Differences in genotype and phenotype are most likely to occur in populations that have become isolated at the periphery of the range (Lesica and Allendorf 1995; Mayr 1970; Safriel et al. 1994). Isolated populations lack or have greatly reduced levels of immigration and, consequently, may diverge from central populations due to genetic drift and natural selection. Peripheral populations often have reduced levels of genetic variability relative to central populations (Lesica and Allendorf 1995)

Genes vs. Environment: A False Dichotomy

Assessments of natural variation among populations are generally focused on traits that have a direct genetic basis (i.e., inherited traits), with little emphasis on those that do not (e.g., Vogler and DeSalle 1994). The prevailing view seems to be that because only genetic material is inherited, it represents the essential element of natural variation, selection, and adaptation. In contrast, a phenotype for which no direct genetic basis is known is thought to be of less evolutionary significance and of only minor importance in conservation planning (see Pennock and Dimmick 1997; Rohlf 1994). However, we believe this view to be fundamentally incorrect because phenotypic plasticity (which is itself a genetic trait) and its effects on individual fitness can play a key role in evolutionary processes (Mayr 1970; Pianka 1994).

Natural Selection and Inherited vs. Non-inherited Traits

Evolutionary theory states that populations contain inherited variation that arises by random mutation and recombination and which is acted upon by random genetic drift and natural selection. Natural selection is the differential reproductive success of different phenotypes, a process which slowly changes gene frequencies in populations. Those individuals with phenotypes that are selected against are less successful than others and, eventually, their genes are eliminated from the population.

Traits that are largely influenced by the environment are considered non-inherited. This does not mean that these traits are non-genetic. Most non-inherited traits are under "indirect" genetic control, as it is ultimately the genes of the individual that allow the phenotype to be shaped by the environment. When natural selection acts upon these phenotypes, gene frequencies do not immediately change because there is no direct correlation between the genotype and the phenotype. However, non-genetic modifications of the phenotype that occur in the absence of genetic change can be adaptive, can influence fitness, and may be preserved by indirect genetic mechanisms and learned behaviors (Falconer and Mackay 1996; Grant 1963; Mayr 1970).

The evolutionary significance of phenotypic plasticity has been discussed in many contexts (Baldwin 1896; see also Ancel 1999 and Simpson 1953). Baldwin argued that such responses might permit a population to inhabit an environment to which it is poorly adapted. Through this mechanism, the population may gain the time necessary to acquire, through mutation, genotypes with an adaptive advantage (Grant 1963).

Discriminating between inherited and non-inherited traits is extremely difficult. To determine if a behavioral, physiological, morphological, or biochemical trait is strongly influenced by the environment requires careful laboratory study (e.g., common garden and reciprocal transplant experiments). Such studies are nearly impossible with large, highly mobile organisms like the lynx.

Examples of Strong Environmental Influences on Phenotypic Traits

There are many classic examples of natural selection acting upon heritable traits (e.g., Boag and Grant 1981; Reznick et al. 1990). There appear to be fewer instances where the local environment has been shown to determine a phenotype. In this section, we review several cases where environment plays a large role in shaping the phenotype.

Rhymer (1992) conducted both a reciprocal transplant and a common-garden experiment with mallards from California and Manitoba to see if size variations were inherited. She found that while some differences in the size and morphology of mallards persisted regardless of environment, most of the variation in size was under environmental control. Growth in ducks is not locally adapted as was previously suggested (Lightbody and Ankeny 1984), but was determined by local environmental conditions at the time of rearing (Rhymer 1992).

Red-winged blackbirds show large clinal variation in size and shape. James (1983) conducted a reciprocal transplant experiment with red-winged blackbird eggs from northern and southern Florida and a single transplant experiment from Colorado to Minnesota. She concluded that regional variation in the shape of red-winged blackbirds was largely non-genetic because transplanted eggs produced birds more like the phenotypes typical of their adopted area.

Geist (1991) discussed the taxonomic status of wood bison that were previously thought to be a subspecies distinct from the plains bison. He concluded that observed differences between plains and wood bison were not genetically determined, but were phenotypic differences associated with diet. Thus, differences between wood bison populations appear to be based on phenotypic plasticity.

Learned behaviors also demonstrate the strong influence of the local environment on a trait. Both within and among populations, individuals can exhibit a wide range of learned behaviors. The inheritance of learned behavior is termed *cultural inheritance* (Cavalli-Sforza and Feldman 1973). A well-known example is the learned ability of several species of British birds to open milk bottles. This behavior was first reported in the 1920s and Hinde and Fisher (1951) have subsequently mapped its spread over an extensive area. Recent work by Lefebvre (1995a) indicates that the spread of milk-bottle opening by birds has been accelerating across the United Kingdom (U.K.). However, the behavior is still not found in some U.K. populations, even though it is prevalent in others.

Cultural inheritance has also been reported in primates (see Lefebvre 1995b). Kawamura (1954) noted that neighboring troops of Japanese macaques differed in feeding habits, and others began feeding the macaques to observe their social behavior. One of the foods they provided was wheat grains spread on a sandy beach, a food source that was difficult for the monkeys to handle. One female macaque separated out the wheat grains, which floated, by placing handfuls of sand into puddles of water on the beach. Shortly thereafter, researchers saw other troop members imitate the separation technique (Kawai 1965). Soon, it became a technique unique to members of this troop and not found in other troops.

The key point is that non-inherited traits are often adaptive and therefore can influence fitness and evolution. Accordingly, phenotypic variety must be carefully considered by conservationists regardless of the mechanism by which it was created.

Considerations for Conservation Planning

Reintroductions, Augmentations, and Translocations

Reintroduction entails moving individuals from one or more wild populations to parts of the species' range where local populations no longer exist. Population *augmentation* is the process of moving individuals from one or more wild populations to a different part or parts of the species' range where local populations are precariously small. We refer to any relocation of individuals from an existing wild population into a new environment as a *translocation*.

Augmenting populations with captive-bred animals, or introducing captive-bred individuals into the wild, is generally problematic. Captive-bred animals usually have lower survival rates, a reduced fright response to predators, and may lack other behaviors necessary to survive in the wild (Reinert 1991; Stahl 1981). In addition, adaptation to captivity can occur allowing those genotypes best suited for surviving and reproducing in captivity to increase in frequency, while those genotypes best suited for surviving and reproducing in the wild dwindle (Kohane and Parsons 1988; Allendorf 1993).

When appropriate behaviors are absent in captive-bred individuals, it may mean that those behaviors are learned. Learned behaviors, such as predator avoidance, probably depend on exposure to specific predators which may not occur in the natal ranges of translocated animals. However, the lack of a "hard-wired" genetic basis for these behaviors renders them no less critical with regard to successful reproduction and, ultimately, to fitness (see Bekoff 1989 for a discussion of behavioral development in carnivores).

Translocations may fail for many reasons, including non-inherited differences among populations, limits to phenotypic plasticity, and detrimental stochastic events. Several examples illustrate the problems inherent in translocating animals from one ecosystem to another.

Evans and Williamson (1976) described an attempted introduction of wild turkeys from an arid region of Texas to the wetter areas of eastern Texas. Although the dry-adapted birds survived, high humidity prevented them from nesting successfully, and the introduction failed.

Woodland caribou from two British Columbia (B.C.) populations (west-central and east-central) were transplanted into northern Idaho to augment a small remnant population (Warren 1990; Warren et al. 1996). Transplanted individuals had a tendency to retain the movement and feeding behavior of their original stocks. Caribou from west-central B.C. eat mainly terrestrial lichens in winter, whereas caribou from east-central B.C. eat arboreal lichens because the snow is too deep to dig through. After translocation, more east-central caribou emigrated from the transplant area, in keeping with the tendency of the parent population to emigrate more frequently than west-central caribou. Most west-central caribou died, and apparently starved while digging for lichens in winter, ignoring abundant arboreal lichens in the transplant area.

Lynx translocations have also proven to be problematic. Eighty-three lynx were translocated from the Yukon Territory into the Adirondack Mountains of New York in the late 1980s (Chapter 13). Nearly half the animals died within two years of being released and, in spite of considerable search effort, there is no recent evidence of lynx occurrence in the Adirondacks (K. Gustafson, personal communication). An ongoing lynx reintroduction effort involving the translocation of animals from Yukon and Alaska into Colorado has been fraught with problems, including the starvation of several individuals (Kloor 1999). Translocations are most likely to succeed between populations whose environments and ecological relationships are similar, especially with regard to climate, habitat, and community composition. We believe that translocation of closely related populations, with similar local adaptations, will have the highest probability of success. Furthermore, we believe that relocation from the core to the periphery of a species range will usually entail significant risk.

Outbreeding Depression

Interbreeding between two populations may result in a reduction in number, viability, or fitness of offspring, a phenomenon known as *outbreeding depression* (Templeton 1986; Waser and Price 1994). There are two mechanisms responsible for outbreeding depression: mixing of locally adapted populations, and disruption of *co- adapted gene complexes*, which are sets of genes that increase fitness when all are present in the individual (Templeton et al. 1986).

The first mechanism, interbreeding of animals from two locally adapted populations, produces offspring that may not be adapted to either location. There are several examples of translocation failures resulting from mixing locally adapted populations (Grieg 1979; Templeton 1986; Turcek 1951). Populations of the Tatra Mountain ibex in central Europe were supplemented with ibex from Turkey and the Sinai during the 1960s. The hybrids of these ibex rutted in early autumn instead of in winter (as the native ibex did), and the females gave birth in February in Czechoslovakia during the coldest time of the winter. The entire population went extinct because of the mixing of these groups (Grieg 1979).

A second mechanism that can cause outbreeding depression is the disruption of co-adapted gene complexes. The mixing of gene pools (e.g., by translocation of individuals with one set of co-adapted gene complexes to another population with a different set) can break down these gene complexes and cause a reduction in fitness (Dobzhansky 1948).

Natural Variation and Lynx Conservation

Resource managers have the complex task of applying the concepts discussed in this chapter within a legal context. The Endangered Species Act (ESA) will allow listing of "any subspecies of fish or wildlife or plants, and any distinct population segment of any species of vertebrate fish or wildlife which interbreeds when mature." Only two subspecies of lynx have been described in North America: one in Newfoundland (*L.c. subsolanus*), and the other throughout the remainder of Canada, Alaska, and the contiguous United States (*L.c. canadensis*; Werdelin 1981). Thus, determining whether distinct population segments occur within this region is a critical conservation issue.

Evolutionarily Significant Units

The first U.S. management agency that comprehensively addressed the problem of defining distinct population segments was the National Marine Fisheries Service (NMFS). One of the missions of NMFS is to manage Pacific salmon, a species group with high levels of phenotypic variation (Allendorf et al. 1997). Waples (1991) proposed that a population be considered "distinct" if it represents an Evolutionarily Significant Unit (ESU) of the species (a term first coined by Ryder in 1986 with regard to prioritizing species for captive propagation efforts). To be considered an ESU, a population must be reproductively isolated from conspecific populations, and it must represent an important component of the evolutionary legacy of the species. According to Waples (1995) the evolutionary legacy of the species is "the genetic variability that is a product of past evolutionary events and that represents the reservoir upon which future evolutionary potential depends."

When NMFS was asked to evaluate the status of spring-, summer-, and fall-run chinook salmon in the Snake River, they applied the ESU concept (USDC 1991; USDI and USDC 1996; Waples 1995). Large genetic differences separated fall from spring and summer fish, but it was unclear what the contribution of the Snake River fall-run chinook was to the "ecological-genetic diversity" of the species (Waples 1995). Water characteristics such as temperature and turbidity differ dramatically between the Snake River and the adjoining Columbia River, and it was believed that Snake River fall-run chinook had developed either physiological or behavioral adaptations to its river environment. These data, along with different oceanic distributions of the Columbia and Snake River fish, were used to classify Snake River fall-run chinook as an ESU. The spring and summer runs were distinct from the Columbia River chinook. However, the timing of the run (spring versus summer) explained less than 10% of the genetic variation in the sample. Consequently, spring and summer runs were classified as one ESU.

In 1994, the U.S. Fish and Wildlife Service (USFWS) drafted a policy regarding the recognition of distinct vertebrate population segments under the ESA (USDI and USDC 1994). The goal was to use criteria similar to NMFS for defining a distinct population segment (i.e., an ESU). The USFWS proposed that distinct population segments would be defined according to the discreteness and significance of the population segment relative to the remainder of the species (USDI and USDC 1994, 1996). This policy has only recently been adopted (USDC 1996).

The ESU approach has been criticized from both biological and legal perspectives as being not biologically meaningful, too subjective, too specific to salmon, and relying too heavily on genetics (Rohlf 1994; Vogler and DeSalle 1994; see Waples 1995, 1998 for responses). A wide range of solutions have been proposed to address both the problem of subjectivity (see Moritz 1994) and reliance on DNA-based analyses (see Vogler and DeSalle 1994). All participants in this debate appear to agree that understanding observable variation in nature is critical to identifying distinct population segments for conservation.

Because we are often unable to tell if adaptive traits are inherited, an ESU policy that focuses only on inherited traits will fail to identify potentially important distinct population segments. We recommend that all aspects of the natural history of lynx be considered when evaluating potential ESUs for lynx. This includes not only data on neutral genetic markers (e.g., microsatellite DNA), but also potentially adaptive traits inferred from physiological, behavioral, morphological, and ecological studies.

Implications for Lynx Conservation

We know virtually nothing about levels of natural variation in lynx populations. However, we do know that the geographic range of lynx covers a broad range of environmental conditions, especially with regard to habitat structure, habitat ecology, and predator/prey communities (Chapter 14). Additionally, the environment at the core of the lynx range is very different ecologically from the environment at the southern periphery of the species range (Chapter 3). We also know, however, that individual lynx are capable of long-range movements, and that all populations are restricted to boreal forest habitats and appear to rely on snowshoe hares as prey.

Understanding the nature of variation among lynx populations and its implications for conservation will require studies of the genetic structure of subpopulations, estimates of historical and current gene flow between peripheral and core populations, and studies of comparative ecology throughout the range of lynx. Until we understand the nature of geographic variation in lynx populations, it would seem prudent to assume the existence of important genetic and non-genetic differences among populations, especially those that are distant and/or relatively isolated.

Conclusions

In this review, we have attempted to show that (1) natural variation among populations is prevalent in nature, (2) conservation assessments and plans need to explicitly address patterns of natural variation among populations, whether it is inherited or not and (3) such assessments need to be concerned not only with genotypes, but also with the plasticity of those genotypes to produce different phenotypes. The preservation of natural variation will, in part, be concerned with the conservation of genetic diversity and genetic adaptations to local environments. Protection of this type of diversity is mandated by the ESA and can be addressed through the Evolutionarily Significant Unit (ESU) policy recently adopted by the Departments of Interior and Commerce. However, implementation of this policy should include explicit consideration of both inherited and non-inherited variation.

Some non-inherited traits that vary between populations are *ultimately* under genetic control. Traits such as phenotypic plasticity allow species to respond to changing environments and to potentially different environmental conditions found at the periphery of a species' range. Phenotypes which are products of specific environments become endangered if we lose or modify those environments. It would be naive to think that we could re-create an extinct phenotype by taking a similar genotype and subjecting it to comparable environmental conditions. Similarly, we may disrupt adaptive phenotypic responses by introducing individuals to the population that lack the genetic potential to make appropriate phenotypic adjustments. And finally, culturally inherited behaviors are likely to be especially important in higher vertebrates having complex behavioral patterns and socially or parentally facilitated behavioral development.

Traits that are genetically determined and those that are largely determined by the environment are part of a continuum and, in many cases, it may be impossible to distinguish between the two. Does it matter if differences are genetic, if such differences improve fitness and convey a selective advantage by improving reproductive success? The answer is a qualified "no." In the case of genetic adaptations, this advantage is more or less fixed over intermediate time periods (e.g., hundreds of years given a more or less stable environment), thus contributing to the long-term evolutionary potential of the species. In the case of non-genetic differences, the potential for change over the short term may mediate survival rates leading to long-term change. For example, new behaviors learned in response to new environmental challenges could result in improved survival, allowing populations to persist and acclimate to changing conditions. In this scenario, if environments change quickly and dramatically, as is often the case when translocating animals, a lack of behavioral plasticity could lead to increased mortality rates and, eventually, local extirpation.

Similarly, management decisions made on the basis of observed habitat relationships in one population could result in detrimental effects on another population occupying a substantially different environment. For example, forest management practices determined to be beneficial to lynx in the taiga may not be appropriate in southern boreal forests of the western montane region, where ecological conditions are dramatically different. In other words, the translocation of scientific knowledge from one population to another can be as risky as the physical translocation of animals. In either case, the risk of undesirable results will increase with ecosystem dissimilarities and/or geographic distance.

Implications for Management

Because translocations and reintroductions are inherently risky even under optimal conditions, they should be used only when other management options have failed. Conservation objectives are more likely to be met by maintaining and/or enhancing habitat conditions for lynx to provide opportunities for them to recolonize former portions of their range. If deemed necessary, reintroductions into peripheral populations should be done with lynx from other peripheral populations, neighboring populations, or genetically similar populations. It is risky to use individuals from captive, distant, or ecologically dissimilar populations.

Neutral genetic markers can detect the structuring of populations and aid in the identification of source populations for translocated individuals. However, we caution that analyses of neutral markers cannot detect differences in adaptive traits between populations. Thus, even if no subdivision of populations is detected with such analyses, adaptive genetic differences may still exist between populations.

Lastly, it is critical to consider both inherited and non-inherited variation when manipulating lynx populations or managing their habitat. We recommend that managers assume the existence of important genetic and non-genetic differences between distant and/or relatively isolated lynx populations until proven otherwise.

Acknowledgments

We thank Kevin McKelvey, Kermit Ritland, John McKay, Fred Allendorf, and Scott Mills for helpful suggestions on previous versions of this manuscript.

Literature Cited

Allendorf, F. W. 1993. Delay of adaptation to captive breeding by equalizing family size. Conservation Biology 7:416-419.

Allendorf, F. W., D. Bayles, D. L. Bottom, K. P. Currens, C. A. Frissell, D. Hankin, J. A. Lichatowich, W. Nehlsen, P. C. Trotter, and T. H. Williams. 1997. Prioritizing Pacific salmon stocks for conservation. Conservation Biology 11:140-152.

Ancel, L. W. 1999. A quantitative model of the Simpson-Baldwin effect. Journal of Theoretical Biology 196:197-209.

Baldwin, J. M. 1896. A new factor in evolution. American Naturalist 30:441-451.

Bekoff, M. 1989. Behavioral development in terrestrial carnivores. Pages 89-124 *in* J. L. Gittleman, Editor. Carnivore behavior, ecology, and evolution. Cornell University Press, New York, NY.

Boag, P. T and P. R. Grant. 1981. Intense natural selection in a population of Darwin's finches (Geospinzinae) in the Galapagos. Science 214:82-85.

Britten, H.B., P. F. Brussard, D. D. Murphy, and P. R. Ehrlich. 1995. A test for isolation-by-distance in Central Rocky Mountain and Great Basin populations of Edith's checkerspot butterfly (*Euphydryas editha*). Journal of Heredity 86:204-210.

Buskirk, S. W. and L. F. Ruggiero. 1994. American marten. Pages 7-37 *in* The scientific basis for conserving forest carnivores: american marten, fisher, lynx, and wolverine in the Western United States. USDA Forest Service, General Technical Report RM-254.

Carson, H. L. 1959. Genetic conditions that promote or retard the formation of species. Cold Spring Harbor Symposium in Quantitative Biology 23:291-305.

Cavalli-Sforza, L. L. and M. W. Feldman. 1973. Cultural versus biological inheritance: phenotypic transmission from parent to children (a theory of the effect of parental phenotypes on children's phenotypes). American Journal of Human Genetics 25:618-637.

Diamond, J. M. 1975. The island dilemma: lessons of modern biogeographic studies for the design of nature reserves. Biological Conservation 7:129-146.

Dobzhansky, T. 1948. Genetics of natural populations. XVIII. Experiments on chromosomes of *Drosophila pseudoobscura* from different geographical regions. Genetics 33:588-602.

Endler, J. A. 1986. Natural selection in the wild. Princeton University Press, Princeton, NJ.

Evans, P. and L. Williamson. 1976. Return of the eastern turkey. Texas Parks and Wildlife July:2-5.

Falconer, D. S. and T. F. C. Mackay 1996. Introduction to quantitative genetics, 4th Edition. Longman, Essex, England.

Futuyma, D. J. 1986. Evolutionary Biology. Sinauer, Sunderland, MA.

Futuyma, D. J. 1998. Evolutionary Biology. Sinauer, Sunderland, MA.

Geist, V. 1991. Phantom subspecies: the wood bison *Bison bison "athabascae"* Rhoads 1897 is not a valid taxon, but an ecotype. Arctic 44:283-300.

Grant, V. 1963. The origin of adaptations. Columbia University Press, New York, NY.

Grieg, J. C. 1979. Principles of genetic conservation in relation to wildlife management in Southern Africa. South African Journal of Wildlife Research 9:57-78.

Halloran, A. F. and Glass, B. P. 1959. The carnivores and ungulates of the Wichita Mountains Wildlife Refuge. Journal of Mammalogy 40:360-370.

Hartl, D. L. and Clark A. G. 1989. Principles of population genetics, 2nd Edition. Sinauer Associates, Sunderland, MA.

Hinde, R. A. and J. Fisher. 1951. Further observations on the opening of milk bottles by birds. British Birds 44:393-396.

James, F. C. 1983. Environmental component of morphological differentiation in birds. Science 221:184-186.

Kawai, M. 1965. Newly acquired pre-cultural behavior of a natural troop of Japanese monkeys on Koshima Island. Primates 6:1-30.

Kawamura, S. 1954. On a new type of feeding habit which developed in a group of wild Japanese macaques. Seibustu Shinka 2:11-13.

Kloor, K. 1999. Lynx and biologists try to recover after disastrous start. Science 285:320-321.

Kirkpatrick, M. and N. H. Barton. 1997. Evolution of a species' range. American Naturalist 150:1-23.

Kohane, M. J. and P. A. Parsons. 1988. Domestication: evolutionary change under stress. Evolutionary Biology 23:31-48.

Lefebvre, L. 1995a. The opening of milk bottles by birds: evidence for accelerating learning rates, but against the wave-of-advance model of cultural transmission. Behavioural Processes 34:43-54.

Lefebvre, L. 1995b. Culturally-transmitted feeding behaviour in primates: evidence for accelerating learning rates. Primates 36:227-239.

Lesica, P. and F. W. Allendorf. 1995. When are peripheral populations valuable for conservation? Conservation Biology 9:753-760.

Lightbody, J. P. and C. D. Ankney. 1984. Seasonal influences on the strategies of growth and development on canvasback and lesser scaup ducklings. Auk 101:121-133.

Lott, D. F. 1991. Intraspecific variation in the social systems of wild vertebrates. Cambridge University Press, New York, NY.

Mallet, J. 1995. A species definition for the modern synthesis. Trends in Ecology and Evolution 10:294-299.

Mayr, E. 1970. Populations, species, and evolution. Harvard University Press, Cambridge, MA.

Mills, L. S. and F. W. Allendorf. 1996. The one-migrant-per-generation rule in conservation and management. Conservation Biology 10:1509-1518.

Moritz, C. 1994. Defining "evolutionarily significant units" for conservation. Trends in Ecology and Evolution 9:373-375.

Pennock, D. S. and W. W. Dimmick. 1997. Critique of the evolutionarily significant unit as a definition for "Distinct Population Segments" under the U.S. Endangered Species Act. Conservation Biology 11:611-619.

Pianka, E. R. 1994. Evolutionary ecology. Harper and Row, New York, NY.

Reinert, H. K. 1991. Translocation as a conservation strategy for amphibians and reptiles: some comments, concerns, and observations. Herpetologica 47:357- 363.

Reznick, D. N. Bryga, H., J. A. Endler. 1990. Experimentally induced life-history evolution in a natural population. Nature (London) 346:357-359.

Rhymer, J. M. 1992. An experimental study of geographic variation in avian growth and development. Journal of Evolutionary Biology 5:289-306.

Ricklefs, R. E. 1990. Ecology. W. H. Freeman, New York, NY.

Rohlf, D. J. 1994. Pacific salmon. There's something fishy going on here: a critique of the National Marine Fisheries Service's definition of species under the Endangered Species Act. Environmental Law 24:617-671.

Roughgarden, J. 1979. Theory of population genetics and evolutionary ecology: an introduction. MacMillan, New York, NY.

Ruggiero, L. F., R. S. Holthausen, B. G. Marcot, K. B. Aubry, J. W. Thomas, and E. C. Meslow. 1988. Ecological dependency: the concept and its implications for research and management. Transactions of the Fifty-third North American Wildlife and Natural Resources Conference 53:115-126.

Ryder, O. A. 1986. Species conservation and systematics: the dilemma of subspecies. Trends in Ecology and Evolution 1: 9-10.

Safriel, U. N., S. Volis, S. Kark. 1994. Core and peripheral populations and global climate change. Israel Journal of Plant Sciences 42: 331-345.

Simpson, G. G. 1953. The Baldwin effect. Evolution 7:110-117.

Stahl, G. 1981. Genetic differentiation among natural populations of Atlantic salmon (*Salmo salar*) in northern Sweden. Ecological Bulletin (Stockholm) 34:95-105.

Storfer, A. 1999. Gene flow and endangered species translocation: a topic revisited. Biological Conservation 87:173-180.

Templeton, A. R. 1986. Coadaptation and outbreeding depression. Pages 105-116 *in* M. Soule, Editor. Conservation biology: the science of scarcity and diversity. Sinauer, Sunderland, MA.

Templeton, A. R., H. Hemmer, G. Mace, U. S. Seal, W. M. Shields, and D. S. Woodruff. 1986. Local adaptation, coadaptation, and population boundaries. Zoo Biology 5:115-125.

Turcek, F. J. 1951. Effect of introductions on two game populations in Czechoslovakia. Journal of Wildlife Management 15:113-114.

U.S. Department of Commerce. 1991. Interim policy on applying the definition of species under the Endangered Species Act to Pacific salmon. Federal Register 56: 10542-10544.

U.S. Department of the Interior and U.S. Department of Commerce. 1994. Draft joint policy regarding the recognition of distinct vertebrate populations under the ESA. Federal Register 59:65884-65885.

U.S. Department of the Interior and U.S. Department of Commerce. 1996. Policy regarding the recognition of distinct vertebrate population segments under the Endangered Species Act. Federal Register 61:4722-4725.

Vogler, A. P. and R. DeSalle. 1994. Diagnosing units of conservation management. Conservation Biology 8:354-363.

Waples, R. S. 1991. Pacific salmon, *Onchorhynchus* spp., and the definition of "species" under the Endangered Species Act. U.S. National Marine Fisheries Service Marine Fisheries Review 53:11-22.

Waples, R. S. 1995. Evolutionary significant units and the conservation of biological diversity under the endangered species act. Pages 8-27 *in* Nielsen, J. L., Editor. Evolution and the aquatic ecosystem: defining unique units in population conservation. American Fisheries Society, Bethesda MD.

Waples, R. S. 1998. Evolutionarily significant units, distinct population segments, and the Endangered Species Act: reply to Pennock and Dimmick. Conservation Biology 12: 718-721.

Warren, C. D. 1990. Ecotypic response and habitat use of woodland caribou translocated to the southern Selkirk Mountains, northern Idaho. Unpublished M.S. Thesis, University of Idaho, Moscow, ID.

Warren, C. D., J. M. Peek, G. L. Servheen, and P. Zager. 1996. Habitat use and movements of two ecotypes of translocated caribou in Idaho and British Columbia. Conservation Biology 10:547-553.

Waser, N. M. and M. V. Price. 1994. Crossing-distince effects in *Delphinium nelsonii*: outbreeding and inbreeding depression in progeny fitness. Evolution 48:842-852.

Werdelin, L. 1981. Evolution of lynxes. Annales Zoologici Fennici 18:37-71.

Wright, S. 1943. Isolation by distance. Genetics 28:114-138.

Wright, S. 1969. Evolution and the genetics of populations. Volume 2: The theory of gene frequencies. University of Chicago Press, Chicago, IL.

Chapter 6

The Ecology of Snowshoe Hares in Northern Boreal Forests

Karen E. Hodges, Centre for Biodiversity Research,
    University of British Columbia, 6270 University Boulevard,
    Vancouver, BC V6T 1Z4, Canada

Abstract—Snowshoe hares exhibit eight to 11 year population fluctuations across boreal North America, typically with an amplitude of 10 to 25 fold. These fluctuations are synchronous across the continent, with the most recent peak densities occurring in 1990 and 1991. The numeric cycle is driven by changes in survival and reproduction, with annual survival of adults ranging from approximately five to 30% and annual natality ranging from approximately six to 20 leverets/female. These parameters show cyclic changes because of functional and numerical responses of predators and changes in food supply. Predator densities show approximately two to 10 fold fluctuations during the hare cycle. The cyclicity of hares may be partly explained by regular behavioral shifts, with repercussions on their physiology, availability to predators, reproduction, and survival. However, this hypothesis needs more empirical support before it can be accepted.

Introduction

In this chapter, I discuss the ecology of cyclic populations of snowshoe hares in the boreal forests of North America. I emphasize the demographic changes leading to changes in numbers of hares, the habitats that hares use, the impacts of nutrition, physiology, and parasite loads on hares' susceptibility to predation, and the effects of disturbance (fire, logging, fragmentation, and regeneration) on snowshoe hares' behavior and demography. I address what is known about the causes of the cycle and cyclic synchrony among regions. For demographic data, I focus on data sets that show variation through a cycle in one location; I use demographic results from shorter studies to examine the factors that influence demography, rather than trying to infer cyclic or geographic patterns from them.

Magnitude and Synchrony of Northern Hare Cycles

Snowshoe hares show cyclic fluctuations in density across northern North America, with peak densities every eight to 11 years. It was thought that only northern populations of hares cycle (Green and Evans 1940; Finerty 1980; Smith 1983; Keith 1990), but recent evidence suggests that hare in their southern range—through the Cascades, Rockies, and Alleghenies to California, New Mexico, and Virginia—may also cycle (Chapter 7). Hares were introduced into Newfoundland in the 1860s and 1870s. Their numbers increased rapidly, crashed, and have since shown a 10-year cycle (Bergerud 1983).

During the last four decades, the cycle has been largely synchronous across Canada and into Alaska (Table 6.1). Cyclic peaks have occurred roughly at the turn of each decade (1960 to 1961, 1970 to 1971, 1980 to 1981, 1990 to 1991), with lowest densities typically occurring three years later (1963 to 1964, 1973 to 1974, 1983 to 1984, 1993 to 1994). These patterns support previous surveys that concluded that the cycle is synchronous (MacLulich 1937; Keith 1963; Finerty 1980; Smith 1983; Sinclair et al. 1993; Sinclair and Gosline 1997). In the last four decades, peak and low density years have been synchronous across the continent, whereas cycles in the early and middle parts of the century were synchronous at peak densities but not necessarily at low densities (Sinclair and Gosline 1997). There have also been debates about whether hares in the central part of Canada (i.e., Alberta, Saskatchewan, and Manitoba) reach peak densities earlier than in other locations, followed by a wave of peaks that extends north, west, and east (Bulmer 1974; Smith 1983; Ranta et al. 1997). The data from the last three cycles do not support this idea.

There are a few areas in which hares may not cycle in synchrony. The hunting data from Newfoundland suggest that cyclic peaks are asynchronous with those in mainland Canada (S. Mahoney, unpublished). Harvest

Table 6.1.–The snowshoe hare cycle: synchrony, densities, and amplitude. Peak or low years coinciding with the beginning or termination of a study should be viewed with skepticism because of the inability to see what the hare population did in the previous or subsequent years. Density estimates are not comparable because of different field and statistical techniques applied to their generation; they and cyclic amplitude are presented to give an order of magnitude. Cyclic amplitude is rounded to the nearest 5. The data collated into this table are roughly post-1960 and most are within the taiga provinces of the polar domain (Bailey 1997). (S) is spring enumeration. (F) is fall enumeration. No data are indicated by –.

Location	Years of study	Peak	Low	Peak density (hares/ha)	Low density (hares/ha)	Amplitude	Methods	Reference
Newfoundland	1990-1993	1990	1993	–	–	–	Track counts	Thompson & Curran 1995
Newfoundland	1954-1998	1960, 1969, 1976, 1983, 1998[a]	–	–	–	–	Harvest records[a]	Dodds 1965; S. Mahoney, unpublished
Manitouwadge, Ontario	1980-1985	1980	1984	–	–	–	Track counts	Thompson & Colgan 1987; Thompson et al. 1989
Narcisse Wildlife Mgmt Area, Manitoba	1991-1993	–	–	–	0.3-0.4	–	Live-trapping	Murray et al. 1998
Narcisse Wildlife Mgmt Area, Manitoba	1971-1973	–	1973 (S)	–	–	–	Sightings along transects	Rusch et al. 1978
Long Point Peninsula, Manitoba	1971-1987	1971 (F) 1980 (F)	1974 (F) 1985 (F)	4.4	0.2	25	Live-trapping	Koonz 1988, unpublished
Saskatchewan	1958-1987	1960 1970 1980	1963 1973 1984	–	–	–	Observation[b]	Houston 1987; Houston & Francis 1995
Rochester, Alberta	1961-1984	1962 (S) 1971 (S) 1981 (S)	1966 (S) 1975 (S)	5.9-11.8 (F)	0.13-0.26 (S)	25 (S)	Live-trapping	Keith & Windberg 1978; Keith 1983; Keith et al. 1984
Westlock, Alberta woodlot fragments	1970-1974	1970 (F)	1973 (F)	5.6 (F)	0.8 (F)	5	Live-trapping	Windberg & Keith 1978
Prince George, B.C.	1979-1983 1988-1991	1979 (F) 1990 (F)	–	16.4 (F) 4.2-5.2 (F)	–	–	Live-trapping	Sullivan & Sullivan 1988b; Sullivan 1994
Mackenzie Bison Sanctuary, NWT	1989-1996	1989-1990	1992-1993	4.6	0.34	15	Pellet plots[c] Track counts	Poole 1994; K. Poole, unpublished
Ft. Simpson, NWT	1993-1996	–	1994-1995	–	0.17	–	Pellet plots[c]	Poole & Graf 1996; K. Poole, unpublished
Ft. Smith, NWT	1989-1996	1989-1990	1992-1993	2.0	0.09	20	Pellet plots[c]	Poole & Graf 1996; K. Poole, unpublished
Norman Wells, NWT	1989-1997	1989-1990	1992-1993	1.9	0.14	15	Pellet plots[c]	Poole & Graf 1996; K. Poole, unpublished
Yellowknife, NWT	1989-1996	1989-1990	1993-1994	3.4	0.28	10	Pellet plots[c]	Poole & Graf 1996; K. Poole, unpublished

(con.)

Table 6.1–Con.

Location	Years of study	Peak	Low	Peak density (hares/ha)	Low density (hares/ha)	Amplitude	Methods	Reference
Inuvik, NWT	1989-1996	1995-1996	1988-1989	2.0	0.43	5	Pellet plots[c]	K. Poole, unpublished
Dawson, Yukon	1988-1991	1989-1990	–	1.3-4.3[d]	–	–	Pellet plots[c] Track counts	Mowat et al. 1997, unpublished
Whitehorse, Yukon	1988-1991	1990-1991	–	0.9-4.4[d]	–	–	Pellet plots[c] Track counts	Mowat et al. 1997, unpublished
Snafu Lake, Yukon	1988-1993	1990-1991	1986-1987 1993-1994	7.5	0.8-1.1	5-10	Pellet plots[c]	Mowat et al. 1997, unpublished; Slough & Mowat 1996
Kluane Lake, Yukon	1976-1998	1980-1981 1989-1990	1984-1985 1993-1994	2.9 (S) 1.5 (S)	0.16 (S) 0.08 (S)	20	Live-trapping	Krebs et al. 1986b; Krebs et al. 1995; Hodges et al., in press; C. J. Krebs, unpublished
Tanana Valley & s. of Fairbanks, Alaska	1995-1998	–[e]	1994-1995[e]	–	–	–	Aerial surveys	M. McNay, unpublished[e]
Wrangell-St. Elias, Alaska	1991-1998	1990-1991	1993-1994	2.9-5.5[f]	0.12-0.43[f]	20-25[f]	Pellet plots[c]	C. D. Mitchell, unpublished
Fairbanks, Alaska	1986-1996	1988-1989	1992-1993	0.5	0.02	25	Pellet plots[c]	L.A. Viereck & P.C. Adams Bonanza Creek LTER, unpublished
Fairbanks, Alaska	1971-1977	1971 (F)	1975 (F)	~5.9[g]	0.12	50[g]	Live-trapping Pellet plots	Wolff 1980
Fairbanks, Alaska	1955-1961	1961	1955	–	–	–	Live-trapping Pellet plots	Trapp 1962; O'Farrell 1965
Fairbanks, Alaska	1970-1973	1971	–	6.0-6.5	–	–	Live-trapping	Ernest 1974
Kenai Peninsula, Alaska	1971-1974	1973-1974	–	–	–	–	Observations	Oldemeyer 1983
Kenai Peninsula, Alaska	1983-1998	1984-1985	1989-1992	0.8-3.0[h]	0-0.4[h]	5-25[h]	Live-trapping[h]	Bailey et al. 1986; Staples 1995; T. Bailey, unpublished

[a] There does not appear to have been a distinct peak in the late 1980s. Lows are difficult to infer from the data because of variation in hunter effort. (M. O'Donoghue, personal communication).

[b] Peaks are from Houston 1987 and generally correspond to the next to the last year of "high" densities in Houston & Francis (1995). Low values are the 4th of the "low" years from Houston & Francis (1995).

[c] Densities from pellet plots are calculated using a regression equation derived from hare density information from 1976 to 1996 (C.J. Krebs, unpublished):ln(hares/ha) = 0.888962*ln(pellets)-1.203391, corrected for bias by multiplying with 1.57 following Sprugel (1983). Pellets is pellets/0.155m². The current equation uses more information.

[d] The range of values is the range that occurred in five different habitat types.

[e] M. McNay also reports that hare populations were highest in 1988 to 1989 or 1989 to 1990, and may have been at their lowest densities in 1993 to 1994.

[f] For most years, four sites were surveyed and ranges of values indicate sites. In 1991, only two sites were surveyed.

[g] The peak density was inferred from 1971 peak densities in similar habitats in interior Alaska by Ernest (1974).

[h] Density estimates are for adult hares only, trapped in summer. Ranges indicate the extreme values for the five study sites.

data and observations suggest that there may not have been a cyclic peak in the late 1980s or early 1990s (M. O'Donoghue, personal communication), although track surveys in western Newfoundland showed a pronounced decline from 1990 to 1993 (Thompson and Curran 1995). Human impacts on hares are severe in Newfoundland and probably influence hare dynamics (M. O'Donoghue and T. Joyce, personal communication).

The hare population around Inuvik, NWT, is asynchronous. The highest densities were in 1995 and 1996 and the lowest densities were in 1988 and 1989 (out of eight years of collecting pellet-plot data) (K. Poole, unpublished). The Kenai Peninsula in Alaska also is asynchronous, with hares reaching peak densities in 1984 and 1985 with low densities from 1989 to 1992 (Oldemeyer 1983; Bailey et al. 1986; Staples 1995; T. Bailey, unpublished). There has been speculation that hare populations are out of phase throughout Alaska, which allows predators to travel the state in search of locally abundant hares. The available data suggest that is not the case. With the exception of the Kenai Peninsula, hares cycle in synchrony in Alaska (H. Golden, unpublished; Chapter 9).

It has been hypothesized that synchrony is modulated by sunspot activity (Sinclair et al. 1993; Sinclair and Gosline 1997). Sunspot activity is correlated with weather patterns, fire, snowfall, and, potentially, plant growth. Regular changes in one or several of these patterns at a continental scale could synchronize population cycles that are occurring because of biological interactions (Meslow and Keith 1971; Fox 1978; Finerty 1980). The Inuvik and Kenai populations of hares are at the edges of snowshoe hare distribution, and both are coastal. The coastal influence has pronounced effects on the weather patterns, which may change the synchrony in these populations.

The question of whether there is geographic variation in peak and low densities is more difficult to answer because of the array of field and statistical methodologies used for density estimation and the problem of determining what area of land was sampled. There is no obvious north-south or east-west gradient in densities; indeed, during the 1990 to 1991 peak, Yukon had the lowest (1.4 hares/ha at Kluane Lake) (Krebs et al. 1995) and the second-highest (7.3 hares/ha at Snafu Lake) (Slough and Mowat 1996) recorded peak densities. Estimates of low densities range from <0.1 to 1.0 hares/ha. Most estimates of amplitude are five to 25 fold, which is somewhat lower than those inferred by Keith (1990). Hare densities vary within different habitat types (Fuller and Heisey 1986; Koonz 1988, unpublished; Mowat et al. 1997, unpublished; Chapter 7), so estimates may also reflect sampling effort in different habitats.

Natural History of Snowshoe Hares

Adult snowshoe hares range in weight from approximately 1,200 to 1,800 g (Rowan and Keith 1959; Newson and de Vos 1964; C. J. Krebs, unpublished). Sex ratios are fairly even at all ages (Dodds 1965; Keith 1990; Hodges et al., in press). Hares do not breed until the summer following their birth, with very rare exceptions (Keith and Meslow 1967; Vaughan and Keith 1980). Breeding is restricted to the summer, and each female has one to four litters per summer (Keith et al. 1966; Cary and Keith 1979). Anywhere from one to 14 leverets are born per litter; the first litter of the summer has a mean of approximately three leverets, the second litter is largest with a mean of five to six, and the later litters are intermediate in numbers (Cary and Keith 1979; O'Donoghue and Krebs 1992; Jardine 1995; Stefan 1998). Females breed synchronously, perhaps to reduce leveret mortality (O'Donoghue and Boutin 1995). Mating occurs immediately post-partum and gestation lasts 35 to 37 days (Meslow and Keith 1968; Stefan 1998). The early litters are weaned at about 24 to 28 days of age, but the last litter of the season may be nursed for up to 40 days (O'Donoghue and Bergman 1992). The young are precocial; they hide together under deadfall, at the base of a bush, in tangled grasses, or under lupines for the first three to five days, and then hide separately, coming together for their once-a-day nursing (Rongstad and Tester 1971; Graf and Sinclair 1987; O'Donoghue and Bergman 1992; O'Donoghue 1994).

Most North American predators eat snowshoe hares, and most hares die of predation (Keith 1990; Hodges et al., in press). Boreal predators display size selection for hares. Small predators, such as Harlan's hawks, hawk owls, kestrels, and weasels, eat leverets and small juveniles (Stefan 1998; Rohner et al. 1995; F. I. Doyle, unpublished), while larger predators, such as lynx and coyotes, eat large juveniles and adult hares (Keith 1990; Hodges et al., in press). Great horned owls and goshawks eat hares of all sizes (Hodges et al., in press). Most mortality occurs before hares reach breeding age, and leveret survival is lower than juvenile survival. Although wild hares can reach five to six years of age, typically over 70% of the spring breeding population is composed of yearlings (Keith 1990; Hodges et al., in press).

In summer, hares eat forbs, grasses, leaves of shrubs, and some woody browse (Wolff 1978; Grisley 1991; P. Seccombe-Hett, unpublished). In winter, they mainly eat twigs and some bark of bushes and trees (de Vos 1964; Wolff 1978; Keith 1990), but they will also dig through shallow snow for forbs and grasses (Gilbert 1990; Hodges 1998). Hares usually select smaller twigs and are selective about which species they browse (Wolff 1978; Pease et al. 1979; Rogowitz 1988; Smith et al. 1988). Diet selection may be based on protein or fibre content, secondary compounds, energy content, or digestibility (Bryant 1981a; Schmitz et al. 1992; Rodgers and Sinclair 1997; Hodges 1998).

The Community Cycle

Many snowshoe hare predators also display cyclic dynamics, often with a lag of one to three years behind the hare cycle (Keith et al. 1977; Keith 1990; Royama 1992; Boutin et al. 1995). Lynx, coyotes, goshawks, and great horned owls display numerical and functional responses to the changes in hare densities, with numeric responses of two to 10 fold (Brand et al. 1976; Adamcik et al. 1978; Brand and Keith 1979; Todd et al. 1981; Parker et al. 1983; Poole 1994; Doyle and Smith 1994; Houston and Francis 1995; Slough and Mowat 1996; Rohner 1996; O'Donoghue et al. 1997, 1998). Other predators, such as red foxes, marten, fisher, eagles, wolverine, wolves, bobcats, hawk owls, and Harlan's hawks, may show functional responses to hare densities (Keith 1963; Bulmer 1974; Litvaitis et al. 1986; Raine 1987; Kuehn 1989; Theberge and Wedeles 1989; Dibello et al. 1990; Rohner et al. 1995; Hodges et al., in press; F. I. Doyle, unpublished). Foxes, wolverine, marten, and fisher may also exhibit numeric responses to the snowshoe hare cycle (Bulmer 1975; Thompson and Colgan 1987; Kuehn 1989; Slough et al. 1989; Poole and Graf 1996).

Other small herbivores in the boreal forest also demonstrate cyclic dynamics, perhaps resulting from competition with hares for limited food or from being the alternate prey when hares densities are low (Keith 1963; Boutin et al. 1995). Spruce grouse and ruffed grouse show a 10-year fluctuation (Rusch et al. 1978; Keith and Rusch 1988; Boutin et al. 1995), while red squirrels do not (Keith and Cary 1991; Boutin et al. 1995; Boonstra et al., in press), and Arctic ground squirrels may cycle in part of the boreal forest (Boonstra et al., in press). Mice and voles do not have regular 10-year fluctuations (Krebs and Wingate 1985; Boutin et al. 1995), even though several predators prey more heavily on small mammals when hares are scarce (Raine 1987; Giuliano et al. 1989; O'Donoghue et al. 1998).

Hares affect their woody browse species in several ways through the cycle. At peak densities, hares may eat a large proportion of the standing shrub biomass (Pease et al. 1979; Keith 1983; Smith et al. 1988), which will not necessarily kill the plants. Hares also girdle the woody stems of trees and shrubs (Sullivan and Sullivan 1982a; Hodges 1998), which will kill the trees. However, some shrubs resprout from the ground, and girdling may stimulate new growth (Smith et al. 1988). Browsing by hares may affect successional dynamics (Bryant 1987; Rossow et al. 1997), disrupt attempts at reforestation (Sullivan and Moses 1986; Radvanyi 1987, unpublished), and influence the amount of secondary compounds that plants produce and their palatability to hares (Bryant 1981a, 1981b; Fox and Bryant 1984; Bryant et al. 1985).

Demographic Changes Through the Cycle

The numeric hare cycle results from demographic changes. The main demographic changes in order of importance are post-weaning juvenile survival, adult survival, and leveret survival (Krebs 1996; Haydon et al. 1999; Hodges et al., in press). Leveret survival and dispersal contribute the least to cyclic dynamics (Haydon et al. 1999), even though they also vary through the cycle (Boutin et al. 1985; Keith 1990; Stefan 1998).

Reproduction

Two long-term studies in Yukon and Alberta have shown that snowshoe hares have the highest reproductive output during the early increase phase of the cycle (16 to 19 leverets/female) and the lowest reproductive output during the decline phase (six to eight leverets/female), with maximum annual reproductive output about 2.5 fold higher than the lowest reproductive output (Fig. 6.1a,b) (Cary and Keith 1979; O'Donoghue and Krebs 1992; Krebs et al. 1995; Stefan 1998). This pattern is the result of changes in the proportion of females pregnant for each litter group, the number of litters that females have in the summer, and the number of leverets per litter (Table 6.2). In Yukon, hares had only two litters during the decline phase, but had four in the early increase phase (Stefan 1998). In Alberta, in contrast, at least a few hares had a fourth litter in every year of the cycle, but during decline years most hares had only three litters (Keith and Windberg 1978; Cary and Keith 1979). Hares in Alaska had a higher pregnancy rate for the third litter during the peak than during the decline (Ernest 1974). In both Yukon and Alberta, litter size varied more for litters two to four than for litter one; mean size for the first litter varied by approximately 0.5 leverets per litter through the cycle. Means for later litter groups varied by one to two leverets per litter through the different phases.

The factors influencing hares' reproductive output are not well known. Snowshoe hares exhibit cyclic changes in stress levels, indexed by several blood chemistry traits such as cortisol and testosterone concentrations (Boonstra and Singleton 1993; Boonstra et al. 1998a). Stress might cause reproductive changes either by affecting females' reproductive output directly or through maternal effects on the offspring (Boonstra et al. 1998b). Reproduction does not seem to be affected by levels of parasitic infestation (Bloomer et al. 1995; Sovell and Holmes 1996; Murray et al. 1998). Physically, mass, skeletal size, and body condition (indexed by mass corrected for skeletal size) do not appear to affect number of litters or litter size (Hodges et al. 2000, in press; Hodges et al., in press). Older, heavier individuals may have higher ovulation rates than younger, lighter hares (Newson 1964), but

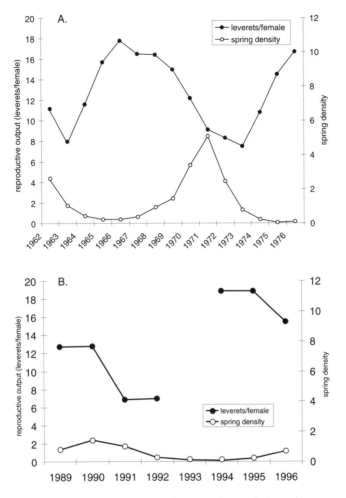

Figure 6.1—Reproductive output in two cyclic populations of hares: Alberta (1A) (Keith & Windberg 1978; Cary & Keith 1979) and Yukon (1B) (Stefan 1998). Total annual natalities were calculated by summing pregnancy rates x mean litter sizes for each litter.

this difference cannot account for the cyclic changes because the lowest reproduction occurs in the decline phase of the cycle when the proportion of adults is highest and average body mass is also high (Hodges et al. 1999; Hodges et al., in press).

Hares regularly lose mass overwinter (Newson and de Vos 1964). Keith (1981, 1990; Keith et al. 1984; Vaughan and Keith 1981) has argued that food shortage leads to the overwinter mass loss and negatively affects total natality in the subsequent summer. However, there is no clear link between

Table 6.2–Reproductive attributes of snowshoe hares from two cyclic populations.

Alberta[a]	Low 1964-1966 1975-1976	Increase 1967-1969	Peak 1961 1970-1971	Decline 1962-1963 1972-1974
Number of litters	4	4	3 to 4[b]	3 to 4[b]
Litter 1				
Range of parturition dates	30 April-15 May	29 April-15 May	4 May-20 May	15 May-20 May
Pregnancy rate	87.2	96.2	92.1	82.3
Mean litter size	3.0	2.8	2.6	2.7
Litter 2				
Range of parturition dates	4 June-19 June	3 June-19 June	8 June-24 June	19 June-24 June
Pregnancy rate	95.7	94.0	85.6	89.8
Mean litter size	5.7	5.3	4.8	4.4
Litter 3				
Range of parturition dates	9 July-24 July	8 July-24 July	13 July-29 July	24 July-29 July
Pregnancy rate	88.0	91.9	72.2	71.0
Litter size	5.1	5.6	4.6	3.7
Litter 4				
Range of parturition dates	13 Aug- 28 Aug	12 Aug-28 Aug	17 Aug-2 Sept	28 Aug-2 Sept
Pregnancy rate	77.3	63.9	14.5	5.7
Litter size	3.7	4.8	4.2	4.0

Yukon[c]	Low 1993-1994[d]	Increase 1995-1996	Peak 1989-1990	Decline 1991-1992
Number of litters	3 to 4[d]	3 to 4[d]	3	2
Litter 1				
Range of parturition dates	9 May-17 May	16 May-2 June	20 May-29 May	27 May-11 June
Pregnancy rate	100	100	89.9	87.5
Mean litter size	3.2	3.4	3.8	3.3
Litter 2				
Range of parturition dates	14 June-24 June	13 June-4 July	21 June-7 July	26 June-11 July
Pregnancy rate	100	100	96.4	90.1
Mean litter size	5.9	6.2	5.9	4.2
Litter 3				
Range of parturition dates	20 July-2 Aug	28 July-5 Aug	28 July-13 Aug	–
Pregnancy rate	100	100	84.5	0
Mean litter size	6.4	5.9	4.3	–

[a]Data are from Cary & Keith (1979) and Keith & Windberg (1978). Parturition dates are the range of mean dates for the years given and were calculated by adding 35 days per litter to the conception dates presented in Keith & Windberg (1978). Pregnancy rates were calculated from necropsies and palpation of live hares; litter sizes from necropsies.
[b]In 1971, 1972, and 1974, hares had only three litters. Average fourth litter pregnancy rates are calculated including these years.
[c]Data are from O'Donoghue & Krebs (1992) and Stefan (1998). Parturition dates are the range of dates from individual hares held in captivity for each litter. Pregnancy rates were calculated by palpation and litter sizes from hares held in captivity until birthing.
[d]Although there were four litters in Yukon during some years, no data were collected on the fourth litter or in 1993.

mass loss and total annual natality. Changes in total annual natality come from changes in pregnancy rates and litter sizes for later litters, whereas the effects of overwinter mass loss might be expected to be most pronounced for the first litter of the season. Hares do not store fat readily and are most nutritionally stressed when food is limited rather than showing delayed effects (Whittaker and Thomas 1983; Thomas 1987). Additionally, studies in the Yukon have not been able to demonstrate a relationship between either mass or mass loss and total annual reproductive output (O'Donoghue and Krebs 1992; Stefan 1998; C. I. Stefan and K. E. Hodges, unpublished). Neither the Yukon studies nor an Alberta study (Vaughan and Keith 1981) found an effect of mass loss on the size of the first litter.

Across both the cycle and the continent, the consistent patterns in reproductive output are: (1) The percentage of females pregnant declines with each successive litter group. Most females have at least two litters, but pregnancy rates for the third and fourth litters are highly variable. (2) Litter two is usually the largest and litter one the smallest. (3) Total annual natality is highest in the low phase, followed by increase, peak, and decline phases. The magnitude of variation is around 2.5 fold. (4) Reproductive output does not appear to be affected by the mother's skeletal size, mass, or parasite load. Age of the mother may affect ovulation rates. Stress levels are correlated temporally with and may contribute to reproductive changes. Overwinter mass loss and limited winter food supplies may reduce reproductive output through reductions in pregnancy rates and litter sizes, but the data are contradictory.

Survival and Causes of Death

Almost all hares die of predation. During the 1990 cycle in Yukon, 95% of the hares for whom cause of death could be positively identified were killed by predators, with approximately half of all deaths due to mammalian predators (Table 6.3) (Hodges et al., in press). Slightly lower estimates of predation were derived from previous cycles in Yukon (Table 6.4) (Boutin et al. 1986) and Alberta (Keith et al. 1977), but these analyses incorporated hares for whom cause of death could not be determined, which would lower the predation estimate. The 1980 and 1990 Yukon cycles showed that starvation and other non-predation deaths occurred during the late increase and peak and into the decline phases, counter to observations in Alberta that most starvation deaths occurred during the decline phase (Keith et al. 1984; Keith 1990). Most leverets that die are killed by predators (81% through a cycle) (O'Donoghue 1994; Stefan 1998), with deaths from exposure or maternal abandonment (starvation) occurring mainly during the decline phase.

The main predators of adult hares are coyotes, lynx, goshawks, and great horned owls (Table 6.3) (Keith et al. 1977; O'Donoghue et al. 1997; Gillis 1997, 1998; Hodges et al., in press). In contrast, leverets are predominantly preyed upon by small raptors (boreal owls, Harlan's hawks, kestrels, hawk owls) and small mammals (red squirrels, ground squirrels, weasels). No leveret kills by lynx or coyotes were observed during a cycle in Yukon (O'Donoghue 1994; Stefan 1998).

Table 6.3–Causes of death for hares near Kluane Lake, Yukon, 1988 through 1996. Years are counted from 1 April through 31 March. Values are percentages of the deaths of radiocollared juvenile and adult hares for which the cause was identifiable (and non-human caused) attributable to each mortality source. The mammalian, avian, and predation categories include kills by marten, weasels, wolves, eagles, hawk-owls, Harlan's hawks, and kills for which predation was certain but the predator species could not be identified. Non-predation deaths are hares that died of starvation, injury, or some other non-predation cause. Data are from C. J. Krebs, unpublished, and Hodges et al., in press.

	1988-89 increase	1989-90 peak	1990-91 decline	1991-92 decline	1992-93 decline	1993-94 low	1994-95 low	1995-96 increase
					Percent			
Coyote	20	27	6	51	18	57	48	26
Lynx	0	14	13	17	25	21	7	17
Goshawk	13	14	19	5	14	7	10	14
Great horned owl	0	5	15	12	11	0	2	6
Mammalian	7	0	2	0	11	0	10	14
Avian	20	5	22	4	4	7	5	6
Predation	13	23	9	11	18	7	19	14
Non-predation	27	14	15	0	0	0	0	3
% predation	73	86	85	100	100	100	100	97
n dead	15	22	54	107	28	14	42	35

Table 6.4–Snowshoe hare mortality data from 1978-1988, Kluane Lake, Yukon. Predator species were not identified for hare kills. Winter (November-April) 1986-1987 and summer (May-October) 1987-1988 data are from Krebs et al. 1992. The remaining data are from Trostel et al. 1987 (winter, December-May; summer, June-November). Data were recalculated to exclude hares for which the cause of death was unidentifiable. Values are the percentage of hares dead of each cause.

Summer	1978 increase	1979 increase	1980 peak	1981 peak	1984 low	1985 low	1987 increase	1988 increase
					Percent			
Mammalian	14	0	23	20	13	0	50	19
Avian	29	33	11	12	38	50	13	16
Predation	57	50	54	64	25	50	13	53
Non-predation	0	17	11	4	25	0	25	13
% predation	100	83	89	96	75	100	75	87
n dead	7	6	35	25	8	6	8	32

Winter	1978 increase	1979 increase	1980 peak	1981 peak	1984 low	1985 low	1986 increase	1987 increase
					Percent			
Mammalian	8	7	26	17	47	45	60	47
Avian	15	20	9	10	0	18	40	27
Predation	62	40	55	40	33	27	0	13
Non-predation	15	33	9	33	20	9	0	13
% predation	85	67	91	67	80	91	100	87
n dead	13	30	53	30	15	11	5	15

Hare survival rates have been measured from either trapping or radiotelemetry data. The trapping data yields less reliable estimates (Boutin and Krebs 1986). This method typically underestimates survival rates because hares are hard to trap (Trapp 1962; Boulanger 1993; Sullivan 1994) and have variable and sometimes high dispersal rates (Boutin et al. 1985; O'Donoghue and Bergman 1992; Gillis 1997; Hodges 1998). Survival estimates from trapping may also be biased by different amounts through the cycle, especially when comparing adult to juvenile survival or when estimating seasonal survival. These biases occur because dispersal and trapability vary seasonally, cyclically, and with age (Boutin et al. 1985, 1986; Krebs et al. 1986b; Boulanger 1993; Hodges 1998).

Snowshoe hare survival estimates from trapping suggest that survival is higher in the increase and peak phases than in the decline and low phases (Fig. 6.2a,b) (Krebs et al. 1986b; see also Keith and Windberg 1978). These data indicate that juvenile hares have lower survival than adults, and that whereas adult hares have lower overwinter survival than summer survival, juveniles may have lower survival during the summer. Snowshoe hare survival data from radiotelemetry only partially confirm these patterns (Fig. 6.3) (Krebs et al. 1995; Hodges et al., in press). Adult survival is indeed lower in the decline phase than at other times, but survival in the low phase is not noticeably different than survival in the increase and peak phases (Hodges et al. 1999). The survival estimates from radiotelemetry are much higher and more biologically reasonable; positive growth rates essentially cannot occur when 30-day survival is lower than 0.90 (corresponding to 25% survival through the year) (Hodges et al., in press), and the estimates from trapping therefore do not come close to an accurate estimation. Furthermore, even radiotelemetry estimates may be biased low (Haydon et al. 1999; C. J. Krebs and W. Hochachka, unpublished).

Survival of leverets to weaning is higher in the increase phase than in the decline phase (Stefan 1998). Post-weaning juvenile survival seems to depend on the litter group: in one year of an increase phase, juveniles in litters one and two survived as well as adults, whereas juveniles from litters three and four fared much worse (Gillis 1997, 1998). In this instance, most of the deaths occurred in the fall, when hares from later litters were simultaneously growing, changing coat color, and switching from forbs to woody browse. Snowshoe hare survival rates and causes of death are typically seasonal (Tables 6.3 and 6.4; Fig. 6.2) (Gillis 1998; Hodges et al., in press). Of the adult hares killed by lynx during a cycle in Yukon, 80% were killed between November and March (Hodges et al., in press). Most coyote predation occurred in October and November, and non-predation deaths occurred most often in late winter.

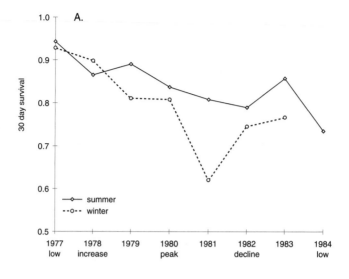

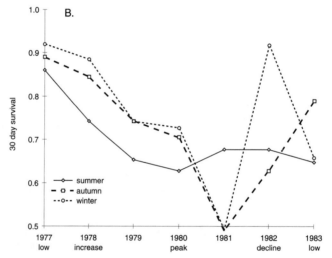

Figure 6.2—Snowshoe hare survival in Yukon, indexed by trapping. These data are mean survival values (2A) from four control areas, calculated from Jolly-Seber estimates using data in Krebs et al. 1986b. For adults, summer is April-September and winter is October-March; juvenile survival (2B) is broken into May-September (summer), October-December (autumn), and January-March (winter).

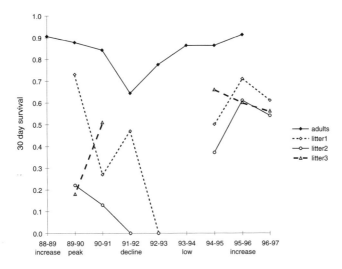

Figure 6.3—Radiotelemetry estimates of snowshoe hare survival in Yukon. Adult 30-day survival is based on the full year, whereas leveret survival is from birth to 30 days. The data are from Stefan 1998 and Hodges et al., in press.

There are anecdotal reports of massive overwinter die-offs, typically during the winter following peak fall densities (Severaid 1942; Keith 1963; C. Silver, unpublished; E. Hofer, personal communication; D. Henry, personal communication). Unfortunately, these reports are non-numeric, but they suggest that starvation or deaths due to disease are prevalent during that initial winter of decline. In some cases, dying hares had infections, some of which were due to *Staphylococcus aureus* (MacLulich 1937). There are hints that these die-offs occur following particularly high cyclic peaks. If such a pattern does exist, these cyclic declines may not be initiated by predation.

In addition to the cyclic patterns of survival, which are largely due to the numerical and functional responses of predators (Keith et al. 1977; Royama 1992; O'Donoghue et al. 1997, 1998), several other factors have been considered for their effects on the survival of hares (Table 6.5). The data on the effect of habitat type on hare survival are equivocal. In several studies, no effect of habitat on hare survival has been detected (Keith and Bloomer 1993; Cox et al. 1997), but other studies have observed lower survival in more open habitat types (Dolbeer and Clark 1975; Sievert and Keith 1985). Small patch size is associated with reduced survival in Wisconsin (Keith et al. 1993).

Avian predators kill hares in open areas more often than expected from the distribution of habitat types (Table 6.5) (Rohner and Krebs 1996; Cox et al.

Table 6.5–Correlates of snowshoe hare mortality. The following studies examined snowshoe hare survival or causes of death with respect to an individual factor to test whether the factor affected hare survival.

Factor and test	Effect of factor	Location	Reference
Habitat			
Deciduous vs. coniferous forest	No statistical effect on survival; potentially lower survival in deciduous habitat in Nov.-Dec.	Wisconsin	Keith & Bloomer 1993
Percent of hares killed by lynx in 4 densities of spruce, deciduous, and shrub habitats	No effect relative to habitat use by lynx	Yukon	Murray et al. 1994
Percent of hares killed by coyotes in 4 densities of spruce, deciduous, and shrub habitats	No effect relative to habitat use by coyotes in 2 yr; in 1 yr, more kills than expected in dense spruce	Yukon	Murray et al. 1994
Percent of hare kills in closed spruce, open spruce, and shrub habitats	More kills in shrub habitats with low canopy cover relative to availability	Yukon	Hik 1994, 1995
Percent hares killed by owls in 5 densities of spruce	More owl kills in open habitats relative to availability	Yukon	Rohner & Krebs 1996
Lynx hunting success in 4 densities of spruce, deciduous, and shrub habitats (kills/chase)	No effect	Yukon	Murray et al. 1995 (see also Murray et al. 1994)
Coyote hunting success in 4 densities of spruce, deciduous, and shrub habitats (kills/chase)	More successful in dense spruce than in open spruce	Yukon	Murray et al. 1995 (see also Murray et al. 1994)
Dense vs. sparse understory cover	Lower survival in areas with low understory cover	Wisconsin	Sievert & Keith 1985
Patch size (7 areas, 5-28 ha)	Lower survival in smaller patches	Wisconsin	Keith et al. 1993
Microhabitat: ≥2 brush piles/ha added to sites	No effect on hare survival rates	Wisconsin	Cox et al. 1997
Vertical foliage density	Coyote kill sites similar to habitat availability; raptor kill sites had lower foliage density	Wisconsin	Cox et al. 1997
Food addition			
Ad lib. Rabbit Chow added year-round to 36 ha areas	No effect on post-weaning juvenile survival	Yukon	Gillis 1997
Ad lib. Rabbit Chow added year-round to 36 ha areas	No effect on leveret or adult survival	Yukon	O'Donoghue 1994; Hodges et al., in press
Ad lib. Rabbit Chow added year-round to 9 ha areas	Survival higher in increase & peak, but lower in decline	Yukon	Krebs et al. 1986b
Downed spruce trees added to a 9 ha area	No effect on survival	Yukon	Krebs et al. 1986a
Ad lib. Rabbit Chow added to 25 ha areas over winter	No effect in 3 time periods; higher survival of fed hares in 1 time period	Manitoba	Murray et al. 1997
2.9-5.8 ha pens stocked with hares; 4/8 had food added; avian predators had access	Higher overwinter survival in pens with food added	Alberta	Vaughan & Keith 1981
Reproductive synchrony			
Days away from mean parturition date	Leverets near mean survived better	Yukon	O'Donoghue & Boutin 1995
Parasite load			
Hares given Ivermectin (anti-nematode) vs. control hares	No effect on survival in 3 time periods; higher survival of parasite-reduced hares in 1 time period	Manitoba	Murray et al. 1997

(con.)

Table 6.5–Con.

Factor and test	Effect of factor	Location	Reference
Hares given Ivermectin & Droncit (anti-cestode) vs. control hares	No effect on survival	Wisconsin	Bloomer et al. 1995
Hares given Ivermectin vs. control hares	No effect on survival	Yukon	Sovell 1993
Other hares			
2.9-5.8 ha pens stocked with hares; 4/8 had food added; avian predators had access	Survival lower at higher densities	Alberta	Vaughan & Keith 1981
Adults and 1st litter juveniles removed from 9 ha grids	Removal of adults improved juvenile survival in summer & fall	Yukon	Boutin 1984a
Body condition			
Condition and foot size smaller than mean for population	Lower survival of poor condition and smaller hares	Wisconsin	Sievert & Keith 1985
Bone marrow of hares killed by owls vs. shot hares	Owl killed hares were in better condition	Yukon	Rohner & Krebs 1996
Age			
2.9-5.8 ha pens stocked with hares; 4/8 had food added; avian predators had access	Juveniles survived less well than adults	Alberta	Vaughan & Keith 1981
% of the hares killed by owls in each age class	Owls preferred juvenile hares over adults relative to age structure in population	Yukon	Rohner & Krebs 1996
Season			
May-August, Sept-Dec, Jan-April	No effect of season on survival in low phase	Yukon	Hodges 1998
April-September, October-March	Adult survival higher in summer than in winter	Yukon	Krebs et al. 1986b

1997; Hodges 1998). Coyotes and lynx have kill rates comparable to the amount of time they spend in each habitat (Murray et al. 1994; O'Donoghue 1997), and their hunting success rates may vary with cover type (Murray et al. 1995). These predators select habitats, but it is unclear whether they select habitats that have the highest prey densities (Ward and Krebs 1985; Theberge and Wedeles 1989; Koehler 1990a; Murray et al. 1994; Poole et al. 1996) or habitats that are easier for them to traverse or hunt in (Murray and Boutin 1991; Murray et al. 1995; O'Donoghue 1997). Although these analyses suggest that hare survival may vary among habitat types, the definitive test for hares is per capita survival in each habitat. Hare survival in each habitat depends on hare density, predator presence, and the hunting success of predators within each habitat. Evaluating these parameters simultaneously will address the question of per capita hare survival as a function of habitat type.

The effect of food supply on hare survival has been studied by adding supplemental food to areas and comparing hare survival on these areas to survival of hares on non-supplemented areas (Table 6.5). Relative to control populations, hare populations on food-supplemented sites have shown reduced survival (Krebs et al. 1986b; Hodges et al., in press), similar survival (Krebs et al. 1986a; O'Donoghue 1994; Gillis 1998; Hodges et al., in press), and increased survival (Vaughan and Keith 1981; Krebs et al. 1986b; Murray et al. 1997). The potential effects of food supply on survival are two-fold: the distribution of food affects feeding locations and hare availability to predators, while the quality and abundance of the food affect physiology and starvation. The effects of food supply on hare survival may therefore depend upon the predation pressure. Starvation deaths mainly occur during and just after peak densities (Boutin et al. 1986; Keith 1990; Hodges et al., in press), which corresponds to the time when there is the least browse available (Smith et al. 1988; Keith 1990), but it is unclear whether starvation deaths are compensatory or additive to predation deaths. If the distribution of food forces hares into habitats that are riskier (as argued by Wolff 1980, 1981; Hik 1994, 1995), survival rates could be reduced, but there is a lack of consensus on the safety of various habitats for hares.

Snowshoe hare mortality patterns are: (1) Most hares of all ages are killed by predators, predominantly coyotes, goshawks, lynx, and great horned owls. (2) Starvation is most prevalent during high densities and into the decline phase. Anecdotal evidence of die-offs indicate that some declines involve more non-predation deaths than others; these die-offs may be linked to especially high cyclic peaks. (3) Survival is lowest during the decline phase and is typically lower in winter than in summer. Mortality rates are highest for leverets, intermediate for juveniles, and lowest for adults. Post-weaning juveniles from early litters may survive as well as adults. (4) Predators' hunting patterns and hunting success vary with habitat type, but few if any studies have shown clearly that per capita survival of hares varies among habitat types.

Dispersal

Snowshoe hares are known to disperse for distances up to 20 km (O'Farrell 1965; Keith et al. 1993; Gillis 1997; Hodges 1998). Assuming a home range size of 10 ha, a hare that relocated to an adjacent area would have to travel only 350 to 400 m from the center of the original range. This definition is probably inadequate because both juvenile and adult hares have been observed traveling >500 m a night but later returning to their home ranges. These forays away from home ranges last anywhere from overnight up to four to five weeks. It is unknown whether these trips are for mating, are precursors to dispersal, or are for some other purpose (O'Donoghue and Bergman 1992; Chu 1996; Gillis 1997; Hodges 1998). Given this range of types of long-distance movements, defining dispersal for hares is problematic.

Estimates of hare dispersal rates (movement greater than a given distance, or movement into trapping and/or removal grids) suggest that there may not be much difference in dispersal rate through the cycle (Table 6.6). Although immigration indices are biased because they may sample animals that were present but previously untrapped and because removal grids may attract animals (Dobson 1981; Boutin et al. 1985; Koenig et al. 1996), neither capture-recapture data nor the more reliable radiotelemetry data show a clear cyclic pattern in dispersal. Snowshoe hares have no clear season nor age of dispersal. The youngest recorded dispersers were 31 and 32 days old (respectively, Gillis 1997; O'Donoghue and Bergman 1992), and adults as old as three and four years have also dispersed (K. E. Hodges, unpublished). Both juveniles and adults disperse throughout the year, and there does not appear to be a sex bias in dispersal (Windberg and Keith 1976; Boutin 1979; Boutin et al. 1985; Keith et al. 1984, 1993; Hodges 1998). Hares that disperse appear to survive as well as hares that remain resident (Boutin 1984a; Keith 1990; Gillis 1997), but in an experiment transplanting hares to simulate dispersal, survival was lower for the first week following transplantation (Sievert and Keith 1985).

Table 6.6–Indices of dispersal rates of snowshoe hares. The trapping data may include animals that were resident but previously untrapped. The radiotelemetry data include animals that moved more than two home-range diameters and animals that died outside their observed home ranges.

Location	Method	Low	Increase	Peak	Decline	Reference
Alberta	Net ingress[a] (% of hares trapped new at time t & present at $t + 1$)	0-21	0-37	0-35	0-41	Keith & Windberg 1978
Yukon	% of hares new in spring population	52	40	42	40	Hodges et al., in press
Yukon	% of radiocollared hares dispersing	– [b]	4.0	2.8	2.7	Boutin et al. 1985
Yukon	% of radiocollared hares dispersing	4.7 (m); 8.4 (f)				Hodges 1998
Yukon	% of radiocollared post-weaning juveniles dispersing	– [b]	50	– [b]	– [b]	Gillis 1997

[a]Ranges are for multiple years within each phase.
[b]No data.

The proximate causes of hare dispersal are unknown, but several potential correlates have been examined. Keith et al. (1993) found little effect of habitat patch size on dispersal rates. Food addition treatments tend to attract immigrants, but there is no indication that hares on control areas disperse at a greater rate than do hares on food addition areas (Boutin 1984b; Hodges et al., in press). Hares that disperse may be lighter than hares that do not disperse (Windberg and Keith 1976; Boutin et al. 1985). That pattern could arise due to sampling (i.e., if juveniles and adults are not readily distinguished morphologically and more juveniles disperse), or it could indicate that lighter hares move to find better food resources or to avoid aggressive encounters (see also Graf 1985; Sinclair 1986; Ferron 1993). Settling rates of dispersing hares are higher when residents are few or have been removed, which could be due to aggression or through hares' assessment of resource availability (Keith and Surrendi 1971; Windberg and Keith 1976; Boutin 1984a).

Snowshoe Hare Behavior

Habitat Use Patterns

Because snowshoe hares eat conifers, they have been studied by foresters to minimize hare damage to naturally regenerating stands or plantations (Aldous and Aldous 1944; Cook and Robeson 1945; Borrecco 1976, unpublished; Radvanyi 1987, unpublished). Other studies have considered how to manage for snowshoe hares as a game species or as food for forest carnivores (Brocke 1975; Carreker 1985, unpublished; Thompson 1988; Koehler and Brittell 1990). These studies often have not considered the availability of different habitat types, thus making it impossible to determine hare habitat selection.

Most studies of hare habitat use have used fecal pellet plots, but some have used numbers per plot and others have used presence/absence per plot; the bias in the latter method may depend on the phase of the cycle. Additionally, hares excrete their pellets while they are active (Hodges 1998), so fecal pellet plots do not sample the resting habitats of hares, even though hares may spend approximately one-third of their time resting (Keith 1964; Hodges 1998). Other studies have used track transects and live trapping as indices of hares' habitat use patterns. Track transects assume that distance traveled is correlated with time spent, which may not be true if hares are traveling through certain habitats and spending time eating (and not creating tracks) in other habitats. Trapping may create a bias by attracting hares to baits. The three methods describe similar patterns of habitat use by hares (Litvaitis et al. 1985a), but the numeric estimates vary with the technique used.

Radiotelemetry may allow a more accurate estimation of hares' habitat use patterns, because it samples locations of active and inactive hares. However, triangulation does not allow fine-scale analysis of habitat use and walking to find hares visually may be slightly biased by startling hares into particular types of habitat (but see Hodges 1998).

Nonetheless, a fairly consistent picture of hare habitat use emerges from the various techniques (Table 6.7). Snowshoe hares typically use coniferous forests and often use areas with dense understory cover (Wolff 1980; Orr and Dodds 1982; Parker 1984, 1986; Thompson et al. 1989; Hik 1994; St-Georges et al. 1995). Hares' use of different stand types appears to be based primarily on the cover afforded by the stand, which varies with species composition and age, and secondarily on the palatability of the species present in the stand (Wolff 1980; Hik 1994). Hares essentially avoid clear-cuts, young stands of regrowth, and open areas. Hares also are more likely to use

Table 6.7–Snowshoe hares' use of regenerating forests. < and > indicate significance of $p < 0.05$.

Location	Measure	Species	Results	Reference
Stand age				
Ontario	Track transects	*Picea* spp. *Betula papyrifera* *Populus tremuloides* *Abies balsamea*	Use of 20 and 30 yr old stands >10 yr old & uncut stands > clearcuts and stands younger than 5 yr	Thompson et al. 1989; Thompson 1988
New Brunswick	Pellet plots Browsed twigs	*Picea mariana* *Pinus banksiana* *Pinus resinosa*	Jack pine: use in 8 yr old stands > 13 yr old Black spruce: use in 13 yr old stands > 8 yr old	Parker 1986
New Brunswick	Live-trapping Pellet plots	*Picea* spp.	Use of 10-17 yr old stands >uncut stands and stands younger than 10 yr	Parker 1984
Newfoundland	Track transects	*Abies balsamea*	Use of 40 yr stands >60 yr stands and uncut	Thompson & Curran 1995
Species				
New Brunswick	Pellet plots Browsed twigs	*Picea mariana* *Pinus banksiana* *Pinus resinosa*	Use of jack pine >black spruce >red pine (8 yr-old stands) Use of black spruce >jack pine (13 yr-old stands)	Parker 1986
Stand density				
Nova Scotia	Damage to trees	*Abies balsamea*	Use of dense stand (~32,000 stems/ha) >use of open stand (7,000 stems/ha)	Lloyd-Smith & Piene 1981, unpublished
British Columbia	Live-trapping Damage to trees	*Pinus contorta*	More hares caught & more trees damaged in heavily stocked stands (regressions, $p < 0.05$ for both)	Sullivan & Sullivan 1983; Sullivan & Sullivan 1988
British Columbia	% of trees damaged Number of wounds	*Pinus contorta*	Higher % damaged and more wounds/tree with increasing stocking density (regressions $p < 0.05$ for both)	Sullivan & Sullivan 1982a,b

regrowing stands with dense understory cover than uncut or even-aged stands with little understory cover (Monthey 1986; Thompson 1988; Thompson et al. 1989; Koehler 1990a,b). Conroy et al. (1979) suggested that habitat interspersion increased hares use of areas. Studies that have compared the distribution of hares to the availability of the various habitat types have found that hares actively select habitats with dense cover and avoid open habitats (O'Donoghue 1983; Litvaitis et al. 1985b; Hik 1994; St-Georges et al. 1995; Hodges 1998).

Several other factors may influence habitat use by hares. Hares may be more likely to use deciduous cover in summer than in winter because the presence of leaves helps to protect them from detection (Wolff 1980; O'Donoghue 1983; Litvaitis et al. 1985b). Similarly, hares are more likely to use areas of sparse cover when it is dark and moonless (Gilbert and Boutin 1991). Hares appear to use roughly the same habitats when active as when resting, although resting hares often use denser microhabitats (e.g., brushpiles, deadfall) (Ferron and Ouellet 1992; Cox et al. 1997; Hodges 1998). A few studies have found limited differences in habitat use between the sexes (Litvaitis 1990; Hik 1994). Several authors have suggested that juveniles use more open habitats than adults do (Dolbeer and Clark 1975; Boutin 1984a). This pattern could result from social interactions because juveniles are subordinate to adults (Graf 1985; Graf and Sinclair 1987).

Several authors have suggested that the densest habitats provide hares with refuges that protect them from predators during the low phase (leading to relatively dense pockets of hares) and that hares then disperse into more open habitats as their densities increase (Keith 1966; Wolff 1980, 1981; Hik 1994, 1995). The spatial scale of this phenomenon has not been well articulated, and studies of multi-annual patterns of habitat use have typically focused on small scale habitat shifts (i.e., m^2 rather than ha or km^2). That approach could be problematic if refugia are at a larger scale such as the patchiness that results from fires (Fox 1978; Finerty 1980).

The current evidence about refugia is equivocal. Several studies over three to five years have shown shifts in hare habitat use, typically with hares using more dense habitats as the population moves from the peak into decline years (Keith 1966; Wolff 1980; Hik 1994; Mowat et al. 1996). Two longer studies, however, although showing interannual variation, did not show regular cyclic patterns in hare habitat use (Fuller and Heisey 1986; Koonz 1988, unpublished). In Manitoba, very different proportions of hares were caught in each of four habitats through 16 years (Fig. 6.4) (Koonz 1988, unpublished), but neither the two low phases nor the two decline phases showed the same pattern of hare habitat use. Furthermore, the refugium hypothesis predicts that open habitats will not be used when hare densities

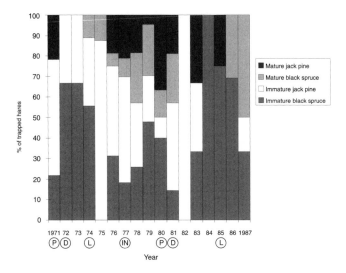

Figure 6.4—Snowshoe hare habitat use through the cycle. Koonz (1988 unpublished) trapped four grids in Manitoba, one in each habitat type; each grid was four ha. The y-axis gives the percentage of hares trapped in each habitat in each year, P = peak, D = decline, L = low, IN = increase.

are low, but several studies have shown that hares do use open habitats during population lows (Fuller and Heisey 1986; Hodges 1998). The refugium hypothesis also suggests that hare habitat shifts arise either through predation on hares in open habitats (Keith 1966) or through behavioral shifts by the hares (Wolff 1980). Yet experimental reduction of predation (and consequently predation risk) did not lead to differential habitat use or selection by hares during the low phase (Hodges 1998).

Only a few studies have explicitly considered hare demography within different habitat types or fragments of habitat. Hare survival may be higher in coniferous than in deciduous cover, especially in winter when deciduous trees lose their leaves (Keith and Bloomer 1993). Similarly, hares may have lower survival in habitats with little understory cover (Sievert and Keith 1985; Sullivan and Moses 1986), but spraying herbicides to reduce the cover of shrubs and ground vegetation and to encourage coniferous growth does not appear to affect hare densities, survival, or reproduction (Sullivan 1994, 1996). In Alberta, hares in fragmented woodlots displayed a numeric decline of reduced amplitude and had slightly higher total annual natalities than hares in nearby contiguous forest in two of four years, but both adult and juvenile survival showed no consistent differences between the fragmented and non-fragmented areas (Windberg and Keith 1978). In another study, Keith et al. (1993) examined demography in fragments of different sizes (5 to 28 ha); hare density and reproduction were unrelated to patch size, whereas survival was lower on small fragments. In all of these studies, predation was the main cause of death.

In summary: (1) Hares' habitat use is linked to dense understory cover rather than to canopy closure. (2) Hares appear to select habitats for cover rather than for food, but cover and food often covary. (3) Predator abundance does not appear to affect the habitat selection patterns of hares. (4) There is no clear shift of habitat use or selection through the cycle, counter to the suggestion that hares may concentrate in refugia during the low phase. Determining the appropriate scale for measuring refugia would help to substantiate this conclusion. (5) There is limited evidence to suggest that hares' survival and reproduction vary among different habitats, but the evidence is so patchy that this idea needs corroboration and further testing.

Diets and Food Limitation

Snowshoe hares eat a variety of coniferous and deciduous woody plants through the winter (Table 6.8) (see also Chapter 7). Regional studies have determined preferences of hares for certain plant species (Bryant and Kuropat 1980; Parker 1984; Bergeron and Tardif 1988; Smith et al. 1988; Hodges 1998), but because hares are distributed across the continent, their preferences vary with the local plant community. Studies on the diet selection of snowshoe hares indicate that hares choose species and twig sizes by responding to some combination of the nutritive and defensive chemistry of the twigs. Protein, fibre, secondary compounds, digestibility, and specific nutrients have all been suggested as arbiters of choice, and hares may be able to balance negative and positive attributes of the various food plants (Bryant and Kuropat 1980; Bryant 1981a,b; Belovsky 1984; Fox and Bryant 1984; Sinclair and Smith 1984b; Reichardt et al. 1984; Schmitz et al. 1992; Rodgers and Sinclair 1997; Hodges 1998).

Snowshoe hares survive on low-protein browse by eating a lot of it, passing it through the digestive system quickly, excreting fibrous pellets, and reingesting soft pellets to extract additional protein and other nutrients (Cheeke 1983, 1987; Sinclair and Smith 1984a). A corollary to this strategy is that hares tend to eat the same amount of food daily (Holter et al. 1974; Pease et al. 1979; Sinclair et al. 1982), and reductions in dietary energy or digestibility therefore lead to mass loss (Rodgers and Sinclair 1997). Additionally, hares have small fat reserves that are capable of maintaining them for only four to six days without eating (Whittaker and Thomas 1983), so mass loss occurs soon after hares start eating inadequate diets. Hares appear to need

Table 6.8—Diet of snowshoe hares and diameters of browsed twigs through the population cycle.

Index	Location	Species	Low	Increase	Peak	Decline	Reference
Mean diameter (mm) of browsed twigs[a]	Yukon	Salix glauca Betula glandulosa Picea glauca	2.4 1.7-2.4 2.1	2.0-2.7 1.8-2.1 2.2	3.3-3.6 2.3-2.5 1.8-2.9	1.5-2.8 1.7 2.1	Smith et al. 1988
Mean diameter (mm) of browsed twigs[a]	Yukon	Salix glauca Betula glandulosa Picea glauca	2.0-3.5 2.0-2.2 2.6-3.7				Hodges 1998
Mean diameter (mm) of browsed twigs[b]	Alaska	Shrubs, mainly Alnus crispa, Salix spp., Betula spp.	yr 1: 2.7-4.8 yr 2: 2.7-3.3	yr 1: 2.7-3.2	–	yr 1: 8.6-13.6 yr 2: 6.2-11.9 yr 3: 2.6-7.5	Wolff 1980
% surveyed twigs that were browsed over-winter on 11 sites[b]	Alaska	Shrubs, mainly Alnus crispa, Salix spp., Betula spp.	yr 1: 0-99; 7/11 sites 0-4 yr 2: 0-50; 7/11 sites 0-3	–	–	yr 1: 100 yr 2: 91-100 yr 3: 3-99	Wolff 1980
% of tagged twigs eaten by hares overwinter[a]	Yukon	Betula glandulosa Salix glauca Picea glauca Shepherdia canadensis	–	7-36 10-24 4-21 5-17	71-82 27 8-13 23-26	4 2 3 1	Smith et al. 1988
% of trees with damage[a]	British Columbia	Pinus contorta		35	57-69	25-54	Sullivan & Sullivan 1988

[a]Ranges are for years within each phase.
[b]Ranges are for sites within each year; yr 1, yr 2, yr 3 refer to the first, second, and third year within each phase.

about 300 g of browse daily, and are better able to maintain their mass on 300 g of small rather than large twigs (Pease et al. 1979). Diets in which the mean twig diameter is >3 mm lead to mass loss, while diets composed of twigs with a mean diameter ≤ 3 mm are thought to be sufficient for hares to maintain their mass (Pease et al. 1979).

Despite this apparent threshold for identifying adequate food for hares, determining food availability is next to impossible (Sinclair et al. 1982, 1988). Hares' dietary composition fluctuates through the cycle (Table 6.8) and classifying food availability is difficult because twigs that a hare would not eat in the low phase are readily consumed during the peak phase. Snowshoe hares can maintain themselves for extended periods of time on sub-optimal foods (Sinclair et al. 1982) and overwinter mass loss is common (Newson and de Vos 1964; Keith 1990), so dietary stress is difficult to measure. Another problem is that hares may not use foods in habitats with high predation risk (Hik 1994), and many food plants show cyclic changes in secondary compound content, with high levels deterring hares from eating those twigs (Bryant 1981a; Fox and Bryant 1984; Sinclair et al. 1988). It is therefore difficult to define food for hares, let alone measure it.

When consistent food indices are applied across a cycle at any one site, most studies show cyclic fluctuations with food least abundant during the peak and early decline phases and becoming abundant during the low phase (Pease et al. 1979; Wolff 1980; Smith et al. 1988; Keith 1990). Some researchers have used such data coupled with estimates of hares' dietary needs to infer absolute food shortage at peak densities (Pease et al. 1979; Keith 1990), while other researchers have not found absolute food shortage (Smith et al. 1988; Sinclair et al. 1988). It is difficult to interpret the results of such studies because of the large error associated with browse estimation and the underlying problem of what food requirements are for hares. A similar difficulty applies to the question of whether hares might be relatively food limited during particular phases of the cycle.

An alternative to the food estimation problems has been to examine hares' dietary intake, physiology, or starvation rates as measures that might indicate nutritional stress. Hare diets do show cyclic fluctuations, with hares eating more large twigs during cyclic peaks (Table 6.8). Hares seldom eat bark at low densities, but will eat it when densities are high; most girdling of trees in conifer plantations occurs when hare densities are high (Radvanyi 1987, unpublished; Hodges 1998). There are also cyclic changes in hare mass losses overwinter (Keith and Windberg 1978; Keith 1990), but it is unclear whether overwinter mass loss is a regular facet of snowshoe hare biology or a sensitive reflection of food shortage. Neither the dietary shifts nor the mass loss patterns necessarily indicate food shortage of a magnitude that would affect demography. The strongest indication of potential food shortage is that starvation rates are higher at high hare densities and into the decline phase, but starvation deaths typically are a small proportion of total mortality and it is unknown if they are additive to or compensatory with predation deaths (Tables 6.3 and 6.4) (Keith et al. 1984; Trostel et al. 1987; Keith 1990; Krebs et al. 1992; Hodges et al., in press).

Food addition experiments circumvent some of these interpretation problems by artificially creating areas of abundant food. These studies have shown little to no effect of food addition on hare survival, reproduction, or cyclic dynamics, leading to the conclusion that food shortage is not a necessary component of cyclic declines (O'Donoghue and Krebs 1992; Stefan 1998; Krebs et al. 1986a,b, 1995; Hodges et al., in press; but see Vaughan and Keith 1981). It is possible that food addition treatments may attract hares (Boutin 1984b; Hodges et al., in press), thus leading to higher hare densities; it is therefore possible that the per capita food supply is still limiting.

Assessing per capita food supply and the effects of food limitation are difficult for snowshoe hares but overall the following patterns seem to hold: (1) Hares eat most woody species, selecting smaller twigs and twigs with fewer chemical defenses. There is a clear cycle in the size of twigs in hare diets, with the largest twigs eaten during high hare densities. (2) Hares at peak densities are capable of consuming a large proportion of the available browse, and hares may girdle trees when densities are high. (3) Food supplementation experiments have been unable to stop cyclic declines, and hare survival and reproduction are similar between food-supplemented and control sites. (4) Absolute food shortage does not appear to occur during hare cycles, but relative food shortage and changes in food quality may occur. (5) Starvation deaths do not seem to occur during the low and increase phases of the cycle, but starvation deaths may reflect either relative or absolute food shortage.

Movements, Home Ranges, and Activity

Snowshoe hares' home range sizes cannot be compared directly among studies because data have been collected differently. Locations have been obtained from trapping records (O'Farrell 1965; Tompkins and Woehr 1979; Wolff 1980), flushing hares repeatedly (Keith et al. 1993), triangulating on radiocollared animals (Boutin 1979, 1984c; Boulanger 1993; Hik 1994), and walking in to observe radiocollared hares (Ferron and Ouellet 1992; Allcock 1994; Chu 1996; Jekielek 1996; Hodges 1998). Additionally, researchers have used varying numbers of locations and time periods for estimating home ranges, the statistical methods of calculating home ranges are not comparable (Worton 1987; Harris et al. 1990), and different software packages may have different algorithms for the "same" statistical method (Lawson and Rodgers 1997). The following generalizations are therefore based on conclusions derived in each paper rather than on a reappraisal of numeric estimates.

Most home range estimates for snowshoe hares indicate that they use areas that are five to 10 ha, and often hares are located within a small subset of their total range (O'Farrell 1965; Wolff 1980; Hodges 1998). Males, but not females, appear to choose resting spots within a smaller area than the area in which they feed, but for both sexes there is a high degree of overlap between areas used for these different activities (Ferron and Ouellet 1992). Hares do not have territories and overlapping home ranges are common, but they may try to avoid encountering each other (Adams 1959; Boutin 1980, 1984c).

Female hares have smaller home ranges than males (Bider 1961; Ferron and Ouellet 1992; Hik 1994; Hodges 1998). Some authors have concluded that the sexes have similar home range sizes, but typically this conclusion is based on trapping data (O'Farrell 1965; Tompkins and Woehr 1979; Wolff 1980; see also Keith et al. 1993; Boulanger 1993). However, males appear to use much more area (assessed by radiotelemetry) than their trapping records indicate, whereas females are more likely to be trapped throughout their observed radiotelemetry ranges (Hodges, in press). The equal home range sizes in the trapping studies are therefore probably the result of a methodological bias that reduces the observed home range size of males.

Snowshoe hares may modify their home range sizes in response to breeding, food supply, population density, and predators. Females constrict the areas they use when they have very young litters (Bider 1961; Graf and Sinclair 1987; O'Donoghue and Bergman 1992; Allcock 1994; Jekielek 1996). Because mating is usually within 24 hours post-partum and females are synchronous breeders (O'Donoghue and Boutin 1995), males increase their movements and the area covered (about 5 fold) around the time when females are oestrous (Bider 1961; Chu 1996). Hares may have smaller home ranges at higher densities (Boutin 1984c; Hik 1994), but hares on sites with supplemental food do not appear to have smaller home ranges than hares on unsupplemented sites, despite higher densities (Boutin 1984b; Hodges 1998) and contrary to the typical pattern for other small mammals (Boutin 1990). Hares in predator exclosures may have smaller home ranges than unprotected hares (Hodges 1998), but Small and Keith (1992) found no differences in hares' home range sizes before and after red foxes were introduced to islands.

Hares are mostly active in twilight, although during summer in high latitudes they are active in daylight (Keith 1964; Boulanger 1993; Boulanger and Krebs 1996; Hodges 1998). Movement rates are high in summer, which may be related to breeding. Winter movement rates are low, possibly to minimize exposure to the cold (Hodges 1998). In both winter and summer, foraging movements do not appear to be related to hare density, and males have higher movement rates than females (Boulanger 1993; Hik 1994; Hodges 1998). Hares on food addition sites have movement patterns similar to hares on control sites, whereas hares protected from predators may respond by decreasing movements (Hodges 1998).

In summary: (1) Home ranges for hares are not well defined; hares often make extra-range movements, especially during the breeding season, and home-range overlap is high among hares. (2) Male hares move more and use larger areas than do females. (3) Neither food supply nor predator abundance have clear effects on hares' movement patterns and home ranges. (4) Hare density does not appear to have a strong effect on hares' movements.

Physiological Changes Through the Cycle

Several authors have argued that cyclic changes in hares' physiology (parasitic infestation, mass or mass loss, hematology, immunochemistry, fat reserves) might be partially causal of cyclic reproductive or survival changes (Keith et al. 1985; Boonstra et al. 1998a). For any of these factors to be causal, it must demonstrate the appropriate cyclicity and its impact on reproduction or survival should be of a magnitude comparable to the observed changes in these parameters.

Hares exhibit cycles in mass, overwinter mass loss, and mass-based condition indices (Newson and de Vos 1964; Keith and Windberg 1978; Hodges et al. 2000, in press). Mean spring mass of hares varied by approximately 200 g through the 1990 cycle in Yukon (K. E. Hodges and C. J. Krebs, unpublished). The lowest average mass was during the low phase and highest average mass was during the peak and early decline phases (see also Keith and Windberg 1978; Cary and Keith 1979). Keith and Windberg (1978) suggested that survival was lower for lower-mass individuals, but their use of trapping data for this point does not allow them to distinguish among dispersal, death, and low trapability. Elsewhere, lower-mass individuals were thought to have higher dispersal rates (Windberg and Keith 1976). Keith (1990) has suggested that hares with high overwinter mass loss have reduced reproductive output, but studies in Yukon have failed to find an impact of mass (or mass corrected for skeletal size) on reproductive output (Hodges et al. 2000, in press; C. I. Stefan and K. E. Hodges, unpublished).

Bone marrow fat content may be a more sensitive indicator of body condition, but it can only be ascertained after death. Hares dying of starvation have low marrow fat relative to hares in the rest of the population (Keith et al. 1984; Murray et al. 1997), and hares killed by predators may have lower marrow fat than hares in the population at large (Keith et al. 1984), but in some cases their marrow fat content is similar (Murray et al. 1997). Hares killed by great horned owls in Yukon had a slightly higher marrow fat content than did hares in the rest of the population (Rohner and Krebs 1996). Furthermore, food addition does not necessarily lead to higher marrow fat, despite the presumably better nutrition of hares on food-added sites (Murray et al. 1998). Other fat indices, such as kidney fat, may be better indicators of body condition than bone marrow fat content if they respond continuously to hare body condition rather than having some maximum value as bone marrow appears to.

Hares that are stressed might have reduced reproduction or survival rates. Chronic exposure to predators, nutritional limitation, or aggressive interactions potentially may lead to deleterious feedbacks in the hypothalamic-pituitary-adrenal system (Feist 1980; Boonstra and Singleton 1993; Boonstra et al. 1998a). Adrenal hypertrophy could index such stress, but the mass of adrenals show neither a cyclic pattern nor a clear relationship with hare density (Windberg and Keith 1976; Höhn and Stelfox 1977; Cary and Keith 1979), although food shortage can lead to lighter adrenals (Vaughan and Keith 1981). More sensitive examinations of the biochemistry (e.g., free cortisol levels, leucocyte counts, testosterone levels) indicate that hares are more stressed during the peak and decline phases than during the low phase (Dieterich and Feist 1980; Boonstra and Singleton 1993; Boonstra et al. 1998a). These biochemical responses have yet to be shown to be causally linked to changes in reproductive output or survival rates of hares.

Snowshoe hares are parasitized by many nematode and cestode species. *Trichuris leporis*, *Obeliscoides cuniculi*, *Dirofilaria scapiceps*, *Trichostrongylus* spp., *Nematodirus triangularis*, *Passalurus nonanulatus*, *Taenia pisiformis*, and *Eimeria* spp. can have relatively high infestation rates and/or show cyclic fluctuations (Erickson 1944; Bookhout 1971; Cary and Keith 1979; Keith et al. 1985; Sovell 1993). Juvenile hares often have heavier parasite infestations than adults (Maltais and Ouellette 1983; Keith et al. 1985; Keith et al. 1986; but see Erickson 1944). Theoretically, the presence of a cycle in parasite abundance can enhance the hare population cycle through sublethal effects (Ives and Murray 1997). Empirically, however, both correlative analyses and experimental manipulations of parasite load have failed to link parasite infestation levels and reproductive output (Cary and Keith 1979; Sovell 1993; Bloomer et al. 1995; Murray et al. 1998) or survival (Sovell 1993; Bloomer et al. 1995; but see Murray et al. 1997).

Explanations for the Cycle

Given the variety of physiological and demographic cycles that occur during the numeric hare cycle, not to mention the plant and predator cycles, it is no surprise that many explanations exist to explain the hare cycle. There are two basic tiers of explanation: (1) Describing the regular changes in reproduction, survival, and dispersal that contribute to the numeric cycle. (2) Explaining the factors that lead to changes in each of these demographic parameters. This second class of explanation is broadly divided into trophic interactions and behavioral and physiological effects.

Most of the numeric change is driven by changes in juvenile survival, followed by changes in adult survival and leveret survival (Keith 1990; Krebs 1996; Haydon et al. 1999). Adult survival is more important than juvenile survival during the decline phase, when juvenile survival is so low that small changes in it have little impact on the dynamics (Haydon et al. 1999). Changes in reproductive output and dispersal do not have a very large effect on numeric changes because hares are short-lived and have high fecundity. The breeding population is therefore determined more by recruitment than by adult survival (see also Lebreton and Clobert 1991). Because the young hares have to survive for six to nine months before breeding, their survival rates have more impact on the population than do their starting numbers.

Explaining the changes in each of the demographic parameters is the next step of explaining the numeric hare cycle, and it is here that many different stories are told (for reviews, see Finerty 1980; Keith 1990; Krebs et al. 1992; Boonstra et al. 1998b). Although hypotheses invoking intrinsic regulation, hare-plant interactions, or hare-predator interactions have been proposed (Chitty 1967; Krebs 1978; Finerty 1980; Bryant 1981a; Fox and Bryant 1984; Trostel et al. 1987), available evidence suggests that hares' interactions with both food plants and predators are integral to demographic changes (Keith 1963; Krebs et al. 1992, 1995, 1996; Hodges et al., in press). Keith (1974, 1981, 1990) has proposed that food shortage at peak densities initiates the decline through an increase in starvation rates, and that the high mortality that characterizes the decline phase is then largely imposed by predators. Recent experimental work in the Yukon does not substantiate the argument that food shortage initiates the decline, but shows instead that the cycle is most likely due to interactions of food plants, hares, and predators throughout the cycle (Smith et al. 1988; Sinclair et al. 1988; Krebs et al. 1986b, 1995; Hodges et al., in press). In Yukon, single factor manipulations of food and predators increased hare densities but failed to alter either the numeric cycle or the cyclic changes in survival and natality. However, the simultaneous addition of food and reduction of predators resulted in a hare population with higher

survival, higher annual natality, and higher densities than control populations (Krebs et al. 1995; Hodges et al., in press).

Recent models have attempted to unify behavior, physiology, trophic
interactions, and demographic changes. Hik (1994, 1995) proposed that
hares change habitat types when faced with high predation risk, with safer
habitats also being poorer in food. Under this scenario, the combination of
high predation risk and voluntary dietary restriction cause low survival and
poor reproduction during the decline phase. When risk is reduced and hares
again use better habitats, survival and reproduction rebound (see also Keith
1966; Wolff 1980). Boonstra et al. (1998a) have expanded this model to
suggest that hares also experience physiological stress (that may or may not
be food linked) as a result of high predation risk, and that the stress can
impact reproduction directly and through maternal effects. These models
putatively explain the prolonged low phase of the cycle: hare densities stay
low for several years, even after food plants have regrown and predator
numbers have declined (Smith et al. 1988; Boonstra et al. 1998b; Hodges et al.
1999). If hares affect their nutrition and stress by behavioral changes, or if
they experience maternal effects from mothers who were stressed during the
decline phase, both reproduction and survival could be depressed (Hik 1994;
Boonstra et al. 1998b). Another scenario invokes the sub-lethal impacts of
parasites, suggesting that cyclic changes in parasite infestation rates and
loads impact hare survival and reproduction (Ives and Murray 1997; Murray
et al. 1997). These scenarios are worth testing; at present they are based
mostly on chains of correlation and linking population level analyses
together. To substantiate these arguments, it is critical to examine individual
hares to determine the impacts of predation risk, nutrition, stress, and
parasite load on hare survival and reproduction.

Conclusion

In the north, snowshoe hares undergo regular population cycles of five to
25 fold amplitude. Survival and reproductive changes are responsible for the
numeric changes, but there is uncertainty about the relative impacts of the
factors (food supply, stress, habitats, parasites) affecting these survival and
reproductive changes. Differences in amplitude and duration of the cycle
could possibly be due to variation in hare behavior or habitat characteristics,
if these do affect demography. It would be valuable to develop models that
show how much and what kinds of demographic variation are necessary to
create cycles of different amplitudes and durations. Field studies that can
explain patterns of demographic variation would also be useful.

Acknowledgments

I have enjoyed the opportunity to delve into the snowshoe hare, boreal ecology, and population cycle literatures more thoroughly. I am indebted to the Lynx Science Team for giving me the opportunity to do so. This chapter has benefited greatly from discussion with and comments from C. J. Krebs, A. R. E. Sinclair, J. L. Ruesink, and G. Koehler. Three anonymous reviewers offered helpful suggestions. I am indebted to the following people, who have graciously and generously allowed me access to unpublished data and observations: T. Bailey, F. I. Doyle, H. Golden, D. Henry, W. Hochachka, C. J. Krebs, S. Mahoney, M. McNay, C. D. Mitchell, G. Mowat, K. Poole, P. Seccombe-Hett, C. I. Stefan, L. A. Viereck, and P. C. Adams. T. Karels provided technical assistance.

Literature Cited

Adamcik, R. S., A. W. Todd, and L. B. Keith. 1978. Demographic and dietary responses of great horned owls during a snowshoe hare cycle. Canadian Field-Naturalist 92:156-166.

Adams, L. 1959. An analysis of a population of snowshoe hares in northwestern Montana. Ecological Monographs 29:141-170.

Aldous, C. M. and S. E. Aldous. 1944. The snowshoe hare—a serious enemy of forest plantations. Journal of Forestry 42:88-94.

Allcock, K. 1994. Do predation risk and food affect the home ranges of snowshoe hares? BSc Thesis. University of British Columbia, Vancouver.

Bailey, R. G. 1997. Ecoregions map of North America. USDA Forest Service. Scale 1:15000000.

Bailey, T. N., E. E. Bangs, M. F. Portner, J. C. Malloy, and R. J. McAvinchey. 1986. An apparent overexploited lynx population on the Kenai Peninsula, Alaska. Journal of Wildlife Management 50:279-290.

Banfield, A. W. F. 1974. The mammals of Canada. University of Toronto Press, Toronto.

Belovsky, G. E. 1984. Snowshoe hare optimal foraging and its implications for population dynamics. Theoretical Population Biology 25:235-264.

Bergeron, J.-M. and J. Tardif. 1988. Winter browsing preferences of snowshoe hares for coniferous seedlings and its implication in large-scale reforestation programs. Canadian Journal of Forest Research 18:280-282.

Bergerud, A. T. 1983. Prey switching in a simple ecosystem. Scientific American 249:130-141.

Bider, J. R. 1961. An ecological study of the hare *Lepus americanus*. Canadian Journal of Zoology 39:81-103.

Bloomer, S. E. M., T. Willebrand, I. M. Keith, and L. B. Keith. 1995. Impact of helminth parasitism on a snowshoe hare population in central Wisconsin: a field experiment. Canadian Journal of Zoology 73:1891-1898.

Bookhout, T. A. 1971. Helminth parasites in snowshoe hares from northern Michigan. Journal of Wildlife Diseases 7:246-248.

Boonstra, R., S. Boutin, A. Byrom, T. Karels, A. Hubbs, K. Stuart-Smith, M. Blower, and S. Antpoehler. In press. The role of red squirrels and Arctic ground squirrels in the boreal forest. *in* C. J. Krebs, S. Boutin, R. Boonstra, editors. Vertebrate community dynamics in the boreal forest.

Boonstra, R., D. Hik, G. R. Singleton, and A. Tinnikov. 1998a. The impact of predator-induced stress on the snowshoe hare cycle. Ecological Monographs 79:371-394.

Boonstra, R., C. J. Krebs, and N. C. Stenseth. 1998b. Population cycles in small mammals: the problem of explaining the low phase. Ecology 79:1479-1488.

Boonstra, R. and G. R. Singleton. 1993. Population declines in the snowshoe hare and the role of stress. General and Comparative Endocrinology 91:126-143.

Borrecco, J. E. 1976. Controlling damage by forest rodents and lagomorphs through habitat manipulation. Proceedings: Seventh Vertebrate Pest Conference, ed. C. S. Siebe, March 9-11, 1976, Monterey, CA.

Boulanger, J. 1993. Evaluation of capture-recapture estimators using a cyclic snowshoe hare population. MSc Thesis. University of British Columbia, Vancouver.

Boulanger, J. G., and C. J. Krebs. 1996. Robustness of capture-recapture estimators to sample biases in a cyclic snowshoe hare population. Journal of Applied Ecology 33:530-542.

Boutin, S. 1979. Spacing behavior of snowshoe hares in relation to their population dynamics. MSc Thesis. University of British Columbia, Vancouver.

Boutin, S. 1980. Effect of spring removal experiments on the spacing behavior of female snowshoe hares. Canadian Journal of Zoology 58:2167-2174.

Boutin, S. 1984a. The effect of conspecifics on juvenile survival and recruitment of snowshoe hares. Journal of Animal Ecology 53:623-637.

Boutin, S. 1984b. Effect of late winter food addition on numbers and movements of snowshoe hares. Oecologia 62:393-400.

Boutin, S. 1984c. Home range size and methods of estimating snowshoe hare densities. Acta Zoologica Fennica 171:275-278.

Boutin, S. 1990. Food supplementation experiments with terrestrial vertebrates: patterns, problems, and the future. Canadian Journal of Zoology 68:203-220.

Boutin, S., B. S. Gilbert, C. J. Krebs, A. R. E. Sinclair, and J. N. M. Smith. 1985. The role of dispersal in the population dynamics of snowshoe hares. Canadian Journal of Zoology 63:106-115.

Boutin, S., and C. J. Krebs. 1986. Estimating survival rates of snowshoe hares. Journal of Wildlife Management 50:592-594.

Boutin, S., C. J. Krebs, R. Boonstra, M. R. T. Dale, S. J. Hannon, K. Martin, A. R. E. Sinclair, J. N. M. Smith, R. Turkington, M. Blower, A. Byrom, F. I. Doyle, C. Doyle, D. Hik, L. Hofer, A. Hubbs, T. Karels, D. L. Murray, M. O'Donoghue, C. Rohner, and S. Schweiger. 1995. Population changes of the vertebrate community during a snowshoe hare cycle in Canada's boreal forest. Oikos 74:69-80.

Boutin, S., C. J. Krebs, A. R. E. Sinclair, and J. N. M. Smith. 1986. Proximate causes of losses in a snowshoe hare population. Canadian Journal of Zoology 64:606-610.

Brand, C. J. and L. B. Keith. 1979. Lynx demography during a snowshoe hare decline in Alberta. Journal of Wildlife Management 43:827-849.

Brand, C. J., L. B. Keith, and C. A. Fischer. 1976. Lynx responses to changing snowshoe hare densities in central Alberta. Journal of Wildlife Management 40:416-428.

Brocke, R. H. 1975. Preliminary guidelines for managing snowshoe hare habitat in the Adirondacks. Transactions of the Northeast Section, The Wildlife Society, Northeast Fish and Wildlife Conference 32:46-66.

Bryant, J. P. 1981a. The regulation of snowshoe hare feeding behavior during winter by plant antiherbivore chemistry. Pages 720-731 *in* K. Myers and C. D. MacInnes, editors. Proceedings of the World Lagomorph Conference. University of Guelph, Guelph.

Bryant, J. P. 1981b. Phytochemical deterrence of snowshoe hare browsing by adventitious shoots of four Alaskan trees. Science 213:889-890.

Bryant, J. P. 1987. Feltleaf willow-snowshoe hare interactions: plant carbon/nutrient balance and floodplain succession. Ecology 68:1319-1327.

Bryant, J. P. and P. J. Kuropat. 1980. Selection of winter forage by subarctic browsing vertebrates: the role of plant chemistry. Annual Review of Ecology and Systematics 11:261-285.

Bryant, J. P., G. D. Wieland, T. Clausen, and P. Kuropat. 1985. Interactions of snowshoe hare and feltleaf willow in Alaska. Ecology 66:1564-1593.

Bulmer, M. G. 1974. A statistical analysis of the 10-year cycle in Canada. Journal of Animal Ecology 43:701-718.

Bulmer, M. G. 1975. Phase relations in the ten-year cycle. Journal of Animal Ecology 44:609-621.

Carreker, R. G. 1985. Habitat suitability index models: snowshoe hare. U.S. Fish and Wildlife Service Biological Report 82 (10.101).

Cary, J. R., and L. B. Keith. 1979. Reproductive change in the 10-year cycle of snowshoe hares. Canadian Journal of Zoology 57:375-390.

Cheeke, P. R. 1983. The significance of fiber in rabbit nutrition. Journal of Applied Rabbit Research 6:103-106.

Cheeke, P. R. 1987. Rabbit feeding and nutrition. Academic Press, Inc., Orlando.

Chitty, D. 1967. The natural selection of self-regulatory behaviour in animal populations. Proceedings of the Ecological Society of Australia 2:51-78.

Chu, T. K. Y. 1996. Fluctuations in home range size of male snowshoe hares during summer breeding season. BSc Thesis. University of British Columbia, Vancouver.

Conroy, M. J., L. W. Gysel, and G. R. Dudderar. 1979. Habitat components of clear-cut areas for snowshoe hares in Michigan. Journal of Wildlife Management 43:680-690.

Cook, D. B. and S. B. Robeson. 1945. Varying hare and forest succession. Ecology 26:406-410.

Cox, E. W., R. A. Garrott, and J. R. Cary. 1997. Effect of supplemental cover on survival of snowshoe hares and cottontail rabbits in patchy habitat. Canadian Journal of Zoology 75:1357-1363.

de Vos, A. 1964. Food utilization of snowshoe hares on Manitoulin Island, Ontario. Journal of Forestry 62:238-244.

Dibello, F. J., S. M. Arthur, and W. B. Krohn. 1990. Food habits of sympatric coyotes, *Canis latrans*, red foxes, *Vulpes vulpes*, and bobcats, *Lynx rufus*, in Maine. Canadian Field-Naturalist 104:403-408.

Dieterich, R. A. and D. D. Feist. 1980. Hematology of Alaskan snowshoe hares (*Lepus americanus mcfarlani*) during years of population decline. Comparative Biochemistry and Physiology 66A:545-547.

Dobson, F. S. 1981. An experimental examination of an artificial dispersal sink. Journal of Mammalogy 62:74-81.

Dodds, D. G. 1965. Reproduction and productivity of snowshoe hares in Newfoundland. Journal of Wildlife Management 29:303-315.

Dolbeer, R. A. and W. R. Clark. 1975. Population ecology of snowshoe hares in the central Rocky Mountains. Journal of Wildlife Management 39:535-549.

Doyle, F. I. and J. N. M. Smith. 1994. Population responses of northern goshawks to the 10-year cycle in numbers of snowshoe hares. Studies in Avian Biology 16:122-129.

Erickson, A. B. 1944. Helminth infections in relation to population fluctuations in snowshoe hares. Journal of Wildlife Management 8:134-153.

Ernest, J. 1974. Snowshoe hare studies. Final Report, Alaska Dept. Fish Game.

Feist, D. D. 1980. Corticosteroid release by adrenal tissue of Alaskan snowshoe hares in a year of population decline. Journal of Mammalogy 61:134-136.

Ferron, J. 1993. How do population density and food supply influence social behaviour in the snowshoe hare (*Lepus americanus*)? Canadian Journal of Zoology 71:1084-1089.

Ferron, J. and J.-P. Ouellet. 1992. Daily partitioning of summer habitat and use of space by the snowshoe hare in southern boreal forest. Canadian Journal of Zoology 70:2178-2183.

Finerty, J. P. 1980. The population ecology of cycles in small mammals. Yale University Press, New Haven.

Fox, J. F. 1978. Forest fires and the snowshoe hare-Canada lynx cycle. Oecologia 31:349-374.

Fox, J. F. and J. P. Bryant. 1984. Instability of the snowshoe hare and woody plant interaction. Oecologia 63:128-135.

Fuller, T. K. and D. M. Heisey. 1986. Density-related changes in winter distribution of snowshoe hares in northcentral Minnesota. Journal of Wildlife Management 50:261-264.

Gilbert, B. S. 1990. Use of winter feeding craters by snowshoe hares. Canadian Journal of Zoology 68:1600-1602.

Gilbert, B. S. and S. Boutin. 1991. Effect of moonlight on winter activity of snowshoe hares. Arctic and Alpine Research 23:61-65.

Gillis, E. A. 1997. Natal dispersal and post-weaning survival of juvenile snowshoe hares during a cyclic population increase. MSc Thesis. University of British Columbia, Vancouver.

Gillis, E. A. 1998. Survival of juvenile snowshoe hares during a cyclic population increase. Canadian Journal of Zoology 76:1949-1956.

Giuliano, W. M., J. A. Litvaitis, and C. L. Stevens. 1989. Prey selection in relation to sexual dimorphism of fishers (*Martes pennanti*) in New Hampshire. Journal of Mammalogy 70:639-641.

Graf, R. P. 1985. Social organization of snowshoe hares. Canadian Journal of Zoology 63: 468-474.

Graf, R. P. and A. R. E. Sinclair. 1987. Parental care and adult aggression toward juvenile snowshoe hares. Arctic 40:175-178.

Green, R. G. and C. A. Evans. 1940. Studies on a population cycle of snowshoe hares on the Lake Alexander area. I. Gross annual censuses, 1932-1939. Journal of Wildlife Management 4:220-238.

Grisley, K. J. 1991. Summer plant food preferences of snowshoe hares (*Lepus americanus*) and its implications on juvenile growth. BSc Thesis. University of British Columbia, Vancouver.

Harris, S., W. J. Cresswell, P. G. Forde, W. J. Trewhella, T. Woollard, and S. Wray. 1990. Home-range analysis using radio-tracking data—a review of problems and techniques particularly as applied to the study of mammals. Mammal Review 20:97-123.

Haydon, D. T., E. A. Gillis, C. I. Stefan, and C. J. Krebs. 1999. Biases in the estimation of the demographic parameters of a snowshoe hare population. Journal of Animal Ecology 68:501-512.

Hik, D. S. 1994. Predation risk and the 10-year snowshoe hare cycle. Ph.D. Dissertation. University of British Columbia, Vancouver.

Hik, D. S. 1995. Does risk of predation influence population dynamics? Evidence from the cyclic decline of snowshoe hares. Wildlife Research 22:115-129.

Hodges, K. E. 1998. Snowshoe hare demography and behaviour during a cyclic population low phase. Ph.D. Dissertation. University of British Columbia, Vancouver.

Hodges, K. E. In press. Proximate factors affecting snowshoe hare movements during a cyclic population low phase. Ecoscience.

Hodges, K. E., C. J. Krebs, and A. R. E. Sinclair. 1999. Snowshoe hare demography during a cyclic population low. Journal of Animal Ecology 68:581-594.

Hodges, K. E., C. I. Stefan, and E. A. Gillis. 1999. Does body condition affect fecundity in a cyclic population of snowshoe hares? Canadian Journal of Zoology 77:1-6.

Hodges, K. E., C. E. Doyle, C. I. Stefan, E. A. Gillis, D. S. Hik, and C. J. Krebs. In press. Snowshoe hare demography. *in* C. J. Krebs, S. Boutin, R. Boonstra, editors. Vertebrate community dynamics in the boreal forest.

Höhn, E. O. and J. G. Stelfox. 1977. Snowshoe hare adrenal weights in relation to population density. Canadian Journal of Zoology 55:634-637.

Holter, J. B., G. Tyler, and T. Walski. 1974. Nutrition of the snowshoe hare *Lepus americanus*. Canadian Journal of Zoology 52:1553-1558.

Houston, C. S. 1987. Nearly synchronous cycles of the great horned owl and snowshoe hare in Saskatchewan. *in* R. W. Nero, R. J. Clark, R. J. Knapton, and R. H. Hamre, editors. Biological conservation of northern forest owls. Gen. Tech. Rep. RM-142. Fort Collins, CO: USDA Forest Service, Rocky Mountain Forest and Range Experiment Station: 56-58.

Houston, C. S. and C. M. Francis. 1995. Survival of great horned owls in relation to the snowshoe hare cycle. Auk 112:44-59.

Ives, A. R. and D. L. Murray. 1997. Can sublethal parasitism destabilize predator-prey population dynamics? A model of snowshoe hares, predators and parasites. Journal of Animal Ecology 66:265-278.

Jardine, C. 1995. A comparison of a cyclic and non-cyclic population of snowshoe hares in Kluane, Yukon. MSc Thesis. University of British Columbia, Vancouver.

Jekielek, J. 1996. Changes in spatial distributions and movement rates of female snowshoe hares during the breeding season. BSc Thesis. University of British Columbia, Vancouver.

Keith, I. M., L. B. Keith, and J. R. Cary. 1986. Parasitism in a declining population of snowshoe hares. Journal of Wildlife Diseases 22:349-363.

Keith, L. B. 1963. Wildlife's ten-year cycle. University of Wisconsin Press, Madison.

Keith, L. B. 1964. Daily activity pattern of snowshoe hares. Journal of Mammalogy 45: 626-627.

Keith, L. B. 1966. Habitat vacancy during a snowshoe hare decline. Journal of Wildlife Management 30:828-832.

Keith, L. B. 1974. Some features of population dynamics of mammals. Proceedings of the International Congress of Game Biologists 11:17-58.

Keith, L. B. 1981. Population dynamics of hares. Pages 395-440 *in* K. Myers, and C. D. MacInnes, editors. Proceedings of the World Lagomorph Conference. University of Guelph, Guelph.

Keith, L. B. 1983. Role of food in hare population cycles. Oikos 40:385-395.

Keith, L. B. 1990. Dynamics of snowshoe hare populations. Pages 119-195 *in* H. H. Genoways, editor. Current Mammalogy. Plenum Press, New York.

Keith, L. B. and S. E. M. Bloomer. 1993. Differential mortality of sympatric snowshoe hares and cottontail rabbits in central Wisconsin. Canadian Journal of Zoology 71:1694-1697.

Keith, L. B., S. E. M. Bloomer, and T. Willebrand. 1993. Dynamics of a snowshoe hare population in fragmented habitat. Canadian Journal of Zoology 71:1385-1392.

Keith, L. B. and J. R. Cary. 1991. Mustelid, squirrel, and porcupine population trends during a snowshoe hare cycle. Journal of Mammalogy 72:373-378.

Keith, L. B., J. R. Cary, O. J. Rongstad, and M. C. Brittingham. 1984. Demography and ecology of a declining snowshoe hare population. Wildlife Monographs 90:1-43.

Keith, L. B., J. R. Cary, T. M. Yuill, and I. M. Keith. 1985. Prevalence of helminths in a cyclic snowshoe hare population. Journal of Wildlife Diseases 21:233-253.

Keith, L. B. and E. C. Meslow. 1967. Juvenile breeding in the snowshoe hare. Journal of Mammalogy 48:327.

Keith, L. B., O. J. Rongstad, and E. C. Meslow. 1966. Regional differences in reproductive traits of the snowshoe hare. Canadian Journal of Zoology 44:953-961.

Keith, L. B. and D. H. Rusch. 1988. Predation's role in the cyclic fluctuations of ruffed grouse. Acta XIX Congress of International Ornithologists 699-732.

Keith, L. B. and D. C. Surrendi. 1971. Effects of fire on a snowshoe hare population. Journal of Wildlife Management 35:16-26.

Keith, L. B., A. W. Todd, C. J. Brand, R. S. Adamcik, and D. H. Rusch. 1977. An analysis of predation during a cyclic fluctuation of snowshoe hares. Proceedings of the International Congress of Game Biologists 13:151-175.

Keith, L. B. and L. A. Windberg. 1978. A demographic analysis of the snowshoe hare cycle. Wildlife Monographs 58:1-70.

Koehler, G. M. 1990a. Population and habitat characteristics of lynx and snowshoe hares in north central Washington. Canadian Journal of Zoology 68:845-851.

Koehler, G. M. 1990b. Snowshoe hare, *Lepus americanus*, use of forest successional stages and population changes during 1985-1989 in north-central Washington. Canadian Field-Naturalist 105:291-293.

Koehler, G. M. and J. D. Brittell. 1990. Managing spruce-fir habitat for lynx and snowshoe hares. Journal of Forestry 88(10):10-14.

Koenig, W. D., D. Van Vuren, and P. N. Hooge. 1996. Detectability, philopatry, and the distribution of dispersal distances in vertebrates. Trends in Ecology and Evolution 11: 5154-5157.

Koonz, W. H. 1988. Red-backed vole and snowshoe hare populations in relation to four boreal forest community types on Long Point Peninsula, Manitoba, 1971-1987. Department of Natural Resources Technical Report 88-04.

Krebs, C. J. 1978. A review of the Chitty hypothesis of population regulation. Canadian Journal of Zoology 56:2463-2480.

Krebs, C. J. 1996. Population cycles revisited. Journal of Mammalogy 77:8-24.

Krebs, C. J., R. Boonstra, S. Boutin, M. Dale, S. Hannon, K. Martin, A. R. E. Sinclair, J. N. M. Smith, and R. Turkington. 1992. What drives the snowshoe hare cycle in Canada's Yukon? Pages 886-896 *in* D. R. McCullough and R. H. Barrett, editors. Wildlife 2001: populations. Elsevier Applied Science, London.

Krebs, C. J., S. Boutin, R. Boonstra, A. R. E. Sinclair, J. N. M. Smith, M. R. T. Dale, K. Martin, and R. Turkington. 1995. Impact of food and predation on the snowshoe hare cycle. Science 269:1112-1115.

Krebs, C. J., S. Boutin, and B. S. Gilbert. 1986a. A natural feeding experiment on a declining snowshoe hare population. Oecologia 70:194-197.

Krebs, C. J., B. S. Gilbert, S. Boutin, and R. Boonstra. 1987. Estimation of snowshoe hare population density from turd transects. Canadian Journal of Zoology 65:565-567.

Krebs, C. J., B. S. Gilbert, S. Boutin, A. R. E. Sinclair, and J. N. M. Smith. 1986b. Population biology of snowshoe hares. I. Demography of food-supplemented populations in the southern Yukon, 1976-84. Journal of Animal Ecology 55:963-982.

Krebs, C. J., A. R. E. Sinclair, and S. Boutin. 1996. Vertebrate community dynamics in the boreal forest of north-western Canada. Pages 155-161 *in* R. B. Floyd, A. W. Sheppard, and P. J. DeBarro, editors. Frontiers of population ecology. CSIRO Publishing, Melbourne.

Krebs, C. J. and I. Wingate. 1985. Population fluctuations in the small mammals of the Kluane Region, Yukon Territory. Canadian Field-Naturalist 99:51-61.

Kuehn, D. W. 1989. Winter foods of fishers during a snowshoe hare decline. Journal of Wildlife Management 53:688-692.

Lawson, E. J. G. and A. R. Rodgers. 1997. Differences in home-range size computed in commonly used software programs. Wildlife Society Bulletin 25:721-729.

Lebreton, J.-D. and J. Clobert. 1991. Bird population dynamics, management, and conservation: the role of mathematical modelling. Pages 105-125 *in* C. M. Perrins, J.-D. Lebreton, and G. J. M. Hirons, editors. Bird population studies: relevance to conservation and management. Oxford University Press, Oxford.

Litvaitis, J. A. 1990. Differential habitat use by sexes of snowshoe hares (*Lepus americanus*). Journal of Mammalogy 71:520-523.

Litvaitis, J. A., J. A. Sherburne, and J. A. Bissonette. 1985a. A comparison of methods used to examine snowshoe hare habitat use. Journal of Wildlife Management 49:693-695.

Litvaitis, J. A., J. A. Sherburne, and J. A. Bissonette. 1985b. Influence of understory characteristics on snowshoe hare habitat use and density. Journal of Wildlife Management 49:866-873.

Litvaitis, J. A., J. A. Sherburne, and J. A. Bissonette. 1986. Bobcat habitat use and home range size in relation to prey density. Journal of Wildlife Management 50:110-117.

Lloyd-Smith, J. and H. Piene. 1981. Snowshoe hare girdling of balsam fir on the Cape Breton highlands. Maritime For. Res. Centre, Fredericton, NB. Information Report M-X-124. Canadian Forest Service.

MacLulich, D. A. 1937. Fluctuations in the numbers of the varying hare (*Lepus americanus*). University of Toronto Studies, Biological Series, No. 43.

Maltais, P. M. and E. A. Ouellette. 1983. Helminth parasites of the snowshoe hare, (*Lepus americanus*) in New Brunswick. Le Naturaliste Canadien 110:103-105.

Meslow, E. C. and L. B. Keith. 1968. Demographic parameters of a snowshoe hare population. Journal of Wildlife Management 32:812-834.

Meslow, E. C. and L. B. Keith. 1971. A correlation analysis of weather versus snowshoe hare population parameters. Journal of Wildlife Management 35:1-15.

Monthey, R. W. 1986. Responses of snowshoe hares, *Lepus americanus*, to timber harvesting in northern Maine. Canadian Field-Naturalist 100:568-570.

Mowat, G., B. G. Slough, and S. Boutin. 1996. Lynx recruitment during a snowshoe hare population peak and decline in southwest Yukon. Journal of Wildlife Management 60:441-452.

Mowat, G., J. A. Staniforth, and V. A. Loewen. 1997. The relationship between vegetative cover and snowshoe hare abundance in south and central Yukon. Unpublished report, Yukon Fish and Wildlife Branch, Department of Renewable Resources.

Murray, D. L. and S. Boutin. 1991. The influence of snow on lynx and coyote movements: does morphology affect behavior? Oecologia 88:463-469.

Murray, D. L., S. Boutin, and M. O'Donoghue. 1994. Winter habitat selection by lynx and coyotes in relation to snowshoe hare abundance. Canadian Journal of Zoology 72: 1444-1451.

Murray, D. L., S. Boutin, M. O'Donoghue, and V. O. Nams. 1995. Hunting behaviour of a sympatric felid and canid in relation to vegetative cover. Animal Behavior 50:1203-1210.

Murray, D. L., J. R. Cary, and L. B. Keith. 1997. Interactive effects of sublethal nematodes and nutritional status on snowshoe hare vulnerability to predation. Journal of Animal Ecology 66:250-264.

Murray, D. L., L. B. Keith, and J. R. Cary. 1998. Do parasitism and nutritional status interact to affect production in snowshoe hares? Ecology 79:1209-1222.

Newson, J. 1964. Reproduction and prenatal mortality of snowshoe hares on Manitoulin Island, Ontario. Canadian Journal of Zoology 42:987-1005.

Newson, R. and A. de Vos. 1964. Population structure and body weights of snowshoe hares on Manitoulin Island, Ontario. Canadian Journal of Zoology 42:975-986.

O'Donoghue, M. 1983. Seasonal habitat selection by snowshoe hare in eastern Maine. Transactions of the Northeast Section, Wildlife Society, Fish and Wildlife Conference 40:100-107.

O'Donoghue, M. 1994. Early survival of juvenile snowshoe hares. Ecology 75:1582-1592.

O'Donoghue, M. 1997. Responses of coyotes and lynx to the snowshoe hare cycle. Ph.D. Dissertation. University of British Columbia, Vancouver.

O'Donoghue, M. and C. M. Bergman. 1992. Early movements and dispersal of juvenile snowshoe hares. Canadian Journal of Zoology 70:1787-1791.

O'Donoghue, M. and S. Boutin. 1995. Does reproductive synchrony affect juvenile survival rates of northern mammals? Oikos 74:115-121.

O'Donoghue, M., S. Boutin, C. J. Krebs, and E. J. Hofer. 1997. Numerical responses of coyotes and lynx to the snowshoe hare cycle. Oikos 80:150-162.

O'Donoghue, M., S. Boutin, C. J. Krebs, G. Zuleta, D. L. Murray, and E. J. Hofer. 1998. Functional responses of coyotes and lynx to the snowshoe hare cycle. Ecology 79:1193-1208.

O'Donoghue, M. and C. J. Krebs. 1992. Effects of supplemental food on snowshoe hare reproduction and juvenile growth at a cyclic population peak. Journal of Animal Ecology 61:631-641.

O'Farrell, T. P. 1965. Home range and ecology of snowshoe hares in interior Alaska. Journal of Mammalogy 46:406-418.

Oldemeyer, J. L. 1983. Browse production and its use by moose and snowshoe hares at the Kenai Moose Research Center, Alaska. Journal of Wildlife Management 47:486-496.

Orr, C. D. and D. G. Dodds. 1982. Snowshoe hare habitat preferences in Nova Scotia spruce-fir forests. Wildlife Society Bulletin 10:147-150.

Parker, G. R. 1984. Use of spruce plantations by snowshoe hares in New Brunswick. Forestry Chronicle 60:162-166.

Parker, G. R. 1986. The importance of cover on use of conifer plantations by snowshoe hares in northern New Brunswick. Forestry Chronicle 62:159-163.

Parker, G. R., J. W. Maxwell, L. D. Morton, and G. E. J. Smith. 1983. The ecology of the lynx (*Lynx canadensis*) on Cape Breton Island. Canadian Journal of Zoology 61:770-786.

Pease, J. L., R. H. Vowles, and L. B. Keith. 1979. Interaction of snowshoe hares and woody vegetation. Journal of Wildlife Management 43:43-60.

Poole, K. G. 1994. Characteristics of an unharvested lynx population during a snowshoe hare decline. Journal of Wildlife Management 58:608-618.

Poole, K. G. and R. P. Graf. 1996. Winter diet of marten during a snowshoe hare decline. Canadian Journal of Zoology 74:456-466.

Poole, K. G., L. A. Wakelyn, and P. N. Nicklen. 1996. Habitat selection by lynx in the Northwest Territories. Canadian Journal of Zoology 74:845-850.

Radvanyi, A. 1987. Snowshoe hares and forest plantations: a literature review and problem analysis. Canadian Forest Service, Northern Forestry Centre, Edmonton, Alberta. Information Report NOR-X-290.

Raine, R. M. 1987. Winter food habits and foraging behaviour of fishers (*Martes pennanti*) and martens (*Martes americana*) in southeastern Manitoba. Canadian Journal of Zoology 65:745-747.

Ranta, E., J. Lindstrom, V. Kaitala, H. Kokko, H. Linden, and E. Helle. 1997. Solar activity and hare dynamics: a cross-continental comparison. American Naturalist 149:765-775.

Reichardt, P. B., J. P. Bryant, T. P. Clausen, and G. D. Wieland. 1984. Defense of winter-dormant Alaska paper birch against snowshoe hares. Oecologia 65:58-69.

Rodgers, A. R. and A. R. E. Sinclair. 1997. Diet choice and nutrition of captive snowshoe hares (*Lepus americanus*): interactions of energy, protein, and plant secondary compounds. Ecoscience 4:163-169.

Rogowitz, G. L. 1988. Forage quality and use of reforested habitats by snowshoe hares. Canadian Journal of Zoology 66:2080-2083.

Rohner, C. 1996. The numerical response of great horned owls to the snowshoe hare cycle: consequences of non-territorial 'floaters' on demography. Journal of Animal Ecology 65:359-370.

Rohner, C. and C. J. Krebs. 1996. Owl predation on snowshoe hares: consequences of antipredator behavior. Oecologia 108:303-310.

Rohner, C., J. N. M. Smith, J. Stroman, and M. Joyce. 1995. Northern hawk owls in the nearctic boreal forest: prey selection and population consequences of multiple prey cycles. Condor 97:208-220.

Rongstad, O. J. and J. R. Tester. 1971. Behavior and maternal relations of young snowshoe hares. Journal of Wildlife Management 35:338-346.

Rossow, L. J., J. P. Bryant, and K. Kielland. 1997. Effects of above-ground browsing by mammals on mycorrhizal infection in an early successional taiga ecosystem. Oecologia 110:94-98.

Rowan, W. and L. B. Keith. 1959. Monthly weights of snowshoe hares from north-central Alberta. Journal of Mammalogy 40: 221-226.

Royama, T. 1992. Analytical population dynamics. Chapman & Hall, London.

Rusch, D. H., M. M. Gillespie, and D. I. McKay. 1978. Decline of a ruffed grouse population in Manitoba. Canadian Field-Naturalist 92:123-127.

Schmitz, O. J., D. S. Hik, and A. R. E. Sinclair. 1992. Plant chemical defense and twig selection by snowshoe hare: an optimal foraging perspective. Oikos 65:295-300.

Severaid, J. H. 1942. The snowshoe hare: its life history and artificial propagation. Maine Department of Inland Fisheries and Game.

Sievert, P. R. and L. B. Keith. 1985. Survival of snowshoe hares at a geographic range boundary. Journal of Wildlife Management 49:854-866.

Sinclair, A. R. E. 1986. Testing multi-factor causes of population limitation: an illustration using snowshoe hares. Oikos 47:360-364.

Sinclair, A. R. E. and J. M. Gosline. 1997. Solar activity and mammal cycles in the Northern hemisphere. American Naturalist 149:776-784.

Sinclair, A. R. E., J. M. Gosline, G. Holdsworth, C. J. Krebs, S. Boutin, J. N. M. Smith, R. Boonstra, and M. Dale. 1993. Can the solar cycle and climate synchronize the snowshoe hare cycle in Canada? Evidence from tree rings and ice cores. American Naturalist 141:173-198.

Sinclair, A. R. E., C. J. Krebs, and J. N. M. Smith. 1982. Diet quality and food limitation in herbivores: the case of the snowshoe hare. Canadian Journal of Zoology 60:889-897.

Sinclair, A. R. E., C. J. Krebs, J. N. M. Smith, and S. Boutin. 1988. Population biology of snowshoe hares. III. Nutrition, plant secondary compounds and food limitation. Journal of Animal Ecology 57:787-806.

Sinclair, A. R. E. and J. N. M. Smith. 1984a. Protein digestion in snowshoe hares. Canadian Journal of Zoology 62:520-521.

Sinclair, A. R. E. and J. N. M. Smith. 1984b. Do plant secondary compounds determine feeding preferences of snowshoe hares? Oecologia 61:403-410.

Slough, B. G., W. R. Archibald, S. S. Beare, and R. H. Jessup. 1989. Food habits of martens, *Martes americana*, in the south-central Yukon Territory. Canadian Field-Naturalist 103:18-22.

Slough, B. G. and G. Mowat. 1996. Lynx population dynamics in an untrapped refugium. Journal of Wildlife Management 60:946-961.

Small, R. J. and L. B. Keith. 1992. An experimental study of red fox predation on arctic and snowshoe hares. Canadian Journal of Zoology 70:1614-1621.

Smith, C. H. 1983. Spatial trends in Canadian snowshoe hare, *Lepus americanus*, population cycles. Canadian Field-Naturalist 97:151-160.

Smith, J. N. M., C. J. Krebs, A. R. E. Sinclair, and R. Boonstra. 1988. Population biology of snowshoe hares. II. Interactions with winter food plants. Journal of Animal Ecology 57:269-286.

Sovell, J. R. 1993. Attempt to determine the influence of parasitism on a snowshoe hare population during the peak and initial decline phases of a hare cycle. MSc Thesis. University of Alberta, Edmonton.

Sovell, J. R. and J. C. Holmes. 1996. Efficacy of ivermectin against nematodes infecting field populations of snowshoe hares (*Lepus americanus*) in Yukon, Canada. Journal of Wildlife Diseases 32:23-30.

Sprugel, D. G. 1983. Correcting for bias in log-transformed allometric equations. Ecology 64: 209-210.

St-Georges, M., S. Nadeau, D. Lambert, and R. Décarie. 1995. Winter habitat use by ptarmigan, snowshoe hares, red foxes, and river otters in the boreal forest - tundra transition zone of western Quebec. Canadian Journal of Zoology 73:755-764.

Staples, W. R. III. 1995. Lynx and coyote diet and habitat relationships during a low hare population on the Kenai Peninsula, Alaska. MSc Thesis. University of Alaska, Fairbanks.

Stefan, C. I. 1998. Reproduction and pre-weaning juvenile survival in a cyclic population of snowshoe hares. MSc Thesis. University of British Columbia, Vancouver.

Sullivan, T. P. 1994. Influence of herbicide-induced habitat alteration on vegetation and snowshoe hare populations in sub-boreal spruce forest. Journal of Applied Ecology 31:717-730.

Sullivan, T. P. 1996. Influence of forest herbicide on snowshoe hare population dynamics: reproduction, growth, and survival. Canadian Journal of Forest Research 26:112-119.

Sullivan, T. P. and R. A. Moses. 1986. Demographic and feeding responses of a snowshoe hare population to habitat alteration. Journal of Applied Ecology 23:53-63.

Sullivan, T. P. and D. S. Sullivan. 1982a. Barking damage by snowshoe hares and red squirrels in lodgepole pine stands in central British Columbia. Canadian Journal of Forest Research 12:443-448.

Sullivan, T. P. and D. S. Sullivan. 1982b. Influence of fertilization on feeding attacks to lodgepole pine by snowshoe hares and red squirrels. Forestry Chronicle 58:263-266.

Sullivan, T. P. and D. S. Sullivan. 1983. Use of index lines and damage assessments to estimate population densities of snowshoe hares. Canadian Journal of Zoology 61: 163-167.

Sullivan, T. P. and D. S. Sullivan. 1988. Influence of stand thinning on snowshoe hare population dynamics and feeding damage in lodgepole pine forest. Journal of Applied Ecology 25:791-805.

Telfer, E. S. 1972. Browse selection by deer and hares. Journal of Wildlife Management 36:1344-1349.

Theberge, J. B. and C. H. R. Wedeles. 1989. Prey selection and habitat partitioning in sympatric coyote and red fox populations, southwest Yukon. Canadian Journal of Zoology 67:1285-1290.

Thomas, V. G. 1987. Similar winter energy strategies of grouse, hares and rabbits in northern biomes. Oikos 50:206-212.

Thompson, I. D. 1988. Habitat needs of furbearers in relation to logging in boreal Ontario. Forestry Chronicle 64:251-261.

Thompson, I. D. and P. W. Colgan. 1987. Numerical responses of martens to a food shortage in northcentral Ontario. Journal of Wildlife Management 51:824-835.

Thompson, I. D. and W. J. Curran. 1995. Habitat suitability for marten of second-growth balsam fir forests in Newfoundland. Canadian Journal of Zoology 73:2059-2064.

Thompson, I. D., I. J. Davidson, S. O'Donnell, and F. Brazeau. 1989. Use of track transects to measure the relative occurrence of some boreal mammals in uncut forest and regeneration stands. Canadian Journal of Zoology 67:1816-1823.

Todd, A. W., L. B. Keith, and C. A. Fischer. 1981. Population ecology of coyotes during a fluctuation of snowshoe hares. Journal of Wildlife Management 45:629-640.

Tompkins, D. B. and J. R. Woehr. 1979. Influence of habitat on movements and densities of snowshoe hares. Transactions of the Northeast Section, Wildlife Society, Fish and Wildlife Conference 36:169-175.

Trapp, G. R. 1962. Snowshoe hares in Alaska. II. Home range and ecology during an early population increase. MSc Thesis. University of Alaska, Fairbanks.

Trostel, K., A. R. E. Sinclair, C. J. Walters, and C. J. Krebs. 1987. Can predation cause the 10-year hare cycle? Oecologia 74:185-192.

Vaughan, M. R. and L. B. Keith. 1980. Breeding by juvenile snowshoe hares. Journal of Wildlife Management 44:948-951.

Vaughan, M. R. and L. B. Keith. 1981. Demographic response of experimental snowshoe hare populations to overwinter food shortage. Journal of Wildlife Management 45:354-380.

Ward, R. M. P. and C. J. Krebs. 1985. Behavioural responses of lynx to declining snowshoe hare abundance. Canadian Journal of Zoology 63:2817-2824.

Whittaker, M. E. and V. G. Thomas. 1983. Seasonal levels of fat and protein reserves of snowshoe hares in Ontario. Canadian Journal of Zoology 61:1339-1345.

Windberg, L. A. and L. B. Keith. 1976. Experimental analyses of dispersal in snowshoe hare populations. Canadian Journal of Zoology 54:2061-2081.

Windberg, L. A. and L. B. Keith. 1978. Snowshoe hare populations in woodlot habitat. Canadian Journal of Zoology 56:1071-1080.

Wolff, J. O. 1978. Food habits of snowshoe hares in interior Alaska. Journal of Wildlife Management 42:148-153.

Wolff, J. O. 1980. The role of habitat patchiness in the population dynamics of snowshoe hares. Ecological Monographs 50:111-130.

Wolff, J. O. 1981. Refugia, dispersal, predation, and geographic variation in snowshoe hare cycles. Pages 441-449 *in* K. Myers and C. D. MacInnes, editors. Proceedings of the World Lagomorph Conference. University of Guelph, Guelph.

Worton, B. J. 1987. A review of models of home range for animal movement. Ecological Modelling 38:277-298.

Chapter 7

Ecology of Snowshoe Hares in Southern Boreal and Montane Forests

Karen E. Hodges, Centre for Biodiversity Research, University of British
Columbia 6270 University Boulevard, Vancouver, BC V6T 1Z4 Canada

Abstract—Snowshoe hares occur in many of the montane and sub-boreal forests of the continental United States, as well as throughout the boreal forests of Canada and Alaska. Population dynamics in their southern range were previously thought to be noncyclic, in contrast to the strong 10-year fluctuation that typifies boreal populations of snowshoe hares. Time series data and studies of hare demography indicate that northern and southern populations of hares may instead have similar population dynamics. Hares in southern areas appear to experience two- to 25-fold fluctuations in numbers with peaks eight to 11 years apart. Peak and low densities may be lower in southern areas than in northern ones; in the south, peak densities are commonly one to two hares/ha, whereas northern hare populations commonly have peak densities up to four to six hares/ha. Demographically, survival estimates (30-day) range from approximately 0.65-0.95 in Wisconsin, with lowest survival occurring as populations decline; these values parallel those of cyclic hares in Yukon. Annual reproductive output may vary regionally, but interpretation of this pattern is hindered by noncomparable methodologies.

The southern range of snowshoe hares is roughly delineated by the range of suitable forested habitats. Along the eastern seaboard, hares use spruce/fir and deciduous forests as far south as Tennessee and the Virginias. Around the Great Lakes, hares occur throughout the sub-boreal coniferous forests. In the Rockies and westward, hares mainly use the coniferous forests that extend along the mountains down into New Mexico and California. Throughout their range, hares are predominantly associated with forests that have a well-developed understory that provides protection from predation and supplies them with food. Such habitat structure is common in early seral stages but may also occur in coniferous forests with mature but relatively open overstories or in eastern deciduous forests.

Introduction

Snowshoe hares occur throughout much of North America and have a regular 10-year population cycle in the northern part of their range. Dynamics of southern hare populations, in contrast, have been described as cyclic, cyclic with reduced amplitude, noncyclic but fluctuating, and noncyclic (Howell 1923; Chitty 1950; Finerty 1980; Bittner and Rongstad 1982; Smith 1983; Keith 1990). During the northern hare cycle, hares have both regular numeric changes and regular changes in survival, reproduction, and possibly dispersal (Cary and Keith 1979; Bittner and Rongstad 1982; Keith 1990; Krebs et al. 1995; Hodges et al. in press). The habitats in which hares occur in northern and southern forests vary in terms of species composition, stand structure, and amount of disturbance (from fire or from harvest), leading to speculation that hare dynamics are related to habitat structure and degree of interspersion of different habitat types (Dolbeer and Clark 1975; Wolff 1980, 1981; Buehler and Keith 1982; Sievert and Keith 1985; Keith 1990).

In this chapter, I therefore examine the demography and numeric patterns of southern hare populations, describe patterns of habitat use by hares in southern areas, and discuss the linkages between hare demography and habitat. Throughout, I compare results from southern areas to patterns in northern hare populations. I compile the information with explicit reference to methodology, to ensure that comparisons among regions are made using comparable data. I ask first whether hares display numeric cycles in the southern parts of their range. Second, I examine demographic parameters (reproduction, survival, and dispersal) to see if they show cyclic fluctuations in southern hare populations. Third, I address the dietary and habitat associations of snowshoe hares. I conclude with a discussion of the relationship of hare population dynamics to habitats, and whether refugia, habitat fragmentation, and increases in numbers of facultative (multiple-prey) predators can explain the variation in demographic parameters observed among hare populations.

Distribution and Population Trends

Hares in "the south" occur in four general areas—through the western mountains of Washington and Oregon down into California, through the Rockies into New Mexico, around the Great Lakes, and from the Maritimes down through the Alleghenies and Appalachians into Virginia and West Virginia (Bittner and Rongstad 1982; Fies 1993, unpublished; Hoefler and Duke 1996, unpublished; G. Schmidt, personal communication; J. Rieffenberger, personal communication) These four areas are biologically and climactically diverse (Bailey 1997), so there is good reason to expect that hares might display differing dynamics in each of these regions. With the exception of the mixed deciduous and coniferous forests that cover the nonmountainous areas from the Great Lakes eastward through the Maritimes, most areas containing snowshoe hares in the United States are montane. In contrast, the boreal forests—where hares display a clear population cycle—provide a more contiguous and less mountainous swath of hare habitat (Keith 1990; Bailey 1997).

We have extremely limited knowledge about hares in many of the states where they occur. Distribution records exist for hares in Maryland, Rhode Island, New Jersey, Delaware, Virginia, Tennessee, North Carolina, Ohio, Oregon, California, and New Mexico (Keith 1963; Godin 1977; Bittner and Rongstad 1982; Nagorsen 1985), but I am not aware of any harvest or other time series data for these states. The status and distribution of hares in these states are not well known (Bailey 1971; Godin 1977; Verts and Carraway 1998; G. Schmidt, personal communication), but snowshoe hares are thought to be extirpated from Ohio (D. Scott, personal communication), and in Virginia and California snowshoe hares are a species of special management concern (Handley 1978; Williams 1986, unpublished; Fies 1991; Hoefler and Duke 1996, unpublished; Brylski et al. 1997).

In areas for which time series exist, it is possible to address the issue of cyclicity. There are four possibilities for hare population dynamics: *cyclic*, like northern populations, which display cycles with amplitudes of five to 25 and eight to 11 years between peak populations (Chapter 6); *reduced-amplitude cyclic*, demonstrating the eight- to 11-year periodicity but with amplitudes lower than five-fold; *fluctuating*, with amplitudes similar to those in northern populations, but lacking an eight- to 11-year periodicity; or *noncyclic*, lacking both high-amplitude fluctuations and the eight- to 11-year periodicity in numeric change.

Empirically, applying these definitions requires arbitrary decisions, such as defining the amplitudes at which cyclic populations become cyclic with reduced amplitude or fluctuating populations become noncyclic. It is similarly difficult to know what to do with interpeak durations of less than eight or greater than 11 years, especially in time series recording only two or three peaks. Because even long time series record only a few potential cycles, the power to determine differences in amplitude and duration among time series is low. This difficulty is compounded by the use of indices of abundance (tracks, sightings, harvest records) for which the relationship to actual hare densities is unknown. Because of these problems, I simply present the time series and describe the observed amplitude and interpeak durations of each, but I do not analyze these values statistically (Table 7.1). I consider peaks to be local maxima separated by at least two years and lows are similarly local minima. I calculated amplitudes by dividing each peak value by the subsequent low value, and I present the range of these amplitudes.

Table 7.1–Snowshoe hare population trends in southern parts of their range. Amplitude is rounded to the nearest whole number. Amplitude was calculated by dividing peaks by subsequent lows. I also present the total amplitude for the entire series (max/min) because some series show large overall fluctuations. If only amplitude is given, max/min was the same; if only max/min is given, it was impossible to match peaks and lows. Peak years are given only for series >5 years long, but peaks for series <10 years long should be regarded with suspicion, as should peak years that occur at the beginning or end of a study. Most of these rubrics indicate overwinter estimates; for peak year, I indicate the year that started the winter (e.g., 1990 implies winter 1990-1991).

Location	Survey period (# of years)	Amplitude (max/min)	Years between peaks	Peak years	Reference
Fecal pellet plots (n/plot)[a]					
Montana	1986-1998 (13)	2	7	1990 1997	J. Malloy, unpublished
Utah[b]	1974-1978 (5)	2	–	–	Wolfe et al. 1982
Washington	1986-1989 (3)	2[c]	–	–	Koehler 1990a, 1990b
West Virginia	1942-1953 (12)	10	9	1942 1951	Brooks 1955
Quebec (southern)	1991-1996 (6)	4	–	1991	Ferron et al. 1998
(% plots with pellets)					
Minnesota	1969-1984 (16)	3	–	1978	Fuller & Heisey 1986
Live trapping					
Minnesota	1932-1942 (11)	15	–	1933	Green & Evans 1940a Keith 1963
New Brunswick	1967-1970 (4)	7	–	–	Wood & Munroe 1977
Harvest records					
Nova Scotia (Long Island)	1950-1964 (14)	4	9	1951 1960	Dodds & Thurber 1965
Nova Scotia	1990-1998 (8)	(4)	–	1996	M. Boudreau, unpublished
New Brunswick	1984-1990 (7)	(40)	–	1984	K. Eagle, unpublished

(con.)

Table 7.1–(Con.)

Location	Survey period (# of years)	Amplitude (max/min)	Years between peaks	Peak years	Reference
Maine	1955-1983 (29)	2 (4)	7 to 9	1948 1957 1966 1973 (1972)[d] 1981 (1982)[d]	C. McLaughlin, unpublished Keith 1963
New York	1932-1951 (19) 1960-1968 (7) 1982-1998 (16)	2-6 (24)	8 to 13	1932 1940 1950 1963 (no data) 1982 1995	Keith 1963 G. Batchelar & A. Jacobson, unpublished
Massachusetts	1958-1986 (15)	(12)	–[e]	–[e]	J. Cardoza, unpublished
Pennsylvania	1930-1997 (64)	4-12 (48)	7 to 11	1931 1942 1949 1959 (1967)[f] 1982 (1992)[f]	Diefenbach 1998, unpublished
Connecticut	1923-1955 (32)	2-3 (3)	9 to 10	(1933)[g] 1942 1952	Sondrini 1950 Keith 1963
Ontario (southern, one trapline)	1931-1943 (13)	(17)	9	1933 1942	Hess 1954
Michigan	1937-1997 (61)	1.5-4 (7)	5 to 12	1939 1949 (1954)[h] 1959 1964 1976 1988	G. Karasek, unpublished Keith 1963
Harvest records Wisconsin	1931-1997 (57)	3-11 (30)	8 to 10	1932 1941 1949 1957 (no data) 1978 1988	B. Dhuey, unpublished
Minnesota	1941-1997 (56)	2-24 (29)	8 to 11	1941 1952 1960 1971 1980 1991	Berg 1998, unpublished
Colorado	1955-1960 1968-1970 (9)	(2)	–	1956	Dolbeer 1972a, 1972b
Washington	1988-1997 (9)	(6)	–	1988	D. Ware, unpublished
Idaho	1986-1992 (7)	(5)	–	1988	C. Harris, unpublished
Harvest/area Quebec	1979-1997 (19)	3-9 (14)	7 to 9	1980 1989	R. Lafond, unpublished Fortin and Huot 1995, unpublished

(con.)

Table 7.1–(Con.)

Location	Survey period (# of years)	Amplitude (max/min)	Years between peaks	Peak years	Reference
Harvest/hunter					
Prince Edward Island	1971-1984 1993-1997 (19)	2 (4)	–	1978	R. Dibblee, unpublished
Harvest/hunter-day					
Utah	1975-1996 (22)	3 (5)	12	1978 1990	D. Mitchell, unpublished
Hare sighting indices					
Minnesota	1974-1996 (23)	14-70 (70)[i]	9	1980 1989	B. Berg 1998, unpublished
Minnesota	1946-1959 (13)	(75)	–	1950	Marshall 1954 Keith 1963
Michigan (Isle Royale)	1974-1997 (24)	9-27 (38)[i]	8	1980 1988	Peterson 1998, unpublished
Ontario (Manitoulin Island)	1959-1962	–	–	1959	Newson & de Vos 1964
Manitoba (southeastern)	1974-1979 (5)	9	–	1978	Leonard 1980; Raine 1987
Track transects[j]					
Wisconsin (%)	1977-1998 (21)	2-17 (17)	12	1977 1989	Glenzinski & Dhuey 1998, unpublished
Maine (%)	1994-1997 (4)	2	–	–	C. McLaughlin, unpublished
Montana (#)	1992-1998 (7)	10	–	1991	D. Dziak, unpublished
Wyoming (#)	1987-1996 (10)[k]	(45)[k]	–	–	L. Ruggiero, unpublished

[a]Densities from pellet plots were calculated using a regression equation derived from hare density information from 1976 to 1996 (C.J. Krebs unpublished): ln(hares/ha)=0.888962*ln(pellets)-1.203391, corrected for bias by multiplying with 1.57 following Sprugel (1983). Pellets is pellets/0.155m^2. The methodology and rationale were derived in Krebs et al. (1987), and the current equation simply uses more information.

[b]This time series is for pellet counts in Douglas-fir stands.

[c]Values are based on pellet counts in fall; values for fall 1997 were calculated by summing values for two sampling periods within the year.

[d]From 1972 through 1983, there were also estimates of numbers of hunters. Harvest per hunter indicates the peak years given in parentheses.

[e]The years that have data are sporadic, making it impossible to determine peak years.

[f]Harvest estimates from 1967-1970 were 6,000, 4,000, 5,000, 5,000; although I've given the peak as 1967, it could have been later. From 1982 through 1997, hare harvests have generally declined, with a higher harvest in 1992 than in the preceding two years or subsequent five years.

[g]The early peak is not as clear as the others; for several years, high and low values alternated.

[h]One method of harvest estimation was used from 1937 to 1953, and another from 1954 forward. Although the 1954 harvest estimate represents a local peak, it is difficult to interpret because it lies on the cusp of the two methods.

[i]The amplitudes and max/min ignore one 0 value.

[j]Each track transect methodology is somewhat different; I present them in two broad classes: counts of number of tracks (#) and proportions of transect segments containing any hare tracks (%).

[k]These numbers were derived from transect J, including only years when the transect was run ≥2 times; the amplitude reflects just maximum/minimum rather than trying to match a low to its preceding peak.

The most reliable time series are from live-trapping data or counts of fecal pellets, because density estimates can be derived from these methods (Table 7.1). Based on short time series (three to 13 years), fecal pellet plots have shown density differences of two-fold in Montana, Utah, and Washington (J. Malloy, unpublished; Wolfe et al. 1982; Koehler 1990a,b), four-fold in southern Quebec (Ferron et al. 1998), and 10-fold in West Virginia (Brooks 1955). These surveys indicate peak hare densities of approximately 1-2 hares/ha (see also Table 7.5), which is considerably lower than observed peak densities of approximately 4-6 and sometimes higher in northern areas (Chapter 6). The two longest pellet plot time series showed nine years between peaks in West Virginia (Brooks 1955) and seven years in Montana (J. Malloy, unpublished). Live-trapping in Minnesota and New Brunswick have indicated fluctuations of seven- to 15-fold, with peak densities of approximately 1.6 hares/ha (Green and Evans 1940a; Wood and Munroe 1977).

Most southern time series for snowshoe hares are harvest data. Harvest data are unlikely to indicate either amplitude or peak and low density years accurately. Harvest data provide a true reflection of population dynamics if and only if the same proportion of hares are caught in each year, which almost certainly does not occur because of socioeconomic as well as biological reasons. Furthermore, the harvest data we have reflect various survey techniques (phone and mail surveys, hunter licensing, pelt or carcass sales) and are often based on a small proportion of the hunters (e.g., 5-10%), hence calling into question the ability of the data to record the actual harvest.

As an additional complication, several of the harvest time series show an overall fluctuation of approximately 20-50-fold, but have distinct periods of low or high average harvest. For example, in Pennsylvania, harvests ranged between 8,600-26,200 from 1930 to 1935; 550 to 6,000 from 1937 to 1979; and 1,400-21,800 from 1980 to 1997 (Diefenbach 1998, unpublished). The entire time series has an amplitude of 48, but matching lows to their previous peaks yields amplitudes of four- to 12-fold. It is difficult to partition that variation into anthropogenic versus hare demographic changes without additional information such as area exploited or hunter effort. As an example of the effect of knowing hunter effort: 22 years of Utah harvest data showed a high correlation between total hare harvest and hares per hunter ($r = 0.87\,p < 0.05$), but the magnitude of difference over the entire time series for total harvest was 20-fold whereas for hares per hunter it was only 4.3-fold (D. Mitchell, unpublished). Furthermore, these two indices showed the same peak year, but were off by a year for their lows. Harvest data should therefore not be relied upon for determining the population dynamics of hares. Regular 10-year cycles are unlikely to arise in the harvest data solely because of anthropogenic factors, however; so if harvest data show cycles, they probably reflect hare population dynamics even if absolute duration and amplitude cannot be correctly inferred.

Harvest records from New England, southeastern Canada (Quebec eastward through the Maritimes), and the eastern seaboard show amplitudes ranging from two to 12, with 78% of the interpeak lengths between eight and 10 years (Table 7.1, Fig. 7.1A-D). These data may be confounded by programs of stocking hares for hunters, which has occurred in at least Connecticut, New York, Massachusetts, Pennsylvania, West Virginia, and

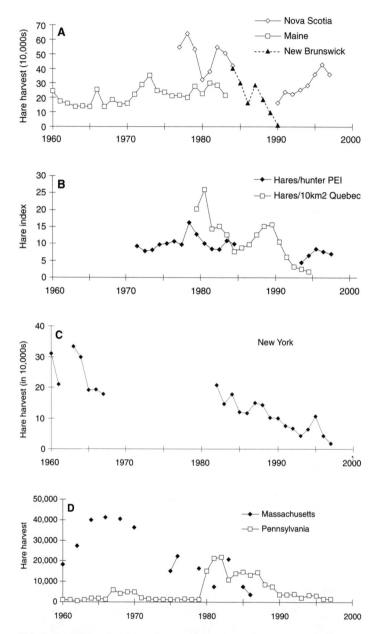

Figure 7.1—Records of snowshoe hare population trends. All records are from sources cited in Table 7.1. (A) Hare harvests from the Maritimes and Maine. (B) Hares per hunter and hares killed per unit area from Prince Edward Island and Quebec. (C) Hare harvests from New York. (D) Hare harvests from Massachusetts and Pennsylvania. (E) Hare harvests in the Midwest. (F) Hare sighting indices in the Midwest. (G) Pellet and track records of hares in the Midwest. (H) Hare harvests and hares per hunter-day in the western states.

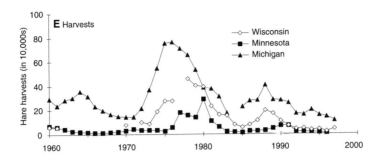

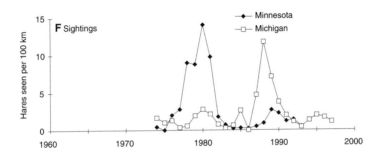

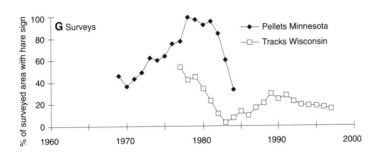

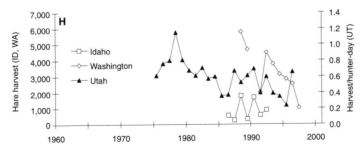

Figure 7.1 (Con.)

Virginia (Brooks 1955; Boyle 1955; Fitzpatrick 1957; Behrend 1960, unpublished; August 1974; Richmond and Chien 1976; Schultz 1980; Brown 1984). Analyses of these programs indicate that <10% of the stocked hares are actually killed by hunters (Fitzpatrick 1957; Schultz 1980), but it is unknown what demographic effects the stocking programs have had.

Around the Great Lakes, harvest data show eight- to 10-year fluctuations of two- to 25-fold amplitude (Table 7.1, Fig. 7.1E-G; see also Keith 1990). These cyclic patterns are confirmed by records of hare sightings in Minnesota (B. Berg, unpublished) and Michigan (Peterson 1998, unpublished; see also Johnson 1969). Pellet plots in Minnesota (Fuller and Heisey 1986) and tracking surveys in Wisconsin (Glenzinski and Dhuey 1998, unpublished) show roughly the same pattern of highs and lows as the harvest data do. Keith (1963, 1990; Buehler and Keith 1982; Sievert and Keith 1985) has argued that hares have become noncyclic in Wisconsin since the 1950s, but the tracking surveys and harvest records are equally suggestive that the cycles have continued.

Population trends of hares from the Rockies westward are not well known (Fig. 7.1H). The harvest records from Idaho, Colorado, and Washington are short compared to the 10-year cycle (i.e., seven to nine years of records), making it difficult to tell if the harvests have the typical 10-year periodicity (Dolbeer 1972b; D. Ware, unpublished; C. Harris, unpublished). Within those years, the amplitudes of fluctuation are two- to six-fold. In Utah, harvest per hunter-day had an amplitude of three-fold and an interpeak duration of 12 years through 22 years of data (D. Mitchell, unpublished). Pellet plots in Utah, Montana, and Washington show two-fold fluctuations in hare density (J. Malloy, unpublished; Wolfe et al. 1982; Koehler 1990a, b). In Wyoming, track counts showed 45-fold variation (L. Ruggiero, unpublished), while Montana track counts showed four- to 10-fold variation (D. Dziak, unpublished; Giddings 1998, unpublished).

The existing time series do not show a strong synchrony. For example, five time series showed a peak in 1988, three in 1989, two in 1990, and two in 1991 (Table 7.1). Throughout the century, there tend to be three- to four-year clusters of peak densities, typically close to the turn of each decade. There are occasional time series that miss peaks or show peaks in years that no other series matches (e.g., New York, which shows a peak in 1995). Southern hare populations may therefore be genuinely asynchronous or the synchrony may only be at a scale of three to four years. As another possibility, the harvest data in particular may be off a year or two relative to the actual hare densities, which would make detection of synchrony difficult.

There are likely to be differences of opinion about how deviant hare populations have to be in amplitude and interpeak duration in order to disqualify them as cyclic or to class them as reduced-amplitude cyclic. In my opinion, the existing evidence is strongly suggestive that southern hare populations are cyclic—amplitudes in the various indices vary from two to 70, and in the longer time series (>10 years) approximately 75% of interpeak intervals are between eight and 11 years. At a minimum, these patterns suggest that studies of hares in southern areas should explicitly address population dynamics. Additional analyses of the existing time series data are unlikely to resolve the cyclicity debate because of the methodological difficulties; we require more time series that are density estimates rather than harvests or other indices.

Snowshoe Hare Demography

Reproduction

Female snowshoe hares can have up to four litters in a season, with one to 14 young per litter; they breed synchronously, leading to distinct litter groups (Cary and Keith 1979; O'Donoghue and Boutin 1995; Stefan 1998). Regionally, there has been some suggestion that hares in southern populations have more but smaller litters than do hares in northern populations, leading to a lower total annual natality (Rowan and Keith 1956; Keith et al. 1966; Ernest 1974; Keith 1981, 1990). Many of the data used to infer this latitudinal pattern were derived using Green and Evans' (1940c) method— calculating average number of litters from the number of females observed to be pregnant throughout the summer corrected for days of observable pregnancy, and calculating mean litter size from all litters combined (often with uneven sampling effort across litter groups). This method has three problems: the average number of litters has often been calculated on a multi-year basis thus conflating cyclic phase, and both pregnancy rates and litter sizes are not calculated independently for each litter group. A much more reliable approach derives pregnancy rate and litter size estimates for each litter group separately, and then sums the litter groups for total annual natality (e.g., Dolbeer and Clark 1975; O'Donoghue and Krebs 1992).

Much of the variation in total annual natality actually seems to be better explained by cyclic phase than by latitude, especially when methodological issues are considered. In Figure 7.2, the dark symbols indicate estimates derived from assessment of each litter group; these show a strong effect of cyclic phase on hares' natality. Data collected using Green and Evans' (1940c) method (open symbols and crosses) do not pick up this cyclic pattern, except in short-term studies, which are less biased by conflation of years. Additionally, this method is likely to bias estimated annual natality downward, because first litters are smaller than later litters (Keith 1990; Stefan

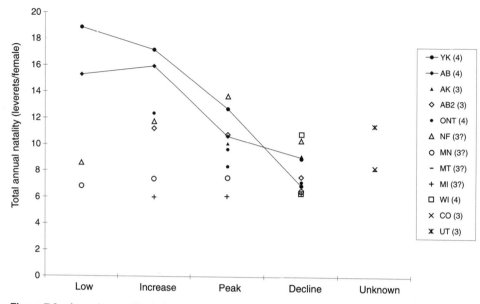

Figure 7.2—Annual reproductive output of snowshoe hares at different phases of the population cycle. Filled symbols are for natalities analyzed as percent pregnant x mean litter size, summed for each litter group. Open symbols are for natalities calculated by Green & Evan's (1940c) method, as mean litter size (litter groups not distinguished) x average litter number (often calculated from many years of data, with phase not distinguished). The first method is much more reliable. When a study had more than one year of data for a phase, annual values were averaged. The number given with each region indicates the maximum number of litter groups observed in that area; ? indicates that the number of litters was not specified in the reference. Wisconsin and Michigan data were assigned to cyclic phases based on trend data from Glenzinski and Dhuey (1998, unpublished) and Karasek (unpublished), while the other references provided information on the population trends in different years. The unknown cyclicities are from Montana, Utah, and Colorado. Sources: YK, Stefan 1998, Hodges et al. in press; AB, Keith & Windberg 1978, Cary & Keith 1979; AK, Ernest 1974; AB 2, Rowan & Keith 1956; ONT, Newson 1964; WI, Kuvlesky & Keith 1983; NF, Dodds 1965; MN, Green & Evans 1940b; MT, Adams 1959; CO & UT, Dolbeer & Clark 1975; MI, Bookhout 1965a.

1998). Thus the smaller and less cyclic annual natalities shown for southern populations are probably due to methodological biases rather than to a true latitudinal gradient. The two strongest data sets, from Alberta and Yukon (symbols with lines) (Cary and Keith 1979; Stefan 1998), offer weak support to the latitudinal pattern, in that Alberta hares tended to have four litters whereas Yukon hares had two to four, but larger litter sizes in Yukon yielded slightly larger total annual natalities in all phases except the decline. Hares in Alaska show trends similar to those of Yukon hares (Ernest 1974). The largest annual natality is approximately 2.5 times greater than the lowest for hares in Yukon and Alberta. The southern hare studies that have calculated annual natality on a per litter basis have been too short to assess the range of reproductive values through a cycle (Newson 1964; Dolbeer and Clark 1975), but three six- to seven-year studies using Green and Evans' (1940c) method show approximately 1.5-fold fluctuation in annual natality (Green and Evans 1940c; Bookhout 1965a; Dodds 1965).

The Alberta and Yukon data sets (Cary and Keith 1979; Stefan 1998) also show that hares consistently have smaller first litters than later litters, and that first litters have a smaller range of variation through the cycle (approximately 0.5 leverets/litter; Chapter 6). If regional differences in litter size exist, they may therefore be easier to detect in the first litter than in later litters, especially if the variation among regions is higher than 0.5 leverets/litter. Additionally, we currently have more data on first litters than on later litter groups. For populations that are known to be cyclic, there does appear to be a latitudinal gradient in the size of the first litter (Fig. 7.3). Within each phase of the cycle, hares in southern populations have smaller first litters (by up to approximately 1.5 leverets) than do hares in northern populations. Hares in Utah and Colorado do not fit this pattern, however; their first litter sizes of approximately 3-4 (Dolbeer and Clark 1975) are comparable to those of hares in Yukon, Alaska, and central Alberta (Ernest 1974; Windberg and Keith 1978, Stefan 1998).

There is a weak latitudinal difference in the dates when hares have their litters (Keith 1981). The onset of hare reproduction is affected by gonadotropin levels, which are affected by daylength (Davis and Meyer 1972, 1973). The beginning of reproduction is also affected by the beginning of spring (Meslow and Keith 1971; Keith 1990), so hares in northern latitudes begin breeding somewhat later than do hares in more southerly latitudes. Nonetheless, most hares have their first litter of the season in May (Keith 1981; Keith 1990; Hodges et al. in press), and the number of litters per season does not seem to depend on when the first litter is born (Stefan 1998; Hodges et al. in press). Additionally, within a region, parturition dates can vary by two to three weeks among years (Cary and Keith 1979; Stefan 1998), which is as great as the purported difference among regions (Keith 1981, 1990).

Survival and Causes of Death

Our estimates of snowshoe hare survival have come from trapping and radiotelemetry, and both of these types of data have been analyzed using various statistical methods (Fig. 7.4). Inferring patterns of regional and even cyclic differences in survival is therefore complicated because the data are not truly comparable. Boutin and Krebs (1986) compared two trapping and two radiotelemetry estimates of 28-day survival using five years of Yukon hare data and found that the radiotelemetry estimates were consistently higher than both trapping estimates, sometimes by as much as 30%. Radio-

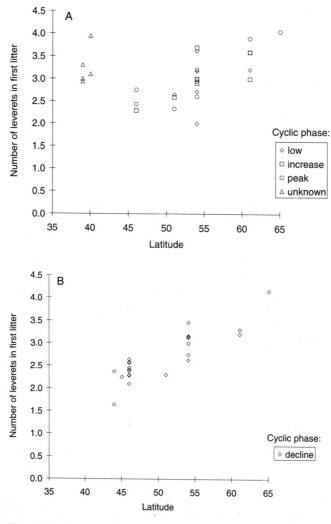

Figure 7.3—The correlation between size of first litter and latitude. Each point represents mean first litter size in one year. Cyclic phases are shown separately because of evidence from Alberta and Yukon that litter size varies through the cycle (Cary and Keith 1979; Stefan 1998). Wisconsin data were assigned to cyclic phases based on trend data from Glenzinski and Dhuey (1998, unpublished) and Karasek (unpublished), and the other references provided information on the population trends in different years; the "unknown" points are for Colorado and Utah (Dolbeer and Clark 1975). Sources: AB, Keith & Windberg 1978, Windberg & Keith 1978, Cary & Keith 1979, Keith et al. 1984; MB, Criddle 1938; ONT, Newson 1964; NB, Wood and Munroe 1977; YK, O'Donoghue and Krebs 1992, Stefan 1998; AK, Ernest 1974; WI, Kuvlesky and Keith 1983; UT, Dolbeer & Clark 1975; and CO, Dolbeer & Clark 1975. The regression of litter size during the decline phase on latitude is highly significant ($F_{1,23} = 71.4$, $p < 0.001$, $r^2 = 0.76$).

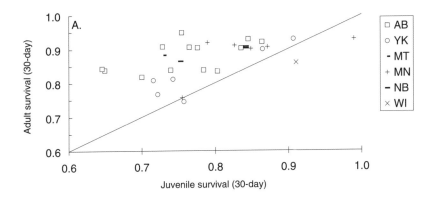

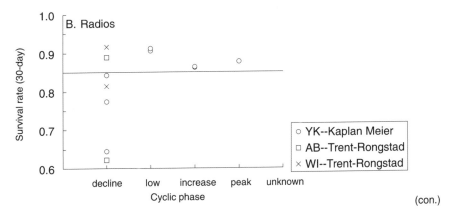

(con.)

Figure 7.4—Snowshoe hare survival estimates. Wisconsin data were assigned to cyclic phases based on trend data from Glenzinski and Dhuey (1998, unpublished), and the other references provided information on the population trends in different years. Panel A shows studies in which juvenile survival (from birth through the following spring, or overwinter) was contrasted with adult annual (or overwinter) survival. The diagonal line indicates identical 30-day survival rates. Each point represents one overwinter or annual period. Sources: AB, Keith & Windberg 1978; YK, Krebs et al. 1986; MT, Adams 1959; MN, Green & Evans 1940b; NB, Wood and Munroe 1977; and WI, Keith et al. 1993. Panels B (radiotelemetry) and C (trapping) show adult overwinter or annual survival broken down regionally and methodologically. Lines are given at 0.85 for comparative purposes. Kaplan-Meier and Trent-Rongstad refer to survival calculated following methodologies in Pollock et al. (1989) and Trent & Rongstad (1974) respectively. Jolly-Seber estimation is described in Krebs (1989), recatch estimation in Keith & Windberg (1978), and age ratios in Green and Evans (1940b). Minimum estimation simply calculates individuals caught at time t that are recaught at time t+1. Sources for panel B: YK, Hodges et al. in press; AB, Keith et al. 1984; and WI, Sievert & Keith 1985. Data for panel C: YK, Krebs et al. 1986; AB, Keith & Windberg 1978; BC, Sullivan & Moses 1986, Sullivan 1996; MN, Green & Evans 1940b; MT, Adams 1959; NB, Wood & Munroe 1977; WI, Kuvlesky & Keith 1983; CO, Dolbeer 1972a; and OR, Black 1965.

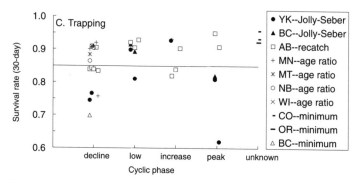

Figure 7.4 (Con.)

telemetry estimates are more likely to be accurate (Chapter 6); survival estimates based on trapping are hampered by the low trappability and potentially high dispersal rates of hares, both of which vary with season, sex, age, phase of cycle, and possibly region and habitat (Trapp 1962; Boutin et al. 1985; Boulanger 1993; Sullivan 1994; Gillis 1997; Hodges 1998).

Trapping studies suggest that juvenile survival is lower than adult survival (Fig. 7.4). This pattern may not be always true, however; using radiocollars, Gillis (1997) found that post-weaning juveniles survived as well as adults during an increase year in Yukon, and Keith et al. (1993) found that juvenile survival was comparable to or higher than adult survival during winter in Wisconsin. Within any given locality, both adult and juvenile survival are lower during population declines (Green and Evans 1940b; Keith and Windberg 1978; Krebs et al. 1986; Hodges et al. in press).

For regional comparisons, I consider only radiotelemetry estimates because of methodological concerns with the trapping data (Table 7.2). Hares

Table 7.2–Survival rates of hares, assessed from radiotelemetry. Where several values are given, they indicate the range among study sites and/or years.

Location	Phase & years	30-day survival rate	Reference
Virginia[a]	unknown 1989-1990	0.63 (>14 days[a]) 0.86 (>60 days[a])	Fies 1993 unpublished
Wisconsin	decline 1988-1991	0.66-0.95	Keith et al. 1993[b] Keith & Bloomer 1993[b] Bloomer et al. 1995[b]
Wisconsin	decline (Dec-Feb) 1994-1995	0.93	Cox et al. 1997
Wisconsin	decline 1982-1983	0.86	Sievert & Keith 1985

[a]Hares were released in a reintroduction program. Estimates are for days post-release.
[b]Approximately half of these hares were treated with antihelminthic drugs, and hares were distributed among seven patches of habitat ranging in size from five to 28 ha. I present survival rates recalculated from Table 5 of Keith et al. 1993.

in Wisconsin had 30-day survival rates ranging between 0.66 and 0.95, with lowest survival occurring as the population declined (Sievert and Keith 1985; Keith et al. 1993; Cox. et al. 1997). These 30-day survival estimates are similar to those from a cyclic population of hares in Yukon, where the lowest monthly survival (0.64) occurred during the decline phase and highest survival (0.91) occurred as the population increased (Hodges et al. in press). In Virginia, imported hares were released in a restocking program; their survival in the first two weeks was low (17 of 26 died), but their survival rates thereafter were similar to those of hares in Wisconsin and Yukon (Fies 1993, unpublished). These results are comparable to those of Sievert and Keith (1985) and evaluations of stocking programs for hunters (Fitzpatrick 1957; Schultz 1980), all of which conclude that transplanted hares have much higher mortality rates within the first several weeks after release.

Most hares in southern populations are killed by predators (Table 7.3) (Fies 1993, unpublished; Sievert and Keith 1985; Keith et al. 1993; Cox et al. 1997; Murray et al. 1997). These studies indicate that predation is responsible for >90% of all hare deaths, a figure comparable to the predation rates found for northern hare populations (Boutin et al. 1986; Krebs et al. 1995; Hodges et al. in press). Both studies of hare mortality patterns and studies of predators indicate that southern hares are preyed upon by lynx, coyotes, bobcat, grey fox, great-horned owls, red fox, weasels, mink, marten, fisher, and goshawks (Zielinski et al. 1983; Litvaitis 1986; Halpin and Bissonette 1988; Giuliano et al. 1989; Kuehn 1989; Dibello et al. 1990; Koehler 1990a; Erdman et al. 1998). Southern forests also contain predators such as raccoons, skunks, feral cats and dogs, and snakes, but the extent to which these predators prey upon hares is unknown. In boreal forests, very young hares are also susceptible to predation by small predators such as red and ground squirrels and some of the smaller hawks (O'Donoghue 1994; Rohner et al. 1995; Stefan 1998; F. Doyle, unpublished), but the southern predators on young hares are unknown.

Dispersal

Radiotelemetry provides the most reliable assessment of dispersal rates (Boutin et al. 1985; Gillis 1997; Chapter 6). There are few such estimates for southern hare populations, but during a population decline in Wisconsin, 2.6% of the hares dispersed and another 5.2% were found dead far enough away from their original locations to suggest possible dispersal (Keith et al. 1993). During a decline in Yukon, 2.7% of hares dispersed (Boutin et al. 1985). Keith et al. (1993) argue that the dispersal rate is higher from smaller habitat patches, but their sample size of dispersers is small (five known dispersers plus 10 animals found dead).

Table 7.3—Causes of mortality for snowshoe hares. Values are % of deaths due to each cause.

Location	Phase & years	Avian	Mammalian	Unknown predator	Non-predation	Unknown	n dead	Observed predators	References
Virginia[a]	unknown 1989 & 1990	8.3	41.7	33.3	16.7[a]	0	24	bobcat grey fox great-horned owl	Fies 1993, unpublished
Manitoba (southern)	decline 1991-1993	32.3	33.3	29.2	5.0	0	318	–	Murray et al. 1997
Wisconsin	decline 1982-1983	26.7	48.3	16.7	8.3	0	60[b]	red fox coyote long-tailed weasel mink great-horned owl goshawk	Sievert & Keith 1985
Wisconsin	decline 1988-1991	10	55	31	4	0	122	–	Keith et al. 1993[c] Keith & Bloomer 1993[c] Bloomer et al. 1995[c]
Wisconsin	decline 1994-1995	14	64	0	7	14	14	coyote	Cox et al. 1997

[a] Hares were relocated from West Virginia into Virginia during January-April in each year. Most died within two weeks of release, and deaths in this period are thought to be related to handling and release into unfamiliar habitat.
[b] I excluded deaths from handling, hunting, and dogs.
[c] Approximately half of these hares were treated with antihelminthic drugs, and hares were distributed among seven patches of habitat ranging in size from five to 28 ha.

Experiments in which hares are transplanted show that hares have re-duced survival immediately following release (Schultz 1980; Sievert and Keith 1985; Fies 1993, unpublished), which Sievert and Keith (1985) inter-preted to mean that dispersers suffer higher mortality than non-dispersers. Although both transplanting and dispersal lead to habitat unfamiliarity, the process of catching, transporting, and releasing hares is very different than what occurs as hares disperse naturally, making it hard to judge from these experiments what factors lead to the higher mortality rate.

Comparative Demography Between Northern and Southern Hare Populations

The available evidence suggests that demographic patterns are largely similar between hares in northern and southern areas. Most hares are killed by predators and the limited data we have on survival in southern areas (Sievert and Keith 1985; Keith et al. 1993; Fies 1993, unpublished; Cox et al. 1997) suggest that northern and southern hares have similar survival. Because the southern regions potentially have a larger suite of predators, particularly for young hares, it is possible that there are regional differences in leveret and juvenile survival rates. Although there appear to be differ-ences in reproduction, with northern hares having larger litters but some-times not as many litters in a season, it is unclear what effect this variation has on the cycle. Analyses of snowshoe hare population dynamics suggest that juvenile and adult survival have more impact on the numeric change than does natality (Keith 1990; Krebs 1996; Haydon et al. 1999). More long-term studies of demography and modeling of the effects of variable survival and reproductive rates would help in our understanding of why hare populations display different lengths and amplitudes of fluctuation.

Snowshoe Hare Behavior

Diets

Hares eat many plant species (Table 7.4). The variability in number of species eaten in the different regions is an amalgam of how speciose the different areas are, hares' likings for the different species, and sampling effort.The short list for the north reflects fewer species in boreal forests than in temperate ones, whereas the relatively short western list may be due instead to less intensive sampling. Although many species preferences have been identified (e.g., Telfer 1972; Bryant and Kuropat 1980; Scott and Yahner 1989; Thomas et al. 1997, unpublished), these depend on the plant

Table 7.4–Food plants used by snowshoe hares in different regions. Because of the variety of analytic techniques and the different floristic communities, I have not attempted to separate species into degrees of utilization or preference.

Conifers	Deciduous trees	Shrubs	References
Maritimes & Maine			
Abies balsamea	*Acer pensylvanicum*	*Corylus cornuta*	Telfer 1972 (NB)
Picea spp.	*Acer rubrum*	*Gaylussaccia baccata*	Litvaitis 1984 (ME)
Picea rubens	*Acer saccharum*	*Hamamelis virginiana*	
Pinus strobus	*Acer spicatum*	*Kalmia* spp.	
Thuja occidentalis	*Alnus rugosa*	*Myrica gale*	
Tsuga canadensis	*Alnus crispa*	*Nemopanthus mucronata*	
	Betula alleghaniensis	*Rhododendron canadense*	
	Betula papyrifera	*Vaccinium* spp.	
	Betula populifolia	*Viburnum* spp.	
	Comptonia peregrina		
	Fagus grandifolia		
	Quercus rubra		
Eastern: Appalachians & Alleghanies			
Picea glauca	*Acer pensylvanicum*	*Juniperus communis*	Rogowitz 1988 (NY)
Picea rubens	*Acer rubrum*	*Kalmia latifolia*	Cook & Robeson 1945 (NY)
Pinus resinosa	*Acer saccharum*	*Rhododendron lapponicum*	Brooks 1955 (VA)
Pinus strobus	*Betula alleghaniensis*	*Rubus alleghaniensis*	Scott & Yahner 1989 (PA)
Pinus sylvestris	*Betula lenta*	*Rubus hispidus*	Walski & Mautz 1977 (NH)
Thuja occidentalis	*Betula lutea*	*Vaccinium erythrocarpum*	Brown 1984 (PA)
Tsuga canadensis	*Betula papyrifera*	*Viburnum dentatum*	
	Fagus grandifolia		
	Fraxinus americana		
	Populus tremuloides		
Midwest: Great Lakes			
Abies balsamea	*Acer pensylvanicum*	*Amelanchier* spp.	Bider 1961 (Que)
Larix laricina	*Acer rubrum*	*Chamaedaphne calyculata*	Grange 1932 (WI)
Picea abies	*Acer saccharum*	*Corylus cornuta*	Bookhout 1965b (MI)
Picea glauca	*Acer spicatum*	*Juniperus communis*	Conroy et al. 1979 (MI)
Picea mariana	*Alnus crispa*	*Ledum groenlandicus*	De Vos 1964 (ONT)
Pinus banksiana	*Alnus rugosa*	*Lonicera* spp.	Grigal & Moody 1980 (MN)
Pinus divaricata	*Betula alba*	*Rhamnus alnifolia*	Johnson 1969 (MI)
Pinus resinosa	*Betula papyrifera*	*Rosa* spp.	Bergeron & Tardif 1988 (Que)
Pinus strobus	*Betula pumila*	*Rubus* spp.	
Thuja occidentalis	*Fagus grandifolia*	*Salix* spp.	
Tsuga canadensis	*Ostrya virginiana*	*Shepherdia canadensis*	
	Populus grandidentata	*Viburnum* spp.	
	Populus pensylvanica		
	Populus tremuloides		
	Populus virginiana		
	Prunus pensylvanica		
	Prunus serotina		
	Prunus virginiana		
	Pyrus malus		
	Quercus rubra		
	Sorbus americana		
	Ulmus americana		
Western: Rockies, Cascades & Intermountain West			
Pinus contorta		*Amelanchier alnifolia*	Adams 1959 (MT)
Pinus ponderosa		*Arctostaphylus uva-ursi*	Koehler 1990a (WA)
Pseudotsuga menziesii		*Ceanothus* spp.	Radwan & Campbell 1968 (WA)
Tsuga heterophylla		*Juniperus scopulorum*	Thomas et al. 1997, unpublished (WA)
		Mahonia repens	Sullivan and Sullivan 1983 (BC)
		Rosa spp.	Borrecco 1976 (WA)
		Rubus spp.	Black 1965 (OR)
		Salix coulteri	
		Symphoricarpus albus	
		Vaccinium spp.	
North: Boreal Forests			
Picea glauca	*Alnus crispa*	*Amelanchier alnifolia*	Smith et al. 1988 (YK)
Picea mariana	*Alnus rugosa*	*Betula glandulosa*	Wolff 1978 (AK)
	Betula papyrifera	*Corylus cornuta*	Bryant 1981 (AK)
	Populus balsamifera	*Ledum decumbens*	
	Populus tremuloides	*Rosa* spp.	
		Salix spp.	
		Shepherdia canadensis	

community where each study is conducted. Hares also eat many nonwoody species (Adams 1959; Radwan and Campbell 1968; Thomas et al. 1997, unpublished; Hodges 1998).

Browse damage by hares can slow regeneration of conifers after logging, especially if hares eat the bark of the young trees (Cook and Robeson 1945; Borrecco 1976; Krefting 1975, unpublished; Sullivan and Sullivan 1986; Bergeron and Tardif 1988). When hares are at high density, they are more likely to eat bark and large twigs than during years when hare densities are lower (de Vos 1964; Lloyd-Smith and Piene 1981, unpublished; Fox and Bryant 1984). Hares can affect young trees by slowing their growth rate, destroying the apical meristem, and even killing them (Corson and Cheyney 1928; Cook and Robeson 1945; Krefting 1975, unpublished; Black et al. 1979).

In the north, food availability has been addressed because of its potential role in the generation of cycles (Vowles 1972; Pease et al. 1979; Bryant 1981; Keith 1983; Smith et al. 1988). In the south, more effort has been placed on describing potential competition for food between hares and deer or moose (Dodds 1960; Dodds 1962, unpublished; Bookhout 1965b; Telfer 1972; Krefting 1975, unpublished). These studies have generally agreed that these herbivores often eat the same plants but do not appear to be limiting each other's numbers, although this pattern has not been thoroughly examined. There is at present no evidence suggesting food limitation in southern hare populations.

Analyzing Snowshoe Hare Habitat Use

In the following discussion, I focus on describing the habitats hares use. I avoid using the terms "habitat needs" and "habitat requirements." These terms are designed to address whether particular habitats are so critical to a species that without them the species cannot survive (these may be "source" habitats [sensu Pulliam 1988] or they may be habitats critical to a particular life-stage, such as habitat for lambing). For a species like the snowshoe hare that uses many habitat types, it is difficult to know what criteria to employ to designate a habitat as "required." Density may not be a good index because in some cases higher densities can occur in "sink" habitats (Van Horne 1983), and hares have no obvious need for particular habitats for reproduction. I similarly avoid discussing "habitat quality" because this phrase does not have a precise definition. In all of these cases, it is more valuable to discuss and to quantify habitat-specific demography.

Hare habitat use patterns have been measured by estimates of density (from trapping or from pellet counts; e.g., Litvaitis et al. 1985b; Krebs et al. 1987; Eaton 1995), direct estimates of relative use (from trapping or radio-telemetry locations of marked hares; e.g., Dolbeer and Clark 1975; Ferron and Ouellet 1992), and indirect estimates of relative use (from browsing intensity or hare tracks; e.g., Monthey 1986; Rogowitz 1988). Of these, density estimates are the most informative, because they can indicate amplitude of change through time or magnitude of difference among habitats. Direct estimates of relative use can be valuable for showing how individuals split their time among different habitats (Manly et al. 1993). Indirect estimates of relative use (indices) are difficult to interpret, because the amplitudes of difference among habitats or years have an unknown relationship to the actual differences in hare densities (Hartman 1960; Thomas et al. 1997, unpublished). Additionally, different protocols (e.g., how to count hare runways) make it difficult to compare results from different studies.

Patterns of Habitat Use by Snowshoe Hares

Density estimates show that hares use certain seral stages more than others, and this pattern appears to be most correlated with horizontal understory cover from approximately 1 to 3 m (Table 7.5). Newly clear-cut areas are essentially not used (Ferron et al. 1998). In Washington, younger lodgepole pine stands support higher densities of hares than do older stands, which is associated with the higher stocking density of the younger stands (Koehler 1990a, b). Typically, forest stands that are densely stocked support higher hare densities than do lightly stocked stands (Litvaitis et al. 1985b; Brocke et al. 1993, unpublished). Similarly, stands with dense understory cover tend to be used more by hares than are stands with little understory cover (Orr and Dodds 1982; Wolfe et al. 1982). Deciduous forests can support reasonable densities of hares, especially if they have well-developed understories (Orr and Dodds 1982; Wolfe et al. 1982; Reed et al. 1999, unpublished).

These patterns of habitat use by hares are supported by studies that employed direct or indirect estimates of relative use (Tables 7.6 and 7.7). The most consistent finding is that hares' use of habitats is correlated with understory cover—stands with shrubs, stands that are densely stocked, and stands at ages where branches have more lateral cover are more heavily used by hares (Black 1965; Dolbeer and Clark 1975; Wolfe et al. 1982; Litvaitis et al. 1985a, b; Monthey 1986; Parker et al. 1983; Koehler 1990a; Swayze 1994, unpublished; Thomas et al. 1997, unpublished). Overstory cover is sometimes correlated with hare habitat use patterns, but typically in cases where it is also significantly correlated with understory cover (Richmond and Chien 1976; Orr and Dodds 1982; Parker et al. 1983; Rogowitz 1988). The species composition in a stand appears to be less correlated with hare habitat use than is understory structure (Ferron and Ouellet 1992; Thomas et al. 1997, unpublished). Stand age per se does not appear to be critical, again

Table 7.5–Snowshoe hare densities in different habitat types. Density estimates are derived either from pellet plots [a] or from live-trapping data.

Location	Year/season	Method	Habitat type	Hare density (hares/ha)	Reference
Stand age/height Nova Scotia	1976	pellet plots	_forests with ≥50% spruce-fir._ _height classes (m):_ 4.5-9.2 4.5-15 9.4-12.3 12.5-15.2	0.59 0.52 0.60 0.36	Orr & Dodds 1982
Quebec (southern)	1993-1996	pellet plots	uncut black spruce forest clear-cut black spruce forest	0.12-0.25 0.01-0.02	Ferron et al. 1998
Washington	1986-1989	pellet plots[b]	~25-yr-old lodgepole pine ~45-yr-old lodgepole pine >80-yr-old lodgepole pine >100-yr-old Englemann fir- subalpine spruce	_1986 / 1987 / 1989_ 1.04 / 1.79 / 0.99 0.86 / 0.45 / 0.39 0.43 / – / 0.22 0.09 / 0.27 / 0.12	Koehler 1990a, b
Species Composition Nova Scotia	1976	pellet plots	spruce-fir maple/birch alder	0.49 0.22 0.69	Orr & Dodds 1982
Utah	1976-1978[c]	pellet plots	aspen–sparse understory aspen–dense understory aspen-conifer edge Douglas-fir subalpine fir Engelmann spruce	0.01 0.22 0.17 0.57 0.99 0.19	Wolfe et al. 1982
Utah	1976-1978	live-trapping	_Englemann spruce-subalpine fir_ July 1976 July 1977 May 1978	1.0 1.8 2.7	Andersen et al. 1980
Colorado	1998	pellet plots[d]	aspen Douglas-fir subalpine fir lodgepole pine Gambel oak Ponderosa pine Engelmann spruce	0.26 0.37 0.37 0.35 0.05 0.18 0.46	Reed et al. 1999, unpublished
% cover Nova Scotia	1976	pellet plots	_forests with ≥50% spruce-fir._ canopy cover classes: 10-40 41-60 61-100	0.62 0.49 0.38	Orr & Dodds 1982
New Hampshire	1990	pellet plots[e]	_spruce-fir-birch-ash-maple_ 9,221 stems/ha (90% conifer) 26,028 stems/ha (99% conifer) 8,512 stems/ha (82% conifer) 6,533 stems/ha (90% conifer)	1.34 1.27 0.74 0.40	Brocke et al. 1993, unpublished
Maine	1982-1983 spring	live-trapping	_total understory stems/ha_ _(total conifer stems/ha):_ 31,490 (2,580) 20,350 (16,150) 18,980 (8,580) 16,440 (4,360)	_1982 / 1983_ 0.4 / 0.6 1.2 / 1.7 0.6 / 0.5 0.2 / 0.1	Litvaitis et al. 1985b

[a]Densities from pellet plots were recalculated from the original papers using a regression equation derived from hare density information from 1976 to 1996 (C.J. Krebs, unpublished): $\ln(\text{hares/ha})=0.888962*\ln(\text{pellets})-1.203391$, corrected for bias by multiplying with 1.57 following Sprugel (1983). Pellets is pellets/0.155m^2. The methodology and rationale were derived in Krebs et al. (1987), and the current equation simply uses more information.

[b]Fall 1987 pellet values were calculated from Koehler 1990a by adding the winter and summer counts.

[c]Values are from the three years in which all habitats were sampled; the values given are averages across years.

[d]Only cover types with >15 pellet plots are shown here.

[e]Pellet counts were transformed to hare densities using the Krebs (1998, unpublished) equation rather than reporting the densities in this reference, which were calculated according to another formula.

Table 7.6–Proportional occurrence of snowshoe hares in different habitat types. The data in this table show the proportion of locations of hares in each habitat type, from locations gathered via radiotelemetry or live-trapping. Live-trapping data are included here instead of in Table 7.5 if the data were presented as number of captures of animals in each habitat type.

Location	Year/season	Method	Habitat type	Proportional use by hares	Reference
Species composition					
Quebec (southeastern)	1987 summer	radiotelemetry (feeding and resting observations combined)	overstory composition: conifer deciduous mixed none understory composition: conifer or none deciduous mixed	19 37 29 15 4 80 16	Ferron and Ouellet 1992
Oregon	1960-1962	trapping[a]	~15-yr Douglas-fir stands open (clear-cut and fire)	78.3 / 74.4[a] 21.7 / 25.6	Black 1965
% cover					
Nova Scotia (Cape Breton Island)	1977-1979	trapping[b]	fir/spruce/birch forests: open mature closed mature regeneration (16-30 yr) regeneration (5-15 yr)	47.2 9.3 22.3 21.2	Parker et al. 1983
Maine	1981-1983 October-May	trapping[c]	understory density: < 700 stems/ha 700-7,000 stems/ha 7,000-20,000 stems/ha >20,000 stems/ha	0 / 6.8[c] 13.7 / 15.6 30.1 / 27.9 56.3 / 49.7	Litvaitis 1984 Litvaitis et al. 1985a
Colorado	1969-1971 July-August	trapping	open (scattered trees) forested (spruce-fir-pine)	9.7 (A) / 25.5 (J)[d] 90.3 (A) / 74.5 (J)	Dolbeer 1972a Dolbeer & Clark 1975

[a]Values are for the same sites but for periods with different numbers of traps.
[b]Values are % of live captures/1,000 trap nights.
[c]Values are for two sites.
[d]A refers to adults, J to juveniles.

because of the importance of stand structure, but several studies have indicated that younger stands may support more hares than do older mature stands (C. Grove, unpublished; Johnson 1969; Koehler 1990a,b; Byrne 1998, unpublished).

Fires and harvesting both return land to early seral stages but may differ in their effects on hares. Spatial scale of the two disturbances may differ, and whereas fire often leaves some standing trees, both dead and alive, clear-cuts and even some selective cuts remove much of the overstory and often understory as well (Chapter 3). Several authors have argued that fire contributes to the cyclicity of hares, by providing regenerating areas rich in food and cover (Howell 1923; Grange 1965; Fox 1978), but there are comparatively few studies of hares' use of burned stands of various ages. In Colorado, pellet plots showed that hares used an eight-year-old burn of lodgepole pine forest much less than the adjacent unburned forest (Roppe and Hein 1978). In Michigan, hares used a 30-year-old burned site

Table 7.7—Indices of relative use by hares of different habitat types. Statistical significance (at $p < 0.05$) is taken directly from the analyses performed by the authors: > shows statistical significance, ≥ shows a trend but no statistical significance, = shows no trend and no statistical significance. In cases where no statistics were performed, the comparable symbols ⊃, ⊇, and ≈ are used to indicate trends. (0) indicates little or no sign of hares in the habitat.

Location	Year/season	Methods[a]	Snowshoe hare habitat use	Reference
Stand age/height				
Maine	1974-1977 winter	tracks (%)	*conifer regrowth:* 12-15 yr > 7-9 yr > 1-3 yr	Monthey 1986
Vermont	winter	tracks	*deciduous:* stands younger than 60 yr ⊃ stands older than 60 yr[b]	C. Grove, unpublished
New York	1972-1974 March	tracks (#)	saw timber ⊃ seedling/sapling ⊇ pole timber ⊃ old field (0)	Richmond and Chien 1976
Pennsylvania	1984-1985 winter	tracks (%)	successful deciduous regeneration > unsuccessful deciduous regeneration[c]	Scott & Yanner 1989
Colorado	1997-1998 winter	tracks (#)	mature ⊇ sapling/pole ⊇ old-growth ⊃ shrub/seedling ⊃ open	Byrne 1998, unpublished
Stand composition				
Maine	1974-1977	tracks (%)	spruce/fir > mixed > maple/beech/birch	Monthey 1986
Maine	1981	tracks (#) pellets	deciduous > spruce/fir > mixed	O'Donoghue 1983
Vermont	winter	tracks	conifer ≈ deciduous ≈ mixed ≈ open[d]	C. Grove, unpublished
Connecticut	1958-1959 winter	tracks trapping[e]	conifer plantation = deciduous > mixed > old field	Behrend 1960, unpublished
New York	1972-1974 March	tracks (#)	Norway spruce ≈ white pine ⊃ stands without these species	Richmond and Chien 1976
New York	1980 January/March	food offerings pellets	spruce > pine-shrub, spruce-shrub > deciduous (0), open (0)	Rogowitz 1988
Pennsylvania	1977 Feb-March	tracks (#)	deciduous regeneration (8 yrs old) ⊃ laurel ⊃ hemlock	Brown 1984
Michigan	1976 Jan-March	browsing intensity	cedar/fir ⊃ ash/elm ⊇ alder ⊃ oak/pine ⊃ clear-cut	Conroy et al. 1979
Michigan (Isle Royale)	1963-1968	pellets	1936 burn > conifer, deciduous > 100-yr-old burn (0)[f]	Johnson 1969

(con.)

Table 7.7 (Con.)

Location	Year/season	Methods[a]	Snowshoe hare habitat use	Reference
Stand composition				
Wisconsin	1978-1979 winter	tracks (#)	spruce-cedar-tamarack > pine-oak, alder, aspen-birch, pine-maple, maple-basswood (0) spruce-pine plantations > pine-oak, alder, maple-basswood (0) spruce-pine plantations ≥ aspen-birch, pine-maple	Buehler & Keith 1982
Utah	1972-1973 June-July	pellets	spruce/fir ≥ lodgepole pine > aspen	Clark 1973
Montana	1977	tracks (#)	lodgepole ⊃ grass islands in lodgepole stands ⊃ subalpine fir-Engelmann spruce ⊃ conifer islands in grassland	Koehler et al. 1979
Colorado	1974	pellets	unburned lodgepole > 8-yr-old burned lodgepole	Roppe & Hein 1978
Colorado	1997-1998 winter	tracks (#)	lodgepole ≈ white fir ≈ limber pine ≥ Douglas-fir ≥ Engelmann spruce ≈ ponderosa pine ⊃ aspen ⊃ willow ⊃ oak ⊃ open	Byrne 1998, unpublished
% cover				
Maine	1981-1983	tracks (%) pellets	*understory density:* 20,000+ stems/ha > 7,000-20,000 > 700-7,000 > below 700 stems/ha	Litvaitis 1984 Litvaitis et al. 1985a
Maine	1981	tracks (#) pellets	*understory density:* dense > moderate > open > sparse	O'Donoghue 1983
New York	1970-1974 fall-winter	tracks (#) trapping	*fir/spruce:* 20,900 stems/ha > 5,900 stems/ha	Brocke 1975
Connecticut	1958-1959 winter	tracks trapping[e]	*understory cover from 0-6 ft:* 61-100% > 21-60%	Behrend 1960, unpublished
Washington	1994	pellet plots	*23-yr-old lodgepole pine regeneration* *stand density:* ~100,000 stems/ha > ~20,000 stems/ha = ~1000 stems/ha	Swayze 1994, unpublished
Washington	1974-1975	damage to seedlings (live-trapping)	*sites with Douglas-fir regeneration:* clearcuts > clear-cuts treated with herbicides to eliminate herbaceous growth	Borrecco 1976

[a]For methods, *tracks (%)* means track counts where the proportion of transect segments with tracks was calculated, *tracks (#)* means tracks were actually counted along transects, *pellets* indicates pellet plots where the collection design or the presentation do not allow for conversion to density estimates, and *browsing intensity* and *food offerings* indicate observations of browse use.

[b]Stands were evaluated for presence/absence of hares only. For this analysis, I excluded stands containing trees of ages overlapping these two groups.

[c]Successful regeneration: >70% of 20 1.83-m radius plots containing ≥2 stems that are ≥1.5 m tall.

[d]Stands were evaluated for presence/absence of hares only. 82-86% of deciduous, mixed, and coniferous stands contained hare sign; 100% of open sites did as well, but only four open sites were sampled compared to 37-99 stands of the other types.

[e]Behrend presented tracks and live captures together in the analysis of habitat use.

[f]The 1936 burn had a variety of habitat types within it, including alder, jack pine, white birch, aspen.

more than a 100-year-old burned site (Johnson 1969). In the Northwest Territories, hares used a burned site during the first winter post-fire, to eat the bark of the burned black spruce trees (Stephenson 1985).

Hares may show seasonal shifts in habitat use, using more or denser coniferous cover in winter than in summer, which suggests that winter cover may be more important than summer cover (O'Donoghue 1983; Parker et al. 1983; Litvaitis et al. 1985b; Swayze 1994, unpublished). Additionally, hare habitat use may vary with regional density; in Minnesota, hares' use of areas with little cover was higher when population densities were high, even though the rank order of hare habitat use remained basically the same as at low densities (Fuller and Heisey 1986). Juvenile hares may use more open habitats than do adult hares (Dolbeer and Clark 1975), and there may be differences in habitat use between males and females (Litvaitis 1990).

Regionally, hares appear more likely to use deciduous forests in the east than in the west (Tables 7.5 through 7.8). On the east coast, where both deciduous and coniferous stands are present, hares may use the coniferous stands more (Richmond and Chien 1976; Orr and Dodds 1982; Rogowitz 1988), but in some cases hares make equal or more use of the deciduous

Table 7.8–Habitat survey results. Forest managers were requested to indicate the top two habitats in which they would find hares. The numbers indicate responses for different national forests; in some cases, one forest manager responded for multiple forests. Clearly, some forest types occur only in one of the regions; the more valuable comparison is within a region to see which habitat types managers consider to contain more hares.

Forest type	Oregon & Washington	Intermountain West	Great Lakes & eastern U.S.
Engelmann spruce-subalpine fir	2	15	–
Interior Douglas-fir	6	4	–
Western larch	1	3	–
Grand fir	5	3	–
White fir	3	–	–
Balsam fir	–	–	5
Mountain hemlock	3	–	–
Coastal fir-hemlock	2	–	–
Red cedar-hemlock	2	1	–
Western red cedar	–	1	–
White cedar	–	–	2
Lodgepole pine	7	14	–
Whitebark pine	–	1	–
Red pine	–	–	2
Jack pine	–	–	1
Ponderosa pine	1	–	–
Red spruce	–	–	1
White spruce	–	–	1
Spruce-tamarack	–	–	1
Spruce-birch	–	–	1
Cottonwood/willow	1	1	–
Aspen	1	4	2
Birch	–	–	2

stands (Behrend 1960, unpublished; O'Donoghue 1983; Brown 1984; Litvaitis et al. 1985b). On the east coast, many deciduous forests have dense understories of shrubs and immature trees and these forest types are commonly used by hares (Tompkins and Woehr 1979; O'Donoghue 1983; Brown 1984; Scott and Yahner 1989; Ferron and Ouellet 1992). Western deciduous forests—such as aspen or poplar stands—may lack this understory growth, and these stands do not show as much use by hares (Clark 1973; Wolfe et al. 1982; Byrne 1998, unpublished; Reed et al. 1999, unpublished). This pattern again highlights the association between hares and understory cover. On the west coast, lodgepole pine, Douglas-fir, and Englemann-spruce/subalpine fir stands are common habitats for hares. On the east coast, the common cover types for hares are spruce/fir, pine, and deciduous.

Habitat interspersion may be valuable to hares by providing them access to habitats with different protective abilities and food availabilities (Conroy et al. 1979; Krenz 1988; Koehler and Brittell 1990; Beauvais 1997; Thomas et al. 1997). Krenz (1988) found that hares in Minnesota were more likely to use deciduous shrub cover if it was clumped (at a scale of circles of 168 m radius), whereas hares were more likely to use coniferous cover that was more evenly distributed. Additionally, the size of habitat patches can affect hare densities. In Washington, stands ≥32 ha had roughly double the number of hare pellets as occurred in stands <16 ha (Thomas et al. 1997), and in Wisconsin there was a trend for larger forest stands to be more likely to have hares present within them (Buehler and Keith 1982). Thomas et al. (1997, unpublished) also found that the amount of disturbed habitat (talus, meadows, or heavily thinned mature forest) in a 600 m strip around each habitat patch was negatively correlated with the number of hare pellets within the patch. In Maine, an area managed with clear-cutting had higher track counts than did areas that were partially harvested or entirely uncut, suggesting that the habitat matrix affects hare abundance (Monthey 1986). In Minnesota, hare habitat use was more correlated with habitat interspersion than with stand type, and hares used the edges more than centers of the heavily used stand types (Conroy et al. 1979). In Wyoming, snowshoe hare presence in stands was correlated with the degree of interspersion with clear-cuts and riparian areas (Beauvais 1997).

The bulk of evidence suggests that habitats affect hares' survival rates because vulnerability to predation and predator density vary among habitats (O'Donoghue 1997; Murray et al. 1994, 1995). Fecundity may possibly vary with habitat as well, perhaps mediated by dietary differences (Hik 1994) or the effects of predation risk on stress levels (Boonstra et al. 1998). At a stand level, then, demography is likely to vary with cover and food availability. At the level of multiple stands, however, hares may be able to switch back and forth between different types of stands (Conroy et al. 1979;

Krenz 1988; Hik 1994), or different age classes of hares may use different stand types (Dolbeer and Clark 1975; Boutin 1984). Hare dynamics within the set of stands will therefore depend on the densities of hares within each stand as well as the survival and fecundity rates typical of each stand type. The size of each stand and the degree of interspersion are likely to affect hare dynamics as well—an array of large stands may have different overall dynamics than a quilt of small stands because the movement of hares between stands is easier when each stand is smaller. Additionally, if certain predators require large stands of particular habitat types, they may not occur in landscapes where the same amount of habitat is dispersed in smaller patches.

The habitat use patterns of southern snowshoe hares are similar to those of hares in northern boreal forests. Hares in northern forests also are often associated with early seral forests, again with understory cover or stand density as good correlates with hare habitat use patterns (Wolff 1980; Sullivan and Sullivan 1982a,b, 1983; Hik 1994, 1995; O'Donoghue 1997). Northern forests are predominantly coniferous, and the deciduous aspen and poplar stands typically do not support a thick shrub understory; hares in northern forests do not use these deciduous stands extensively (Hodges 1998).

Discussion

The predominant snowshoe hare story in this century has been that snowshoe hares are strongly cyclic in the north but show reduced or no cycles in their southern distribution (Howell 1923; MacLulich 1937; Criddle 1938; Keith 1963, 1990; Grange 1965; Finerty 1980; Bittner and Rongstad 1982; Smith 1983). This paradigm has arisen from two main fronts: analyses of time series data (mainly harvest records) and comparisons of demographic patterns among regions. I have so far presented time series that support the possibility that hares are cyclic in southern areas, although with peak and low densities lower than those in northern areas. I have similarly argued that the comparable data we have from southern and northern hare populations indicate similar demography among regions. In this final section, I argue that it is time to emphasize analyses that address why snowshoe hare fluctuations vary in amplitude, maximum density, and duration both within and among regions. There is an extensive literature discussing the linkages of hare behavior, habitats, and demography, and this framework may prove useful for evaluating the mechanisms leading to different dynamics and densities in different times or areas.

The dominant model of the effect of hare habitat use patterns on their demography has been used to explain both cyclic dynamics and the previously hypothesized noncyclicity in the southern range of hares (Keith 1966, 1990; Dolbeer and Clark 1975; Wolff 1980, 1981; Buehler and Keith 1982; Sievert and Keith 1985; Hik 1994, 1995). The refugium model was most clearly articulated by Wolff (1980, 1981) as follows: hares selectively use dense, safe habitats until high hare densities force some hares into poor habitats, which exposes them to higher predation risk, thus contributing to the numeric and functional responses of predators and the cyclic decline. The habitats with densest cover, meanwhile, provide refugia to hares, thus allowing a source population during the low phase. In this model, reproductive declines are thought to originate because food supply in the densest habitats is lower, or poorer quality, leaving hares with a trade-off between nutrition and survival (Hik 1994, 1995). Alternatively, recent evidence suggests that reproductive declines may be due to the stress of encounters with predators, which is highest as hare populations decline (Boonstra and Singleton 1993; Boonstra et al. 1998).

The refugium model has also been used to explain the putative lack of cycles in the south (Dolbeer and Clark 1975; Wolff 1980, 1981). In this case, the basic argument is that southern habitats are more patchy due to being montane (and with greater human impacts). The implication is that hares that disperse from refugia are even less likely to survive, especially since there are noncyclic facultative predators able to prey on the hares. Within each southern habitat patch, therefore, cyclic dynamics are liable to be subdued because of the smallness of the patch and the survival sink awaiting dispersers from the patch.

This refugium model can be broken down into a number of testable components:

(1) refuge habitats exist, in which hares have higher survival than in other habitat types;

(2) the distribution of hares relative to habitats changes through the cycle, with a higher proportion of hares in refugia during the low phase;

(3) hare reproduction varies with habitat, with hares in refugia showing the lowest reproductive output.

If hares in southern populations have dynamics that differ from those of hares in northern populations, then two additional propositions are relevant:

(4) hares in southern populations have lower survival in non-refuge habitats than do hares in northern non-refuge habitats (or in the north refugia comprise a larger proportion of the habitat available than in the south); and

(5) hares in southern populations have lower survival overall than do hares in northern populations, thus stabilizing the cycle.

A similar model has been proposed for Fennoscandian microtine cycles that emphasizes the role of facultative predators in the southern noncyclic range of microtine rodents (Erlinge et al. 1983; Hansson and Henttonen 1985; Hansson 1987; Erlinge 1987; Hanski et al. 1991; Lindström 1994). This model is similar to the refugium model in that a critical element is the increased mortality that occurs in noncyclic prey populations relative to cyclic ones. Habitat is invoked more in the role of enabling facultative predators and alternative prey to be present, rather than in the role of changing the accessibility of the cyclic prey species to the predators. The same argumentation could be applied to the snowshoe hares: if the facultative predation model is true, we would expect to see (A) overall higher mortality rates of snowshoe hares in their southern range, and (B) a higher proportion of deaths by facultative predators in southern populations than in northern populations. Although both models need higher hare mortality in the southern populations (requirements 5 and A), it is possible that hares could have higher mortality rates in the south without the other requirements of either model being upheld, in which case other hypotheses would need to be constructed to explain why the mortality rates differed. It is also possible that per capita predation rates on hares may be similar among regions, but that the predators are compensatory with each other (Stenseth et al. 1997; Hodges et al. in press), thus making the proportion of kills due to each predator interesting from a community organization perspective but irrelevant to the dynamics of hares.

At present, our evaluation of these two predation models can be little more than conjectural (Table 7.9). We have limited data that address only requirements 1 and 2 of the refugium model. A few studies have indicated small differences in hare survival (measured with radiotelemetry) among habitats (Sievert and Keith 1985; Keith and Bloomer 1993), and predators choose particular habitat types and may have differential success rates in each type (Hik 1994; Murray et al. 1994, 1995; Rohner and Krebs 1996; Cox et al. 1997). There is, however, no clear cyclic pattern in snowshoe hares' use of the available habitat types (Fuller and Heisey 1986; Chapter 6), counter to the refugium hypothesis. Experimental work in Yukon has shown that hares protected from predators still prefer dense cover and do not show much greater use of open cover than unprotected hares (Hik 1994; Hodges 1998), which argues against the idea that high predation pressure forces hares into dense habitats.

To evaluate the roles of habitat structure and predation on hare cycles among regions properly, we need precise definitions of refugia and nonrefugia and our data from hare populations in different regions need to be comparable. Given the evidence from Alberta and Yukon that shows that both food and predation are necessary components of the cycle (Keith 1990;

Table 7.9–Evaluation of the refugium and facultative predation hypotheses for snowshoe hare cycles. Requirements 1-5 belong to the refugium hypothesis, and A-B to the facultative predation hypothesis. Support for any of 4a-4c would be adequate; only one is needed to support that requirement of the refugium model. If requirements 1 & 2 are met, but 4 & 5 are not, refugia can help explain northern cyclicity but cannot explain dynamics in southern populations. Requirement 3 is not strictly necessary, but would support the argument that habitat affects hare demography.

Model requirements	Evidence	Questions that need to be resolved
1. differential survival in different habitat types	see chapter 6; 2 Wisconsin studies found differential survival	What magnitude of difference is necessary?
2. hare distribution in habitats varies cyclically (higher % of hares in refuges during low phase)	see chapter 6; no clear cyclicity in hare habitat use	What magnitude of difference is necessary? Does the % of mortalities/hare/habitat vary? (is a refugium a physical place?)
3. differential reproduction in different habitat types	no data available	Is habitat a proxy for nutrition or maternal stress?
4a. survival in southern non-refuges < survival in northern non-refuges	no comparable data available	Critical to define well and make comparable between regions.
4b. survival in southern refuges < survival in northern refuges	no comparable data available	Critical to define well and make comparable between regions. Can "refuge" habitats be defined by vegetation type and/or structure or are they defined by having higher survival within them?
4c. lower % of refuge habitat in south than in north	"refuge" habitat needs definition first	Critical to define well and make comparable between regions. Can "refuge" habitats be defined by vegetation and/or structure or are they defined by having higher survival within them?
5 & A. lower survival rate in south than in north	comparable data suggest similar survival rates	What period of the cycle should be used for comparison? What magnitude of difference is necessary? Is it sufficient if survival differs in only one age class or season?
B. higher % of deaths by facultative predators in south than in north	no comparable data available	Definitions needed of facultative vs. obligate for N. American predators of hares. Is it sufficient if this requirement applies to only one age class? What magnitude of difference is necessary?

Krebs et al. 1995), it is distressing that the dominant models for explaining cycles and potential regional differences in cycles focus on predation. Reproductive changes occur cyclically and possibly regionally yet are given only minor attention in these models of hare dynamics. Even though hare survival appears to have more effect on numeric changes, explicit hypotheses should be developed that incorporate hares' food supply and reproductive changes. Furthermore, the degree of interspersion and the size of each habitat patch may matter as much to hare demography as does the actual proportion of each habitat type, so spatially explicit analyses need to be conducted.

Conclusions

Currently, our knowledge of snowshoe hares in their southern range is dominated by information on distribution and habitat use patterns. Our knowledge of hare numeric patterns is derived mainly from harvest records, and our knowledge of hare demographic patterns in their southern range tend to come from short-term studies (<5 years). All of these data sets are stronger in the northeast and around the Great Lakes than in the southern and western range of snowshoe hares. Time series of snowshoe hare density will be valuable throughout the range of snowshoe hares, but especially in the western and southern regions where few time series exist. The existing demographic studies suggest that patterns may be similar from north to south, but southern records tend to be shorter in duration; it will be valuable to assess the range of variation in demography in southern sites across a range of densities and population trends. The consensus of many studies from north to south is that hares utilize habitats with dense understories and many overstory species, but we do not yet have a complete understanding of how the degree of interspersion or spatial scale of fragmentation affect hare densities and population dynamics. Our future research should emphasize the interrelationship between habitats—at multiple scales and in various spatial arrays—and snowshoe hare population dynamics.

Acknowledgments

I wish I had more space to acknowledge the consistent and patient support of G. Koehler and C.J. Krebs; this chapter is much better than it would have been sans their support and their insightful comments. Three anonymous reviewers and members of the Lynx Science Team offered comments on the manuscript that have greatly strengthened it. S. Clark was indispensible: she was incredibly useful in contacting people and acquiring references for me, an effort that L. Moffatt additionally aided. This chapter relies on the generosity of many people who were willing to provide me with their unpublished, reports, and observations. I am extremely grateful to the following people for doing so: M. Boudreau, C. McLaughlin, K. Eagle, D. Dziak, G. Batchelar, A. Jacobson, J. Cardoza, G. Karasek, D. Ware, R. Lafond, R. Dibblee, D. Mitchell, J. Malloy, L. Ruggiero, G. Schmidt, C. Harris, J. Rieffenberger, C. Krebs, and D. Scott. I additionally benefitted from seeing an unpublished manuscript by D. Murray.

Literature Cited

Adams, L. 1959. An analysis of a population of snowshoe hares in northwestern Montana. Ecological Monographs 29:141-170.

Andersen, D. C., J. A. MacMahon, and M. L. Wolfe. 1980. Herbivorous mammals along a montane sere: community structure and energetics. Journal of Mammalogy 61:500-519.

Anonymous. 1985. Small game harvest trends. Conservation Nova Scotia 9(2):8.

August, J. B. 1974. A study of liberation of snowshoe hare on ancestral range in Virginia. MSc. Thesis. Virginia Polytechnic Institute and State University, Blacksburg.

Bailey, V. 1971. Mammals of the Southwestern United States. Dover Publications Inc., New York.

Bailey, R. G. 1997: Ecoregions map of North America. USDA Forest Service. Scale 1:15000000.

Beauvais, G. P. 1997. Mammals in fragmented forests in the Rocky Mountains: community structure, habitat selection, and individual fitness. Ph.D. Dissertation, University of Wyoming, Laramie.

Behrend, D. F. 1960. An analysis of snowshoe hare habitat on marginal range. Unpublished Report.

Berg, B. 1998. Minnesota grouse and hares, 1998. Unpublished report, Minnesota Department of Natural Resources.

Bergeron, J.-M. and J. Tardif. 1988. Winter browsing preferences of snowshoe hares for coniferous seedlings and its implication in large-scale reforestation programs. Canadian Journal of Forest Research 18:280-282.

Bider, J. R. 1961. An ecological study of the hare *Lepus americanus*. Canadian Journal of Zoology 39:81-103.

Bittner, S. L., and O. J. Rongstad. 1982. Snowshoe hare and allies. Pages 146-163 *in* J. A. Chapman and G. A. Feldhamer, editors. Wild mammals of North America: biology, management, and economics. Johns Hopkins University Press, Baltimore.

Black, H. C. 1965. An analysis of a population of snowshoe hares, *Lepus americanus washingtonii* Baird, in western Oregon. Ph.D. Dissertation, Oregon State University, Corvallis.

Black, H. C., E. Dimock II, J. Evans, and J. Rochelle. 1979. Animal damage to coniferous plantations in Oregon and Washington—Part I. A survey, 1963-1975. Forest Research Laboratory, Oregon State University, Corvallis. Research Bulletin 25.

Bloomer, S. E. M., T. Willebrand, I. M. Keith, and L. B. Keith. 1995. Impact of helminth parasitism on a snowshoe hare population in central Wisconsin: a field experiment. Canadian Journal of Zoology 73:1891-1898.

Bookhout, T. A. 1965a. Breeding biology of snowshoe hares in Michigan's upper peninsula. Journal of Wildlife Management 29:296-303.

Bookhout, T. A. 1965b. Feeding coactions between snowshoe hares and white-tailed deer in northern Michigan. Transactions of the North American Wildlife and Natural Resources Conference 30:321-335.

Boonstra, R., D. Hik, G. R. Singleton, and A. Tinnikov. 1998. The impact of predator-induced stress on the snowshoe hare cycle. Ecological Monographs 79:371-394.

Boonstra, R. and G. R. Singleton. 1993. Population declines in the snowshoe hare and the role of stress. General and Comparative Endocrinology 91:126-143.

Borrecco, J. E. 1976. Controlling damage by forest rodents and lagomorphs through habitat manipulation. Proceedings: Seventh Vertebrate Pest Conference, ed. C. S. Siebe, March 9-11 1976, Monterey, CA.

Boulanger, J. 1993. Evaluation of capture-recapture estimators using a cyclic snowshoe hare population. MSc Thesis, University of British Columbia.

Boutin, S. 1984. The effect of conspecifics on juvenile survival and recruitment of snowshoe hares. Journal of Animal Ecology 53:623-637.

Boutin, S., B. S. Gilbert, C. J. Krebs, A. R. E. Sinclair, and J. N. M. Smith. 1985. The role of dispersal in the population dynamics of snowshoe hares. Canadian Journal of Zoology 63:106-115.

Boutin, S. and C. J. Krebs. 1986. Estimating survival rates of snowshoe hares. Journal of Wildlife Management 50:592-594.

Boutin, S., C. J. Krebs, A. R. E. Sinclair, and J. N. M. Smith. 1986. Proximate causes of losses in a snowshoe hare population. Canadian Journal of Zoology 64:606-610.

Boyle, J. D. 1955. An evaluation of stocking New Brunswick hare, *Lepus americanus*, in Massachusetts mixed forest habitat. MSc Thesis, University of Massachusetts, Amherst.

Brocke, R. H. 1975. Preliminary guidelines for managing snowshoe hare habitat in the Adirondacks. Transactions of the Northeast Section, The Wildlife Society, Northeast Fish and Wildlife Conference, 32:46-66.

Brocke, R. H., J. L. Belant, and K. A. Gustafson. 1993. Lynx population and habitat survey in the White Mountain National Forest, New Hampshire. US Forest Service and State of New Hampshire Fish & Game Department, unpublished report.

Brooks, M. 1955. An isolated population of the Virginia varying hare. Journal of Wildlife Management 19:54-61.

Brown, D. F. 1984. Snowshoe hare populations, habitat, and management in northern hardwood forest regeneration areas. MSc Thesis, Pennsylvania State University, Collegeville.

Bryant, J. P. 1981. The regulation of snowshoe hare feeding behaviour during winter by plant antiherbivore chemistry. Pages 720-731 *in* K. Myers and C. D. MacInnes, editors. Proceedings of the World Lagomorph Conference. University of Guelph, Guelph.

Bryant, J. P. and P. J. Kuropat. 1980. Selection of winter forage by subarctic browsing vertebrates: the role of plant chemistry. Annual Review of Ecology and Systematics 11:261-285.

Brylski, P. V., P. W. Collins, E. D. Pierson, W. E. Rainey, and T. E. Kucera. 1998. Mammal species of special concern in California. California Department of Fish and Game, Wildlife Management Division.

Buehler, D. A. and L. B. Keith. 1982. Snowshoe hare distribution and habitat use in Wisconsin. Canadian Field-Naturalist 96:19-29.

Byrne, G. 1998. A Colorado winter track survey for snowshoe hares and other species. Colorado Division of Wildlife, unpublished report.

Cary, J. R. and L. B. Keith. 1979. Reproductive change in the 10-year cycle of snowshoe hares. Canadian Journal of Zoology 57:375-390.

Chitty, H. 1950. The snowshoe rabbit enquiry, 1946-1948. Journal of Animal Ecology 19:15-20.

Clark, W. R. 1973. Reproduction, survival and density of snowshoe hares in northeastern Utah. MSc. Thesis, Utah State University, Logan.

Conroy, M. J., L. W. Gysel, and G. R. Dudderar. 1979. Habitat components of clear-cut areas for snowshoe hares in Michigan. Journal of Wildlife Management 43:680-690.

Cook, D. B. and S. B. Robeson. 1945. Varying hare and forest succession. Ecology 26:406-410.

Corson, C. W. and E. G. Cheyney. 1928. Injury by rabbits to coniferous reproduction. Journal of Forestry 26:539-543.

Cox, E. W., R. A. Garrott, and J. R. Cary. 1997. Effect of supplemental cover on survival of snowshoe hares and cottontail rabbits in patchy habitat. Canadian Journal of Zoology 75:1357-1363.

Criddle, S. 1938. A study of the snowshoe rabbit. Canadian Field-Naturalist 52:31-40.

Davis, G. J. and R. K. Meyer. 1972. The effect of day length on pituitary FSH and LH and gonadal development of snowshoe hares. Biology of Reproduction 6:264-269.

Davis, G. J. and R. K. Meyer. 1973. FSH and LH in the snowshoe hare during the increasing phase of the 10-year cycle. General and Comparative Endocrinology 20:53-60.

de Vos, A. 1964. Food utilization of snowshoe hares on Manitoulin Island, Ontario. Journal of Forestry 62:238-244.

Dibello, F. J., S. M. Arthur, and W. B. Krohn. 1990. Food habits of sympatric coyotes, *Canis latrans*, red foxes, *Vulpes vulpes*, and bobcats, *Lynx rufus*, in Maine. Canadian Field-Naturalist 104:403-408.

Diefenbach, D. R. 1998. Game take and furtaker surveys. Pennsylvania Game Commission, Bureau of Wildlife Management Research Division, Annual Project Report, Project Job 11101.

Dodds, D. G. 1960. Food competition and range relationships of moose and snowshoe hare in Newfoundland. Journal of Wildlife Management 24:52-60.

Dodds, D. G. 1962. A preliminary survey of forest wildlife conditions in Nova Scotia. Wildlife Division, Nova Scotia Department of Lands and Forests.

Dodds, D. G. 1965. Reproduction and productivity of snowshoe hares in Newfoundland. Journal of Wildlife Management 29:303-315.

Dodds, D. G. and H. G. Thurber. 1965. Snowshoe hare (*Lepus americanus struthopus*) harvests on Long Island, Nova Scotia. Canadian Field-Naturalist 79:130-133.

Dolbeer, R. A. 1972a. Population dynamics of the snowshoe hare in Colorado. Ph.D. Dissertation, Colorado State University, Fort Collins.

Dolbeer, R. A. 1972b. The snowshoe hare in the Western United States: its status and potential as a game animal. Pages 331-342 *in* Proceedings of the 52nd Annual Conference of the Western Association, State Game & Fish Commission, Portland, OR.

Dolbeer, R. A. and W. R. Clark. 1975. Population ecology of snowshoe hares in the central Rocky Mountains. Journal of Wildlife Management 39:535-549.

Eaton, B. R. 1995. Estimates of snowshoe hare abundance from pellet plot counts: a critical evaluation. MSc Thesis, Acadia University, Wolfville.

Erdman, T. C., D. F. Brinker, J. P. Jacobs, J. Wilde, and T. O. Meyer. 1998. Productivity, population trend, and status of northern goshawks, *Accipiter gentilis atricapillus, in* northeastern Wisconsin. Canadian Field-Naturalist 112:17-27.

Erlinge, S. 1987. Predation and noncyclicity in a microtine population in southern Sweden. Oikos 50:347-352.

Erlinge, S., G. Goransson, L. Hansson, G. Hogstedt, O. Liberg, I. N. Nilsson, T. Nilsson, T. von Schantz, and M. Sylven. 1983. Predation as a regulating factor on small rodent populations in Southern Sweden. Oikos 40:36-52.

Ernest, J. 1974. Snowshoe hare studies. Final Report, Alaska Dept. Fish Game, W-17-4, W-17-5, W-17-6.

Ferron, J. and J.-P. Ouellet. 1992. Daily partitioning of summer habitat and use of space by the snowshoe hare in southern boreal forest. Canadian Journal of Zoology 70:2178-2183.

Ferron, J., F. Potvin, and C. Dussault. 1998. Short-term effects of logging on snowshoe hares in the boreal forest. Canadian Journal of Forest Research 28:1335-1343.

Fies, M. L. 1991. Snowshoe hare. Pages 576-578 *in* K. Terwilliger, editor. Virginia's endangered species: proceedings of a symposium. McDonald and Woodward Publishing Company, Blacksburg, VA.

Fies, M. L. 1993. Survival and movements of relocated snowshoe hares in western Virginia. Virginia Department of Game & Inland Fisheries Research Report.

Finerty, J. P. 1980. The population ecology of cycles in small mammals. Yale University Press, New Haven.

Fitzpatrick, W. A. 1957. The survival and movements of live trapped and introduced hares (*Lepus americanus*, Erxleben) in Massachusetts. MSc. Thesis. University of Massachusetts, Amherst.

Fortin, C. and J. Huot. 1995. Ecologie comparee du Coyote, du Lynx du Canada et du Renard roux au parc national Forillon. Universite Laval, Ste-Foy, Quebec.

Fox, J. F. 1978. Forest fires and the snowshoe hare-Canada lynx cycle. Oecologia 31:349-374.

Fox, J. F. and J. P. Bryant. 1984. Instability of the snowshoe hare and woody plant interaction. Oecologia 63:128-135.

Fuller, T. K. and D. M. Heisey. 1986. Density-related changes in winter distribution of snowshoe hares in northcentral Minnesota. Journal of Wildlife Management 50:261-264.

Giddings, B. 1998. Montana Division of Fish, Wildlife, and Parks. Unpublished report.

Gillis, E. A. 1997. Natal dispersal and post-weaning survival of juvenile snowshoe hares during a cyclic population increase. MSc Thesis, University of British Columbia, Vancouver.

Giuliano, W. M., J. A. Litvaitis, and C. L. Stevens. 1989. Prey selection in relation to sexual dimorphism of fishers (*Martes pennanti*) in New Hampshire. Journal of Mammalogy 70:639-641.

Glenzinski, B. and B. Dhuey. 1998. Wisconsin wildlife surveys. Unpublished, Wisconsin Department of Natural Resources.

Godin, A. J. 1977. Wild mammals of New England. Johns Hopkins Press, Baltimore.

Grange, W. B. 1932. Observations on the snowshoe hare, *Lepus americanus phaeonotus* Allen. Journal of Mammalogy 13:1-19.

Grange, W. B. 1965. Fire and tree growth relationships to snowshoe rabbits. Fire Ecology Conference 4:110-125.

Green, R. G. and C. A. Evans. 1940a. Studies on a population cycle of snowshoe hares on the Lake Alexander area. I. Gross annual censuses, 1932-1939. Journal of Wildlife Management 4:220-238.

Green, R. G. and C. A. Evans. 1940b. Studies on a population cycle of snowshoe hares on the Lake Alexander area. II. Mortality according to age groups and seasons. Journal of Wildlife Management 4:267-278.

Green, R. G. and C. A. Evans. 1940c. Studies on a population cycle of snowshoe hares on the Lake Alexander area. III. Effect of reproduction and mortality of young hares on the cycle. Journal of Wildlife Management 4:347-358.

Grigal, D. F. and N. R. Moody. 1980. Estimation of browse by size classes for snowshoe hare. Journal of Wildlife Management 44:34-40.

Halpin, M. A. and J. A. Bissonette. 1988. Influence of snow depth on prey availability and habitat use by red fox. Canadian Journal of Zoology 66:587-592.

Handley, C. J. 1978. Mammals. Pages 483-621 *in* D. W. Linzey, editor. Proceedings of the symposium on endangered and threatened plants and animals of Virginia. Virginia Polytechnic Institute and State University, Blacksburg.

Hanski, I., L. Hansson, and H. Henttonen. 1991. Specialist predators, generalist predators, and the microtine rodent cycle. Journal of Animal Ecology 60:353-367.

Hansson, L. 1987. An interpretation of rodent dynamics as due to trophic interactions. Oikos 50:308-318.

Hansson, L. and H. Henttonen. 1985. Gradients in density variations of small rodents: the importance of latitude and snow cover. Oecologia 67:394-402.

Hartman, F. H. 1960. Census techniques for snowshoe hares. MSc Thesis, Michigan State University, Lansing.

Haydon, D. T., E. A. Gillis, C. I. Stefan, and C. J. Krebs. 1999. Biases in the estimation of the demographic parameters of a snowshoe hare population. Journal of Animal Ecology in press.

Hess, Q. F. 1946. A trapper's record of animal abundance in the Oba-Hearst area of Ontario for the years 1931-1944. Canadian Field-Naturalist 60:31-32.

Hik, D. S. 1994. Predation risk and the 10-year snowshoe hare cycle. Ph.D. Dissertation, University of British Columbia,Vancouver.

Hik, D. S. 1995. Does risk of predation influence population dynamics? Evidence from the cyclic decline of snowshoe hares. Wildlife Research 22:115-129.

Hodges, K. E. 1998. Snowshoe hare demography and behaviour during a cyclic population low phase. Ph.D. Dissertation. University of British Columbia, Vancouver.

Hodges, K. E., C. J. Krebs, D. S. Hik, C. I. Stefan, E. A. Gillis, and C. E. Dagle. In press. Snowshoe hare demography. *in* C. J. Krebs, S. Boutin, R. Boonstra, editors. Vertebrate community dynamics in the boreal forest.

Hoefler, G. and R. Duke. 1996. Snowshoe hare. California Wildlife Habitat Relationships System, California Interagency Wildlife Task Group & California Department of Fish and Game.

Howell, A. B. 1923. Periodic fluctuations in the numbers of small mammals. Journal of Mammalogy 4:149-155.

Johnson, W. J. 1969. Food habits of the Isle Royale red fox and population aspects of three of its principal prey species. Ph.D. Dissertation, Purdue, West Lafayette.

Keith, L. B. 1963. Wildlife's ten-year cycle. University of Wisconsin Press, Madison.

Keith, L. B. 1966. Habitat vacancy during a snowshoe hare decline. Journal of Wildlife Management 30:828-832.

Keith, L. B. 1981. Population dynamics of hares. Pages 395-440 *in* K. Myers and C. D. MacInnes, editors. Proceedings of the World Lagomorph Conference. University of Guelph, Guelph.

Keith, L. B. 1983. Role of food in hare population cycles. Oikos 40:385-395.

Keith, L. B. 1990. Dynamics of snowshoe hare populations. Pages 119-195 *in* H. H. Genoways, editor. Current mammalogy. Plenum Press, New York.

Keith, L. B. and S. E. M. Bloomer. 1993. Differential mortality of sympatric snowshoe hares and cottontail rabbits in central Wisconsin. Canadian Journal of Zoology 71:1694-1697.

Keith, L. B., S. E. M. Bloomer, and T. Willebrand. 1993. Dynamics of a snowshoe hare population in fragmented habitat. Canadian Journal of Zoology 71:1385-1392.

Keith, L. B., J. R. Cary, O. J. Rongstad, and M. C. Brittingham. 1984. Demography and ecology of a declining snowshoe hare population. Wildlife Monographs 90:1-43.

Keith, L. B., O. J. Rongstad, and E. C. Meslow. 1966. Regional differences in reproductive traits of the snowshoe hare. Canadian Journal of Zoology 44:953-961.

Keith, L. B. and L. A. Windberg. 1978. A demographic analysis of the snowshoe hare cycle. Wildlife Monographs 58:1-70.

Koehler, G. M. 1990a. Population and habitat characteristics of lynx and snowshoe hares in north-central Washington. Canadian Journal of Zoology 68:845-851.

Koehler, G. M. 1990b. Snowshoe hare, *Lepus americanus,* use of forest successional stages and population changes during 1985-1989 in North-central Washington. Canadian Field-Naturalist 105:291-293.

Koehler, G. M. and J. D. Brittell. 1990. Managing spruce-fir habitat for lynx and snowshoe hares. Journal of Forestry 88(10):10-14.

Koehler, G. M., M. G. Hornocker, and H. S. Hash. 1979. Lynx movements and habitat use in Montana. Canadian Field-Naturalist 93:441-442.

Krebs, C. J. 1989. Ecological methodology. HarperCollins, New York.

Krebs, C. J. 1996. Population cycles revisited. Journal of Mammalogy 77:8-24.

Krebs, C. J., S. Boutin, R. Boonstra, A. R. E. Sinclair, J. N. M. Smith, M. R. T. Dale, K. Martin, and R. Turkington. 1995. Impact of food and predation on the snowshoe hare cycle. Science 269:1112-1115.

Krebs, C. J., B. S. Gilbert, S. Boutin, and R. Boonstra. 1987. Estimation of snowshoe hare population density from turd transects. Canadian Journal of Zoology 65:565-567.

Krebs, C. J., B. S. Gilbert, S. Boutin, A. R. E. Sinclair, and J. N. M. Smith. 1986. Population biology of snowshoe hares. I. Demography of food-supplemented populations in the southern Yukon, 1976-84. Journal of Animal Ecology 55:963-982.

Krefting, L. W. 1975. The effect of white-tailed deer and snowshoe hare browsing on trees and shrubs in northern Minnesota. Agricultural Experiment Station, University of Minnesota, Technical Bulletin 302-1975, Forestry Series 18.

Krenz, J. D. 1988. Effect of vegetation dispersion on the density of wintering snowshoe hares (*Lepus americanus*) in northern Minnesota. MSc Thesis. University of Minnesota, Duluth.

Kuehn, D. W. 1989. Winter foods of fishers during a snowshoe hare decline. Journal of Wildlife Management 53:688-692.

Kuvlesky, W. P. J. and L. B. Keith. 1983. Demography of snowshoe hare populations in Wisconsin. Journal of Mammalogy 64:233-244.

Leonard, R. D. 1980. The winter activity and movements, winter diet, and breeding biology of the fisher (*Martes pennanti*) in southeastern Manitoba. MSc Thesis, University of Manitoba, Winnipeg.

Lindström, E. R. 1994. Vole cycles, snow depth and fox predation. Oikos 70:156-160.

Litvaitis, J. A. 1984. Bobcat movements in relation to prey density. Ph.D. Dissertation. University of Maine, Orono.

Litvaitis, J. A. 1990. Differential habitat use by sexes of snowshoe hares (*Lepus americanus*). Journal of Mammalogy 71:520-523.

Litvaitis, J. A., J. A. Sherburne, and J. A. Bissonette. 1985a. A comparison of methods used to examine snowshoe hare habitat use. Journal of Wildlife Management 49:693-695.

Litvaitis, J. A., J. A. Sherburne, and J. A. Bissonette. 1985b. Influence of understory characteristics on snowshoe hare habitat use and density. Journal of Wildlife Management 49:866-873.

Litvaitis, J. A., J. A. Sherburne, and J. A. Bissonette. 1986. Bobcat habitat use and home range size in relation to prey density. Journal of Wildlife Management 50:110-117.

Lloyd-Smith, J. and H. Piene. 1981. Snowshoe hare girdling of balsam fir on the Cape Breton highlands. Maritime Forest Research Centre, Fredericton, NB. Information Report M-X-124. Canadian Forest Service.

MacLulich, D. A. 1937. Fluctuations in the numbers of the varying hare (*Lepus americanus*). University of Toronto Studies, Biological Series, No. 43.

Manly, B. F. J., L. L. MacDonald, and D. L. Thomas. 1993. Resource selection by animals: statistical design and analysis for field studies. Chapman & Hall, London.

Marshall, W. H. 1954. Ruffed grouse and snowshoe hare populations on the Cloquet Experimental Forest, Minnesota. Journal of Wildlife Management 18:109-112.

Meslow, E. C. and L. B. Keith. 1971. A correlation analysis of weather versus snowshoe hare population parameters. Journal of Wildlife Management 35:1-15.

Monthey, R. W. 1986. Responses of snowshoe hares, *Lepus americanus*, to timber harvesting in northern Maine. Canadian Field-Naturalist 100:568-570.

Murray, D. L., S. Boutin, and M. O'Donoghue. 1994. Winter habitat selection by lynx and coyotes in relation to snowshoe hare abundance. Canadian Journal of Zoology 72:1444-1451.

Murray, D. L., S. Boutin, M. O'Donoghue, and V. O. Nams. 1995. Hunting behaviour of a sympatric felid and canid in relation to vegetative cover. Animal Behaviour 50:1203-1210.

Murray, D. L., J. R. Cary, and L. B. Keith. 1997. Interactive effects of sublethal nematodes and nutritional status on snowshoe hare vulnerability to predation. Journal of Animal Ecology 66:250-264.

Nagorsen, D. W. 1985. A morphometric study of geographic variation in the snowshoe hare (*Lepus americanus*). Canadian Journal of Zoology 63:567-579.

Newson, J. 1964. Reproduction and prenatal mortality of snowshoe hares on Manitoulin Island, Ontario. Canadian Journal of Zoology 42:987-1005.

Newson, R. and A. de Vos. 1964. Population structure and body weights of snowshoe hares on Manitoulin Island, Ontario. Canadian Journal of Zoology 42:975-986.

O'Donoghue, M. 1983. Seasonal habitat selection by snowshoe hare in eastern Maine. Transactions of the Northeast Section, Fish & Wildlife Conference 40:100-107.

O'Donoghue, M. 1994. Early survival of juvenile snowshoe hares. Ecology 75:1582-1592.

O'Donoghue, M. 1997. Responses of coyotes and lynx to the snowshoe hare cycle. Ph.D. Dissertation. University of British Columbia, Vancouver.

O'Donoghue, M. and S. Boutin. 1995. Does reproductive synchrony affect juvenile survival rates of northern mammals? Oikos 74:115-121.

O'Donoghue, M. and C. J. Krebs. 1992. Effects of supplemental food on snowshoe hare reproduction and juvenile growth at a cyclic population peak. Journal of Animal Ecology 61:631-641.

Orr, C. D. and D. G. Dodds. 1982. Snowshoe hare habitat preferences in Nova Scotia spruce-fir forests. Wildlife Society Bulletin 10:147-150.

Parker, G. R., J. W. Maxwell, L. D. Morton, and G. E. J. Smith. 1983. The ecology of the lynx (*Lynx canadensis*) on Cape Breton Island. Canadian Journal of Zoology 61:770-786.

Pease, J. L., R. H. Vowles, and L. B. Keith. 1979. Interaction of snowshoe hares and woody vegetation. Journal of Wildlife Management 43:43-60.

Peterson, R. O. 1998. Ecological studies of wolves on Isle Royale, Annual Report 1997-98.

Pulliam, H. R. 1988. Sources, sinks, and population regulation. American Naturalist 132:652-661.

Radwan, M. A. and D. L. Campbell. 1968. Snowshoe hare preference for spotted catsear flowers in western Washington. Journal of Wildlife Management 32:104-108.

Raine, R. M. 1987. Winter food habits and foraging behaviour of fishers (*Martes pennanti*) and martens (*Martes americana*) in southeastern Manitoba. Canadian Journal of Zoology 65:745-747.

Reed, D. F., G. Byrne, and J. Kindler. 1999. Snowshoe hare density/distribution estimates and potential release sites for reintroducing lynx in Colorado. Colorado Division of Wildlife Report, unpublished.

Richmond, M. E. and C.-Y. Chien. 1976. Status of the snowshoe hare on the Connecticut Hill wildlife management area. New York Fish and Game Journal 23:1-12.

Rogowitz, G. L. 1988. Forage quality and use of reforested habitats by snowshoe hares. Canadian Journal of Zoology 66:2080-2083.

Rohner, C. and C. J. Krebs. 1996. Owl predation on snowshoe hares: consequences of antipredator behaviour. Oecologia 108:303-310.

Rohner, C., J. N. M. Smith, J. Stroman, and M. Joyce. 1995. Northern hawk-owls in the nearctic boreal forest: prey selection and population consequences of multiple prey cycles. Condor 97:208-220.

Roppe, J. A. and D. Hein. 1978. Effects of fire on wildlife in a lodgepole pine forest. Southwestern Naturalist 23:279-288.

Rowan, W. and L. B. Keith. 1956. Reproductive potential and sex ratios of snowshoe hares in northern Alberta. Canadian Journal of Zoology 34:273-281.

Schultz, W. C. 1980. Extent and causes of mortality in stocked snowshoe hares. Journal of Wildlife Management 44:716-719.

Scott, D. P. and R. H. Yahner. 1989. Winter habitat and browse use by snowshoe hares, *Lepus americanus*, in a marginal habitat in Pennsylvania. Canadian Field-Naturalist 103:560-563.

Sievert, P. R. and L. B. Keith. 1985. Survival of snowshoe hares at a geographic range boundary. Journal of Wildlife Management 49:854-866.

Smith, C. H. 1983. Spatial trends in Canadian snowshoe hare, *Lepus americanus*, population cycles. Canadian Field-Naturalist 97:151-160.

Smith, J. N. M., C. J. Krebs, A. R. E. Sinclair, and R. Boonstra. 1988. Population biology of snowshoe hares. II. Interactions with winter food plants. Journal of Animal Ecology 57:269-286.

Sondrini, W. J. 1950. Estimating game from licensee reports. Connecticut State Board of Fisheries and Game, Hartford.

Sprugel, D. G. 1983. Correcting for bias in log-transformed allometric equations. Ecology 64:209-210.

Stefan, C. I. 1998. Reproduction and pre-weaning juvenile survival in a cyclic population of snowshoe hares. MSc Thesis, University of British Columbia, Vancouver.

Stenseth, N. C., W. Falck, O. N. Bjørnstad, and C. J. Krebs. 1997. Population regulation in snowshoe hare and Canadian lynx: asymmetric food web configurations between hare and lynx. Proceedings of the National Academy of Science, USA 94:5147-5152.

Stephenson, D. E. 1985. The use of charred black spruce bark by snowshoe hare. Journal of Wildlife Management 49:296-300.

Sullivan, T. P. 1994. Influence of herbicide-induced habitat alteration on vegetation and snowshoe hare populations in sub-boreal spruce forest. Journal of Applied Ecology 31:717-730.

Sullivan, T. P. 1996. Influence of forest herbicide on snowshoe hare population dynamics: reproduction, growth, and survival. Canadian Journal of Forest Research 26:112-119.

Sullivan, T. P. and R. A. Moses. 1986. Demographic and feeding responses of a snowshoe hare population to habitat alteration. Journal of Applied Ecology 23:53-63.

Sullivan, T. P. and D. S. Sullivan. 1982a. Barking damage by snowshoe hares and red squirrels in lodgepole pine stands in central British Columbia. Canadian Journal of Forest Research 12:443-448.

Sullivan, T. P. and D. S. Sullivan. 1982b. Influence of fertilization on feeding attacks on lodgepole pine by snowshoe hares and red squirrels. Forestry Chronicle 58:263-266.

Sullivan, T. P. and D. S. Sullivan. 1983. Use of index lines and damage assessments to estimate population densities of snowshoe hares. Canadian Journal of Zoology 61:163-167.

Sullivan, T. P. and D. S. Sullivan. 1986. Impact of feeding damage by snowshoe hares on growth rates of juvenile lodgepole pine in central British Columbia. Canadian Journal of Forest Research 16: 1145-1149.

Swayze, L. A. 1994. Snowshoe hare use patterns in selected lodgepole pine stands in north-central Washington. Unpublished report, Okanogan National Forest, Washington.

Telfer, E. S. 1972. Browse selection by deer and hares. Journal of Wildlife Management 36:1344-1349.

Thomas, J. A., J. G. Hallett, and M. A. O'Connell. 1997. Habitat use by snowshoe hares in managed landscapes of northeastern Washington. Washington Department of Fish & Wildlife, USDA Forest Service.

Tompkins, D. B. and J. R. Woehr. 1979. Influence of habitat on movements and densities of snowshoe hares. Transactions of the Northeast Section, Wildlife Society, Fish & Wildlife Conference 36:169-175.

Trapp, G. R. 1962. Snowshoe hares in Alaska. II Home range and ecology during an early population increase. MSc Thesis, University of Alaska, Fairbanks.

Trent, T. T. and O. J. Rongstad. 1974. Home range and survival of cottontail rabbits in southwestern Wisconsin. Journal of Wildlife Management 38:459-472.

Van Horne, B. 1983. Density as a misleading indicator of habitat quality. Journal of Wildlife Management 47:893-901.

Verts, B. J. and L. N. Carraway. 1998. Land mammals of Oregon. University of California Press, Berkeley.

Vowles, R. H. 1972. Snowshoe hare-vegetation interactions at Rochester, Alberta. MSc. Thesis, University of Wisconsin, Madison.

Walski, T. W. and W. W. Mautz. 1977. Nutritional evaluation of three winter browse species of snowshoe hares. Journal of Wildlife Management 41:144-147.

Williams, D. F. 1986. Mammalian species of special concern in California. California Department of Fish and Game, Admininstrative Report 86-1.

Windberg, L. A. and L. B. Keith. 1978. Snowshoe hare populations in woodlot habitat. Canadian Journal of Zoology 56:1071-1080.

Wolfe, M. L., N. V. Debyle, C. S. Winchell, and T. R. McCabe. 1982. Snowshoe hare cover relationships in northern Utah. Journal of Wildlife Management 46:662-670.

Wolff, J. O. 1978. Food habits of snowshoe hares in interior Alaska. Journal of Wildlife Management 42:148-153.

Wolff, J. O. 1980. The role of habitat patchiness in the population dynamics of snowshoe hares. Ecological Monographs 50:111-130.

Wolff, J. O. 1981. Refugia, dispersal, predation, and geographic variation in snowshoe hare cycles. Pages 441-449 *in* K. Myers and C. D. MacInnes, editors. Proceedings of the World Lagomorph Conference. University of Guelph, Guelph.

Wood, T. J. and S. A. Munroe. 1977. Dynamics of snowshoe hare populations in the Maritime Provinces. Canadian Wildlife Service, Occasional Paper number 30.

Zielinski, W. J., W. D. Spencer, and R. H. Barrett. 1983. Relationship between food habits and activity patterns of pine martens. Journal of Mammalogy 64:387-396.

Chapter 8

History and Distribution of Lynx in the Contiguous United States

Kevin S. McKelvey, USDA Forest Service, Rocky Mountain Research Station, 800 E. Beckwith, Missoula, MT 59807

Keith B. Aubry, USDA Forest Service, Pacific Northwest Research Station, 3625 93rd Ave. SW, Olympia, WA 98512

Yvette K. Ortega, USDA Forest Service, Rocky Mountain Research Station, 800 E. Beckwith, Missoula, MT 59807

Abstract—Using written accounts, trapping records, and spatially referenced occurrence data, the authors reconstructed the history and distribution of lynx in the contiguous United States from the 1800s to the present. Records show lynx occurrence in 24 states. Data over broad scales of space and time show lynx distribution relative to topography and vegetation. For all three study regions (Northeastern states, Great Lakes and North-Central states, and Western Mountain states), high frequencies of occurrence were in cool, coniferous forests, with occurrences at primarily higher elevations in the West.

Introduction

Understanding the geographic distribution of an organism can provide important insights into its ecology. In this chapter we compile and analyze occurrence data for lynx in the contiguous United States. We've organized our analyses into three sections. In the first, we evaluate available information on the history of lynx occurrence. Because data were generally collected independently by each state, this analysis is presented state-by-state. In the second, we evaluate the extent to which population dynamics of lynx in the states adjacent to Canada are associated with Canadian population dynamics and investigate the nature of observed relationships. In the third section, we identify the broadly defined vegetation cover types and elevation zones that encompass the majority of lynx occurrence records and examine the spatial relationships of records occurring outside these core areas.

The Nature of the Data

The analyses and discussion presented in this chapter are based on a variety of data from many sources. We believe they represent most of what is known concerning where and when lynx have occurred within the contiguous United States. We divide these data into three types. The first type is written accounts describing the occurrence patterns of lynx. For many of these accounts, and particularly the older ones, data are not presented to support the written statements. Because of the paucity of other information, our understandings of the historical distribution of lynx prior to the 20th century rely heavily on these accounts.

The second type of data are state- and province-level trapping records. These data are recorded in Novak et al. (1987) for all states and Canadian provinces that maintained records. The strength of trapping data is that it has been collected annually for many years using similar methods. These data have been used to analyze time trends (Elton and Nicholson 1942; Ranta et al. 1997), but there are several problems associated with using these data in this manner. A general problem with trapping data is that they do not represent constant effort: More lynx trapped could be due to more trapper effort rather than more lynx. A particular problem associated with lynx is confusion with bobcats, especially large, pale bobcats that were often referred to as "lynx-cats" (Novak et al. 1987). For these reasons, we limit our analysis of trapping data to those states for which we could confirm that lynx and bobcat harvest records were tabulated separately.

Lastly we have spatially referenced occurrence data. These data come from many sources: the primary literature, unpublished reports, museum specimens, state survey efforts, and casual observations (See Appendix 8.1). These data, because of their sources and types, have varying reliability. Although these data carry a reliability index, the index is not constant across data sets. Even if it were, reliability at the level of the individual observation does not necessarily infer overall reliability for a data set. Reliability of the data set depends not only on the intrinsic reliability of each datum, but also on the rarity of the organism. That is, as an organism becomes more rare, the proportion of false positives increases. For example, we know that bobcats are sometimes misidentified as lynx. If lynx were correctly identified 100% of the time and bobcats correctly identified 99% of the time, we have very reliable identification at the level of the individual observation. However, if 1,000 bobcats are seen for every lynx, then for every 1,000 wildcat identifications 10 will be classified as lynx, but on average only one will actually be a lynx. Even if lynx were extirpated from the area in question, these data would still include 10 "lynx." While we note the number of "reliable" points by type for each state (Table 8.1), we do no formal analyses based on these designations. Rather, for analyses where high reliability for each occurrence is essential, we used a subset of these data we call "verified records." We considered a record to be verified only if it was represented by a museum specimen or a written account in which a lynx was either in someone's possession or observed closely, i.e., where a lynx was killed, photographed, trapped and released, or treed by dogs. Information obtained from snow-tracking surveys conducted by trained individuals are discussed where appropriate, but neither tracks nor sighting reports were considered to represent a verified record.

Data quantity and quality vary greatly from state to state (Table 8.1). Because none of these data, with the possible exception of trapping records, represent anything like a census, using numbers of occurrences to infer numbers of lynx in an area during a specific time period or to make comparisons between states is not appropriate. Assessing changes in occurrence at the state level can be attempted from the verified records, but we caution that inferences derived from those data are potentially unreliable. We know, for instance, that a lynx was killed in New Hampshire in 1992. This does not, however, lead to any conclusions concerning the current status of lynx populations in New Hampshire. Similarly, simply because we have no verified records for lynx in Michigan after 1985 does not mean that lynx are currently absent from Michigan.

In most states, the majority of the data consist of physical remains or track data collected by state agencies. In the West, however, Colorado and Oregon have a high proportion of visual data (Table 8.1), and the patterns in these states should be considered to be less reliable. In the Great Lakes states, Wisconsin has a high proportion of visual sightings, but the areas in which they occur also contain physical specimens and particularly tracks.

Table 8.1—Lynx occurrence data used in this chapter. R means reliable, U means of unknown reliability. See text for a discussion of data types and reliability. Unknown occurrences were often older records in existing databases where data other than the location were not retained. In the western states, many records of unknown reliability are associated with locations reported by Maj and Garton (1994) that are not duplicated in other databases.

State	Spatially referenced occurrences[a] Physical[b] R	U	Tracks R	U	Visual R	U	Unknown	Total	Trapping[c] Time period	Number	Verified records[d] Time period	Number
Colorado	33	0	25	25	26	45	42	196			1878-1974	17
Connecticut	0	0	0	0	0	0	0	0			1839	1
Idaho	96	0	74	1	58	4	1	234			1874-1991	74
Illinois	0	0	0	0	0	0	0	0			1842	1
Indiana	0	0	0	0	0	0	0	0			1832	1
Iowa	1	0	0	0	0	0	0	1			1869-1963	6
Maine	15	4	6	1	0	2	0	28			1862-1999	35
Massachusetts	0	0	0	0	0	0	0	0			1855-1918	5
Michigan	32	23	8	5	2	2	9	81			1842-1983	44
Minnesota	179	6	7	4	4	6	81	287	1930-1983	5,585	1892-1993	76
Montana	588	0	518	24	63	7	342	1,542	1950-1997	3,012	1887-1999	84
North Dakota	7	0	0	0	0	0	1	8			1850-1963	16
Nebraska	4	0	0	0	0	0	4	8			1890-1983	13
New Hampshire	40	1	7	5	3	6	0	62	1928-1964	139	1860-1992	5
Nevada	2	0	0	0	0	0	0	2			1916	2
New York	13	2	0	0	1	0	1	17			1877-1973	24
Oregon	15	5	0	1	9	27	15	72			1897-1993	12
Pennsylvania	1	1	0	0	0	0	0	2			1903-1926	4
South Dakota	3	0	0	0	0	0	3	6			1875-1973	10
Utah	11	1	2	0	4	4	5	27			1916-1991	10
Vermont	4	0	0	0	0	0	0	4			1928-1965	4
Washington	144	7	384	107	43	23	57	765	1960-1989	215	1896-1999	134
Wisconsin	12	32	7	42	4	65	0	162			1870-1992	29
Wyoming	83	5	92	7	113	18	43	361			1856-1999	30

[a] Only data spatially referenced to at least the county level are included in these totals.

[b] Physical remains data also include photographs, radiotelemetry collared animals, and recent hair samples. These other occurrence types generally make up a tiny proportion of the total.

[c] Trapping data are presented for those states where we confirmed the reliability of these data.

[d] Verified records are spatially referenced to the state and in some cases contain additional records not in the spatially referenced occurrence data.

History of Lynx Occurrence in the Contiguous United States

In previously published distribution maps for lynx in North America, the lynx's range in the United States is depicted as marginal or peninsular extensions of the northern taiga into the western mountains, Great Lakes region, and Northeast (Burt 1946; Seton 1929; Hall 1981; McCord and Cardoza 1982). As explained in Chapter 3, these regions represent southern extensions of boreal forest in the United States, each of which has unique tree species composition, natural disturbance regimes, and histories of human-mediated changes in the composition, extent, and juxtaposition of available habitats. In the next section, we review the history of lynx occurrence and abundance in each of these three regions on a state-by-state basis. Although state boundaries generally do not correspond to ecological ones, lynx populations are managed by individual state wildlife or game agencies, and published literature is often limited to reporting or summarizing information from a particular state.

To evaluate the history of lynx occurrence in the contiguous United States, we compiled verified records from each state by obtaining data on museum specimens and reviewing published literature and unpublished state agency reports and harvest records. If there was a discrepancy between published tabulations of harvest data (Novak et al. 1987) and records obtained directly from state or provincial agencies, we assumed the latter to be more reliable and used those data in our analyses. To obtain museum specimen records of lynx in the contiguous United States, we contacted 88 museums or private collections in North America, including all mammal collections with >10,000 specimens, any museum from which lynx specimens had been reported, and at least one major museum from each state in which lynx have been reported to occur. We located 343 museum records of lynx in the contiguous United States from 41 museums or private collections, dating from 1842 to 1993.

Northeastern States

Maine—We located 35 museum specimens from Maine: 15 have no date associated with them and 12 were collected between 1862 and 1897. Only eight were obtained during this century: one in 1903, four in 1948, two in 1954, and one in 1993. Among these specimens, seven are kittens that either have no date of collection or were collected in the 1860s, verifying that a breeding population of lynx occurred in Maine during historical times. Reproduction of lynx in Maine during recent times was verified in 1964, when three kittens were presented to the state for bounty; additional verified records are known from 1966, 1973 (2 lynx), 1987, 1989, 1990, 1993, and 1998 (Hunt 1974; Jakubus 1997; Maine Dept. of Inland Fisheries and Wildlife, unpublished). Anecdotal evidence suggests that lynx were also breeding in the state during the 1970s; Chief Warden Alanson Noble reported seeing an adult lynx and kitten on the Southwest Branch of the St. John River in March 1976 (Jakubus 1997). Snow-tracking surveys have been conducted by the Maine Dept. of Inland Fisheries and Wildlife in areas with historical lynx records each winter since 1994-1995. Lynx tracks were found in all years to date except 1995-1996 and 1996-1997 (Jakubus 1997; C. McLaughlin, personal communication). Radiotelemetry research on lynx was initiated by the state in 1999; to date (September 1999), one female and one male lynx have been trapped and radio-collared. In June 1999, radiotelemetry monitoring of the female led researchers to a den with 2 kittens, verifying reproduction of lynx in Maine for the first time since 1964 (C. McLaughlin, personal communication).

Written records of Manly Hardy, a trapper and fur buyer in northern and eastern Maine during the late 1800s, indicate that during this time lynx occurred only in the northern portion of the state, and were not abundant; Manly also noted that lynx numbers varied greatly in different years, suggesting that population fluctuations may have occurred historically (Jakubus 1997, unpublished). According to Palmer (1937, unpublished), lynx had not been found in extreme southwestern Maine since the time of European colonization; by the 1930s, lynx only occurred in the northern half of the state. By the mid-1960s, lynx were reportedly absent from all but the north and northwestern portion of the state, where they were considered scarce (Hunt 1964). In 1967, the Maine legislature repealed the lynx bounty payment and gave the species complete protection from hunting or trapping.

New Hampshire—New Hampshire is the only state in the Northeast with a long and detailed history of commercial lynx harvest: From 1928 to 1964, 139 lynx were harvested in New Hampshire (Orff 1985, unpublished). In the 10-year period from 1928 to 1939, 114 lynx were harvested (mean = 10.4 per year, range 1-20), but the population appears to have declined significantly in the late 1930s; only 25 lynx were taken from 1940 to 1964 (mean = 1.0 per year, range 0-3), when trapping of lynx in the White Mountain National Forest was prohibited (Fig. 8.1). According to data compiled by Clark Stevens of the University of New Hampshire, 97% of lynx bountied from 1931 to 1954 were killed in the White Mountains of northern New Hampshire in Coos, Grafton, and Carroll Counties (Silver 1974). In 1965, the bounty was repealed by the State legislature but was reinstituted outside the

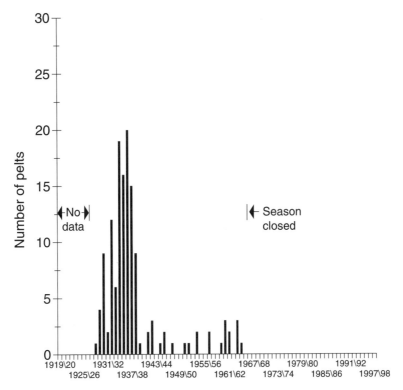

Figure 8.1—Lynx harvest data from New Hampshire, 1928-1964.

White Mountains in 1967 (Siegler 1971). In 1971, the lynx was protected from all harvest in New Hampshire; in 1980 it was listed as a state endangered species (Orff 1985, unpublished).

Except for harvest data, there are few verified records of lynx from New Hampshire; only four museum specimens are known: one undated and one each from 1860, 1947, and 1948. Only two recent verified records are known from New Hampshire; both were adult males that were road-killed in 1966 and 1992 (Litvaitis 1994; E. Orff, personal communication). From January to March 1986, Litvaitis et al. (1991) surveyed approximately 100 km^2 of the White Mountain National Forest on snowshoes (20 transects 2.5-10.0 km long) 24-96 hours after snowfall but found no lynx tracks. They concluded that their failure to find tracks and the scarcity of recent verified detections indicated that a viable population of lynx did not occur in New Hampshire at that time. We found no direct evidence of lynx breeding in New Hampshire in either historic or recent times.

The history of lynx in New Hampshire has been summarized in detail by several authors (Litvaitis et al. 1991; Siegler 1971; Silver 1974). Information on lynx occurrence and population status prior to the early 1900s is fragmentary and difficult to interpret because lynx and bobcat were typically considered together as "wildcat" in early records and reports (Silver 1974). From the late 1920s through the 1930s, lynx harvests in New Hampshire were relatively high (from 1934 to 1937, ≥15 lynx were trapped/year) and fluctuated strongly in number, reaching a peak in the mid-1930s that was coincident with a population peak recorded in Quebec (Figs. 8.1 and 8.2; Litvaitis et al. 1991). After 1940, lynx harvests remained low (0-3 trapped/year) until the trapping season was closed in 1965 (Fig. 8.1). Based on these records, Litvaitis et al. (1991) argued that historic populations of lynx in New Hampshire (and, probably, Maine) and Quebec were continuous at one time, and that immigrating lynx entered New Hampshire on a regular basis. They further speculated that large-scale timber harvesting for agricultural and residential development north of the Saint Lawrence Seaway in southern Quebec resulted in the isolation of lynx populations in New England, which were unable to remain viable without occasional immigrations of lynx from the north.

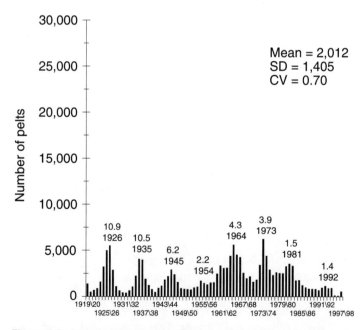

Figure 8.2—Lynx harvest data for Quebec, 1919-1997; peak years are indicated, as well as a measure of amplitude calculated by dividing the peak harvest value by the previous low harvest value.

Vermont—Published distribution maps for lynx in New England include Vermont within the range of lynx (Hamilton 1943; Godin 1977), but only four records verifying their occurrence at any time in the state could be found. Only one museum specimen is known from Vermont, a lynx collected in 1965 from Royalton in northern Windsor County. A lynx was reportedly killed in 1928 in Windam, Windam County (Osgood 1938); another was taken in Ripton, Addison County in 1937 (Hamilton and Whittaker 1979), and a third was trapped in the town of St. Albans, Franklin County in 1968 (Anonymous 1987, unpublished). In 1987, the Vermont Agency of Natural Resources classified the lynx as a state endangered species.

Massachusetts and Connecticut—No museum specimens of lynx could be found from Massachusetts or Connecticut, and verified records of lynx occurrence in these states are extremely rare. Parker (1939) describes a mounted specimen in the Worcester Museum of Natural History taken in Princeton in the winter of 1884-1885, but we were unable to locate this specimen. A lynx was reportedly killed in Concord, Middlesex County about 1855 (F.C.B. 1878), one was trapped about 1865 in Goshen, Hampshire County (Barrus 1881), one was killed in 1905 in Lanesborough, Berkshire County (Central 1905), and another was captured in 1918 near Mt. Greylock, also in Berkshire County (Eaton 1919). Crane (1931) considered the lynx to be "very rare" in western Massachusetts and quoted a report from 1840 that stated, "[The lynx] was once common in the State, but appears now only in the depth of winter, and as a straggler." The lynx is now considered extirpated from Massachusetts (Cardoza, in press). Only one verified record of lynx in Connecticut was found: one was shot at Southington, Hartford County in 1839 (Goodwin 1935). Goodwin (1935) concluded that the "lynx is now a very rare animal in Connecticut, and it probably never was very common."

New York—The history of lynx in New York was described in detail by Bergstrom (1977, unpublished) and Brocke (1982, unpublished), and much of the following account comes from these sources. Historical records suggest that the lynx was once relatively common in New York, but that its range retreated northeastward as early as the mid- to late-1800s. Rafinesque (1817) observed lynx in the Catskill, Allegheny, and Adirondack Mountains, and a lynx was killed near Rhineback on the Hudson River in the eastern foothills of the Catskill Mountains in southeastern New York during the winter of 1877-1878 (Mearns 1899). A report on the zoology of New York in 1842, however, failed to note the lynx's presence in the southern portion of the state, describing its range as "not uncommon in the northern districts of the state [presumably the Adirondack Mountains]" (DeKay 1842). Anecdotal reports gathered by Harper (1929) indicated that the lynx was fairly common in the Adirondacks in the 1880s and 1890s, but a report on the mammals of the Adirondack region in 1884 described the lynx as rare and occurring mostly in the eastern portions of the region (Merriam 1884). By the turn of the century, Miller (1899) speculated that, although the lynx still occurred in the Adirondacks and may still occur in the Catskills, the species was rapidly approaching extinction in New York.

Verified evidence of the occurrence of lynx in New York after 1900 consists of 23 records scattered in time from 1907 to 1973 (Table 8.2). All but four of these records are from the Adirondack Mountains, an area of boreal forest adjacent to the Green Mountains of Vermont and the White Mountains of New Hampshire. These high-elevation boreal zones may have served as a corridor of suitable habitat, providing connectivity among areas occupied by lynx in the northeastern United States with those in southeastern Canada (see map in Bailey 1998). Until 1970, the lynx was an unprotected species in New York and bounty payments were made for their pelts. The bounty was removed in 1970, but the lynx remained unprotected until 1976, when it was declared a game animal with closed hunting and trapping seasons. The New York Department of Environmental Conservation considers the lynx to be extirpated as a breeding species in the State, and has recommended that it be listed as a state endangered species (Bergstrom 1977, unpublished).

In response to a lack of evidence for the continued presence of lynx in the State, a program to reintroduce lynx to the Adirondack Mountains was initiated in the late 1970s (Brocke et al. 1990). A feasibility study (Brocke 1982,

Table 8.2–Verified records of lynx in New York.

Date	Record	Reference
Unknown	1 specimen from Jefferson County (western Adirondacks)	Academy of Natural Sciences of Philadelphia
1877-88	1 killed near Rhinebeck on the Hudson River (southeastern New York)	Mearns 1899
1907	2 killed in Willseyville, Tioga County (south-central New York)	Seagers 1948
1908	1 killed in Nine Mile Swamp, near North Brookfield (Adirondacks)	Whish 1919
1908	3 killed in the Quaker Bridge region (Adirondacks)	Whish 1919
1909	5 killed near Lowville, Lewis County (western Adirondacks)	Whish 1919
1916	1 killed in Oneida County (southwestern Adirondacks)	Anonymous 1952
1918	1 trapped near Upper Jay, Essex County (northeastern Adirondacks)	Anonymous 1918
1928	1 killed on Hogback Mountain, Essex County (northeastern Adirondacks)	Anonymous 1952
1930	1 taken alive near Elizabethtown, Essex County (northeastern Adirondacks)	Seagers 1948
Late 1930s	1 killed near Azure Mountain, Waverly, Franklin County (northern Adirondacks)	Bergstrom 1977, unpublished
1951	1 shot on Battle Hill, Washington County (eastern New York)	Seagers 1951
1961	1 shot near Sherman Lake, Crown Point, Essex County (northeastern Adirondacks)	Bergstrom 1977, unpublished
1962	1 trapped on Black Cat Mountain in Arietta, Hamilton County (central Adirondacks)	Anonymous 1963
1964	1 killed near Croghan, Lewis County (western Adirondacks)	Fountain 1976
Winter 1965-66	1 trapped on Pine Mountain, near Wells, Hamilton County (central Adirondacks)	Anonymous 1966
1968	1 specimen from Catskill, Delaware County (southeastern New York)	American Museum of Natural History
1973	1 trapped in Altona, Clinton County (northeastern Adirondacks)	Bergstrom 1977, unpublished

unpublished) indicated that a suitable colonization area for lynx existed in the Adirondacks above 800 m where bobcats (a potential competitor) were rare and where snowshoe hare populations were dense enough to support lynx. Between 1989 and 1991, after about 10 years of planning and public input, 83 lynx ranging in age from <1 to 10.5 years were translocated from the Whitehorse area of the Yukon Territory in Canada, radio-collared, and released in the High Peaks area of the Adirondack Mountains (Brocke et al. 1991; K. Gustafson, personal communication). These animals were monitored for two years until the transmitter batteries failed; recorded mortality was high: 37 of 83 were known to have died, 16 of which were road-killed. Available evidence indicates that the reintroduction was unsuccessful; since the last radiotracking season in the winter of 1992-1993, there have been no verified records of lynx in the Adirondacks and no indication that any reintroduced lynx bred after they were released (K. Gustafson, personal communication).

Pennsylvania—A comprehensive review of paleontological, historical, and specimen records of lynx in Pennsylvania was conducted by Williams et al. (1985). Surprisingly, they report 26 records of lynx being killed in Pennsylvania from 1790 to 1900. Bobcats and lynx were often confused in reports from the 18th and 19th centuries, however, so we view these records with caution. Recent records are extremely scarce: Only one museum specimen exists, a lynx collected near Antrium, Tioga County in 1923. A lynx was reportedly killed in 1903 in Clinton County and two others in 1926 in Monroe County (Shoemaker 1929; Grimm and Whitebread 1952, unpublished). The majority of records reported by Williams et al. (1985) are from the northern counties where unbroken, mature boreal forest existed prior to extensive logging of Pennsylvania forests in the latter half of the 19th century. This area also represents the southwestern-most extension of mixed deciduous-coniferous forest in the northeastern United States (Bailey 1998).

Great Lakes and North-Central States

Michigan—Historical accounts of varying reliability, summarized by Burt (1946) and Baker (1983), suggest that in the 1800s lynx may have been widely distributed in both the Lower and Upper Peninsulas of Michigan. However, six of seven verified records from the 1800s are from the Upper Peninsula near the Wisconsin border; a lynx killed in Washtenaw County in 1842 and five lynx trapped along the Au Sable River in Oscoda County in 1917 represent the only verified records of lynx from the Lower Peninsula (Table 8.3). Verified records of lynx occurrence in Michigan in the early 1900s are extremely scarce: five specimens were collected on Isle Royale in 1904

Table 8.3–Verified records of lynx in Michigan.

Date	Record	Reference
Unknown	1 specimen from Michigan.	Zoology Museum, University of Michigan
(1842)[a]	1 taken near Petersburg, Monroe County (LP)[b]	Wood and Dice 1924
1842	1 killed in Washtenaw County (LP)	Wood 1922
(1844)[a]	1 killed along the Au Sable River, Oscoda County (LP)	Wood and Dice 1924
Prior to 1874	3 specimens from Marquette, Marquette County (UP)[c]	Peabody Museum, Yale University
1874	1 specimen from Gogebic County (UP)	Milwaukee Public Museum
(1875)[a]	Several caught at headwaters of Manistique River, Schoolcraft County (UP)	Wood and Dice 1924
1889	1 specimen from Ishpening, Marquette County (UP)	Milwaukee Public Museum
1890-91	1 taken near Gogebic Lake, Gogebic County (UP)	Dice and Sherman 1922
(1894)[a]	1 taken 18 miles east of Cadillac, Wexford County (LP)	Wood and Dice 1924
(1894-95)[a]	34 killed in Mackinac County (UP)	Wood and Dice 1924
(1903)[a]	1 trapped at Big Creek, Oscoda County (LP)	Wood and Dice 1924
1904-05	5 collected on Isle Royale, Keneenaw County (UP)	Zoology Museum, University of Michigan
1910	1 taken at Rudyar, Chippewa County (UP)	Wood and Dice 1924
1912	1 taken near Sault Ste. Marie, Chippewa County (UP)	Wood and Dice 1924
1917	5 trapped along the Au Sable River near Luzerne, Oscoda County (LP)	Harger 1965
1923	1 specimen from Mackinac County (UP)	National Museum of Natural History
1928	1 trapped in Ontonagon County (UP)	Baker 1983
1940	1 trapped on Bois Blanc Island, Mackinac County (UP)	Harger 1965
1949	1 trapped at Engadine, Mackinac County (UP)	Harger 1965
1953	1 specimen from Dunbar, Marquette County (UP)	Erickson 1955; Zoology Museum, University of Michigan
1955	1 specimen from Marquette County (UP)	Grand Rapids Public Museum
1958	1 specimen from Rockview, Chippewa County (UP)	Michigan State University Museum
1960	1 shot near Rockview, Chippewa County (UP)	Harger 1965
1960	1 specimen from Trout Lake, Chippewa County (UP)	Michigan State University Museum
1961	1 specimen from Pickford, Chippewa County (UP)	Zoology Museum, University of Michigan
1961	1 shot near Dafter, Chippewa County (UP)	Harger 1965
1962	1 shot near Pickford, Chippewa County (UP)	Harger 1965
1962	1 shot near Nun's Creek, Mackinac County (UP)	Harger 1965
1962	1 trapped near Channing, Dickinson County (UP)	Harger 1965
1962	1 shot 7 mi. N of Iron Mountain, Dickinson County (UP)	Harger 1965
1962	1 specimen from Dunbar, Chippewa County (UP)	Michigan State University Museum
1962	1 shot in Ontonagon County (UP)	Harger 1965
1962	1 shot near Sagola, Dickinson County (UP)	Harger 1965
1962	1 shot near Trout Lake, Chippewa County (UP)	Harger 1965
1962	1 shot near Manistique, Schoolcraft County (UP)	Harger 1965
1962	1 shot between Topaz and Matchwood, Ontonagon County (UP)	Harger 1965
1962	1 specimen from Sault Ste. Marie, Chippewa County (UP)	Michigan State University Museum
1962	1 shot near Dafter, Chippewa County (UP)	Harger 1965
1966	1 specimen from Schoolcraft County (UP)	Michigan State University Museum
1983	1 killed in Mackinac County (UP)	Michigan Dept. of Natural Resources

[a]Wood and Dice (1924) caution that there is a strong possibility that some of these records may be of bobcats; we therefore consider these records to be probable, but not verified, records of lynx in Michigan.
[b]LP = Lower Peninsula.
[c]UP = Upper Peninsula.

and 1905, and mortality records from the Upper Peninsula are known only from 1910, 1912, 1923, and 1928 (Table 8.3). By 1928, the Michigan Department of Conservation reported the lynx to be extirpated from the Lower Peninsula and nearly so from the Upper Peninsula; by 1938, the lynx was declared on the verge of extinction throughout Michigan and, in later reports, was not even mentioned (Harger 1965).

By the mid-1940s, Burt (1946) considered the lynx to be "probably gone from the fauna of Michigan," but there are verified records from 1940, 1949, 1953, 1955, and 1958 (Table 8.3). From 1960 to 1962, 16 lynx were killed on the Upper Peninsula, including 12 in 1962, following an unusually large irruption of lynx in south-central Canada during the early 1960s (Adams 1963; Gunderson 1978). Harvest records from Ontario, Manitoba, and Saskatchewan clearly depict the irruption of lynx during this time and its unusually high amplitude (Fig. 8.3), which was several times greater than during previous peaks recorded this century. Since the early 1960s, however, only two verified records of lynx in Michigan could be found: one in 1966 and another in 1983 (Table 8.3). The lynx has been fully protected in Michigan since 1983, when it was classified as a threatened species; it was reclassified as a state endangered species in 1987.

Wisconsin—The history of lynx in Wisconsin was reviewed in detail by Thiel (1987), including a comprehensive compilation of specimen and mortality records. Only 11 verified records of lynx in Wisconsin prior to

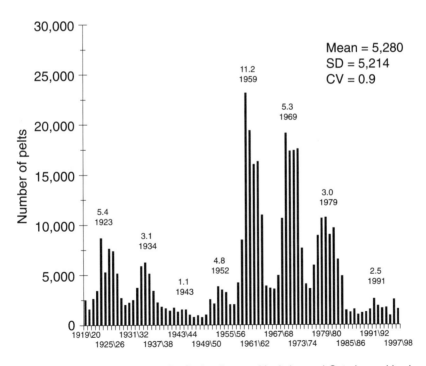

Figure 8.3—Lynx harvest data for Saskatchewan, Manitoba, and Ontario combined, 1919-1997; peak years are indicated, as well as a measure of amplitude calculated by dividing the peak harvest value by the previous low harvest value.

1962 are known, including eight records dating from 1870 to 1926 and three specimens collected in 1946, 1954, and 1955 (Table 8.4). The lynx is reported to have always occurred most frequently in the northern portion of Wisconsin (Jackson 1961), and the distribution of verified records supports this assertion. Only three records are known from the southernmost counties near the Illinois border; the last of these was in 1946. The last known occurrence of the lynx in central Wisconsin was in 1972, and all but a few records since 1965 are from counties located near the borders of northern Minnesota and the Upper Peninsula of Michigan (Table 8.4). An unusual increase in lynx mortalities occurred in Wisconsin during the 1960s and early 1970s (Table 8.4; Thiel 1987). The number of verified records of lynx being killed (16) in Wisconsin during this time period exceeded those from the previous 100 years (Table 8.4). Similar increases in lynx mortalities during these same time periods have been reported for Minnesota, North Dakota, and Montana (Adams 1963; Gunderson 1978; Mech 1973, 1980).

Table 8.4–Verified records of lynx in Wisconsin.

Date	Record	Reference
1870	1 specimen from Jefferson County	Zoological Museum, University of Wisconsin, Madison
1899	2 specimens from Iron County	Zoological Museum, University of Wisconsin, Madison
1901	1 specimen from Gordon, Douglas County	Zoological Museum, University of Wisconsin, Madison
1907	1 killed in Middleton, Dane County	Schorger 1947
1908	1 specimen from Edson, Chippewa County	Museum of Natural History, Wisconsin State University, Stevens Point
1917	1 trapped in La Crosse, La Crosse County	Milwaukee Public Museum
1926	1 shot in Shell Lake, Washburn County	Stouffer 1961 (cited in Thiel 1987)
1946	1 specimen from Spring Green, Sauk County	Zoological Museum, University of Wisconsin, Madison
1954	1 specimen from Hurley, Iron County	Zoological Museum, University of Wisconsin, Madison
1955	1 specimen from Richland, Rusk County	Zoological Museum, University of Wisconsin, Madison
1962	1 shot in Rusk County	Thiel 1987
1963	1 shot in Douglas County	Thiel 1987
1964	1 killed in Jackson County	Thiel 1987
1965 or 1968	1 killed in Pierce County	Thiel 1987
1965	1 killed in Green Lake County	Thiel 1987
1965	1 killed by a train near Viroqua, Pierce County	Thiel 1987
1965	1 specimen shot while swimming at the mouth of the St. Louis River, Douglas County	University of Wisconsin, Superior
1971	1 shot in Trempealeau County	Thiel 1987
1972	1 shot in Trempealeau County	Thiel 1987
1972	1 specimen from Woodruff, Vilas County	Zoological Museum, University of Wisconsin, Madison
1972	1 killed by car in Oneida County	Thiel 1987
1972	1 trapped in Price County	Thiel 1987
1972	1 specimen from Lake Noquebay, Marinette County	Technical Center, University of Wisconsin, Marinette
1972	1 shot in Tomahawk, Lincoln County	Thiel 1987
1973	1 trapped in Iron County	Thiel 1987
Winter 1972-1973	1 specimen from Oneida or Vilas County	Zoological Museum, University of Wisconsin, Madison
1992	1 specimen from Burnette County	Museum of Natural History, Wisconsin State University, Stevens Point
1992	1 specimen from St. Croix County	Museum of Natural History, Wisconsin State University, Stevens Point

Since that time, only two records of lynx being killed in Wisconsin are known; both were in 1992. Lynx tracks were detected by the Wisconsin Department of Natural Resources during wolf surveys from 1993 to 1997, but all were within six to seven miles of each other, suggesting that they may represent the same individual (Wydeven 1998, unpublished). Lynx have been completely protected in Wisconsin since 1957, when harvest seasons and bounty payments were eliminated; in 1972, the lynx was placed on the state endangered species list.

Indiana, Illinois, Ohio, and Iowa—Lyon (1936) reviewed published reports of lynx from Indiana in the 1800s and concluded that none could be considered verified records, given the confusion over terms used for cougar, bobcat, and lynx in these sources. Mumford (1969) believed that some of these records might be authentic, however, and cited a report of a lynx being killed at Bicknell, Knox County in southwestern Indiana in 1832. Records from Illinois are similarly scanty; Kennicott (1855) included the lynx in his list of mammals occurring in Cook County (now metropolitan Chicago), and specimen records of the Academy of Natural Sciences of Philadelphia include a lynx collected in Illinois that was obtained by the museum in June 1842 (this specimen is now missing from the collection). No verified records of lynx from Ohio could be found, but Smith et al. (1973) included the species in a list of mammals that once bred in Ohio but which have now been extirpated. Historical records of lynx in Iowa are more prevalent; Spurrell (1917) reported that three lynx were trapped in Sac County in northwestern Iowa in 1869 and one in 1875; another lynx was apparently killed in Iowa in 1906 (Gunderson 1978). In July 1963, a lynx was shot in Shelby County in west-central Iowa (Rasmussen 1969); none has been reported since that time.

Minnesota—Published historical information on lynx in Minnesota is virtually nonexistent. In an early monograph on the mammals of Minnesota, Herrick (1892) was uncertain if the lynx was even a member of the state's fauna at that time. Hunters consistently told him that two species of wildcats occupied the state but all specimens he examined, including those presented to him as "lynx," proved to be bobcats. Although lynx were apparently not common at that time, their presence in Minnesota during the late 1800s is confirmed by the existence of eight museum specimens dating from 1892 to 1900. Two of these specimens are from Sherbourne County in south-central Minnesota and the remainder are from Itaska County in the north-central portion of the state. Verified records prior to the south-central Canadian population peak of 1959 are scarce: a lynx was collected in Sherbourne County in 1927, one in Morrison County in 1928, one in St. Louis County in 1951, one in Aitkin County in 1953, and one in Lake of the Woods County in 1955.

The only other documented information on lynx in Minnesota prior to 1960 are harvest records published by the state Department of Natural Resources (Fig. 8.4; Henderson 1978). However, these records should be considered with caution; data from 1930 to 1976 do not represent reports of catch or carcass records obtained during the year of harvest but, rather, are estimates of harvest obtained in later years by mail survey. These records indicate, however, that lynx have been harvested in relatively high numbers in Minnesota in most years since 1930 (mean = 103 per year, range = 0-400). Peaks in the harvest record that occurred in 1962 and 1973 are also reflected in museum specimen records. All other specimens from Minnesota are from the early 1960s and early 1970s: one from 1960, one from 1961, four from 1962, 14 from 1963, one from 1964, 25 from 1972, and one from 1973. During this time, Mech (1980) trapped 14 lynx in northeastern Minnesota: five in 1972, three in 1973, four in 1974, and two in 1975.

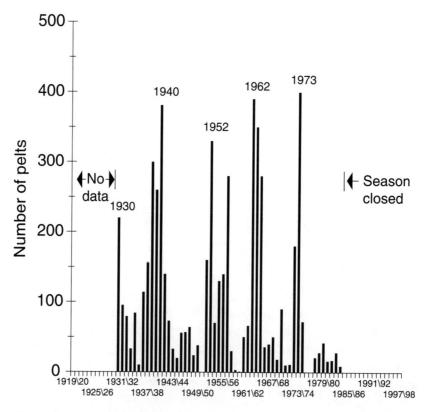

Figure 8.4—Lynx harvest data from Minnesota, 1930-1983; years of peak harvest values are indicated.

The continued occurrence of lynx in Minnesota in the late 1970s and early 1980s is verified by state records dating from 1977 to 1983, which represent reports of catch from hunters and trappers at the close of each trapping season. Altogether, 161 lynx were harvested in Minnesota during this period (mean = 23, range = 9-42). When expected increases in lynx numbers failed to occur in the early 1980s, the state closed the harvest season for lynx; it has not been reopened. Since the closure of lynx harvests, only three verified lynx records are known: one trapped in Cook County in 1992, and one illegal possession in Anoka County and one road-kill in St. Louis County in 1993 (DonCarlos 1994, unpublished). The only documented records of lynx breeding in Minnesota are two females that gave birth to kittens in the spring of 1972 (Mech 1973).

North Dakota—The northern Great Plains are generally not included in the range of lynx (Burt 1946; McCord and Cardoza 1982; Quinn and Parker 1987; Seton 1929), yet there are a surprising number of historical specimen records from this region. Bailey (1926) reports numerous anecdotal accounts of lynx being trapped in North Dakota in the 1800s and lists three specimen records: one collected at Fort Union (now Buford, North Dakota, on the Montana border) in 1850, one at Arrowhead Lake in east-central North Dakota in 1907, and one at Cannonball near the south-central border in 1915. Other reports include several lynx that were killed in the northeastern portion of the state, including one at Lakota in 1915 and two near Grafton in 1909 and 1911. Bailey (1926) makes several references to periodic increases in lynx numbers in this region, noting that "in some years, the lynx is common over the northern portion of North Dakota," and that many lynx were captured in north-central North Dakota and brought into taxidermists' shops in 1908 and 1909, when they were apparently "wandering in search of new hunting fields." Two lynx were bountied during the winter of 1954-1955 in the northeastern corner of North Dakota (Adams 1963; Gunderson 1978). In addition, many lynx apparently were killed in North Dakota during the lynx irruptions of the 1960s and 1970s (Adams 1963). According to records of the North Dakota Game and Fish Department, 53 lynx were harvested from 1962 to 1965 and another 24 from 1972 to 1973. With the exception of eight museum specimens collected in 1962 and 1963, no other verified lynx records from North Dakota could be found.

South Dakota and Nebraska—The earliest records of lynx in South Dakota are both from the southeastern corner of the state, near the borders of Minnesota and Iowa: One lynx was taken above Sioux City in 1875 and a museum specimen was collected at Bullhead, Corson County in 1925. Other reports include one killed in Meade County and two in Pennington County in 1944; one near Briton, Chamberlain County in 1962; one near Marindahl,

Yankton County in 1962; one near Chamberlain, Brule County in 1963 (Gunderson 1978; Turner 1974); a museum specimen collected in northeastern South Dakota in 1965; and, according to federal Animal Damage Control records, one killed in 1973 on the Cheyenne River in Pennington County. Records from Nebraska are of a similar nature: a museum specimen was collected in 1890 near Norfolk in Madison County, and Jones (1964) reports that a lynx was killed in 1915 near Bassett in north-central Nebraska, another along the North Platte River near Keystone in 1917, and a third near Ewing in 1958. All other verified records are associated with mid-continent lynx irruptions in the early 1960s, 1970s, and 1980s: five from 1963 to 1964; three from 1972 to 1974; and a specimen collected near Herman, Washington County in 1983 (Nebraska Game and Parks records).

Western Mountain States

Montana—Available information on the history of lynx in Montana in the late 1800s and early 1900s consists of 12 museum specimens collected between 1887 and 1921; published information on the recent or historical status of Montana mammals is limited (Hoffmann et al. 1969). Four specimens were collected in Rosebud and Musselshell Counties in southeastern Montana in 1887, one in 1895 at upper St. Mary Lake in Glacier National Park, three in the Bitterroot Mountains in 1910 (two at Bass Creek and one at Elk Lake), two in 1916 (one without a specific collecting locality and another at Deer Lodge, Powell County in west-central Montana), one in 1918 at Kintla Lake in Glacier National Park, and one in 1921 in northwestern Montana near Plains, Sanders County. The status of lynx in the Glacier Park area of northwestern Montana during the early 1900s was reviewed by Bailey (1918), who considered the lynx "more or less common throughout the Glacier Park region." He noted, however, that "during years when rabbits are abundant, [lynx] too, become abundant, and when there are few rabbits, they are correspondingly scarce." Five specimens were collected in northwestern Montana in the 1940s and 1950s: one in Lincoln County in 1941, two in Flathead County in 1954 and 1956, one in Missoula County in 1958, and one from an unknown locality in the late 1950s.

As in the Great Lakes and north-central States, most later specimen records are associated with lynx irruptions in the early 1960s and 1970s. The remaining 19 specimens include 14 obtained from 1962 to 1966 and five from 1971 to 1976. Data on lynx harvests in the state have been kept since 1950, however, and show continuous presence of lynx in the state (Fig. 8.5); since 1977, over 475 lynx were harvested in Montana. Smith (1984, unpublished) and Brainerd (1985, unpublished) captured 10 lynx during radiotelemetry studies in western Montana in the 1980s, and an ongoing

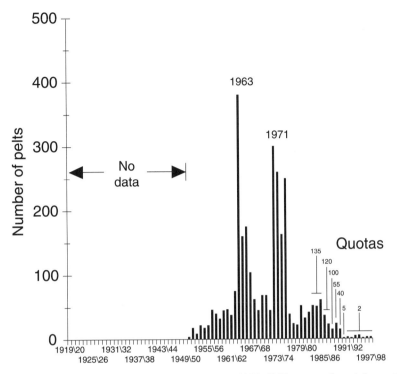

Figure 8.5—Lynx harvest data from Montana, 1950-1997; years of peak harvest values are indicated.

study begun in 1998 in the area around Seeley Lake (Chapter 11) has captured 18 lynx to date (June 1999). Although reliable data on lynx reproduction in Montana are scarce, Brainerd (1985, unpublished) examined 20 trapper-killed lynx carcasses, including several kittens, and found a pregnancy rate for all ages of 70.6%. As was noted for New Hampshire, lynx harvest data from Montana is cyclic in nature, with peaks corresponding closely in time and magnitude with those occurring in western Canada, especially for 1963 and 1971 (Figs. 8.5 and 8.6).

Idaho—Specimen records of lynx in Idaho during the early 1900s are relatively common; there are 22 museum specimens dating from 1874 to 1917, all of which were collected in the northern and central montane regions of Idaho north of the Snake River Plain. Specimens were later collected in central Idaho in 1939 on the Payette National Forest in Valley County and in 1940 in Idaho County. The only other museum records are both from the northern panhandle region: one from Bonner County in 1954 and one from

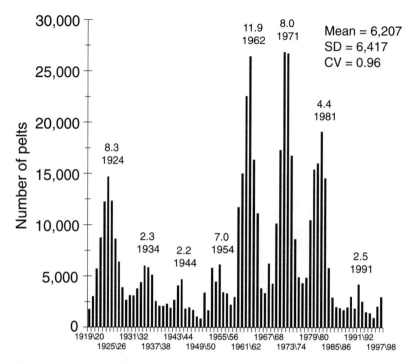

Figure 8.6—Lynx harvest data for British Columbia and Alberta combined, 1919-1997; peak years are indicated, as well as a measure of amplitude calculated by dividing the peak harvest value by the previous low harvest value.

Shoshone County in 1955. Other verified records prior to 1960 include one from Shoshone County in 1901, one from Boundary County in 1919, one from Idaho County in 1936, one from northwest Idaho in 1939, one from Clearwater County in 1942, five from Caribou County in 1947, two from Bonneville County in 1955, and one from Idaho County in 1947 (Anonymous 1999, unpublished; Dalquest 1948). With the exception of Caribou and Bonneville Counties, which are located along the Wyoming border, all of these records are from the north-central and northern regions of the state.

In an early account of the mammals of Idaho, Davis (1939) described lynx occurring "in the mountainous regions north and east of the Snake River Plain." Rust's (1946) assessment of the status of lynx in northern Idaho is similar: "While nowhere abundant in northern Idaho, the Canadian lynx is fairly well distributed throughout the wooded areas of eight of the 10 northern counties, largely in the Canadian and Hudsonian zones." He noted that 25-30 lynx are usually taken by local trappers in addition to those killed by predator control agents.

There are 35 verified records from 1960 to 1991: four from 1962 to 1969, 18 from 1970 to 1979, 10 from 1982 to 1989, and three from 1990 to 1991; there are no verified records of lynx in Idaho since 1991 (Anonymous 1999, unpublished). Although most of these records are from the northern and central regions of Idaho where lynx occurred historically, six are from counties in the Snake River Plain, in areas where forest types occupied by lynx are absent or very fragmentary in extent (see "Lynx Associations with Broad Cover Types"). These include records from Blaine, Butte, Jerome, and Twin Falls Counties in 1972; one from Blaine County in 1984; and one from Power County in 1990. As in other western and midwestern states, there are a number of anecdotal accounts of lynx being killed or captured in anomalous, low-elevation habitats during lynx irruptions in the 1960s and 1970s (Lewis and Wenger 1998). These accounts are derived from interviews initiated in 1997, however, and the lack of similar reports from the 1980s or 1990s suggests that these records represent transient lynx.

Lynx harvest records for Idaho from 1934 to 1981 are available (Novak et al. 1987), but state biologists consider these data to be unreliable prior to the late 1980s due to the inclusion of large, pale bobcats in these totals. This concern appears to be valid; after 1981, when a mandatory pelt-tagging program was instituted, no lynx was harvested for the next seven trapping seasons (Anonymous 1999, unpublished). The lynx was unprotected in Idaho before 1977, when it was classified as a furbearer and harvest was restricted to a one-month trapping season and a three-month pursuit season. In 1990, a state-wide quota of three lynx per year was imposed; the season was closed in 1996.

Washington—Verified records of lynx in Washington are numerous and well-distributed since the late 1800s. There are 78 museum specimens of lynx from Washington—more than any other state in the contiguous United States. The earliest records are represented by 10 specimens collected in 1896 and 1897 on Mt. Adams in the southern Cascade Range near the border of Oregon. All but a few subsequent specimen records, however, are from the north-central and northeastern portions of the state near the Canadian border, including 32 from 1916 to 1920, three from 1928 to 1930, four from 1939 to 1940, eight from 1951 to 1959, one in 1965, and 17 from 1976 to 1983. In addition, there are three specimens from southeastern Washington: one from the Blue Mountains in 1931 and two from arid grassland habitats in 1962 and 1963. A lynx was reportedly trapped near the southern boundary of Mt. Rainier National Park "some years" prior to 1927 (Taylor and Shaw 1927) and nine lynx were trapped west of Oroville in Okanogan County in 1938 (photo in Dalquest 1948). According to Dalquest (1948), each of several trappers regularly took a dozen or more lynx from remote areas of northeastern Washington each year. No verified records of lynx are known from coastal areas west of the Cascade Range. Lynx populations in Washington have been studied in the field more than anywhere else in the contiguous United States, and most of what is known of lynx ecology in southern boreal forests comes from these studies (Chapter 13; Koehler and Aubry 1994). Thirty lynx were studied with radiotelemetry in north-central Washington from 1981 to 1988 (Brittell et al. 1989, unpublished; Koehler 1990), including two radio-collared females that each gave birth to kittens in 1986 and 1987; snow-tracking indicated that a third, uncollared female also had a litter of kittens in 1986 (Koehler 1990). From 1995 to 1999, 16 remote-camera photographs of lynx were taken at bait stations in north-central Washington (J. Rohrer and M. Skatrud, personal communication).

Management of lynx in Washington began in 1933, when the Washington Department of Game was established and the lynx was classified as a fur-bearer that could only be harvested by trapping; the first lynx trapping season was in the winter of 1934-1935. Monitoring of the lynx harvest did not begin until 1961, however, at which time trappers were required to submit reports of catch to the Department of Game. In 1978, the state initiated mandatory tagging of lynx pelts within 10 days of the close of each trapping season (Brittell et al. 1989, unpublished). Washington harvest data from 1961 to 1984 (Fig. 8.7) suggests that Washington lynx populations may also exhibit cyclic patterns of abundance. During the peak harvest of 1969, 26 of the 31 lynx taken were from the Kettle Range in Ferry County. Only a few were harvested in this area from 1970 to 1974, but 14 of 19 lynx taken in Washington in 1975 and 17 of 39 taken in 1976 came from this area. Of the 25 lynx harvested since that time, only two were from Ferry County. Although trapper effort and pelt prices undoubtedly influence these data, the lynx population in the Kettle Range appears to have undergone several dramatic increases and decreases in number from 1961 to 1977. Snow-tracking surveys conducted from 1992 to 1996 in the Kettle Range resulted in only two sets of tracks: one in 1991-1992 and one in 1995-1996 (Washington Dept. of Fish and Wildlife, unpublished data). Trapping seasons lasted 2-2.5 months from 1961 to 1977 but were shortened to about one month beginning in 1978; in 1987, a restricted permit system was implemented. Thus, harvest data after 1977 are not directly comparable to previous data. A statewide closure of the lynx trapping season was implemented in 1990, and the lynx was classified as a threatened species in Washington in 1993.

Oregon—The presence of lynx in Oregon in the late 1800s and early 1900s is documented by nine museum specimens collected from 1897 to 1927. Verified records after that time, however, are extremely rare. Only three

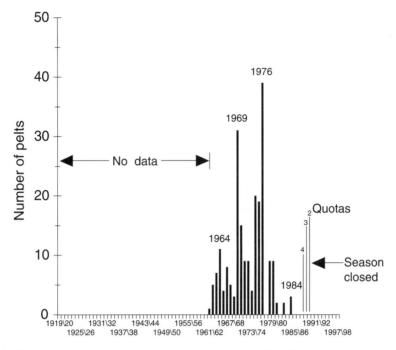

Figure 8.7—Lynx harvest data from Washington, 1960-1989; years of peak harvest values are indicated.

recent specimens are known, and all were collected in anomalous habitats within several years of lynx population peaks in western Canada (see "Lynx Associations With Broad Cover Types"): one in bunchgrass-rimrock habitat in Wallowa County in 1964, one in a suburban residential area in Benton County in 1974 (Verts and Carraway 1998), and a third in Harney County in southeastern Oregon in 1993, where there are only small fragments of forest types associated with lynx occurrence (see "Lynx Associations With Broad Cover Types"). Although Bailey (1936) describes early anecdotal reports of lynx in western Oregon, the 1974 specimen is the only verified record of lynx west of the Cascade Crest in Oregon.

Wyoming—Reeve et al. (1986, unpublished) conducted a thorough and comprehensive review of existing information on lynx in Wyoming, including verified records and information obtained through a mail and telephone survey of knowledgeable individuals in the state. The only verified record not located by these authors was a museum specimen obtained at Fort Frederick Steele in Carbon County in southeastern Wyoming sometime prior to 1872. There are three specimen records from the 1800s, including another from southeastern Wyoming in 1856 and one collected near the headwaters of the Wind River in northwestern Wyoming in 1893. All other early specimens were from the northwestern portion of the state: one from the Big Horn Mountains in 1919, two from the Wind River Range in 1908 and 1919, and seven collected from 1904 to 1920 in the area in and around Yellowstone National Park in what is now referred to as the "Greater Yellowstone Ecosystem" (GYE). In an early monograph on the animal life of Yellowstone Park, Bailey (1930) wrote that lynx "were said to be common and generally distributed throughout the timbered region." There are no recent verified records from the GYE.

Verified records of lynx in Wyoming after 1920 are rare; there are nine verified records from 1940 to 1957, and all were lynx killed near the west-central border of the state. A lynx was collected in 1940 at Hoback Rim in northwestern Sublette County and another in 1949 near Afton, Lincoln County. The remaining seven records are described by Halloran and Blanchard (1959) and include five lynx trapped by state predator control agents in northern Lincoln County from 1952 to 1955, a specimen collected in northwestern Sublette County in 1954, and a kitten collected in southwestern Teton County in 1957. The only other verified records are a lynx taken in Albany County in the Laramie Range of southeastern Wyoming in 1963 (Long 1965), and one from an anomalous locality near Douglas, Converse County in east-central Wyoming in 1983 (Reeve et al. 1986). A radiotelemetry study was initiated in western Wyoming in 1996, resulting in the capture of two lynx: a male in December 1996 and a female in March 1997; the female produced a litter of four kittens in May 1998 (Chapter 11). Prior to 1973, when the lynx was given full protection in Wyoming, it was considered a predator that could be harvested legally anytime of year without a license; consequently, no reliable harvest records are available from Wyoming.

Colorado—A thorough review of the history of documented lynx records in Colorado was conducted by Halfpenny et al. (1989, unpublished) and, except for the discovery of several more historical specimen records, little new information has become available since their analysis. Unlike other western montane regions considered thus far, boreal forest habitat in Colorado is insular in nature and isolated from similar habitat in Utah and Wyoming by more than 150 km of lower elevation habitats in the Green River Valley and Wyoming Basin (Findley and Anderson 1956). All but a few specimen records are from the center of this island of boreal forest habitat in west-central Colorado. There are four specimens from the late 1800s: one without a specific collecting locality, one from Cumbres County near the New Mexico border, one from Breckenridge, Summit County, and one from Colorado Springs, El Paso County. Halfpenny et al. (1989, unpublished) reported that Edwin Carter's taxidermy notes in the Denver Museum of Natural History included a lynx trapped in Soda Gulch, Clear Creek County in 1878. Museum specimens were also found from Grand Lake, Grand County in 1904-1905; Jefferson, Park County in 1912; and southwestern Gunnison County in 1925. Terrell (1971) reported one lynx trapped at Red Cliff, Eagle County in 1929 and one at Marble, Gunnison County in 1931. Through interviews with trappers, Halfpenny et al. concluded that reports of three lynx being trapped in Eagle County in 1930 and 1936 were reliable.

After 1936, no lynx specimens or reports of kills are known until 1969, when a specimen was trapped near Leadville, Lake County, and others were reportedly shot on the Frying Pan River, Pitkin County (Terrell 1971) and on the south side of Vail Mountain, Eagle County (Halfpenny et al. 1989, unpublished). In 1972, a lynx specimen was trapped on Guanella Pass, Clear Creek County and, in 1974, two were trapped (one is preserved as a specimen) on the north side of Vail Mountain, Eagle County. Since that time, only tracks have been found, including three sets on the Frying Pan River, Eagle and Pitkin Counties and five sets near Mt. Evans, Clear Creek County (Halfpenny et al. 1989, unpublished). There are no verified records of lynx in Colorado since 1974, despite large-scale snow-tracking efforts (Carney 1993, unpublished). The management history of lynx in Colorado is similar to that reported for Wyoming: The lynx was designated an unprotected predator until 1970, when all harvest of lynx was prohibited; in 1973, it was classified as a state endangered species.

Utah—Our understanding of the distribution and status of lynx in Utah comes entirely from scattered mortality records. Barnes (1927) reported that 103 lynx were trapped in a number of counties in Utah in 1915 and 1916, but Durrant (1952) questioned the validity of these records and believed that most were actually large bobcats. The relative scarcity of early specimen records supports this conclusion. Only three specimens of lynx from Utah in the early 1900s were found in museums, including one collected in 1916 from Wasatch County, one in 1931 from Sanpete County, and one in 1937 from Daggett County. Later records are all from the northwestern portion of Utah near the southern borders of Wyoming and Idaho. Those records include one museum specimen collected in 1957 from Daggett County, mortality reports from Uintah County in 1958 and Summit County in 1958 and 1962 (McKay 1991, unpublished), one specimen from Summit County in 1963, a mortality report from the north slope of the Uinta Mountains in 1972 (McKay 1991, unpublished) and a lynx trapped in Cache County in 1991 (R. McKay, personal communication). No verified records are known after this time. The lynx is listed as a sensitive species in Utah and has been protected from all intentional harvest since 1974.

Nevada—There are two museum specimens from Nevada; both were collected in 1916 in Elko County in north-central Nevada near the Oregon border (Schantz 1947). These specimens represent the southernmost records of lynx occurrence west of the Rocky Mountains and are the only verified records of lynx from Nevada. Three of the 12 specimens from Oregon were also collected in 1916, suggesting that this may have been a year during which lynx were dispersing south of their primary range; peaks in lynx pelt returns from British Columbia and southern Alberta were recorded in 1915 and 1916, respectively (Elton and Nicholson 1942; p. 229).

Synchrony Between United States and Canadian Trapping Data

Lynx populations in the contiguous United States occur at the southern margin of a large, interconnected distribution whose geographic center lies in the northern taiga (McCord and Cardoza 1982; Quinn and Parker 1987). It has been suggested that the persistence of some lynx populations in the contiguous United States may be dependent upon the periodic immigration of lynx into the United States during the crash of northern lynx populations (Thiel 1987). In the following section, we analyze harvest data, occurrence data, and verified records from the United States in relation to lynx cycles in Canada to address the following questions: (1) Are lynx records in the contiguous United States associated with cyclic population highs in Canada? and (2) If so, do similar patterns occur repeatedly across time and space?

In southern boreal forests, lynx are believed to occur at relatively low population densities (Koehler and Aubry 1994), and throughout the 20th century, harvest records for lynx in Canada have been two to three orders of magnitude larger than those for the contiguous United States (Novak et al. 1987). In the taiga, long-range emigrations from core populations are associated with the crash of snowshoe hare populations; when prey becomes scarce, home ranges dissolve and lynx become nomadic (Chapter 9). Thus, it is possible that periodic immigrations of lynx into the United States from southern Canadian provinces may occur during such events.

Thiel (1987) argues that periodic immigrations of lynx into the United States from Canada will produce large increases in lynx records in the United States occurring several years after cyclic highs in Canada, the lag being the immigration time. Additionally, we would expect many of these records to occur in cover types generally not used by lynx and in geographic areas in which lynx records are generally scarce. However, lagged dynamics and unusual occurrence patterns, while suggestive, do not necessarily mean that such occurrences are directly attributable to transients. Complex asynchronous dynamics are predicted by predator/prey diffusion reaction models (see Hastings and Harrison 1994 for a review) and occur due to the interactions between local population dynamics and changes due to dispersal. Mowat et al. (Chapter 9), for instance, suggest that lynx dynamics in the taiga exhibit lagged synchrony and that the lynx cycle in Canada "emanates" from central Canada with the patterns in Yukon, Alaska, and Quebec lagged several years behind those of Saskatchewan and Manitoba. Correlation analyses of Canadian trapping data (Ranta et al. 1997) also indicate that, on a continental scale, patterns are least synchronous at intermediate distances and most synchronous when comparing locations that are either very close or very far.

Methods

We evaluated Mowat et al.'s (Chapter 9) hypothesis by comparing data from the central provinces of Alberta and Saskatchewan with data from areas to the northwest (Alberta + Saskatchewan ➔ Yukon ➔ Alaska) and the east (Alberta + Saskatchewan ➔ Manitoba ➔ Ontario ➔ Quebec). We computed correlation coefficients between trapping data for the provinces of Alberta and Saskatchewan and the other provinces and Alaska incrementally shifted back in time 0-5 years, noted the time lag associated with the highest correlation, and tested whether lagging the data caused significant changes in correlation coefficients (Zar 1996, pp. 384-386).

For states with reliable and long-term lynx harvest data (New Hampshire, Minnesota, Montana, and Washington), we repeated the correlation analyses (above) to determine the extent to which these data were correlated with harvest data from Canadian provinces and whether these data were lagged. For these analyses we correlated state trapping data with those Canadian provinces which, due to their proximity, were most likely to contribute to the local populations. For each state, we visually examined the data using the most correlated lag time to determine if the patterns appeared synchronous.

Because our primary data are trapping records, which may show patterns and synchrony that result solely from social and economic factors, we looked to other data to provide a check on the trapping records as well as to provide information for times and places where trapping data were absent. Occurrence data and the verified records are not directly associated with trapping activity and are available for states such as Michigan and Wisconsin where we have no state-level trapping data. For comparisons of Canadian trapping data with verified records and general occurrence data, we used the most correlated lag times for the Canadian data from the analyses of trapping data described above. Because occurrence data are often sparse and erratic, we used visual methods to identify potential associations between these data sets. For Michigan and Wisconsin, where we lacked trapping data, we compared patterns in the occurrence of verified lynx records to peaks in harvest data from the Canadian provinces using the lag time that was most correlated with the Minnesota trapping data. For the Great Lakes region we estimated the degree to which general occurrence patterns in data other than harvest records were correlated with Canadian harvest data lagged as indicated by correlation with Minnesota trapping records.

Another line of inquiry concerns the degree to which patterns in the lynx data are correlated with local patterns of hare abundance. For the Great Lakes region, hare data were available and were highly correlated within the region (Chapter 7). For Minnesota, we were able to check these data against independently collected hare occurrence data and the relationship was strong ($r = 0.89$, Fig. 8.8). Local lynx populations should respond to changes in local hare abundances, and the resultant patterns, therefore, may allow separation of local and dispersal dynamics. We compared lynx trapping and

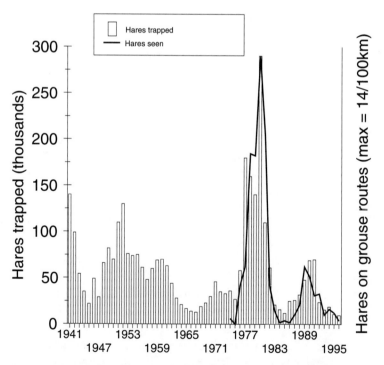

Figure 8.8—A comparison between snowshoe hare trapping data and numbers of hares observed on grouse drumming routes in Minnesota. Unpublished data provided by the Minnesota Department of Natural Resources.

occurrence data in the Great Lakes region with local patterns of hare abundance for the period in which hare-trapping was recorded. We used hare-trapping data from Minnesota because it is complete, is highly correlated with data from Wisconsin and Michigan, and has been independently verified for the last 22 years. Additionally we could compare it directly to lynx harvest records in Minnesota. Specifically, we were looking for local increases in hare harvest associated with the peak lynx harvests in the 1960s and 1970s and a response in lynx occurrence data to a large increase in hare abundance between 1975 and 1983 (Fig. 8.8). This increase was thought to be unusually large, perhaps representing the highest densities of hares in that region during the 20th century (Fig. 8.8; B. Berg, personal communication); thus, if resident lynx populations were present, they should have responded numerically to this large irruption in primary prey populations.

Results

Trapping data—Lagging provincial and Alaskan trapping data 0-2 years produced the highest correlations when compared with the central provinces of Alberta and Saskatchewan (Table 8.5). With the exception of Yukon,

Table 8.5–Pearson correlation coefficients (r) between trapping data from central Canada and states in the United States and provinces to the northwest and east. Correlations are to central Canadian data shifted 0-5 years. The best fit for each state or province is indicated in bold type. In the contiguous United States, correlation coefficients are only significantly different (Zar 1996, pp. 384-386) for Montana.

Comparison	Time period	Shifted						Significance
		0 years	1 year	2 years	3 years	4 years	5 years	
Contiguous U.S.								
New Hampshire with Quebec	1928-1964	**0.23**	0.20	0.02	−0.13	−0.20	−0.18	0.273
Minnesota with Ontario + Manitoba + Saskatchewan	1930-1983	−0.10	0.12	0.22	**0.32**	0.24	0.00	0.240
Montana with Alberta + British Columbia	1950-1989	0.35	0.69	**0.74**	0.62	0.35	0.05	<0.001
Washington with Alberta + British Columbia	1961-1977	−0.24	−0.29	−0.05	0.17	**0.25**	0.21	0.538
Northwest								
Yukon with Alberta + Saskatchewan	1934-1996	0.08	0.28	**0.36**	0.26	0.06	−0.12	0.070
Alaska with Alberta + Saskatchewan	1934-1996	0.30	0.63	**0.79**	0.77	0.60	0.31	<0.001
East								
Manitoba with Alberta + Saskatchewan	1924-1997	**0.92**	0.68	0.38	0.11	−0.04	−0.01	<0.001
Ontario with Alberta + Saskatchewan	1924-1997	0.74	**0.77**	0.64	0.39	0.12	−0.06	<0.001
Quebec with Alberta + Saskatchewan	1924-1997	0.38	0.60	**0.71**	0.68	0.53	0.33	<0.001

lagging the data caused significant ($p < 0.05$) changes in the correlation coefficients. The correlation patterns to the east were consistent with Mowat et al.'s "emanation" hypothesis. Manitoba was synchronous with Alberta and Saskatchewan, Ontario lagged one year, and Quebec lagged two years (Table 8.5). Patterns to the northwest were not as clear. Both Yukon and Alaska had the highest correlations when lagged two years, and Alaska was much more highly correlated than was Yukon (Table 8.5).

For those states and years for which reliable annual trapping data were recorded, correlations between harvest totals from the United States and adjacent Canadian provinces were generally modest (Table 8.5), Montana being the exception. New Hampshire was the only state for which non-lagged data provided the strongest correlation. Correlations between United States and Canadian harvest data for the other three states were all improved by shifting the Canadian data back in time: two years gave the best fit for Montana, three years for Minnesota, and four years for Washington. Visual inspection of these data suggests that increases in correlation coefficients were due to improved alignment of the oscillations in numbers of lynx trapped (Figs. 8.9-8.12).

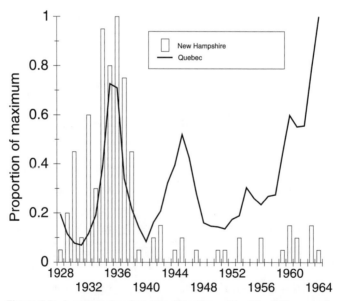

Figure 8.9—Lynx trapping data from New Hampshire (Fig. 8.1) overlaid on lynx trapping data from Quebec (Fig. 8.2). The strongest correlation between these data sets was with no lag between New Hampshire and Quebec.

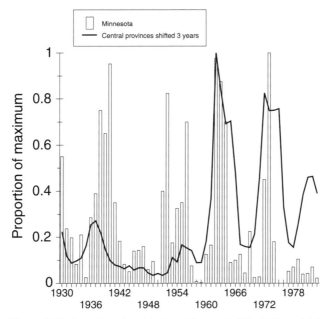

Figure 8.10—Lynx trapping data from Minnesota (Fig. 8.4) overlaid on lynx trapping data from Ontario, Manitoba, and Saskatchewan combined (Fig. 8.3). The strongest correlation between these data sets was with a three-year lag between Minnesota and south-central Canada.

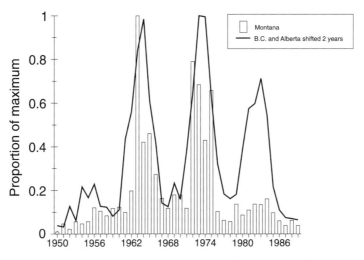

Figure 8.11—Lynx trapping data from Montana (Fig. 8.5) overlaid on lynx trapping data from Alberta and British Columbia combined (Fig. 8.6). The strongest correlation between these data sets was with a two-year lag between Montana and southwestern Canada.

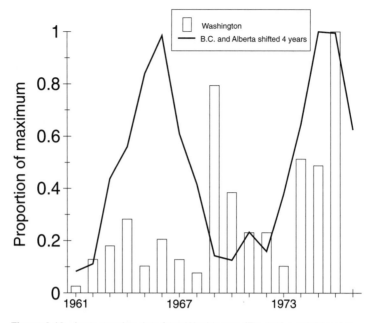

Figure 8.12—Lynx trapping data from Washington (Fig. 8.7) overlaid on lynx trapping data from Alberta and British Columbia combined (Fig. 8.6). The strongest correlation between these data sets was with a four-year lag between Washington and southwestern Canada.

One reason that the correlations were not stronger between states and adjacent provinces was that the patterns were not constant over time. For example, in New Hampshire, raw data for the first 12 years (1928-1939) are highly correlated with populations in Quebec ($r = 0.76$), when an average of 10 lynx were harvested each year; after this period, however, harvest records declined to only 0-3 lynx per year and the data become erratic and difficult to interpret (Fig. 8.9). In Minnesota, a three-year lag with data from the south-central Canadian provinces resulted in a strong correlation for the most recent period ($r = 0.73$, 1960-1983) but the pattern is out of phase in the previous 26 years (Fig. 8.10).

Occurrence data—Trapping data were removed from the general lynx occurrence database (Table 8.1) to produce as independent a data set as possible. Visual inspection of occurrence data from the Great Lakes region suggest that these fluctuations were aligned with trapping data from the south-central Canadian provinces with a three-year lag (Fig. 8.13). The verified lynx occurrences for Michigan and Wisconsin (Tables 8.3 and 8.4), for the period 1934-1997, are a subset of the occurrence data presented above and, in some years, make up the bulk of these data. These data are also

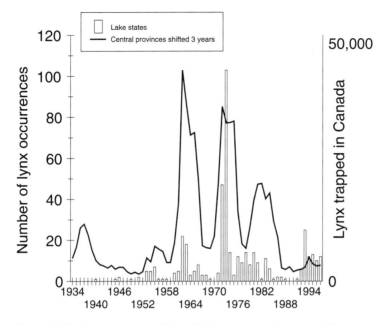

Figure 8.13—Lynx occurrence data, with trapping records removed (see Table 8.1), for the states of Wisconsin, Minnesota, and Michigan combined overlaid on lynx trapping data from Saskatchewan, Manitoba, and Ontario combined (Fig. 8.3). Canadian data were lagged three years based on the best fit to Minnesota trapping data (Table 8.5, Fig. 8.10).

concordant with the general occurrence data and are aligned with trapping data from the south-central provinces with a three-year time lag (Fig. 8.14).

Hare densities—To look for responses to the regional increase in hare populations in the Great Lakes states during the late 1970s and early 1980s (Fig. 8.8), we compared hare harvest data from Minnesota with general occurrence data from the Great Lakes region. Based on these data, there appears to be no relationship between this recent increase in hare density and numbers of lynx observed (Fig. 8.15). We also compared hare and lynx harvest data for the state of Minnesota (Fig. 8.16). The large peaks in lynx harvest in the 1960s and 1970s, which occurred three years after similar irruptive dynamics in central Canada, do not appear to be associated with increases in local hare harvest.

Discussion

The idea that lynx population dynamics emanate from the center of the taiga outward toward the periphery is supported by these analyses.

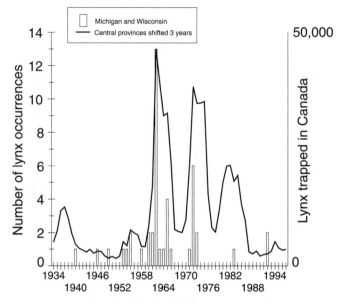

Figure 8.14—Verified lynx records for Wisconsin and Michigan combined (Tables 8.3 and 8.4) overlaid on lynx trapping data from Saskatchewan, Manitoba, and Ontario combined (Fig. 8.3). Canadian data were lagged three years based on the best fit to Minnesota trapping records (Table 8.5, Fig. 8.10). Note that verified records for these states are weak, with a maximum number per year of 13 in 1962.

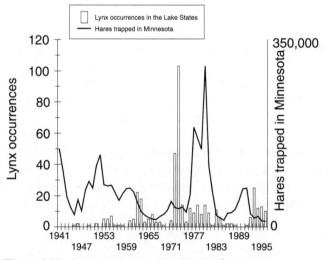

Figure 8.15—Lynx occurrence data for the Great Lakes region (Fig. 8.13) overlaid on snowshoe hare harvest data for Minnesota.

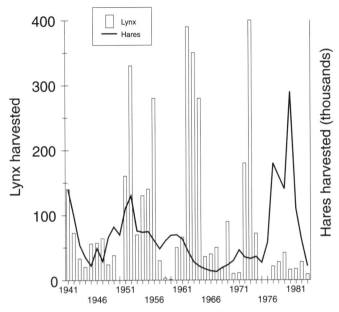

Figure 8.16—Lynx and hare harvest data for Minnesota.

Patterns in the contiguous United States, while weaker, are consistent with the patterns observed within Canada and between Canada and Alaska. With the exception of the northeastern United States, both correlation metrics (for those data where we applied them) and visual inspection suggested that lagging the Canadian data forward by two to four years improved the correlation with United States data. While there are several nonbiological factors that could lead to these patterns, the consistency of lagged correlations between the trapping data and the occurrence data and across various states and regions suggests that these patterns are biologically based.

For the Canadian provinces and Alaska, correlation patterns were generally very strong and were consistent across the entire time series (>60 years in all cases). In the United States, correlations were generally weak and, with the exception of New Hampshire, were primarily associated with the large irruptive peaks in the 1960s and 1970s.

If we assume that observed patterns indicate general changes in numbers of lynx, then there are several hypotheses that could explain these patterns. One is the immigration hypothesis presented above, another is that local populations are responding to the same factors that are controlling northern populations and, hence, are in synchrony, and a third is that the dynamics are some combination of the two.

In the Canadian provinces, Alaska, Montana, and Washington, we know that there are local reproductive populations, knowledge that invalidates a pure immigration hypothesis. For these areas, we can only state that they appear to be a part of a population in which lagged synchronous dynamics occur. Because we do not know why these dynamics occur, we cannot say to what extent they are affected by changes in local dynamics and the role that immigration might play.

For the most recent decades, dynamics in the Great Lakes region may be strongly driven by immigration. Though the data are weak, the lack of a response in the occurrence data to an extremely large regional increase in hares that peaked in 1980 coupled with low hare densities during the lynx peaks in the 1960s and 1970s suggest these irruptive dynamics may not be local in origin. This does not tell us whether or not there are local populations present, however; it merely indicates that the large "spikes" that dominate recent temporal patterns of lynx occurrence in the Lake States are at least partially Canadian in origin.

Given this, we find puzzling the lack of lynx occurrence records associated with a large population peak occurring in the central provinces during the early 1980s. This population peak was higher than any recorded in the 20th century prior to 1959, but there was no evidence from museum specimens, verified mortality records, or anecdotal observations that unusual numbers of lynx occurred in any portion of its range in the contiguous United States. In 1984, after the expected increase in lynx numbers in Minnesota failed to occur, the state closed the lynx harvest (DonCarlos 1994, unpublished).

The "explosions" of lynx in the early 1960s and 1970s were unprecedented events in the 20th century (Fig. 8.3). Many lynx observed during these "explosions" were found in anomalous habitats and geographic regions, exhibited abnormal behavior, and suffered high mortality (Gunderson 1978; Thiel 1987). Mech (1980) reported that lynx numbers declined dramatically in Minnesota after the 1972 influx; trapping records also indicate that post-irruptive populations were low: 215 were trapped in 1972, 691 in 1973, 88 in 1974, and 0 in 1975 and 1976. Lynx occurrence records in Michigan and Wisconsin similarly declined to very low levels within a few years after the peak irruptive periods (Thiel 1987; Fig. 8.14). It may be that the correlations which we observed between lynx occurrences in the northern United States and Canada following these irruptions are historically unusual as well.

Lynx Associations With Broad Cover Types

By considering lynx occurrence data over broad scales of space and time, we can describe patterns in the distribution of occurrences relative to topography and vegetation to elucidate the nature of their range in the contiguous United States (Fig. 8.17). Because of the irregularities in the data, we do not use the data themselves to define the bounding polygons as one would for home range data (White and Garrott 1990). Instead, we simply ask: Which cover types and elevation zones contain most of the occurrences?

To examine the distribution of lynx occurrences by elevation, we used data from a Digital Elevation Model (1,040 m/pixel) re-coded into 250-m elevation classes. For the Northeast and Great Lakes states, we used provinces from Bailey's (1998) ecoregion classification to describe vegetation at the broader scale, and subsection-level "potential dominant vegetation-1" (Keys et al. 1995) at the finer scale. For western states, Bailey's ecoregions were overly broad, and we lacked a subsection-level map. We therefore characterized western vegetation using Küchler (1964), with the form classification representing a large-scale cover class, and "vegetation type" representing a finer-scale class of potential vegetation.

All occurrences with at least county-level resolution within the three regions (Table 8.1) were included in these habitat analyses. In the Northeast and Great Lakes states, where most of the data were at county-level resolution, counties were assigned to vegetation and elevation classes using a majority-area rule, and occurrences with county-level resolution were then assigned to these county-level classes. To describe the distribution of occurrences by habitat type, we emphasized the classes of vegetation and elevation which encompassed at least 75% of the occurrences in a region and referred to them as "primary" types. The distribution of occurrences was also compared to the areal distribution of the types within each region. Because elevational relationships are likely to vary among states along ecological gradients, we also considered elevation distributions on a state-by-state basis.

Habitat Patterns Associated With Lynx Occurrences

West—Elevations in the West are variable, ranging from 0 to 4,180 m. Lynx occurrences generally occurred at higher elevations than is reflected by the areal distribution of elevation zones: 70% of occurrences fell within the 1,500-2,000-m class, which comprised only 42% of the area. This pattern is highly influenced by variation among states in the number of occurrences: 95% of the occurrences in the 1,250-2,000-m range are from Montana and Washington. However, frequency distributions for the individual states continue to demonstrate peak numbers of occurrences at mid-elevations that deviate from the areal distribution of elevation classes (Fig. 8.18). Additional patterns emerge from the state-by-state distributions. Examining elevation patterns across the region, both point and area distributions

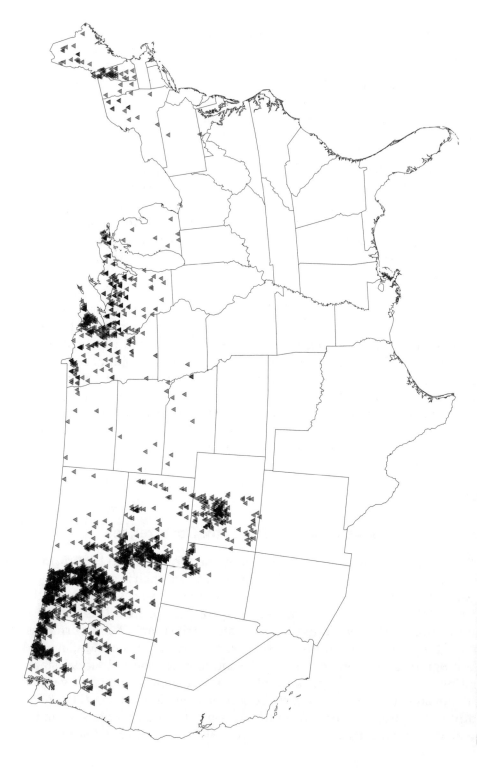

Figure 8.17—Spatial distribution of lynx occurrence data from 1842 to 1998 (Table 8.1).

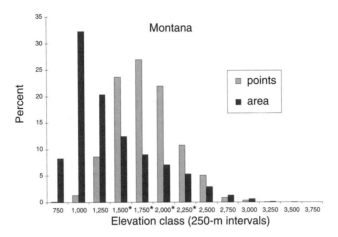

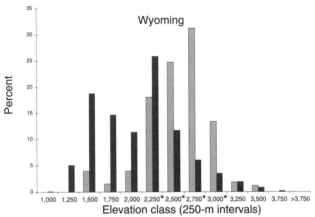

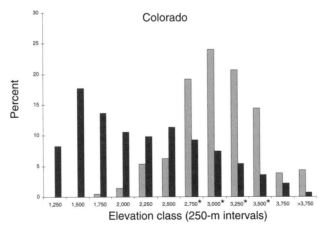

Figure 8.18—Relationships between lynx occurrence and elevation for Montana, Wyoming, and Colorado. Elevation zones marked with a (★) were included in the definition of primary areas of occurrence.

shift to increasingly higher elevations as one moves southward from Idaho and Montana to Wyoming, Utah, and Colorado (Fig. 8.18).

Vegetation types are also effective in characterizing the distribution of occurrences. At the larger vegetation scale, Rocky Mountain Conifer Forest contains 83% of the occurrences but represents only 27% of the area in the region (Fig. 8.19). The other conifer-dominated class in the region, PNW Conifer Forest, had the second highest point frequency (7%), which was generally equivalent to its areal frequency, but occurrences were located only in areas adjacent to Rocky Mountain Conifer Forest. Less than 3% of the occurrences were located in each of the remaining classes, with decreasing frequencies of occurrences with greater distance from areas of Rocky Mountain Conifer Forest (Fig. 8.19). On the finer scale of vegetation classification, the distribution of occurrences also differed significantly from the areal distribution of types. The primary types, Douglas-fir and western spruce/fir forests of the Rocky Mountain Conifer class, and fir/hemlock of the PNW Conifer class, encompass 79% of the occurrences but only 15% of the area. Occurrences are rare within the remaining vegetation types, which include both non-forest and drier forest types.

Areas that encompass primary classes of both elevation and vegetation contain 67% of the occurrences, including a majority of the occurrences within most states (Fig. 8.20). The area within this combined habitat type generally increases from south to north. From Montana southeast to Utah and Colorado, clusters of this combined habitat type become increasingly isolated. From Washington to Oregon, the width of the strip representing primary habitat narrows as one moves southward.

Great Lakes region—Elevations in this region are low and of low variability, ranging from 170 to 660 m. The distribution of occurrences parallels the areal distribution of elevations in the region, with 80% of occurrences falling in the mid-elevation zone of 250-500 m, which represents 78% of the total area. This relationship also holds within the individual states; thus, elevation was not important in characterizing the distribution of occurrences in this region.

The locations of lynx records in these states were associated with vegetation type, however. At the coarser vegetation scale, 88% of occurrences are within Mixed Deciduous-Coniferous Forest, which accounts for <50% of the area (Fig. 8.21). The remaining 12% of occurrences were located in Broadleaved Continental Forests and Forest-Steppes and Prairies. At the finer vegetation scale, the seven vegetation types containing occurrences encompassed 73% of occurrences but only 32% of the area; of the seven types, sugar maple-basswood, jack pine, and white pine-red pine forest types had the highest frequencies of occurrences (each >15%). All of these

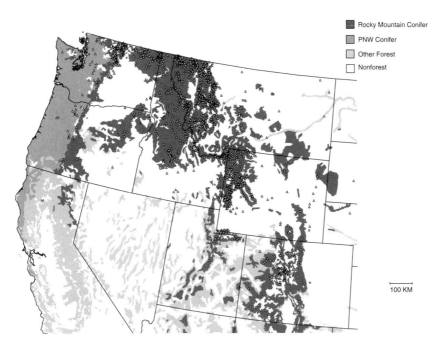

Figure 8.19—Lynx occurrence data overlaid on Küchler (1964) vegetation classes in the western United States. The Rocky Mountain Conifer cover-type enclosed 83% of lynx occurrences.

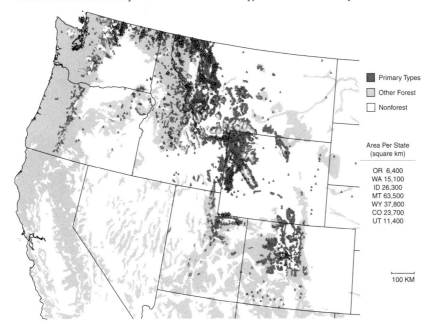

Figure 8.20—Areas of primary lynx occurrence are those areas that (1) consist of a cover type associated with at least 75% of lynx occurrences and (2) lie within an elevation zone enclosing at least 75% of lynx occurrences in each state; 67% of lynx records fell within this area.

247

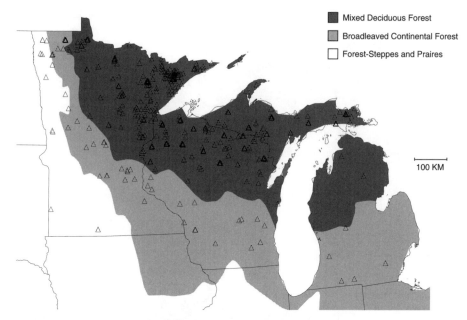

Figure 8.21—Lynx occurrence data overlaid on Bailey (1998) vegetation classes in the Great Lakes region. The Mixed Deciduous-Coniferous Forest type enclosed 88% of lynx records.

primary types are classified as Mixed Deciduous-Coniferous Forest, except for the sugar maple-basswood type which falls into Broadleaved Continental Forest. The distribution of these primary vegetation types occurs primarily in northern Wisconsin and Minnesota, with <15% within Michigan (Fig. 8.22). Conversely, areas lacking occurrences are found in southern areas and represent mostly non-conifer or unforested types.

Northeast—Elevations in the Northeast range from 0 to 1,745 m. The distribution of occurrences by elevation is shifted toward higher elevations compared to the areal distribution of elevations in the region: 77% of occurrences were at mid-elevations ranging from 250 to 750 m, which comprises 59% of the total area. The 0-250-m class has the greatest difference between occurrences and area with only 20% of occurrences compared to 39% of the area. These patterns also hold within Maine, New Hampshire, and New York, but Vermont, Massachusetts, and Pennsylvania had too few occurrences to allow comparison (Table 8.1).

Vegetation also serves to describe the distribution of lynx occurrences in the region (Fig. 8.23). At the broader scale, the most northerly and mountainous class in the region, Mixed Forest-Coniferous Forest-Tundra, encompasses 88% of the occurrences compared to only 29% of the area, and the remaining occurrences fell into five other provinces. At the finer scale,

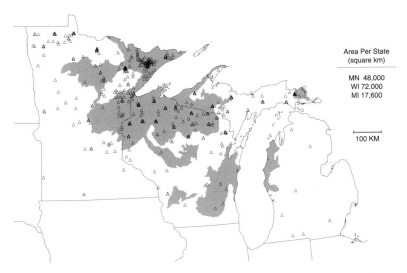

Figure 8.22—Areas of primary lynx occurrence in the Great Lakes region are those areas that enclose 73% of lynx records based on potential dominant vegetation types (Keys et al. 1995). Elevation was not used to define areas of primary occurrence in this region.

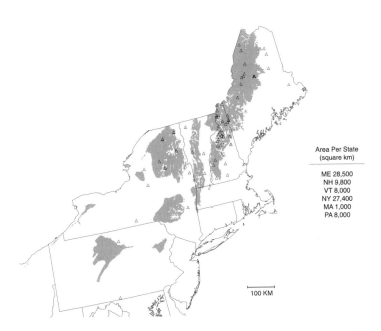

Figure 8.23—Areas of primary lynx occurrence in the northeastern states based on potential dominant vegetation types (Keys et al. 1995) and elevations >250 m; 70% of lynx records fell within these areas.

249

occurrences are located within 10 vegetation types, with the highest frequency in red spruce-balsam fir/sugar maple-birch-beech forest (53%). The primary types also include sugar maple-birch-beech forest and red spruce-balsam fir forest; the three types together comprise 84% of occurrences compared to 29% of the area and are found within Mixed Forest-Coniferous Forest-Tundra. The types that include spruce-fir are absent south of Vermont and the northern Adirondack Mountains. In general, lynx occurrences were rare within areas typed as dry forest or non-forest.

Intersecting the primary vegetation classes with the primary elevation classes left an area that is primarily contained within Mixed Forest-Coniferous Forest-Tundra, includes 70% of the occurrences, and encompasses a majority of the occurrences within each state (Fig. 8.23). More than 60% of this area occurs in Maine and New York, followed by Vermont, New Hampshire and Pennsylvania, with trace amounts in Massachusetts. From Maine south to Pennsylvania, areas of primary occurrence become increasingly disjunct.

Implications of Habitat Relationships

Because our analyses of habitat associations were conducted with data that varied greatly among states (Table 8.1), observed patterns within a region are heavily weighted by those states with the most occurrences. However, even in states with relatively few occurrences, the locations generally fell within the predicted habitat classes. In the Northeast, most of the occurrences were in the White Mountains of New Hampshire; but predicted vegetation associations that were based largely on these data include most of the locations in New York and Maine (Fig. 8.23). Thus, broad-scale patterns in vegetation and elevation effectively capture regional patterns in the distribution of lynx occurrences. The consistency across states within a region adds support to the idea that these patterns reflect general habitat use patterns of lynx.

For all three regions, high frequencies of occurrence records correspond to cool, coniferous forests in northern areas. For the western and northeastern regions, these forests occur at mid-elevations in montane areas; frequencies of occurrences decrease from these areas toward the more maritime zones. In all three regions, areas of primary occurrence become increasingly rare and fragmented as one moves away from these northerly concentrations of coniferous forests and, in the West, primary forest types also occur at higher elevations along this gradient. The range of the snowshoe hare, the primary prey of lynx, is also coincident with montane areas in the West and Northeast and northern areas in the Great Lakes region (Chapter 7).

Ephemeral locations and dispersal potential—Although the primary vegetation classes encompassed the majority of occurrences, many occurrences fell into other vegetation classes. Occurrences could be associated with these types because of location or vegetation classification errors or dispersal movements, or they could be indicative of small resident populations. While we cannot differentiate between these causes in an absolute sense, we can use the spatial distributions of these locations to explore the most likely explanations.

For those 349 occurrences in the focal states of the West that were located outside of the Rocky Mountain or PNW Conifer classes (Fig. 8.19), we calculated the nearest straight-line distance to a conifer-type polygon. We compared these distances to those of random locations placed within the non-conifer types using a X^2 homogeneity test. Data from the northeastern and Great Lakes regions were not analyzed because of their limited spatial resolution (generally only at county level).

Both error and dispersal occurrences should be close to source types, whereas occurrences from resident populations may be distributed randomly with respect to source areas. Occurrences representing errors are generally concentrated in a narrow "epsilon band" around the source type (Blakemore 1984; Dunn et al. 1990) due to granularity along the boundary. Such an error distribution should decline very quickly with distance from the source. In contrast, a simple dispersal model of constant probability of detection with distance (usually through mortality) should show exponential decline with distance.

Points located in non-conifer types are significantly closer to conifer forest types than expectation ($p < 0.001$), indicating that they are associated with conifer forests. Most of the occurrences are extremely close to a conifer type (Fig. 8.24), and 79% (274 of 349) are within 10 km of conifer forest. Undoubtedly, many of these occurrences actually occurred within conifer forests and lie outside of these types due to errors in location and vegetation mapping, while others may be associated with normal within-home range or short-range exploratory movements. Assuming that many of the non-conifer locations within 10 km of conifer types may be due to mapping error, we are left with 75 locations >10 km from conifer forest whose distance distribution generally declines exponentially with distance from conifer forests (Fig. 8.25).

These remaining occurrences are reasonably distant from the nearest area typed as conifer forest, at an average distance of 39 km and maximum distance of 259 km, and are probably in non-conifer, and generally non-forested types. In addition, because most of the non-conifer types in the region are non-forest (Fig. 8.19), these distances represent conservative

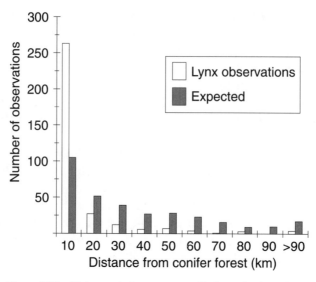

Figure 8.24—Distances to the nearest conifer forest for those lynx occurrences in non-conifer cover types in the West. Lynx occurrences were significantly closer to conifer types than would be expected based on random placement within non-conifer types.

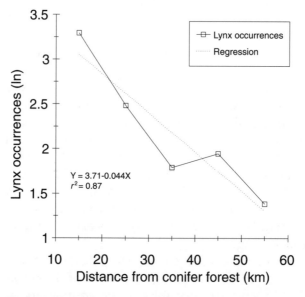

Figure 8.25—Lynx occurrences in areas that are >10 km from a conifer type decline exponentially with distance. An exponential distribution is transformed to a linear relationship by taking the log of the dependent variable.

estimates of the amount of non-forested landscape crossed by lynx prior to detection. We also have 20 records of lynx locations in Nevada and the Plains states (Table 8.1) that probably represent much longer dispersals across open lands. However, our data suggest that long-distance dispersals are relatively rare, as only four of 3,803 occurrences in the Western region were >100 km from conifer forest.

Conclusions

There are records of lynx occurrence in 24 states. Generally, verified records extend to the mid 1800s, and, due to confusion with bobcats, earlier accounts are often suspect. For four of these states—Minnesota, Montana, New Hampshire, and Washington—we have reliable trapping data, and for Minnesota and Montana, fairly large numbers of lynx were trapped in the 20th century (5,585 and 3,012, respectively). For most states, data are too fragmentary to infer much concerning lynx beyond simple occurrence. In the states where we have trapping data, dynamics appear to be associated with patterns of lagged synchrony that occur across Canada and Alaska, but the mechanisms that underlie these dynamics are unknown. Given our current lack of understanding of these dynamics, their presence increases our uncertainty concerning the meaning of an occurrence, or even many occurrences. In Minnesota, for instance, the 5,585 lynx trapped in the 20th century could have been produced by a local population, or as some researchers have hypothesized, be mostly immigrants or any combination of local lynx and dispersers.

Lynx occurrences in the 20th century are closely associated with conifer forest types associated with the southern extensions of the boreal forest, a pattern that conforms to our biological understandings of lynx habitat (Chapter 13). There is little evidence of occurrence in other types such as pure deciduous forests in the East or shrub-steppe types in the West. Where occurrences are in unusual types, most of the locations are immediately adjacent to the conifer cover types containing most of the occurrences.

Literature Cited

Adams, A. W. 1963. The lynx explosion. North Dakota Outdoors 26:20-24.

Anonymous. 1918. The Canadian lynx. The Conservationist 10:157.

Anonymous. 1952. Another lynx. The New York State Conservationist 6:34.

Anonymous. 1963. The lynx in New York. The Conservationist 17:39.

Anonymous. 1966. Another lynx. The Conservationist 20:41.

Anonymous. 1987. Endangered and threatened species of plants and animals in Vermont. Unpublished, Vermont Agency of Natural Resources, North Springfield, Vermont.

Anonymous. 1999. Canada lynx in Idaho: species conservation assessment. Unpublished Idaho Conservation effort: USDI Bureau of Land Management, Idaho Department of Fish and Game, Idaho Department of Parks and Recreation, U.S. Fish and Widlife Service, USDA Forest Service.

Bailey, R. G. 1998. Ecoregions map of North America: explanatory note. USDA Forest Service, Miscellaneous Publication No. 1548.

Bailey, V. 1918. Wild animals of Glacier National Park: the mammals. USDI National Park Service, Washington, DC.

Bailey, V. 1926. A biological survey of North Dakota. North American Fauna 49:1-229.

Bailey, V. 1930. Animal life of Yellowstone National Park. Charles C. Thomas Publisher, Springfield, IL.

Bailey, V. 1936. Mammals and life zones of Oregon. North American Fauna 55:1-416.

Baker, R. H. 1983. Michigan mammals. Michigan State University Press, Lansing, MI.

Barnes, C. T. 1927. Utah mammals. Bulletin of the University of Utah 17:1-88.

Barrus, H. 1881. History of the town of Goshen, Hampshire County, Massachusetts. Published by the author in Boston, MA.

Bergstrom, A. S. 1977. The status of the lynx in New York (*Lynx canadensis*). Unpublished, U.S. Fish and Wildlife Service, Endangered and Threatened Wildlife and Plants.

Blakemore, M. 1984. Generalization of error in spatial databases. Cartographica 21:131-139.

Brainerd, S. M. 1985. Reproductive ecology of bobcats and lynx in western Montana. Unpublished M.S. Thesis, University of Montana, Missoula, MT.

Brittell, J. D., R. J. Poelker, S. J. Sweeney, and G. M. Koehler. 1989. Native cats of Washington, Section III: lynx. Unpublished, Washington Department of Wildlife, Olympia, WA.

Brocke, R. H. 1982. Restoration of the lynx *Lynx canadensis* in Adirondack Park: a problem analysis and recommendations. Unpublished, Federal Aid Project E-1-3 and W-105-R. New York State Department of Environmental Conservation Study XII, Job 5.

Brocke, R. H., K. A. Gustafson, and A. R. Major. 1990. Restoration of the lynx in New York: biopolitical lessons. Transactions of the North American Wildlife and Natural Resources Conference 55:590-598.

Brocke, R. H., K. A. Gustafson, and L. B. Fox. 1991. Restoration of large predators: potentials and problems. Pages 303-315 *in* Challenges in the conservation of biological resources. a practitioner's guide. D. J. Decker, M. E. Krasny, G. R. Goff, C. R. Smith, and D. W. Gross, eds. Westview Press, Boulder, CO.

Burt, W. H. 1946. The mammals of Michigan. University of Michigan Press, Ann Arbor, MI.

Cardoza, J. E. In press. Lynx. *in* T. W. French and J. E. Cardoza, eds. Rare vertebrates of Massachusetts. Massachusetts Audubon Society, Lincoln, MA.

Carney, I. M. 1993. Colorado lynx study: winter 1993. Unpublished, Colorado Division of Wildlife, Glenwood Springs, CO.

Central. 1905. In Massachusetts. Forest and Stream 64:30-31.

Crane, J. 1931. Mammals of Hampshire County, Massachusetts. Journal of Mammalogy 12:267-273.

Dalquest, W. W. 1948. Mammals of Washington. University of Kansas Publications in Natural History 2:1-444.

Davis, W. B. 1939. The recent mammals of Idaho. The Caxton Printers, Ltd., Caldwell, ID.

DeKay, J. E. 1842. Natural history of New York. Part I. Zoology. D. Appleton and Co., New York.

Dice, L. R. and H. B. Sherman. 1922. Notes on the mammals of Gogebic and Ontonogon Counties, Michigan, 1920. Occasional Papers of the Museum of Zoology, University of Michigan 109:1-47.

DonCarlos, M. W. 1994. Fact sheet: management of the lynx (*Felis lynx*) in Minnesota. Unpublished, Minnesota Department of Natural Resources, St. Paul, MN.

Dunn, R., A. R. Harrison, and J. C. White. 1990. Positional accuracy in digital databases of land use: an empirical study. International Journal of Geographical Information Systems 4:385-398.

Durrant, S. D. 1952. Mammals of Utah: taxonomy and distribution. University of Kansas Publications, Museum of Natural History 6:1-549.

Eaton, W. P. 1919. Big game returning to New England hills. Bulletin of the American Game Protection Association 8:11.

Elton, C. and M. Nicholson. 1942. The ten-year cycle in numbers of the lynx in Canada. Journal of Animal Ecology 11:215-244.

Erickson, A. W. 1955. A recent record of lynx in Michigan. Journal of Mammalogy 36:132-133.

F. C. B. 1878. Lynxes in Massachusetts. Forest and Stream 1:531.

Findley, J. S. and S. Anderson. 1956. Zoogeography of the montane mammals of Colorado. Journal of Mammalogy 37:80-82.

Fountain, E. A., Jr. 1976. The Canada lynx. The Conservationist 31:2.

Godin, A. J. 1977. Wild mammals of New England. Johns Hopkins University Press, Baltimore, MD.

Goodwin, G. G. 1935. The mammals of Connecticut. State Geological and Natural History Survey, Bulletin No. 53.

Grimm, W. C. and R. Whitebread. 1952. Mammal survey of northeastern Pennsylvania. Unpublished, Pittman-Robertson Project 42-R:1-82.

Gunderson, H. L. 1978. A mid-continent irruption of Canada lynx, 1962-63. Prairie Naturalist 10:71-80.

Halfpenny, J.C., S. J. Bissell, and D. M. Nead. 1989. Status of the lynx (*Felis lynx*, Felidae) in Colorado with comments on its distribution in Western United States. Unpublished, Institute of Arctic and Alpine Research, University of Colorado, Boulder, CO.

Hall, E. R. 1981. The mammals of North America, 2nd Edition. John Wiley and Sons, New York.

Halloran, A. F. and W. E. Blanchard. 1959. Lynx from western Wyoming. Journal of Mammalogy 40:450-451.

Hamilton, W. J., Jr. 1943. The mammals of the Eastern United States. Comstock Publishing Co., Ithaca, NY.

Hamilton, W. J., Jr., and J. O. Whittaker, Jr. 1979. Mammals of the Eastern United States, 2nd edition. Cornell University Press, Ithaca, NY.

Harger, E. M. 1965. The status of the Canada lynx in Michigan. The Jack-Pine Warbler 43:150-153.

Harper, F. 1929. Notes on mammals of the Adirondacks. New York State Museum Handbook No. 8, New York State Museum, Albany, NY.

Hastings, A. and S. Harrison. 1994. Metapopulation dynamics and genetics. Annual Review of Ecology and Systematics 25:163-184.

Henderson, C. 1978. Minnesota Canada lynx report, 1977. Minnesota Wildlife Research Quarterly 38:221-242.

Herrick, C. L. 1892. The mammals of Minnesota. Geological and natural history survey of Minnesota, Bulletin No. 7.

Hoffmann, R. S., P. L. Wright, and F. E. Newby. 1969. The distribution of some mammals in Montana: I. Mammals other than bats. Journal of Mammalogy 50:583-604.

Hunt, J. H. 1964. The lynx. Maine Fish and Game Magazine 6:14.

Hunt, J. H. 1974. The little-known lynx. Maine Fish and Game Magazine 16:28.

Jackson, H. H. T. 1961. The mammals of Wisconsin. University of Wisconsin Press, Madison, WI.

Jakubus, W. J. 1997. Lynx in Maine. Unpublished, Maine Department of Inland Fisheries and Wildlife, Bangor, ME.

Jones, J. K., Jr. 1964. Distribution and taxonomy of mammals of Nebraska. University of Kansas Publications, Museum of Natural History 16:1-356.

Keith, L. B. 1963. Wildlife's ten-year cycle. University of Wisconsin Press, Madison, WI.

Kennicott, R. 1855. Catalogue of animals observed in Cook County, Illinois. Transactions of the Illinois State Agricultural Society 1:577-595.

Keys, J., Jr., C. Carpenter, S. Hooks, F. Koenig, W. H. McNab, W. Russell, and M. L. Smith. 1995. Ecological units of the Eastern United States - first approximation (cd-rom), Atlanta, GA. U.S. Department of Agriculture, Forest Service. GIS coverage in ARC/INFO format, selected imagery, and map unit tables.

Koehler, G. M. 1990. Population and habitat characteristics of lynx and snowshoe hares in north central Washington. Canadian Journal of Zoology 68:845-851.

Koehler, G. M. and K. B. Aubry. 1994. Lynx. Pages 74-98 in L. F. Ruggiero, K. B. Aubry, S. W. Buskirk, L. J. Lyon, and W. J. Zielinski, tech. eds. The scientific basis for conserving forest carnivores: American marten, fisher, lynx and wolverine in the Western United States. USDA Forest Service General Technical Report RM-254.

Küchler, A. W. 1964. Potential natural vegetation of the conterminous United States (map and manual). American Geographical Society Special Publication 36.

Lewis, L. and C. R. Wenger. 1998. Idaho's Canada lynx: pieces of the puzzle. Idaho Bureau of Land Management Technical Bulletin No. 98-11.

Litvaitis, J. A. 1994. New Hampshire's wild felines. New Hampshire Wildlife Journal 6:4-7.

Litvaitis, J. A., D. Kingman, Jr., J. Lanier, and E. Orff. 1991. Status of lynx in New Hampshire. Transactions of the Northeast Section of the Wildlife Society 48:70-75.

Long, C. A. 1965. The mammals of Wyoming. University of Kansas, Museum of Natural History Publication 14:493-758.

Lyon, M. W., Jr. 1936. Mammals of Indiana. The American Midland Naturalist 17:1-384.

Maj, M. and E. O. Garton. 1994. Fisher, lynx, wolverine summary of distribution information. Appendix B *in* L. F. Ruggiero, K. B. Aubry, S. W. Buskirk, L. J. Lyon and W. J. Zielinski, tech. eds. The scientific basis for conserving forest carnivores: American marten, fisher, lynx and wolverine in the Western United States. USDA Forest Service General Technical Report RM-254.

McCord, C. M. and J. E. Cardoza. 1982. Bobcat and lynx. Pages 728-766 *in* J. A. Chapman and G. A. Feldhamer, eds. Wild mammals of North America. Johns Hopkins University Press, Baltimore, MD.

McKay, R. 1991. Biological assessment and inventory plan for the North American lynx (*Felis lynx canadensis*) in the Uinta Mountains. Unpublished, Ashley National Forest and Utah Natural Heritage Program, Utah Department of Natural Resources, Salt Lake City, UT.

Mearns, E. A. 1899. Notes on the mammals of the Catskill Mountains, New York, with general remarks on the fauna and flora of the region. Proceedings of the U.S. National Museum 21:341-360.

Mech, L. D. 1973. Canadian lynx invasion of Minnesota. Biological Conservation 5:151-152.

Mech, L. D. 1980. Age, sex, reproduction, and spatial organization of lynxes colonizing northeastern Minnesota. Journal of Mammalogy 61:261-267.

Merriam, C. H. 1884. The mammals of the Adirondack region, northeastern New York. L. S. Foster Press, New York.

Miller, G. S., Jr. 1899. Preliminary list of the mammals of New York. Bulletin of the New York State Museum 6:339-340.

Mumford, R. E. 1969. Distribution of the mammals of Indiana. The Indiana Academy of Sciences, Indianapolis, IN.

Novak, M., M. E. Obbard, J. G. James, R. Newman, A. Booth, A. J. Satterthwaite, and G. Linscombe. 1987. Furbearer harvests in North America, 1600-1984. Ministry of Natural Resources, Ontario, Canada.

Orff, E. P. 1985. Lynx (*Felis lynx*) status report. Unpublished, New Hampshire Fish and Game Department, Concord, NH.

Osgood, F. L., Jr. 1938. The mammals of Vermont. Journal of Mammalogy 19:435-441.

Palmer, R. S. 1937. Mammals of Maine. Unpublished M.S. Thesis, University of Maine, Orono, ME.

Parker, H. C. 1939. A preliminary list of the mammals of Massachusetts. Proceedings of the Boston Society of Natural History 41:403-415.

Quinn, N. W. S. and G. Parker. 1987. Lynx. Pages 682-695 *in* Wild furbearer management and conservation in North America. M. Novak, J. A. Baker, M. E. Obbard, and B. Malloch, eds. Ministry of Natural Resources, Ontario, Canada.

Rafinesque, C. S. 1817. Description of seven new genera of North American quadrupeds. American Monthly Magazine 2:44-46.

Ranta, E., V. Kaitala, and J. Lindstrom. 1997. Dynamics of Canadian lynx populations in space and time. Ecography 20:454-460.

Rasmussen, J. L. 1969. A recent record of the lynx in Iowa. Journal of Mammalogy 50:370-371.

Reeve, A., F. Lindzey, and S. Buskirk. 1986. Historic and recent distribution of the lynx in Wyoming. Unpublished, Wyoming Cooperative Fishery and Wildlife Research Unit, Laramie, WY.

Ruggiero, L. F., K. B. Aubry, S. W. Buskirk, L. J. Lyon, and W. J. Zielinski, tech. eds. 1994. The scientific basis for conserving forest carnivores: American marten, fisher, lynx and wolverine in the Western United States. USDA Forest Service General Technical Report RM-254.

Rust, H. J. 1946. Mammals of northern Idaho. Journal of Mammalogy 27:308-327.

Schantz, V. 1947. Record of *Lynx canadensis canadensis* in Nevada. Journal of Mammalogy 28:292-293.

Schorger, A. W. 1947. Canada lynx taken in Sauk County, Wisconsin. Journal of Mammalogy 28:186-187.

Seagers, C. 1948. Missing New Yorkers. The New York State Conservationist 2:32.

Seagers, C. 1951. The lynx is back. The New York State Conservationist 6:40.

Seton, E. T. 1929. Lives of game animals. Doubleday, Doran, and Co., Inc., Garden City, NY.

Shoemaker, H. W. 1929. The wild animals of Clinton County, Pennsylvania. Pennsylvania Alpine Club Wild Life Bulletin 10:1-110.

Siegler, H. R. 1971. The status of wildcats in New Hampshire. Pages 38-45 *in* S. E. Jorgensen and L. D. Mech, eds. Proceedings of a symposium on the native cats of North America: their status and management. U.S. Fish and Wildlife Service, Twin Cities, MN.

Silver, H. 1974. A history of New Hampshire game and furbearers, 2nd edition. New Hampshire Fish and Game Department, Survey Report 6, Concord, NH.

Smith, D. S. 1984. Habitat use, home range, and movements of bobcats in western Montana. Unpublished M.S. Thesis, University of Montana, Missoula, MT.

Smith, H. G., R. K. Burnard, E. E. Good, and J. M. Keener. 1973. Rare and endangered vertebrates of Ohio. The Ohio Journal of Science 73:257-271.

Spurrell, J. A. 1917. An annotated list of the mammals of Sac County. Proceedings of the Iowa Academy of Science 24:274-275.

Stouffer, A. L. 1961. The story of Shell Lake. The Washburn County Historical Society Register, Shell Lake, WI.

Taylor, W. P. and W. T. Shaw. 1927. Mammals and birds of Mount Rainier National Park. USDI National Park Service, U.S. Government Printing Office, Washington, DC.

Terrell, B. 1971. Lynx. Colorado Outdoors 20:19.

Thiel, R. P. 1987. The status of Canada lynx in Wisconsin, 1865-1980. Wisconsin Academy of Sciences, Arts and Letters 75:90-96.

Turner, R. W. 1974. Mammals of the Black Hills of South Dakota and Wyoming. University of Kansas, Museum of Natural History, Miscellaneous Publication No. 60.

Verts, B. J. and L. N. Carraway. 1998. Land mammals of Oregon. University of California Press, Berkeley, CA.

Whish, J. D. 1919. Lynx in the Adirondacks. Forest and Stream 89:353.

White, G. C. and R. A. Garrott. 1990. Analysis of wildlife radio-tracking data. Academic Press, San Diego, CA.

Williams, S. L., S. B. McLaren, and M. A. Burgwin. 1985. Paleo-archaeological and historical records of selected Pennsylvania mammals. Annals of Carnegie Museum 54:77-188.

Wood, N. A. 1922. The mammals of Washtenaw County, Michigan. Occasional Papers of the Museum of Zoology, University of Michigan, Ann Arbor, No. 123.

Wood, N. A. and L. R. Dice. 1924. Records of the distribution of Michigan mammals. Papers of the Michigan Academy of Science, Arts, and Letters 3:425-445.

Wydeven, A. P. 1998. Lynx status in Wisconsin, 1998. Unpublished, Wisconsin Department of Natural Resources, Madison, WI.

Zar, J. H. 1996. Biostatistical analysis. Prentice Hall, Upper Saddle River, NJ.

Appendix 8.1

Sources for Lynx Occurrence Data in the United States

Colorado: The Colorado Natural Heritage Program maintains a state database that is a compilation of museum records, Colorado Division of Wildlife harvest records, sightings reported to the Division, and published reports. The White River National Forest reported five visual observations and Rocky Mountain National Park reported one. Museum specimen records were obtained from the Denver Museum of Natural History, Academy of Natural Sciences of Philadelphia, Milwaukee Public Museum, and the National Museum of Natural History. Records from the database compiled by O.S. Garton and Mary Maj and previously published in Ruggiero et al. (1994) are also included.

Idaho: The state database for Idaho is maintained by the Idaho Fish Conservation Data Center (IDFG CDC) and is a compilation of museum records, IDFG harvest records, sightings of animals and tracks reported to the CDC and interviews of knowledgeable hound hunters and trappers. Visual observations and/or tracks were reported by the following National Forests: Beaverhead-Deerlodge, Bitterroot, Idaho Panhandle, Nez Perce, and Sawtooth. Museum specimen records were obtained from Harvard Museum of Comparative Zoology, National Museum of Natural History, University of Colorado Museum, and the Slater Museum of Natural History at the University of Puget Sound. Records from the database compiled by O.S. Garton and Mary Maj and previously published in Ruggiero et al. (1994) are also included.

Illinois: We have only one record for the state of Illinois and that is of a mounted skin from the Academy of Natural Sciences of Philadelphia.

Iowa: The one Iowa record we have is from a mounted skin belonging to the private collection of Jerry L. Rasmussen of Rock Island, Illinois.

Maine: Museum specimen records were obtained from the Harvard Museum of Comparative Zoology, the Museum of Zoology at the University of Michigan, and the National Museum of Natural History. Also included are harvest records as published in Ontario's Ministry of Natural Resources "Furbearer harvests in North America 1600-1984" by Milan Novak et al. Winter track counts were conducted from 1994 to 1997 by the State of Maine Department of Inland Fisheries and Wildlife, and track observations during the winter of 1994-1995 are reflected here. This same agency compiled records of incidental takings and historical observations.

Massachusetts: The only records for Massachusetts are from state harvest reports and bounty records kept by the Massachusetts Division of Fisheries and Wildlife.

Michigan: Museum specimen records were obtained from the following: Michigan State University Museum, Peabody Museum at Yale, Grand Rapids Public Museum, Milwaukee Public Museum, Museum of Zoology at the University of Michigan, and the National Museum of Natural History. Various sightings compiled by both the Michigan Department of Natural Resources and the Michigan Natural Heritage Natural Features Inventory are reported here as well as historical data from two articles, Elsworth M. Harger's 1965 "The Status of the Canada Lynx in Michigan" and "Michigan Mammals" by Rollin H. Baker, published in 1983. Dean Beyer (University of Northern Michigan) compiled a database of approximately 45 lynx records that includes sightings, tracks, and museum specimen records from various sources. One visual observation was reported by the Ottawa National Forest.

Minnesota: Data points for Minnesota include harvest records and records of confiscated carcasses and accidental lynx mortalities obtained from the Minnesota Department of Natural Resources (MNDNR). The MNDNR also provided us with records they had compiled of personal reports of sightings and tracks, reports from newspaper articles, and shootings. Two surveys were done by the MNDNR that yielded data points, a winter track survey conducted 1991 through 1997 (one observation of tracks), and a predator and furbearer scent post census 1975 through 1997 (four detections). L. David Mech trapped and radio-collared a number of lynx from 1972 through 1978 and published the results in "Age, Sex, Reproduction, and Spatial Organization of Lynxes Colonizing Northeastern Minnesota" in 1980. The capture points of those lynx are reflected here. Additionally, Mech kept autopsy records for lynx trapped, shot, or otherwise killed from 1972 to 1974, and those data points are included in our database. Museum specimen records were reported by the following: Bell Museum of Natural History; National Museum of Natural History; the Bird and Mammals Collection at University of California, Los Angeles; the Illinois State Museum, the University of Wisconsin Zoological Museum; and the Los Angeles County Museum.

Montana: The Montana state database is maintained by the Montana Department of Fish, Wildlife and Parks (MDFWP). Occurrence records for this database were obtained from MDFWP harvest records, logbooks, occurrence reports by individuals, and winter track surveys. A number of National Forests reported visual observations, tracks, and physical remains.

These forests include Flathead, Beaverhead-Deerlodge, Gallatin, Kootenai, Lewis and Clark, and Lolo National Forests. Glacier National Park also reported visual observations and tracks. Museum specimen records were obtained from the following: American Museum of Natural History, The Glacier Collection at Glacier National Park, University of Nebraska State Museum, University of North Dakota, Illinois State Museum, National Museum of Natural History, and the Philip Wright Zoological Museum. Records from the database compiled by O.S. Garton and Mary Maj and previously published in Ruggiero et al. (1994) are also included.

Nebraska: The U.S. Fish and Game, South Dakota Field Office provided seven confirmed lynx records. Museum specimen records were obtained from the University of Nebraska State Museum.

Nevada: Nevada has only two records; both were obtained from the National Museum of Natural History.

New Hampshire: The New Hampshire Fish and Game provided harvest/ bounty reports as well as a compilation of records from various sources such as personal accounts of observations and newspaper articles. From the White Mountain National Forest we obtained a compilation of records from personal reports and responses to questionnaires. The Audubon Society of New Hampshire provided points from their Endangered Species Program database. Museum specimen records were obtained from the Museum of Comparative Zoology at Harvard, Cornell University Vertebrate Collections, and the University of Maine.

New York: The majority of the data points for New York came from the U.S. Fish and Wildlife Service report, "The Status of the Lynx in New York (*Lynx canadensis*)" by A.S. Bergstrom (1977, unpublished). The New York State Department of Environmental Conservation reported two rather recent lynx occurrences, one shot and one sighted. Museum specimen records were obtained from the American Museum of Natural History and the Academy of Natural Sciences of Philadelphia.

North Dakota: Most of the North Dakota points are from museum specimen records from the Los Angeles County Museum, University of North Dakota, the Museum of Southwestern Biology at the University of New Mexico, and the National Museum of Natural History. The North Dakota Game and Fish Department reported the total number of lynx taken for two time periods, 1962-65 and 1972-73, on a statewide basis.

Oregon: The Oregon Department of Fish and Wildlife (ODFW) maintains a state database made up of ODFW harvest records, published reports, and sightings reported to the ODFW. Three National Forests reported visual observations: Malheur, Umatilla, and Willamette. Museum specimen records in the database are from the following museums: National Museum of Natural History, Oregon State University, the private collection of Wendell Weaver, the University of Kansas Museum of Natural History, and the Slater Museum of Natural History at University of Puget Sound. Records from the database compiled by O.S. Garton and Mary Maj and previously published in Ruggiero et al. (1994) are also included.

Pennsylvania: The Nature Conservancy's Pennsylvania Science Office reported the "last known record" of naturally occurring lynx. One museum specimen record was obtained from the Reading Public Museum and Art Gallery.

South Dakota: Six records of lynx observations were obtained from the South Dakota Department of Game, Fish and Parks, which manages the South Dakota Natural Heritage Data Base. Museum specimen records were obtained from South Dakota State University and the National Museum of Natural History.

Utah: Records were obtained from the Utah Division of Wildlife Resources (UDWR) Rare Mammal Sighting Program, UDWR harvest records, other UDWR records, published reports, and interviews with various organizations and private individuals. These records make up the state database that is maintained by the UDWR Utah Natural Heritage Program. Museum specimen records were obtained from the Carnegie Museum of Natural History, Utah Museum of Natural History, and the National Museum of Natural History. Ashley National Forest reported five visual observations. Records from the database compiled by O.S. Garton and Mary Maj and previously published in Ruggiero et al. (1994) are also included.

Vermont: The points for Vermont come from two sources: the Vermont Department of Fish and Wildlife (historical records of lynx taken) and the Dartmouth College Museum.

Washington: Details of the Washington state database are lacking and as such, many of the sources are listed as "unknown." Sources that are listed include the U.S. Forest Service, U.S. Bureau of Land Management, the Washington Department of Natural Resources, and data from local counties. We received point data directly from the Okanogan National Forest. These observations were from winter track surveys and camera/bait stations during 1981-1988. Other survey data included here are from a telemetry study done by the Washington Department of Fish and Game, 1981-1988. The Idaho Panhandle and Mount Baker-Snoqualmie National Forests and North Cascades National Park reported a variety of visual observations, tracks, and physical remains. A number of museums contained specimens, including the Conner Museum at Washington State University, National Museum of Natural History, University of Washington Burke Museum, the Museum of Vertebrate Zoology at Berkeley, the University of Massachusetts, and the Slater Museum of Natural History at the University of Puget Sound. Records from the database compiled by O.S. Garton and Mary Maj and previously published in Ruggiero et al. (1994) are included.

Wisconsin: The Wisconsin Department of Natural Resources (WIDNR) provided data points from harvest records, trapper questionnaires, and confirmed personal accounts. Richard Thiel (Bureau of Endangered Resources, WIDNR) compiled quite an extensive collection of lynx/lynx sign observations from sources such as newspaper articles, hunter-trapper questionnaires, museum records, and personal accounts. This "raw data" is summarized in Thiel's 1987 publication "The Status of Canada Lynx in Wisconsin, 1865-1980." Another report by the WIDNR from which data points were taken is Adrian Wydeven's 1998 report, "Lynx Status in Wisconsin." The Nicolet National Forest ran winter track surveys 1993 through 1998, and track observations from that study are included here. Lastly, museum specimen records were obtained from the following: University of Wisconsin at Madison Zoological Museum, Museum of Natural History at the University of Wisconsin at Stevens Point, the Milwaukee Public Museum, the University of Wisconsin at Superior, and the University of Wisconsin Tech Center at Marinette.

Wyoming: The Wyoming state database is maintained by the Wyoming Department of Game and Fish (WDGF) and is a compilation of data from the following sources: WDGF records, publications, federal agency records, interviews with trappers, and a lynx research project in the Wyoming Range of southwestern Wyoming. A number of records were compiled by Reeve et al. (1986, unpublished) and some of the more recent records were compiled by Tom Laurion (WDGF). Three visual observations were reported by Yellowstone National Park. Museum specimen records were obtained from Harvard Museum of Comparative Zoology, University of Kansas Museum of Natural History, National Museum of Natural History, University of Wyoming Museum of Zoology, and the Carnegie Museum of Natural History. Records from the database compiled by O.S. Garton and Mary Maj and previously published in Ruggiero et al. (1994) are included.

Chapter 9

Ecology of Lynx in Northern Canada and Alaska

[1]Garth Mowat, Fish and Wildlife Division, Timberland Consultants Ltd.,
    P. O. Box 171, Nelson, British Columbia V1L 5P9 Canada

[1]Kim G. Poole, Fish and Wildlife Division, Timberland Consultants Ltd.,
    P. O. Box 171, Nelson, British Columbia V1L 5P9 Canada

Mark O'Donoghue, Fish and Wildlife Branch, Dept. of Renewable Resources,
    Box 310, Mayo, Yukon Territory Y0B 1M0 Canada

[1]Order of the first two authors decided by the toss of a coin

Abstract—We review the ecology of lynx in the northern part of its range, drawing heavily on the results of recent research from that region. Snowshoe hares form the bulk of prey items in essentially all studies and at all periods in the cycle, but use of alternative prey, often red squirrel, increases as hares become scarce. Caching of freshly killed prey is rare, although carrion is consumed, primarily during periods of food shortage. Habitat use by lynx varies geographically, but tends to track that of snowshoe hares. Lynx prefer older (>20 years old) regenerating forest stands. Mature forest stands are often used but rarely selected. Most lynx dens found to date have been associated with blowdown or deadfall trees in regenerating stands. Lynx maintain mostly exclusive intrasexual territories, based on social intolerance and mutual avoidance. Male home ranges tend to be larger than female ranges. There appears to be no linear relationship between hare abundance and lynx home range size, although lynx do increase their home range size dramatically following the cyclic hare crash. Male and female home ranges generally overlap completely while within-sex overlap is usually modest; related females may tolerate greater overlap. Lynx numbers fluctuate in synchrony over vast areas and generally lag behind the snowshoe hare cycle by about one year. Peak densities of 30-45 lynx/100 km^2 have been observed in regenerating stands, and 8-20/100 km^2 in mature forest and more southern ranges. Population densities during the low are <3 lynx/100 km^2. Growth in lynx populations is a result of high fecundity, high kit survival, and low adult mortality. The decline is due to increased dispersal, high natural mortality, and a collapse in recruitment. During hare abundance, adult fecundity is high, litter size averages four to five, and yearling lynx give birth. During the cyclic low, recruitment essentially fails for about two years, and is followed by several years of modest recovery. Although trapping is an important mortality source in many areas, natural causes (primarily starvation and predation) account for most detected mortality during the first two years after the hare decline. Fifteen straight-line dispersal distances of 500-1,100 km have been recorded from recent studies in the two northern territories. Dispersal of adults was highest during and following the decline in hare densities. Trapping can reduce lynx populations and can have the greatest impact during the cyclic low, but the long-term impact of trapping on subsequent cycles is unclear. Despite reduced harvests in all jurisdictions and localized overharvest in some areas, no permanent decrease in range has been detected in contiguous northern populations.

Introduction

The primary purpose of this chapter is to synthesize relevant information on lynx ecology in northern Canada and Alaska. We have followed the ecoregion domains of Bailey (1998) to divide work covered in this chapter from work conducted in "southern boreal forests" (Chapter 13); here we review research conducted in the polar domain (Bailey 1998). Our intention was to review studies done in a northern boreal environment, as opposed to those done in more southern forests (reviewed by Koehler and Aubry 1994). Much new research on lynx has been conducted over the past decade, most of it from the northern boreal region. This chapter will emphasize these recent studies and will update previous reviews of lynx ecology (e.g., McCord and Cardoza 1982; Tumlison 1987; Quinn and Parker 1987; Hatler 1988, unpublished; Koehler and Aubry 1994). We refer briefly to snowshoe hare ecology primarily as it directly relates to lynx; more comprehensive examinations of the ecology of both northern and southern hare populations are provided in Chapters 6 and 7.

There has been much casual discussion among lynx researchers and managers regarding the similarity of ecological dynamics, processes, and relationships of northern populations of lynx to those residing in montane environments. We make limited comparisons between northern and southern populations here; this will be covered in greater detail in Chapter 13. Here we review lynx behavior in terms of prey selection, foraging patterns, habitat selection, and social organization. We summarize information regarding population dynamics including recruitment, survival, dispersal, and population densities. All topics are presented with respect to the relationship between lynx and snowshoe hare population dynamics. The relationship between lynx and other carnivores of the boreal community are presented elsewhere (Chapter 4).

Description

The Canada lynx is a medium-sized cat with a flared facial ruff, black ear tufts, large padded feet, and a short, black-tipped tail (Banfield 1974; Quinn and Parker 1987). Lynx show mild sexual dimorphism in size, males (averaging 80-90 cm long and 9-10.5 kg in weight) being 13-25% larger than females (76-84 cm long and 8-9 kg; Quinn and Parker 1987). In the north, lynx are found to the northern limit of trees in Alaska, Yukon, and mainland Northwest Territories (NWT). Lynx are widespread and cyclically abundant in the North and the lynx harvest is an important source of income for many northern residents. In recent times lynx, along with marten, have provided the principal source of income for northern trappers (Slough et al. 1987).

Food Habits

Snowshoe hares form most of the diet of lynx across North America. Hares comprise from one-third to nearly all of prey items identified for lynx (for food habits summaries see Quinn and Parker 1987:686; Koehler and Aubry 1994:75; O'Donoghue et al. 1998b). Other common prey items include red squirrels, mice and voles, flying squirrels, ground squirrels, beaver, muskrat, grouse and ptarmigan, and other birds. Ungulates, including deer, caribou, moose, Dall's sheep, and bison, are eaten as carrion and occasionally, excluding bison and moose, as prey (Saunders 1963a; Bergerud 1971; Parker et al. 1983; Stephenson et al. 1991; K. Poole, unpublished). Predation on ungulates is generally restricted to calves, although adults are taken (Stephenson et al. 1991). Use of ungulates appears to be greater during winter and during cyclic low hare abundance. Predation by lynx on red fox and other lynx also occurs, again mostly during periods of low hare numbers (Stephenson et al. 1991; O'Donoghue et al. 1995).

Several trends are evident when examining data on lynx diets. In lynx populations reliant on highly cyclic populations of snowshoe hares, the proportion of hares in the diet generally declines and use of alternative prey increases as hares become scarce (Brand et al. 1976; Stephenson et al. 1991; O'Donoghue et al. 1998b; K. Poole, unpublished). In southwestern Yukon, red squirrels became increasingly important (20-44% biomass) during the years of lowest hare density compared to almost no use (0-4% biomass) during years of high hare densities (O'Donoghue et al. 1998b). Similarly, during years of hare scarcity, use of carrion, red squirrel, ruffed grouse, and other birds increased in central Alberta (Brand et al. 1976), and in southwestern NWT, red squirrels and birds were found more frequently (K. Poole, unpublished data). Red squirrels in particular appear to be an important alternative food source for lynx throughout the North during periods of low hare abundance.

Lynx diets in summer generally have less snowshoe hare and more alternative prey than in winter (Quinn and Parker 1987; Koehler and Aubry 1994). On the Kenai Peninsula in Alaska, Staples (1995) found 64% and 38% hare and 11% and 28% red squirrel in winter and summer lynx scats, respectively. In the Gaspé region of Québec, Fortin and Huot (1995) found hares formed 58% of the diet of lynx during the snow-free period and 85% during winter, with small mammals and red squirrels being important secondary prey during both periods. The lynx diet in southwest Yukon in summer contained a greater diversity of prey, primarily because of the addition of ground squirrels (O'Donoghue et al. 1998c). Other common alternative prey used by lynx during summer include ducks, passerines and other birds, ungulates, and carrion (Saunders 1963a; van Zyll de Jong 1966; Nellis et al. 1972; Brand et al. 1976; Parker et al. 1983). It is unclear whether the greater abundance of alternative prey in lynx diets during summer is a result of decreased hunting success on hares or an increase in the availability of alternative prey.

To our knowledge, differences in diets of lynx by age and sex class have not been reported. At high hare densities, when lynx eat almost solely hares, few inter-class differences in diet would be expected. At lower hare densities, however, some partitioning in resources might be expected. Pulliainen et al. (1995) found no differences in diet between sexes or age categories of European lynx in east Finland where hares dominated the diet. However, in southwest Finland, where hares and white-tailed deer were consumed equally, male lynx consumed more deer and fewer hares than females.

Foraging Ecology and Hunting Behavior

Due to their heavy dependence on hares for food, morphological adaptations to hunting hares (Murray and Boutin 1991), and almost complete overlap of geographic range with hares (Banfield 1974), lynx are usually considered hare specialists. Accordingly, their foraging behavior is characterized by hunting tactics and movement patterns appropriate for hunting hares.

Lynx hunt by either stalking and rushing at their prey, or ambushing them from "ambush beds" established near the trails of prey (Murray et al. 1995; O'Donoghue et al. 1998a). In the southwest Yukon, the frequency of ambush beds along lynx trails increased nine-fold from the cyclic peak to the low (O'Donoghue et al. 1998a). This corresponded to a switch in diet (*sensu* Murdoch 1969) from hares to red squirrels and the establishment of more ambush beds near squirrel middens. During this period, lynx also initiated progressively more chases of hares from ambush beds (from about 4% to 36% of all chases), although their hunting success was about the same as from stalks for hares, and slightly lower for squirrels (O'Donoghue et al. 1998a). Frequent use of ambush beds by lynx has been noted in one other study (Saunders 1963a, 1963b), but elsewhere lynx seldom ambushed hares (Nellis and Keith 1968; Parker 1981). The costs and benefits of ambushing rather than stalking prey likely depend on prey abundance and behavior as well as the physiological state of the predator (see, for example, Davies 1977 and Formanowicz and Bradley 1987). Ambushing prey when their availability is low may be more energetically efficient for lynx than actively searching for them (O'Donoghue et al. 1998a).

Lynx typically prefer feeding on freshly killed prey over scavenging (Parker 1981; O'Donoghue et al. 1998b). In the southwest Yukon, lynx cached the whole carcasses of only 1.6% of the radio-collared hares they killed, compared to 37.0% of those killed by coyotes (O'Donoghue et al. 1998b). Lynx caches were formed on the surface of the snow by the lynx pulling snow over them. All of the caches that were monitored and retrieved by lynx were consumed in less than two days. Observations of lynx scavenging hares (Nellis and Keith 1968; Parker 1981) and the carcasses of ungulates (see Food Habits) have been made as well, but this appears to occur most often during times of food shortage.

While typically solitary, lynx regularly hunt in mother-kit family groups. Families usually spread out while hunting hares in good habitat, and hares flushed by one animal are often killed by another (Saunders 1963a; Parker 1981; Mowat and Slough 1998; O'Donoghue et al. 1998a). This behavior undoubtedly increases the foraging efficiency of family groups, but likely due to the inexperience of kits, calculated per-individual kill rates of lynx hunting as families were 50-60% lower than those of adults hunting alone (O'Donoghue et al. 1998a). Groups of two or three adult lynx foraging together were recorded in the southwest Yukon during the cyclic decline and low (O'Donoghue et al. 1998a). Very limited data from the latter study suggest that the kill rates of animals in these groups may have been equal to or higher than those of lynx foraging by themselves. Several other authors have recorded small groups of adult lynx together (Carbyn and Patriquin 1983; Poole 1995; Staples 1995; Mowat and Slough 1998), and Barash (1971) recorded adult lynx hunting and feeding together. Aldama and Delibes (1991) recorded similar behavior in Iberian lynx.

Lynx-Prey Relationships

Although the boreal forest has relatively low species diversity, the food web of boreal vertebrates appears to be more complex than was once recognized (Krebs and Boutin 1998, unpublished). The close relationship between population fluctuations of lynx and snowshoe hares is well documented. Lynx respond both numerically, through changes in their rates of survival, recruitment, and movements, and functionally, through changes in their kill rates, to the hare cycle. The lags in these responses, and in the combined "total response" (which expresses changes in the proportion of the prey population killed relative to prey density), contribute to the cyclic behavior of the system by introducing a delayed density dependent effect (May 1981; Korpimäki and Krebs 1996; Sinclair and Pech 1996).

Numbers of lynx may vary from three to 17-fold during a cyclic fluctuation (Keith et al. 1977; Poole 1994; Slough and Mowat 1996; O'Donoghue et al. 1997). Peak densities are typically reached one year after the cyclic peak for hares, thus the numerical responses of lynx to changing densities of hare show delayed density dependence (Sinclair and Pech 1996; O'Donoghue et al. 1997).

The functional responses of lynx to the hare cycle have only been estimated in two studies. In Alberta, lynx killed about three times as many hares at cyclic peaks as they did when the abundance of hares was low; maximum kill rates were estimated to be about 0.8 hares per day (Keith et al. 1977). Based on their data from snow-tracking, these authors estimated that lynx showed a Type-2 functional response (*sensu* Holling 1959b), or one in which kill rates increase at a monotonically decreasing rate to an asymptotic maximum. Kill rates of hares by lynx varied four to five-fold in the southwest Yukon during a hare cycle, and the estimated maximum kill rates were higher than those in Alberta at about 1.6 hares per day (O'Donoghue et al. 1998b, 1998c). A Type-2 functional response also fit the observed data well for this study. The calculated kill rates in Alberta may have been underestimates, due to the assumptions made that lynx only rested once per day (Brand et al. 1976; Keith et al. 1977), which is questionable (Parker 1981; O'Donoghue et al. 1998b).

Changes in the kill rates of hares by lynx are accompanied by behavioral changes that likely change the "components" (Holling 1959a, 1966) of the functional responses. Lynx chased hares for longer distances when hares were rare than when they were abundant in the southwest Yukon, so "reactive distances" of lynx may have changed as well (O'Donoghue et al. 1998b). The reported success of lynx in catching hares once they had initiated chases has varied from 19% to 57% (Saunders 1963a; Brand et al. 1976; Parker 1981; Major 1989; O'Donoghue et al. 1998b), but it does not seem to be directly related to density of hares (Brand et al. 1976; O'Donoghue et al. 1998b). In the southwest Yukon, the travel rates and total activity time also varied little over the course of the cycle (O'Donoghue et al. 1998b), while activity rates did seem to increase with lower densities of hares densities in the NWT (K. Poole, unpublished). However, switches in prey selection (from hares to red squirrels) and hunting tactics at low hare numbers both likely contributed to the functional responses in the southwest Yukon. Kill rates by lynx and other predators may only decline once hares are concentrated in largely inaccessible habitats, or "refugia" (Wolff 1980; Hik 1995). Refugia for prey species typically act to stabilize predator-prey relationships (Taylor 1984), and a relatively invulnerable subpopulation of hares in very dense cover likely allows them to persist at higher densities through cyclic lows.

The total impact of predation by lynx on the dynamics of hare populations is determined by combining their numerical and functional responses (Solomon 1949; Messier 1995). Based on their calculated responses, Keith et al. (1977) estimated that lynx killed from 2 to 13% of the hares present each winter in Alberta, with peak predation rates occurring two to four years after the hare cyclic high. Likewise, lynx killed an estimated 4 to 32% of hares over winter in the southwest Yukon, with the highest predation rates one to three years after the cyclic peak (O'Donoghue et al. 1998c). Again, the lag in the effect of predation on numbers of hares would contribute to the cyclic dynamics, and throughout the cycle in abundance of hares, lynx are one of the most important predators of hares. Exclusion of lynx and coyotes from experimental areas in the southwest Yukon, when combined with food addition, resulted in densities of hares approximately 11 times higher than those on control areas, and this effect was most pronounced during the cyclic low (Krebs et al. 1995; Krebs and Boutin 1998).

While the effects of predation by lynx on hares may be considerable, lynx likely have little impact on other alternative prey in the boreal forest. Grouse were the main alternative prey of lynx in Alberta (Brand et al. 1976), but they never represented more than an estimated 12% of the total biomass in the diets of lynx. Keith et al. (1977) attributed synchronous fluctuations in numbers of grouse and hares to changes in predation rates on grouse by raptors. In the southwest Yukon, red squirrels were the most important alternative prey for lynx during years of low abundance of hares (O'Donoghue et al. 1998b). However, even when squirrels represented 79% of kills by lynx during winter, the total impact of predation by lynx was less than 4% of the estimated population of squirrels (O'Donoghue et al. 1998c). The negligible impact of predation by all terrestrial predators on red squirrels was also confirmed experimentally in the Yukon (Stuart-Smith and Boutin 1995). Throughout their range, lynx appear unable to persist at high densities when numbers of snowshoe hares are low. This both limits the effect of their predation on alternative prey, and allows numbers of hares to recover from cyclic lows.

Habitat Selection and Use

At the largest spatial scale, lynx occupy the boreal, subboreal and western montane forests of North America (McCord and Cardoza 1982; Quinn and Parker 1987). They occur in many forest types that are not truly boreal, although all of the forests they occupy are relatively simple in terms of physical structure and species composition (Koehler and Aubry 1994). Lynx are absent or uncommon in the wet coastal forests of western Canada and Alaska. Lynx are more or less ubiquitous residents of northern forests, with their distribution becoming more discontinuous toward the south. Legendre et al. (1978) demonstrated that lynx were most abundant in the boreal forest of their northeast Québec study area, and that lynx distribution was associated with the distribution of the hare. Lynx were also found in the sub-arctic forest, which was dominated by balsam fir and paper birch. Lynx were not found in the more open subarctic forests and tundra to the north. Dwyer et al. (1989) concluded that lynx in central Ontario were primarily associated with upland boreal forest and, to a lesser extent, marshlands with black spruce, alder and willow. Lynx avoided wetlands with cattails, oak, maple, and hemlock. Quinn and Thompson (1987) found that lynx were abundant in both the boreal and mixed-wood boreal zones in central Ontario; these authors compared several population parameters among the two zones and found no strong indication to suggest differences in fitness or density. In western Canada, Hatler (1988) reported that the majority of the lynx harvest in British Columbia (B.C.) came from the only area of true boreal forest in the province.

At the stand level, lynx prefer regenerating forest stands like those of its main prey, the snowshoe hare (Thompson 1988; Koehler and Aubry 1994). Throughout the north, lynx select older regenerating stands (greater than about 20 years of age) both of human and fire origin at all points in the hare cycle (Kesterson 1988; Thompson et al. 1989; Major 1989; Perham 1995; Staples 1995). Lynx do not frequently use younger regenerating stands (Thompson et al. 1989; Golden 1993; Perham 1995; Staples 1995). It appears climax shrub stands are also avoided (Staples 1995), even when they contain sizeable hare populations (Murray et al. 1994), although the work of Major (1989) suggests these stands may receive greater use in summer. Many authors have demonstrated use (though not selection) of mature forest stands, and indeed one study team (Murray et al. 1994 and O'Donoghue et al. 1998a) worked where all forested stands were mature. It is interesting to note that these authors reported a persistent lynx population in this area, even during a cyclic population low (O'Donoghue et al. 1997). Kesterson (1988) and Staples (1995) both demonstrated strong selection for mature stands included within a mid-seral burn, but they demonstrated strong selection against mature forest when it was the matrix habitat. We conclude that mature coniferous habitat can support lynx in the North, although the quality of mature habitat may vary regionally. Major (1989) and Mowat et al. (1998, unpublished) demonstrated that mature aspen, white spruce, and black spruce stands in three areas of Yukon contained significant quantities of browse and horizontal cover, and contained modest numbers of hares during all phases of the cycle.

Do lynx and hares show similar patterns of habitat selection? We suggest yes, with two exceptions. First, hares appear to select more dense stands than lynx (O'Donoghue et al. 1998a). Presumably lynx are unable to hunt in the densest stands and are hence excluded. This suggestion is consistent with the observations of many researchers (e.g., Wolff 1980) that hares survive in pockets of dense habitat during the cyclic low. Second, hares appear to select dense shrubs with little aerial cover, at least during periods of reasonable abundance, whereas lynx rarely use such stands. Keith (1990) suggested that hares need dense understory cover but that "overstory characteristics are of doubtful significance in habitat selection." It is unclear, however, whether lynx avoid some shrub stands because they lack aerial cover or because they are simply too dense to hunt in successfully. Based on observations of hares using denser cover than lynx in forested stands, we suggest that the latter explanation is correct.

Only one study has measured lynx and hare habitat use over the course of a cyclic fluctuation (O'Donoghue et al. 1998a). In the southwest Yukon study, the pattern of habitat selection by lynx roughly followed that of hares though, on average, hares used denser stands in all years. Lynx and hares used habitats with the densest vegetative cover during the cyclic decline, while both used more open habitats when hares were abundant (O'Donoghue et al. 1998a). This study was conducted in a mature forest matrix and it is unclear whether lynx also move to denser habitats in regenerating stands when hares are scarce. Within years, lynx may demonstrate broader habitat choice during summer when alternative foods are more abundant (Major 1989; Fortin and Huot 1995).

Kesterson (1988) and Staples (1995) both demonstrated selection for a relatively rare habitat, which they describe as mature stands within a burned forest matrix. Both these authors suggested that lynx tend to hunt along the edge of this habitat. Major (1989) also suggested that lynx hunted edge habitats—in this case, the edge of dense riparian willow stands. The use of habitat edges may be an important hunting strategy for lynx, which may allow them to hunt hares that live in habitats that are normally too dense to hunt effectively. Several authors have shown that lynx select against openings such as water or open meadows, although some use of terrestrial openings was always detected (Murray et al. 1994; Fortin and Huot 1995; Poole et al. 1996). Most openings have few if any resident hares, so this result is not surprising, especially in winter. This does not indicate that lynx will not cross openings; indeed the fact that lynx were occasionally located in openings, including farmland (Fortin and Huot 1995), suggests they are not against entering them. We found lynx regularly crossed several hundred meter wide openings during our work in NWT and Yukon; occasionally, lynx crossed frozen lakes and rivers >1 km across (K. Poole and G. Mowat, personal observation).

While relatively few lynx dens have been described in the North, all had similar structural aspects regardless of their stand types. Berrie (1974) described three dens located in central Alaska; two were in tangles of spruce blowdown, and the other was in a tangle of spruce roots washed up on the bank of a creek. Stephenson (1986) located one den site in a mature spruce-birch stand, with the den located in an area of numerous deadfall trees. Kesterson (1988) stated that "lynx seemed to select den sites in or near mature habitats dominated by large quantities of wind-felled trees." Hatler (1988) described a den found in logging debris and blowdown on the edge of a six to eight-year-old cut-block in northern B.C. Slough (in press) located 39 lynx dens in south-central Yukon. One of these den sites was in a mature spruce stand, one was in a mature subalpine fir stand, and 37 were in regenerating stands about 30 years in age. Three dens were under young, bushy subalpine fir trees, two were in dense copses of mature willow, and 34 were under blowdown, usually dense tangles of trees. Poole (1992) located five lynx den sites in southwestern NWT. Den sites were characterized as areas of moderate to heavy deadfall located in mature conifer or regenerating mixed conifer and deciduous stands. In summary, female lynx appear to select den sites in a number of forest types in the North. Lynx do not appear constrained to select specific stand types; rather, the feature that was consistently chosen was the structure at the site itself. Wind-felled trees were the most common form of protection selected by female lynx, although other structures such as roots and dense live vegetation were also used. The importance of proximity to areas with high prey density to den site selection has not been examined.

Wildfire, which is the most important factor in the dynamics of the northern boreal forest ecosystem (Kelsall et al. 1977; Viereck 1983), is a major habitat modifier (Johnson et al. 1995). Johnson et al. (1995) and Paragi et al. (1997) suggest that optimum habitat for hare and lynx can be achieved in interior Alaska by frequent and numerous but relatively small fires, or large patchy fires with abundant unburned inclusions. However, the effects of spatial heterogeneity and juxtaposition of habitats on behavior and population dynamics of lynx are unstudied.

Logging, which is also an important factor in the dynamics of many boreal forests, restarts the succession necessary to create optimum hare and lynx habitat, but often removes the structure needed for denning by lynx. Whether the regrowth on a logged area becomes usable hare habitat will depend on site level factors and silviculture treatment post-harvest (Thompson 1988; Koehler and Brittell 1990). Thompson (1988) suggested that planted and tended boreal sites are used less by hares and lynx than naturally regenerating sites. Thompson (1988) further suggested that increased hare and lynx populations would occur with logging plans that incorporate numerous small stands of mature forest, hence increasing the amount of uncut forest-successional edge. There may be a limit to the benefit of edges for hares because predation on hares may increase in small habitat patches (Chapter 6); very small patches may present predation risks that are not sustainable for hares. We conclude that logging will only provide quality lynx habitat if a dense understory of coniferous or deciduous vegetation results. Because hares select habitat based more on understory cover than browse (Chapter 6), plant species appear to be of secondary importance. Except for extremely dense stands, silvicultural prescriptions such as pre-commercial thinning or herbicide application that thin or remove the understory probably reduce habitat quality for lynx (but see Sullivan 1994, 1996). Leaving groups of standing and downed trees may allow for denning opportunities within the cutting area and not force female lynx to search out den sites in mature forest, as suggested by Koehler and Brittell (1990). Denning structure must be scattered about the landscape because female lynx probably establish temporary dens throughout their home range during the period when kittens are old enough to travel but not hunt (Bailey 1981). Several of the above authors have suggested that good lynx habitat includes both late and early seral components; we conclude that lynx can survive in single habitat types, such as early seral or mature forests, as long as the features to support both hares and denning by lynx exist.

Spatial Organization, Social Behavior

The lynx spacing mechanism is functionally similar to that of other Carnivora such as mustelids and ursids. Brittell et al. (1989) suggested that lynx have a social organization similar to that of bobcats and cougars, consisting of social intolerance and mutual avoidance (Seidensticker et al. 1973; Bailey 1974). Powell (1979) described this land tenure system as "intrasexual territories" and Kesterson (1988) also used this description for lynx. In this system, resident individuals maintain intra-sexually exclusive territories, and males may or may not have larger home ranges than females. Lynx are territorial, but not according to the strictest definitions (see Hornocker et al. 1983 for a related discussion of this topic). Scent-marking using feces, sprayed urine, or anal secretions may be used to mark home ranges and to provide both spatial and temporal information that may reduce confrontations (Saunders 1963b; Mellen 1993; Staples 1995). Lynx also show strong range fidelity, often over many years (Poole 1995; O'Donoghue et al. 1998c), have core range areas that seldom overlap (Poole 1995; O'Donoghue et al. 1998c), and appear to avoid contact among individuals (Poole 1995) and violent encounters (Poole 1995; Mowat and Slough 1998). Poole's (1995) work suggests that some sort of spacing mechanism was operating to keep same-sex animals separated in time and space. However, the tendency toward neutral indices of dynamic interactions (the degree to which two animals avoid, ignore, or attract each other [Macdonald et al. 1980]) indicated little or no active avoidance or overt defense of areas between overlapping or adjacent pairs, suggesting that this spacing was upheld by relatively passive means. Conflict among individuals is rare in lynx (Poole 1995; Mowat and Slough 1998) and perhaps in other solitary felids as well (Hornocker and Bailey 1986). Aggressive lynx-lynx encounters do occur, however, and occasionally result in cannibalism, primarily during years of food shortage (Poole 1994; O'Donoghue et al. 1995; Mowat and Slough 1998).

Lynx home range sizes vary among areas, sexes, seasons, and cyclical phases. It is difficult to compare home range sizes among studies because of differing methods of data collection, sample sizes, and analysis techniques. Many studies did not determine the ages of the individuals tracked and could not identify subadults. Further, the home range size of breeding lynx may increase (Kesterson 1988), hence yearly home ranges may vary depending on when the data were collected, especially when sample sizes are small.

Koehler and Aubry (1994) summarized home range sizes for lynx. Dramatic variation in home range size has been reported for lynx across their North American range (8-738 km^2), not all of which can be explained by differences in measurement and analysis techniques. Male home range sizes are usually larger than female ranges (Kesterson 1988; Koehler and Aubry 1994; Fortin and Huot 1995; Perham 1995; Slough and Mowat 1996; O'Donoghue et al. 1998c, but see Ward and Krebs 1985 and Poole 1994). In the south-central Yukon, yearling lynx had similar home range sizes to adults (Slough and Mowat 1996), while Noiseux and Doucet (1987) found that yearling home ranges were generally smaller than adult home ranges in southern Québec. Philopatry to home ranges has been reported among individuals of both sexes resident over several years, but home range shifts and abandonment are also common (Breitenmoser et al. 1993b; Poole 1994; Perham 1995; Slough and Mowat 1996; O'Donoghue et al. 1998c).

Poole (1994), Slough and Mowat (1996), and O'Donoghue et al. (1998c) showed that lynx range size increased dramatically after the sudden decrease in hare abundance in the North. Perham (1995) studied lynx after a hare decrease in Alaska and found great variation in home range size of males, several of which had ranges >200 km^2. Poole (1994) and Slough and Mowat (1996) presented data for several years before the hare decrease and home range size changed little during this period. Ward and Krebs (1985) suggested lynx home range size changed with hare abundance; however, they used a categorical analysis (with three categories of hare abundance) to test this relationship, and only the largest and the smallest categories differed significantly from one another (p <0.05). Therefore, their data could also be interpreted to show similar home range sizes through the lynx cycle followed by an increase after the sudden hare population decrease. The only researchers to empirically test for a linear relationship between lynx home range size and hare abundance were Brand et al. (1976) and Slough and Mowat (1996). Brand et al. (1976) used only eight home range sizes across five different winters and were further forced to pool the sexes for their analysis; these limitations aside, they did not find a linear relationship between lynx home range size and hare abundance. Slough and Mowat (1996) had larger sample sizes across eight years and found no liner relationship for either sex.

It may be more appropriate to test lynx home range size against hare abundance the previous year because there appears to be a one year lag in the numeric response of lynx to hares (Krebs et al. 1995; O'Donoghue et al. 1997). We used correlation analysis and published data from Poole (1994) and Slough and Mowat (1996) to test for a linear relationship between lynx home range size and hare density the previous year. We used mean yearly home range sizes for each sex because of the large variation in sample size among years (n = 1-15 individuals per year). These conservative tests suggest there was no linear relationship between lynx home range size and hare density the previous year for both sexes and study areas (p >0.3, df 3-7 in all cases; Fig. 9.1a,b).

Lynx did increase their home range sizes dramatically following the hare crash, and as mentioned above, it would further appear that home range size changes relatively little during years of high hare abundance. There appears to be a threshold hare density below which lynx home range size increases (Fig. 9.1a,b). We did not compare yearly changes in home range size for individual lynx; perhaps some individuals do alter their home range size with hare abundance in a more linear fashion.

Home ranges vary seasonally in lynx. Females hunt alone while the kittens are young, making solitary forays from the den site. As kittens get older they begin to travel with the female, although it is assumed they are cached at temporary den sites when she is hunting (Kesterson 1988), as has been recorded for bobcats (Bailey 1979). Kesterson (1988) and Mowat and Slough (1998) observed that female home ranges were very small during the denning period; range size increased appreciably in mid-summer once the kittens were large enough to begin leaving the den site. By early fall, female home range size expands to reoccupy the area used before birth, and we assume that the kittens travel with the female, even while hunting (Bailey 1979; Winegarner and Winegarner 1982; Kesterson 1988). Kittens remain with the mother throughout the winter. Family groups begin to break-up in early March (Saunders 1963b; Brand et al. 1976; Parker et al. 1983; Poole 1995; Mowat et al. 1996b). Kittens appear to be closely associated with their

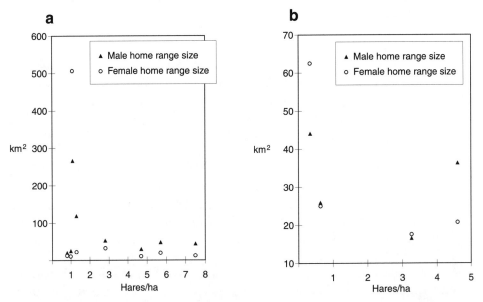

Figure 9.1—The relationship between lynx home range size (n = 1-15) and hare density the previous year across: (a) eight years of a hare cycle in south-central Yukon (Slough and Mowat 1996), and (b) four years of a hare cycle in southwest NWT (Poole 1994; K. Poole, unpublished).

mothers until February or early March, when the association weakens; natal dispersal begins in late April and early May (Poole 1995; Mowat et al. 1996b). Some juvenile kittens disperse immediately (Poole 1995; Slough and Mowat 1996), while others remain in the natal area for up to one year after their first winter (Kesterson 1988; Slough and Mowat 1996). Similar behavior has been recorded for bobcats (McCord and Cardoza 1982) and Iberian lynx (Aldama and Delibes 1991). Dispersal from the mother's home range can be sudden or it can be a more gradual process (Kesterson 1988; Poole 1994; Mowat and Slough 1998). Separation of the kittens and mother may be hastened by the subsequent breeding of the adult female (McCord and Cardoza 1982); however, Mowat and Slough (1998) documented a female and male lynx together for several days in the company of the female's 10-month-old kittens. Kesterson (1988) noted no strong trend toward increased home range size of males during the breeding season in his study population, though a few individuals did appear to increase their range size while breeding.

Home range overlap is often used to assess social patterns in mammals. This parameter is probably measured even more inaccurately than home range size because it is affected by all the constraints mentioned above for home range and is further complicated by the fact that errors can be made during interpretation of the measurement when relatedness of individuals is unknown. Unfortunately, relatedness of individuals is rarely known in field studies. Given the above constraints, it is not surprising great variation in overlap has been shown for both sexes (Ward and Krebs 1985). In the NWT, Poole (1995) recorded variable amounts of overlap among lynx during peak and declining densities of snowshoe hares. Much of the overlap was among females and was attributed to several pairs of females that showed large overlap in home range, often for several years. These females were assumed to have been related. This observation shows the weakness in measuring range overlap when individual relationships are unknown. Researchers working on other species of lynx have also recorded variable home range overlap within sexes (Breitenmoser et al. 1993a; Jedrzejewski et al. 1996; Ferreras et al. 1997). Generally, male and female home ranges overlap completely while within-sex overlap is usually modest or may be confined to one or two pairs of individuals per study (e.g., Poole 1995). Home range exclusiveness may be a function of degree; some overlap may occur at the 90 or 95% home range contour level, but, as noted in Poole (1995), little may occur among the 50% contour core areas.

Felids are said to have a social system based on matrilineal descent (Kleiman and Eisenberg 1973; Kerby and Macdonald 1988). This theory would suggest that pair bonds between females, either mother-daughter or sibling pairs, persist and that these relationships form the basis for the organization of social structure. This theory is difficult to test in solitary species, but there is evidence suggesting that female pair bonds do persist in Canada lynx and other lynx. Female kittens sometimes establish home ranges within those of their mothers (Kesterson 1988; Breitenmoser et al. 1993b; Slough and Mowat 1996). Kesterson (1988) found that three female kittens remained in or near their natal ranges during the entire period for which they were monitored. This trend has been noted in other solitary felids (Eisenberg 1981; Sundquist 1981; Ross and Jalkotzy 1992) and suggested by Poole (1994) and Staples (1995) for Canada lynx. Secondly, adult females may retain amicable contact with their female offspring throughout their life. Barash (1971) witnessed a group of two adult and one yearling lynx hunt and share a ground squirrel. Carbyn and Patriquin (1983) located two different female and kit groups together five times over a 30-day period. Staples (1995) recorded two different adult females together, each with a single yearling female offspring, a total of 15 times. O'Donoghue et al. (1998a) witnessed several adult animals hunting together through three winters during the cyclic hare decline and low. Mowat and Slough (1998) often recorded related adult females together during their study of lynx in south-central Yukon, even when both females had accompanying kittens. Mowat and Slough (1998) also reported an incident where an adult female and her yearling offspring gave birth within 800 m of each other. Both Poole (1995) and O'Donoghue et al. (1997) found female home ranges with large overlap, although this was not the norm on either study area; both groups felt that these females were likely related.

The persistence of female bonds has important implications for lynx conservation. Matrilineal groups may confer greater fitness on their members by allowing group hunting at certain times (O'Donoghue et al. 1998a), the possibility of adoption of orphaned kittens (Carbyn and Patriquin 1983; Mowat and Slough 1998), and a reduction in the investment in territorial defense. In addition, populations with related individuals may attain higher density because territoriality may be relaxed among relatives.

Behavioral Responses of Lynx to Humans

Staples (1995) presented data on lynx responses to close encounters with humans. As suggested by earlier authors, he found that lynx were generally tolerant of humans. The work of Staples (1995) and other anecdotal accounts of lynx behavior suggests that lynx can tolerate human disturbance and even continued presence. Trappers will relate that lynx are relatively easy to capture; they appear to have little fear of human scent, they respond to baits and lures, and can be attracted using visual attractants.

Humans may exert potentially negative influences on lynx by building residences and roads in and through lynx habitat, by altering and modifying existing habitats, and by direct disturbance through recreation or travel in areas inhabited by lynx. Our anecdotal experiences suggest that lynx will tolerate moderate levels of snowmobile traffic through their home ranges. We could not detect changes in lynx movement patterns or home range in our northern studies despite constant, repetitive and daily travelling through the study areas to check traps and locate animals. Lynx appeared to readily cross highways, and several animals in southwestern NWT established home ranges adjacent to roads. Lynx are also regularly sighted sitting along roadsides in the North. Lynx tracks were regularly observed adjacent to residential areas in both Yukon and NWT, although we do not know if these animals were residents. Lynx may tend to avoid areas with higher levels of disturbance or greater fragmentation of habitat from development, although this has not been rigorously tested. Several studies of lynx have occurred in areas with reasonably dense rural human populations and interspersed agricultural areas, which further suggests lynx can tolerate daily human use and presence in an area (Brand and Keith 1979; Fortin and Huot 1995). Both these studies demonstrated resident lynx populations of about $10/100$ km^2.

Although lynx will generally flee when closely approached, they appear to become bolder and less wary of people during periods of low prey abundance. Anecdotal observations include a lynx eyeing a dog on the edge of a mid-summer wedding celebration in the NWT, another killing a dog outside a trapline cabin while the trapper was present, and a third defending a fox caught in a trap while the trapper approached. Several incidences of lynx stalking domestic animals throughout the Yukon during low prey abundance have been recorded (Mowat and Slough 1998).

Population Dynamics

Lynx numbers fluctuate in response to population levels of snowshoe hare, and the decline in lynx numbers generally lags one year behind the decline in hare numbers (Elton and Nicholson 1942; Butler 1953; Keith 1963; Brand and Keith 1979; Boutin et al. 1995). Lynx populations, as indexed by harvest data, (Fig. 9.2) fluctuate in synchrony over vast geographic areas, showing roughly similar trends in timing and amplitude of cyclic peaks and lows across the continent (Ranta et al. 1997). The lynx cycle appears to initiate and emanate from central Canada, following similar trends in the hare cycle (Smith 1983), such that peak lynx harvests in Saskatchewan and Manitoba from 1960 to 1980 occurred around the turn of the decade, and two to four years later in Yukon, Alaska, and Québec. Long-distance dispersal of

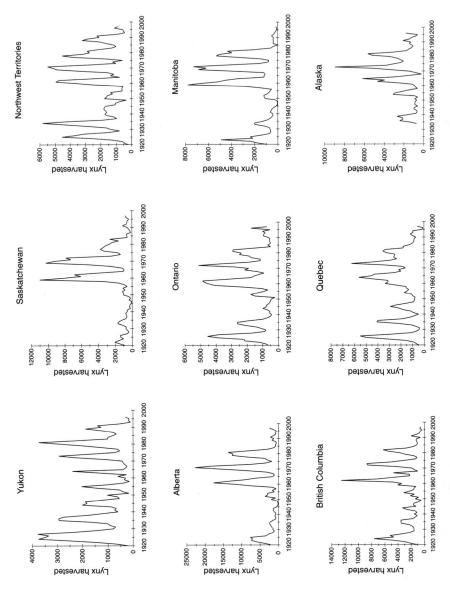

Figure 9.2—Lynx harvest from 1920 to 1997 for eight Canadian territories and provinces and Alaska. Data from 1920 to 1983 were primarily from Novak et al. (1987). Data from 1984 to 1997 were obtained from the individual provinces and territories and from the State of Alaska.

lynx and other predators during cyclic declines could act as a synchronizing element of the hare cycle (Butler 1953; Lack 1954; Korpimäki and Krebs 1996). In a recent analysis of time series data for hare and lynx, Stenseth et al. (1997) suggest that the dominant community linkages are three dimensional for the hare cycles, and two dimensional for the lynx cycles. The hare appears to be regulated from below and above (thus both the vegetation-hare and hare-predator interactions must be considered to understand hare dynamics), whereas the lynx seems to be regulated only from below (thus, for the lynx, the hare-lynx interaction dominates). This lack of a third dimension suggests that lynx social structure is not a major factor limiting lynx population growth.

Akçakaya (1992) built a mathematical prey-predator model such that trophic functions are modeled as functions of prey-to-predator ratios rather than as functions of prey density only (functions of per capita resources). This model developed limit cycles consistent with changes in a south to north gradient and predicted a periodicity of around 10 years. Both of these patterns are consistent with the true dynamics of the cycle. This paper demonstrates the need to consider both lynx and hare population size when considering lynx population dynamics.

The cycle in lynx and hare numbers is often broken into phases. The low period typically lasts three to five years and is denoted by low population density and a mild decline and recovery in numbers through the period (Poole 1994; Slough and Mowat 1996; O'Donoghue et al. 1997). During the increase phase, about three years in duration, lynx numbers increase quickly (Poole 1994; Slough and Mowat 1996; O'Donoghue et al. 1997). The peak phase is usually a two-year period of high lynx density with modest or no population growth (Poole 1994; Slough and Mowat 1996; O'Donoghue et al. 1997). The decline or crash phase of the hare cycle is one to two years in duration; lynx numbers decline dramatically during this phase of the cycle.

Quinn and Parker (1987) and Koehler and Aubry (1994) have summarized lynx densities. More recent work suggests that peak densities in lightly or unharvested areas in the North may range between 30-45 lynx/100 km^2 in recent burns (Poole 1994; Slough and Mowat 1996). Peak densities in a mature forest matrix in the North or in the more southern part of the lynx's range are typically lower, at 8-20 lynx/100 km^2 (Parker et al. 1983; Banville 1986; Kesterson 1988; Noiseux and Doucet 1987; Fortin and Huot 1995; O'Donoghue et al. 1997). Brand et al. (1976) estimated 10 lynx/100 km^2 during a hare peak in central Alberta in a mixed forest matrix with inclusions of agriculture. Population densities during the low are typically less than 3 lynx/100 km^2, regardless of habitat quality (Brand et al. 1976; Poole 1994; Staples 1995; Slough and Mowat 1996; O'Donoghue et al. 1997). In south-central Yukon, Slough and Mowat (1996) calculated a finite rate of increase (λ) of 2.03 to the peak, stable numbers during the first year of declining hare populations (λ = 1.01), and λ = 0.01 during the decline. It should be noted that all densities presented here are rough figures, and although they are adequate to demonstrate general temporal and spatial trends, they combine several different methods, none of which are based on a sampling methodology or present confidence intervals.

As may be expected, age structure changes with population size in lynx. Lynx populations are dominated by young animals during the late increase, peak, and early decline phases of the cycle, leaving an aging adult cohort through the low phase (Nellis et al. 1972; Brand et al. 1976; Poole 1994; Slough and Mowat 1996; O'Donoghue et al. 1997). Average age increases through the low phase due to lack of recruitment, and the oldest age structure is in the first part of the increase phase, before new recruits are added (Slough and Mowat 1996). There is less evidence for cyclic variation in sex ratios. Sex ratios of kittens do not differ from equality (Poole 1994; Slough and Mowat 1996). Sex ratios of adults and yearlings did not differ from unity in any year in south-central Yukon (Slough and Mowat 1996), but in southwestern NWT there appeared to be a shift in sex ratio from greater numbers of males at peak population levels to more females during low levels (Poole 1994). Lembeck (1986) also documented a shift from predominantly males to more females in an unharvested bobcat population during a population decrease, and suggested this resulted from a population control mechanism linked to females. Smaller individuals may be better able to survive under conditions of low food abundance, hence the shift to a population composed of more females during low levels. Trapping also tends to remove males in greater proportion to their abundance because they have larger home ranges and may disperse more often.

Most lynx harvests are biased toward males (Berrie 1974; Quinn and Thompson 1987), but even sex ratios (Brand and Keith 1979) or proportionately more females (Bailey et al. 1986) have been observed. The observation of more females in the harvest by Bailey et al. (1986) was coupled with a harvest that exceeded replacement. Age structure of untrapped populations would presumably be composed of older-aged animals compared to harvested populations (Knick 1990; Poole 1994; Slough and Mowat 1996). Harvests of lynx in the area surrounding an untrapped study area in south-central Yukon had 36% fewer kits, 40% more yearlings, and 4% fewer adults than were present on the study area (Slough and Mowat 1996). Yearlings were greatly over-represented and kits under-represented in the harvest, as suggested in other areas (Brand and Keith 1979; Quinn and Thompson 1985).

Lynx dispersal, immigration, survival, and recruitment are closely linked throughout the snowshoe hare cycle. Population growth in lynx is a result of a high percentage of breeding females, large litters, high kit survival, low mortality, and immigration rates that balance or even exceeded losses to emigration. The lynx population decline is due to increased dispersal, high natural mortality, and a collapse in recruitment and immigration. In lynx studies in southwestern Yukon and southwestern NWT, all collared lynx resident prior to or during the decline in hare abundance dispersed or died by the end of the first winter of low hare densities (Poole 1994, 1997; O'Donoghue et al. 1995, 1997). In south-central Yukon, only two previously resident lynx remained after the hare decline from a population peak of over 130 animals (including residents, non-residents and all age classes; Slough and Mowat 1996).

Recruitment

Canada lynx breed through March and April in the North (Quinn and Parker 1987). Breeding pairs may remain together for several days (Poole 1994; Mowat and Slough 1998) and it is assumed females only breed with one male, but this assumption has not been tested (McCord and Cardoza 1982). It is unclear whether female lynx are induced or spontaneous ovulators (Quinn and Parker 1987). Gestation is approximately 70 days (Crowe 1975; Quinn and Parker 1987). In south-central Yukon, the mean date of birth for litters to adult females was 26 May (range 12 May-7 June) and did not differ among years (Mowat et al. 1996b; Slough and Mowat 1996). In southwestern NWT, date of birth appeared to be predominantly in the last 10-12 days of May (K. G. Poole 1992, unpublished). Kittens are born altricial; their eyes open at 10-14 days of age, though their vision is significantly impaired by large cataracts for several weeks thereafter (McCord and Cardoza 1982; G. Mowat, personal observation). Den sites are usually surface scrapes; the female usually scrapes back the ground cover and places the kittens on dry ground (Mowat 1993; Slough, in press).

During the period when hares are most abundant, yearling lynx give birth (Brand and Keith 1979; Quinn and Thompson 1987; Slough and Mowat 1996). In one study, yearling females gave birth approximately two to three weeks later than adults (Mowat et al. 1996b; Slough and Mowat 1996). Male lynx are thought to be incapable of breeding in their first year (McCord and Cardoza 1982; Quinn and Parker 1987).

During the cyclic hare low, lynx pregnancy rates vary from 0 to 100% (see review in Koehler and Aubry 1994), but sample sizes are often very small during this period, hence estimates tend to be unreliable. Adult in utero litter size averages three to four during the low period (Brand and Keith 1979; O'Connor 1984; Slough and Mowat 1996). Birth rate, the proportion of females that give birth, has been measured twice during the first year of the low phase and Poole (1994) and Slough and Mowat (1996) suggested, on the basis of few observations, that live births were few or nonexistent. Few yearling females conceive during the low phase (Brand and Keith 1979; O'Connor 1984), and Mowat et al. (1996b) argued that few or no yearlings successfully give birth. All studies report no kittens present during the second winter following the hare crash (Brand et al. 1976; Poole 1994; Slough and Mowat 1996; O'Donoghue et al. 1997); the few kittens born generally have little chance of survival. However, kittens have been reported throughout the cycle in the Klondike Valley in southwestern Yukon (J. Fraser, personal communication) and in the Mackenzie River Delta in northwestern NWT (K. Poole, unpublished); these exceptions may point to areas of optimum hare and lynx habitat. It is unclear how long the period of no or low recruitment continues; many authors have argued that recruitment fails for three to five years (Brand and Keith 1979; Parker et al. 1983; Mowat et al. 1996b). In southwestern NWT, no kittens were present among collected carcasses ($n = 69$) during the two years following the hare decline (Poole 1994). In south-central Yukon, Slough and Mowat (1996) found no kittens in a sample of seven carcasses during the first year of low hare numbers; however, Slough (1996) analyzed pelts ($n = 45$) collected from a broader area for the same year and found 13% kittens. Slough (1996) believed that this overestimate was caused by a decline in lynx body size (and hence pelt length) during the crash.

Female lynx may begin to give birth before hare densities start to increase. Brand et al. (1976) saw live litters in summer during two different years of the cyclic low in hare abundance in central Alberta. Slough and Mowat (1996) found that three females gave birth to litters during the latter part of the low phase on their study area. The authors suggested that two other females may have done so as well. Perhaps the most convincing evidence of recruitment during the latter part of the low phase comes from the analysis of trapper samples. Slough and Mowat (1996) found 13 ($n = 33$) and 25% ($n = 29$) kittens in a carcass collection during the last two years of low hare and lynx densities before the hare increase. Clearly, some young lynx are recruited to the trappable population during the hare low, especially in the latter years of the low (Slough and Mowat 1996).

As hare numbers increase, yearling females begin to breed and adult litter sizes increase (Brand and Keith 1979; O'Connor 1984; Slough and Mowat 1996). Pregnancy and birth rates range from 73 to 100% for adults and 33 to 100% for yearlings during this period (Poole 1994; Mowat et al. 1996b; and see Table 3 in Mowat et al. 1996a:438). Adult litter size averages four to five during periods of hare abundance (Mowat et al. 1996a:438). Kitten survival is high (50-83%) during the increase and peak phase of hare cycle (Brand et al. 1976; Poole 1994; Slough and Mowat 1996). However, survival of kittens of yearling mothers was low (<26%) even in high quality habitat at all times of the hare cycle in south-central Yukon (Mowat et al. 1996b; Slough and Mowat 1996). These authors suggest yearlings contribute little to recruitment but the generality of this pattern is unclear. Lynx have large litters in comparison to other carnivores of their size (Mowat et al. 1996b) and this, combined with high kitten survival, generates rapid population growth during the increase and peak phases of the cycle (Slough and Mowat 1996).

The birth rate of adults and yearlings is reduced the spring following the hare decline (Poole 1994; Slough and Mowat 1996). Kitten survival also declines to near zero the year after hare numbers crash (Brand et al. 1976; Parker et al. 1983; Poole 1994); this decline was delayed one year in south-central Yukon (Slough and Mowat 1996). Here, most adult females gave birth to large litters while densities of hares were declining precipitously, but their birth rate declined to zero one year after the hare crash (Slough and Mowat 1996). In utero pregnancy rates and litter sizes declined little during the first year of the lynx crash and continued to overestimate reproduction and recruitment during the decline and low (Mowat et al. 1996a), making these measurements weak estimators of recruitment and poor predictors of the lynx decline.

In summary, lynx reproduction is closely tied to hare abundance in northern populations. Kitten survival declines to zero shortly after the hare crash, although some lynx continue to breed and possibly give birth for one more year (Poole 1994; Mowat and Slough 1998). Conception by adults continues through the low phase but very few live litters are born, especially during the two years following the lynx decline. In utero litter size declines through the low, which results in lower litter sizes early in the increase phase. Lynx may begin to recruit juveniles at least two years before appreciable recovery in hare numbers. We suggest the perception that lynx recruitment is zero during hare lows is overstated, at least in the far North. Northern lynx populations do recruit some individuals when hares are scarce and these individuals may be important in maintaining lynx populations through a hare low phase.

Mortality and Survival

Survival rates of lynx vary tremendously as snowshoe hare abundance changes through the cycle. Not surprisingly, the level of trapping in and around the population under study influences survival rates. Annual survival rates of adults during the increase and peak phase of the hare cycle were >0.70 in a lightly trapped population in southwestern Yukon

(O'Donoghue et al. 1997), and >0.89 in largely untrapped populations in southwestern NWT and south-central Yukon (Poole 1994; Slough and Mowat 1996). Annual survival rates of adult lynx remained high (0.78-0.95) (Poole 1994; Slough and Mowat 1996) or declined slightly (0.45-0.63) (O'Donoghue et al. 1997) through the one- or two-year hare decline. The first year of very low hare numbers was characterized by low adult survival (0.09-0.40), followed by higher survival in the one to two subsequent years of low hare densities (0.63-0.82) (Poole 1994; Slough and Mowat 1996,; O'Donoghue et al. 1997). A similar decline in the annual survival of bobcats was observed during a decline in jackrabbit density in Idaho (Knick 1990).

Survival tends to be lowest in winter. In southwestern NWT, cumulative survival summed over four years was higher during summer than during winter (0.91 vs. 0.08; Poole 1994). Most mortality during low hare abundance occurred during mid-December to mid-February, and most natural mortality (primarily starvation) appeared to coincide with <-35 °C temperatures, when metabolic requirements would be greatest (Poole 1994; O'Donoghue et al. 1995).

Causes of lynx mortality vary greatly across studies. Brand et al. (1976) noted that starvation of adult lynx seemed unlikely in all but the most pristine areas, suggesting that nutritionally stressed lynx are first predisposed to mortality related to humans. Ward and Krebs (1985) summarized studies to the mid-1980s of tagged lynx (n = 36) and found 95% of all lynx deaths were human related (mostly from fur-trapping), and only 5% of deaths were from natural causes. However, this result is probably biased by the fact that trappers provided their principal mode of recovery of dead animals. In interior Alaska, Stephenson (1986) estimated that annual mortality rates from trapping ranged from 55-100% of radio-marked lynx. On the Kenai Peninsula in Alaska, Bailey et al. (1986) suggested trapping was directly or indirectly involved in all nine lynx deaths on their study area during two years of high hare density, with trapping removing 80% of individuals over one year of age. On the same study area during a trapping closure, Staples (1995) observed that no adult male lynx died of natural causes during periods of low hare densities. Trapping mortality rates appear to be related to trapping pressure (generally driven by fur prices); seasonal trapping mortality in central Alberta increased two- to four-fold with a doubling of pelt prices (Brand and Keith 1979).

Earlier studies showed high trap-related mortality and essentially no natural mortality in lynx populations. On the basis of modeling population changes from combined harvest and field data, Brand and Keith (1979) concluded that trapping mortality of lynx tended to be additive. However, the authors' field samples were relatively small, and they could not distinguish between undetected mortality and dispersal (Hatler 1988). The recent Yukon (O'Donoghue et al. 1995, 1997; Slough and Mowat 1996) and NWT (Poole 1994) studies have documented significant natural mortality (primarily starvation) of lynx during the first two winters of hare scarcity (or second or third year of hare decline), which suggests that, at this period in the cycle, trapping mortality may be primarily compensatory to natural mortality at least in lightly or untrapped areas. The annual death rate from trapping (0.08) was higher than from natural causes (0.02) during peak and declining hare numbers in southwestern NWT (Poole 1994). However, during low hare numbers the death rate was far higher from natural causes (0.48) than trapping (0.20). In south-central Yukon, the annual survival rate on the study area was 0.40 in the first full year of low hare densities, with all detected mortality from natural causes (Slough and Mowat 1996). However, 20 marked lynx (27% of all emigrants) were trapped after dispersal, and 92% ($n = 25$) of known emigrant deaths were human-caused, primarily by trappers (Slough and Mowat 1996). Comparing survival rates among studies can be problematic because rates can be affected by how researchers dealt with emigrants. Trapping returns alone will bias mortality rates, since little natural lynx mortality is detected (e.g., Ward and Krebs 1985).

Causes of natural mortality of lynx are difficult to determine; a radiocollar and tufts of hair provide little basis for inference. Ideally, mortality factors should also be identified as proximate or ultimate causes. Starvation (and related conditions) and cases of cannibalism of lynx have been recorded, primarily during periods of low prey abundance (Poole 1994; O'Donoghue et al. 1995; Slough and Mowat 1996). Predation on lynx by wolverine, wolf and coyote have also been confirmed (Slough and Mowat 1996; O'Donoghue et al. 1995; 1997; Chapter 4). Lynx host a diverse parasitic fauna, including nematodes, cestodes, trematodes, lice, and fleas (van Zyll de Jong 1966; McCord and Cardoza 1982; Smith et al. 1986; Quinn and Parker 1987), but parasite influence on lynx health and survival is unknown.

In summary, northern lynx populations subject to cyclic hare densities and differing trapping pressures exhibit large differences in mortality rates and causes. In lightly trapped or untrapped populations, population growth is characterized by high kit and adult survival that extends into the decline in hare numbers, followed by an increase in natural mortality (starvation, predation, and cannibalism) coupled with high dispersal (see next section) (Poole 1994; Slough and Mowat 1996; O'Donoghue et al. 1997). This pattern may be disrupted in areas with heavier and consistent trapping pressure, resulting in natality rates insufficient to maintain normal cyclic changes in populations through an entire cycle (Bailey et al. 1986).

Movements and Dispersal

Daily movements of lynx within their range vary greatly and appear to be affected by environmental conditions, primarily prey densities and snow characteristics (Nellis and Keith 1968; Ward and Krebs 1985). Daily travel distances are generally calculated by three methods: (1) snow-tracking to determine cumulative distance moved over a 24-hour period (e.g., Brand et al. 1976; O'Donoghue et al. 1998b); (2) radiotelemetry to determine either straight-line distances between midday locations in successive days (e.g., Ward and Krebs 1985; Poole 1994); or (3) between paired fixes separated by 0.25-2 hours (Parker et al. 1983; Breitenmoser et al. 1991). Based on snow-tracking, average daily cruising distance ranges from 5-9 km (study means from Saunders 1963b; Nellis and Keith 1968; Parker 1981). Daily cruising distances provided by sequential (one to two hours) telemetry locations from a study on Cape Breton Island, Nova Scotia, were slightly greater in summer (about 9 km) than in winter (8 km; Parker et al. 1983). However, daily travel distances of lynx of 12.9-13.5 km in summer and 20.5 km in winter were measured during one year of the cyclic decline in the southwest Yukon (Breitenmoser et al. 1991). It may be assumed that females with young kittens have more restricted movements (Kesterson 1988; Mowat and Slough 1998).

The causes of changes to or differences in movement patterns of lynx are unclear. Studies in Alberta found increases in daily movements with increased hare density; Nellis and Keith (1968) speculated that the observed differences were due to differences in snow characteristics. However, Ward and Krebs (1985) documented a doubling of daily cruising radius (straight-line distance between successive 24-hour locations) from 2.7 to 5.4 km during moderate to high and low hare densities (<0.5 hares/ha), respectively, which they interpreted as increased foraging effort with decreased prey abundance. Similar conclusions can be drawn in southwestern NWT; daily travel distances as determined by radiotelemetry (24-hour locations) generally were greater (p <0.001) after the decline in hare numbers (Poole 1994). Standardized track counts conducted daily on the same trails provide additional support; track counts tripled between years of similar lynx densities but from peak to declining hare densities (K. Poole, unpublished). However, studies in the southwest Yukon detected no significant changes in the percent time spent active by lynx during a cyclic decline (O'Donoghue et al. 1998b), highlighting the inconsistency of results among studies.

Most information on long-distance movements by lynx comes from animals caught by trappers. The number and locations of returns from trappers are affected by the density and distribution of trapping around study areas, and by behavioral differences in trap vulnerability among age and sex classes of lynx (Bailey et al. 1986; Quinn and Thompson 1987; Slough and Mowat 1996; Poole 1997). Therefore, all dispersal rates and distances reported must be considered potentially biased.

Long distance (>100 km) movements of lynx were once thought of as anomalies (Nellis and Wetmore 1969; Mech 1977), but are now considered characteristic (Ward and Krebs 1985; Brittell et al. 1989; Perham et al. 1993; O'Donoghue et al. 1995, 1997; Slough and Mowat 1996; Poole 1997). Documented straight-line dispersal distances range up to 1,100 km, with 15 documented cases of dispersal >500 km (Ward and Krebs 1985; Slough and Mowat 1996; O'Donoghue et al. 1997; Poole 1997; Fig. 9.3). Relatively intensive radiotelemetry efforts up to 200 km from the NWT study area center detected a uniform dispersal direction for female lynx, and a male dispersal favoring south and west (Poole 1997). Dispersing lynx crossed roads and large rivers and lakes, sometimes during the snow-free season. The minimum daily travel rate during dispersal averaged 4.6 km/day

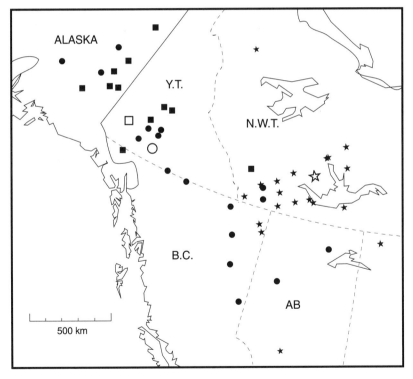

Figure 9.3—Dispersal of lynx >100 km from three areas in the NWT and Yukon. Data are taken from: ■ = Ward and Krebs (1985) (3) and O'Donoghue et al. (1997) (8); ● = Slough and Mowat (1996) (17); and ★ = Poole (1997) (19). Hollow symbols denote study area centers.

(range 1.7-8.3; n = 3; Ward and Krebs 1985), 4.2 km/day (0.3-23.6; n = 8; Slough and Mowat 1996), and 2.7 km/day (range 1.0-8.4, n = 10, Poole 1997) in three studies in the Yukon and NWT. These data suggest that dispersing lynx do not travel any farther per day than resident lynx.

Although emigration and immigration of lynx occurs throughout the hare cycle (Slough and Mowat 1996; O'Donoghue et al. 1997), a cyclic pattern is apparent. The rapid increase phase in lynx populations in south-central Yukon was at least partially due to immigration rates (21-38%) balancing or exceeding losses to emigration (0-33%; Slough and Mowat 1996). Emigration rates (52-79%) increased and exceeded immigration (12-50%) during the two-year decline in hare abundance and the first full year of low hare densities. In southwestern NWT, annual probability of dispersal for adult lynx was low (<24%) at peak hare densities and up to the spring after the hare crash (Poole 1997). Dispersal of adults primarily occurred in the spring after the rapid decline in hare abundance and during the first two winters of low hare numbers (78-100%; n = 9-16), and then stabilized during the third and fourth winters of low hare densities (<20%; n = 10) (Poole 1997). In southwestern Yukon, all three long-distance dispersals of resident adults occurred at the end of the snowshoe hare decline, with movements stabilizing during the subsequent winter (Ward and Krebs 1985). During a study of the same population a decade later, six of 15 collared lynx dispersed during the first year of a two-year snowshoe hare decline (O'Donoghue et al. 1995). Similar patterns of dispersal have been observed in bobcats (Hornocker and Bailey 1986; Knick 1990).

Annual timing of dispersal varies. Timing of dispersal may be related to the type of dispersal being observed. One type is juveniles dispersing from natal areas ("innate dispersal": a spontaneous movement related to the genetics of the dispersing individual). Another type is adults dispersing in response to an environmental "catastrophy" ("environmental dispersal": a behavioral response to unfavorable conditions; Howard 1960), such as the hare decline faced by northern lynx populations every 10 years. Juveniles would tend to disperse primarily in the spring, soon after independence. In lynx populations, we would expect most environmental dispersal to occur during the period of greatest nutritional stress, generally mid-winter. The period of greatest dispersal was March-June in south-central Yukon (Slough and Mowat 1996), and during mid-winter of the second year of the hare decline in southwestern Yukon (O'Donoghue et al. 1995). In southwestern NWT, most dispersal took place during March-June after the winter hare decline and during mid-winter of the subsequent two winters (Poole 1997).

Known immigrants to the south-central Yukon study area were more often adult males (Slough and Mowat 1996). During increasing, peak, and the initial decline in hare abundance, independent kittens 10-12 months of age and yearlings form the bulk of emigrants. Adults are most of dispersers during the latter portion of the decline and initial years of low hare densities (Slough and Mowat 1996; Poole 1997). Although male lynx have larger home ranges and hence increased mobility, male-biased dispersal rates in adult lynx have not been documented (Slough and Mowat 1996; Poole 1997). In addition, there were no differences in dispersal distances between sexes, or between kitten/yearling and adult age classes (Poole 1997). We do not feel we can conclude juvenile dispersal is even among the sexes due to lack of data.

Although emigration was apparently not sex-biased in the south-central Yukon study, 14 of 17 detected dispersals >100 km were by males (Slough and Mowat 1996). Most of these samples were from trapping returns, which are inherently biased toward males (Bailey et al. 1986; Quinn and Thompson 1987). Dispersal rates or distances are generally greater for males than females of most mammalian species (Greenwood 1980; Wolff 1994).

Annual survival rates did not differ for dispersing vs. non-dispersing lynx in southwestern NWT for any interval between the peak and the fourth year of low hare densities (Poole 1997). Survival of dispersing lynx was high (85-91%) during the peak and initial decline in hare abundance and the second to fourth years of low hare densities, and poor (29%) during the first full year of low hare densities (Poole 1997). Natural causes (largely starvation) accounted for over twice as many deaths of dispersing lynx than human-related causes (13 vs. six). Many lynx apparently died of natural causes en route, shortly after initiating dispersal, which suggests that the strategy used by lynx was to maintain residency until a critical starvation "stress point" was reached and then seek to disperse (O'Donoghue et al. 1995; Poole 1997). Initiation of dispersal often appeared to coincide with temperatures <-35 °C, a period when metabolic requirements would be greatest and prey diversity would be minimal, thereby increasing nutritional stress (O'Donoghue et al. 1995; Poole 1997). Given the regional extent of low snowshoe hare densities (Keith 1990; Poole and Graf 1996) many lynx never reached areas of higher prey density.

Some dispersing lynx survived the hare population low and re-established home ranges some distance from their point of dispersal (verified at 65-85 km, potentially up to 1,000 km; Slough and Mowat 1996, O'Donoghue et al. 1997; Poole 1997). These successful re-establishments of home ranges are difficult to detect using conventional study methods and are likely underreported. Long-distance dispersal of lynx and other predators during cyclic declines could act as a synchronizing element of the hare cycle (Butler 1953; Lack 1954; Korpimäki and Krebs 1996; O'Donoghue et al. 1997).

Recent studies have documented the dispersal patterns of adult lynx during much of the cycle. More research is needed to examine dispersal of juveniles, which likely occurs throughout the cycle, but peaks when both hare and lynx numbers are increasing or high (Hatler 1988; Slough and Mowat 1996; Poole 1997). Further understanding of the factors affecting juvenile dispersal, such as the influence of sex and matrilineal relationships and prey density, will have implications for harvest management and the expansion and maintenance of more southern, non-cyclic lynx populations. Similarly, an understanding of the influence of habitat availability and connectivity (including forest fragmentation caused by timber harvest) on both juvenile and adult lynx dispersal will aid in management of southern populations.

Harvest Management

Trapping mortality may be primarily compensatory to natural mortality during the first two years of lynx decline when natural mortality rates are high, but not during other periods of the cycle (Poole 1994; O'Donoghue et al. 1995, 1997; Slough and Mowat 1996). While the effects of harvest during the cyclic low could be severe, sustainable harvests can be high during the later cyclic increase and peak phases because growth rates are large (Poole 1994; Mowat et al. 1996b; Slough and Mowat 1996).

Lynx harvest records show a harvest cycle that varied dramatically in pattern over the past two centuries (Fig. 9.4). The harvest cycle can be

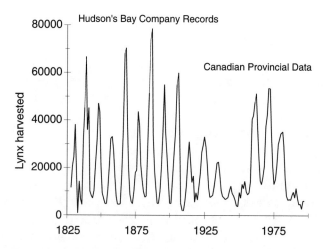

Figure 9.4—Lynx harvest in Canada from 1825 to 1997. Data prior to 1919 are from the Hudson's Bay Company and therefore do not represent the entire lynx harvest for Canada. After 1919, data were collected for each province and territory. (Data for 1827-1908; 1919-1983 from Novak et al. 1987. Data for 1910-1918 from Elton and Nicholson 1942. Data for 1984-1997, unpublished.)

characterized as having uniform high amplitude through to the early 1900s, declining amplitude from the 1920s to the 1950s, three fairly "normal" harvest cycles from the late 1950s to the early 1980s, and reduced amplitude during the 1990s peak. The cyclic pattern through the 20th century was relatively similar among jurisdictions, although the two northern territories had a slightly more distinct 1990 cyclic peak (Fig. 9.2).

Citing declining harvest returns and anecdotal information, De Vos and Matel (1952) noted a decrease in lynx numbers and distribution in Canada between 1920 and 1950. They cited overtrapping and ecological changes in habitat, primarily as a result of forest harvesting, as the main factors responsible for the decrease. We believe overtrapping may be the more probable explanation because forest harvesting as conducted in the early part of the century (high-grading) was unlikely to have caused a widespread decline in lynx numbers and distribution. Similarly, several authors have suggested local populations were overexploited during the cyclic low of the 1980s (Todd 1985; Bailey et al. 1986; Hatler 1988). There is little doubt that trapping can reduce lynx populations. Todd (1985) argued that recovery from low population levels may be prolonged, and that it took more than one hare cycle for lynx to recover from the suspected over-harvest during the 1920s and 1930s. However, harvest returns are affected by the host of factors influencing trapper effort and success, including changes in socioeconomic conditions, season length, quota and trap type restrictions, fur prices, subsidies, mode of transportation, and ease of access. Fur prices likely affect harvest effort over the short term (Brand and Keith 1979), but it may not be valid to compare and contrast inflation-adjusted prices and harvests that occurred decades apart. Harvest returns, therefore, may be roughly indicative of, but do not directly represent, real population changes.

There remains considerable debate whether lynx were significantly over-harvested during the 1980s and early 1990s (Todd 1985; Hatler 1988; Nowell and Jackson 1996). Interestingly, this period came after three cycles from 1960 to 1980 characterized by relatively high peak harvests, and, possibly more importantly, relatively high harvest levels during the cyclic lows (Fig. 9.4). Peak harvests (summing the five-year harvest around each peak) from 1960 to 1980 were similar to peak harvests during the classic cycles of the late 1800s, but the five-year harvest during the lows of 1960 to 1980 were about 25% higher than the lows of the late 1800s. Snowmobiles became readily available in the late 1950s and early 1960s, likely influencing trapper coverage, access, and attitudes. Whether or not these increased harvest levels during the cyclic lows had a significant cumulative impact on subsequent population levels is unknown. Harvest levels during the 1990 peak were significantly below earlier peaks observed during the 1960s and 1970s, which, in our opinion, is not unexpected given the 10-fold decrease in pelt prices over the last half of the 1980's, and hence lower trapper effort. This decrease in trapper effort was real; for example, NWT trappers told us that they were not interested in spending money on gas and equipment for a $60 lynx pelt when they received over $600 per pelt only a few years earlier. Many turned to wage jobs rather than trapping; the number of trappers in the NWT dropped from about 3,200 in the mid-1980s to 1,400 in the early 1990s (NWT Department of Renewable Resources, unpublished). Thus the decrease in harvest was at least partially due to decreased trapper effort in an area where lynx numbers appeared to be cycling normally (Poole 1994). In addition, based on community fur returns and local knowledge, no decrease in range has been detected in the two northern territories or Alaska through the 1990s (K. Poole, B. Slough, H. Golden, unpublished). Although we acknowledge that the amplitude of lynx abundance may have been decreased somewhat through the 1980s and 1990s, based on this coarse analysis we have no evidence to conclude that there was a long-term impact to contiguous northern lynx populations due to over-harvest during the low of the 1980s.

The long-term impact of high harvest pressure during the mid-1980s low phase in the lynx cycle on more southerly populations or where trapping intensity was severe may have been more significant (Todd 1985; Bailey et al. 1986; Hatler 1988). Ease of access in some areas (such as seismic lines spaced at one kilometer intervals blanketing parts of central and northern Alberta and British Columbia) coupled with extreme trapping pressure driven by high pelt prices during low lynx abundance may have reduced or eliminated lynx from some areas. In response to concerns about overharvest of lynx during the 1980s low, most Canadian provinces and Alaska implemented season reductions, reduced quotas, or harvest closures in at least portions of their jurisdictions in the late 1980s. The reduced harvest levels observed during the lynx cyclic peak of the early 1990s (Figs. 9.2, 9.4) were likely due to a combination of decreased trapper effort resulting from reduced pelt prices, and harvest restrictions that remained in place through much of the early 1990s; overharvest during the 1980 cyclic low may also have been a contributing factor. Given continuing low lynx pelt prices and trapper effort, we contend that in time, dispersal by lynx from adjacent healthy populations will likely repopulate many depopulated areas. However, the amplitude of the recovery to normal cyclic populations may be reduced for more than one cycle.

Although lynx populations in some areas have been over-harvested, we suggest that despite limited harvest management over the past half century, normal cycles have persisted throughout much of their northern range. This observation does not negate the need for more intensive harvest management in areas of high trapping pressure or marginal habitat, especially during the cyclic low. Harvest management options include implementation of a tracking harvest strategy (Caughley 1977; Brand and Keith 1979) where trapping is curtailed or eliminated for three to four years following the lynx decline; maintenance of permanent untrapped habitat or refugia (Slough and Mowat 1996); and season or quota restrictions (Parker et al. 1983; Todd 1985; Bailey et al. 1986; Poole 1994; Slough and Mowat 1996).

A tracking harvest strategy has management appeal because the only information required to implement the system is crude knowledge of the timing of the lynx decline. This information can be inferred from harvest records. However, measuring pelt length is relatively cheap and yields information on juvenile recruitment leading to greater certainty in the timing of cyclic events (Slough 1996). In healthy populations, we recommend managers consider curtailing harvest beginning two years after lynx populations begin to decline. In areas where distribution is more constrained or harvest more intense, managers may prefer to restrict harvest starting one year after lynx numbers begin to decline. Harvest should be restricted for three to four years or until there is evidence of significant juvenile recruitment and population increase; track counts may be a cost-effective monitoring method (Thompson et al. 1989).

A refugia management strategy has less utility where harvest pressure is fairly continuous throughout the landscape. Large movements and home ranges by lynx during low hare densities dictate that individual traplines are often not large enough to support even one lynx, and therefore management activities must be prescribed on a regional basis. Protecting a viable population in a refuge would require planning at the scale of thousands of square kilometers because lynx persist at such low densities during the low phase, and trapping effort on the edge of a refuge could remove lynx that reside tens of kilometers inside the refuge (Carbyn and Patriquin 1983). We suggest that attempting to conserve lynx by establishing permanently untrapped refugia is only advisable where very large reserves currently exist; even then lynx may be overharvested from substantial areas outside the reserve if harvest effort is intense. Further, establishing a network of reserves is politically difficult.

Season restrictions are necessary in all areas for the traditional reasons of avoiding harvest during breeding activities and timing harvest to the period when pelts are prime. Further, restricting trapping for lynx until December or even January may reduce the chance that orphaned juveniles die after their mother is trapped, providing greater sustainable harvests and less risk to the population (Bailey 1981; Parker et al. 1983; Mowat 1993).

This effort may be particularly important in low-density populations. In heavily harvested areas or where lynx are at low densities or discontinuous distributions, quotas may be the only means to adequately limit harvest. Because of the ease with which lynx are trapped, even very short seasons such as one month will not necessarily ensure appropriate harvest levels. Quotas give the managers the greatest control over harvest levels; however, setting reasonable quotas requires information about population size and habitat quality. Few managers have this kind of information for an entire management jurisdiction. For most managers in the northern part of the range of Canada lynx some sort of tracking harvest strategy will offer adequate protection to lynx populations at an achievable cost. However, the most effective management option will depend upon a host of factors specific to each region, including the spatial distribution of trapping effort, lynx density and cyclic dynamics, habitat quality and distribution, and socio-political factors.

Acknowledgments

We thank the many researchers, technicians, government personnel, and harvesters who have helped advance our knowledge of lynx in the northern boreal forest over the past decade. The NWT Department of Renewable Resources, the Yukon Department of Renewable Resources, and the Natural Sciences and Engineering Research Council of Canada provided the bulk of funding for much of the recent research from the two northern territories summarized here. Research from Kluane, Yukon, was conducted as a part of the Kluane Boreal Forest Ecosystem Project headed by C. J. Krebs. We thank B. G. Slough for providing his data on lynx den site characteristics. Lastly, we thank L. Ruggiero for inviting us to write this paper.

Literature Cited

Akçakaya, H. R. 1992. Population cycles of mammals: evidence for a ratio-dependent predation hypothesis. Ecological Monographs 62:119-142.

Aldama, J. J. and M. Delibes. 1991. Observations of feeding groups in the Spanish lynx (*Felis paradina*) in the Doñana National Park, SW Spain. Mammalia 55: 143-147.

Bailey, R. G. 1998. Ecoregions map of North America: Explanatory note. Miscellaneous Publications Number 1548. Washington, DC: U.S. Department of Agriculture, Forest Service.

Bailey, T. N. 1974. Social organization in a bobcat population. Journal of Wildlife Management 38:435-446.

Bailey, T. N. 1979. Den ecology, population parameters and diet of eastern Idaho bobcats. Pages 62-69 *in* P. C. Escherich and L. Blum, editors. Proceedings of the 1979 bobcat research conference. National Wildlife Federal Science and Technology Series 6.

Bailey, T. N. 1981. Factors of bobcat social organization. Pages 984-1000 *in* J. A. Chapman and D. Pursley, editors. Proceedings of the worldwide furbearer conference. Frostburg, MD.

Bailey, T. N., E. E. Bangs, M. F. Portner, J. C. Malloy, and R. J. McAvinchey. 1986. An apparent overexploited lynx population in the Kenai Peninsula, Alaska. Journal of Wildlife Management 50:279-290.

Banfield, A. W. F. 1974. The mammals of Canada. University of Toronto Press, Toronto, Canada.

Banville, D. 1986. Étude écologique du lynx du Canada sur la haute Côte-Nord. Québec Ministerè du Loiser, de la Chasse et de la Pêche, Québec.

Barash, D. P. 1971. Cooperative hunting in the lynx. Journal of Mammalogy 52:480.

Berrie, P. M. 1974. Ecology and status of the lynx in interior Alaska. Pages 4-41 *in* R. L. Eaton, editor. The world's cats. Volume 1. World Wildlife Safari, Winston, OR.

Bergerud, A. T. 1971. The population dynamics of the Newfoundland caribou. Wildlife Monographs 25:1-55.

Boutin, S., C. J. Krebs, R. Boonstra, M. R. T. Dale, S. J. Hannon, K. Martin, A. R. E. Sinclair, J. N. M. Smith, R. Turkington, M. Blower, A. Byrom, F. I. Doyle, C. Doyle, D. Hik, L. Hofer, A. Hubbs, T. Karels, D. L. Murray, V. Nams, M. O'Donoghue, C. Rohner, and S. Schweiger. 1995. Population changes of the vertebrate community during a snowshoe hare cycle in Canada's boreal forest. Oikos 74:69-80.

Brand, C. J., L. B. Keith, and C. A. Fischer. 1976. Lynx responses to changing snowshoe hare densities in Alberta. Journal of Wildlife Management 40:416-428.

Brand, C. J. and L. B. Keith. 1979. Lynx demography during a snowshoe hare decline in Alberta. Journal of Wildlife Management 43:827-849.

Breitenmoser, U., C. Breitenmoser, and G. A. Zuleta. 1991. Lynx; progress report September 1991. Kluane Boreal Forest Ecosystem Project, Kluane, Yukon.

Breitenmoser, U., P. Kavczensky, M. Dötterer, C. Breitenmoser-Würsten, S. Capt, F. Bernhart, and M. Liberek. 1993a. Spatial organization and recruitment of lynx in a re-introduced population in the Swiss Jura Mountains. Journal of Zoology 231:449-464.

Breitenmoser, U., B. G. Slough, and C. Breitenmoser-Würsten. 1993b. Predators of cyclic prey: is the Canada lynx victim or profiteer of the snowshoe hare cycle? Oikos 66:551-554.

Brittell, J. D., Poelker, R. J., Sweeney, S. J., and G. M. Koehler. 1989. Native cats of Washington. Section III: Lynx. Washington Department of Wildlife, Olympia.

Butler, L. 1953. The nature of cycles in populations of Canadian mammals. Canadian Journal of Zoology 31:242-262.

Carbyn, L. N. and D. Patriquin. 1983. Observations on home range sizes, movements and social organization of lynx, *Lynx canadensis*, in Riding Mountain National Park, Manitoba. Canadian Field-Naturalist 97:262-267.

Caughley, G. 1977. Analysis of vertebrate populations. John Wiley and Sons, New York.

Crowe, D. M. 1975. Aspects of aging, growth, and reproduction of bobcats from Wyoming. Journal of Mammalogy 56:177-198.

Davies, N. B. 1977. Prey selection and search strategy of the spotted flycatcher (*Muscicapa striata*), a field study on optimal foraging. Animal Behaviour 25:1016-1033.

De Vos, A. and S. E. Matel. 1952. The status of the lynx in Canada, 1929-1952. Journal of Forestry 50:742-745.

Dwyer, P. M., F. F. Mallory, and J. R. Pitblado. 1989. Preliminary assessment of lynx habitat and distribution during cyclic population lows in northern Ontario. Musk-ox 37:129-136.

Eisenberg, J. F. 1981. Life history strategies of the Felidae: Variations on a common theme. Pages 293-303 *in* S. D. Miller and D. D. Everett, editors. Cats of the world: biology, conservation, and management. Washington, DC: National Wildlife Federation.

Elton, C. and M. Nicholson. 1942. The ten year cycle in numbers of lynx in Canada. Journal of Animal Ecology 11:215-244.

Ferreras, P., J. F. Beltran, J. J. Aldama, and M. Delibes. 1997. Spatial organization and land tenure system of the endangered Iberian lynx. Journal of the Zoological Society of London 243:163-189.

Formanowicz, D. R. and P. J. Bradley. 1987. Fluctuations in prey density: effects on the foraging tactics of scolopendrid centipedes. Animal Behaviour 35:453-461.

Fortin, C. and J. Huot. 1995. Ecologie comparee du Coyote, du Lynx du Canada et du Renard roux au parc national Forillon. Rapport Final for Parcs Canada, Departement de Biologie, Universite Laval, Québec.

Golden, H. 1993. Furbearer track count index testing and development. Alaska Department of Fish and Game, Research Progress Report W-24-1.

Greenwood, P. J. 1980. Mating systems, philopatry and dispersal in birds and mammals. Animal Behaviour 28:1140-1162.

Hatler, D. F. 1988. A lynx management strategy for British Columbia. Wildlife working report WR-34. B.C. Ministry of Environment and Parks, Victoria.

Hik, D. S. 1995. Does risk of predation influence population dynamics? Evidence from the cyclic decline of snowshoe hares. Wildlife Research 22:115-129.

Holling, C. S. 1959a. Some characteristics of simple types of predation and parasitism. Canadian Entomologist 91:385-398.

Holling, C. S. 1959b. The components of predation as revealed by a study of small-mammal predation of the European pine sawfly. Canadian Entomologist 91:293-320.

Holling, C. S. 1966. The functional response of vertebrate predators to prey density. Memoirs of the Entomological Society of Canada 48:1-86.

Hornocker, M. G., J. P. Messick, and W. E. Melquist. 1983. Spatial strategies in three species of Mustelidae. Acta Zoologica Fennica 174:185-188.

Hornocker, M. and T. Bailey. 1986. Natural regulation in three species of felids. Pages 211-220 *in* S. D. Miller and D. D. Everett, editors. Cats of the world: biology, conservation, and management. Washington, DC,. National Wildlife Federation.

Howard, W. E. 1960. Innate and environmental dispersal of individual vertebrates. American Midland Naturalist 63:152-161.

Jedrzejewski, W., B. Jedrzejewska, H. Okarma, K. Schmidt, A. N. Bunevich, and L. Milkowski. 1996. Population dynamics (1869-1994), demography, and home ranges of the lynx in Bialowieza Primeval forest (Poland and Belarus). Ecography 19:122-138.

Johnson, W. N., T. F. Paragi, and D. D. Katnik. 1995. The relationships of wildland fire to lynx and marten populations and habitat in interior Alaska. Final Report. Galena, AK: U.S. Fish and wildlife Service.

Keith, L. B. 1963. Wildlife's ten-year cycle. University of Wisconsin Press, Madison.

Keith, L. B. 1990. Dynamics of snowshoe hare populations. Pages 119-195 in H. H. Genoways, editor. Current mammalogy. Plenum Press, New York.

Keith, L. B., A. W. Todd, C. J. Brand, R. S. Adamcik, and D. H. Rusch. 1977. An analysis of predation during a cyclic fluctuation of snowshoe hares. Proceedings of the International Congress of Game Biologists 13:151-175.

Kelsall, J., Telfer, E. S., and T. D. Wright. 1977. The effects of fire on the ecology of the boreal forest, with particular reference to the Canadian north: a review and selected bibliography. Canadian Wildlife Service, Occasional Paper No. 32, Ottawa, Ontario.

Kerby, G. and D. W. Macdonald. 1988. Cat society and the consequences of colony size. Pages 67-81 in D. C. Turner and P. Bateson, editors. The domestic cat: the biology of its behavior. Cambridge University Press, Cambridge.

Kesterson, M. B. 1988. Lynx home range and spatial organization in relation to population density and prey abundance. M.S. Thesis, University of Alaska, Fairbanks.

Kleiman, D. G. and J. F. Eisenberg. 1973. Comparisons of canid and felid social systems from an evolutionary perspective. Animal Behaviour 21:637-659.

Knick, S. T. 1990. Ecology of bobcats relative to exploitation and a prey decline in southeastern Idaho. Wildlife Monograph 108:1-42.

Koehler, G. M. and J. D. Brittell. 1990. Managing spruce-fir habitat for lynx and snowshoe hares. Journal of Forestry Oct 90:10-14.

Koehler, G. M. and K. B. Aubry. 1994. Lynx. Pages 74-98 in L. F. Ruggiero, K. B. Aubry, S. W. Buskirk, L. J. Lyon, and W. J. Zielinski, editors. The scientific basis for conserving forest carnivores: American marten, fisher, lynx, and wolverine in the Western United States. Gen. Tech. Rep. RM-254. Fort Collins, CO: U.S. Department of Agriculture, Forest Service, Intermountain Forest and Range Experiment Station.

Korpimäki, E. and C. J. Krebs. 1996. Predation and populations cycles of small mammals. BioScience 46:754-764.

Krebs, C. J. and S. Boutin, editors. 1998. Vertebrate community dynamics in the boreal forest - The Kluane Project. Unpublished manuscript.

Krebs, C. J., S. Boutin, R. Boonstra, A. R. E. Sinclair, J. N. M. Smith, M. R. T. Dale, K. Martin, and R. Turkington. 1995. Impact of food and predation on the snowshoe hare cycle. Science 269:1112-1115.

Lack, D. 1954. Cyclic mortality. Journal of Wildlife Management 18:25-37.

Legendre, P., F. Long, R. Bergeron, and J-M. Levasseur. 1978. Inventaire aerien de la faune dans le Moyen Nord quebecois. Canadian Journal of Zoology 56:451-462.

Lembeck, M. 1986. Long term behavior and population dynamics of an unharvested bobcat population in San Diego County. Pages 305-310 *in* S. D. Miller and D. D. Everett, editors. Cats of the world: biology, conservation and management. National Wildlife Federation, Washington, DC.

Macdonald, D. W., F. G. Ball, and N. G. Hough. 1980. The evaluation of home range size and configuration using radio-tracking data. Pages 405-424 *in* C. J. Amlaner, Jr. and D. W. Macdonald, editors. A handbook on biotelemetry and radio tracking. Pergamon Press, Oxford, England.

Major, A. R. 1989. Lynx, *Lynx canadensis canadensis* (Kerr) predation patterns and habitat use in the Yukon Territory, Canada. M.S. Thesis, State University of New York, Syracuse.

May, R. M. 1981. Models for single populations. Pages 78-104 *in* R. M. May, editor. Theoretical ecology. Principles and applications. Second Edition. Sinauer, Sunderland, MA.

McCord, C. M. and J. E. Cardoza. 1982. Bobcat and lynx. Pages 728-766 *in* J. A. Chapman and G. A. Feldhamer, editors. Wild mammals of North America. The Johns Hopkins University Press, Baltimore, MD.

Mech, L. D. 1977. Record movement of a Canadian lynx. Journal of Mammalogy 58:676-677.

Mellen, J. D. 1993. A comparative analysis of scent-marking, social and reproductive behavior in 20 species of small cats (*Felis*). American Zoologist 33:151-166.

Messier, F. 1995. On the functional and numerical responses of wolves to changing prey density. Pages 187-197 *in* L. N. Carbyn, S. H. Fritts, and D. R. Seip, editors. Ecology and conservation of wolves in a changing world. Canadian Circumpolar Institute, Occasional Publications No. 35, Edmonton, Alberta, Canada.

Mowat, G. 1993. Lynx recruitment in relation to snowshoe hare density. M.S. Thesis, University of Alberta, Edmonton.

Mowat, G., S. Boutin, and B. G. Slough. 1996a. Using placental scars to estimate litter size and pregnancy rate in lynx. Journal of Wildlife Management 60:430-440.

Mowat, G., B. G. Slough, and S. Boutin. 1996b. Lynx recruitment during a snowshoe hare population peak and decline in southwest Yukon. Journal of Wildlife Management 60:441-452.

Mowat, G. and B. G. Slough. 1998. Some observations on the natural history and behavior of the Canada lynx, *Lynx canadensis*. Canadian Field-Naturalist 112:32-36.

Mowat, G., J. Staniforth, and V. Loewen. 1998. The relationship between vegetative cover and snowshoe hare abundance in south and central Yukon. Yukon Fish and Wildlife Branch, Final Report. Whitehorse, Yukon.

Murdoch, W. W. 1969. Switching in generalist predators: experiments on predator specificity and stability of prey populations. Ecological Monographs 39:335-354.

Murray, D. L. and S. Boutin. 1991. The influence of snow on lynx and coyote movements: does morphology effect behavior? Oecologia 88:463-469.

Murray, D. L., S. Boutin, and M. O'Donoghue. 1994. Winter habitat selection by lynx and coyotes in relation to snowshoe hare abundance. Canadian Journal of Zoology 72:1444-1451.

Murray, D. L., S. Boutin, M. O'Donoghue, and V. O. Nams. 1995. Hunting behaviour of a sympatric felid and canid in relation to vegetative cover. Animal Behaviour 50:1203-1210.

Nellis, C. H. and L. B. Keith. 1968. Hunting activities and success of lynxes in Alberta. Journal of Wildlife Management 32:718-722.

Nellis, C. H. and S. P. Wetmore. 1969. Long-range movements of lynx in Alberta. Journal of Mammalogy 50:640.

Nellis, C. H., S. P. Wetmore, and L. B. Keith. 1972. Lynx-prey interactions in central Alberta. Journal of Wildlife Management 36:320-329.

Noiseux, F. and G. J. Doucet. 1987. Étude de la population du lynx du Canada (*Lynx canadensis*) de la Réserve Faunique des Laurentides, Québec. Québec Minister du Loisir, de la Chasse et de la Pêche, Québec.

Nowell, K. and P. Jackson. 1996. Wild cats: status survey and conservation action plan. IUCN/SSC Cat Specialist Group, Gland, Switzerland.

Novak, M, M. E. Obbard, J. G. Jones, R. Newman, A. Booth, A. J. Satterthwaite, and G. Linscombe. 1987. Furbearers harvests in North America, 1600-1984. Ministry of Natural Resources, Ontario, Canada.

O'Connor, R. M. 1984. Population trends, age structure and reproductive characteristics of female lynx in Alaska, 1963 through 1973. M.S. Thesis, University of Alaska, Fairbanks.

O'Donoghue, M., E. Hofer, and F. I. Doyle. 1995. Predator versus predator. Natural History 104(3):6-9.

O'Donoghue, M., S. Boutin, C. J. Krebs, and E. J. Hofer. 1997. Numerical responses of coyotes and lynx to the snowshoe hare cycle. Oikos 80:150-162.

O'Donoghue, M., S. Boutin, C. J. Krebs, D. L. Murray, and E. J. Hofer. 1998a. Behavioral responses of coyotes and lynx to the snowshoe hare cycle. Oikos 82:169-183.

O'Donoghue, M., S. Boutin, C. J. Krebs, G. Zuleta, D. L. Murray, and E. J. Hofer. 1998b. Functional responses of coyotes and lynx to the snowshoe hare cycle. Ecology 79:1193-1208.

O'Donoghue, M., S. Boutin, D. L. Murray, C. J. Krebs, E. J. Hofer, U. Breitenmoser, C. Breitenmoser-Würsten, G. Zuleta, C. Doyle, and V. O. Nams. 1998c. Coyotes and lynx. Chapter 13 *in* C. J. Krebs and S. Boutin, editors. The Kluane Boreal Forest Ecosystem Project. Unpublished manuscript.

Paragi, T. F., W. N. Johnson, and D. D. Katnik. 1997. Selection of post-fire seres by lynx and snowshoe hares in the Alaskan taiga. Northwest Naturalist 78:77-86.

Parker, G. R. 1981. Winter habitat use and hunting activities of lynx (*Lynx canadensis*) on Cape Breton Island, Nova Scotia. Pages 221-248 *in* J. A. Chapman and D. Pursley, editors. Worldwide Furbearer Conference proceedings, Aug. 3-11, 1980. Frostburg, MD.

Parker, G. R., J. W. Maxwell, L. D. Morton, and G. E. J. Smith. 1983. The ecology of the lynx (*Lynx canadensis*) on Cape Breton Island. Canadian Journal of Zoology 61:770-786.

Perham, C., T. Doyle, and B. Route. 1993. Mortality factors, home range characteristics, and habitat preferences of lynx inhabiting Tetlin National Wildlife Refuge and Wrangell-St. Elias National Park and Preserve. U.S. Fish and Wildlife Service, Tetlin National Wildlife Refuge, Tok, AK.

Perham, C. T. 1995. Home range, habitat selection, and movements of lynx in eastern interior Alaska. M. Sc. Thesis, University of Alaska, Fairbanks.

Poole, K. G. 1992. Lynx research in the Northwest Territories, 1991-92. Report number 68, NWT Renewable Resources, Yellowknife. Unpublished Manuscript.

Poole, K. G. 1994. Characteristics of an unharvested lynx population during a snowshoe hare decline. Journal of Wildlife Management 58:608-618.

Poole, K. G. 1995. Spatial organization of a lynx population. Canadian Journal of Zoology 73:632-641.

Poole, K. G. 1997. Dispersal patterns of lynx in the Northwest Territories. Journal of Wildlife Management 61:497-505.

Poole, K. G. and R. P. Graf. 1996. Winter diet of marten during a snowshoe hare decline. Canadian Journal of Zoology 74:456-466.

Poole, K. G., L. A. Wakelyn, and P. N. Nicklen. 1996. Habitat selection by lynx in the Northwest Territories. Canadian Journal of Zoology 74:845-850.

Powell, R. A. 1979. Mustelid spacing patterns: variations on a theme by *Mustela*. Zoologica Tierpsychologica 50:153-165

Pulliainen, E., E. Lindgren, and P. S. Tunkkari. 1995. Influence of food availability and reproductive status on the diet and body condition of the European lynx in Finland. Acta Theriologica 40:181-196.

Quinn, N. W. S. and G. Parker. 1987. Lynx. Pages 683-694 *in* M. Novak, J. A. Baker, M. E. Obbard, and B. Malloch, editors. Wild furbearer management and conservation in North America. Ontario Trappers Association, North Bay.

Quinn, N. W. S. and J. E. Thompson. 1985. Age and sex of trapped lynx, *Felis canadensis*, related to period of capture and trapping technique. Canadian Field-Naturalist 99:267-269.

Quinn, N. W. S. and J. E. Thompson. 1987. Dynamics of an exploited Canada lynx population in Ontario. Journal of Wildlife Management 51:297-305.

Ranta, E., V. Kaitala, and J. Lindström. 1997. Dynamics of Canadian lynx populations in space and time. Ecography 20:454-460.

Ross, P. I. and M. G. Jalkotzy. 1992. Characteristics of a hunted cougar population in southwestern Alberta. Journal of Wildlife Management 56:417-426.

Saunders, J. K. 1963a. Food habits of lynx in Newfoundland. Journal of Wildlife Management 27:384-390.

Saunders, J. K. 1963b. Movements and activities of lynx in Newfoundland. Journal of Wildlife Management 27:390-400.

Seidensticker, J. C., IV, M. G. Hornocker, W. V. Wiles, and J. P. Messick. 1973. Mountain lion social organization in the Idaho Primitive Area. Wildlife Monographs 35:1-60.

Sinclair, A. R. E. and R. P. Pech. 1996. Density dependence, stochasticity, compensation and predator regulation. Oikos 75:164-173.

Slough, B. G., R. H. Jessup, D. I. McKay, A. B. Stephenson. 1987. Wild furbearer management in Western and Northern Canada. Pages 1062-1076 *in* M. Novak, J. A. Baker, M. E. Obbard, and B. Malloch, editors. Wild furbearer management and conservation in North America. Ontario Trappers Association, North Bay.

Slough, B. G. 1996. Estimating lynx population age ratio with pelt length data. Wildlife Society Bulletin 24:495-499.

Slough, B. B. In press. Characteristics of Canada lynx, *Lynx canadensis*, maternal dens and denning habitat. Canadian Field-Naturalist.

Slough, B. G. and G. Mowat. 1996. Population dynamics of lynx in a refuge and interactions between harvested and unharvested populations. Journal of Wildlife Management 60:946-961.

Smith, C. H. 1983. Spatial trends in Canadian snowshoe hare, *Lepus americanus*, population cycles. Canadian Field-Naturalist 97:151-160.

Smith, J. D., E. M. Addison, D. G. Joachim, and L. M. Smith. 1986. Helminth parasites of Canada lynx (*Felis canadensis*) from northern Ontario. Canadian Journal of Zoology 64:358-364.

Solomon, M. E. 1949. The natural control of animal populations. Journal of Animal Ecology 18:1-35.

Staples, W. R. 1995. Lynx and coyote diet and habitat relationships during a low hare population on the Kenai Peninsula, Alaska. M.S. Thesis, University of Alaska, Fairbanks, AK.

Stenseth, N. C., W. Falck, O. N. Bjornstad, and C. J. Krebs. 1997. Population regulation in snowshoe hare and Canadian lynx: asymmetric food web configurations between hare and lynx. Proceedings of the National Academy of Science, USA. 94:5147-5152.

Stephenson, R. O. 1986. Development of lynx population estimation techniques. Alaska Dep. Fish and Game. Federal Aid in Wildlife Restoration. Final Report, Project W-22-5, Job 7.12R. Juneau.

Stephenson, R. O., D. V. Grangaard, and J. Burch. 1991. Lynx, *Felis lynx*, predation on red foxes, *Vulpes vulpes*, caribou, *Rangifer tarandus*, and Dall sheep, *Ovis dalli*, in Alaska. Canadian Field-Naturalist 105:255-262.

Stuart-Smith, A. K. and S. Boutin. 1995. Predation on red squirrels during a snowshoe hare decline. Canadian Journal of Zoology 73:713-722.

Sullivan, T. P. 1994. Influence of herbicide-induced habitat alteration on vegetation and snowshoe hare populations in sub-boreal spruce forest. Journal of Applied Ecology 31:717-730.

Sullivan, T. P. 1996. Influence of forest herbicide on snowshoe hare population dynamics: reproduction, growth, and survival. Canadian Journal of Forest Research 26:112-119.

Sundquist, M. 1981. The social organization of tigers (*Panthera tigris*) in Royal Chitawan National Park, Nepal. Smithsonian Contribution to Zoology #336. Smithsonian Institute Press, Washington, DC.

Taylor, R. J. 1984. Predation. Chapman and Hall, London.

Thompson, I. D. 1988. Habitat needs of furbearers in relation to logging in boreal Ontario. The Forestry Chronicle 64:251-261.

Thompson, I. D., I. J. Davidson, S. O'Donnell, and F. Brazeau. 1989. Use of track transects to measure the relative occurrence of some boreal mammals in uncut forest and regeneration stands. Canadian Journal of Zoology 67:1816-1823.

Todd, A. W. 1985. The Canada lynx: ecology and management. Canadian Trapper 13:15-20.

Tumlison, R. 1987. *Felis lynx*. Mammalian Species 269:1-8.

van Zyll de Jong, C. G. 1966. Food habits of the lynx in Alberta and the Mackenzie District, N.W.T. Canadian Field-Naturalist 80:18-23.

Viereck, L.A. 1983. The effects of fire in black spruce ecosystems of Alaska and northern Canada. Pages 201-220 *in* R.W. Wein and D.A. MacLean, editors. The role of fire in northern circumpolar ecosystems. John Wiley and Sons, Toronto, Ontario.

Ward, R. M. P. and C. J. Krebs. 1985. Behavioral responses of lynx to declining snowshoe hare abundance. Canadian Journal of Zoology 63:2817-2824.

Winegarner, C. E. and M. S. Winegarner. 1982. Reproductive history of a bobcat. Journal of Mammology 63:680-682.

Wolff, J. O. 1980. The role of habitat patchiness in the population dynamics of snowshoe hares. Ecological Monographs 50:111-130.

Wolff, J. O. 1994. More on juvenile dispersal in mammals. Oikos 71:349-352.

Chapter 10

Canada Lynx Habitat and Topographic Use Patterns in North Central Washington: A Reanalysis

Kevin S. McKelvey, USDA Forest Service, Rocky Mountain Research Station, Forestry Science Lab, 800 E. Beckwith, Missoula, MT 59807

Yvette K. Ortega, USDA Forest Service, Rocky Mountain Research Station, Forestry Science Lab, 800 E. Beckwith, Missoula, MT 59807

Gary M. Koehler, Washington Department of Fish and Wildlife, 600 Capitol Way N., Olympia, WA 98501

Keith B. Aubry, USDA Forest Service, Pacific Northwest Research Station, 3625 93rd Ave. SW, Olympia, WA 98512

J. David Brittell, Washington Department of Fish and Wildlife, 600 Capitol Way N., Olympia, WA 98501

Abstract—We examined habitat selection by 22 lynx on the Okanogan National Forest in Washington, analyzing radiotelemetry data collected during two previous studies, 1981 through 1988. At a coarse scale, lynx showed little use of areas below 1,400 m or above 2,150 m. Within the zone between 1,400 and 2,150 m, lynx used areas with slopes <10% and moderate stream densities in winter. Selection for combinations of physical variables and vegetation types was stronger in winter versus summer, and lynx showed strong selection for lodgepole pine cover types in winter. Relative abundance of snowshoe hares measured from pellet counts on plots within the study area were highest within lodgepole pine and lowest within Douglas-fir cover types, and winter selectivity may have been influenced by abundance and distribution of hares. In summer, lynx avoided Douglas-fir cover types and selected northeast aspects; Douglas-fir tended to occur on southwest aspects, especially at higher elevations. Road densities in the study area did not have a significant effect on habitat selection, and lynx crossed roads at frequencies that did not differ from random expectation.

Introduction

Little is known about habitat use patterns of Canada lynx at the southern periphery of their range, and relevant telemetry studies are particularly limited. Koehler et al. (1979) found that two radio-tracked lynx in Montana used densely stocked stands of lodgepole pine almost exclusively, but results were based on only 29 telemetry locations. Smith (1984) found that approximately 80% of locations obtained from four lynx radio-tracked for two years in Montana were within areas classified in the subalpine fir series (Pfister et al. 1977). Neither Koehler et al. (1979) nor Smith (1984) compared use patterns to the distribution of available forest types. Other telemetry-based studies in the contiguous United States include Mech (1980), who monitored 14 lynx in Minnesota, and Brainerd (1985), who tracked seven lynx in Montana, but neither reported habitat use. Three telemetry-based studies of lynx are in progress in the western United States and Southwest Canada (see Chapters 11, 12).

Most information on habitat relationships of lynx in the contiguous United States has been derived from two telemetry studies conducted on the Okanogan National Forest, Washington. Brittell et al. (1989) obtained 540 locations for 17 lynx between 1981 and 1983, and Koehler (1990) recorded 302 locations for seven lynx between 1984 and 1988 (Table 10.1). Koehler (1990) reported that home ranges contained a higher proportion of lodgepole pine and a lower proportion of Douglas-fir cover types than the overall study area (a zone surrounding the lynx locations and confined to elevations above 750 m). He also found more pellets of snowshoe hares within lodgepole pine forests than within other cover types used by lynx and concluded that lynx selected habitat based on hare densities. Additionally, Koehler (1990) found that cover types associated with low-elevation grass-lands or alpine areas were rare within home ranges and that the average elevation of telemetry locations in winter was lower than that in summer. In contrast, Brittell et al. (1989) reported that lynx home ranges did not differ

Table 10.1.—Telemetry data for the 22 lynx sampled by Brittell et al. (1989) and Koehler (1990). Two lynx were monitored during both studies.

Lynx ID	Sex	n	Start (mo/yr)	Stop (mo/yr)	Duration (days)	Avg. days between locations	Locations by month												Study[a]	Sampled[b]
							J	F	M	A	M	J	J	A	S	O	N	D		
1	M	23	10/81	7/82	274	12	4	2	3	3	2	5	2	0	0	1	1	0	B	B
3	F	31	10/81	8/82	298	10	5	2	4	3	3	5	4	2	0	1	1	1	B	B
4	M	19	8/82	3/83	227	12	2	2	4	0	0	0	0	4	0	3	2	2	B	W
6	M	64	4/82	9/83	534	8	2	2	4	7	7	10	6	8	9	4	2	3	B	B
7	M	47	11/81	3/83	483	10	4	4	7	2	4	5	4	4	3	3	3	4	B	B
11	M	60	4/82	9/83	534	9	2	2	4	7	5	10	5	8	9	3	2	3	B	B
14	F	47	5/82	9/83	506	11	1	2	3	1	4	8	4	6	9	4	2	3	B	B
16	M	49	7/82	9/83	431	9	2	2	4	4	4	5	4	9	9	3	0	3	B	B
17	F	18	7/82	1/83	177	10	2	0	0	0	0	0	2	2	3	4	2	3	B	B
18	F	18	7/82	1/83	169	9	2	2	4	0	0	0	1	4	3	3	2	3	B	B
20	F	41	10/82	9/83	338	8	2	2	4	4	4	5	3	5	6	2	0	0	B	S
21	M	25	4/83	9/83	169	7	0	0	0	2	4	5	3	5	6	0	0	0	B	S
24	F	12	7/83	9/83	65	5	0	0	0	0	0	0	1	5	6	0	0	0	B	S
31	M	11	7/83	9/83	65	6	0	0	0	0	0	0	0	5	5	0	0	0	B	S
33	F	16	5/82	6/82	53	3	0	0	0	0	6	10	0	0	0	0	0	0	B	B
55087	M	28	2/87	2/88	345	12	0	5	9	0	6	4	2	0	1	1	0	0	K	S
59011	M	28	6/85	6/86	384	14	3	5	4	1	2	6	0	5	1	0	0	1	K	B
104090	M	88	7/82;6/86	9/83;9/87	883	10	7	8	9	4	4	15	8	10	12	3	4	4	B;K	B
109062	M	37	2/86	10/87	721	19	1	8	7	2	1	6	3	1	4	1	2	1	K	B
111167	F	103	8/83;6/85	9/83;10/87	927	9	6	1	4	6	3	21	13	12	17	3	5	1	B;K	B
112071	F	33	3/86	10/87	595	18	1	3	2	2	3	7	6	0	3	1	4	1	K	B
195058	M	44	11/84	7/86	606	14	0	1	4	2	3	3	7	8	9	2	3	2	K	B
Total		842					46	51	72	46	65	130	79	102	115	42	37	38		

[a]B = Brittell et al.; K = Koehler.
[b]Sampled in both (B) seasons, or exclusively in winter (W) or summer (S).

significantly from the study area in terms of slope, aspect, elevation, and vegetation type.

Considering the scarcity of information on habitat use by lynx and the conflicting results described above, we reexamined data from Brittell et al. (1989) and Koehler (1990). Because these two studies occurred in the same area and used the same methods, they represent a continuum of data collection amounting to 842 locations for 22 lynx (Table 10.1). By combining these data, and by taking advantage of current GIS and statistical technologies, we were able to evaluate habitat relationships in greater detail than had been possible in the past.

Using the combined telemetry locations of Brittell et al. (1989) and Koehler (1990) as well as spatial data describing vegetation, topography, roads and streams, we evaluated habitat selection by lynx in the study area considering multiple spatial scales. Additionally, we considered location data from road-based track and camera surveys recently conducted by the State of Washington and the Okanogan National Forest. Because lynx locations derived from such surveys are sometimes used to infer lynx habitat relationships, we assessed the concordance between these locations and the telemetry data. We also used hare data from Koehler (1990) to examine the relationship between habitat use by lynx and hare densities.

Methods

Study Area

Lynx studies were conducted by Brittell et al. (1989) and Koehler (1990) in a 1,800-km^2 area of Okanogan County in the northeastern Cascade Range of Washington (48° 15' to 49° N., 119° 45' to 120° 15' W.) where elevations range from 750 to 2,540 m. Road densities averaged 800 m/km^2 (±STD of 870 m/km^2; range 0-3,400 m/km^2), and >90% of the length consisted of narrow, unpaved roads. Annual precipitation averaged 51 cm at 660 m, and snow depth exceeded 1 m above 1,980 m during November through March (Koehler 1990). Douglas-fir and ponderosa pine dominated forests below 1,370 m and southern aspects at higher elevations. High elevation forests above 1,370 m were dominated by Engelmann spruce, subalpine fir, and lodgepole pine (Koehler 1990).

Available Data

Telemetry locations were obtained by Brittell et al. (1989) and Koehler (1990) for 13 adult male and nine adult female lynx from 1982 to 1988 (Table 10.1). Lynx were captured in leg-hold and box-type live traps.

Under ketamine hydrochloride anesthesia, lynx were marked with ear tags, and fitted with activity-sensitive transmitter collars (Telonics, Mesa, AZ). Movements of radio-collared animals were monitored from aircraft at seven to 15 day intervals, depending on weather, and at one to five day intervals from the ground. Lynx were approached to within 200 m for ground monitoring and attempts were made to obtain ≥2 locations at ~90° direction from the animal. Locations were plotted on 1:62,500 U.S. Geological Survey topographic maps to the nearest 50 m. Telemetry error averaged 200 m for data collected 1982 through 1986 (Koehler 1990) but was not estimated for other years.

For examination of habitat selection by lynx, we obtained three GIS vegetation layers: one used by Koehler (1990) that was designed to model areas of equivalent fuel loading (Fuels), another generated for the Okanogan National Forest by Pacific Meridian Resources, Inc. (PMR), and a third resulting from the North Cascades Grizzly Bear Ecosystem Evaluation (NCGBEE) (Almack et al. 1993). The maps were derived from various LANDSAT images dating from the early to mid-1980s and had similar resolution (pixel size ~50 m). Because the maps were classified with differing methods into different vegetation classes (Table 10.2), their depiction of vegetation in the study area also varied. Labeling of vegetation classes must be considered primarily nominal: it is unknown to what extent class label reflects actual vegetation in a given area. For these reasons, we considered each vegetation coverage separately in examinations of habitat selection, describing our results in terms of the classes in each coverage. In the discussion, we look for common patterns among these analyses, making inferences about the types of vegetation selected by lynx (Table 10.2).

Our analyses of habitat selection by lynx also incorporated physical variables including road and stream densities, elevation, slope, and aspect. Coverages of roads and streams developed from 1:24,000-scale data were converted to density maps by rasterizing the lines and using Arc/INFO's FOCALSUM function (ESRI 1997) to index densities. Densities were computed within a fixed neighborhood extending 2.3 km, equivalent to the average radius of the 50% adaptive kernel home range estimate for lynx with >50 locations (Table 10.1). Used in this way, FOCALSUM produces a raster-map in which the value of each raster is the sum of the number of "road" or "stream" rasters within 2.3 km.

One problem with using this approach to calculate densities is that all roads or streams within the 2.3 km neighborhood contribute equally regardless of distance from the "focal" raster. Not only is it likely that roads or streams close to a location influence habitat use more than distant ones, but the area within the neighborhood is concentrated at the edge, away from the focal raster. Unless this is corrected, the road or stream densities

Table 10.2– Vegetation classes within the study area as defined by the Fuels (A), PMR (B), and NCGBEE (C) layers (see text for explanation). Also listed are labels for vegetation types used in the text Discussion section to refer to important classes. Species names are: subalpine fir (*Abies lasiocarpa*), subalpine larch (*Larix lyallii*), lodgepole pine (*Pinus contorta*), whitebark pine (*Pinus albicaulis*), Engelmann spruce (*Picea engelmannii*), ponderosa pine (*Pinus ponderosa*), Douglas-fir (*Psuedotsuga menziesii*), western larch (*Larix occidentalis*), PUTR (*Purshia tridentata*), VACA (*Vaccinium caespitosum*), VADE (*Vaccinium deliciosum*), VASC (*Vaccinium scoparium*).

Original class label	Class definitions for meso-scale analyses	Vegetation type	Area (%)	Mean elevation (meters)	STD elevation (meters)
A					
Lodgepole pine	Lodgepole pine	Lodegepole pine	32.6	1,705	209.8
Engelmann spruce	Engelmann spruce	Spruce-fir	8.9	1,840	151.1
Engelmann spruce/subalpine fir/other	Engelmann spruce/subalpine fir/other		9.6	1,780	161.5
Ponderosa pine/Douglas-fir/western larch	Ponderosa pine/Douglas-fir/western larch	Douglas-fir	13.0	1,388	199.6
Lodgepole pine/other	Lodgepole pine/other		7.4	1,780	221.8
Douglas-fir/ponderosa pine	Douglas-fir/ponderosa pine		6.9	1,307	205.6
Grass, rock	Grass, rock		8.0	1,835	368.7
Hardwood/hardwood conifer	Other		1.9	1,294	257.3
Subalpine larch	Other		4.7	2,085	100.5
Mountain hemlock/silver fir	Other		1.2	1,934	132.7
Whitebark pine	Other		1.3	2,125	140.8
Ponderosa pine	Other		2.7	1,047	252.7
Shrub, grass/conifer	Other		1.8	1,453	332.0
B					
Douglas-fir	Douglas-fir	Douglas-fir	6.1	1,382	307.8
Douglas-fir/mix conifer	Douglas-fir/mix conifer		9.5	1,504	243.7
Lodgepole pine	Lodgepole pine	Lodgepole pine	20.4	1,776	230.1
Mix-various conifer species	Mix-various conifer species		10.8	1,503	310.7
Subalpine fir	Subalpine fir		17.7	1,782	220.1
Subalpine fir/Engelmann spruce	Subalpine fir/Engelmann spruce		5.1	1,668	219.1
Subalpine fir/Douglas-fir	Subalpine fir/other		0.7	1,558	231.7
Subalpine fir/lodgepole pine	Subalpine fir/other		2.6	1,854	248.8
Subalpine fir/mix conifer	Subalpine fir/other		1.8	1,835	177.4
Grass	Grass		9.0	1,662	435.6
Douglas-fir/lodgepole pine	Other		0.5	1,557	305.3
Engelmann spruce/mix conifer	Other		1.0	1,775	227.6
Less than 25% any species	Other		6.2	1,508	391.5
Lodgepole pine/mix conifer	Other		0.8	1,788	196.9
Pacific silver fir	Other		1.2	1,865	195.6
Pacific silver fir/mix conifer	Other		0.1	1,949	66.2
Ponderosa pine	Other		1.5	1,325	274.6
Shrub	Other		3.9	1,684	418.6

(con.)

Table 10.2 (Con.)

Original class label	Class definitions for meso-scale analyses	Vegetation type	Area (%)	Mean elevation (meters)	STD elevation (meters)
B (con.)					
Subalpine larch/mix conifer	Other		0.0	2,115	0.0
Various hardwood species	Other		0.1	1,480	96.9
Western larch/mix conifer	Other		0.6	1,472	148.1
Whitebark pine/mix conifer	Other		0.3	1,853	183.6
Agriculture and developed	Absent		<0.1	380	0.0
Ponderosa pine/Douglas-fir	Absent		0.2	967	192.1
C					
Subalpine fir-Engelmann spruce-lodgepole pine–east	Subalpine fir-Engelmann spruce-lodgepole pine	Lodgepole pine	60.3	1,751	172.9
Douglas-fir-mixed conifer–east	Douglas-fir-mixed conifer		14.7	1,396	252.5
Subalpine larch	Other forest		2.3	2,128	65.5
Non-riparian deciduous–east	Other forest		0.8	1,730	179.9
Whitebark pine	Other forest		1.5	2,130	57.3
Engelmann spruce riparian	Other forest		1.8	1,540	361.5
Riparian deciduous forest–east	Other forest		0.2	1,273	406.6
Subalpine - alpine VASC - VACA meadow	Subalpine meadow		2.8	2,028	177.2
Subalpine heather-VADE meadow	Subalpine meadow		0.4	2,192	200.8
Subalpine lush meadow–southwest	Subalpine meadow		0.5	2,102	138.0
Subalpine meadow -messic to dry–east	Subalpine meadow		1.2	1,708	143.9
Subalpine mosaic–east	Subalpine meadow		0.9	1,653	98.9
Alpine meadow–east	Other open		0.7	2,244	89.0
Bare and rock	Other open		0.5	1,964	365.7
Montane herbaceous–east	Other open		2.7	1,315	149.9
Montane mosaic–east	Other open		1.6	1,263	151.8
Montane shrub–east	Other open		0.2	1,708	372.3
Agriculture - fallow and dry pasture	Absent		0.1	433	73.3
Lush shrub elev. herbaceous–east	Absent		0.1	813	281.0
Ponderosa pine	Absent		0.5	756	111.4
Ponderosa pine-Douglas-fir	Absent		5.1	1,046	139.0
Shrub steppe - herbaceous	Absent		0.7	987	163.5
Shrub steppe - PUTR	Absent		0.5	888	175.5
Wet soil and gravel	Absent		0.0	2,152	0.0

computed for a location using FOCALSUM will be dominated by land conditions 2 km away and will be relatively insensitive to adjacent roads or streams. We therefore applied a linear distance-weighting function to the neighborhood: adjacent road or stream rasters contributed 3.0 to the FOCALSUM, and roads or streams at distances of 1.15 and 2.3 km contributed 1.5 and 0.0, respectively.

The digital elevation model (pixel size ~32 m) that we obtained contained systematic errors, or bands, which produced ridges and trenches along the cardinal directions. We removed the bands using Arc/INFO's FOCALMEAN function (Brown and Barra 1994) and used the resultant grid to obtain elevation, slope, and aspect data (ESRI 1997). Because aspect may be most relevant to the biology of the lynx through its influence on temperature and moisture gradients, we transformed aspect from a circular statistic into a measure of angular distance from northeast. Redefined aspect values ranged from 0 on the coldest, wettest slopes (due northeast) to 180 on the warmest, driest slopes (due southwest). We also assigned flat areas a value of 180 because they receive high radiant energy loads.

Evaluating Habitat Use

Methods developed to evaluate habitat selection for populations compare the distribution of animal locations relative to that of available habitat types. When a habitat type is used at a proportion significantly greater than its availability, we state that it is selected, while we infer that the opposite inequality indicates avoidance of the type (White and Garrott 1990). However, the definition of available habitat is problematic: whether or not analysis indicates that a particular type is selected depends, in part, on the degree to which underused types are included in the definition of available habitat, and results are therefore somewhat arbitrary (Johnson 1980; White and Garrott 1990; Rosenberg and McKelvey 1999).

Established methods for evaluating population-level habitat selection include two approaches that view the population and available universe differently (Manly et al. 1993). In one approach, data from all individuals are pooled, and available habitat is generally defined as the study area (e.g., Neu et al. 1974). However, given that lynx in our data set were sampled unevenly, with the number of locations per individual ranging from 11 to 103 (Table 10.1), simple pooling would give unsatisfactory results because depiction of habitat selection for the population would be skewed toward those heavily sampled individuals. Pooling may also suppress habitat selection patterns of individuals or classes of individuals (White and Garrott 1990). An alternate approach is to compute resource use functions for individuals and then combine these into a population-level statistic.

In this case, available habitat is defined by the home range (Manly et al. 1993; White and Garrott 1990). However, these methods are only meaningful when applied to well-sampled individuals. Of the 22 lynx for which we had data, most had too few points for meaningful calculation of individual use patterns, and only four had >50 locations (Table 10.1).

Given the nature of our sample and the problems associated with established methods, we developed an approach for evaluating habitat selection that combined principles of the approaches described above. Because habitat use may vary by season, we first split the location data into winter (October-March) and summer (April-September) periods for which we conducted separate analyses. We chose these six-month seasons because of convenience and because they distinguished the period of significant snow cover (winter) from that of breeding activity (summer). For each season, we pooled data across individuals, but used sub-sampling to obtain an equivalent number of points per animal so that habitat choices of each could be equally represented. A subset of points was generated by randomly picking five points per animal. By picking a relatively small number of points per individual, we could incorporate lynx with few points and minimize sequential autocorrelation and potential pseudo-replication (Swihardt and Slade 1985). We generated multiple subsets ($n = 20$) of points for which we conducted separate analyses of habitat selection, allowing us to consider the robustness of derived habitat relationships among potential subsamples.

Rather than limiting the analysis to one definition of availability, we evaluated habitat selection at multiple spatial scales, clearly defining available habitat at each scale such that statements concerning selection could be qualified. We began analyses at a coarse scale to consider patterns within the study area that we defined as the 100% minimum convex polygon for all the locations buffered by the diameter (4.8 km) of the average 50% adaptive kernel home range (Fig. 10.1). Because most habitat variables were highly correlated with elevation, we limited analysis at this scale to evaluation of selection among broad elevation classes. We used resultant understandings to delineate a more restricted zone of available habitat that excluded those elevation classes with little or no use, allowing us to examine meso-scale habitat selection.

For categorical data describing elevation and vegetation, we compared use to availability for each subset by computing χ^2 goodness-of-fit statistics and Bonferroni confidence intervals (Neu et al. 1974). We assessed the overall significance of results as follows: if χ^2 tests for at least 75% of subsets showed that use of a class significantly exceeded availability ($p < 0.05$), then we inferred strong selection for that class; if analysis showed that at least 50% of subsets demonstrated use that was significantly greater than

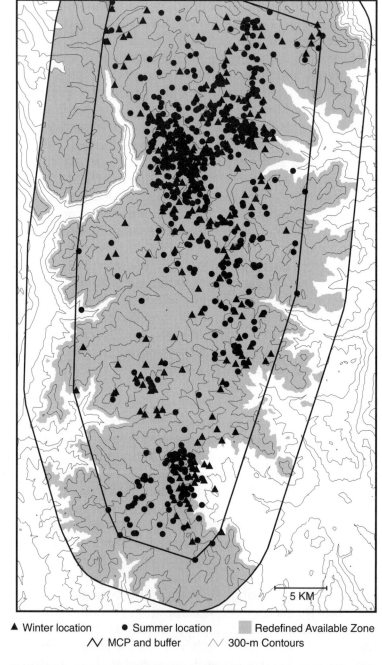

▲ Winter location   ● Summer location   ▨ Redefined Available Zone

/\/ MCP and buffer   /\/ 300-m Contours

Figure 10.1—The study area on the Okanogan National Forest in north-central Washington showing the distribution of 836 lynx telemetry locations collected 1981 through 1988. Also pictured are zones of availability used for coarse and meso-scale analyses of habitat selection.

availability, we inferred marginal selection for the class. Avoidance was assessed in the same manner.

To incorporate continuous physical variables into analyses of meso-scale selection, we developed logistic regression models for each subset that compared lynx locations to random points within the available zone. Vegetation patterns are correlated to physical variables: drier forests are typically located on lower, south-facing slopes. To assess the degree to which lynx selection patterns indicated by the physical models reflected selection for vegetation types, we developed combined models that included vegetation class as a design variable to consider whether vegetation was an important indicator of use when physical features were accounted for.

Overall significance of regression results was assessed as follows: if a variable was statistically significant (Wald χ^2 test, $p <0.05$) in logistic regression models derived for at least 75% of the subsets, then we described the variable as either strongly selected or strongly avoided, depending on the sign of its coefficient. Statistical significance of models was evaluated with the Score test ($p <0.05$), and models were compared using Akiake's Information Criterion (AIC), with lower AIC scores indicating better models (SAS 1990).

To consider patterns that may have been masked by pooling the data, we used χ^2 tests of homogeneity to compare use of vegetation classes between sexes. Similarly, we tested for differences in use of vegetation classes between the two time periods of study, 1981 through 1983 (Brittell et al. 1989) and 1984 through 1988 (Koehler 1990), and descriptive statistics were used to assess similarity of use patterns among the 22 lynx. When we found significant differences between sexes or time periods, we repeated the χ^2 analyses (above) on these subsets.

For evaluation of fine-scale habitat selection, we examined use within home ranges of lynx with >50 locations. For each of these lynx, the distribution of available types was defined by a 100% minimum convex polygon that surrounded its locations. We evaluated selection of vegetation classes using χ^2- goodness-of-fit statistics and Bonferroni confidence intervals.

To examine whether roads may have had direct affects on fine-scale habitat use, we considered the degree to which lynx crossed roads. Sequential telemetry locations on opposite sides of a road should indicate that the road was crossed unless the road ended within the home range, thereby enabling the animal to move between the points without crossing the road. Most roads in the study area passed through lynx home ranges rather than ending within them (Fig. 10.2). For each individual with >50 locations, we tested whether line segments defined by sequential telemetry

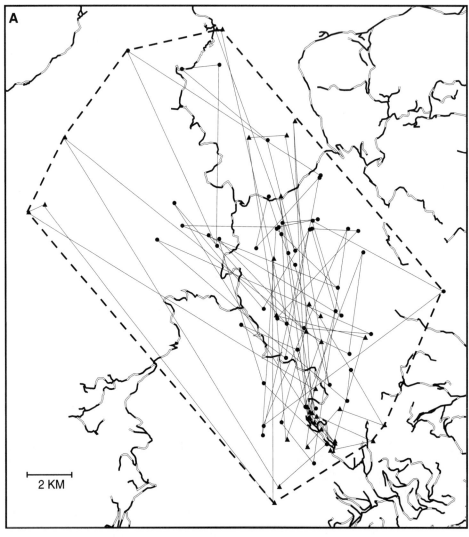

▲ Winter location   • Summer location   ╱ ↙ Home Range
∿ Potential Movement   ⋀ Road

Figure 10.2—Methodology used to evaluate rates at which lynx crossed roads. The frequency of road intersections for lines between sequential telemetry locations (A) was compared to that for randomly generated lines (B, page 319).

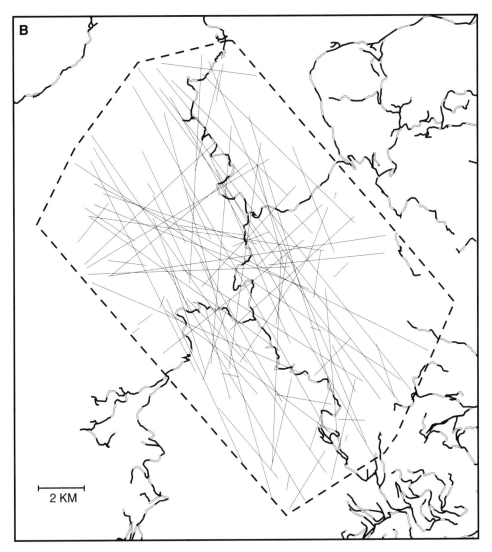

B

2 KM

/✔ Home Range ⌒ Potential Movement ⌒ Road

locations intersected roads more or less than expected. To generate the null expectation for each lynx, we first computed the distances between successive telemetry locations. Line segments of length chosen randomly from this set of distances were placed at random locations and azimuths within the home range so that they fit entirely within its boundary (Fig. 10.2). Because we generated a large number of random lines per lynx ($n = 8,000$), we treated the proportion that intersected roads as a known expectation (no variance) and used χ^2-goodness-of-fit statistics for comparison to the proportion of road intersections indicated by telemetry locations.

Okanogan National Forest Road Surveys

For comparison to telemetry-based findings, we considered the types of habitat where lynx were detected by remote camera and track surveys conducted on the Okanogan National Forest 1994-1998 (J. Rohrer, unpublished). These detections were obtained at baited stations located at non-random points along roads. Still, because lynx are not thought to be drawn long distances to baits (Robert Naney personal communication; John Weaver personal communication), we reasoned that lynx may have been detected in habitat types similar to those used by radio-tracked lynx. We therefore examined the distribution of detections among elevation and vegetation classes, but limited our analyses to descriptive statistics.

Hares

Koehler (1990) sampled pellets of snowshoe hares within the study area to consider the distribution of hares among habitat types used by lynx. Transects ($n = 68$) were partitioned among cover types in proportion to their abundance within the study area (Koehler 1990). However, because transects were placed perpendicular to roads, they did not constitute a representative sample of the study area. To allow data to be independent among transects, transects were spaced ≥325 m apart based on the assumption that home range sizes for hares were <8.8 ha (Wolff 1980; Chapters 6 and 7). Pellets were counted within 10, 1-m-radius circular plots spaced at 10 m intervals along each transect, and counts were summed per transect. Pellets were counted and cleared from plots during September 1986 and counted again on cleared plots in May and June 1987. Habitat measurements were also taken on the sample plots (Koehler 1990), allowing us to examine relative abundance of hares among forest cover types and elevation classes. Because pellet samples were non-representative, we confined analyses to descriptive statistics.

Results

For the combined data set, most lynx were sampled across several seasons, and in some cases several years (Table 10.1). Locations were distributed through time such that the average interval between sampling was >2 days for all 22 lynx, but more locations were recorded in summer than winter.

Coarse-Scale Habitat Selection

Six telemetry locations fell beyond our maps of habitat features, leaving 836 telemetry locations (n = 305 and 531 for winter and summer, respectively) for analyses of habitat selection. When buffered, the minimum convex polygon formed by these points defined an area of available habitat of 166,620 ha (Fig. 10.1). The majority of telemetry locations fell at elevations between 1,700 and 2,000 m (Fig. 10.3). Lynx strongly avoided (100% of subsets) areas <1,100 m, 1,100-1,250 m, and 1,250-1,400 m in both seasons (Fig. 10.3). Seasonal differences in habitat selection were apparent for

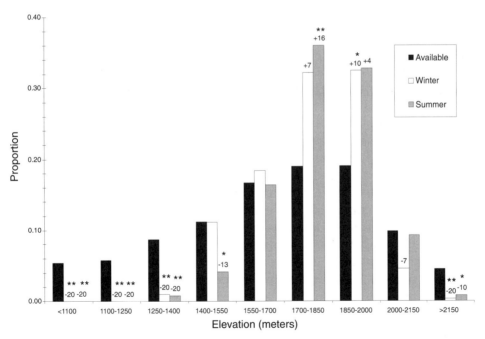

Figure 10.3—Coarse-scale use of elevation classes summarized across locations for 22 lynx. Above each bar is the number of subsets for which use was greater (+) or less (–) than availability (p <0.05). Classes with marginal (*) or strong (**) selection patterns (see text) are marked accordingly.

higher elevations: use of the 1,400-1,550-m class did not differ from availability in winter, but lynx showed marginal avoidance of this zone in summer (65% of subsets; Fig. 10.3). Similarly, avoidance of the >2,150-m class was strong in the winter (100% of subsets), but marginal in the summer (50% of subsets; Fig. 10.3).

Meso-Scale Habitat Selection

Based on coarse-scale patterns of habitat use, we redefined available habitat to exclude elevation classes that were avoided in both seasons (Fig. 10.3). Removal of zones <1,400 m and >2,150 m reduced the available area by 25% (Fig. 10.1), eliminated several vegetation classes (Table 10.2), and left 98.6% of the locations (301 and 523 for winter and summer, respectively).

Vegetation classes—Selection of vegetation classes within the redefined area was similar for the three vegetation layers. Using the Fuels map, the majority of telemetry locations fell within the lodgepole pine class: 53% in winter and 48% in summer, compared to 39% of the available area (Fig. 10.4A). Each of seven remaining classes had ≤15% of locations. Lynx showed strong selection for the lodgepole pine class in winter (85% of subsets), and strong avoidance of the ponderosa pine/Douglas-fir/western larch class in summer (85% of subsets; Fig. 10.4A).

Using the PMR classification, the majority of lynx points fell into the lodgepole pine class: 39% in winter and 33% in summer, compared to an availability of 24% (Fig. 10.4B). The subalpine fir class contained 25% of locations, and each of the remaining seven classes had <15%. Lynx showed marginal selection for the lodgepole pine class in winter (55% of subsets), avoidance of the Douglas-fir class in both winter (100% of subsets) and summer (50% of subsets), and strong avoidance of the Douglas-fir/ mixed conifer class in both seasons (≥95% of subsets; Fig. 10.4B).

More than 80% of lynx locations fell into the subalpine fir-Engelmann spruce-lodgepole pine class of the NCGBEE map, with <10% in each of the four remaining classes (Douglas-fir-mixed conifer, other forest, subalpine meadow, other open). Lynx showed marginal selection for the subalpine fir-Engelmann spruce-lodgepole pine class in summer (65% of subsets). However, the NCGBEE map was coarse at this scale, with 78% of the available area falling into this class, and we did not include this map in subsequent analyses.

Physical variables—Correlation among pairs of physical variables (road and stream densities, elevation, aspect, and slope) was low (Pearson r <0.5). Logistic regression models that included all five variables were significant

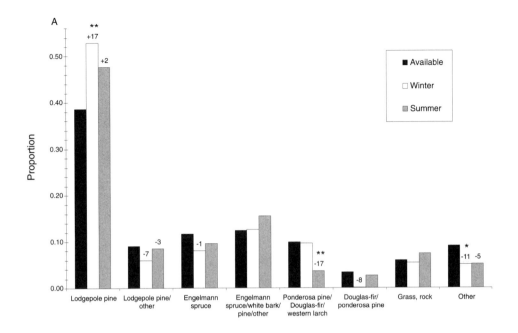

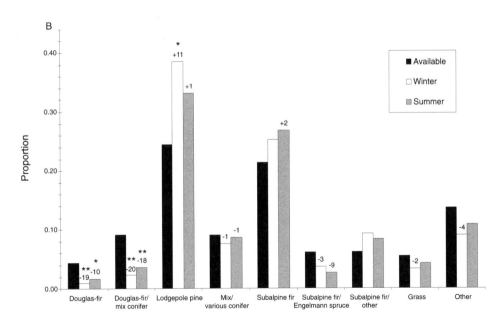

Figures 10.4—Meso-scale use of vegetation classes summarized across locations for 22 lynx using the Fuels (A) and PMR (B) vegetation layers (see Table 10.2 and text for explanation). Above each bar is the number of subsets for which use was greater (+) or less (-) than availability (*p* <0.05). Classes with marginal (*) or strong (**) selection patterns (see text) are marked accordingly.

for all subsets (χ^2 >11.5, df = 5, p <0.05), with better models in winter (AIC = 766-792) compared to summer (AIC = 848-876). In winter, selection patterns were strong for slope and stream density: probability of lynx use increased significantly with decreasing slope (χ^2 >4.2, df = 1, p <0.04 for 80% of subsets; Fig. 10.5A) and increasing stream density (χ^2 >4.2, df = 1, p <0.04 for 80% of subsets; Fig. 10.5B). In summer, selection patterns were strong for elevation and aspect: probability of lynx use increased significantly with increasing elevation (χ^2 >4.4, df = 1, p <0.04 for 70% of subsets; Fig. 10.5C) and decreasing aspect (χ^2 >5.1, df = 1, p <0.025 for 85% of subsets; Fig. 10.5D). However, for stream density and elevation, selection did not follow a linear pattern: use deviated most from availability at intermediate values of these variables (Fig. 10.5B, C). Use also deviated from availability at low to intermediate road densities (Fig. 10.5E), although selection patterns were weak (winter: χ^2 <3.4, df = 1, p >0.06 for 100% of subsets; summer: χ^2 <3.8, df = 1, p >0.05 for 55% of subsets).

Combined models of vegetation and physical variables—Vegetation class was a significant predictor of probability of lynx use, even when physical variables were accounted for within logistic regression models. Using the Fuels map, models that included vegetation class were better (χ^2 >21.8, df = 12, p <0.05) than models with only physical variables for 80% of winter subsets (AIC = 764-790) and 60% of summer subsets (AIC = 837-877). The lodgepole pine class was strongly selected in the winter (χ^2 >4.3, df = 1, p <0.04 for 80% of subsets) and marginally selected in the summer (χ^2 >5.3, df = 1, p<0.03 for 50% of subsets). The addition of vegetation to the model did not significantly change relationships between habitat use and the physical variables described above: in winter, flatter slopes were strongly selected (χ^2 >4.7, df = 1, p <0.04 for 80% of subsets), as were areas with higher stream densities (χ^2 >5.0, df = 1, p <0.03 for 90% of subsets). In summer, northern aspects were strongly selected (χ^2 >4.1, df = 1, p <0.05 for 85% of subsets), but elevation was significant for only 40% of subsets (χ^2 >4.0, df = 1, p <0.05).

Logistic regression models that included vegetation classes from the PMR layer (χ^2 >23.0, df = 13, p <0.04) were better (χ^2 >23.0, df = 13, p <0.04) than models with only physical variables for 100% of winter subsets (AIC = 741-786) and 10% of summer subsets (AIC = 850-873). Selection for the lodgepole pine class was strong in the winter (χ^2 >4.0, df = 1, p <0.05 for 100% of subsets) and marginal in the summer (χ^2 >4.0, df = 1, p <0.05 for 60% of subsets). As with the Fuels map, relationships between habitat use and physical variables generally did not change with the addition of vegetation class to the model: in winter, flatter slopes were marginally selected (χ^2 >4.5, df = 1, p <0.04 for 50% of subsets), and selection was

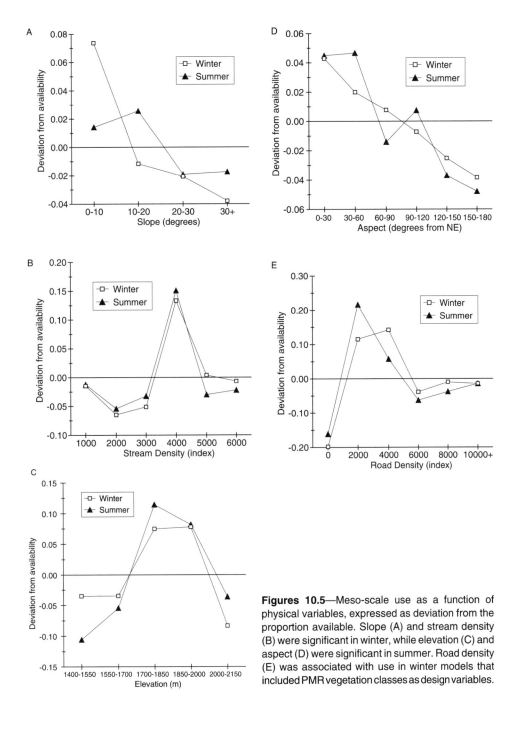

Figures 10.5—Meso-scale use as a function of physical variables, expressed as deviation from the proportion available. Slope (A) and stream density (B) were significant in winter, while elevation (C) and aspect (D) were significant in summer. Road density (E) was associated with use in winter models that included PMR vegetation classes as design variables.

strong ($\chi^2 > 5.0$, df = 1, $p < 0.03$ for 80% of subsets) for areas with higher stream densities. Road density also showed a strong association ($\chi^2 > 4.1$, df = 1, $p < 0.05$ for 80% of subsets) with lynx use in winter. In summer, northern aspects were strongly selected ($\chi^2 > 5.5$, df = 1, $p < 0.02$ for 80% of subsets), but elevation was significant for only 30% of subsets ($\chi^2 > 3.9$, df = 1, $p < 0.05$).

To examine the degree to which selection for physical variables by lynx was associated with specific vegetation classes, we built logistic regression models that used physical variables to predict the occurrence of vegetation classes that were strongly selected or avoided. Because selection patterns were similar for the two vegetation layers, we limited these analyses to the Fuels map. Occurrence of the lodgepole pine type decreased along slope and aspect gradients, and increased with stream density ($\chi^2 > 4.1$, df = 1, $p < 0.05$) for each parameter; model $\chi^2 = 35.0$, df = 5, $p = 0.0001$, AIC = 3485). Therefore, this class tended to occur in flatter areas with northeast aspects and higher stream densities. Occurrence of the ponderosa pine/Douglas-fir/western larch class increased with aspect and decreased with elevation and road density ($\chi^2 > 6.4$, df = 1, $p < 0.02$ for each parameter; model $\chi^2 = 475.0$, df = 5, $p = 0.0001$, AIC = 1262). Therefore, this class tended to occur within lower elevation areas with southwest aspects and lower road densities.

Additional factors—To examine whether patterns in habitat use for the combined population were consistent within various subgroups, we compared the distribution of locations among vegetation classes defined by the Fuels map for the two time periods of study, 1981 through 1983 and 1984 through 1988. Annual and summer use patterns between time periods were significantly different ($\chi^2 = 14.6$, df = 7, $p = 0.04$ and $\chi^2 = 18.5$, df = 7, $p = 0.01$, respectively), but winter patterns did not differ ($\chi^2 = 9.6$, df = 7, $p = 0.21$; Fig. 10.6).

Because use of vegetation classes differed significantly between time periods, we split the locations by time period and repeated tests for mesoscale selection for each period separately. Tests for winter selection showed stronger patterns in 1984 through 1988 compared to 1981 through 1983. Lynx selected the lodgepole pine class marginally (65% of subsets) in 1984 through 1988 but did not show selection (10% of the subsets) in 1981 through 1983. Similarly, avoidance of Douglas-fir classes in winter was stronger in 1984 through 1988 versus 1981 through 1983 (ponderosa pine/ Douglas-fir/western larch: 25% versus 0%; Douglas-fir/ponderosa pine: 100% versus 45%). Results for summer were comparable between time periods with selection for lodgepole pine shown for 5% (1981 through 1983) and 0% (1984 through 1988) of subsets, and avoidance of ponderosa pine/ Douglas-fir/western larch shown for 60% and 50% of subsets.

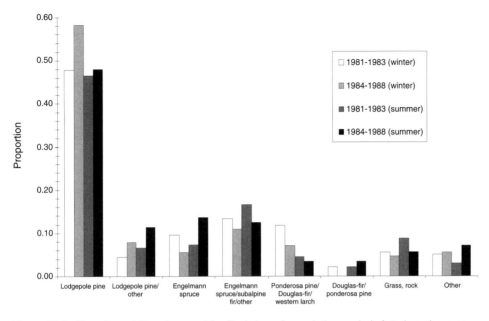

Figure 10.6—Use of vegetation classes of the Fuels layer for each time period of study and season.

Distribution of locations among vegetation classes also differed by sex ($\chi^2 = 19.8$, df = 7, $p = 0.006$), and this difference applied to winter ($\chi^2 = 19.7$, df = 7, $p = 0.006$) but not summer ($\chi^2 = 8.2$, df = 7, $p = 0.31$; Fig.10.7). To assess whether these differences in use between sexes indicated differences in habitat selection, we split the subsets by sex and repeated tests for meso-scale selection. Selection by season for each sex followed results obtained for the combined population (Fig. 10.4A). Both sexes showed selection for the lodgepole pine class and avoidance of the ponderosa pine/Douglas-fir/western larch class: in winter, selection for lodgepole pine was shown for 50% of subsets for females compared to 10% for males; avoidance of ponderosa pine/Douglas-fir/western larch was shown for 10% of subsets for females versus 0% for males and avoidance of Douglas-fir/ponderosa pine for 45% versus 100%. In summer, selection for lodgepole pine was shown for 5% of subsets for females compared to 10% for males; avoidance of ponderosa pine/Douglas-fir/western larch was shown for 85% of subsets for females versus 40% for males.

Proportions of locations in each vegetation class defined by the Fuels map were similar across the 22 lynx (Fig. 10.8). Use of lodgepole pine by the group was relatively high (49 ± STD of 13.0%), and 19 lynx had a higher proportion of locations in this class than the proportion available. Use of

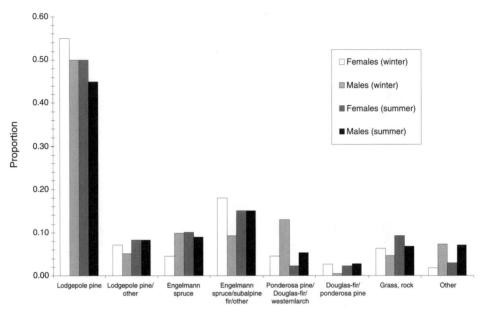

Figure 10.7—Use of vegetation classes of the Fuels layer for each sex and season.

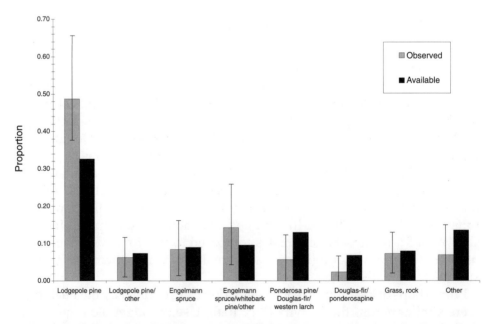

Figure 10.8—The average (± STD) proportion of locations in each vegetation class defined by the Fuels layer for 22 lynx. Availability of each class is shown for comparison.

ponderosa pine/Douglas-fir/western larch was relatively low (6 ± STD of 3.9%), and 18 lynx had a lower proportion of locations in this class than the proportion available.

Fine-Scale Selection Patterns

Four lynx had >50 locations distributed across seasons and covering >500 days (Table 10.1). Only one of these lynx showed use of vegetation classes that differed significantly from availability within its home range: lynx 104090 selected the lodgepole pine class (Fuels map) in winter ($\chi^2 = 6.0$, df = 1, p <0.02) and avoided the subalpine fir class (PMR map) in summer ($\chi^2 = 4.5$, df = 1, p <0.04). However, relatively few classes (2-6 and 2-7 classes for the Fuels and PMR maps, respectively) could be tested for selection because of their low representation within home ranges of individual lynx. For each of the four lynx, frequency of road crossings did not differ from random expectation ($\chi^2 = 0.4, 0.7, 1.6$, and 3.2; df = 1; $p = 0.08, 0.21$, 0.39, and 0.55).

Okanogan National Forest Road Surveys

Lynx detections from road surveys were in different habitat types than predicted by telemetry data. The majority (48%) of detections occurred at lower elevations (1,400 to 1,700 m). Although 28% of detections were within the lodgepole pine class, 34% fell into the ponderosa pine/Douglas-fir/western larch and Douglas-fir/ponderosa pine classes of the Fuels layer. Similarly, 43% of detections occurred in Douglas-fir classes of the PMR layer with 10% in the lodgepole pine class. To further examine these patterns, we compared the vegetation classes occurring along survey roads to those of the surrounding landscape. Roads tended to pass through Douglas-fir classes while the landscape was dominated by lodgepole pine classes. For example, in the southwest portion of the Okanogan National Forest (Fig. 10.9), the lodgepole pine class of the Fuels layer covered 41% of the area and the ponderosa pine/Douglas-fir/western larch and Douglas-fir/ponderosa pine classes covered 21%. In contrast, only 20% of the road's length passed through the lodgepole class and 21% passed through Douglas-fir classes. Similarly, 21% of lynx detections in this area fell within lodgepole pine and 36% within the Douglas-fir classes. However, those detections that fell within non-lodgepole pine classes were generally adjacent and proximal to patches of the lodgepole pine class (Fig. 10.9).

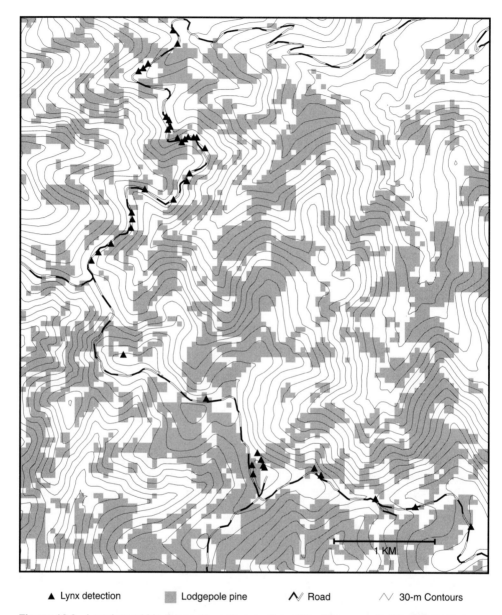

▲ Lynx detection   ▦ Lodgepole pine   〜 Road   〜 30-m Contours

Figure 10.9—Locations within the southwestern portion of the Okanogan National Forest where lynx were detected during road surveys. Lynx locations are not distributed uniformly along the road, but conform more to the habitat characteristics of the road than of the surrounding landscape.

Hares

Hare abundance broadly followed patterns of selection by lynx. Forest types and elevation zones with the highest densities of hares corresponded to those classes strongly selected by lynx (Fig. 10.10A,B). However, only

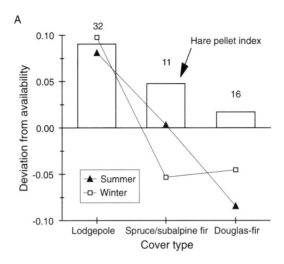

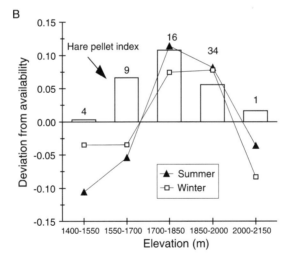

Figure 10.10—Standardized abundance of hare pellets (bars) and use by lynx (lines) as a function of cover type (A) and elevation (B). Pellet counts from the first (unswept) sample were averaged across the number of transects shown above each bar. Use of cover types by lynx, expressed as deviation from the proportion available, was defined by the distribution of locations across corresponding vegetation classes of the Fuels layer.

four hare samples were taken between 1,250 and 1,550 m, and they were all within Douglas-fir cover types that had lower hare densities across elevation zones. In addition, only 36% of the available area between 1,400 and 1,550 m consisted of Douglas-fir classes (Fuels map), whereas lodgepole pine classes composed 26% of the area. Douglas-fir was similarly over-represented in pellet samples taken in the 1,550 to 1,800-m zone.

Discussion

Our multi-scale analyses of habitat selection provide strong support for Koehler's (1990) original findings that lynx use lodgepole pine more than expected and Douglas-fir less than expected. Even when our models were limited to the elevation zone used by lynx, and we accounted for the physical attributes of the landscape, selection for lodgepole pine was still statistically significant. Vegetation classes defined by lodgepole pine were important in meso-scale comparisons of use to availability using all three vegetation layers (Table 10.2), and the inclusion of lodgepole classes as design variables significantly improved models of habitat use derived from physical variables. Lynx avoided areas defined by Douglas-fir (Table 10.2), although Douglas-fir classes were not important in models of habitat use that included other habitat variables. Physical features associated with occurrence of lodgepole pine and Douglas-fir were the same features associated with habitat selection by lynx, suggesting that these physical features were primarily indicators of selection for vegetation types.

Selection of northeast aspects in the summer, however, may have been independent of selection for vegetation. In winter, the proportional use of northeast aspects was greater than availability (Fig. 10.5D), but aspect was not significant when considered along with the other habitat variables. However, in summer, models combining physical and vegetation variables indicated that northeast aspects were strongly selected. Douglas-fir was associated with southwest aspects in a logistic regression model, and avoidance of Douglas-fir in summer was the most strong and consistent pattern among analyses of selection for the combined population, and for sex and time periods separately, with at least 45% of subsets demonstrating avoidance in each case. Therefore, avoidance of Douglas-fir in summer may have been associated with the tendency of lynx to select areas with northeast aspects. Preliminary summer telemetry data for lynx in the Seeley Lake area in Montana also suggest selection of north-facing aspects where 80% of locations fell (John Squires personal communication). Lynx habitat in the Seeley Lake area differs significantly from that on the Okanogan National Forest, and it is unlikely that topographic correlates to vegetation would be the same for the two areas. Thermoregulation provides a plausible explanation for the apparent selection of aspects with wetter, cooler conditions in the summer.

Use of lower elevations in the winter described by Koehler (1990) was also apparent for the broader population of 22 lynx. We detected a seasonal elevation shift: decreased use of the 2,000 to 2,150-m zone and increased use of areas 1,400 to 1,550 m in winter. Selection for vegetation types also varied with season. Lynx showed stronger selection for lodgepole pine in winter compared to summer for the combined population, and for both sexes and time periods. These shifts also translated into an increased proportion of locations on flatter slopes with higher road densities (Figs. 10.5A, E). Use of Douglas-fir also increased in winter, although only according to the Fuels map. This pattern may have related to increased adjacency of lodgepole and Douglas-fir classes at lower elevations where the latter type becomes more prevalent and less associated with southwest aspects. Overall, comparisons of logistic regression models indicated that selection for combinations of physical and vegetation variables was stronger in winter than in summer.

Patterns in habitat use by lynx also corresponded to relative abundance of snowshoe hares as measured by pellet counts. The elevation zones and cover type with the highest hare indices were those selected by lynx. This association was evident despite the high variability in the hare data (Table 3 in Koehler 1990) and that cover types representing hare habitat were based on ground-based assessments (Koehler 1990) whereas lynx habitat was represented by broad vegetation classes defined from LANDSAT imagery. Because the hare data were derived from non-representative samples, caution must be exercised when interpreting the apparent relationship between elevation and hare density. However, given the strong use patterns that Koehler (1979) observed in Montana, we suspect that the observed correlation between lynx and hare patterns indicates a strong causal relationship. A review of studies of lynx at northern latitudes (Chapter 10.9) shows similar patterns of lynx selecting habitats where hares are more plentiful. From snow tracking studies of lynx among white spruce forests in the Yukon, Murray et al. (1994) found that lynx selected densely stocked stands of white spruce where hares were most abundant during one year, but used spruce stands according to availability the next year, when hare numbers were similar among habitats.

Given the variability of hare densities in time and space and the apparent sensitivity of lynx to these fluctuations, the overall difference in habitat use observed between the periods of study is not surprising. Lynx showed relatively high use of lodgepole pine and low use of Douglas-fir in both 1981 through 1983 and 1984 through 1988. However, use was more skewed toward lodgepole pine and away from Douglas-fir in winter 1984 through 1988 versus winter 1981 through 1983 (Fig. 10.6). Similarly, comparisons of use to availability indicated that selection for lodgepole pine was much stronger for winter 1984 through 1988 versus winter 1981 through 1983, as was avoidance of Douglas-fir classes. Selection patterns for summer were similar between time periods.

Koehler (1990) characterized hare densities measured during his study as low, and these data also indicated that hares were concentrated within areas of lodgepole pine. Lower hare densities may lead to a more patchy distribution of hares and subsequent stronger habitat selection by lynx (Murray et al. 1994), particularly in winter when lynx have fewer opportunities to use alternate prey (Chapter 13).

Our analyses also indicated a neutral relationship between habitat selection and roads. A significant positive association between road density and habitat use was observed for winter locations, but only when the vegetation classes of the PMR layer were combined in models with physical variables. We suspect that this statistical relationship reflects a correlation between the classification of vegetation and the prevalence of roads. Therefore, road density, as computed within home-range-sized areas, did not appear to have significant effects on habitat selection for the combined population. Our analysis of habitat use at a finer scale indicated that frequency of road crossing for each of four lynx did not differ from expected. We acknowledge that our results are based on a small number of lynx within a limited geographic area, but can state that we found no evidence that habitat use by lynx was affected by narrow, forest roads at the relatively low densities that characterized the study area. However, we caution that our analyses did not address potential indirect effects of roads on habitat quality for lynx (Chapter 4).

Road-based surveys did not provide a representative sample of the surrounding landscape, and patterns of use appear to have been influenced by composition of adjacent habitat types (i.e., prevalence of lodgepole). We therefore believe simple examination of the distribution of the resulting detections—including comparisons to the surrounding landscape, to areas along survey roads, or to surveyed locations where lynx were not detected—should not be used to make inferences about habitat use.

Overall, our results suggest that habitat selection by lynx may be driven by differing mechanisms in summer compared to winter. In summer, lynx showed more general use of cover types but consistently avoided warm, dry slopes: behavior that may have been associated with thermoregulation. Although habitat selection was stronger in winter for all sets of analyses, use of vegetation in this season was not constant across time periods. Habitat selection in winter may be more influenced by hares and therefore more sensitive to variability in hare distribution and abundance. To develop understandings of mechanisms that underlie habitat requirements for lynx in the contiguous United States, further examination of habitat selection that includes consideration of fluctuations in availability of snowshoe hares is needed.

Literature Cited

Almack, J. A., W. L. Gaines, R. H. Naney, P. H. Morrison, J. R. Eby, G. F. Wooten, M. C. Snyder, S. H. Fitkin, and E. R. Garcia. 1993. North Cascades grizzly bear ecosystem evaluation. Report to Interagency Grizzly Bear Committee. Denver, CO.

Brainerd, S. M. 1985. Reproductive ecology of bobcats and lynx in western Montana. Missoula, MT: University of Montana M.S. Thesis.

Brittell, J. D., R. J. Poelker, S. J. Sweeney, and G. M. Koehler. 1989. Native cats of Washington. Unpublished. Olympia, WA, Washington Department of Wildlife.

Brown, D. G. and T. J. Barra. 1994. Recognition and reduction of systematic error in elevation and derivative surfaces from 7 1/2-minute DEMs. Photogrammetric Engineering and Remote Sensing 60:189-194.

Environmental Systems Research Institute, Inc. (ESRI) 1997. ARC/INFO version 7.1.2. Redlands, CA.

Johnson, D. H. 1980. The comparison of usage and availability measurements of evaluating resource preferences. Ecology 61:65-71.

Koehler, G. M. 1990. Population and habitat characteristics of lynx and snowshoe hares in north central Washington. Canadian Journal of Zoology 68:845-851.

Koehler, G. M., M. G. Hornocker, and H. S. Hash. 1979. Lynx movements and habitat use in Montana. Canadian Field-Naturalist 93(4):441-442.

Manly, B. F. J., L. L. McDonald, and D. L. Thomas. 1993. Resource selection by animals. Chapman and Hall, New York.

Mech. L. 1980. Age, sex reproduction, and spatial organization of lynxes colonizing northeastern Minnesota. Journal of Mammalogy 61: 261-267.

Murray, D. L., S. Boutin, and M. O'Donoghue. 1994. Winter habitat selection by lynx and coyotes in relation to snowshoe hare abundance. Canadian Journal of Zoology 72:1444-1451.

Neu, C. W., C. R. Byers, and J. M. Peek. 1974. A technique for analysis of utilization-availability data. Journal of Wildlife Management 38:541-545.

Pfister, R. D., B. L. Kovalchik, S. F. Arno, and R. C. Presby. 1977. Forest habitat types of Montana. Intermountain Forest and Range Experiment Station, USDA Forest Service, General Technical Report INT-34.

Rosenberg, D. K. and K. S. McKelvey. 1999. Estimation of habitat selection for central place organisms. Journal of Wildlife Management 63:1028-1038.

SAS Institute. 1990. SAS/STAT user's guide. Version 6. 4th edition. SAS Institute Inc., Cary, NC.

Smith, D. S. 1984. Habitat use, home range, and movements of bobcats in western Montana. Missoula, MT: University of Montana. M.S. Thesis.

Swihardt, R. K. and N. A. Slade. 1985. Testing for independence of observations in animal movement. Ecology 66:4 1176-1184.

White, G. C. and R. A. Garrott. 1990. Analysis of wildlife radio-tracking data. Academic Press, New York.

Wolff, J. O. 1980. The role of habitat patchiness in the population dynamics of snowshoe hares. Ecological Monographs 50: 111-130.

Chapter 11

Lynx Home Range and Movements in Montana and Wyoming: Preliminary Results

John R. Squires, University of Montana, Forestry Science Laboratory, 800 E. Beckwith, Missoula, MT 59807

Tom Laurion, Wyoming Game and Fish Dept., 260 Buena Vista, Lander, WY 82520

Abstract—Preliminary telemetry data suggest that lynx in Montana and Wyoming have large home ranges; this result supports the Koehler and Aubry (1994) contention that lynx from southern lynx populations have large spatial-use areas. Annual home ranges of males were larger than females. Straight-line, daily travel distance averaged 2 to 4 km, which is similar to northern populations. Four males in Montana, and the male and female in Wyoming, made exploratory movements of 20 to 30 km. The extent of these movements may be underestimated because we could not locate all lynx that traveled extensively. We do not know if these movements were exploratory or if the home ranges of these animals include widely dispersed use-areas. The female in Wyoming denned in a mature subalpine fir forest with high horizontal cover from coarse woody debris.

Introduction

Our knowledge of lynx ecology for southern populations is limited to only seven studies (Koehler et al. 1979; Mech 1980; Smith 1984; Brainerd 1985; Brittell et al. 1989; Koehler 1990; Chapter 12), two of which focused primarily on bobcats (Smith 1984; Brainerd 1985). Thus, land managers are in the difficult position of having to manage lynx habitat based on little data. In this chapter, we present preliminary data from ongoing studies in western Montana and northwestern Wyoming. Research objectives for the Montana study are to determine habitat use of lynx at multiple spatial scales, to describe dispersal and movements, to investigate population vital rates to the extent possible given a limited sample size, and to document seasonal food habits.

In Wyoming, the initial research goal was to determine the distribution of lynx in the state. Surveys confirmed earlier reports that lynx were present in the Wyoming Range located in western Wyoming; trappers, in 1971-1972, harvested 18 lynx in a small portion of the Wyoming Range (B. Neely and J. Welch, personal communication). In 1996, the Wyoming Game and Fish Department intensified its research efforts to address the following objectives: to quantify hare population trends from 1997 to 2001, to describe lynx movements in the Wyoming Range, and to obtain genetic and demographic data to the extent possible, given the small populations. Understanding the ecology of lynx in Wyoming is critical to conservation planning because these animals represent the southernmost known population.

In this chapter, we describe the spatial-use patterns of lynx based on preliminary data. We acknowledge that home range sizes, by themselves, are difficult to interpret and have limited utility (White and Garrott 1990). However, these data facilitate conservation planning in at least two ways. First, monitoring southern populations of lynx requires a basic understanding of spatial-use patterns. For example, the number and placement of monitoring stations within landscapes depend on the spatial-use patterns of lynx. Second, given the lack of existing data, any additional information that describes the movements of lynx from southern populations may help identify ecological differences between northern and southern populations. Understanding the ecology of southern lynx populations is especially important, given the species' proposed listing under the Endangered Species Act (Federal Register vol. 63:36994-37013).

Study Areas

The study area in Montana is located in the Clearwater River drainage, near the town of Seeley Lake. This area is about 1,800 km^2, extending east to west from the Swan Range to the Mission Mountains, and north to south from Lindbergh Lake to Salmon Lake. Lynx harvests (1977-1994) and track surveys suggest this area may support the highest density of lynx in Montana (Brian Giddings, personal communication). The study area includes state, federal, and private lands that support intensive commercial forestry. An extensive road network associated with timber harvest, and a high snow pack, attract private and commercial snowmobile operators. The Bob Marshall and Mission Mountain Wilderness areas flank the east and west sides of the study area, respectively. Elevations on the Seeley Lake study area are about 1,200 to 2,100 m.

The warm and dry forests at lower elevations are dominated by Douglas-fir, western larch, lodgepole pine, and ponderosa pine on south to west aspects—usually as mixed forests—although Douglas-fir may form pure stands (U.S. Forest Service 1997). Low-elevation forests are open or park-like, but dense stands occur where fire has been absent. Frequent, low-intensity fire is the primary natural disturbance (average = 42 years, Fischer and Bradley 1987). Fires eliminate small-diameter trees, producing a park-like structure. Based on 1930 photos, forest patches with moderately open overstories were several hundred to thousands of hectares in size (U.S. Forest Service 1997). Timber harvest and fire suppression have shifted the open mature forests that were once most prevalent on low-elevation sites to forests of small-diameter, densely stocked stands. Low-elevation sites are usually less than 35% slope.

Mid-elevations support primarily cool and moist to dry conifer forests. Dominant tree species include seral Douglas-fir, western larch, and lodgepole pine in mixed to single-species forest stands. Low frequency, stand-replacing fires create even-aged stands that form a mosaic of early seral to old-growth forests (Fischer and Bradley 1987). Slopes at mid-elevations are often greater than 35%.

Upper elevation forests are mostly subalpine fir, whitebark pine, and Engelmann spruce with lesser components of lodgepole pine, Douglas-fir, and western larch. Subalpine forests are multi-storied and multi-aged, often with a dense shrub understory. Fire disturbances are infrequent and vary from small spot to large stand-replacement fires depending on climatic conditions. Riparian vegetation varies from riparian grasses and sedges to communities composed of dogwood, willow, alder, and mixed conifer forests. Forested riparian areas are primarily subalpine fir, Engelmann spruce, Douglas-fir and black cottonwood.

In Wyoming, the study area is located in the Wyoming Range, near Big Piney. Topography is steep to rolling and elevations are about 2,400 to 3,100 m. Forest cover on drier sites is primarily homogeneous stands of lodgepole pine. Spruce-fir forests are generally restricted to north aspects and compose 19% of vegetative cover. About 9% of forests are aspen, which are declining from encroachment by conifers. Vegetation on south slopes is mainly sagebrush and wheatgrasses with patches of aspen and conifer; the area is about 20% non-forest and 8% riparian. During the late 19th century, forests in the Wyoming Range were harvested for railroad ties. Road densities are high; the density of roads open to public travel is about 0.3 km/km^2.

Methods

In Montana, lynx were captured using Victor™ #3 soft-catch traps and Fremont snares placed near tracks. Sets were baited with carrion or one of several scent compounds (beaver castor, Pacific Call™, Cat Passion™). Most "cubby" sets were constructed from small branches so that trapped lynx could knock them down without injury (G. Mowat, personal communication). Some traps were placed in large, permanent "cubbies" that were large enough to prevent trapped animals from entangling the trap on the sides of the set. We checked traps daily and stopped trapping in mid-April to avoid capturing pregnant females. In Wyoming, lynx were captured using Walker hounds that pursued and treed lynx after being released on tracks.

In Montana, immobilization drugs (10 mg/kg body wt. Ketaset®, concentration 100mg/mL; and Xylazine, 1mg/kg body wt., concentration 100mg/mL) were administered from pressurized syringe-darts using either a Telinject™ CO_2-powered blow tube or syringe pole. This dose produced predictable immobilization periods (20-30 minutes) and stable vital signs. Animals were weighed, sexed, ear tagged, and fitted with Lotek™ radio collars (175 g). After processing, we placed lynx inside a large, hard-sided box to recover fully from drug effects before release. Treed lynx, in Wyoming, were immobilized (5 mg/kg Telazol®, Fort Dodge Labs, Poole et al. 1993) using a pressurized syringe-dart fired from an air rifle (Dan-Inject™, Denmark). Drugged lynx were then either caught as they fell from the tree with a large net held by two or three people (T. Bailey, personal communication), or lowered with a rope. Lynx were fitted with transmitters (Telonics™, Mesa, AZ), were weighed, were measured, and had blood and hair samples taken.

We monitored the movements of radio-collared lynx in Montana using both aerial and ground telemetry. Aerial locations were taken weekly using a Cessna 185 with wing-mounted "H" antennas. Aerial locations were determined using a non-differentially correctable GPS on board the aircraft. In addition, two two-person teams located up to four lynx per day to augment aerial locations. A "priority" lynx was selected for each monitoring day to reduce variation across animals. Transmitters were equipped with activity switches so that observers could monitor the animal's behavior to minimize disturbance. Ground tracking was coordinated using hand-held radios to ensure bearings crossed at about 90°. Antenna locations were determined using a differentially correctable GPS (Trimble Corporation®). Relocations were taken from 5:00 to 22:00 to ensure that locations were taken throughout the day; lynx were not tracked at night. We used aerial telemetry to track two males that moved to the Bob Marshall Wilderness Area; these animals received less monitoring effort compared to lynx that remained on the study area. During May, females were located almost daily to check for denning activity. In Wyoming, radio-collared lynx were located one or two times weekly, mostly from the ground with limited use of aircraft.

On the Seeley Lake study area, hare abundance during summer (May to August) was estimated on two trap grids established in four general cover types. These types included: (1) open young, <50% canopy closure, tree dbh <23 cm; (2) open older, <50% canopy closure, dbh >23 cm; (3) closed young, >50% canopy closure, dbh <23 cm; and (4) closed older, >50% canopy closure, dbh >23 cm. Each grid consisted of 50 traps (24 x 24 x 66 cm, Tomahawk™) in a 10 x 5 array with 50-m spacing. Traps were baited with apple and alfalfa pellets. Hare density was estimated using mark-recapture methods (Pollock 1982; Pollock et al. 1990). In Wyoming, hare abundance was estimated from fecal counts on five 600-m transects located within lynx home ranges (Krebs et al. 1987). As a comparison to the Wyoming Range, hare abundance was also estimated near Dubois, WY (four, 750-m transects) and in the Beartooth Mountains (four, 700-m transects) in areas believed suitable for lynx. Quadrats (5.08 x 305 cm, $n = 300$ total) were spaced at 30-m intervals. All quadrats were cleared of hare feces when transects were established and then were counted and cleared once per year in June.

For both study areas, we used the computer program Ranges V (Kenward and Hodder 1996) to estimate home range using 95%, 90% and 50% minimum convex polygons (MCP, Hayne 1949). We used MCP home ranges because this method was most appropriate given the limited number of lynx relocations and for comparability with the literature. However, home range estimates using minimum convex polygons are sensitive to sample size (White and Garrott 1990:148). Incremental-area plots suggest the area of most (five of six lynx >30 relocations) home ranges was asymptotic when estimated with greater than 30 locations; Poole (1994) found >20 points were adequate for lynx in Northwest Territories, Canada. Core-use areas within home-ranges were defined as the 50% MCP (Ackerman et al. 1989). Home range overlap was calculated according to Poole (1995). We calculated straight-line travel distances for animals located on consecutive days as an index to hunting effort for comparison with other populations (Brand et al. 1976; Ward and Krebs 1985; Poole 1994).

Results

Trapping Success

In Montana, we captured 13 lynx (four females, nine males) from January through April 1998; trap success averaged 0.5 lynx/100 trap nights. Two additional lynx escaped from traps. From 15 December 1998 to 15 March 1999, we captured five additional lynx (two males, one female, one male kitten) and recaptured three from the previous winter. Trap success was 0.6 lynx/100 trap nights for all captures and 0.4 captures/100 trap nights, for new captures. The only non-target forest carnivore we captured was a female wolverine; a second wolverine escaped from the trap.

In Wyoming, one male and one female lynx were captured on 7 December 1996 and 15 March 1997, respectively. The female was recaptured on 19 November 1997 to replace the collar and the male was recaptured on 20 December 1997 but was injured in the process. This animal received veterinary care until 4 February 1998, when it was released.

Daily Movements

In Montana, the mean daily straight-line distance traveled by male lynx averaged 2.8 km (SD = 0.4, range = 2.5-3.3 km, n = 4, Table 11.1) during summer (mid-May to August 1998). The mean of two females without young during the same period averaged 3.2 km per day (SD = 1.0, range = 2.5-3.9 km, Table 11.1). In Wyoming, the mean daily-travel distance of the male averaged 4.1 km during summer (range = 1.3-7.2 km, n = nine consecutive travel days, Table 11.2) compared to 2.7 km during winter (SD = 1.9, range = 0.7-9.5 km, n = 22). The daily travel distance of the Wyoming female was similar during both summer (mean = 2.4 km, SD = 1.9, range = 0.3-5.2 km, n = 8) and winter (mean = 2.2 km, SD = 1.4, range = 0.2-3.8 km, n = 7).

Table 11.1–Straight-line daily travel distances of lynx during the summer (May-August, 1998); n = number of days consecutive locations were obtained.

Lynx ID	Average distance	SD	Range
	km		km
Male 4 (n = 9)	3.3	1.2	1.5-5.7
Male 6 (n = 13)	2.5	2.0	0.8-7.0
Male 26 (n = 13)	2.7	1.5	0.2-5.5
Male 28 (n = 8)	2.6	1.4	0.9-4.4
Average male (n = 4 males)	2.8	0.4	2.5-3.3
Female 10 (n = 11)	3.9	2.2	1.2-7.7
Female 14 (n = 25)	2.5	1.7	0.1-6.5
Average female (n = 2 females)	3.2	1.0	2.5, 3.9

Table 11.2–Straight-line daily travel distances of a single male and female lynx in western Wyoming during summer (May-August) and winter (December-April); n = number of days consecutive locations were obtained.

Lynx ID	Average distance	SD	Range
	km		km
Male (summer, $n = 9$)	4.1	1.9	1.3-7.2
Male (winter, $n = 22$)	2.7	1.9	0.7-9.5
Female (summer, $n = 8$)	2.4	1.9	0.3-5.2
Female (winter, $n = 7$)	2.2	1.4	0.2-3.8

Home Ranges

In Montana, annual home ranges (90% convex polygon) averaged 220 km^2 (SE = 95, $n = 4$) for males and 90 km^2 (SE = 32, $n = 2$) for females (Table 11.3). Seasonal ranges of males were 127 km^2 (SE = 54, $n = 4$) during winter and 125 km^2 (SE = 42, $n = 6$) during summer (Table 11.3). Seasonal ranges of females were approximately half the size of males; home ranges of females averaged 51 km^2 (SE = 22, $n = 4$) during winter and 42 km^2 (SE = 9, $n = 2$) during summer.

In Wyoming, the male's 90% MCP home range from December 1996 to May 1999 was 116 km^2 ($n = 279$ relocations) compared to 105 km^2 ($n = 149$) for the female from March 1997 to May 1999 (Table 11.4). During winter, the male's 90% MCP home range averaged 63 km^2 (n = three winters) compared to 50 km^2 for the female (n = two winters). During summer, the male's 90% MCP home range averaged 81 km^2 (n = two summers) compared to 57 km^2 for the female (n = 2 summers).

In Montana, seasonal home ranges (90% MCP) of females overlapped 62% (SE = 26, $n = 2$) between winter and summer and males overlapped 56% (SE = 6, $n = 4$, Table 11.5). Core-use areas of females as delineated by 50% MCP overlapped extensively (68%, SE = 1, $n = 2$) between winter and summer, but males shifted their core-use areas between seasons with little overlap (17%, SE = 5, $n = 4$). In Wyoming, the female's annual home range (1997-1998) overlapped the male's by about 88%; the degree of overlap varied from 85% in winter to 43% in summer.

Exploratory Movements

In Montana, four males engaged in exploratory movements outside their established home ranges, mostly during mid-summer. Male 4 (four to six years old based on tooth wear and staining) left its home range on

Table 11.3–Seasonal home range size of lynx, Seeley Lake, March 1998 to March 1999.

Lynx ID	Number of relocations	Minimum convex polygon (km^2)		
		95%	90%	50%
Winter, female				
F01	15	15	15	2
F10	27	56	52	19
F14	27	129	114	16
F18	23	26	23	8
Average (SE)		57 (26)	51 (22)	11 (4)
Winter, male[a]				
M02	28	190	137	80
M04	27	84	67	24
M06	29	283	275	36
M26	23	33	30	12
Average (SE)		148 (56)	127 (54)	38 (15)
Summer, female				
F10	40	53	50	17
F14	54	52	33	12
Average (SE)		53 (1)	42 (9)	15 (3)
Summer, male				
M02	23	318	189	53
M04	38	66	64	33
M06	40	178	173	117
M20	18	534	274	41
M26	41	20	19	11
M28	36	38	32	10
Average (SE)		192 (82)	125 (42)	44 (16)
Annual, female[b]				
F10	67	65	58	24
F14	81	164	121	16
Average (SE)		115 (50)	90 (32)	20 (4)
Annual, male[c]				
M02	51	483	448	114
M04	65	132	102	33
M06	69	303	299	157
M26	64	32	29	11
Average (SE)		238 (99)	220 (95)	79 (34)

[a]M20 excluded, <10 relocations.
[b]F09 excluded, <10 relocations.
[c]M03, M05, M07, M08, M12, M16, and M22 excluded, <10 relocations.

Table 11.4–Seasonal home ranges of a single male and female lynx in western Wyoming.

Lynx ID	Number of relocations	Minimum convex polygon (km^2)		
		95%	90%	50%
Winter				
Male (10/1996-3/1997)	39	71	64	17
Male (10/1997-3/1998)	20	66	64	19
Male (10/1998-3/1999)	26	134	60	11
Female (10/1997-3/1998)	23	66	38	6
Female (10/1998-3/1999)	30	66	62	29
Summer				
Male (4/1996-9/1996)	40	88	68	17
Male (4/1997-9/1997)	15	94	94	21
Female (4/1997-9/1997)	41	69	68	11
Female (4/1998-9/1998)	22	67	45	16
Annual				
Male (12/1996-5/1999)	279	137	116	54
Female (3/1997-5/1999)	149	114	105	59

Table 11.5–Percent overlap between winter (October 1998 to March 1999) and summer (April 1998 to September 1998) home ranges.

	Minimum convex polygon:		
	95%	90%	50%
	Female overlap		
F10	84	88	67
F14	35	36	68
Average (SE)	60 (25)	62 (26)	68(1)
	Male overlap		
M02	40	48	6
M04	39	42	14
M06	71	70	15
M26	69	63	31
Average (SE)	55 (9)	56 (6)	17 (5)

21 July and traveled 28 km southwest. After about four days, it returned to its home range on 28 July. Male 6 (two to four years old) left its home range on 29 July and traveled south for 24 km and remained on the new area for the summer. The daily travel speed of this male while traveling averaged 5.8 km/day (n = three travel days). Male 20 (one to two years old) moved extensively throughout the spring and summer. On 18 March, this male traveled west 22 km and was back near the center of its activity area by 2 April. On 21 July, Male 20 was located in the Bob Marshall Wilderness. By 28 July, this male had traveled a straight-line distance of 39 km to a site near Ovando, MT. He had to cross a two-lane highway and the Blackfoot River (about 30-40 m wide) during the movement. Male 20 remained near Ovando for two days before it moved again and could no longer be located from an aircraft. On 12 August, we relocated Male 20 47 km north of Ovando and by 20 August the animal moved 17 km back to the center of its home range. Male 28 (three to five years old) left its home range on about 6 July and was not relocated, even with extensive aerial searching. He returned to his home range on 3 August where he remained throughout the summer.

In Wyoming, both the male and female made exploratory movements during summer 1998. The male left his home range on about 19 June and remained away until 4 September when he was relocated back on his home range. The female left her home range on about 4 July and returned on about 10 August. Neither animal was located during an extensive aerial search, so their exploratory movements remain unknown. Between 15 May and 15 June 1999, the male made two exploratory movements to the same general area about 30 km northeast of his home range; he returned to his home range in late June.

Hare Density

In Montana, preliminary estimates of summer snowshoe hare density averaged 0.9 hares/ha in closed old forests, 1.9/ha in closed young forests, 0.6/ha in open old forests, and 0.7/ha in open-young forests (S. Mills and C. Henderson, personal communication). Hare densities in the Wyoming Range were 0.8 hares/ha in 1997 and 1.4/ha in 1998. This compared to 0.9 (1997) and 1.0/ha (1998) near Dubois, WY, and 0.6/ha in the Beartooth Mountains (1998).

Mortality

In Montana, we documented six deaths (necropsies conducted by Montana Department of Fish, Wildlife, and Parks); three animals died of starvation, two were killed by mountain lions, and one died of unknown causes.

Denning

In Montana, two females failed to centralize their activities with home ranges during May 1998, suggesting they did not give birth. We were unable to relocate a third female from when she was captured during the winter until 22 September when we located her near the original trap site. This female had two kittens but we do not know whether the radio failed temporarily or she moved off the study area to den. During May 1999, three of four females centralized their movements within home ranges. Two females produced two kittens each that we ear-tagged at four weeks of age. The third female selected a den, but she failed to give birth or her kittens died before we visited the site when the kittens would have been one month old. The female that produced kittens the year before failed to den in 1999.

In Wyoming, the female produced a litter of four kittens (two males, two females) on about 27 May 1998; all kittens were alive on 14 June 1998 when they were ear-tagged. However, based on snow tracking, the kittens were not with the female in November and presumably had died. In May 1999 the same female produced two additional kittens.

The natal den in Wyoming was located in a mature subalpine fir forest with co-dominant lodgepole pine. The den site was on a moderately steep slope (36%) with a west aspect (282°). The den was located in a cave-like tree well 1.5 m wide, 2.5 m long and 0.5 m deep. Three downed logs crisscrossed above the opening to 1.5 m in height. Trees surrounding the den ($n = 4$) averaged 32 cm dbh and 22 m in height. Canopy closure was 48%. Coarse woody debris (downed logs) was abundant around the den, covering 28% of the forest floor. Sapling subalpine firs (<7.5 cm dbh) were abundant (sapling <1.4 m in height = 2,800 stems/ha; saplings >1.4 m = 800/ha). The abundant woody debris and high sapling density provided high horizontal cover, averaging (four cover-board readings at 10 m) 78% between 0-1.5 m. Shrubs were sparse on the site.

Immediately after the kittens were marked in mid-June, the female moved her litter to a maternal den located approximately 200 m from the natal den. This den was located in a depression (0.5 m x 0.5 m wide, 0.3 m deep) beside a fallen tree. Trees surrounding the den (n = 3) averaged 50 cm dbh and 30 m in height. Canopy closure was 54%. Coarse woody debris (logs) also was high, covering 13% of the forest floor. Sapling (<7.5 cm dbh) density was high, averaging 5,800 stems/ha (sapling <1.4 m in height = 5,000/ha; saplings >1.4 m = 780/ha). Horizontal cover was also high at this den averaging 86% cover between 0-1.5 m.

We have not rigorously quantified the habitat characteristics of dens (n = 4) located in 1999. However, we can say that all dens were associated with coarse woody debris.

Discussion

Our findings generally support Koehler and Aubry's (1994:93) contention that lynx living at the southern extent of the species' range have large home ranges. In Montana, annual 95% MCP home ranges of males averaged 238 km^2 (SE = 99, n = 4) and 115 km^2 (SE = 50, n = 2) for females; the sizes of these home ranges are similar to those of males (277 km^2, SD = 71, n = 3) and females (135 km^2, SD = 124, n = 3) in the southern Canadian Rocky Mountains (Chapter 12). Similarly, the annual home ranges of the male (110 km^2) and female (90 km^2) lynx in Wyoming were also large compared to northern populations (Chapter 13). The home range sizes we report are probably underestimates given that we could not locate some animals during a portion of the summer. As with most populations (Brainerd 1985; Koehler 1990; Poole 1994; Slough and Mowat 1996), males in Montana and Wyoming tend to have much larger home ranges than females.

Parker et al. (1983) found that daily activity and travel patterns of lynx are primarily a function of hunting succes. Given that lynx in Montana and Wyoming have relatively large home ranges, daily movement patterns of lynx in Montana and Wyoming should be large relative to northern populations, especially since hare densities are low. However, daily-travel distances of lynx in Montana and Wyoming (about 2-4 km/day) were generally similar to those in Alaska (Kesterson 1988) and southwest Yukon (about 2-4 km) when hare density was above 0.5 hares/ha (Ward and Krebs 1985), but appear greater than lynx in Washington (about 1 km, Brittell et al. 1989). Although travel distances (i.e., foraging effort) are partially a function of prey density, daily movements tend to be insensitive to changing prey abundance as long as hare densities remain above 1.0 hares/ha (Ward and Krebs 1985). For example, in southwest Yukon, daily-travel distances of lynx were similar whether hares were abundant (at 15 hares/ha, daily travel of lynx = 2.7 km, 95% CI 1.8-3.7) or relatively scarce (at 1.0 hares/ha, daily travel of lynx = 2.4 km, 95% CI 2.0-2.9; Ward and Krebs 1985). However, when hare densities declined to 0.5 hares/ha daily, travel distance increased to 3.3 km (95% CI 2.8-3.7); at 0.2 hares/ha lynx traveled 5.4 km (95% CI 3.9-7.0) per day. Thus, if southern and northern populations are comparable, daily movements of lynx in Wyoming and Montana suggest that prey are above the threshold where movements greatly expand.

Lynx in Montana and Wyoming engaged in exploratory movements of 20 to 30 km; exploratory distances are probably underestimated given our inability to locate all lynx that traveled extensively. We do not know if these movements were truly exploratory or if the home ranges of these individuals include use-areas that are very widely dispersed. It is interesting that all four lynx in Montana that engaged in exploratory movements did so at about the same time; all animals moved in late July. In Wyoming, the male initiated its exploratory movement on about 19 June and the female on 4 July. Lynx in northern populations become nomadic when prey are scarce (Ward and Krebs 1985; Slough and Mowat 1996). This explanation seems unlikely during the summer in Montana and Wyoming, given the seasonal abundance of young hares and ground squirrels.

The natal den in Wyoming was located in a mature subalpine fir forest with high horizontal cover from coarse woody debris and saplings. In Washington, Koehler (1990) described the habitat associated with four dens (of two females) as mature (≥250 years) forests of Engelmann spruce, subalpine fir, and lodgepole pine. These dens were in sites with high woody debris (40 downfall logs/50 m) that the kittens were using as escape cover. The structural components—mature forests and high woody debris—associated with the natal den in Wyoming were similar to those associated with dens in Washington.

Literature Cited

Ackerman, B. B., F. A. Leban, E. O. Garton, and M. D. Samuel. 1989. User's manual for program HOME RANGE. 2nd ed. Tech. Rep. No. 15. Forestry, Wildlife, and Range Experiment Station, University of Idaho, Moscow.

Brainerd, S. M. 1985. Reproductive ecology of bobcats and lynx in western Montana. University of Montana, Missoula.

Brand, C. J., L. B. Keith, and C. A. Fischer. 1976. Lynx responses to changing snowshoe hare densities in central Alberta. Journal of Wildlife Management 40:416-28.

Brittell, J. D., R. J. Poelker, S. J. Sweeney, and G. M. Koehler. 1989. Native cats of Washington. Olympia, WA: Washington Department of Wildlife (unpublished).

Fischer, W. C. and A. F. Bradley. 1987. Fire ecology of western Montana forest habitat types. Gen. Tech. Rep. INT-223. Ogden, UT: U.S. Department of Agriculture, Forest Service, Intermountain Research Station.

Hayne, D. W. 1949. Calculation of size of home range. Journal of Mammalogy 30:1-18.

Kenward, R. E. and K. H. Hodder. 1996. Ranges V: an analysis system for biological location data. Institute of Terrestrial Ecology, Furzebrook Research Station, Wareham, Dorset UK.

Kesterson, M. B. 1988. Lynx home range and spatial organization in relation to population density and prey abundance. University of Alaska, Fairbanks.

Koehler, G. M., K. B. Aubry. 1994. Lynx. Pages 74-98 In L. F. Ruggiero, K. B. Aubry, S. W. Buskirk, J. L. Lyon, W. J. Zielinski, tech. eds. The scientific basis for conserving forest carnivores: American marten, fisher, lynx and wolverine in the Western United States. Gen. Tech. Rep. RM-254. Fort Collins, CO: U.S. Department of Agriculture, Forest Service, Rocky Mountain Forest and Range Experiment Station.

Koehler, G. M., M. G. Hornocker, and H. S. Hash. 1979. Lynx movements and habitat use in Montana. Canadian Field-Naturalist 93:441-2.

Koehler, G. M. 1990. Population and habitat characteristics of lynx and snowshoe hares in north central Washington. Canadian Journal of Zoology 68:845-51.

Krebs, C. J., G. S. Gilbert, S. Boutin, and R. Boonstra. 1987. Estimation of snowshoe hare population density from turd transects. Canadian Journal of Zoology 65:565-7.

Mech, L. D. 1980. Age, sex, reproduction, and spatial organization of lynxes colonizing northeastern Minnesota. Journal of Mammalogy 61:261-7.

Pollock, K. H. 1982. A capture-recapture design robust to unequal probability of capture. Journal of Wildlife Management 46:752-757.

Pollock, K. H., J. D. Nichols, C. Brownie, and J. E. Hines. 1990. Statistical inference for capture-recapture experiments. Wildlife Monographs 100:1-97.

Parker, G. R., J. W. Maxwell, and L. D. Morton. 1983. The ecology of the lynx (Lynx canadensis) in Cape Breton Island. Canadian Journal of Zoology 61:770-86.

Poole, K. G. 1994. Characteristics of an unharvested lynx populations during a snowshoe hare decline. Journal of Wildlife Management 58:608-18.

Poole K. G. 1995. Spatial organization of a lynx population. Canadian Journal of Zoology 73(4):632-41.

Slough, B. G. and G. Mowat. 1996. Lynx population dynamics in an untrapped refugium. Journal of Wildlife Management 60:946-61.

Smith, D. S. 1984. Habitat use, home range, and movements of bobcats in western Montana. University of Montana, Missoula.

Ward, R. M .P and C. J. Krebs. 1985. Behavioural responses of lynx to declining snowshoe hare abundance. Canadian Journal of Zoology 63:2817-24.

White, G. C. and R. A. Garrott. 1990. Analysis of wildlife radio-tracking data. Academic Press, Inc., New York.

U.S. Forest Service. 1997. Rice Ridge ecosystem management area and watershed analysis vegetation report. U.S. Forest Service, Lolo National Forest, Seeley Lake, MT (unpublished).

Chapter 12

Space-Use, Diet, Demographics, and Topographic Associations of Lynx in the Southern Canadian Rocky Mountains: A Study

Clayton D. Apps, Aspen Wildlife Research
2331 – 7th Ave. N.W., Calgary, Alberta, T2N 1A1, Canada

Abstract—Snowshoe hares are considered the primary prey of Canada lynx throughout their range. Relative to northern populations, hares occurring in mountainous regions at southern latitudes are thought to remain at low and stable densities through time. Hence, the ecology of associated southern lynx populations is expected to resemble that of northern populations during the low phase of the hare population cycle. The space use, diet, and demographics of lynx in the Rocky Mountains of southeastern British Columbia and southwestern Alberta are consistent with this hypothesis, based on data collected from 10 lynx, including six (three males, three females) resident adults, during two years of an assumed increase phase of a hare cycle. Mean hare densities were low, ranging from 0.01 to 0.47/ha among cover types and landscapes. Lynx winter diet ($n = 137$ kills) was diverse and included hares (52%), red squirrels (30%), northern flying squirrels (5%), grouse (3%), martens (3%), and voles (3%). Kitten recruitment to winter was zero among adult females for four lynx-years. Family groups that did occur in the study area during winter were associated with small litters of two. Survival among resident

USDA Forest Service Gen Tech. Rep. RMRS-GTR-30. 1999

351

adults was 100%, but three of four subadults monitored during winter did not survive to mid-May. Home ranges were large, with annual 95% adaptive kernel utilization distributions averaging 381 and 239 km² for resident males and females respectively. Minimum daily movements averaged 3.8 and 3.0 km respectively. Two juvenile dispersals were short (44 and 17 km) and ended in starvation.

Space use by lynx may also relate to physiography, the influence of which may vary seasonally in mountainous landscapes. Most lynx selected mid elevations (1,550-1,850 m) and moderate to gentle slopes (<40%) within home ranges. Residents used higher elevations, and some used steeper slopes during summer than during winter. Highways were crossed less than random expectation within home ranges, suggesting that they influenced lynx movements. Sexual differences in home range size were not significant, but daily movements of males were greater than those of females, indicating that they used space more extensively.

Introduction

The ecology of northern Canada lynx populations varies temporally with snowshoe hare densities, as demonstrated with respect to population characteristics (Brand et al. 1976; Brand and Keith 1979; Poole 1994; Mowat et al. 1996; Slough and Mowat 1996; O'Donoghue et al. 1997), food habits and foraging behavior (Brand et al. 1976; O'Donoghue et al. 1998a; O'Donoghue et al. 1998b), space-use and movements (Ward and Krebs 1985; Poole 1994; Slough and Mowat 1996), and dispersal (Poole 1997). However, it appears that hare populations of southern latitudes and mountainous regions remain at relatively low and stable densities through time, possibly a result of a more patchy habitat distribution, greater competition, and a greater suite of predators (Dolbeer and Clark 1975; Wolff 1980). Hence, Koehler (1990) theorized that the ecology of southern lynx populations resembles that of northern populations during cyclic hare lows. Assuming that any variation of hare density will be synchronous throughout their range (Smith and Davis 1981), it follows that several hypotheses would hold true during the increase and high phase of the cycle. Relative to results reported for northern populations during hare lows, southern lynx populations should be associated with: (1) hare densities that are as low, (2) diet of as much alternate prey, (3) resident home ranges that are as large, (4) daily foraging movements that are as long, (5) reproduction and survival that are as low, and (6) dispersal rates that are as great.

Space use by lynx may also relate to physiography (Koehler and Aubry 1994), the influence of which may vary seasonally in mountainous landscapes. For example, open habitats that occur in conjunction with higher elevations and rugged topography are associated with several prey species that would be available only during snow-free months (Scotter and Ulrich 1995). Snow conditions that may restrict lynx movements and/or increase expended energy (Murray and Boutin 1991) are also more likely at higher elevations. Thus, individuals occurring in mountainous terrain can be expected to use lower elevations and gentler slopes, make shorter daily movements, and use smaller home ranges when snow is present. Near southern range extents, lynx can also be expected to use cooler, north and east aspects more often during snow-free months. This assumes that they are more susceptible to heat stress during summer because the species is better adapted physiologically to northern regions more central to its geographic range. Finally, just as physiography may affect space use of resident lynx, landscape features may also influence dispersal, and in highly mountainous terrain, movements can be expected to align with major valleys. Lynx movements may also be negatively influenced by highways due to habitat fragmentation and direct avoidance, an important consideration for their conservation (B. Ruediger 1996, unpublished). If highways restrict lynx movements, they should be crossed less than random expectation where they occur within home ranges.

Among solitary carnivores, it is assumed that female spacing patterns will reflect the distribution of resources, whereas space use by males also will conform to the distribution of females (Sandell 1989). Accordingly, home ranges of female lynx are generally smaller than those of males, and spatial overlap between sexes is extensive (Koehler and Aubry 1994; Poole 1995; Slough and Mowat 1996). Because social tolerance is expected among solitary foragers where resources are dispersed (Carr and McDonald 1986), these relationships should also hold true among southern lynx populations persisting in mountainous regions, where habitat is patchy and female home ranges are not necessarily contiguous. The more extensive space use expected from males also should be reflected in daily movements greater than those of females.

In this paper, I examine the hypotheses outlined above with research conducted in the southern Canadian Rocky Mountains between November 1996 and October 1998. Results are of an unexploited, southern lynx population, occurring in a highly mountainous region, during the increase phase of a snowshoe hare cycle in other regions (C. J. Krebs, personal communication).

USDA Forest Service Gen Tech. Rep. RMRS-GTR-30. 1999

353

Study Area

The study area (>3,000 km^2) is centrally located within the Shining Mountains ecoprovince (Demarchi 1994), and most of it lies within the East Kootenay Wildlife Management Sub-region of southeastern British Columbia. It is defined by the Beaverfoot and upper Kootenay drainages on provincial land and straddles the Continental Divide of British Columbia and Alberta to include the Vermilion, Middle Bow, and Kicking Horse valleys within Kootenay, Banff, and Yoho National Parks.

Characteristic of the Canadian Rockies, much of the area is rock, ice, and other inherently unsuitable lynx habitat, and high peaks separate broad valleys incised by narrow tributary valleys. Elevations (1,200 to over 3,000 m) span three biogeoclimatic zones (Meidinger and Pojar 1991). Below 1,500 m, the Montane Spruce Zone is characterized by a climax overstory of hybrid Engelmann/white spruce and subalpine fir. The Engelmann Spruce-Subalpine Fir Zone occurs at higher elevations but below 2,300 m, where Engelmann spruce and subalpine fir dominate the climax overstory up to the Alpine Tundra Zone at highest elevations. Sub-climax stands throughout the study area are dominated by lodgepole pine. The macroclimate is continental, with mean temperatures ranging from –18°C (January) to 23°C (July) and 42-63% of the 51-81 cm mean annual precipitation falling as snow (Achuff et al. 1984). Natural and human conditions vary throughout the study area, and linear features include two- to four-lane paved highways with annual (1994) average daily traffic volumes of 1,119-8,322 vehicles per day (A. Clevenger, personal communication, Banff, AB), as well as industrial road networks, a twin-tracked railway, and trail systems.

Other predators and potential competitors with lynx include coyote, wolf, black bear, grizzly bear, marten, wolverine, cougar, at least three hawk species, golden eagle, and the great-horned owl. Fishers and red fox are rare, and bobcats are not resident (Poll et al. 1984). Potential lynx prey include snowshoe hares, red squirrels, northern flying squirrels, gallinaceous birds, microtine rodents, hoary marmots, ground squirrels, bushy-tailed woodrats, and beavers. Potential ungulate prey include moose, elk, bighorn sheep, mountain goat, mule deer, and white-tailed deer.

Despite a limited season in British Columbia, lynx have not been legally harvested on the provincial section of the study area for at least 15 years. Based on this, and the 68 years of protection that lynx have received in the national parks (Poll et al. 1984), I consider the resident population in the study area to be unexploited.

Methods

Hare Densities

I determined a range of snowshoe hare densities by counting fecal pellets during September 1998 in established 305 x 5.1 cm quadrats (Krebs et al. 1987). Ten quadrats were spaced at 30.5 m intervals along each of 61 transects. Transects were placed randomly among early- (20-60 years), mid- (60-120 years), and late- (>120 years) successional stands but were spaced by ≥500 m. Sampling was further stratified among three landscapes within the study area, representing geographically distinct areas where I consider terrain conditions conducive to supporting lynx. Hare densities were calculated with a modified version of the Krebs et al. (1987) regression equation, using the HARETURD program (C. J. Krebs, personal communication).

Lynx Capture

Study animals were captured during the winters of 1996-1997 and 1997-1998, with efforts focused in landscapes where lynx signs had been reported in recent years. Hounds trained to pursue felids were used to tree lynx, following methods described for cougars and bobcats (Hornocker 1970; Apps 1996). Live trapping was also carried out using Soft Catch® (Woodstream Corp., Litiz, PA.) #3 padded foot-hold traps in cubby sets (Hawbaker 1974) with modifications (Mowat et al. 1994). Captured lynx were immobilized with ketamine hydrochloride and xylazine hydrochloride at 10.0 and 2.5 mg/kg estimated body mass (Woodbury 1996), administered intramuscularly with an extendable pole-syringe or a *Cap-chur*® (Palmer Chemical and Equipment Co. Inc., Douglasville, GA.) Powder Projector dart gun. Anesthesia was occasionally maintained with an additional ketamine injection of 6.0 mg/kg. Immobilized lynx were sexed, and age was subjectively classed (adult: >2 years; juvenile: 1-2 years; kitten: <1 year) based on skeletal measurements and tooth wear. Study animals were fitted with motion/mortality sensing whip antennae radiocollars (Lotek Eng. Inc., Newmarket, ON.) and allowed to recover before release. Recovery was expedited on three occasions using atipamezole hydrochloride to reverse xylazine at twice the dosage of the latter (Woodbury 1996).

Radiotelemetry

Radiolocations were obtained throughout the year, at least weekly for all animals, and at least four days per week for most animals. Radiotelemetry was conducted from the ground and fixed-wing aircraft using standard

USDA Forest Service Gen Tech. Rep. RMRS-GTR-30. 1999

355

techniques (Samuel and Fuller 1996). Ground locations were estimated from three bearings taken within 1.5 hours, with origins located using hand-held Eagle Explorer® GPS receivers (Eagle Electronics, Catoosa, OK). Bearings were taken <2 km from the animal's estimated location 69% of the time. Two azimuths intersected at 70-110° for 88% of error polygons, and 89% of error polygons were <25 ha. Lynx were mostly inactive during 71% of ground locations, and I expect that time delays between bearings had a negligible effect on accuracy. Universal Transverse Mercator coordinates of radiolocations were referenced to ±50 m from 1:20,000 orthophoto or 1:50,000 National Topographic System (NTS) maps. Positional error associated with 95% of aircraft radiolocations was considered to be ±150 m (M. Gibeau, personal communication).

Food Habits

Study animals were snow-tracked during both years when possible, and kills and scavenging were documented over 759 km of trails. Prey remains were sufficient for positive species identification in most cases, although some kills may have been missed due to recent snow or for small prey. Tracks were directly observed wherever possible to minimize missed kills.

Population Attributes

Lynx carcasses and/or radiocollars were retrieved as soon as possible after mortality. Probable cause of death was determined from necropsies (Shury Veterinary Services, Canmore, AB) and field evidence. Female study animals were snow-tracked pre- and post-capture to determine whether kittens were present. When encountered, family groups of uncollared lynx were also snow-tracked to count kittens. The movements of females exhibiting strong site fidelity during May through July were radiotracked daily.

Space Use and Movements

I defined resident lynx as those associated with one activity center subjectively determined over at least three months. Home ranges of resident adults were estimated seasonally and annually over both years using the program CALHOME (Kie et al. 1996). I defined summer and winter seasons by the typical six-month snow and snow-free periods beginning and ending 1 November and 1 May. The late-February to early-April breeding period (Koehler and Aubry 1994) occurred in winter. To facilitate comparison with other research, I calculated the 100% and 95% minimum convex polygon (MCP) (Hayne 1949) and 95%, 75%, and 55% adaptive kernel utilization distributions (UD) using optimal smoothing parameters (Worton 1989). Lynx movements indicated that home ranges could be traversed within 24 hours, thus only radiolocations that were temporally independent by this interval were used (*sensu* Swihart and Slade 1985). Among all animals, the 95% UD area appeared to asymptote at 43 to 55 radiolocations (Apps, unpublished). I compared UD levels between sexes and seasons using multivariate analysis of variance (MANOVA; $\alpha = 0.05$). Static interaction between lynx known to have neighboring or contiguous home ranges was inferred from spatial home range overlap (Macdonald et al. 1980).

I defined minimum daily movements (MDM) as the distance between sequential radiolocations separated by 18-36 hours ($\bar{x} = 24$ hours). Mean MDM were compared among resident lynx of each sex using analysis of variance (ANOVA; $\alpha = 0.05$), and between seasons and sexes using unpaired Student's t-tests ($\alpha = 0.025$). I assumed that lynx exhibiting consistent, linear movements were transient or dispersing animals. Where possible, I summarized the movements of these animals with respect to timing of dispersal, direction, distance, MDM, and proximate outcome.

Topographic Selection and Highway Influence

For each resident lynx, I assessed seasonal selection for elevation, slope, and aspect within respective annual home ranges. This corresponds to Johnson's (1980) third-order resource selection and Thomas and Taylor's (1990) Study Design 3, with inferences relevant at the individual level. Digital elevation, slope, and aspect models were derived in a GIS from 1:50,000 NTS elevation contours. Aspect was described by two ratio-scale ($0\rightarrow1$) variables depicting south$\rightarrow$north and west$\rightarrow$east aspects. The raster resolution of each variable was set to 25 ha, roughly corresponding to the maximum spatial error of lynx radiolocations. Topographic attributes used by each animal were estimated from radiolocations temporally independent by at least 24 hours, following rationale described for home range analysis. Available attributes were estimated from an equivalent sample of systematic random locations within each animal's 95% UD. Variables were screened for multicollinearity using Pearson correlation coefficients (Tabachnick and Fidell 1989), and non-redundant ($r < 0.8$) variables were entered into multiple logistic regression to derive probabilistic resource selection functions (Manly et al. 1993). Box-Tidwell transformations (Box and Tidwell 1962) of elevation and slope were significant in some initial models, indicating that lynx selection for these attributes was non-linear (Hosmer and Lemeshow 1989). To facilitate comparisons among animals, I grouped elevation and slope data into three classes for each variable, roughly

USDA Forest Service Gen Tech. Rep. RMRS-GTR-30. 1999

357

corresponding to average 0.33 percentile groupings of available habitat among all animals. I tested the improvement of fitted models over null models by evaluating the reduction in (–2) log-likelihood ratios against a Chi-square distribution (Hosmer and Lemeshow 1989; α = 0.05), and I assessed the explanatory power of each model by regressing actual use against predicted use probabilities to derive coefficients of determination (r^2). The significance of variable coefficients was evaluated using Chi-square tests of Wald statistics (α = 0.05), and the contributions of each variable were assessed from the sign and strength of their partial correlations (r) with each model (Hosmer and Lemeshow 1989; Norusis 1994). From r statistics, I inferred preference where positive, and avoidance where negative. I evaluated differences in seasonal use of each variable using unpaired Student's t-tests (α = 0.0125). I used SPSS 7.0 (SPSS Inc., Chicago, IL) software for statistical analyses.

Paved highways dissected all lynx home ranges relatively linearly. I therefore assumed that a crossing occurred if sequential radiolocations were obtained on opposite sides of a highway (Chapter 10). This facilitated tests of the null hypothesis that lynx movements within home ranges were random with respect to highways. Movements of resident lynx were defined as the minimum distance between sequential radiolocations, and for each, a movement vector of the same length but random location and azimuth was generated within respective 95% UD isopleths. Lynx and random movements were then coded according to their intersection with highways, and differences in lynx vs. random crossing frequencies were evaluated using Chi-square tests (α = 0.05).

Results

Hare Densities

For early-, mid-, and late-successional stands respectively, mean hare densities by landscape were 0.16/ha (95% CI = 0.11-0.24), 0.08/ha (95% CI = 0.05-0.11), and 0.01/ha (95% CI = 0-0.02) in the upper Kootenay Valley; 0.25/ha (95% CI = 0.19-0.35), 0.06/ha (95% CI = 0.04-0.10), and 0.10/ha (95% CI = 0.07-0.15) in the Beaverfoot Valley; and 0.47/ha (95% CI = 0.36-0.62), 0.39/ha (95% CI = 0.26-0.57), and 0.32/ha (95% CI = 0.22-0.46) in the Vermilion Pass.

Food Habits and Population Attributes

Ten lynx, comprising three adult males, three adult females, one juvenile male, two kitten/juvenile females, and one kitten male, were radiocollared, monitored and snow-tracked for 1-23 months between November 1996 and October 1998. Lynx kills ($n = 137$) documented over both years were composed of snowshoe hares (52%), red squirrels (30%), northern flying squirrels (5%), grouse (3%), martens (3%), voles (3%), a northern flicker (<1%), and unknown species (3%). One case of scavenging on an intact mule deer, presumed to have died from a vehicle collision, occurred for 2-4 days before it was usurped by wolves.

None of the three adult females in the study sample were traveling with kittens at the time of their capture in November 1997 or 1998. One uncollared family group was detected in the study area during March 1997, and three uncollared family groups were detected during November and December 1997. I assumed the latter groups were different individuals because each group was separated by a linear distance >30 km, beyond the maximum exploratory movement of radiocollared females (personal observations). Each group contained an adult and two kittens. Both kittens (M/04, F/03) from one family group were subsequently radiocollared, but neither survived to May. Two females that were monitored through March of 1997 (F/01) and 1998 (F/02) were snow-tracked while traveling with males, and F/02 was also directly observed during copulation with an uncollared male on 13 March. Daily radiolocations of F/01 were within 250 m of an activity center between 20 May and 1 June 1997, after which she resumed normal movements and did not revisit the presumed den site. From this, I inferred that she lost or abandoned her litter at or just after parturition. Kittens were also not detected with her during snow-tracking early in the following winter. Radiolocations of F/02 were within 500 m of an activity center on 82% of days between 22 May and 14 July 1998, and she was observed with one kitten in August of that year.

Known survival of resident adults was 100% over both years. A dispersing female kitten (F/03) and a transient, juvenile male (M/05) died of starvation on 15 April and 3 May 1998 respectively. A male kitten (M/04) likely was killed by an uncollared adult male lynx in December 1997 while traveling with his family group and within his natal range. A female kitten (F/05) released to her natal area in April 1998 after four months in captivity due to a capture injury survived at least the following six months.

Space Use and Movements

The mean number of radiolocations used for summer and winter home range estimates was 96 (range = 63-183) and 149 (range = 72-265) respectively. Mean 95, 75, and 55% UD estimates did not significantly differ between seasons for males ($F = 3.66$, 3 df, $p = 0.222$) or females ($F = 1.34$, 3 df, $p = 0.548$). Mean annual UD estimates (Table 12.1) also did not significantly

USDA Forest Service Gen Tech. Rep. RMRS-GTR-30. 1999

359

Table 12.1–Annual minimum convex polygon (MCP) and adaptive kernel utilization distribution (UD) home range estimates (km^2) for resident lynx in the southern Canadian Rocky Mountains, British Columbia and Alberta, 1996-1998.

Lynx sex/ID	Period monitored (m/y)	n	100% MCP	95% MCP	95% UD	75% UD	55% UD
M/01	11/96 – 10/98	448	559	357	337	117	45
M/02	03/97 – 10/98	189	346	224	330	49	24
M/03	03/97 – 06/98	141	388	249	477	150	51
Male mean		3	431	277	381	105	40
Male SD			113	71	83	52	14
F/01	11/96 – 09/97	200	408	276	505	85	31
F/02	11/97 – 10/98	254	133	85	94	25	11
F/04	04/98 – 10/98	103	77	44	87	30	13
Female mean		3	206	135	229	47	18
Female SD			177	124	239	33	11

differ between sex ($F = 2.92$, 3 df, $p = 0.266$). Spatial overlap between the annual 95, 75, and 55% UD areas of M/01 and F/01 was 36, 63, and 60%, respectively. Of their 183 concurrent daily radiolocations, 78% were separated by >3 km. A second adult female was known to occur also within the 50% UD area of these two lynx, as inferred from snow-tracking and radiolocations of her dependent kitten (M/04). In addition, unmarked adult lynx were detected within the 70% UD of all other study animals between 1 November and 15 February 1998.

Minimum daily movement (MDM) (Table 12.2) differed among resident females during summer ($F = 9.81$; 2, 163 df; $p <0.001$) but not winter ($F = 0.43$; 2, 235 df; $p = 0.65$). MDM differed among resident males during both summer ($F = 3.67$; 2, 182 df; $p = 0.027$) and winter ($F = 4.62$; 2, 349 df; $p = 0.010$). Movements were greater during summer for M/01 ($t = 3.48$, 278 df, $p <0.001$) and were greater during winter for F/02 ($t = 2.72$, 125 df, $p = 0.007$), while seasonal differences were not significant among other residents ($t <1.77$, 26-110 df, $p >0.082$). Male movements were greater than those of females during both summer ($t = 5.01$, 347 df, $p <0.001$) and winter ($t = 3.05$, 584 df, $p = 0.002$).

Dispersal

Dispersal movements were documented for three subadult lynx. After he was radiocollared on 19 March 1998, a juvenile male (M/05) made a 44 km southeast movement over 11 days (MDM: $\bar{x} = 3.7$ km, SD = 1.9). He then used one meadow complex intensively (MDM: $\bar{x} = 1.3$ km, SD = 0.9) for the next 31 days before his death on 3 May. After she was radiocollared within her natal range, a female kitten (F/03) rejoined her mother for three days, then moved independently for three days before 28 March when she initiated a

Table 12.2–Minimum daily movements (MDM; km) for resident lynx during summer (1 May–31 October), winter (1 November–30 April), and annually in the southern Canadian Rocky Mountains, British Columbia and Alberta, 1996-1998.

Lynx sex/ID	Summer				Winter				Annual	
	n	Range	Mean	SD	n	Range	Mean	SD	Mean	SD
M/01	124	0.1 – 14.3	4.8	3.2	212	0.5 – 19.3	3.5	3.5	3.9	3.5
M/02	27	0.4 – 13.7	3.3	3.1	45	0.8 – 23.2	5.0	5.2	4.3	4.6
M/03	34	0.4 – 10.9	3.7	2.3	95	0.1 – 19.8	3.0	2.9	3.2	2.7
Males	3		3.9	0.8	3		3.8	1.1	3.8	0.6
F/01	53	0.0 – 10.3	3.0	2.4	101	0.1 – 12.0	2.7	2.5	2.9	2.5
F/02	64	0.0 – 10.9	1.9	2.2	125	0.1 – 10.4	2.8	2.1	2.5	2.2
F/04	49	0.5 – 13.7	3.9	2.8	12	0.8 – 6.1	3.4	1.8	3.9	2.6
Females	3		2.9	1.0	3		3.0	0.4	3.0	0.7

southeast linear movement of 17 km over three days (MDM: $\bar{x}$ = 5.6 km, SD = 0.4). She then used one area intensively (MDM: $\bar{x}$ = 0.9 km, SD = 0.5) for the next 15 days before her death. The movements of both animals followed the major valley in which they occurred and paralleled but did not cross the Trans-Canada Highway. After her 30 April release, a kitten/juvenile female (F/05) used a 75% UD home range of 53 km² for five months, after which she made two separate exploratory movements of a minimum 74 km and 55 km over 24 and 11 days respectively. The second movement continued in a southward dispersal.

Topographic Selection and Highway Influence

Topographic selection within home ranges was apparent among all six resident lynx during summer (χ^2 >21.6, 5-6 df, p <0.002), and among five during winter (χ^2 >35.6, 5-6 df, p <0.001). Among animals, models explained variation (r^2) ranging from 12 to 36% during summer and 19 to 36% during winter. Lynx either avoided or did not select highest (>1,850 m) elevations, preferred or did not avoid mid (1,550-1,850 m) elevations, and although lowest (<1,550 m) elevations were not avoided during winter, two animals did avoid them during summer (Table 12.3). All males and one female used mean elevations 90-133 m higher during summer than during winter (t >2.72, 131-434 df, p <0.008). However, seasonal use of elevations did not differ for two females (t <1.19, 97-237 df, p >0.240). Most lynx avoided or did not select steeper (>40%) slopes, and preferred or did not avoid moderate (20-40%) or gentle (<20%) slopes (Table 12.3). Mean slopes used were 4-9% steeper during summer than during winter for two males and two females (t >2.65, 131-237 df, p <0.009), whereas slope use did not differ between seasons for one male and one female (t <0.95, 97-434 df, p >0.344). Selection for aspect varied among animals (Table 12.3). Among all six lynx, there were

USDA Forest Service Gen Tech. Rep. RMRS-GTR-30. 1999

361

Table 12.3–Significance (p) and partial correlations (r) of variables considered within multiple logistic regression models of topographic selection within home ranges. Results are given for summer (1 May-31 October) and winter (1 November-30 April) for resident lynx in the southern Canadian Rocky Mountains, British Columbia and Alberta, 1996-1998. Preference (+) or avoidance (−) is inferred from r statistics where $p < 0.05$.

Variable		Lynx sex/ID: summer						Lynx sex/ID: winter					
		M/01	M/02	M/03	F/01	F/02	F/04	M/01	M/02	M/03	F/01	F/02	F/04
Elevation (m)	p	<0.001	0.006	0.049	<0.001	0.511	0.196	<0.001	0.071	<0.001	<0.001	0.773	0.547
<1,550	r	−0.20	+0.11	+0.13	−0.20	–	0.00	0.00	+0.12	+0.22	0.00	–	0.0
1,550 − 1,850	r	+0.30	+0.10	0.00	+0.29	0.00	+0.06	+0.26	0.00	0.00	+0.27	0.00	0.00
>1,850	r	0.00	−0.21	−0.11	0.00	0.00	0.00	−0.21	−0.13	−0.20	−0.21	0.00	0.00
Slope (%)	p	<0.001	0.163	0.025	0.038	0.890	0.859	0.018	0.465	0.192	0.015	0.008	0.931
<20	r	+0.07	0.00	−0.18	+0.15	0.00	0.00	+0.09	0.00	0.00	+0.12	0.00	0.00
20 − 40	r	+0.12	+0.09	+0.04	0.00	0.00	0.00	0.00	0.00	0.00	+0.05	+0.13	0.00
>40	r	−0.19	0.00	+0.07	−0.07	0.00	0.00	−0.07	0.00	+0.06	−0.14	−0.11	0.00
S→N aspect	p	0.358	0.002	0.100	0.513	0.333	0.024	0.050	0.345	0.711	0.914	0.057	0.723
	r	0.00	−0.19	−0.06	0.00	0.00	−0.12	−0.051	0.00	0.00	0.00	−0.06	0.00
W→E aspect	p	0.001	0.071	<0.001	0.323	<0.001	0.020	0.973	0.265	<0.001	0.119	<0.001	0.466
	r	+0.13	−0.08	+0.30	0.00	−0.29	−0.123	0.00	0.00	+0.27	+0.04	−0.22	0.00

no significant seasonal differences in the use of northward aspects ($t < 2.26$, 97-434 df, $p > 0.025$), and although one male used eastward aspects greater during summer than during winter ($t = 2.56$, 434 df, $p = 0.011$), seasonal differences were not significant among the other five lynx ($t < 1.93$, 97-237 df, $p > 0.055$). All six resident lynx crossed highways less than random expectation within their home ranges ($x^2 > 139.9$, 1 df, $p < 0.001$).

Discussion

Hare Densities

Hare densities (range = 0.01-0.47/ha) observed in the southern Canadian Rockies during 1996-1998 are comparable to those reported in northern lynx study areas during cyclic hare population lows. Hare densities in the southwest Yukon declined from 8.0 to 10.7/ha to 0.2 to 0.5/ha during one cycle (Ward and Krebs 1985), and another population fell from 7.5/ha to 1.3/ha during the next cycle (Slough and Mowat 1996). Similarly, a population in the Northwest Territories fell from 7 to 9/ha to 0.4 to 1.0/ha during the early 1990s (Poole 1994), and a northern Alberta population declined drastically from about 17/ha to 0.34/ha during the early 1970s (Brand et al. 1976). Because my study period coincided with the increase phase of a hare cycle (C. J. Krebs, personal communication), assuming goegraphic synchrony, my results are consistent with suggestions that hare densities remain relatively low in southern British Columbia and the northwestern United States (Chitty 1950; Dolbeer and Clark 1975; Wolff 1980).

Food Habits

The large proportion (47%) of prey other than snowshoe hares documented during winter in this study to date generally is consistent with observations of opportunistic lynx food habits during hare lows (Koehler and Aubry 1994; Staples 1995; O'Donoghue et al. 1998b). The 35% combined proportion of red squirrel and flying squirrel kills also is roughly consistent with Koehler's (1990) reported 24% occurrence of tree squirrels in lynx scats collected year-round in Washington. Lynx predation on marten has not been previously reported and likely is opportunistic. Despite the substantial numeric quantity of alternate prey in the diet of lynx in this study, hares clearly represent the most important food source when biomass ratios are considered (e.g., 1:5 squirrel:hare; Nellis and Keith 1968), as is consistent with other lynx populations (Koehler and Aubry 1994; Staples 1995; O'Donoghue et al. 1998b). My results, however, may underestimate the diversity of prey used due to missed kills of small species during snow-tracking, as was found by O'Donoghue et al. (1998b) in a comparison of kill-site with scat data. Although lynx in the Yukon cached partially consumed hares (O'Donoghue et al. 1998b), this behavior was not observed in the southern Canadian Rockies.

Reproduction and Recruitment

Kitten production and survival were low during the study period. The apparent lack of recruitment to early winter among study animals is consistent with northern populations after a hare decline, when winter litter sizes were zero (Brand et al. 1976; Poole 1994; Mowat et al. 1996). O'Donoghue et al. (1997) also did not detect family groups in their Yukon study area after the hare decline. Among the four uncollared family groups, litter sizes also were low in comparison to northern populations in the year preceding the hare decline, when mean winter litter sizes were 3.0 ($n = 3$; Poole 1994) and 3.3 ($n = 12$; Mowat et al. 1996). However, the occurrence of some kittens suggests that habitat quality varied among female home ranges within the study area. Among southern populations, Koehler (1990) also reported low (12%) kitten survival to winter from three litters in north-central Washington, and three adult females monitored in Montana from 1982 through 1984 did not produce kittens (Brainerd 1985). Evidence of breeding and den site abandonment of F/01 is consistent with the suggestion by Mowat et al. (1996) that breeding and implantation continues to occur regardless of prey densities.

USDA Forest Service Gen Tech. Rep. RMRS-GTR-30. 1999

363

Survival

Survival of resident adults was high over both years, as was found in another population refugium (Slough and Mowat 1996). During hare lows in northern populations, most natural mortality is due to starvation and is preceded by nomadic movements (Ward and Krebs 1985; Poole 1994; Slough and Mowat 1996), as observed for two lynx in this study. These two deaths occurred during spring, in contrast to Poole's (1994) observation that most natural mortality in his Northwest Territories study area occurred during mid-winter. Evidence of cannibalism that I report has been documented before (Elsey 1954; Nellis et al. 1972; Brittell et al. 1989; Poole 1994; O'Donoghue et al. 1995; Slough and Mowat 1996).

Space Use and Movements

Annual home ranges of resident lynx in the southern Canadian Rockies were considerably larger than those reported for most other studies employing the same estimators, regardless of prey density or geographic locale (Koehler and Aubry 1994; Poole 1994; Slough and Mowat 1996). Minimum convex polygon (MCP) home ranges in my study area were roughly 5-10 times larger than previously reported (Ibid.), although the influence of sample size on this estimator may confound comparisons (White and Garrot 1990). An exception to this was reported for the year after a hare decline in the Yukon, when four female and two male resident lynx maintained larger mean home ranges with high variability (Slough and Mowat 1996). Similarly, MDM mostly were higher than in other studies of comparable methods (Ward and Krebs 1985; Poole 1994), implying greater foraging effort. One exception to this was documented by Ward and Krebs (1985) during a hare decline in the Yukon, when lynx increased their daily movements from 2.4 to 3.3 to 5.4 km/day as hares declined from 1.0 to 0.5 to 0.2/ha, respectively. However, another Yukon study did not find that lynx increased their active time in response to declining hare numbers (O'Donoghue et al. 1998b). Differences between 100 and 95% MCP home ranges reflect exploratory movements that were made throughout the year by all resident study animals. Physiography and the distribution of potential habitat may partially account for lynx home range size differences between geographic areas (Koehler and Aubry 1994). In comparison to other study areas, space use and movements by lynx in the southern Canadian Rocky Mountains therefore may be disproportionately greater relative to prey densities.

Few studies have examined seasonal variation in space-use by lynx. Although I found no significant seasonal differences in UD areas for either sex, tests were based on a low sample size. More extensive space-use during summer was apparent for only one male; however, inclusion of the breeding period within the winter season may have masked seasonal differences among other lynx. Although not statistically tested, in Nova Scotia, individuals of both sexes used areas during summer that were larger than those used during winter (Parker et al. 1983), and two females with young used smaller areas during summer in Alaska (Bailey et al. 1986). In accordance with the latter observation, the only lynx that made smaller daily movements during summer was a female with kittens.

Relative to other study animals, the noticeably smaller UD areas that I report for two females (F/02, F/04) may reflect the distribution and configuration of potential habitat in the landscape where they occur. Still, although samples were small, home range comparisons between sex did not reveal more intensive space use by females as has generally been observed (Koehler and Aubry 1994), perhaps because females were mostly without kittens during the monitoring period. Smaller female home ranges were reported in the Yukon only during years of high kitten survival to 1 March (Slough and Mowat 1996). Poole (1994), however, did not detect home range differences between sexes over four years of variable kitten survival in the Northwest Territories. Regardless of home range comparisons, differences in daily movements suggest that females used space more intensively than males during both seasons.

Differential space use within home ranges may be influenced by habitat features and social interactions (Samuel et al. 1985). Obvious differences between annual UD levels indicate that lynx home ranges were not used homogenously but were associated with distinct core use areas. Poole (1994) also reported the use of obvious core home ranges by lynx (50% vs. 95% MCP). Evidence of intersexual spatial overlap that I report is consistent with most other populations (Koehler and Aubry 1994; Poole 1995). Sharing of home ranges between sexes or related females observed elsewhere also would be expected in the southern Canadian Rockies, considering the heterogeneous distribution of potential lynx habitat (Sandell 1989).

Topographic Selection

Lynx exhibited variable selection for topographic attributes, which may relate to differing associations of topography with habitat, human, and snow conditions; however, there was some consistency in pattern. Avoidance of highest elevations and steepest slopes by lynx in this study area likely is due to unsuitable habitat associations and energetic costs of accessing any habitat that is suitable. Lynx may also use topography to help partition themselves from competing species. Although they used higher mean elevations than coyotes during winter in the Yukon (Murray and Boutin

USDA Forest Service Gen Tech. Rep. RMRS-GTR-30. 1999

365

1991), lynx may not avoid lowest elevations within home ranges if habitat and terrain conditions are otherwise unsuitable for canids. During summer, they may further minimize interference competition with canids by using higher elevations and steeper slopes. The seasonal shift in elevation use that I found is similar to that reported by Koehler (1990) among lynx in the mountains of north-central Washington. Within their home ranges, bobcats occurring sympatric with coyotes in southeast British Columbia preferred mid elevations, avoided slopes <10°, and selected distances <0.75 km from slopes associated with rock outcrops (Apps 1996). Terrain was also a factor in habitat partitioning between bobcats and coyotes in Idaho (Koehler and Hornocker 1991). Regardless of interspecific relationships, the open habitats associated with higher elevations in my study area contain additional prey species not available during winter (Scotter and Ulrich 1995), and snow conditions may increase the energetic cost of travel at higher elevations during much of the winter.

I found no obvious pattern of aspect selection by lynx within home ranges, and use did not differ seasonally among most animals. However, McKelvey et al. (Chapter 10) detected preference for northeast aspects at the scale of their Washington study area. If lynx exhibit aspect preferences in the southern Canadian Rockies, they may occur at broader or finer spatial scales than I considered. Moreover, finer-scale selection for this variable may relate to solar insolation, which will vary greatly within and among days. The individual selection for aspect that did occur may be an artifact of covariation with other habitat and human conditions.

Highway Influence

The likelihood of highway crossings by resident lynx can be expected to vary among home ranges according to proximal habitat conditions, width of road allowance and traffic volume, and perhaps by the animal's sex and reproductive status. Although my analysis did not account for these factors, all lynx crossed highways less than random expectation within their 95% UD home ranges, suggesting that highways influenced lynx movements. Although my analysis only considered the influence of highways within home ranges, they may also influence home range selection just as dominant natural features can (Koehler and Aubry 1994), and this would decrease the substantive influence apparent within home ranges. Although there have been no other reports to date of lynx space use and movements relative to human linear disturbance, four lynx in Washington did not cross logging roads differently from random within home ranges (Chapter 10). However, bobcats in Wisconsin selected home ranges with lower densities of secondary roads and crossed paved highways less than expected, a function of vehicle traffic levels and juxtaposition of preferred habitat to roads (Lovallo and Anderson 1996).

Dispersal

The timing of F/03's dispersal is within the March-June emigration peak observed by Slough and Mowat (1996) in the Yukon but occurred nine days before their earliest female kitten dispersal. The linear movements by this lynx and M/05 are in the lower extremes of those reported for lynx emigrating from northern populations (Slough and Mowat 1996; Poole 1997); however most reported lynx dispersals have been of adults. The orientation of movements relative to terrain and the Trans-Canada Highway suggests that dominant natural and human features may constrain dispersal options in the southern Canadian Rockies. The intensive use of one area exhibited by both lynx before their deaths does not imply residency because dispersing felids have exhibited short-term use of temporary home ranges (Beier 1995; Apps 1996).

Conclusions

Although results are based on limited data, several conclusions specific to the southern Canadian Rocky Mountains can be made. Hare densities, and the diet, space-use and movements, reproduction, subadult survival, and dispersal of lynx were consistent with those of northern populations during hare lows. However, assuming geographic synchrony, the study period coincided with the increase phase of a snowshoe hare cycle, suggesting that lynx populations in the southern Canadian Rocky Mountains are not subject to the dramatic, cyclic pulses in productivity reported for northern populations. The following are also apparent: lynx spacing patterns suggest that resource distribution is patchy; males use space more extensively than females; topography influences habitat potential, with seasonal differences; and highways may negatively influence lynx movements.

Acknowledgments

These first two years of this ongoing study were funded by the British Columbia Habitat Conservation Trust Fund, Parks Canada, the Columbia Basin Fish and Wildlife Compensation Program, and the Habitat and Silviculture Assistance Fund. Field assistance was capably provided by R. Owchar, B. Bertch, S. Stevens, P. Wandeler, S. Hawes, D. Quinn, B. Baxter, C. Darimont, M. Vassal, J. Weaver, J. Bryan, D. Ghekas, and D. Poszig. J. Weaver and G. Mowat also contributed helpful advice on study design

USDA Forest Service Gen Tech. Rep. RMRS-GTR-30. 1999

367

and methods. Project administration and in-kind contributions were provided by A. Dibb of Parks Canada, A. Fontana and R. Neil of the BC Ministry of Environment, Lands and Parks, and J. Krebs of the Columbia Basin Fish and Wildlife Compensation Program. Veterinary services were provided by T. Shury and M. Zehnder. Temporary animal holding and care were facilitated by T. Kinley and N. Newhouse. Constructive input to this manuscript was provided by S. Buskirk and two anonymous reviewers.

Literature Cited

Achuff, P. L., W. D. Holland, G. M. Coen, and K. Van Tighem. 1984. Ecological land classification of Kootenay National Park, British Columbia. Vol. I: Integrated resource description. Alberta Institute of Pedology, University of Alberta, Edmonton, AB.

Apps, C. D. 1996. Bobcat (*Lynx rufus*) habitat selection and suitability assessment in southeast British Columbia. Thesis. Faculty of Environmental Design, University of Calgary, Calgary, AB.

Bailey, T. N., E. E. Bangs, M. F. Portner, J. C. Malloy, and R. J. McAvinchey. 1986. An apparent overexploited lynx population on the Kenai Peninsula, Alaska. Journal of Wildlife Management 50:279-289.

Beier, P. 1995. Dispersal of juvenile cougars in fragmented habitat. Journal of Wildlife Management 59:228-237.

Box, G. E. P., and P. W. Tidwell, 1962. Transformation of the independent variables. Technometrics 4: 531-550.

Brainerd, S. M. 1985. Reproductive ecology of bobcats and lynx in western Montana. Thesis. University of Montana, Missoula, MT.

Brand, C. J., and L. B. Keith. 1979. Lynx demography during a snowshoe hare decline in Alberta. Journal of Wildlife Management 43:827-849.

Brand, C. J., L. B. Keith, and C. A. Fischer. 1976. Lynx responses to changing snowshoe hare densities in central Alberta. Journal of Wildlife Management 40:416-428.

Brittell, J. D., R. J. Poelker, S. J. Sweeney, and G. M. Koehler. 1989. Native cats of Washington. Section III: Lynx. Washington Department of Wildlife, Olympia, WA.

Carr, G., and D. W. MacDonald. 1986. The sociality of solitary foragers: a model based on resource dispersion. Animal Behavior 34:1540-1549.

Chitty, H. 1950. The snowshoe rabbit enquiry, 1946-48. Journal of Animal Ecology 19:15-20.

Demarchi, D. A. 1994. Ecoprovinces of the central North American Cordillera and adjacent plains. Pages 153-167 *in* L. F. Ruggiero, K. B. Aubry, S. W. Buskirk, L. J. Lyon, and W. J. Zielinski, eds. The scientific basis for conserving forest carnivores—American marten, fisher, lynx, and wolverine in the western United States. General Technical Report RM-254. Fort Collins, CO: USDA Forest Service, Rocky Mountain Forest and Range Experiment Station.

Dolbeer, R. A., and W. R. Clark. 1975. Population ecology of snowshoe hares in the central Rocky Mountains. Journal of Wildlife Management 24:52-60.

Elsey, C. A. 1954. A case of cannibalism in Canada lynx (*Lynx canadensis*). Journal of Mammalogy 35:129.

Hawbaker, S. S. 1974. Trapping North American furbearers. Revised 17th Edition. Kurtz Bros., Clearfield, PA.

Hayne, D. W. 1949. Calculation of home range size. Journal of Mammalogy 30:1-18.

Hornocker, M. G. 1970. An analysis of mountain lion predation upon mule deer and elk in the Idaho Primitive Area. Wildlife Monographs 21.

Hosmer, D. W., Jr., and S. Lemeshow. 1989. Applied logistic regression. John Wiley and Sons, New York.

Johnson, D. H. 1980. The comparison of usage and availability measurements for evaluating resource preference. Ecology 61:65-71.

Kie, J. G., J. A. Baldwin, and C. J. Evans. 1996. CALHOME: a program for estimating animal home ranges. Wildlife Society Bulletin 24:342-344.

Koehler, G. M. 1990. Population and habitat characteristics of lynx and snowshoe hares in North Central Washington. Canadian Journal of Zoology 68:845-851.

Koehler, G. M., and K. B. Aubry. 1994. Lynx. Pages 74-98 *in* L. F. Ruggiero, K. B. Aubry, S. W. Buskirk, L. J. Lyon, and W. J. Zielinski, eds. The scientific basis for conserving forest carnivores—American marten, fisher, lynx, and wolverine in the western United States. General Technical Report RM-254. Fort Collins, CO: USDA Forest Service, Rocky Mountain Forest and Range Experiment Station.

Koehler, G. M., and M. G. Hornocker. 1991. Seasonal resource use among mountain lions, bobcats, and coyotes. Journal of Mammology 72: 391-396.

Krebs, C. J., B. S. Gilbert, S. Boutin, and R. Boonstra. 1987. Estimation of snowshoe hare population density from turd transects. Canadian Journal of Zoology 65:565-567.

Lovallo, M. J., and E. M. Anderson. 1996. Bobcat movements and home ranges relative to roads in Wisconsin. Wildlife Society Bulletin 24:71-76.

Macdonald, D. W., F. G. Ball, and N. G Hough. 1980. The evaluation of home range size and configuration using radiotracking data. Pages 405-424 *in* C. J. Amlaner, Jr., and D. W. Macdonald, eds. A handbook on biotelemetry and radiotracking. Pergamon Press, Oxford, England.

Manly, B. F. J., L. L. McDonald, and D. L. Thomas. 1993. Resource selection by animals: statistical design and analysis for field studies. Chapman and Hall, New York.

Meidinger, D. V., and J. Pojar. 1991. Ecosystems of British Columbia. Special Report Series Number 4. British Columbia Ministry of Forests, Victoria, BC.

Mowat, G., B. G. Slough, and R. Rivard. 1994. A comparison of three live capturing devices for lynx: capture efficiency and injuries. Wildlife Society Bulletin 22:644-650.

Mowat, G., B. G. Slough, and S. Boutin. 1996. Lynx recruitment during a snowshoe hare population peak and decline in southwest Yukon. Journal of Wildlife Management 60: 441-452.

Murray, D. L., and S. Boutin. 1991. The influence of snow on lynx and coyote movements: does morphology affect behaviour? Oecologia 88:463-469.

USDA Forest Service Gen Tech. Rep. RMRS-GTR-30. 1999

369

Nellis, C. H., and L. B. Keith. 1968. Hunting activities and successes of lynxes in Alberta. Journal of Wildlife Management 32:718-722.

Nellis, C. H., S. P. Whetmore, and L. B. Keith. 1972. Lynx-prey interactions in central Alberta. Journal of Wildlife Management 36:320-329.

Norusis, M. J. 1994. SPSS advanced statistics 6.1. SPSS Inc., Chicago, Ill.

O'Donoghue, M., E. Hofer, and F. I. Doyle. 1995. Predator versus predator. Natural History 10:6-9.

O'Donoghue, M., S. Boutin, C. J. Krebs, and E. J. Hofer. 1997. Numerical responses of coyotes and lynx to the snowshoe hare cycle. Oikos 80:150-162.

O'Donoghue, M., S. Boutin, C. J. Krebs, D. L. Murray, and E. J. Hofer. 1998a. Behavioural responses of coyotes and lynx to the snowshoe hare cycle. Oikos 82:169-183.

O'Donoghue, M., S. Boutin, C. J. Krebs, G. Zuleta, D. L. Murray, and E. J. Hofer. 1998b. Functional responses of coyotes and lynx to the snowshoe hare cycle. Ecology 79: 1193-1208.

Parker, G. R., J. W. Maxwell, and L. D. Morton. 1983. The ecology of lynx (*Lynx canadensis*) on Cape Breton Island. Canadian Journal of Zoology 61:770-786.

Poll, D. M., M. M. Porter, G. L. Holroyd, R. M. Wershler, and L. W. Gyug. 1984. Ecological land classification of Kootenay National Park, British Columbia. Vol II: Wildlife resource. Canadian Wildlife Service, Edmonton, AB.

Poole, K. G. 1994. Characteristics of an unharvested lynx population during a snowshoe hare decline. Journal of Wildlife Management 58:608-618.

Poole, K. G. 1995. Spatial organization of a lynx population. Canadian Journal of Zoology 73:632-641.

Poole, K. G. 1997. Dispersal patterns of lynx in the Northwest Territories. Journal of Wildlife Management 61:497-505.

Ruediger, B. 1996. The relationship between rare carnivores and highways. Unpublished Report. USDA Forest Service, Missoula, MT. 7p.

Samuel, M. D., and M. R. Fuller. 1996. Wildlife radiotelemetry. Pages 370-418 *in* T. A. Bookhout, ed. Research and management techniques for wildlife and habitats. Fifth ed., rev. The Wildlife Society, Bethesda, MD.

Samuel, M. D., D. J. Pierce, and E. O. Garton. 1985. Identifying areas of concentrated use within the home range. Journal of Applied Ecology 54:11-719.

Sandell, M. 1989. The mating tactics and spacing patterns of solitary carnivores. Pages 164-182 *in* J. L. Gittleman, ed. Carnivore behavior, ecology, and evolution. Cornell University Press, Ithaca, NY.

Scotter, G. W., and T. J. Ulrich. 1995. Mammals of the Canadian Rockies. Fifth House, Saskatoon, SK.

Slough, B. G., and G. Mowat. 1996. Lynx population dynamics in an untrapped refugium. Journal of Wildlife Management 60:946-961.

Smith, C. H., and J. M. Davis. 1981. A spatial analysis of wildlife's ten-year cycle. Journal of Biogeography 8:27-35.

Staples, W. R. 1995. Lynx and coyote diet and habitat relationships during a low hare population on the Kenai Peninsula, Alaska. Thesis. University of Alaska, Fairbanks, AK.

Swihart, R. K., and N. A. Slade. 1985. Influence of sampling interval on estimates of home range size. Journal of Wildlife Management 49:1019-1025.

Tabachnick, B. G., and L. S. Fidell. 1989. Using multivariate statistics. Sec. ed. Harper Collins. Inc., New York, NY.

Thomas, D. L., and E. J. Taylor. 1990. Study designs and tests for comparing resource use and availability. Journal of Wildlife Management 54:322-330.

Ward, R. M. P., and C. J. Krebs. 1985. Behavioural responses of lynx to declining snowshoe hare abundance. Canadian Journal of Zoology 63:2817-2824.

White, G. C., and R. A. Garrott. 1990. Analysis of wildlife radio-tracking data. Academic Press, Inc., Toronto.

Wolff, J. O. 1980. Role of habitat patchiness in the population dynamics of snowshoe hares. Ecological Monographs 50:111-130.

Woodbury, M. R., ed. 1996. The chemical immobilization of wildlife. Canadian Association of Zoo and Wildlife Veterinarians, Winnipeg, MN.

Worton, B. J. 1989. Kernel methods for estimating the utilization distribution in home-range studies. Ecology 70:164-168.

USDA Forest Service Gen Tech. Rep. RMRS-GTR-30. 1999

371

Chapter 13

Ecology of Canada Lynx in Southern Boreal Forests

Keith B. Aubry, USDA Forest Service, Pacific Northwest Research Station, 3625 93rd Ave. SW, Olympia, WA 98512

Gary M. Koehler, Washington Department of Fish and Wildlife, 600 Capitol Way N, Olympia, WA 98501

John R. Squires, USDA Forest Service, Rocky Mountain Research Station, 800 E. Beckwith, Missoula, MT 59807

Abstract—Canada lynx occur throughout boreal forests of North America, but ecological conditions in southern regions differ in many respects from those in Canada and Alaska. To evaluate the extent to which lynx ecology and population biology may differ between these regions, we review existing information from southern boreal forests and compare our findings to information presented in Chapter 9 on lynx in the taiga. Throughout North America, lynx diets in both winter and summer are dominated by snowshoe hares. In southern boreal forests, alternative prey, especially red squirrels, are important constituents of the diet. This reliance on alternative prey may reflect a response to low-density hare populations in southern regions, because alternative prey are also important in the taiga during lows in the snowshoe hare cycle. In addition, limited information on lynx diets during snow-free months indicates that alternative prey are important during summer in both northern and southern populations, regardless of the status of local hare populations. As in the taiga, lynx in southern regions are associated with boreal and sub-boreal forest conditions, including upper elevation, coniferous forests in the western mountains and mixed coniferous-deciduous forests in the Northeast. Throughout their range, lynx are absent or uncommon in dense, wet forests along the Pacific coast. In both northern and southern regions, lynx occur predominantly in habitats where snowshoe hares are abundant, especially early successional stands with high stem densities. However, in southern boreal forests, such habitats appear to be used primarily for hunting; all known den sites in southern regions were located in mature forest stands with large woody debris. As in the taiga during times of hare scarcity, relatively large home ranges appear to be characteristic of lynx in southern boreal forests. Lynx dispersal movements are similar to those reported from the taiga. However, only lynx in southern forests are known to make exploratory movements prior to dispersal. We speculate that such explorations may reflect a more heterogeneous habitat mosaic, and a correspondingly lower probability of successful dispersal in southern regions. Demographic characteristics of southern lynx populations, including low densities, low pregnancy rates, low litter sizes, and high kitten mortality rates are similar to those reported from the taiga during times of hare scarcity. As in the taiga, we found little evidence that roads represented a significant disturbance or mortality factor for lynx. Roads into lynx habitat may, however, provide access to generalist competitors, such as coyotes and bobcats. Although there is little evidence that competition with other predators negatively influences lynx populations, this aspect of their ecology has not been studied in southern boreal forests. In summary, differences in lynx ecology between populations in southern boreal forests and those in the taiga appear to be related primarily to the use of alternative prey species; the effect of habitat patchiness on movements, reproduction, and survival; and the potential effects of different communities of predators and competitors on lynx populations.

Introduction

Canada lynx occur in most boreal forest habitats in North America, including the classic boreal forests or taiga of northern Canada and Alaska, upper elevation coniferous forests of the Rocky Mountains and Cascade Range, and mixed coniferous-deciduous forests of southeastern Canada, New England, and the Great Lakes states (Chapters 3 and 8; McCord and Cardoza 1984; Quinn and Parker 1987). Most of the geographic range of lynx in North America occurs in the taiga, however, where Canada lynx ecology has been studied in greatest detail (Chapter 9). Lynx reach their highest densities in the taiga, where populations undergo dramatic 10-year cycles in delayed synchrony with snowshoe hare populations (Elton and Nicholson 1942; Keith 1963; Chapter 9).

Some authors have argued that lynx populations in the southern portion of their range in the contiguous United States do not cycle in abundance, but occur at relatively stable densities comparable to those found during cyclic lows in the taiga (Keith 1963; Koehler and Aubry 1994). This hypothesis is based largely on the observation that snowshoe hare populations in the southern portions of their range are either stable or have cycles of very low amplitude (Adams 1959; Keith 1963; Dolbeer and Clark 1975; Wolff 1980, 1982). However, Hodges (Chapter 7) has compiled new information on snowshoe hare populations in southern boreal forests that indicates that hares may fluctuate in number more than previously thought, but at much lower amplitudes than those recorded in the taiga. Ecological conditions in southern boreal forests occupied by lynx differ in many ways from those in the taiga (Chapter 3). Thus, the ecology of lynx in southern boreal forests may differ in important ways from that described for populations in the North (see also Chapter 5). If so, such differences would have important implications for lynx conservation in the contiguous United States.

In this chapter, we review existing information on lynx ecology in boreal forests south of the Polar ecoregions (Bailey 1998) and compare and contrast these findings to those presented in Chapter 9 on lynx ecology in northern boreal forests. Information considered here includes all studies of lynx ecology in the contiguous United States, as well as those conducted in Humid Temperate and Dry ecoregions in the southern Canadian Rocky Mountains (Chapter 12) and on Cape Breton Island in Nova Scotia (Parker 1981; Parker et al. 1983).

Food Habits and Relationships With Prey

Throughout North America, the distribution of lynx is virtually coincident with the distribution of snowshoe hares (McCord and Cardoza 1984; Bittner and Rongstad 1984) and, within that range, lynx tend to occur in habitats where snowshoe hares are most abundant (Koehler and Aubry 1994; Chapter 9). In northern regions, lynx prey almost exclusively on snowshoe hares during winter; however, during snow-free seasons or when hares are at low abundances, alternative prey, especially red squirrels, are taken in higher proportions (Chapter 9). Although limited information from studies in the western mountains indicates a similar predominance of snowshoe hares in the diet of lynx (Koehler and Aubry 1994), hare densities are typically low in southern boreal forests compared to northern regions (Chapters 6 and 7).

There have been few studies of lynx food habits in southern boreal forests (Table 13.1). Among 29 lynx scats collected in north-central Washington during winter and summer from 1985 to 1987, 23 (79%) contained snowshoe

Table 13.1– Frequency of occurrence (%) of prey items in diets of Canada lynx in North America. Contents of scats, stomachs, and digestive tracts may contain more than one prey item; thus, total percentages for these analyses may exceed 100%.

Study area	Snowshoe hare	Red squirrel	Other small mammals	Grouse and ptarmigan	Other birds	Ungulates	Other
Southern boreal forests							
North-central Washington; annual (n = 29 scats)[a]	79	24	3			7	
Southern Canadian Rocky Mountains; winter (n = 137 kills found during snow tracking)[b]	52	30	8	3	1		6
Cape Breton Island, Nova Scotia; winter (n = 75 stomachs)[c]	97	1	3	3		5	
Cape Breton Island, Nova Scotia; winter (n = 55 scats)[c]	93		7	4	2	5	
Cape Breton Island, Nova Scotia; summer (n = 441 scats)[c]	70	4	4-5	1	6-7	9	<1
Northern boreal forests during low snowshoe hare densities							
Central Alberta; winter (n = 338 items found in stomachs)[d]	35	12	33	6	6	3	7
Central Alberta; winter (n = 54 kills found during snow tracking)[e]	56	7		15			22
Southwestern Yukon; winter (n = 280 kills found during snow tracking)[f]	20	64	13	1			1
Southwestern Yukon; winter (n = 101 scats)[f]	79	50	21				7
Kenai Peninsula, Alaska; winter (n = 161 scats)[g]	91	15	13	10	1	7	6
Kenai Peninsula, Alaska; winter (n = 16 kills found during snow tracking)[g]	63	19	13	6			
Kenai Peninsula, Alaska; summer (n = 42 scats)[g]	67	50	29	12	10		10
Northern boreal forests during high snowshoe hare densities							
Central Alberta; winter (n = 72 items found in stomachs)[d]	90		5		3		1
Central Alberta; winter (n = 35 kills found during snow tracking)[e]	86	3		6			6
Southwestern Yukon; winter (n = 222 kills found during snow tracking)[f]	89	3	3	4			1
Southwestern Yukon; winter (n = 239 scats)[f]	92	5	16				20
Kenai Peninsula, Alaska; winter (n = 41 scats)[h]	100	5	7		10		
Alberta and Northwest Territories; winter (n = 52 digestive tracts)[i]	79	2	10	10	13	12	2
Alberta and Northwest Territories; summer (n = 23 digestive tracts)[i]	52	9	39	8	26		

[a]Koehler 1990; [b]Apps Chapter 12; [c]Parker et al. 1983; [d]Brand and Keith 1979; [e]Brand et al. 1976; [f]O'Donoghue et al. 1998 (data on frequency of occurrence in scats provided by M. O'Donoghue); [g]Staples 1995, unpublished; [h]Kesterson 1988, unpublished; [i]van Zyll de Jong 1966

hare and seven (24%) contained red squirrels; remains of both species were also found at den sites (Koehler 1990). Using Koehler's (1990) pellet plot data, Hodges (Chapter 7) estimated fall snowshoe hare densities on the study area at 0.09-1.79 hares/ha. Snow tracking along 20.5 km of lynx trails detected eight chases of prey by lynx; snowshoe hares were chased six times and captured twice, whereas red squirrels were unsuccessfully chased twice. Lynx had been observed capturing red squirrels in the study area previously, however (Brittell et al. 1989, unpublished). Other prey items, including remains of a deer fawn, adult deer, and white-footed mouse, were each found in only one scat.

During snow-tracking studies from 1996 to 1998, Apps (Chapter 12) documented 137 lynx kills during winter in the southern Canadian Rocky Mountains. Prey species included 71 (52%) snowshoe hares, 41 (30%) red squirrels, nine (5%) northern flying squirrels, five (3%) martens, voles, and grouse, one northern flicker, and five "unknown." Snowshoe hare densities in the study area were estimated at 0.01-0.47 hares/ha. A radio-marked male lynx scavenged a road-killed mule deer for several days before being driven off by wolves. The only food habits information collected during snow-free months was the observation that a radio-marked juvenile male hunted meadow voles on seven occasions. There are several reported observations of lynx hunting ground squirrels in southern boreal forests. In Wyoming, a male lynx was seen hunting Wyoming ground squirrels in sagebrush habitat in late April, and a female was observed hunting similarly in early July (Chapter 11). Barash (1971) observed two adult and one juvenile lynx cooperatively hunting Columbian ground squirrels during summer in Glacier National Park, Montana.

In contrast to findings from western montane regions, studies in Nova Scotia (Parker 1981; Parker et al. 1983) indicated that alternative prey were relatively unimportant in lynx diets during winter. However, snowshoe hares occurred in the study area at densities higher than most recorded in the taiga (5.8-10 hares/ha; see Chapter 6), suggesting that food habits of lynx in Nova Scotia may not be comparable to those of other lynx populations in southern boreal forests, where hares occur at substantially lower densities (Chapter 7). In addition, although southern red-backed voles, masked shrews, ruffed grouse, and spruce grouse were all considered to be common in the study area, red squirrels were relatively rare. In "advanced" successional stages (16-30 years after cutting), hare densities declined from 10 hares/ha in 1977 to 1.7 hares/ha in 1979. Nevertheless, for all years combined, snowshoe hares were present in 97% of stomachs examined ($n = 75$) and 93% of scats ($n = 55$) collected during winter; red squirrels were found in only one stomach (Parker et al. 1983). Among 200 chases detected during snow tracking in the winter of 1977-1978, 198 were of snowshoe hares that resulted in 34 kills; the remaining two chases were of ruffed grouse (Parker 1981). During summer, however, alternative prey were more important in the diet; only 70% of scats examined (n = 441) contained remains of snowshoe hare. Other foods of lynx during summer included birds, small mammals, and carrion.

Very few studies of lynx food habits during snow-free periods have been conducted in North America (Table 13.1; Chapter 9). Based on available information, however, there appear to be few essential differences in the food habits of the lynx throughout its range. Regardless of geographic location, lynx diets are dominated by snowshoe hares during all seasons of the year. If hares are abundant, lynx subsist almost exclusively on them during winter. In the taiga, alternative prey are important in the winter during lows in the snowshoe hare cycle (Table 13.1; Chapter 9). During summer in northern boreal forests, alternative prey are more abundant in lynx diets regardless of the status of local snowshoe hare populations (Table 13.1). It is unclear, however, whether this shift is related to increased availability of alternative prey or to decreased hunting success on hares during snow-free periods (Chapter 9). Although data are scarce, the red squirrel appears to be the most important alternative prey species throughout the range of lynx, with grouse, small mammals, and carrion of lesser importance in the diet. In southern boreal forests, limited data suggest that because snowshoe hares typically occur at low densities (Chapter 7), alternative prey may always be important components of lynx diets, especially in the western mountains.

Habitat Relationships

Historical and current records show that lynx occur primarily within Douglas-fir, spruce-fir, and fir-hemlock forests at elevations ranging from 1,500 to 2,000 m in the western mountains, boreal forest types at 250-500 m in the Great Lakes region, and mixed forest-coniferous forest-high tundra vegetation types at 250-750 m in the northeastern United States (Chapter 8). However, lynx habitat relationships within these forest types have been studied in only a few locations. Studies that documented habitat use with radiotelemetry have monitored relatively few animals: three lynx in Nova Scotia (Parker et al. 1983), five and two in Montana (Smith 1984, unpublished; Koehler et al. 1979, respectively), and seven in Washington (Koehler 1990). Brittell et al. (1989, unpublished) reported forest cover type and topographic attributes for home range areas of 23 radio-marked lynx in Washington, but such analyses do not provide reliable information on habitat selection. However, McKelvey et al.'s (Chapter 10) reanalysis of telemetry data from

Washington (Brittell et al. 1989, unpublished; Koehler 1990) has provided new information on selection of forest habitats and topographic features by lynx in that region. Intensive snow-tracking studies comparing habitat use with availability have only been conducted in Nova Scotia (Parker 1981; 192 km of trails).

Associations With Forest Types

In the western mountains, Canada lynx occur predominantly within boreal forests (Chapter 8; Koehler and Aubry 1994); elevational zones for these forests vary with latitude, ranging from an average of about 1,400 m in Washington to 2,700 m in Colorado (Chapter 3). The lynx study area in the southern Canadian Rockies (Chapter 12) is dominated by Engelmann spruce-white spruce and subalpine fir forests occurring at elevations between 1,200 and 3,000 m; lodgepole pine is present as a seral species. The area where lynx are being studied in western Montana (Chapter 11) ranges from 1,200 to 2,100 m in elevation and is dominated by Douglas-fir, western larch, and lodgepole pine at lower elevations, and subalpine fir, whitebark pine, and Engelmann spruce at upper elevations. Habitat used by five radio-marked lynx in Montana was described by Smith (1984, unpublished) as occurring within subalpine fir forest associations. The lynx study area in western Wyoming (Chapter 11) is located at 2,600-2,750 m in elevation, where pure stands of lodgepole pine occur on drier sites and spruce-fir is generally restricted to north-facing slopes; south-facing slopes are dominated by sagebrush and wheat grass communities. Halfpenny et al. (1989, unpublished) reported lynx above 2,700 m along edges of dense spruce-fir stands near parklands and aspen stands in Colorado.

Forest cover types selected by lynx in the Cascade Range of north-central Washington (Chapter 10) are similar to those used by lynx in the Rocky Mountains. In the Cascades, lynx selected lodgepole pine cover types at elevations ranging from 1,370 to 2,130 m. During winter, however, lynx shifted their activities to elevations below 1,520 m, avoiding those above 1,980 m. During summer, lynx selected northeast aspects, but whether lynx selected these sites for thermal or other features is not known (Chapter 10). Douglas-fir, ponderosa pine, and western larch stands were used less than expected by lynx.

Lynx are forest dwellers, but historical records (Chapter 8) and recent studies (Chapter 11) show that lynx occur occasionally in non-forested areas, such as shrub-steppe habitats in eastern Montana, Wyoming, and Idaho. However, such observations appear to represent either transient individuals or resident animals searching opportunistically for prey.

Associations of lynx occurrences and forest cover types in the Northeast described in Chapter 8 fit closely with published descriptions of lynx habitat. On Cape Breton Island in Nova Scotia, lynx occupied forested habitats at elevations from 360 to 390 m, where the climax vegetation consisted of balsam fir and black spruce bogs, and alder-bordered streams. Lynx also frequented open spruce-dominated bogs, where multiple tracks and evidence of play activity suggested that such sites may be used for resting and socializing (Parker 1981). Most trapping records from the White Mountains of New Hampshire during the 1960s were from elevations over 1,000 m in forest types dominated by hardwoods and spruce-balsam fir (Litvaitis et al. 1991). Brocke (1982) speculated that the historic distribution of lynx in the Adirondack Mountains of northern New York was associated with spruce-fir forest receiving heavy snowfall at elevations over 900 m. Descriptions of habitat used by lynx in the Great Lakes states are generally anecdotal in nature and provide few insights about lynx ecology in that region.

Forest types occupied by lynx in the taiga are described as boreal, sub-boreal, and montane forests containing snowshoe hares; lynx are absent or uncommon, however, in wet, coastal forests of western Canada and Alaska (Chapter 9). These descriptions of broad forest associations are similar to those reported from southern boreal forests. In the contiguous United States, the range of lynx is essentially coincident with the distribution of boreal forest in the western mountains and northeastern United States (Chapters 3 and 8; McCord and Cardoza 1984); as in Canada and Alaska, lynx are absent from the dense, wet forests along the Pacific coast.

Stand-Scale Habitat Associations

Habitat use by lynx at the stand scale has been studied with both snow tracking and radiotelemetry in many areas of the taiga (Chapter 9), but there are few studies of this kind in southern boreal forests. In Montana, Koehler et al. (1979) reported that 26 of 29 lynx locations for two radio-marked lynx were in densely stocked lodgepole pine stands where hares were abundant; the remainder were in Douglas-fir and western larch stands. Selection by lynx of dense lodgepole pine stands containing high numbers of snowshoe hares has also been demonstrated in north-central Washington (Koehler 1990). Lodgepole pine is a seral, fire-dependent species in boreal forests of the western mountains (Chapter 3) and appears to be preferred by lynx in northern portions of the Cascade Range and Rocky Mountains (Koehler et al. 1979; Koehler 1990; Chapter 10). Average fire frequency in the North Cascades of Washington is 109-137 years (Chapter 3); but within the 1,800 km^2 study area in north-central Washington, fires burned areas >2,500 ha (more than half of an average female's home range) at more frequent intervals (late 1800s, 1929, 1972, and 1994; Okanogan National Forest, unpublished). However, whether the persistence of lynx populations in this area (Chapter 8) is related to relatively short fire-return intervals is not known. Differences in fire ecology between northern and southern boreal forests and resulting implications for management of lynx habitat are discussed in detail in Chapters 3 and 15.

Early successional forests appear to be important for lynx in Nova Scotia. Snow tracking (Parker 1981) and radiotelemetry (Parker et al. 1983) studies on Cape Breton Island indicated that lynx selected early (5-15 years old) and advanced (16-30 years old) successional forests, followed by open mature conifer and open black spruce bog habitat types. Closed mature forests (both conifer and mixed conifer-hardwood), open mature mixed forests, riparian alder swales, and frozen lakes were used less than expected. During summer, use of successional habitat decreased and use of mature conifer habitat increased (Parker et al. 1983).

Parker (1981) found that lynx most strongly selected advanced successional forests, where hares were most abundant. However, among other habitat types, he found no consistent correlation between habitat selection and the relative abundance of snowshoe hares. Mature, mixed conifer-hardwood forests with relatively high hare populations were selected against, whereas open, mature coniferous forests with relatively few hares were used more often than expected. Parker speculated that factors other than prey abundance may influence habitat selection by lynx and suggested that lynx use open mature conifer forests, where hares are relatively scarce, for cover and travel. Parker also speculated that lynx use early and advanced successional stages, where hares are abundant, for hunting.

Koehler and Brittell (1990) described similar habitat use in north-central Washington; snow tracking revealed that lynx generally traveled in straight, non-meandering paths in mature forest stands with sparse understory cover, indicating that lynx were using stands where hares were scarce but not actively hunting in them. Such forest conditions were identified as "travel habitat" that provided security cover when lynx move between foraging or den sites (Koehler and Brittell 1990). From snow tracking, Koehler (1990) found that lynx traveled the edges of meadows but only crossed meadows where openings were less than 100 m wide. During winter, lynx were also observed traveling through silviculturally thinned stands with 420-640 trees/ha (Koehler 1990). From these observations, Koehler and Brittell (1990) speculated that lynx avoid open areas where security cover is lacking but that 420-640 trees/ha could provide adequate travel cover; during snow-free periods, shrub habitats may also be used for travel by lynx.

Koehler (1990) located four maternal den sites used by two females in north-central Washington, all of which were located on north-facing slopes in mature (>250 years) forest stands with an overstory of spruce, subalpine fir, and lodgepole pine that contained an average of 40 logs/50 m. A maternal den in Wyoming was located in a mature subalpine fir stand that had relatively dense understory cover from large woody debris and saplings (Chapter 11).

In the taiga, lynx typically prefer forested stands containing the densest populations of snowshoe hares; such habitats are generally represented by older (>20 years) regenerating stands of both natural and human origin, or mature stands with a dense understory (Chapter 9). However, even if hares are abundant, lynx generally do not occur in forested stands with extremely dense understories or in shrub-dominated sites, probably because lynx cannot hunt effectively in such stands (Chapter 9). Tangles of blowdown in mature forests are used for den sites, but recent work in the Yukon demonstrates that lynx may den in younger, regenerating stands (30 years old) containing blowdown or structures that provide similar cover, such as roots and dense vegetation (Chapter 9). The critical habitat component for maternal dens appears to be understory structure that provides security and thermal cover for kittens. Suitable understory structures are generally found in unmanaged, mature forest stands, but may also occur in early successional forests where windthrow and snags are present.

Although lynx in southern boreal regions generally select forested stands having abundant snowshoe hare populations, they also occasionally use habitats with relatively low numbers of hares. In contrast to findings from the taiga, habitats used by lynx in the southern portion of their range may include those that are used primarily for traveling between foraging sites and others that are used primarily for hunting (Koehler and Brittell 1990; Parker 1981). Although these speculations are based on relatively few data, habitats that contain abundant snowshoe hare populations in southern boreal forests may be more patchy and disjunct in distribution (Dolbeer and Clark 1975; Wolff 1980, 1982), forcing lynx to travel among foraging patches to find adequate prey. Further research on habitat use relative to the abundance of snowshoe hares is needed to evaluate this hypothesis.

Spatial Organization

Home Range

Ten studies (Brainerd 1985, unpublished; Brittell et al. 1989, unpublished; Koehler et al. 1979; Koehler 1990; Mech 1980; Parker et al. 1983; Smith 1984, unpublished; Chapters 11 [two studies] and 12) have documented spatial organization of resident lynx populations in southern regions using radio-telemetry, but most were short-duration studies involving relatively few individuals (n = 1-8; Table 13.2). Home range studies vary considerably in design, implementation, and analysis resulting in many potential sources of bias. These include differences in the sex, age, and reproductive status of study animals, the status of prey populations, season of study, duration of study, sample size, sampling technique, and analytical approach, among others. Consequently, comparisons among studies are problematic and results should be interpreted cautiously.

Table 13.2–Mean home range sizes of Canada lynx in North America.

Location	Mean home range size (km^2)	Calculation method and season	Source
Southern boreal forests			
Southern Canadian Rocky Mountains	277 ± 71[a] (male; n = 3) 135 ± 124 (female; n = 3)	95% Minimum Convex Polygon (MCP), annual	Chapter 12
North-central Washington	49 ± 25 (male; n = 8) 37 ± 26 (female; n = 7)	100% MCP, annual	Brittell et al. 1989, unpublished
North-central Washington	69 ± 28 (male; n = 5) 39 ± 2 (female; n = 2)	100% MCP, annual	Koehler 1990
North-central Montana	36 (male; n = 1)	100% MCP, March-October	Koehler et al. 1979
North-central Montana	133 (male and female; n = 4)	100% MCP, annual	Smith 1984, unpublished
North-central Montana	122 (male; n = 6) 43 (female; n = 3)	100% MCP, annual	Brainerd 1985, unpublished
North-central Montana	238 ± 99 (male; n = 4) 115 ± 50 (female; n = 2)	95% MCP, annual	Chapter 11
West-central Wyoming	90 (male; n = 1) 66 (female; n = 1)	95% MCP, winter	Chapter 11
West-central Wyoming	91 (male; n = 1) 68 (female; n = 1)	95% MCP, summer	Chapter 11
Northeastern Minnesota	194 (n = 2) 87 (n = 2)	100% MCP, annual	Mech 1980
Cape Breton Island, Nova Scotia	26 (male; n = 1) 32 (female; n = 1)	100% MCP[b], summer	Parker et al. 1983
Cape Breton Island, Nova Scotia	12 (male; n = 1) 19 (female; n = 1)	100% MCP[b], winter	Parker et al. 1983
Northern boreal forests during low snowshoe hare densities			
Southwestern Manitoba	221 (male; n = 1) 158 (female; n = 2)	100% MCP[b], annual	Carbyn and Patriquin 1983
South-central Northwest Territories	26 ± 5 (male; n = 8) 44 ± 14 (male; n = 2) 25 ± 5 (female; n = 8) 63 ± 28 (female; n = 2)	95% MCP, annual, 1991-92 95% MCP, annual, 1992-93 95% MCP, annual, 1991-92 95% MCP, annual, 1992-93	Poole 1994

(con.)

Table 13.2–(Con.)

Location	Mean home range size (km^2)	Calculation method and season	Source
South-central Yukon	119 $\pm$ 189 (male; $n = 6$)	95% MCP, annual, 1992-93	Slough and Mowat 1996
	266 $\pm$ 106 (male; $n = 2$)	95% MCP, annual, 1993-94	
	23 $\pm$ 7 (female; $n = 10$)	95% MCP, annual, 1992-93	
	507 $\pm$ 297 (female; $n = 4$)	95% MCP, annual, 1993-94	
Southwestern Yukon	28 $\pm$ 5 (male; $n = 4$)	95% MCP, annual, 1992-93	M. O'Donoghue,
	35 (male; $n = 1$)	95% MCP, annual, 1993-94	personal communication
	40 $\pm$ 11 (male; $n = 2$)	95% MCP, annual, 1994-95	
	24 $\pm$ 16 (female; $n = 3$)	95% MCP, annual, 1992-93	
	34 (female; $n = 1$)	95% MCP, annual, 1993-94	
	45 (female; $n = 2$)	95% MCP, annual, 1994-95	
Interior Alaska	160 $\pm$ 38 (male; $n = 5$)	95% MCP, annual, 1991-92	Perham 1995, unpublished
	183 $\pm$ 66 (male; $n = 6$)	95% MCP, annual, 1992-93	
	30 $\pm$ 9 (female; $n = 3$)	95% MCP, annual, 1991-92	
	47 $\pm$ 23 (female; $n = 23$)	95% MCP, annual, 1992-93	
Northern boreal forests during high snowshoe hare densities			
South-central Northwest Territories	36 $\pm$ 8 (male; $n = 7$)	95% MCP, annual, 1989-90	Poole 1994
	17 $\pm$ 2 (male; $n = 13$)	95% MCP, annual, 1990-91	
	21 $\pm$ 6 (female; $n = 4$)	95% MCP, annual, 1989-90	
	18 $\pm$ 3 (female; $n = 10$)	95% MCP, annual, 1990-91	
Southwestern Yukon	14 $\pm$ 1 (male; $n = 2$)	90% MCP, annual	Ward and Krebs 1985
	13 $\pm$ 7 (female; $n = 2$)		
South-central Yukon	48 $\pm$ 26 (male; $n = 7$)	95% MCP, annual, 1989-90	Slough and Mowat 1996
	44 $\pm$ 23 (male; $n = 12$)	95% MCP, annual, 1990-91	
	20 $\pm$ 9 (female; $n = 4$)	95% MCP, annual, 1989-90	
	13 $\pm$ 4 (female; $n = 13$)	95% MCP, annual, 1990-91	
Southwestern Yukon	24 $\pm$ 9 (male; $n = 7$)	95% MCP, annual, 1990-91	M. O'Donoghue,
	39 $\pm$ 51 (male; $n = 7$)	95% MCP, annual, 1991-92	personal communication
	17 $\pm$ 14 (female; $n = 4$)	95% MCP, annual, 1990-91	
	17 $\pm$ 7 (female; $n = 4$)	95% MCP, annual, 1991-92	
Kenai Peninsula, Alaska	225 $\pm$ 220 (male; $n = 6$)	100% MCP[b], annual	Kesterson 1988,
	107 $\pm$ 53 (female; $n = 8$)		unpublished

[a]Standard deviation, if available from source.
[b]Proportion of points used not specified; assumed to be 100%.

In general, lynx home ranges in southern boreal forests are large compared to those reported from the taiga during times of high snowshoe hare densities (Table 13.2). Using only annual home range estimates from studies with sample sizes ≥ 3 listed in Table 13.2, the average mean home range size for males is 151 km^2 in southern boreal forests, 103 km^2 in the taiga during low hare densities, and 62 km^2 in the taiga during high hare densities. The average mean home range size for females in southern boreal forests is 72 km^2, whereas in the taiga, it is 109 km^2 during hare population lows and 30 km^2 during hare highs.

Use of centrally located "core" home ranges, where activities were concentrated, was reported from north-central Washington and Nova Scotia (Brittell et al. 1989, unpublished; Parker et al. 1983). In most studies, males used vacated territories when a neighboring male died or emigrated, and male ranges overlapped extensively with those of one to three females (Brittell et al. 1989, unpublished; Koehler 1990; Parker et al. 1983; Chapter 11). In Montana, home ranges of juveniles overlapped those of adults regardless of sex (Brainerd 1985, unpublished) but, in Nova Scotia, the home range of a juvenile female was adjacent to those of an adult male and an adult female during both winter and summer (Parker et al. 1983). Although factors affecting the selection of home ranges at the landscape scale are largely unknown, home range boundaries in Washington generally occurred along ridges and major rivers (G. Koehler, unpublished); major highways may also define home range boundaries (Chapter 12).

Few studies have investigated seasonal changes in home range use, and results are inconsistent (Table 13.2). In Wyoming, home ranges for both the male and female lynx were similar in size during winter and summer. In Montana, Brainerd (1985, unpublished) suggested that summer home ranges were much smaller than annual home ranges for both males and females, and Smith (1984, unpublished) reported the largest home ranges during the spring breeding season. However, home ranges for both the male and female lynx studied in Nova Scotia were smaller during winter than in summer, and Koehler (1990) reported that lynx in north-central Washington occupied the same home ranges for two or more consecutive years.

As reported for lynx populations in the taiga (Chapter 9), estimated home range sizes for lynx in southern boreal forests vary substantially and appear to be determined by numerous factors. However, relatively large home ranges appear to be characteristic of southern lynx populations, especially in the western mountains (Table 13.2). Both male and female home ranges in southern boreal forests are comparable to those occurring in the taiga during times of hare scarcity, and are substantially larger than those reported from the taiga during high snowshoe hare densities. In the north, lynx maintain similar-sized home ranges during most phases of the hare cycle but will expand home ranges when hare populations decline to low levels (Chapter 9). In most southern boreal forests, reported hare densities are similar to those occurring during population lows in the north (Chapters 6 and 7; but see Parker et al. 1983). Thus, as in the north after hare populations have crashed, lynx in southern boreal regions probably occupy relatively large home ranges in response to low-density hare populations.

Exploratory Movements

Occasionally, lynx in southern populations make what appear to be "exploratory" movements in which they make long-distance movements beyond their normal home range boundaries and subsequently return to their home range. Among eight lynx (six males, two females) studied in Montana, one juvenile and three adult males made exploratory movements ranging from 17 to 38 km in straight-line distance (Chapter 11). The duration of exploratory movements varied from one week to several months. All adult movements were initiated in July, but the juvenile made two exploratory movements; one between 18 March and 2 April and a second from about 21 July to 20 August. In the Wyoming study, an adult male left his home range in mid-June and returned in early September and an adult female left hers in early July and returned by early August; the geographic extent of these movements is unknown, however (Chapter 11). In the southern Canadian Rockies, a juvenile female made an exploratory movement of 38 km in straight-line distance in the fall prior to dispersing (C. Apps, personal communication).

Exploratory movements of this kind have not been reported from the taiga (Chapter 9). We speculate that in montane boreal forests, the distribution of high-quality lynx habitat is patchy and fragmented due to high amounts of topographic relief and variation in habitat conditions resulting from natural disturbance processes (Chapter 3). Under such conditions, dispersal in different directions would be expected to have varying probabilities of success. Thus, in montane systems with high amounts of spatial heterogeneity, dispersal success may be enhanced by exploratory movements to locate suitable habitat.

Dispersal

Dispersal is the movement of a organism (either juvenile or adult) from a place of residence to its first or subsequent breeding site (Shields 1987). Data on lynx dispersal in southern boreal forests are scanty and anecdotal in nature, and no successful dispersals (i.e., where a lynx has bred after moving to a new location) have been reported from southern boreal forests. Consequently, presumed dispersals may simply represent long-distance movements that were cut short when the animal died. Between late April and November, a female lynx dispersed a distance of 325 km from Montana to British Columbia, where it was trapped (Brainerd 1985, unpublished). A male lynx dispersed 97 km in Montana before it was trapped (Smith 1984, unpublished). In north-central Washington, an adult male and female lynx that were both resident in the study area for at least a year dispersed north into British Columbia, where they were trapped 616 and 80 km north of the study area, respectively (Brittell et al. 1989, unpublished; J. Brittell, personal communication). Apps (Chapter 12) described three dispersal movements in the southern Canadian Rockies, including a juvenile male that dispersed 44 km in March and then remained in the new location for 31 days before his death; a juvenile female that moved 17 km over three days in March and occupied the new area for 15 days before her death; and a juvenile female that dispersed 55 km before contact was lost. Mech (1977) reported a 483-km movement by a female lynx that was radio-marked in northeastern Minnesota in 1974 and trapped in western Ontario in 1977.

Dispersal distances reported from southern boreal forests are comparable to those in the taiga, where movements >100 km are considered typical (Chapter 9). Apps (Chapter 12) suggested that steep terrain and the Trans-Canada Highway may affect dispersal movements. However, four of five lynx that dispersed in Montana, Washington, and Minnesota (Brainerd 1985, unpublished; Brittell et al. 1989, unpublished; Mech 1980; Smith 1984, unpublished) crossed either two- or four-lane highways and major rivers before they were trapped. Mowat et al. (Chapter 9) also reported that dispersing lynx in northern forests often crossed roads and large rivers and lakes, even during the snow-free season.

Demographic Characteristics

The most reliable information available on demographic characteristics for southern lynx populations comes from the successive field studies conducted by Brittell et al. (1989, unpublished) and Koehler (1990) in north-central Washington in the 1980s. Brittell et al. (1989, unpublished) monitored a total of 23 lynx with radiotelemetry in north-central Washington from 1980 to 1983. Among 12 resident females, none were known to have given birth to kittens during the course of the study. However, snow tracking indicated that an unmarked female was accompanied by two kittens in the winter of 1980-1981 and again in 1982-1983; no tracks of kittens were found in 1981-1982. Snow tracking was not conducted in the winter of 1983-1984 but, in August 1984 after field work was terminated, kittens were observed on two separate occasions: one radio-marked and one unmarked female were each accompanied by two kittens in or near the study area. Thus, from 1980 to 1984 at least eight kittens (mean litter size = two) were produced in a population estimated to contain 23 resident lynx each year of the three-year study. The study area was 1,161 km^2 in extent, resulting in an estimated density of 2.0 lynx/100 km^2. Among radio-marked lynx, 12% were identified as transients; thus, total lynx density, including kittens and transients, was estimated at 2.4 lynx/100 km². During the course of this study, three females and one male died from natural causes; the mean annual mortality rate for radio-marked lynx was estimated at 11% (range = 0-29%).

Koehler (1990) continued radiotelemetry work on Brittell et al.'s study area from 1985 to 1987, monitoring a total of seven lynx (five males, two females). During both years of the study, 15 adults were known to occupy the central portion of the study area (648 km²), at an estimated density of 2.3 adults/100 km². No kittens were observed in the study area during winter 1985-1986, but in 1986-1987, snow tracking indicated that four kittens were present in the study area, resulting in an estimated mean annual density for adults and kittens of 2.6 lynx/100 km². In 1986, both radio-marked females had litters of three and four kittens each. Both females gave birth again in 1987, one to a single kitten and the other to at least one kitten (actual litter size could not be determined); thus, mean litter size over both years of the study was at least 2.7 kittens. In addition, an uncollared female was accompanied by three kittens in the winter of 1986-1987. From snow tracking in the winters of 1986-1987 and 1987-1988, Koehler determined that only one of eight kittens from the three litters of known size survived to the following winter, resulting in an estimated kitten mortality rate of 88%. Two radio-marked adult males died during the course of the study, one from predation and another from unknown causes. Annual mortality rates for radio-marked adult lynx were 27% in 1986 and 0% in 1987. Thus, the estimated mortality rate for kittens was six to seven times higher than the mean mortality rate for radio-marked adults.

Both reproductive rates and kitten survival rates appear to be similarly low in other regions of the southern boreal forest where lynx have been studied. None of three adult female lynx captured by Apps (Chapter 12) in the southern Canadian Rockies in November of 1997 or 1998 were travelling with kittens; however, one radio-marked female was observed with a kitten in August 1998. Four unmarked family groups were detected in the study area (>3,000 km²) in 1997, each of which contained two kittens. Both kittens (one male, one female) from one of the family groups were subsequently radio-marked, but neither survived to the spring of 1998. All resident adults survived through both years of the study, but a dispersing female kitten and a transient juvenile male died of starvation in the spring of 1998; a male kitten was killed by a predator in December 1997. None of the three adult female lynx monitored with radiotelemetry by Brainerd (1985, unpublished) in Montana from 1982 to 1984 gave birth to kittens. Only one out of four female lynx monitored during 1998 in Montana was known to have given birth (Chapter 11); after radio contact with this female was lost during the breeding season, she was relocated in late September 1998 with two kittens. The adult female radio-marked in Wyoming (Chapter 11) gave birth to a litter of four kittens (two males, two females) on about 27 May; all four were still alive on 14 June when they were ear-tagged, but none survived into the winter.

Other information on productivity in lynx populations in southern boreal forests comes from carcass studies. Brainerd (1985, unpublished) examined placental scars and corpora lutea in 18 female lynx carcasses from Montana ranging in age from 1.5 to 9.5 years. Based on placental scars, the average litter size increased with age: yearlings had a mean litter size of 1.75 (range = 1-3), whereas mean litter size for adults was 3.25 (range = 1-5). Ovulation rates were also higher for adults, increasing from 3.22 (range = 2-5) for yearlings, to 5.33 (range = 2-9) for adults. The pregnancy rate for adults was 100%, whereas only 44.4% of uteri from yearlings contained placental scars.

Parker et al. (1983) examined 154 lynx carcasses obtained from trappers in Nova Scotia over three winters: 1977-1978 ($n = 42$), 1978-1979 ($n = 57$), and 1979-1980 ($n = 55$). The oldest lynx were 11 years old, but <6% of the sample was older than six years in any year. Over the three years of the study, the percentage of kittens in the sample declined from 29% to 9%, and 2%. Based on counts of placental scars, mean litter size was 3.2 for yearlings and 3.6 for adults; neither differed significantly among years. Overall pregnancy rates were 68% for adults and 27% for yearlings. However, yearling pregnancy rates declined from 67% in 1977-1978 to 29% in 1978-1979 and 0% in 1979-1980, whereas adult pregnancy rates only declined from 75% to 64%. Declines in the overall breeding and recruitment rates, as well as the reproductive success of yearlings, was attributed to a dramatic decrease (about six-fold in the best habitats) in the abundance of snowshoe hares over the course of the study (Parker et al. 1983).

With few exceptions, demographic parameters reported from southern boreal forests are comparable to those occurring in the taiga during times of hare scarcity. The low in-utero litter sizes (3.25-3.6), low yearling pregnancy rates (27-44.4%), low yearling litter sizes (1.75-3.2), low kitten production, high kitten mortality rate (88%), and low lynx densities (Table 13.3) reported from southern populations are all characteristic of northern populations during hare lows. In the North, peak lynx densities vary from eight to 45 lynx/100 km^2 depending on habitat conditions, but drop to <3 lynx/100 km^2 during hare population lows, regardless of habitat quality (Chapter 9). Density estimates for lynx in north-central Washington ranged from 2.0 to 2.6 lynx/100 km^2 and remained relatively constant over the course of the seven-year study (Brittell et al. 1989, unpublished; Koehler 1990). The apparent stability of this low-density population has led to speculation that, because hare populations also occur at low levels in most southern boreal forests, lynx populations in the western mountains may not exhibit the cyclic fluctuations characterisitic of northern populations (Koehler and

Table 13.3–Densities of Canada lynx populations in North America.

Study area	Lynx density (lynx/100 km^2)	Source
Southern boreal forests		
North-central Washington	2	Brittell et al. 1989, unpublished
North-central Washington	3	Koehler 1990
Cape Breton Island, Nova Scotia	20[a]	Parker et al. 1983
Northern boreal forests during low snowshoe hare densities		
Central Alberta	2	Nellis et al. 1972, Brand et al. 1976
South-central Northwest Territories	3	Poole 1994
South-central Yukon	3	Slough and Mowat 1996
Southwestern Yukon	2	O'Donoghue et al. 1997
Kenai Peninsula, Alaska	4[b]	Kesterson 1988, unpublished
Interior Alaska	2-6	Stephenson 1986, unpublished
Northern boreal forests during high snowshoe hare densities		
Central Alberta	10	Nellis et al. 1972, Brand et al. 1976
South-central Northwest Territories	30	Poole 1994
South-central Yukon	45	Slough and Mowat 1996
Southwestern Yukon	17	O'Donoghue et al. 1997
Kenai Peninsula, Alaska	18	Kesterson 1988, unpublished

[a]Snowshoe hare densities were comparable to those occurring during population highs in northern boreal forests.
[b]Calculated from author's description of lynx abundance.

Aubry 1994). However, we caution that data bearing on this hypothesis are extremely limited; furthermore, a recent review of snowshoe hare density data in southern boreal regions (Chapter 7) and lynx trapping records from Washington, Montana, and New Hampshire (Chapter 8) suggest that both snowshoe hare and lynx populations may fluctuate more in number in the south than believed previously. Whether observed patterns reflect changes in resident lynx populations or immigrations from other areas, however, is unknown (Chapter 8). Understanding the nature of lynx population dynamics in southern boreal forests is a critical research need.

Human Impacts

Trapping

Little is known about the effects of trapping or shooting mortality on lynx populations in southern boreal forests. However, in recent years, concern over the conservation status of lynx throughout the contiguous United

States has resulted in severe restrictions on legal harvest; all states except Montana have either given lynx complete protection or closed their trapping season. In Montana, a statewide quota of 135 lynx was imposed in 1982; this quota was lowered steadily until 1991, when it was reduced to two lynx per year. Although legal harvest is no longer a conservation concern, human-caused mortality is believed to be additive in the low-density lynx populations characteristic of southern boreal forests (Koehler 1990; Table 13.3). If so, illegal or incidental harvest could significantly reduce population numbers of lynx in southern regions.

Roads and Trails

Roads into areas occupied by lynx may pose a threat to lynx from incidental harvest or poaching (Koehler and Brittell 1990), increased access during winter for competing carnivores, especially coyotes (Chapter 4), disturbance or mortality from vehicles, and loss of habitat. Although we know little about the indirect effects of roads or trails on lynx, none of the 89 lynx studied with radiotelemetry in Washington (Brittell et al. 1989, unpublished; Koehler 1990), Montana (Brainerd 1985, unpublished; Koehler et al. 1979; Smith 1984, unpublished; Chapter 11), Wyoming (Chapter 11), the southern Canadian Rockies (Chapter 12), Minnesota (Mech 1980), or Nova Scotia (Parker et al. 1983) were killed in vehicle collisions. Among 37 radio-marked animals that died during these studies, 19 were shot or trapped, eight died of starvation, six from predation, and four from unknown natural causes. Vehicle collisions were a significant mortality factor among 83 lynx translocated into the Adirondack Mountains of New York from the Yukon between 1989 and 1991; in the two years that translocated lynx were monitored with radiotelemetry, 16 were road-killed (K. Gustafson, personal communication). However, because translocated lynx may be especially vulnerable to vehicle collisions (Brocke et al. 1991), the high incidence of road-kills among lynx in this reintroduction effort is probably not representative of resident lynx populations in southern boreal forests.

In Nova Scotia, Parker (1981) found from snow tracking that road edges and forest trails were often followed by lynx for considerable distances, and similar observations were made during winter in Washington for roads less than 15 m wide (Koehler and Brittell 1990). From analysis of sequential telemetry locations for lynx in Washington, McKelvey et al. (Chapter 10) concluded that selection or avoidance of roads could not be inferred. Roads in the study area were of primitive standards that received little use in summer but were frequently used by snowmobilers in winter. Ongoing research by Apps (Chapter 12) in the southern Canadian Rockies suggests, however, that paved roads may have an influence on lynx spatial organization.

The 70% adaptive kernel home-range contour for two males and two females coincided with the Trans-Canada Highway; for another male, it coincided with a secondary highway.

Mowat et al. (Chapter 9) reported similar observations concerning roads in northern boreal forests; lynx appeared to tolerate moderate levels of snowmobile traffic, readily crossed highways, and established home ranges in proximity to roads. Several studies of lynx in the taiga have been conducted in areas of relatively dense rural human populations and agricultural development, suggesting that lynx can tolerate moderate levels of human disturbance.

Predation and Competition

Only a few instances of predation on lynx have been reported from southern boreal forests, but all are believed to have been by felids. Two of six mortalities reported from ongoing radiotelemetry studies in Montana were predation by mountain lions; both occurred during the snow-free period, including an adult male killed in May and a juvenile male killed in October (Chapter 11). An adult female lynx found dead in Montana in late January during an earlier study was believed to have been killed by a mountain lion (Koehler et al. 1979). A juvenile female lynx found dead in November in north-central Washington was believed to have died from a bite on the top of her skull by either a bobcat or a lynx (Brittell et al. 1989, unpublished), and an adult male was apparently killed by an unknown predator in January (Koehler 1990). In the southern Canadian Rockies, a male kitten was apparently killed by an un-marked male lynx in December (Chapter 12).

Cannibalism has also been reported from the taiga and generally occurs during periods of low hare abundance. In the north, wolverine, wolves, and coyotes have also been reported to prey on lynx (Chapter 9). Because mountain lions do not occur in most portions of the northern boreal forest or eastern United States (Dixon 1984), the potential effects of predation or competition from mountain lions are unique to lynx populations in the western mountains. Mountain lions are known to occupy high-elevation lynx habitats during both summer and winter. In a comparative study of habitat use by mountain lions, bobcats, and coyotes in central Idaho, Koehler and Hornocker (1991) found that a larger proportion of mountain lion locations (28%) were in high-elevation subalpine fir-whitebark pine habitats during summer than either bobcat (10%) or coyote (3%) locations. They also noted that, because of their body size, mountain lions could negotiate deeper snows than could other predators, enabling the mountain lions to better exploit higher elevations and mesic habitats where deep snows accumulated.

Mountain lions are present in lynx summer home ranges in Montana (Chapter 11), but interactions between them have not been studied.

Lynx and bobcats are generally believed to be spatially separated by snow depth, but several cases of these two species occupying the same area and presumably competing with one another for food and space have been documented in the western mountains (Smith 1984, unpublished; Brittell et al. 1989, unpublished). Parker et al. (1983) reported that the contraction of lynx range on Cape Breton Island in Nova Scotia was coincident with colonization of the lowlands by bobcats; in 1983, lynx only occurred in the highest elevation areas where bobcats had not established themselves. However, this appears to represent the authors' speculations only; no data to support this statement are presented. Although coyotes are potentially significant competitors of lynx (Chapter 4), evidence indicating that coyotes have negatively affected lynx populations in southern boreal forests is lacking.

Competition between lynx and other mammalian or avian predators does not appear to strongly influence lynx populations in the taiga (Chapter 9), probably because of the cyclic nature of snowshoe hare populations (which mediates the effects of exploitation competition), and the relative scarcity of many of the mammalian predators likely to compete strongly with lynx (Chapter 4). Buskirk et al. (Chapter 4) have discussed the potential for detrimental effects on lynx populations from increased competition with generalist predators in landscapes disturbed and/or fragmented by human activities. If such competition can have a significant effect on lynx populations, we speculate that it may be of particular concern in western montane regions of the southern boreal forest. In that area, lynx are sympatric with the three potentially strongest competitors: mountain lions (interference competition), bobcats, and coyotes (exploitation competition), all of which are generally increasing in number (Chapter 4). However, this concern is largely conjectural; data on the effects of sympatric carnivores on lynx populations in southern boreal forests are rare.

Conclusions

In this chapter, we considered all lynx studies conducted south of the Polar Ecoregions in North America (Bailey 1998), including those in Nova Scotia, Minnesota, and the western montane regions. However, results from Nova Scotia differed strongly in many ways from studies conducted in other southern boreal forests (see Tables 13.1, 13.2, 13.3), and were most similar to studies conducted in the taiga during snowshoe hare population peaks. Results from western montane regions, where snowshoe hare populations generally occurred at relatively low densities, were similar among studies, and generally comparable to those reported from the taiga during hare population lows. For these reasons, results from lynx studies in Nova Scotia are probably more representative of taiga populations than those in the western montane regions.

In general, southern lynx populations appear to be distinguished from those in the taiga primarily by differences in the quality and distribution of available habitat: their primary prey, the snowshoe hare, typically occurs at very low densities and, because of differences in topography and natural disturbance regimes, habitats containing abundant snowshoe hare populations are more patchily distributed than in the taiga. As a result, their food habits, home range sizes, densities, and reproductive characteristics are generally comparable to those reported for northern lynx populations during times of hare scarcity. Differences in lynx ecology between populations in the taiga and those occurring in southern boreal forests appear to be related primarily to the use of alternative prey species, the effect of habitat patchiness on movements, reproduction and survival, and the potential effects of different communities of predators and competitors on lynx populations.

Literature Cited

Adams, L. 1959. An analysis of a population of snowshoe hares in northwestern Montana. Ecological Monographs 29:141-170.

Bailey, R. G. 1998. Ecoregions map of North America: explanatory note. USDA Forest Service, Miscellaneous Publication No. 1548.

Barash, D. P. 1971. Cooperative hunting in the lynx. Journal of Mammalogy 52:480.

Bittner, S. L. and O. J. Rongstad. 1984. Snowshoe hare and allies. Pages 146-163 in J. A. Chapman and G. A. Feldhamer, eds. Wild mammals of North America. Johns Hopkins University Press, Baltimore, MD.

Brainerd, S. M. 1985. Reproductive ecology of bobcats and lynx in western Montana. Unpublished M.S. Thesis, University of Montana, Missoula, MT.

Brand, C. J. and L. B. Keith. 1979. Lynx demography during a snowshoe hare decline in Alberta. Journal of Wildlife Management 43:827-849.

Brand, C. J., L. B. Keith, and C. A. Fischer. 1976. Lynx responses to changing snowshoe hare densities in central Alberta. Journal of Wildlife Management 40:416-428.

Brittell, J. D., R. J. Poelker, S. J. Sweeney, and G. M. Koehler. 1989. Native cats of Washington, Section III: lynx. Unpublished, Washington Department of Wildlife, Olympia, WA.

Brocke, R. H. 1982. Restoration of the lynx Lynx canadensis in Adirondack Park: a problem analysis and recommendations. Unpublished, Federal Aid Project E-1-3 and W-105-R. New York State Department of Environmental Conservation Study XII, Job 5.

Brocke, R. H., K. A. Gustafson, and L. B. Fox. 1991. Restoration of large predators: potentials and problems. Pages 303-315 *in* Challenges in the conservation of biological resources. a practitioner's guide. D. J. Decker, M. E. Krasny, G. R. Goff, C. R. Smith, and D. W. Gross, eds. Westview Press, Boulder, CO.

Carbyn, L. N. and D. Patriquin. 1983. Observations of home range sizes, movements and social organization of lynx, *Lynx canadensis*, in Riding Mountain National Park, Manitoba. Canadian Field-Naturalist 97:262-267.

Dixon, K. R. 1984. Mountain lion. Pages 711-727 *in* J. A. Chapman and G. A. Feldhamer, eds. Wild mammals of North America. Johns Hopkins University Press, Baltimore, MD.

Dolbeer, R. A. and W. R. Clark. 1975. Population ecology of snowshoe hares in the central Rocky Mountains. Journal of Wildlife Management 39:535-549.

Elton, C. and M. Nicholson. 1942. The ten-year cycle in numbers of the lynx in Canada. Journal of Animal Ecology 11:215-244.

Halfpenny, J.C., S. J. Bissell, and D. M. Nead. 1989. Status of the lynx (*Felis lynx*, Felidae) in Colorado with comments on its distribution in Western United States. Unpublished. Institute of Arctic and Alpine Research, University of Colorado, Boulder, CO.

Keith, L. B. 1963. Wildlife's ten-year cycle. University of Wisconsin Press, Madison, WI.

Kesterson, B. A. 1988. Lynx home range and spatial organization in relation to population density and prey abundance. Unpublished M.S. Thesis, University of Alaska, Fairbanks, AK.

Koehler, G. M. 1990. Population and habitat characteristics of lynx and snowshoe hares in north central Washington. Canadian Journal of Zoology 68:845-851.

Koehler, G. M. and K. B. Aubry. 1994. Lynx. Pages 74-98 *in* L. F. Ruggiero, K. B. Aubry, S. W. Buskirk, L. J. Lyon, and W. J. Zielinski, eds. The scientific basis for conserving forest carnivores: american marten, fisher, lynx and wolverine in the Western United States. USDA Forest Service General Technical Report RM-254.

Koehler, G. M. and J. D. Brittell. 1990. Managing spruce-fir habitat for lynx and snowshoe hares. Journal of Forestry 88:10-14.

Koehler, G. M. and M. G. Hornocker. 1991. Seasonal resource use among mountain lions, bobcats, and coyotes. Journal of Mammalogy 72:391-396.

Koehler, G. M., M. G. Hornocker, and H. S. Hash. 1979. Lynx movements and habitat use in Montana. Canadian Field-Naturalist 93:441-442.

Litvaitis, J. A., D. Kingman, Jr., J. Lanier, and E. Orff. 1991. Status of lynx in New Hampshire. Transactions of the Northeast Section of the Wildlife Society 48:70-75.

McCord, C. M. and J. E. Cardoza. 1984. Bobcat and lynx. Pages 728-766 *in* J. A. Chapman and G. A. Feldhamer, eds. Wild Mammals of North America. Johns Hopkins University Press, Baltimore, MD.

Mech, L. D. 1977. Record movement of a Canadian lynx. Journal of Mammalogy 58:676-677.

Mech, L. D. 1980. Age, sex, reproduction, and spatial organization of lynxes colonizing northeastern Minnesota. Journal of Mammalogy 61:261-267.

Nellis, C. H., S. P. Wetmore, and L. B. Keith. 1972. Lynx-prey interactions in central Alberta. Journal of Wildlife Management 36:320-329.

O'Donoghue, M., S. Boutin, C. J. Krebs, and E. J. Hofer. 1997. Numerical response of coyotes and lynx to the snowshoe hare cycle. Oikos 80:150-162.

O'Donoghue, M., S. Boutin, C. J. Krebs, G. Zuleta, D. L. Murray, and E. J. Hofer. 1998. Functional response of coyotes and lynx to the snowshoe hare cycle. Ecology 79:1193-1208.

Parker, G. R. 1981. Winter habitat use and hunting activities of lynx (*Lynx canadensis*) on Cape Breton Island, Nova Scotia. Pages 221-248 *in* Worldwide Furbearer Conference proceedings. J. A. Chapman and D. Pursley, eds. Frostburg, MD.

Parker, G. R., J. W. Maxwell, and L. D. Morton. 1983. The ecology of the lynx (*Lynx canadensis*) on Cape Breton Island. Canadian Journal of Zoology 61:770-786.

Perham, C. T. 1995. Home range, habitat selection, and movements of lynx in eastern interior Alaska. Unpublished M.S. Thesis, University of Alaska, Fairbanks, AK.

Poole, K. G. 1994. Characteristics of an unharvested lynx population during a snowshoe hare decline. Journal of Wildlife Management 58:608-618.

Quinn, N. W. S. and G. Parker. 1987. Lynx. Pages 682-695 *in* Wild furbearer management and conservation in North America. M. Novak, J. A. Baker, M. E. Obbard, and B. Malloch, eds. Ministry of Natural Resources, Ontario, Canada.

Shields, W. M. 1987. Dispersal and mating systems: investigating their causal connections. Pages 3-24 *in* Mammalian dispersal patterns: the effects of social structure on population genetics. B. D. Chepko-Sade and Z. T. Halpin, eds. University of Chicago Press, Chicago.

Slough, B. G. and G. Mowat. 1996. Population dynamics of lynx in a refuge and interactions between harvested and unharvested populations. Journal of Wildlife Management 60:946-961.

Smith, D. S. 1984. Habitat use, home range, and movements of bobcats in western Montana. Unpublished M.S. Thesis, University of Montana, Missoula, MT.

Staples, W. R. 1995. Lynx and coyote diet and habitat relationships during a low hare population on the Kenai Peninsula, Alaska. Unpublished M.S. Thesis, University of Alaska, Fairbanks, AK.

Stephenson, R. O. 1986. Development of lynx population estimation techniques. Unpublished, Alaska Department of Fish and Game, Federal Aid in Wildlife Restoration, Final Report, Project W-22-5, Job 7.12R, Juneau, AK.

van Zyll de Jong, C. G. 1966. Food habits of the lynx in Alberta and the Mackenzie District, N.W.T. Canadian Field-Naturalist 80:18-23.

Ward, R. M. P. and C. J. Krebs. 1985. Behavioural responses of lynx to declining snowshoe hare abundance. Canadian Journal of Zoology 63:2817-2824.

Wolff, J. O. 1980. The role of habitat patchiness in the population dynamics of snowshoe hares. Ecological Monographs 50:111-130.

Wolff, J. O. 1982. Refugia, dispersal, predation, and geographic variation in snowshoe hare cycles. Pages 441-449 *in* K. Myers and C. D. MacInnes, eds. Proceedings of the World Lagomorph Conference, University of Guelph, Guelph, Ontario.

Chapter 14

Comparative Ecology of Lynx in North America

Steven W. Buskirk, Department of Zoology and Physiology,
University of Wyoming, P.O. Box 3166, Laramie, WY 82071

Leonard F. Ruggiero, USDA Forest Service, Rocky Mountain Research Station,
800 E. Beckwith, Missoula, MT 59801

Keith B. Aubry, USDA Forest Service, Pacific Northwest Research Station,
3625 93rd Ave. SW, Olympia, WA 98512

Dean E. Pearson, USDA Forest Service, Rocky Mountain Research Station,
800 E. Beckwith, Missoula, MT 59801

John R. Squires, USDA Forest Service, Rocky Mountain Research Station,
800 E. Beckwith, Missoula, MT 59801

Kevin S. McKelvey, USDA Forest Service, Rocky Mountain Research Station,
800 E. Beckwith, Missoula, MT 59801

Abstract—Lynx occur across a large geographic area, but have only been studied in a few locations, and this has led to extrapolation of understandings into areas with very divergent ecologies. We discuss ecological differences across the range of lynx, contrasting the patterns of climate, vegetation, disturbance dynamics and succession, and predator/prey relationships. In all these particulars, areas where lynx occur within the contiguous United States diverge from the well-studied areas of the taiga. We caution against uncritical application of ecological understandings derived from the North to southern lynx and we emphasize the potential importance of late-successional forests as habitat for hares, red squirrels, and lynx in the southern part of the range of the lynx.

Introduction

Our limited knowledge of lynx ecology in North America comes from only a few areas across a broad geographic range (Table 14.1). For example, we have much greater knowledge of lynx ecology in the taiga (Chapters 6, 9) than in southern boreal forests (Chapters 7, 13). Similarly, most of what is known about habitats of snowshoe hares comes from the north-central and northeastern United States. Understandings are therefore extrapolated to other sites that have different climatic, topographic, and vegetative conditions. Such extrapolations may be inappropriate in some cases and result in negative consequences for lynx conservation (Chapter 5). The comparative assessment of lynx ecology presented here explores this potential problem and identifies solutions. Although most extrapolations at issue are along a several thousand-kilometer ecological gradient from north to south, we also address extrapolations along the potentially more complex west-east gradient (for example from northeastern Washington to Colorado or from Montana to Maine).

Table 14.1–Frequently cited lynx studies according to topic and geographic area. Quality code describes the emphasis of the study: 1) primary topic of study, 2) major component of study, 3) minor component of study.

Topic	Alaska	Pacific Northwest	Yukon, NWT Alberta, Manitoba	Rocky Mountain Region	Northeastern and Northcentral U. S., and eastern Canada
Habitat relationships	Perham 1995 - 2 Paragi et al. 1997 - 1	Koehler 1990 - 2	Murray et al. 1994 - 1 Poole et al. 1996 - 1	Koehler et al. 1979 - 3 Smith 1984 - 3	Parker et al. 1983 - 3
Population dynamics and reproduction	O'Connor 1984 - 1		Elton and Nicholson 1942 - 1 Nellis et al. 1972 - 1 Brand and Keith 1979 - 1 Quinn and Thompson 1987 - 1 Poole 1994 - 1 Boutin et al. 1995 - 1 Slough and Mowat 1996 - 1 Mowat et al. 1996 - 1 O'Donoghue et al. 1997 - 1 Ranta et al. 1997 - 1 O'Donoghue et al. 1998b - 1	Brainerd 1985 — 2	Parker et al. 1983 - 2
Movements and home range	Kesterson 1988 - 1 Perham 1995 - 1 Bailey et al. 1986 - 3	Brittell et al. 1989 - 2 Koehler 1990 - 1	Carbyn and Patriquin 1983 - 1 Ward and Krebs 1985 - 1 Poole 1994 - 2 Slough and Mowat 1996 - 2	Smith 1984 - 3 Brainerd 1985 - 2 Chapter 11 - 2 Chapter 12 - 1	Saunders 1963b - 1 Mech 1980 - 1 Parker et al. 1983 - 2

(con.)

Table 14.1–Con.

Topic	Alaska	Pacific Northwest	Yukon, NWT Alberta, Manitoba	Rocky Mountain Region	Northeastern and Northcentral U. S., and eastern Canada
Habitat relationships of snowshoe hares	Bailey et al. 1986	Black 1965 Sullivan and Sullivan 1982, 1983, 1988 Koehler 1990, 1991		Adams 1959 Dolbeer and Clark 1975 Wolfe et al. 1982	Conroy et al. 1979 Orr and Dodds 1982 Buehler and Keith 1982 Parker 1984 Litvaitis et al. 1985 Parker 1986 Fuller and Heisey 1986 Monthey 1986 Rogowitz 1988 Scott and Yahner 1989 Thompson et al. 1989 Thompson and Curran 1995 Ferron and Ouellet 1992 St-Georges et al. 1995
Foraging behavior	Stephenson et al. 1991 - 1		Nellis and Keith 1968 Brand et al. 1976 - 2 Ward and Krebs 1985 Murray et al. 1995 O'Donoghue et al. 1998a		
Food habits	Kesterson 1988 - 2 Staples 1995 - 2	Koehler 1990 - 2	van Zyll de Jong 1966 - 1 Brand et al. 1976 - 1 Brand and Keith 1979 - 2 O'Donoghue et al. 1998a,b - 2	Chapter 12 - 2	Saunders 1963a - 1 Parker et al. 1983 - 2
Dispersal		Brittell et al. 1989 - 3	Ward and Krebs 1985 - 2 O'Donoghue et al. 1995 - 3 Slough and Mowat 1996 - 2 Poole 1997 - 1	Mech 1977 - 3 Brainerd 1985 - 3	
Predator and competitor interactions		Koehler et al. 1979 - 3	Murray and Boutin 1991 - 1 O'Donoghue et al. 1995 - (observations)	Chapter 11 - 3	

As the chapters in this book show, the ecological relationships and population dynamics of the lynx show similarities across its range (Chapters 8, 13). However, they also reflect significant differences in the environments occupied by lynx (Chapters 3, 9, 13), suggesting that there may be important geographical differences in lynx ecology. Therefore, we assess the nature and extent of regional variation in key biotic and abiotic gradients that appear to affect the lynx and its prey. We divide the chapter into five sections:

1. Direct climatic effects
2. Natural disturbance regimes, topography, and resulting landscape patterns
3. Forest successional pathways
4. Patterns of snowshoe hare and red squirrel abundance
5. Predator-prey communities

Direct Climatic Effects

Temperature and moisture regimes appear to limit the distribution of lynx at coarse and fine scales via differential effects on snowfall and habitat structure. In the North (Bailey's [1998] Polar Domain), frozen soils and permafrost generally hold water near the soil surface, favoring high densities of shrubs and young trees. Also, cold air holds relatively little moisture, so that snow is only moderately deep and very dry. These conditions are favorable for lynx and snowshoe hares. However, to the south, soil moisture in summer is lower, higher elevation forests experience higher evaporation rates, and mountain ranges cause patterns of soil moisture and snow deposition to be much more localized. Areas of boreal forest are therefore more patchily distributed in the southern part of the species' range (Chapters 3, 8). This may also mean that lynx favor more mesic north-facing aspects farther south, as was found on the Okanogan Plateau of Washington (Chapter 10).

Snow depths in boreal forests and their southern extensions generally increase from north to south, with the deepest snows generally found in southern Colorado. This is because colder northern air holds relatively less moisture than the warmer air farther south (Pruppacher and Klett 1978, Fig. 4.6). On the other hand, snow in southern lynx habitats may undergo more winter thaws, with subsequent formation of crusts, than snow in the taiga. Crusted snow would tend to remove the competitive advantage held by lynx, with their long limbs and low foot loadings (Chapter 4). Such an advantage or the lack thereof may contribute importantly to the success or failure of lynx populations in some parts of their range. Because of the fragmented nature of landscapes and heterogeneous distribution of topographic, climatic, and vegetative conditions in western forests, lynx and snowshoe hare habitats there are more prone to a metapopulation structure, which has important implications for their population ecology (Chapter 2). This condition is exacerbated by the presumably greater human-caused fragmentation of lynx habitat in the south.

In the East, the climax forest condition of deciduous or mixed deciduous/coniferous trees differs sharply from conditions in the West where succession tends toward coniferous trees. This difference is due to variable influences of climate, specifically the frequency of precipitation and the effects of elevation. But, in eastern North America, human influences have been pervasive so that few eastern forests at temperate latitudes are in a climax condition. As a result, many of the eastern forests that were lynx habitat in presettlement times are younger and mostly deciduous-dominated today.

Natural Disturbance Regimes, Topography, and Resulting Landscape Patterns

Successional stage is commonly regarded as a correlate of habitat quality for snowshoe hares and strongly reflects natural disturbance regimes. The taiga is extensive, has fairly homogeneous climate and physiognomy, and exhibits little topographic relief (Elliot-Fisk 1988). Kelsall et al. (1977) described the remarkably uniform snow depths (mean annual total snowfall = 102-127 cm) across the vast northern boreal forest of Canada. Climax forests of the taiga are dominated by three coniferous tree species: white spruce on well-drained sites, black spruce on sites underlain by permafrost, and, east of the Cordillera, balsam fir (Viereck and Little 1972, Hosie 1973). Trees are relatively short and have crowns that can extend to the ground. Because none of the three tree dominants is thick-barked, climax vegetation in the taiga has little resistance to fire, which is almost always stand-replacing. These trees also are prone to insect outbreaks, which can defoliate large areas. Because of the homogeneous moisture conditions and topography, and because of even-aged stands created by stand-replacing fires, large areas become flammable simultaneously and, when ignition occurs, fires tend to burn until the weather changes (Johnson 1992). In Alaska during the period 1893-1937, over 2.4 million ha of forest were reported burned by just 19 individual fires (Barney 1971), a mean of 128,000 ha per fire. In the taiga, therefore, snow characteristics, disturbance regimes, and resulting vegetation conditions are homogeneous over large areas.

In the Rocky Mountain West, by contrast, site conditions and forest types vary at small scales. Traveling 10 km from plains to mountaintop, one encounters habitats from dry desert or steppe, through montane and subalpine forests, to tundra, rock, and permanent snow. Across this gradient, natural fire-return intervals can vary from less than 10 years in drier types to over 400 years in moist subalpine stands (Chapter 3). In such settings, fires often start at low elevation, then slow and die as they ascend mountains into moister types. Although Rocky Mountain forests have experienced some very large fires (Gruell 1985, Turner et al. 1997), most fires are topographically limited and smaller than those in the North. Even when comparing areas with similar fire regimes (i.e., similar fire-return periods, stand replacing fires, and forest age structures fitting the negative exponential model, Chapters 3, 15), fires in the Rocky Mountain West are generally smaller, with more complex shapes, due to more complex topography and a wider range of forest types per unit area. For example, wet concave areas dominated by Engelmann spruce tend to burn with less frequency and intensity than adjacent dry convex ones dominated by lodgepole pine. Likewise, post-fire succession tends to be strongly affected by local topography: north aspects will tend toward different post-disturbance trajectories than south-facing slopes. All of these factors tend to produce more heterogeneity within fires and post-fire seres in Rocky Mountain forests of the contiguous United States than in the taiga. Some subalpine forests in the West are so moist and dissected by areas of rock that fire is virtually excluded.

Relative to lynx-prey relationships, the heterogeneity of Rocky Mountain forests results in higher densities of edges, possibly of ecotones, and the relatively fine-scaled juxtaposition of forests of various ages. (See Chapter 9 for a discussion of the potential importance of edge in lynx–hare relationships.) Few forested areas in the Rocky Mountain West the size of a lynx home range (about 75 km^2) contain homogeneous vegetation. Rather, such areas tend to feature many stands comprised of several tree and shrub species having a wide range of stem densities and ages. In contrast, a large burn in the taiga could easily homogenize a landscape as large as several lynx home ranges.

The frequency and kinds of disturbance in forested systems generally vary more strongly along east-west than north-south gradients. This is true at both continental and smaller scales: the eastern Cascades are more fire-prone than the western Cascades, and conifer forests of Montana are more fire-prone than those in New England (Chapter 3). By contrast, disturbance events, including fire and avalanches, occur at the northern and southern edges of the distribution of lynx with remarkably similar frequencies (Chapter 3). In the northeastern United States, broad-scale natural disturbance appears to have been infrequent and most forests would have been in climax condition at the time of European contact (Lorimer 1977). However, today those patterns are virtually irrelevant; the disturbance dynamics of these forests are driven mostly by humans, and forests are much younger. In many places this has resulted in a reduced conifer component, so that what were mixed deciduous-coniferous forests 300 years ago are deciduous forests today. The replacement of mixed stands with pure deciduous stands been accelerated in recent years in the Great Lakes States by the increasing importance of aspen as a crop tree (Chapter 3).

Forest Successional Pathways

In boreal forests, succession generally progresses from herbs and crypto-gams soon after disturbance to shrubs, seedlings, saplings, mature trees, and finally to climax forest (Kelsall et al. 1977, Kimmins 1987; Chapter 3). Commonly, after a stand-replacing disturbance, the initial cohort of trees is densely stocked, resulting in self-thinning and low levels of light at the forest floor. Gradually, closed canopies give way to gaps as insect infestation, disease and windthrow kill individual and small groups of trees, allowing light to reach the forest floor. Light gaps encourage shade-intolerant trees, shrubs, and herbs, greatly increasing understory diversity (Pickett and White 1985, Spies et al. 1990, Valverde and Silvertown 1997). However, details of successional pathways will vary according to the nature of local disturbance regimes, tree species composition, and position along major ecological gradients.

Within the taiga, regenerating seres exhibit high stem densities for trees and shrubs for 20-35 years (Foote 1983). The young tree stage that follows features dense deciduous trees with an understory of low shrubs for another 25 years (30-55 years post-fire). This is followed by a conifer-hardwood stage that also maintains an understory shrub component, followed by the climax spruce stage, around 90-150 years post-fire. At this climax stage, understory vegetation is reduced to cryptogams, a few shrubs, and low tree branches. Successional sequences in the taiga, therefore, support understory shrubs and small trees for a long time, perhaps over 60 years. Although understory shrubs mostly disappear in climax spruce forests (Foote 1983), gaps will allow some trees and shrubs to grow, providing some low cover.

In northeastern and Great Lakes boreal forests, successional pathways reflect the strong adaptations of deciduous trees. Hardwoods may dominate entire seral sequences, including climax communities on warm, mesic sites. Here, insects and wind, rather than fire, play important roles in disturbance (Baskerville 1975, Lorimer 1977, Pastor and Mladenoff 1992). Cooler sites, or sites at the extremes of the moisture gradient, follow successional pathways similar to spruce in taiga forests (Dammon 1964, Larsen 1980). The shrub stage often is dominated by dense jack pine and quaking aspen for 5-15 years post-disturbance. After reaching the young tree stage, aspen and pine develop understories of shade-tolerant spruce, fir, maple, and birch until about 40 years post-disturbance. The multistoried climax spruce-fir-mixed hardwood stage is not reached until about 165 years after disturbance (Chapter 3). So, in cooler sites, understory cover will be dense during early shrub stages (5-20 years post-disturbance), then decline and emerge again about 40 years post-disturbance, as climax species grow through the understory. Understory cover then declines again as climax species reach overstory proportions. In hardwood-dominated climax forests, understory cover may be sparse away from canopy gaps, whereas in conifer-dominated climax forests, understory cover tends to be more abundant.

Successional pathways in western montane boreal forests vary dramatically along gradients of moisture and soil nutrients. Climate during the growing season, an important determinant of vegetation, is remarkably similar across the lodgepole pine zone of western forests (Lotan and Perry 1983, table 2). Although total precipitation decreases from west to east across the western contiguous United States, the proportion that falls during the growing season increases so that lodgepole pine forests in Colorado receive about as much summer precipitation as those in the Cascades, which are generally considered more mesic (Lotan and Perry 1983). Of course, sites farther south receive higher incident radiation during the growing season and occur higher on mountains where lower atmospheric pressure causes faster evaporation than near sea level (Knight 1994). Boreal forests with equivalent precipitation will therefore become more xeric farther south.

Soil moisture during the growing season strongly influences shrub and seedling abundance in western coniferous forests. Alexander et al. (1986) described the poor regeneration of lodgepole pine in the Medicine Bow Mountains of southern Wyoming following disturbance on dry sites. However, on some sites, lodgepole pine formed dog-hair stands that persisted for hundreds of years (Alexander et al. 1986:10). In eastern Washington and western Montana, the shrub and young tree stages are distinct but brief (about 5-30 years post-fire), and shrub stem densities are low (Stickney 1981, 1986; Zamora 1982) compared with the taiga (Foote 1983). This pattern becomes more pronounced farther south and east (Colorado and Wyoming), where early seral lodgepole pine tends not to develop a shrub component and tree stem densities can be very low, depending on cone serotiny, fire intensity, elevation, and soils (Alexander et al. 1986).

In subalpine fir climax types in the Pacific Northwest, sapling densities through time are often bimodal (Fig. 14.1, Agee 1993) with peaks occurring in the shrub-sapling stage and again after canopy gaps develop (Spies et al.

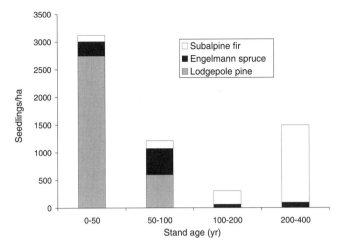

Figure 1—Densities (no./ha) of conifer seedling (< 4 cm dbh) stems in relation to stand age after fire in the Pasayten Wilderness, Washington. Data are from Fahnestock (1976).

1990). Spies and Franklin (1989) reported mean densities of shade-tolerant saplings in moist Douglas-fir forests of Oregon and Washington consistent with this bimodal pattern: 228/ha in young stands, 84/ha in mature stands, and 335/ha in old growth. For understory cover of deciduous shrubs, they reported increasing densities as succession progressed: 6.8% in young stands, 8.9% in mature stands, and 12% in old growth. This bimodal pattern is probably the norm on moist sites. After disturbance, the site will be fully revegetated with deciduous or coniferous tree species and tall deciduous brush. Because moist sites support high leaf areas (Gholz 1982), overstory canopies will be dense, leading to a relative lack of vegetation under the mature canopy and, when the stand is old enough that mortality in the overstory is significant, forest gaps are rapidly colonized. These patterns, however, are far less general on dry sites. On dry sites, tree regeneration after disturbance is extremely variable (Arno et al 1985, Alexander et al. 1986), and these sites often lack tall brush components. As a result, open areas are colonized by grasses or short brush species. Despain (1990), for example, illustrates the small amount of shrub and small tree understory in all but the moistest conifer forest sequences in Yellowstone National Park.

Patterns of Snowshoe Hare and Red Squirrel Abundance

Understanding the successional correlates of wildlife abundance is particularly relevant because many species can be linked to specific seres via forest structure and composition. Forest management alters successional sequences, either by reducing disturbance (fire suppression) or increasing it (timber harvest). However, successional pathways vary greatly in rate, species composition, and physical structure (Pfister et al. 1977, Steele et al. 1981, Moir and Ludwig 1979). Therefore, understanding habitat associations of lynx and their prey must be framed in terms of specific, regional successional trajectories.

Wherever they have been studied, hare densities are positively correlated with densities of small-diameter woody stems (Brock 1975, Wolfe et al. 1982, Pearson 1999, Chapters 6, 7). Density appears to be more important than composition largely because hares consume a wide variety of plant species (Chapter 7). Thus, in general, dense small-diameter stems simultaneously provide both food and cover. Based on these understandings, and lacking site-specific hare density data, we hypothesize that hare densities can be inferred from sapling and tall shrub densities for those forest types known to support hares. In mesic forests, therefore, we argue that hare densities should be bimodal with stand age: highest in early seral conditions, minimal in closed-canopy mature forests, and reaching moderate densities in extremely old gap-phase forests. We do not, however, expect this pattern to be common on dry sites where erratic regeneration and the lack of tall deciduous brush often lead to very open conditions for extensive periods after disturbance. In these stands, hare habitat will only be produced in later seres.

This bimodal association between brushy vegetation and population density has been shown in northwestern California for the shrub-associated dusky-footed woodrat, an important prey of the northern spotted owl. This species is most abundant in dense understory following disturbance, absent from mature forest with scarce shrubs and young trees, and intermediate in abundance in old growth, where increased understory cover accompanies gap succession (Sakai and Noon 1993). Data for snowshoe hares along entire successional sequences are scanty; hares tend to be rare immediately after disturbance, abundant in the shrub-sapling stage, and uncommon in closed-canopy forest (Litvaitis et al. 1985; Koehler 1990a,b; Ferron et al. 1998; Chapters 6,7). In Ontario, Thompson et al. (1989) counted hare tracks on 2 km transects for 5 years. The transects intersected logged stands ≤30 years old and uncut forest 150-200 years old. Average track counts were highest in

20-year-old stands, and abundant and approximately equal numbers of tracks were located in 30-year-old stands and areas of uncut forests. Thompson et al. (1989) attributed the relatively high levels of hare tracks in the old forests to the presence of brush in canopy gaps. Mills and Henderson (unpubl. data) found hares relatively abundant in old-growth forest in northwestern Montana, and Beauvais (1997) found track densities of hares to be positively correlated with variables indicative of late-seral stages in northern Wyoming. Powell (1991 unpubl. data cited in Powell and Zielinski 1994) described a bimodal distribution of snowshoe hare abundance along a successional sequence on the Olympic Peninsula of Washington. These pieces of evidence, while weak, suggest that hares may be relatively abundant in climax conifer forests of the western contiguous United States, and bimodally distributed along successional gradients on mesic sites.

However, in the drier areas within lynx range, including areas in the southern Rocky Mountains of Colorado where regenerating stands develop no shrub stage, suitable hare habitat may only occur in old-growth forests and riparian areas (Lawrence 1955, Dolbeer and Clark 1975). In these areas, snowshoe hare abundance may follow a unimodal distribution that peaks under old-growth conditions with the development of canopy gaps. Two years of snow tracking in a range of stands from young to old growth in northern Wyoming (Beauvais 1997) showed that snowshoe hare tracks were negatively correlated with indices typical of highly fragmented landscapes, such as density of clearcut edge, and positively correlated with indices such as percent of forest cover and percent of spruce-fir cover. Snowshoe hares were also positively correlated with maximum diameters of trees, and with total number of stems within 5 m of sampling points.

Although it is generally acknowledged that early seral stages resulting in dense understory cover provide important habitat for snowshoe hares (Chapters 6, 7), little research has examined the relative importance of gap succession in climax forests for hare habitat. However, the process of gap development, which produces the habitat conditions associated with hares, varies among regions. For instance, gap succession in the Pacific Northwest is driven primarily by single tree mortality, which results in smaller gaps that compose a smaller proportion of the overall forest (Spies et al. 1990). In contrast, in eastern North America wind and insects play larger roles, thereby generating more group-tree mortality, which results in larger gaps and affects a larger proportion of the forest (Kneeshaw and Bergeron 1998). These processes may affect the spatial scales of usable habitat for snowshoe hares within climax or old-growth forests in different regions of North America.

Understanding red squirrel abundances in the context of succession is also important given the role of squirrels as alternative prey for lynx (O'Donoghue et al. 1998b, Chapters 9, 13). Because squirrels eat primarily conifer seeds, in the West their abundance over successional time is linked to cone-producing ages, usually mature (Smith 1970, Obbard 1987) or older (Kemp and Keith 1970, Rusch and Reeder 1978), conifers. Thus, late-successional forest provides habitat within which two prey species important to lynx occur sympatrically and are relatively abundant.

Predator-Prey Communities

The North American distributions of lynx and their two most important prey, snowshoe hares and red squirrels, roughly coincide (Hall 1981). Other potential prey species occupy much smaller geographic ranges, so the availability of alternative prey varies regionally for lynx. In the taiga, these include mice and voles, northern flying squirrels, arctic ground squirrels, beavers, muskrats, grouse and ptarmigan, and a variety of ungulates (Chapter 9). Arctic hares and Alaska hares are tundra dwellers that penetrate forest edges slightly (Hall 1981) and may be eaten in a few areas. In southern boreal forests, however, potential prey communities differ substantially. Medium-sized birds (grouse and ptarmigan), small mammals, and ungulates are relatively abundant throughout the range of lynx, but medium-sized mammal assemblages in southern boreal forests contain many more species than those in the taiga. In montane Colorado, for example, there are four species of leporids: snowshoe hare, white-tailed jackrabbit, mountain cottontail, and desert cottontail (Hall 1981). The coyote, a generalized leporid predator, exploits only snowshoe hares in the North but can switch among various leporids, even those not sympatric in distribution, in southern regions. Although prey-switching by coyotes may seem to ease the competitive pressure on lynx in the southern part of its range, it probably does the opposite. It allows coyotes to switch among leporid species, including snowshoe hares, as seasons, weather, and prey populations change. There is no evidence to suggest that lynx are effective at this kind of prey switching. The greater dietary options available to coyotes in the southern part of the range of lynx may provide a buffer to coyote populations during population lows of hares that is not readily available to lynx and may make coyotes more effective competitors with lynx through time.

Similarly, southern boreal forests during the snow-free season feature diverse medium-sized rodents not present in the taiga, including woodrats, marmots, ground squirrels, fox and eastern gray squirrels, and chipmunks. Although available evidence indicates that snowshoe hares and red squirrels are the most important lynx foods during winter in all portions of their range (Chapters 9, 13), summer diets have scarcely been studied. The influence of this diverse array of alternative prey in the southern portion of the range of lynx is largely unknown.

Lynx also have more potential competitors in the southern part of their range than in the North. In the North, the interference competitors that are likely to be dominant are the wolf and coyote, but coyotes are largely restricted to areas without wolves (Buskirk 1999). In southern boreal forests, by contrast, potential interference competitors of lynx include the coyote, cougar, and bobcat. Data from Montana show that cougars kill lynx and may be a substantial source of mortality (Chapter 13). In the taiga, however, cougars are absent or rare. Coyotes, cougars, and bobcats have expanded their ranges and increased their populations in the contiguous United States within the last 20 years (Chapter 4). Therefore, regional and temporal variation in carnivore communities may contribute to the differential success of lynx populations across North America.

In a few areas of the contiguous United States, wolves are increasing in distribution and numbers, while coyotes are decreasing in response (Crabtree and Sheldon 1999). Lynx should be better able to co-exist with wolves than coyotes, because wolves prey more on ungulates than leporids and are probably too large to be effective interference competitors with lynx (Chapter 4). Accordingly, community conditions for lynx in the Greater Yellowstone Area, where wolf populations are expanding and coyote populations contracting, should improve in coming years.

Broad regional variation in forested landscapes, especially the extent and connectivity of mesic forest types, may mediate competitive interactions involving lynx. Because suitable habitat areas are generally smaller in the southern part of the range, competitors, including those not highly adapted to snow, may be better able to occupy lynx habitat than those in the North (Chapter 4). This process may also be facilitated by human activities, which produce dense systems of roads and trails that probably enable coyotes and other predators to gain access to areas with soft, deep snow (Chapter 4). In general, intensive forest management and concomitant fragmentation of habitat via timber harvesting and road systems are more prevalent in southern boreal forests compared to the taiga. Thus, human-mediated increases in potential competitors and predators may present a more serious threat to lynx populations in southern boreal forests than in the taiga.

Conclusions

Across the vast geographic area occupied by lynx in North America, we observe strong gradients in climate, topography, elevation, soil conditions, snow conditions, plant dominants, disturbance regimes, and successional trajectories. On top of these are added the highly variable influences of humans. Extrapolating information gathered in one part of this region to others must be done with the greatest of care and would be facilitated by additional research. The likelihood of important among-population differences increases with geographical and ecological distances between populations (Chapter 5). This chapter identifies some potentially important ecological differences over the range of lynx and suggests that variation among populations is a key issue for lynx conservation in the contiguous United States.

In the southern range of lynx, the communities of both competitors and prey are more diverse than those in the North. Not only are lynx in the South subject to a different suite of interference competitors, including mountain lions, but exploitation competition with generalists such as coyotes will likely be more significant due to the ability of these predators to prey-switch. The interactions between lynx and competitors in the south is unstudied and represents a major research need.

We question the generalization that the best way to provide habitat for lynx prey, including hares, is to create early-successional forest. On mesic sites, the highest hare densities are generally found in sapling-stage forests after disturbance, but squirrels are absent from these sites. We believe the data, though sparse, also suggest that old gap-phase forests provide a combination of high numbers of squirrels and moderate densites of hares on many sites. Additionally, site moisture appears to be an important correlate of shrub and sapling densities in the early stages following disturbance and, in dry areas of the West where post-disturbance regeneration is erratic, gap-phase old-growth forests may provide relatively higher densities of small-diameter woody stems compared to earlier stages of succession on the same sites.

In areas where boreal forests are highly fragmented, older forests may be an important stabilizing element. Because small areas of boreal forest can be highly altered by single disturbance events, such as fire, hare dynamics associated with post-disturbance conditions will be transient. Older forests are temporally stable, will produce hares in lower but more reliable numbers, and provide squirrels as alternative prey. On dry sites, where young forests do not reliably produce hare habitat, older forests may provide a critical source of hare habitat.

We are cautious in reaching these conclusions because data are so limited. However, the relationship between forest succession and prey abundance is an area of utmost importance to southern lynx conservation. We believe that a well-designed, geographically extensive study to further examine these relationships should be given the highest priority for research. Failure to carefully consider successional trajectories and their structural habitat correlates on a regional and site-specific basis can produce the opposite of intended results, especially with regard to the habitat needs of snowshoe hares. Ultimately, lynx management must take into account unique regional attributes and site conditions relative to disturbance regimes and successional pathways that follow natural disturbance and management events.

Literature Cited

Adams, L. 1959. An analysis of a population of snowshoe hares in northwestern Montana. Ecological Monographs 29:141-170.

Agee, J. A. 1993. Fire ecology of Pacific Northwest forests. Island Press, Washington, DC.

Alexander, R. R., G. R. Hoffman, and J. M. Wirsig. 1986. Forest vegetation of the Medicine Bow National Forest in southeastern Wyoming: a habitat type classification. USDA Forest Service, Research Paper RM-271.

Arno, S. F., D. G. Simmerman, and R. E. Keane. 1985. Forest succession on four habitat types in western Montana. USDA Forest Service, General Technical Report INT-177.

Bailey, R. G. 1998. Ecoregions map of North America: explanatory note. USDA Forest Service, Miscellaneous Publication No. 1548.

Bailey, T. N., E. E. Bangs, M. F. Portner, J. C. Mallory, and R. J. McAvinchey. 1986. An apparent overexploited lynx population on the Kenai Peninsula, Alaska. Journal of Wildlife Management 50:279-290.

Barney, R. J. 1971. Wildfires in Alaska - some historical and projected effects and aspects. Pages 51-59 in C. W. Slaughter, R. J. Barney and G. M. Hansen, editors. Fire in the northern environment - a symposium. USDA Forest Service, Pacific Northwest Forest and Range Experiment Station, Portland, OR.

Baskerville, G. L. 1975. Spruce budworm: super silviculturist. Forestry Chronicle 51: 138-140.

Beauvais, G. P. 1997. Mammals in fragmented forests in the Rocky Mountains: community structure, habitat selection, and individual fitness. Unpublished Ph.D. Dissertation, University of Wyoming, Laramie, WY.

Black, H. C. 1965. An analysis of a population of snowshoe hares, *Lepus americanus washingtonii* Baird. in western Oregon, Unpublished Ph.D. Dissertation, Oregon State University, Corvallis, OR.

Boutin, S., C. J. Krebs, R. Boonstra, M. R. T. Dale, S. J. Hannon, K. Martin, A. R. E. Sinclair, J. N. M. Smith, R. Turkington, M. Blower, A. Byrom, F. I. Doyle, C. Doyle, D. Hik, L. Hofer, A. Hubbs, T. Karels, D. L. Murray, M. O'Donoghue, C. Rohner, and S. Schweiger. 1995. Population changes of the vertebrate community during a snowshoe hare cycle in Canada's boreal forest. Oikos 74:69-80.

Brainerd, S. M. 1985. Reproductive ecology of bobcats and lynx in western Montana. Unpublished M.S. Thesis, University of Montana, Missoula, MT.

Brand, C. J. and L. B. Keith. 1979. Lynx demography during a snowshoe hare decline in Alberta. Journal of Wildlife Management 43:827-849.

Brand, C. J., L. B. Keith, and C. A. Fischer. 1976. Lynx responses to changing snowshoe hare densities in central Alberta. Journal of Wildlife Management 40:416-428.

Brittell J. D., R. J. Poelker, S. J. Sweeney, and G. M. Koehler. 1989. Native cats of Washington, Section III: lynx. Unpublished, Washington Department of Wildlife, Olympia, WA.

Brocke, R. H. 1975. Preliminary guidelines for managing snowshoe hare habitat in the Adirondacks. Transactions of the Northeast Section, The Wildlife Society, Northeast Fish and Wildlife Conference 32:46-66.

Buehler, D. A. and L. B. Keith. 1982. Snowshoe hare distribution and habitat use in Wisconsin. Canadian Field-Naturalist 96:19-29.

Buskirk, S. W. 1999. Mesocarnivores of Yellowstone. Pages 165-187 *in* T. W. Clark, S. C. Minta, P. M. Kareiva, and P. M. Curlee, Editors. Carnivores in ecosystems. Yale University Press, New Haven, CT.

Carbyn, L. N. and D. Partiquin. 1983. Observations on home range sized, movements and social organization of lynx, *Lynx canadensis*, in Riding Mountain National Park, Manitoba. Canadian Field-Naturalist 97:262-267.

Conroy, M. J., L. W. Gysel, and G. R. Dudderar. 1979. Habitat components of clear-cut areas for snowshoe hares in Michigan. Journal of Wildlife Management 43:680-690.

Crabtree, R. L. and J. W. Sheldon. 1999. The ecological role of coyotes on Yellowstone's northern range. Yellowstone Science 7:15-23.

Dammon, A. W. H. 1964. Some forest types of central Newfoundland and their relations to environmental factors. Forest Science Monographs 8.

Despain, D. G. 1990. Yellowstone vegetation. Roberts Rinehart Publishers, Boulder, CO.

Dolbeer, R. A. and W. R. Clark. 1975. Population ecology of snowshoe hares in the central Rocky Mountains. Journal of Wildlife Management 39:535-549.

Elliot-Fisk, D. L. 1988. The boreal forest. Pages 33-62 *in* M. G. Barbour and W. D. Billings, editors. North American terrestrial vegetation. Cambridge University Press, Cambridge, UK.

Elton, C. and M. Nicholson. 1942. The ten year cycle in numbers of lynx in Canada. Journal of Animal Ecology 11:215-244.

Fahnestock, G. R. 1976. Fires, fuel, and flora as factors in wilderness management: The Pasayten case. Tall Timbers Fire Ecology Conference 15:33-70.

Ferron, J. and J. P. Ouellet. 1992. Daily partitioning of summer habitat and use of space by the snowshoe hare in southern boreal forests. Canadian Journal of Zoology 70:2178-2183.

Ferron, J., F. Potvin, and C. Dussault. 1998. Short-term effects of logging on snowshoe hares in the boreal forest. Canadian Journal of Forest Research 28:1335-1343.

Foote, M. J. 1983. Classification, description, and dynamics of plant communities after fire in the taiga of interior Alaska. USDA Forest Service, Research Paper PNW-307.

Fuller, T. K. and D. M. Heisey. 1986. Density-related changes in winter distribution of snowshoe hare in north central Minnesota. Journal of Wildlife Management 50:261-264.

Gholz, H. L. 1982. Enviornmental limits on aboveground net primary production, leaf area, and biomass in vegetation zones of the Pacific Northwest. Ecology 63:469-481.

Gruell, G. E. 1985. Fire on the early western landscape: an annotated record of wildland fires 1776-1900. Northwest Science 59:97-107.

Hall, E. R. 1981. The mammals of North America. John Wiley and Sons, New York.

Hosie, R. C. 1973. Native Trees of Canada, 7th Edition. Canadian Forestry Service, Ottawa, Ontario, Canada.

Johnson, E. A. 1992. Fire and vegetation dynamics: studies from the North American boreal forest. Cambridge University Press, Cambridge, UK.

Kelsall, J. P., E. S. Telfer, and T. D. Wright. 1977. The effects of fire on the ecology of the boreal forest, with particular reference to the Canadian North: a review and selected bibliography. Canadian Wildlife Service, Occasional Paper No. 32, Ottawa, Canada.

Kemp, G. A. and L. B. Keith. 1970. Dynamics and regulation of red squirrel (*Tamiasciurus hudsonicus*) populations. Ecology 51:763-779.

Kesterson M. B. 1988. Lynx home range and spatial organization in relation to population density and prey abundance. Unpublished M.S. Thesis, University of Alaska, Fairbanks, AK.

Kimmins J. P. 1987. Forest ecology. Macmillan Publishing Company, New York.

Kneeshaw, D. D. and Y. Bergeron. 1998. Canopy gap characteristics and tree replacement in the southern boreal forest. Ecology 79:783-794.

Knight, D. H. 1994. Dynamics of subalpine forests. Pages 128-138 *in* G. D. Hayward and J. Verner, editors. Flammulated, boreal, and great gray owls in the United States: a technical conservation assessment. USDA Forest Service, General Technical Report RM-253.

Koehler, G. M. 1990. Population and habitat characteristics of lynx and snowshoe hares in north central Washington. Canadian Journal of Zoology. 68:845-851.

Koehler, G. M. 1991. Snowshoe hare, *Lepus americanus*, use of forest successional stages and population changes during 1985-1989 in north-central Washington. Canadian Field-Naturalist 105:291-293.

Koehler, G. M., M. G. Hornocker, and H. S. Hash. 1979. Lynx movements and habitat use in Montana. Canadian Field-Naturalist 93:441-442.

Larsen, J. A. 1980. The boreal ecosystem. Academic Press. New York.

Lawrence, I. E. 1955. An ecological study of the snowshoe hare, *Lepus americanus bairdii*, Hayden in the Medicine Bow National Forest of Wyoming. Unpublished M.S. Thesis, University of Wyoming, Laramie, WY.

Litvaitis, J. A., J. A. Sherburne, and J. A. Bissonette. 1985. Influence of understory characteristics on snowshoe hare habitat use and density. Journal of Wildlife Management 49: 866-873.

Lorimer, C. G. 1977. The presettlement forest and natural disturbance cycles of northeast Maine. Ecology 58:139-148.

Lotan, J. E. and D. A. Perry. 1983. Ecology and regeneration of lodgepole pine. USDA Forest Service, Agriculture Handbook No. 606. Washington, DC.

Mech, L. D. 1977. Record movement of a Canadian lynx. Journal of Mammalogy 58:676-677.

Mech, L. D. 1980. Age, sex, reproduction, and spatial organization of lynxes colonizing northeastern Minnesota. Journal of Mammalogy 61:261-267.

Moir, W. H. and J. A. Ludwig. 1979. Preliminary classification for the coniferous forest and woodland series of Arizona and New Mexico. USDA Forest Service, Research Paper RM-207.

Monthey, R. W. 1986. Responses of snowshoe hares, *Lepus americanus*, to timber harvesting in northern Maine. Canadian Field-Naturalist 100:568-570.

Mowat, G., B. G. Slough, and S. Boutin. 1996. Lynx recruitment during a snowshoe hare population peak and decline in southwest Yukon. Journal of Wildlife Management 60:441-452.

Murray, D. and L., S. Boutin. 1991. The influence of snow on lynx and coyote movements: does morphology affect behavior? Oecologia 88:463-469.

Murray, D. L., S. Boutin, and M. Odonoghue. 1994. Winter habitat selection by lynx and coyotes in relation to snowshoe hare abundance. Canadian Journal of Zoology 72: 1444-1451.

Murray, D. L., S. Boutin, M. O'Donoghue, and V. O. Nams. 1995. Hunting behavior of a sympatric felid and canid in relation to vegetative cover. Animal Behavior 50:1203-1210.

Nellis, C. H. and L. B. Keith. 1968. Hunting activities and success of lynxes in Alberta. Journal of Wildlife Management 32:718-722.

Nellis, C. H., S. P. Wetmore, and L. B. Keith. 1972. Lynx-prey interaction in central Alberta. Journal of Wildlife Management 36:320-329.

Obbard, M. E. 1987. Red squirrel. Pages 265-281 *in* M. Novak, J. A. Baker, M. E. Obbard, and B. Malloch, eds. Wild furbearer management and conservation in North America. Ontario Ministry of Natural Resources, Ontario, Canada.

O'Connor, R. M. 1984. Population trends, age structure, and reproductive characteristics of female lynx in Alaska, 1961 through 1973. Unpublished M.A. Thesis, University of Alaska, Fairbanks.

O'Donoghue, M., S. Boutin, C. J. Krebs, D. L. Murray, E. J. Hofer. 1998a. Behavioral responses of coyotes and lynx to the snowshoe hare cycle. Oikos 82:169-183.

O'Donoghue, M., E. Hofer, and F. I. Doyle. 1995. Predator versus predator. Natural History 3/95:6-9.

O'Donoghue, M., C. J. Krebs, G. Zuleta, D. L. Murray, E. J. Hofer. 1998b. Functional responses of coyotes and lynx to the snowshoe hare cycle. Ecology 79:1193-1208.

O'Donoghue, M., S. Boutin, C. J. Krebs, and E. J. Hofer. 1997. Numerical responses of coyotes and lynx to the snowshoe hare cycle. Oikos 80:150-162.

Orr, C. D. and D. G. Dodds. 1982. Snowshoe hare habitat preferences in Nova Scotia spruce-fir forests. Wildlife Society Bulletin 10:147-150.

Paragi, T. F., W. N. Johnson, and D. D. Kitnik. 1997. Selection of post-fire seres by lynx and snowshoe hares in the Alaskan taiga. Northwestern Naturalist 78:77-86.

Parker, G. R. 1984. Use of spruce plantations by snowshoe hares in New Brunswick. Forestry Chronicle 60:162-166.

Parker, G. R. 1986. The importance of cover on use of conifer plantations by snowshoe hares in northern New Brunswick. Forestry Chronicle 62:159-163.

Parker, G. R., J. W. Maxwell, and L. D. Morton. 1983. The ecology of the lynx (*Lynx canadensis*) in Cape Breton Island. Canadian Journal of Zoology 61:770-786.

Pastor, J. and D. J. Mladenoff. 1992. The southern boreal-northern hardwood forest border. Pages 216-240 *in* H. H. Shugart, R. Leemans, and G.B. Bonan, editors. A systems analysis of the global boreal forest. Cambridge University Press, Cambridge, UK.

Pearson, D. E. 1999. Small mammals of the Bitterroot National Forest: a literature review and annotated bibliography. UDSA Forest Service, General Technical Report RMRS-GTR-25.

Perham, C. J. 1995. Home range, habitat selection, and movements of lynx (*Lynx canadensis*) in eastern interior Alaska. Unpublished M.S. Thesis, Univiversity of Alaska, Fairbanks.

Pfister, R. D., B. L. Kovalchik, S. F. Arno, and R. C. Presby. 1977. Forest habitat types of Montana. USDA Forest Service, General Technical Report GTR-INT-34.

Pickett, S. T. A. and P. S. White. 1985. The ecology of natural disturbance and patch dynamics. Academic Press, New York.

Poole, K. G. 1994. Characteristics of an unharvested lynx populations during a snowshoe hare decline. Journal of Wildlife Management 58:608-618.

Poole, K. G. 1997. Dispersal patterns of lynx in the Northwest Territories. Journal of Wildlife Management 61:497-505.

Poole, K. G., L. A. Wakelyn, and P. N. Nicklen. 1996. Habitat selection by lynx in the Northwest Territories. Canadian Journal of Zoology 74:845-849.

Powell, R. A. and W. J. Zielinski. 1994. Fisher. Pages 38-73 *in* L. F. Ruggiero, K. B. Aubry, S. W. Buskirk, L. J. Lyon, and W. J. Zielinski, technical editors. The scientific basis for conserving forest carnivores: American marten, fisher, lynx and wolverine in the Western United States. USDA Forest Service, General Technical Report RM-254.

Pruppacher, H. R. and J. D. Klett. 1978. Microphysics of clouds and precipitation. D. Reidel Publishing Company, Boston, MA.

Quinn, N. W. S. and J. E. Thompson. 1987. Dynamics of an exploited Canada lynx population in Ontario. Journal of Wildlife Management 51:297-305.

Ranta, E., V. Kaitala, and J. Lindstrom. 1997. Dynamics of Canadian lynx populations in space and time. Ecography 20:454-460.

Rogowitz, G. L. 1988. Forage quality and use of reforested habitats by snowshoe hares. Canadian Journal of Zoology 66:2080-2083.

Rusch, D. A. and W. G. Reeder. 1978. Population ecology of Alberta red squirrels. Ecology 59:400-420.

Sakai, H. F. and B. R. Noon. 1993. Dusky-footed woodrat abundance in different-aged forests in northwestern California. Journal of Wildlife Management 57:373-382.

Saunders, J. K. 1963a. Food habits of the lynx in Newfoundland. Journal of Wildlife Management 27:384-390.

Saunders, J. K. 1963b. Movements and activities of the lynx in Newfoundland. Journal of Wildlife Management 27:390-400.

Scott, D. P. and R. H. Yahner. 1989. Winter habitat and browse use by snowshoe hares, *Lepus americanus*, in a marginal habitat in Pennsylvania. Canadian Field-Naturalist 103:560-563.

Slough, B. G. and G. Mowat. 1996. Lynx population dynamics in an untrapped refugium. Journal of Wildlife Management 60:946-961.

Smith, C. C. 1970. The coevolution of pine squirrels (*Tamiasciurus hudsonicus*) and conifers. Ecological Monographs 40(3)349-371.

Smith, D. S. 1984. Habitat use, home range, and movements of bobcats in western Montana. Unpublished M.A. Thesis, University of Montana, Missoula, MT.

Spies, T. A. and J. F. Franklin. 1989. Gap characteristics and vegetation response in coniferous forests of the Pacific Northwest. Ecology 70:543-545.

Spies, T. A., J. F. Franklin, and M. Klopsch. 1990. Canopy gaps in Douglas-fir forests of the Cascade Mountains. Canadian Journal of Forest Research 20:649-658.

Staples, W. R. III. 1995. Lynx and coyote diet and habitat relationships during a low hare population on the Kenai Peninsula, Alaska. Unpublished M.S. Thesis, University of Alaska, Fairbanks.

Steele, R., R. D. Pfister, R. A. Ryker, J. A. Kittams. 1981. Forest habitat types of central Idaho. USDA Forest Service, General Technical Report GTR-INT-114.

Stephenson, R. O., D. V. Grangaard, and J. Burch. 1991. Lynx, *Felis lynx*, predation on red foxes, *Vulpes vulpes*, caribou, *Rangifer tarandus*, and dall sheep, *Ovis dalli*, in Alaska. Canadian Field-Naturalist 105:255-262.

St-Georges, M., S. Nadeau, D. Lambert, and R. Décarie. 1995. Winter habitat use by ptarmigan, snowshoe hares, red foxes, and river otters in the boreal forests – tundra transition zone of western Quebec. Canadian Journal of Zoology 73:755-764.

Stickney, P. F. 1981. Vegetative recovery and development. Pages 32-40 *in* N. V. DeByle, editor. Cleacutting and fire in the larch/Douglas-fir forests of western Montana. USDA Forest Service, General Technical Report GTR-INT-99.

Stickney, P. F. 1986. First decade plant succession following the Sundance Forest Fire, northern Idaho. USDA Forest Service, General Technical Report GTR-INT-197.

Sullivan, T. P. and D. S. Sullivan. 1982. Barking damage by snowshoe hares and red squirrels in lodgepole pine stands in central British Columbia. Canadian Journal of Forest Research 12:443-448.

Sullivan, T. P. and D. S. Sullivan. 1983. Use of index lines and damage assessments to estimate population densities of snowshoe hares. Canadian Journal of Zoology 61: 163-167.

Sullivan, T. P. and D. S. Sullivan. 1988. Influence of stand thinning on snowshoe hare population dynamics and feeding damage in lodgepole pine forest. Journal of Applied Ecology 25:791-805.

Thompson, I. D. and W. J. Curran. 1995. Habitat suitability for marten of second-growth balsam fir forests in Newfoundland. Canadian Journal of Zoology 73:2059-2064.

Thompson, I. D., I. J. Davidson, S. O'Donnell, and F. Brazeau. 1989. Use of track transects to measure the relative occurrence of some boreal mammals in uncut forest and regeneration stands. Canadian Journal of Zoology 67:1816-1823.

Turner, M. G., W. H. Romme, R. H. Gardner, and W. W. Hargrove. 1997. Effects of fire size and pattern on early succession in Yellowstone National Park. Ecological Monographs 67:411-433.

Valverde, T. and J. Silvertown. 1997. Canopy closure rate and forest structure. Ecology 78:1555-1562.

van Zyll De Jong, C. G. 1966. Food habits of the lynx in Alberta and the Mackenzie District, N.W.T. Canadian Field-Naturalist 80:18-23.

Viereck, L. A. and E. L. Little, Jr. 1972. Alaska trees and shrubs. U.S. Department of Agriculture Handbook No. 410.

Ward, R. M. P. and C. J. Krebs. 1985. Behavioral responses of lynx to declining snowshoe hare abundance. Canadian Journal of Zoology 63:2817-2824.

Wolfe, M. L., N. V. Debyle, C. S. Winchell, and T. R. McCabe. 1982. Snowshoe hare cover relationships in northern Utah. Journal of Wildlife Management 46:662-670.

Zamora, B. A. 1982. Understory development in forest succession: an example from the Inland Northwest. Pages 63-69 *in* J. E. Means, editor. Forest succession and stand development research in the northwest: Proceedings of the Symposium. Forest Research Laboratory, Oregon State University, Corvallis.

Chapter 15

Lynx Conservation in an Ecosystem Management Context

Kevin S. McKelvey, USDA Forest Service, Rocky Mountain Research Station, 800 E. Beckwith, Missoula, MT 59801

Keith B. Aubry, USDA Forest Service, Pacific Northwest Research Station, 3625 93rd Ave. SW, Olympia, WA 98512

James K. Agee, College of Forest Resources, University of Washington, Box 352100, Seattle, WA 98195

Steven W. Buskirk, Department of Zoology and Physiology, University of Wyoming, P.O. Box 3166, Laramie, WY 82071

Leonard F. Ruggiero, USDA Forest Service, Rocky Mountain Research Station, 800 E. Beckwith, Missoula, MT 59801

Gary M. Koehler, Washington Department of Fish and Wildlife, 600 Capitol Way N., Olympia, WA 98501

Abstract—In an ecosystem management context, management for lynx must occur in the context of the needs of other species, watershed health, and a variety of products, outputs, and uses. This chapter presents a management model based on the restoration of historical patterns and processes. We argue that this model is sustainable in a formal sense, practical, and likely to provide for the needs of a variety of species, including lynx. Because our knowledge of lynx biology and disturbance ecology is limited, implementation of this model will be experimental and must be accompanied by a well-planned monitoring program.

Introduction

Our knowledge of lynx ecology and population dynamics in southern boreal forests is limited and based on information obtained at only a few geographic localities (Chapter 13). Because of these information gaps, the conservation of lynx populations in this region must proceed initially with limited knowledge about their habitat relationships and, consequently, with a limited understanding of how to design forest management strategies that will provide for the persistence of lynx populations in the contiguous United States. However, even if we possessed perfect knowledge, management aimed solely at maintaining or improving habitat conditions for a single species across such a broad geographic area would conflict with many other resource management objectives. Managing habitat for lynx may not provide for the needs of other species of conservation concern, or for biodiversity, watershed health, recreation, grazing, mining, timber, or wilderness uses, yet each has a statutory or regulatory basis and a constituency on public lands.

In addition, the scale at which forest management strategies are defined will be a critical consideration for lynx conservation. Because lynx occupy large home ranges and occur at low densities (about one lynx/50 km^2; Chapter 13), the long-term viability of lynx populations cannot be achieved at the spatial scale of relatively small parcels of public land, or even larger units such as individual National Forests or National Parks. Consequently, we believe that lynx conservation in the contiguous United States can only succeed as part of an ecosystem management strategy that is designed to address the needs of a variety of potentially conflicting resource uses over long periods of time and broad spatial scales. In this chapter, we discuss ways in which lynx conservation could be approached within the context of ecosystem management.

The Concept of Ecosystem Management

The concept of ecosystem management dates back to at least 1988 (Agee and Johnson 1988) and, since that time, a variety of definitions have been published (Grumbine 1994), many of which reflect contrasting areas of emphasis. To various constituencies, ecosystem management represents an emphasis on landscape-scale analysis, on science-based management, on adaptive management, on interagency cooperation, or on ecological integrity (Franklin 1997).

The Ecological Society of America defined ecosystem management as "management driven by explicit goals, executed by policies, protocols, and practices, and made adaptable by monitoring and research based on our best understanding of the ecological interactions and processes necessary to sustain ecosystem structure and function (Christensen et al. 1996)." The central goal or value of ecosystem management is sustainability. We consider the eight components of ecosystem management presented by Christensen et al. (1996) to represent the most useful framework for discussing this concept:

1. Long-term sustainability as a fundamental objective
2. Clear, operational goals
3. Sound ecological models
4. An understanding of complexity and inter-connectedness
5. Recognition of the dynamic nature of ecosystems
6. Attention to context and scale
7. Acknowledgment of humans as ecosystem components
8. A commitment to adaptability and accountability

Sustainability

Long-term ecological, social, and economic sustainability are the central goals of ecosystem management (Christensen et al. 1996). To achieve these goals, management must ensure that ecological resources and processes will be maintained in perpetuity, so that future options for management are not compromised. Operationally, this means keeping all the "pieces" of ecosystem structure, function, and composition, while addressing productivity of wood, water, livestock, minerals, and other resource outputs expected from public lands (Franklin 1993). For example, a forested landscape will only provide a sustainable output of timber if the rate of timber harvest is low enough that the first stands harvested have re-grown to rotation age before the last stand is harvested. It is this aspect of sustainability that is embodied in the ideals of even-aged silviculture and maximum sustained yield. Yet sustainability includes more than timber; it requires maintaining the productivity of the soil (for timber, forage, and other resources) and, more broadly, sustaining ecological function so that native species are perpetuated. Sustainability was once narrowly defined in terms of resource outputs, but the concept now encompasses both the state of the ecosystem and associated resource outputs. The foundation of sustainability is ecological; only by sustaining ecological function can social and economic sustainability be achieved (Committee of Scientists 1999).

Applying a sustainable management model will not necessarily produce a sustainable system, however. Most sustainability paradigms are based on maintaining a state of equilibrium. This is possible in a deterministic world, but seldom occurs at small spatial scales in a stochastic system prone to disturbance, such as in the boreal or subalpine forests typical of lynx habitat. In high-severity fire regimes (Agee 1993), for example, the majority of the land base is burned by only a few large, catastrophic fires (McKelvey and Busse 1996; Minnich 1983). For a system prone to such disturbances to be sustainable, it must be resilient. Resiliency in this context is created by scale; ecosystems are more resilient and, hence, more stable when considered at very large spatial scales. In other words, maintaining ecosystem stability will be most attainable if the size of the extreme events is small in relation to the total area.

Ecosystem Context

One of the primary causes for the loss of ecosystem resiliency (i.e., loss of sustainable character) is loss of context resulting from management activities (Allen and Hoekstra 1992). By this, the authors mean a disparity between the spatial and temporal scales of critical ecosystem processes in the natural system, and the area and planning horizon of management activities. For example, cutthroat trout populations were stable in the western United States during historical times, despite the periodic occurrence of large disturbances within the range of the cutthroat, such as the 1910 fire in northern Idaho and western Montana that burned over 1 million ha. Because this fire occurred in only a portion of the species' range, rivers and streams in disturbed areas that lost cutthroat trout habitat eventually recovered and were recolonized by cutthroat trout. Rivers provided connectivity between disturbed and undisturbed areas. Although trout populations in individual streams were prone to local extirpation from such natural disturbances, they were embedded in the larger context of the western United States cutthroat metapopulation. Thus, even catastrophic disturbances had little impact on the long-term sustainability of this system for cutthroat trout.

The situation is similar for lynx, except that the spatial scale that must be considered is much larger. In southern boreal forests, male and female lynx occupy home ranges that average about 150 km^2 and 75 km^2, respectively (Chapter 13), and interbreeding populations occupy an area many times that size. Throughout most of Canada and Alaska, lynx numbers cycle in abundance every 10 years in a pattern of lagged synchrony within the species' range; population peaks in the center of the continent occur approximately two years before they occur in Alaska or Quebec (Chapter 8; see also Ranta et al. 1997). While it is possible that these patterns are independent of one another and driven by exogenous synchronizing factors, such as climate (Elton and Nicholson 1942), the lagged pattern of synchrony in population dynamics suggests some degree of connectivity through dispersal among northern populations (Chapter 2). At least in the 1960s and 1970s, when Canadian population peaks were unusually high, these patterns of lagged synchrony also appeared in trapping records from Minnesota, Montana, and, more weakly, Washington state (Chapter 8). Thus, it is possible that lynx population dynamics in northern tier states of the contiguous United States are linked to those occurring in Canada.

The potential geographic scope of ecosystem context for lynx populations in the contiguous United States is suggested by the historical analysis of lynx distribution presented in Chapter 8. In Washington, lynx populations have persisted only in relatively large blocks of habitat in north-central and northeastern Washington that are adjacent to lynx habitat in southwestern Canada. Similarly, lynx populations in the Clearwater drainage in western Montana occur in the context of the Bob Marshall Wilderness and direct connections to larger habitat areas in Canada. In addition, the documented decline of lynx in New Hampshire is believed to have resulted more from the loss of large-scale habitat connectivity with Quebec than with the loss or alteration of local habitat conditions (Chapter 8; Litvaitis et al. 1991). Thus, for reasons we do not yet fully understand, ecosystem context for lynx appears to occur at least at the scale of ecoprovinces (Bailey 1998; Chapter 8).

Diversity and Complexity

In natural systems, the age distribution of forest stands varies dramatically from that produced under most forest management models. In natural landscapes, stand age distributions produced by large-scale stochastic events, such as forest fires, are more complex than those that result from deterministic, even-aged models of forest management. In most boreal forest systems, the constant-probability stochastic process model (hereafter referred to as the negative exponential model) results in a distribution of stand ages that approximates a negative exponential curve (Fig. 15.1a). For boreal forests with long fire-return intervals, this model approximates natural stand-age distributions, or at least one that is much closer to natural conditions than the truncated distribution produced by even-aged cutting practices (Fig. 15.1c; see also Chapter 3). By maintaining old-growth forests in the landscape, the negative exponential model also retains mature forests, the most temporally stable element on the landscape. Older forests provide a stabilizing influence that is likely to increase ecosystem resiliency. Resulting landscapes have greater levels of complexity and diversity because all age classes are maintained within the landscape.

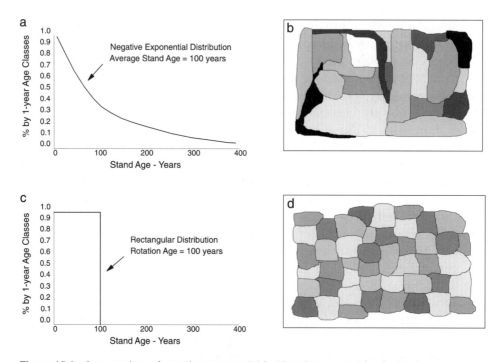

Figure 15.1—A comparison of negative exponential (a, b) and even-aged (c, d) planning paradigms. Graphs on the left depict the stand age distributions, and hypothetical landscape views on the right depict examples of how stands of varying ages, sizes, and shapes could be distributed across the landscape under each planning paradigm. Relative stand age is indicated by increasingly darker shading in the polygons.

Humans as Ecosystem Components

The evaluation of humans as ecosystem components includes both the effects of human perturbations and the needs of society for ecosystem goods and services. Unquestionably, much of the context-based stability that characterized pre-settlement North American ecosystems has been lost. Urbanization and agriculture have increased the isolation and fragmentation of natural areas and reduced the resilience of some parts of those systems to extreme disturbance events; further, this loss of ecosystem context is unlikely to be reversed. We do not believe that a system of reserves maintained by policy or regulation, embedded in a increasingly fragmented and non-natural matrix, can provide for sustainable lynx populations. Inevitable large-scale catastrophes preclude this being a sustainable system from the standpoint of lynx conservation; catastrophes will remove reserves, and there is no mechanism for their replacement or restoration in a reserve/matrix approach. Allen and Hoekstra (1992) have argued that one role of management in sustainable ecosystems is to replace functions that are generally provided in the natural context, but have been lost due to human influences. For this reason, we argue for a system of active management in those land designations where it is permitted. Management of these lands must be cognisant of and limited by the dependency of various species on the condition of these areas given the likelihood of divergent management in adjacent private lands, as well as inevitable natural disturbances.

Simple and rigid prescriptions cannot succeed when the management goals are as complex as maintaining multiple species of wide-ranging vertebrates in natural ecosystems. We simply do not have the knowledge to prescribe procedures that will always achieve these objectives, and we probably never will. Hence, managers cannot be simply technicians; they must be creative thinkers and explorers who use adaptive management to achieve complex and shifting resource management objectives (Walters 1986). We need to build into the system the mechanisms to learn as we go, and the system must be flexible; managers must be able to react quickly to new information to minimize ecosystem damage and maximize conservation opportunities. The necessary regulatory framework must also be in place to allow managers to do so.

Single-Species Habitat Management

Several of the single species-based habitat management models used in the past embodied some of the concepts of ecosystem management because the goal of these approaches was to provide for a broad array of ecological values by ensuring that the habitat needs of key species were met. The National Forest Management Act (NFMA) of 1976, with its attendant planning regulations, included the concept of "indicator" species as a means of maintaining biological diversity on National Forest lands. Most indicator species were chosen on the basis of their presumed sensitivity to ecological changes resulting from management actions. However, the concept was widely criticized as being of little value for monitoring and responding to changes in ecological conditions resulting from management (Patton 1987; Landres et al. 1988), and its use was largely abandoned. "Umbrella" species are conceptually similar to indicators, but their use is based on the assumption that protecting habitat for rare species with large spatial needs will provide for the needs of a variety of more common species with smaller spatial requirements (Berger 1997). Another link between single species with higher levels of biological organization is the concept of "keystone" species (Paine 1969). Keystones are species that make disproportionately large contributions to community or ecosystem function relative to their abundance (Mills et al. 1993).

The Endangered Species Act (ESA) acknowledges the importance of ecosystems, but conservation efforts mandated by the ESA typically have focused on restoring populations of individual species (Christensen et al. 1996). Recently, however, conservation strategies for certain listed species, including the northern spotted owl (USDA and USDI 1994a), bull trout (Rieman and McIntyre 1993), and Pacific salmon stocks (USDA and USDI 1994b), have adopted multi-species habitat conservation approaches. These efforts exemplify the ongoing transformation of endangered species conservation from a focus on individual species, to one that more closely reflects the concepts embodied in ecosystem management. While single-species or "fine-filter" conservation will continue to be mandated by law, we believe that the long-term viability of multiple species will best be addressed with a combination of ecosystem-scale or "coarse-filter" strategies (Haufler et al. 1996; Hunter et al. 1988) and fine-filter strategies for sensitive or rare species whose persistence may require special management actions.

Application of Ecosystem Management to Lynx Conservation

The coarse-filter strategy involves the analysis of pattern and process at large spatial scales. The overall goal is the retention of most biotic diversity and ecological functions through the restoration of ecosystem processes. In this strategy, fine-filter approaches, such as the maintenance of indicator, umbrella, or keystone species, serve as a check on the efficacy of the coarse filter. They also provide insights into modifications that may be necessary to meet the needs of rare or sensitive species not met with a coarse-filter approach. Applying both a coarse and fine filter to the process of ecosystem management increases the probability that key species will be retained, while generating a dynamic and sustainable landscape. For species of concern, such as the lynx, fine-filter measures are mandated by law. The ecosystem management paradigm, when applied to the conservation of lynx, incorporates these species-oriented measures into broad, coarse-filter landscape planning.

Broad-Scale Patterns of Lynx Occurrence

Our analysis of the current and historic distribution of lynx populations in the United States indicates that large, contiguous areas of suitable habitat are necessary for population persistence (Chapter 8). All lynx populations that have long histories of commercial trapping in the contiguous Unites States are those whose geographic range is contiguous with or adjacent to larger areas of suitable habitat north of the Canadian border, including populations in Washington, Montana, and Minnesota. Because individual lynx may disperse >500 km in straight-line distance (Chapter 9), lynx populations in southern boreal forests may be augmented at various times by immigrations from the Canadian taiga. However, the degree to which the persistence of southern populations depends on the rescue effect of immigrations from Canada is unknown (Chapter 8).

We cannot assume that lynx populations in the contiguous United States will be maintained by dispersal of lynx from Canada, nor that connectivity with larger habitat areas in Canada will be maintained in perpetuity. Although cooperative conservation efforts with Canadian land management agencies should be explored in all areas of adjacent lynx habitat, we believe that lynx conservation efforts in the contiguous United States should be addressed at geographic scales that will provide for the persistence of resident populations of lynx, regardless of periodic augmentations that may occur from other areas. Clearly, ecoprovince-wide planning is necessary to provide the broad-scale information necessary for effective conservation of lynx.

The following calculation (included here for illustrative purposes only) provides a sense of the smallest scale at which conservation planning will need to be addressed. The estimated density of a local population of 25 resident lynx in north-central Washington studied with radiotelemetry from 1980 to 1987, was about one lynx per 50 km^2 (Chapter 13; Brittell et al. 1989, unpublished; Koehler 1990). Thus, conservation of this small group of animals, which is probably not viable as a geographically closed population (see Chapter 2), would require a planning area at least 1,250 km^2 in size (25 x 50 km^2). However, this estimate represents a minimum area requirement over a relatively short period of time; to provide sufficient habitat for the population size to fluctuate around a long-term mean of 25 animals, the actual conservation area would need to be considerably larger.

Broad-Scale Habitat Management

Unlike organisms that are tightly linked to a particular forest condition, lynx use a variety of forest age and structural classes (Chapter 13). Preferred prey for lynx are also associated with a variety of forest types. Red squirrels are closely tied to mature, cone-producing forests, whereas snowshoe hares generally reach highest abundance in younger seral stages. Dense horizontal structure appears to be important for snowshoe hares, but such conditions develop at different stages in different forest types (Chapters 6 and 7). These observations suggest that forests managed for lynx should contain a mixture of age classes and structural conditions. How such habitats should be interspersed to benefit lynx, and how to maintain this interspersion in space and time, therefore become central issues in habitat management.

Existing lynx habitat management plans in the contiguous United States are generally focused at relatively small spatial scales, and emphasize the production of young forest to provide foraging habitat, and the maintenance of a few, small patches of older forest to provide denning habitat (e.g., Washington State Department of Natural Resources 1996). These plans are based on the premise that if a few small areas of old-growth forest are provided within the matrix for denning habitat, landscapes managed primarily for a spatial and temporal mosaic of high-quality snowshoe hare habitat will provide for the long-term persistence of lynx populations (Koehler and Brittell 1990). However, this approach is based on untested hypotheses and does not address the divergent needs of other species that inhabit these landscapes. When faced with uncertainty concerning the biological requirements of an organism or of a group of organisms, land management plans must be conservative in their retention of habitat components. Because we know little of the details of lynx habitat relationships at the stand scale or the necessary juxtaposition of stand types, landscape-scale habitat management strategies should provide for a continuum of stand ages in a variety of spatial configurations.

The maintenance of all age classes in commercial forests has been viewed as problematic because even-aged forest management removes all stands older than the rotation age, eliminating both habitat and future management options for organisms associated with late-successional forests. On the other hand, removing all disturbance from a site by suppressing fire and refraining from cutting will, in most areas, preclude stand replacement and impact organisms associated with younger forest conditions. Our challenge, from the perspective of maintaining lynx and their prey in the context of ecosystem management, is to design management strategies that result in dynamic, sustainable landscapes that approximate the composition of natural systems.

Natural Disturbance as a Management Template

Natural disturbance in boreal forests, due to its stochastic nature, tends to generate forests composed of widely varying ages and conditions (Chapter 3). These conditions emerge as a direct consequence of disturbance stochasticity; one drainage may burn frequently, whereas an adjacent drainage may avoid fire for centuries. For example, within a burned drainage variation in wind patterns may leave unburned patches, and diurnal variation in moisture and temperature during a fire may result in some areas having high tree survival, whereas others do not. This stochastic process leads to a landscape with a mosaic of conditions at various spatial scales. A very large, stand-replacing fire has little mosaic within its boundaries (Eberhart and Woodard 1987), but viewed at the spatial scale of the region and the temporal scale of 100 years, it represents a patch in a fire mosaic on the landscape. Such an event produces a large, contiguous area of young forest but, in the larger context, there will be areas of very old forest as well.

Johnson et al. (1995) and Agee (Chapter 3) argue that naturally occurring age distributions in forested landscapes, especially landscapes composed of boreal and subalpine forests (Johnson et al. 1995), often fit negative exponential functions, indicating a constant-probability stochastic process. While this model may not always produce the best fit (Chapter 3), all stochastic processes produce a characteristic signature in the resulting age distribution, including asymptotic "tails" in the older age classes (Fig. 15.1a; Van Wagner 1978; McKelvey and Lamberson 1994). In contrast, cyclic processes, such as even-aged rotation forestry, truncate the age distribution (Fig. 15.1c). In a cyclic system, there is no formal mechanism to generate stands or elements older than rotation age. However, in a forested landscape with a negative exponential stand-age distribution, about 36% of the landscape will be older than the average stand age, about 13% older than twice the average stand age, and about 5% older than three times the average stand age (Table 15.1). Although there is no maximum stand age in this system (Finney 1994), old stands that have not burned will be subject to other sources of mortality, such as insects and disease.

Table 15.1–Equilibrium time since disturbance for forests with a negative exponential stand age distribution. Where time since disturbance exceeds the longevity of individual trees, the stand ages will be younger than are indicated in this table, and the forests will be characterized by "gap" processes due to overstory mortality.

Fire return interval (average stand age)	Percent of area (by age class)				
	<50	50-100	100-200	200-300	>300
100 years	40	24	23	9	4
150 years	29	20	25	`13	13
200 years	23	17	24	14	22
300 years	16	13	20	15	36

The retention of older stands essentially mimics the process of ecological "escape" in systems characterized by large-scale disturbances. In a catastrophic fire, variation in fire intensities and the vagaries of weather allow forest elements at many scales to survive, including individual trees, small groups of trees, stands, or entire watersheds. As multiple fires overlap over many years, there will be small areas embedded in larger areas of younger forest that have, by chance or location, survived multiple fires. This escape of older elements is not effectively mimicked by embedding fixed reserves in a landscape of cyclic management. In a stochastic system, with each new disturbance event, older forests may be destroyed or altered, or they may be left intact; thus, late-successional stands are not spatially assigned and maintained, but emerge dynamically within the disturbance process. A variety of other differences, some of them dramatic, also distinguish fixed-rotation from stochastic systems. For example, if a natural fire-return interval is 100 years, and a 100-year clearcut rotation is implemented to mimic natural rates of disturbance, the average stand age in the managed forest will be 50 years. In a stochastic system with a negative exponential stand-age distribution, however, the same landscape would have an average stand age equal to the fire-return interval, or 100 years.

Assuming that the scale of disturbance corresponds with the movement capabilities of individual lynx, landscapes generated through these stochastic processes would provide an amenable environment for lynx by producing areas of young, dense forest without removing the older elements. If the natural fire regime can be estimated for an area that is to be managed for lynx, then it is logical to use this rate to design management strategies. The overall rate of disturbance would be an aggregate of the cumulative effects of timber harvest, fire, and other natural disturbances (catastrophic windthrow or insect epidemics) on age structure. Therefore, in areas subjected to large wildland fires, or where inholdings are managed for short-rotation timber yield using even-aged management, timber harvest (including salvage) may be inappropriate for decades. In some regions, significant amounts of wilderness or National Park land will be part of the planning area, and management of natural fires must be incorporated into planning. We assume here that fire and timber harvest are similar processes in their capacity to initiate secondary succession. In addition, we would argue for a planned rate of disturbance somewhat less than the historically derived estimate. It is easy to increase the disturbance rate if desirable, but much harder to recover old-growth forests removed through overly aggressive management.

Spatial Patterns Resulting from Natural Disturbance Processes

Applying the negative exponential model has been suggested as an ecosystem management approach (Johnson et al. 1995), and does conform to many of Christensen et al.'s (1996) required properties: it produces sustainable patterns, maintains ecosystem complexity, and is primarily derived from an analysis of natural processes, specifically fire. It does not, however, directly address the larger scale issues of landscape pattern and connectivity. In these regards the model is neutral; it can be applied in a variety of configurations.

In even-aged timber management systems employing clearcutting, harvest units are generally similar in size (Fig. 15.1d). For example, a maximum clearcut size of 40 ac (16 ha) has been mandated on Forest Service lands for many years. Fires come in many sizes, however. In most forested landscapes, the majority of fires are small, whereas the majority of acreage burned has resulted from a few, very large fires (Chapter 3). Although this pattern is probably not feasible or even desirable as a management goal outside of wilderness, there are many advantages associated with producing fewer, larger cutting units. A disturbance pattern characterized by a few large blocks (Fig. 15.1b) is desirable if large areas of interior forest habitat are a management goal, or if processes associated with high edge densities, such as predation, competition, or nest parasitism, are potentially serious problems. It also vastly decreases the number of roads that need to be built. Lower road densities mean less sediment and mass failure into streams, reduced interactions between people and native biota, and slower invasion by exotic weed species. Costs of road construction and maintenance are decreased and, if a site is to be broadcast burned, the cost per acre declines as the area to be burned increases.

Juxtaposition of Habitat

The application of a fixed rotation age, in addition to the negative consequences of truncating the forest age distribution, also produces fixed landscape geometries (Fig. 15.1d). Once an area is cut, it is not scheduled to be re-entered (except for thinning) until it is again at rotation age. Because the adjacent areas will be younger than the rotation age, the next cut will conform to the original boundaries. Even if protected reserves are embedded within an even-aged rotation system, only a relatively small number of age juxtapositions and geometries are possible within each landscape.

However, the juxtaposition of stand ages in a variety of configurations and the edge habitats that result may provide essential ecological complexity at the landscape scale. A predator that needs thermal cover and nest sites in large snags or down logs typically found in old-growth forests, may forage in herbivore-rich early seral stands if they are nearby. For example, northern spotted owls use edge areas between old and young forest preferentially in those areas where young forests contain high concentrations of woodrats (Zabel et al. 1995). Additionally, most organisms have habitat requirements that change seasonally or stochastically; what is optimal in the summer may not be optimal in the winter, and what is optimal in a mild winter may not be useful during extreme conditions. By developing forests with a mixture of young and old stands in a variety of spatial combinations, we are likely to provide habitat requirements for a broad array of organisms.

Stand selection by fire in the taiga is not truly random, but it is more so than in the southern boreal forest types of the contiguous United States. In more southern areas, natural barriers and topographic features such as slope and aspect may provide locations where older forest is more likely to be found. These "refugia" (e.g., Camp et al. 1997) are not permanently fixed on the landscape, but tend to be located in areas that are infrequently disturbed, such as moist sites with topographic protection from wind. Northern aspects and areas near stream confluences are likely to become refuges from fire, whereas steep south- and west-facing slopes are likely to be burned more often. Locally-defined habitat conditions, such as these, should be used to develop spatially explicit landscape configurations.

Heterogeneity at the Local Scale

Although individual lynx may respond to landscape conditions at the scale of 50-100 km^2, their primary prey species respond to much smaller scale patterns, on the order of 1-10 ha. A landscape-scale management strategy that emphasizes stochastic models does not prescribe the size or location of treatments on the landscape, nor does it foreclose options concerning the types of treatments involved; treatments can include either timber harvest or prescribed fire. Additionally, activities on private lands, and naturally occurring events such as lightning fires, wind-throw, insect-induced mortality, etc., also need to be factored into landscape planning. Some of these events and activities may be predictable, while others will be surprises. Accordingly, management strategies must be flexible at several spatial scales.

Snowshoe hares generally occur in areas of dense forest cover, including shrubs and "doghair" thickets of small trees (Chapters 6 and 7). These structures are common in naturally regenerating areas after fire, but do not result from standard, even-aged forestry practices (Daniel et al. 1979). Thus, we believe that natural regeneration and stand development will likely benefit hares and, ultimately, lynx. Creative silviculture is required when management goals extend beyond wood production. This might translate to heavier reliance on natural regeneration after wildland fires. Where harvest mandates artificial regeneration in a short time frame, the planting might be clustered such that the time of early seral dominance will be spatially variable across a unit. If pre-commercial thinning is considered, it should be recognized that the usual objective of increasing the diameter growth of residual trees may be inappropriate for lynx. Leaving some doghair stands may be good for lynx; thinning others so heavily that additional conifer regeneration occurs in the unit may also be appropriate. Because fires leave large amounts of woody material standing and down, management should also leave substantial amounts of woody material in representative size classes, regardless of treatment.

The planning area also needs to encompass transitional areas between what is considered suitable habitat for lynx. Although the role of such areas in maintaining lynx populations is poorly understood, the condition of these areas will likely affect movement and survival during dispersal. For example, in lower elevation zones with mixed-severity fire regimes and fire-resistant trees, such as western larch, it may be appropriate to leave green trees on site. Large units may contain a variety of silvicultural treatments (e.g., clearcuts, as well as areas of green-tree retention at various stem densities) that grade into one another. In these transitional areas, some proportion should be treated with overstory removal significant enough that dense conifer regeneration will result, unless such areas already exist.

Minimum Area and Age-Class Requirements for Applying the Negative Exponential Model

We have argued that effective management of wide-ranging species, such as the lynx, requires planning at large spatial scales. In this context, it is important to note that stochastic disturbance processes only approach equilibrium at large spatial scales. With a negative exponential age distribution, very old forests, which make up a relatively small proportion of the landscape, will be lost by chance alone if planning is done at too small a scale. Johnson et al. (1995) provide equations for estimating the appropriate scale based on fire-return interval, projected age of oldest patch, average patch size, and size of the management unit. Because historic fire-return intervals vary substantially among southern boreal forests (Chapter 3), spatial planning should be based on sub-regional fire-return intervals.

Knowledge of historic patch sizes will enable some rough ideas of minimum area. If stand ages are distributed according to the negative exponential model, the largest patch should be a small proportion of the total landscape. Assuming 10% as the maximum size for a "small" proportion, and applying this to the north-central Washington landscape discussed earlier in this chapter where fires of 20,000 ha have occurred (e.g., the 1988 White Mountain fires), the minimum planning area might be 200,000 ha ($2,000 \text{ km}^2$). If we were less conservative and chose 20%, the minimum area would be $1,000 \text{ km}^2$. This range of 1,000 to 2,000 km^2 compares favorably with the minimum estimate of 1,250 km^2 derived from lynx studies conducted in that area. The size of planning areas need to be based on local conditions and must be linked at broader scales, but these estimates provide a general sense of the scale at which planning would need to take place.

The management approach we have suggested for the conservation of lynx is to imitate the stochastic process of fire by managing for a stand age distribution that approximates the negative exponential model (Fig. 15.1a and 15.1b). Because this model results in an equilibrium distribution of forest age classes, standard methods can be used to estimate sustainable value and volume (McKelvey and Lamberson 1994). This management model is not as difficult to implement as it may seem. The stochastic process being modeled does not need to be randomized in the formal sense; deterministic processes can achieve the same patterns. In fact, within the overall planning area, there is a great deal of freedom concerning the placement and size of management units and the timing of management activities. Any stand can be disturbed at any time as long as the proportions associated with that stand type within the planning area are not exceeded. Accordingly, this strategy is much more spatially flexible than a fixed-rotation system, but it requires larger spatial and temporal frames than have been used historically.

Compatibility of Lynx Conservation with Other Resource Management Objectives

Both the regulatory requirements of state and federal resource management agencies and the concepts embodied in ecosystem management preclude the implementation of a lynx conservation strategy across a broad geographic area that fails to adequately address other resource values, especially the habitat needs of threatened or sensitive species. We propose that other resource management objectives, even those that may conflict in various ways with the needs of lynx, can be accomplished within the context of a habitat management strategy that mimics large-scale stochastic disturbance regimes. A key component of the negative exponential model is that it represents an adaptable and flexible management system, not one with rigid constraints on management options. On the contrary, the dynamic nature of the negative exponential age distribution in both time and space, provides a variety of opportunities for adjusting management actions to meet alternative objectives.

In southern boreal forests, other forest carnivores, including the marten, fisher, and wolverine, are also of conservation concern, but have habitat requirements that differ in many ways from those of the lynx (Ruggiero et al. 1994). Although providing for the habitat needs of these species may conflict with management of lynx habitat at the stand scale, the flexibility inherent in the negative exponential model should enable the attainment of multiple management objectives. In the remainder of this section, we use these three species to present examples of how applying this model to lynx conservation can be compatible with management for species having divergent habitat requirements.

American martens occupy mesic coniferous forests throughout boreal regions of North America, but generally attain their highest densities in late-successional stands with high levels of structural heterogeneity (Buskirk and Powell 1994). In addition, recent work by Hargis et al. (1999) in Utah suggests that interior forest conditions may provide essential breeding habitat for martens. Both martens and lynx occupy habitats characterized by snowy winters, and their ranges overlap extensively in northern portions of the Rocky Mountains, Cascade Range, and northeastern United States. Thus, management of habitat for lynx, especially the creation of early successional stands for snowshoe hare habitat, will impact martens in these regions. Under a stochastic disturbance regime, the resulting successional landscape would provide islands of old-growth habitat nested within an area managed for lynx. However, when applying the negative exponential model, the areal distribution of stand ages is flexible; within the conservation area, a given forest age class could be dispersed, clumped, or a combination of both. Thus, if a primary management objective was to provide habitat for a resident population of martens, or other species closely associated with late-seral forest conditions, older age classes could be clumped so that one or several areas contained high proportions of old growth and interior forest habitat.

Habitats occupied by fishers are similar to martens, but fishers are not as strongly associated with late-successional forests or deep snowpacks (Powell and Zielinski 1994). Fishers occupy a variety of stand ages but prefer forests with high canopy closure and complex structures near the ground. Unlike martens, fishers are not well adapted for traveling or hunting in snow and generally occupy low to mid-elevation forests where deep, soft snow does not accumulate. Although fishers are sympatric with lynx in much of Canada and in some portions of the northeastern United States, historical and current records indicate little overlap in habitats used by these species in the western mountains. Thus, it is unlikely that management of high-elevation boreal forest habitats for lynx will have adverse effects on fisher populations. Because lynx may use lower elevation habitats to move between patches of boreal forest, however, lower elevation zones may contain fisher habitat. Thus, if a management objective was to provide habitat for fishers, a manager might restrict clearcutting or other timber harvest activities designed to create snowshoe hare habitat to upper elevations, where lynx are most likely to occur, but maintain stands at lower elevations in older age classes having high levels of canopy closure. In addition, silvicultural prescriptions designed to provide a diversity of large forest structures in areas of potential fisher habitat would provide den and rest sites and increase prey availability for both martens and fishers.

Wolverines occupy a broader range of vegetation zones than other forest carnivores, including boreal forest, alpine, and tundra habitats. It has been argued that good wolverine habitat is best defined in terms of an adequate food supply in areas of low human density; however, the habitat ecology of wolverines in western montane boreal forests has been studied at only a few localities (Banci 1994; Copeland 1996, unpublished). Because the spatial requirements of wolverine exceed those of lynx (Ruggiero et al. 1994), areas managed for lynx would be smaller than those required for the conservation of wolverine populations. However, because these areas will likely contain components of subalpine and alpine habitats, relatively extensive areas of potential wolverine habitat would be included within areas managed for lynx. Wolverines generally scavenge for ungulates along valley bottoms and forage and den in remote, high-elevation areas (Hornocker and Hash 1981; Magoun and Copeland 1998). Thus, if managers wished to provide habitat for wolverines, they could pay particular attention in the planning process to ungulate winter range and other aspects of habitat quality for ungulates to provide a consistent supply of carcasses for wolverine to scavenge. In addition, wolverines generally avoid areas of human activity. To limit the threat of human-caused disturbance or mortality, managers could also restrict access to portions of the landscape where wolverines are most likely to occur.

Monitoring

The management model we have presented in this chapter represents a conservative approach, but is largely untested. Consequently, the implementation of these ideas should be considered experimental in nature. Because we are relatively ignorant of the ecological and social consequences of this type of approach, a comprehensive monitoring plan must also be established to assess the current status of vegetation and target species within the planning area and to monitor changes to the landscape and the biota that result from the implementation of this management strategy. Unfortunately, most environmental monitoring programs on public lands have not been carried out as planned, nor have they contributed to decision-making by resource managers or the aversion of biological crises (Noon et al. 1999). The primary reasons given by Noon et al. (1999) for the widespread failure of monitoring programs include: a minimal foundation in ecological theory or knowledge, little logical basis for the selection of target species, no required understanding of cause-and-effect, no determination of the magnitude of change that would result in a management response, and no connection between the results of monitoring and decision-making. Lynx conservation in the context of ecosystem management cannot succeed without a scientifically based monitoring strategy that overcomes the shortcomings of previous monitoring efforts.

An important aspect of our suggested approach to lynx conservation in the context of ecosystem management is the resultant flexibility in planning landscape features (i.e., the kinds, amounts, and arrangements of landscape elements) based on outputs of the negative exponential model. As discussed throughout this chapter, these outputs include information about patch sizes and the vegetative composition of modeled landscapes. In many, if not most, instances the appropriate spatial scale for modeling will subsume more than one administrative unit. Thus, model outputs will have to be disaggregated across administrative boundaries. To accomplish this, highly innovative and integrated planning processes will be needed. Innovative approaches to monitoring the consequences of planning decisions will also be required. Indeed, the success of this approach will depend on monitoring the proportions, patch sizes, and arrangements of the vegetation types and successional stages in each planning area. Given the fundamental importance of pattern as an ecological feature, spatially explicit monitoring to ensure conformity to desired patterns will be essential.

Within this framework, more traditional monitoring activities will also need to be performed. Much has been written on this subject (e.g., Goldsmith 1990; Mulder et al. 1999), but the details are beyond the scope of this chapter. Because a primary objective of management actions will be to enhance habitat conditions for both lynx and snowshoe hares, monitoring of hare populations with pellet transects (e.g., Krebs et al. 1987) and lynx populations with snowtracking or other techniques (e.g., Thompson et al. 1981), will likely be critical components of monitoring strategies. Lastly, we emphasize that effective monitoring programs must include pre-defined criteria for determining how to interpret monitoring results, and what actions to take when monitoring indicates the need to modify management direction.

Conclusions

We believe this approach to conserving lynx populations is compatible with the need to provide for other sensitive species and with the coarse-filter approach suggested by ecosystem management. We do not present a detailed template for the implementation of these ideas, because the specific components of management planning will depend on the natural disturbance regime, current conditions within the landscape, the plant and animal species that inhabit it, and other management objectives. In all of the applications of lynx management, however, we recommend the following:

1. Use natural disturbance patterns, in terms of size, frequency, intensity, and stochasticity for guidance concerning the design and management of landscapes.

2. Engage in spatially explicit landscape planning within very large management areas. Lynx metapopulation dynamics operate at regional scales.

3. Manage for landscapes that contain a continuum of age classes, including both very young and very old forest. Not only is this reflected in patterns that result from fire and other natural disturbances, but it represents a prudent conservation policy in the face of uncertainty. In this regard, be especially cautious with older forests and carefully consider the replacement time for each forest type and forest element. A large-diameter log may take hundreds of years to decay; a small clearing can be created in a few weeks.

4. Provide for a variety of regeneration conditions; some areas should be dense and some more open. Treatments that depend on natural regeneration will be more likely to produce these patterns than will planting. Leave individual trees and variable-sized groups of residual elements if natural disturbance processes suggest these structures are appropriate.

5. Practice adaptive management and consider every action on the landscape to be an experiment. Monitor the efficacy of management actions and adapt strategies if desired conditions are not being achieved.

Literature Cited

Agee, J. K. 1993. Fire Ecology of Pacific Northwest Forests. Island Press, Covelo, CA.

Agee, J. K. and D. R. Johnson. 1988. Ecosystem management for parks and wilderness. University of Washington Press, Seattle, WA.

Allen, T. F. H. and T. W. Hoekstra. 1992. Toward a unified ecology. Columbia University Press, New York.

Bailey, R. G. 1998. Ecoregions map of North America: explanatory note. USDA Forest Service, Miscellaneous Publication No. 1548.

Banci, V. 1994. Wolverine. Pages 99-127 *in* L. F. Ruggiero, K. B. Aubry, S. W. Buskirk, L. J. Lyon and W. J. Zielinski, technical editors. The scientific basis for conserving forest carnivores in the Western United States: American marten, fisher, lynx, and wolverine. USDA Forest Service, General Technical Report RM-254.

Berger, J. 1997. Population constraints associated with the use of black rhinos as an umbrella species for desert herbivores. Conservation Biology 11:69-78.

Brittell, J. D., R. J. Poelker, S. J. Sweeney and G. M. Koehler. 1989. Native cats of Washington, Section III: Lynx. Unpublished, Washington Department of Wildlife, Olympia, WA.

Buskirk S. W. and R. A. Powell. 1994. Habitat ecology of fishers and American martens. Pages 283-296 *in* S. W. Buskirk, A. S. Harestad, M. G. Raphael, and R. A. Powell, editors. Martens, sables, and fishers: biology and conservation. Cornell University Press, Ithaca, NY.

Camp, A., C. Oliver, P. Hessburg, and R. Everett. 1997. Predicting late-successional fire refugia pre-dating European settlement in the Wenatchee Mountains. Forest Ecology and Management 95:63-77.

Christensen, N. L., A. M. Bartuska, J. H. Brown, S. Carpenter, C. D'Antonio, R. Francis, J. F. Franklin, J. A. MacMahon, R. F. Noss, D. J. Parsons, C. H. Peterson, M. G. Turner, and R. G. Woodmansee. 1996. The report of the Ecological Society of America Committee on the Scientific Basis for Ecosystem Management. Ecological Applications 6:665-691.

Committee of Scientists. 1999. Sustaining the people's lands: recommendations for stewardship of the National Forests and Grasslands into the next century. USDA Forest Service, Washington, DC.

Copeland, J. P. 1996. Biology of the wolverine in central Idaho. Unpublished M.S. Thesis, University of Idaho, Moscow, ID.

Daniel, T. W., J. A. Helms, and F. S. Baker. 1979. Principles of silviculture, second edition. McGraw-Hill, New York.

Eberhart, K. E. and P. M. Woodard. 1987. Distribution of residual vegetation associated with large fires in Alberta. Canadian Journal of Forest Research 17:1207-1212.

Elton C. and M. Nicholson. 1942. The ten-year cycle in numbers of the lynx in Canada. Journal of Animal Ecology 11:215-244.

Finney, M. A. 1994. The missing tail and other considerations for the use of fire history models. International Journal of Wildland Fire 5:197-202.

Franklin, J. F. 1993. The fundamentals of ecosystem management with applications in the Pacific Northwest. Pages 127-144 *in* G. H. Aplet, V. A. Sample, N. Johnson, and J. T. Olson, editors. Defining sustainable forestry. Island Press, Washington, DC.

Franklin, J. F. 1997. Ecosystem management: an overview. Pages 21-53 *in* M. S. Boyce and A. Haney, editors. Ecosystem management: applications for sustainable forest and wildlife resources. Yale University Press, New Haven, CT.

Goldsmith. F. B., editor. 1990. Monitoring for conservation and ecology. Chapman and Hall, New York.

Grumbine, R. E. 1994. What is ecosystem management? Conservation Biology 8:27-38.

Hargis, C. D., J. A. Bissonette, and D. L. Turner. 1999. The influence of forest fragmentation and landscape pattern on American martens. Journal of Applied Ecology 36:157-172.

Haufler, J. B., C. A. Mehl, and G. J. Roloff. 1996. Using a coarse-filter approach with species assessment for ecosystem management. Wildlife Society Bulletin 24:200-208.

Hornocker, M. G. and H. S. Hash. 1981. Ecology of the wolverine in northwestern Montana. Canadian Journal of Zoology 59:1286-1301.

Hunter, M. L., G. L. Jacobson, Jr., and T. Webb, III. 1988. Paleoecology and coarse-filter approach to maintaining biological diversity. Conservation Biology 2:375-385.

Johnson, E. A., K. Miyanishi, and J. M. H. Weir. 1995. Old-growth, disturbance, and ecosystem management. Canadian Journal of Botany 73:918-926.

Koehler, G. M. 1990. Population and habitat characteristics of lynx and snowshoe hares in north central Washington. Canadian Journal of Zoology 68:845-851.

Koehler, G. M. and J. D. Brittell. 1990. Managing spruce-fir habitat for lynx and snowshoe hare. Journal of Forestry 88:10-14.

Krebs, C. J., B. S. Gilbert, S. Boutin, and R. Boonstra. 1987. Estimation of snowshoe hare population density from turd transects. Canadian Journal of Zoology 65:565-567.

Landres, P. B., J. Verner, and J. W. Thomas. 1988. Ecological uses of vertebrate indicator species: a critique. Conservation Biology 2:316-328.

Litvaitis, J. A., D. Kingman, Jr., J. Lanier, and E. Orff. 1991. Status of lynx in New Hampshire. Transactions of the Northeast Section of the Wildlife Society 48:70-75.

Magoun, A. J. and J. P. Copeland. 1998. Characteristics of wolverine reproductive den sites. Journal of Wildlife Management 62:1313-1320.

McKelvey, K. S. and K. K. Busse. 1996. Twentieth-century fire patterns on Forest Service lands. Pages 1119-1138 *in* Sierra Nevada Ecosystem Project: final report to Congress, Vol. II, Assessments and scientific basis for management options. University of California Press, Davis, CA.

McKelvey, K. S. and R. H. Lamberson. 1994. Random entry forestry: timber management in a time of species conservation. Natural Resource Modeling 8:81-93.

Mills, L. S., M. E. Soule, and D. F. Doak. 1993. The keystone-species concept in ecology and conservation. BioScience 43:219-224.

Minnich, R. A. 1983. Fire mosaics in southern California and northern Baja California. Science 219:1287-1294.

Mulder, B. S., B. R. Noon, T. A. Spies, M. G. Raphael, C. J. Palmer, A. R. Olsen, G. H. Reeves, and H. H. Welsh, technical coordinators. 1999. The strategy and design of the effectiveness monitoring program of the Northwest Forest Plan. USDA Forest Service, General Technical Report PNW-GTR-437.

Noon, B. R., T. A. Spies, and M. G. Raphael. 1999. Conceptual basis for designing an effectiveness monitoring program. Pages 21-48 *in* Mulder, B. S., B. R. Noon, T. A. Spies, M. G. Raphael, C. J. Palmer, A. R. Olsen, G. H. Reeves, and H. H. Welsh, technical coordinators. The strategy and design of the effectiveness monitoring program of the Northwest Forest Plan. USDA Forest Service, General Technical Report PNW-GTR-437.

Paine, R. T. 1969. A note on trophic complexity and community stability. American Naturalist 103:91-93.

Patton, D. R. 1987. Is the use of "management indicator species" feasible? Western Journal of Applied Forestry 2:33-34.

Powell, R. A. and W. J. Zielinski. 1994. Fisher. Pages 38-73 *in* L. F. Ruggiero, K. B. Aubry, S. W. Buskirk, L. J. Lyon, and W. J. Zielinski, technical editors. The scientific basis for conserving forest carnivores in the Western United States: American marten, fisher, lynx, and wolverine. USDA Forest Service, General Technical Report RM-254.

Ranta, E., V. Kaitala, and J. Lindstrom. 1997. Dynamics of Canadian lynx populations in space and time. Ecography 20:454-460.

Rieman, B. E. and J. D. McIntyre. 1993. Demographic and habitat requirements for conservation of bull trout. USDA Forest Service, General Technical Report INT-302.

Ruggiero, L. F., K. B. Aubry, S. W. Buskirk, L. J. Lyon and W. J. Zielinski, technical editors. 1994. The scientific basis for conserving forest carnivores in the Western United States: American marten, fisher, lynx, and wolverine. USDA Forest Service, General Technical Report RM-254.

Thompson, I. D., I. J. Davidson, S. O'Donnell, and F. Brazeau. 1981. Use of track transects to measure the relative occurrence of some boreal mammals in uncut forest and regeneration stands. Canadian Journal of Zoology 67:1816-1823.

USDA and USDI. 1994a. Final supplemental environmental impact statement on management of habitat for late-successional and old-growth related species within the range of the northern spotted owl. USDA Forest Service, Portland, OR.

USDA and USDI. 1994b. Environmental assessment for the implementation of interim strategies for managing anadromous fish-producing watersheds in eastern Oregon and Washington, Idaho, and portions of California. USDA Forest Service and USDI Bureau of Land Management, Washington, DC.

Van Wagner, C. E. 1978. Age-class distribution and the forest fire cycle. Canadian Journal of Forest Research 8:220-227.

Walters, C. 1986. Adaptive management of renewable resources. Macmillan, New York.

Washington State Department of Natural Resources. 1996. Lynx habitat management plan for DNR managed lands. Washington State Department of Natural Resources, Olympia, WA.

Zabel C. J., K. S. McKelvey, and J. P. Ward, Jr. 1995. Influence of primary prey on home-range size and habitat-use patterns of northern spotted owls (*Strix occidentalis caurina*). Canadian Journal of Zoology 73:433-439.

Chapter 16

The Scientific Basis for Lynx Conservation: Qualified Insights

Leonard F. Ruggiero, USDA Forest Service, Rocky Mountain Research
    Station, 800 E. Beckwith, Missoula, MT 59807

Keith B. Aubry, USDA Forest Service, Pacific Northwest Research Station,
    3625 93rd Ave. SW, Olympia, WA 98512

Steven W. Buskirk, Department of Physiology and Zoology, University of
    Wyoming, P.O. Box 3166, Laramie, WY 82071

Gary M. Koehler, Washington Dept. of Fish and Wildlife,
    600 Capitol Way N., Olympia, WA 98501

Charles J. Krebs, University of British Columbia, 6271 University of British
    Columbia, 6270 University Blvd., Vancouver, BC V6T 1Z4

Kevin S. McKelvey, USDA Forest Service, Rocky Mountain Research
    Station, 800 E. Beckwith, Missoula, MT 59807

John R. Squires, Wildlife Biology Program, University of Montana,
    Missoula, MT 59812

Introduction

The information presented in this chapter is based on (1) extant knowledge of lynx ecology, (2) the pertinence of this knowledge to lynx conservation in the contiguous United States, (3) the ecological concepts discussed in the first section of this book, and (4) the collective interpretation and judgment of the authors. We have chosen the term "qualified insights" to indicate that we know very little about lynx ecology in the United States and that understandings based on this state of knowledge are necessarily incomplete. The application of science results in a gradual accretion of understanding as relatively small increments of knowledge are added to existing scientific paradigms. This is not to say that the scientific process is always linear, that intuition and creativity are not crucial aspects of the process, or that paradigm-changing flashes of insight do not occur. All of these are elements of the scientific process, but scientific understandings are generally constructed bit by bit as the result of a sustained commitment to research. It follows that scientists generally ask questions that are tractable given the normal tools of scientific investigation, and that large, complex problems are broken down into manageable pieces. As a corollary to this, it is inappropriate to expect scientists to solve complex problems in a single stroke. Yet this is often what ecologists are called upon to do when land managers and decision-makers find that they lack sufficient understanding to meet legal mandates for environmental protection. For example, understanding how the viability of lynx populations is affected by human actions is an extremely complex problem and, because there has not been a sustained commitment to research, the scientific basis for answering this question is inadequate. No amount of socio-political clamoring for reliable answers will change this; uncertainty will prevail.

In the following pages, we have attempted to distill the state of knowledge regarding lynx ecology along with our interpretations about the kind and quality of understandings that this knowledge conveys. Because the state of the art is poorly developed for lynx ecology, the first section of this book was devoted to a presentation of salient ecological concepts. These concepts provide a partial basis for the scientific interpretations discussed in Chapter 1. Until additional data are collected, we must assume that insights based on well-established concepts are valid.

The eleven topics presented below represent crucial areas of ecological understanding relative to species conservation (Chapter 1). Although we attempted to offer substantive interpretations in each of these areas, a lack of information often prevented us from doing so. We elaborate on these information needs in Chapter 17.

1. Present and Historical Patterns of Lynx Distribution

During the 1800s and early 1900s, lynx occurred in Colorado, Idaho, Maine, Michigan, Minnesota, Montana, New Hampshire, New York, Utah, Washington, Wisconsin, and Wyoming. Relatively few records occur in other states. Based on an extensive review of historical information, including trapping records, New Hampshire, Minnesota, Montana, and Washington appear to have supported the most lynx. A dramatic decline in lynx numbers appears to have occurred in New Hampshire, where recent records are scarce. Although records from New York, Colorado, and Utah have always been scarce, the lack of recent verified records suggest that lynx may have been extirpated from these states (Chapter 8). The status of lynx in the remaining states is unknown.

Extant lynx populations in Washington, Montana, and perhaps Maine occupy habitats that are contiguous with habitats in Canada. It is likely that prior to extensive human development adjacent to the St. Lawrence Seaway, lynx populations in New Hampshire also occurred in habitats that were contiguous with similar habitats in Canada (Litvaitis et al. 1991). In addition, trapping records indicate that lynx populations in Montana, Minnesota, and Washington appear to have cycled in lagged synchrony with lynx populations in Canada during the population highs of the 1960s and 1970s (Chapter 8). The only other known population of lynx is in Wyoming (Chapter 11). This population is thought to be small, is adjacent to extensive park and wilderness areas, and is located within the Greater Yellowstone Ecosystem.

We conclude that extensive areas of contiguous suitable habitat are needed to ensure viable lynx populations. All areas in the contiguous United States where we can state with certainty that lynx currently occur are directly connected to larger habitat areas. Apparently, lynx are unlikely to persist in relatively small, isolated refugia of suitable habitat. In saying this, we acknowledge a very incomplete understanding of what constitutes suitable lynx and hare habitat in the contiguous United States.

2. Factors Limiting the Geographic Distribution of Lynx

Most lynx records in North America are found in boreal forests (Chapter 8). In the Great Lakes states, most records are in the Mixed Deciduous-Coniferous Province, and, in the northeastern states, most records are in the Mixed Forest-Coniferous Forest-Tundra Province (provinces after Bailey 1998). In the western mountains of the United States, most records are in the Douglas-fir, western spruce/fir, and fir/hemlock vegetation types (Kuchler 1964). All of these types can be characterized as mesic coniferous forests with cold snowy winters. Lynx have morphological adaptations for moving and hunting in snow as exemplified by significantly lower foot loadings than most carnivores (Chapter 4). Records from Washington, Wyoming, and Utah/Colorado show that lynx occur at higher elevations as one moves south, with modal elevations of 2,000 m, 2,700 m, and 3000 m, respectively (Chapter 8). In addition, it is generally agreed that lynx distributions are limited by the availability of snowshoe hares (Chapter 9).

Other than cool, snowy, conifer forests and snowshoe hares, we have not identified additional factors that limit the distribution of lynx. However, this does not mean that additional factors do not exist. Indeed, there are geographic areas that appear to have the necessary features to support lynx, yet lynx occurrence records are scarce or absent from these areas. Three such areas are the Cascade and Coast Ranges in the western United States, the southern Rocky Mountains, and the Great Lake States (except for the extreme northeast corner of Minnesota). Assuming that adequate densities of snowshoe hares exist in these areas, the lack of lynx records indicates that there are factors controlling the distribution of lynx that we do not understand.

We conclude that at the broadest geographic scale, lynx distribution is limited to moist, cool boreal forests that support some minimum density of snowshoe hares (e.g., at least 0.5 hares/ha in northwestern Canada but unknown farther south). Lynx are also limited to areas with snowy winters, likely because of their coadaptation with hares and because snow gives lynx a competitive advantage over other carnivores. In the West, lynx are uncommon or absent in coastal forests, possibly due to limiting abiotic factors.

3. Principal Habitat Features Affecting Lynx

At the stand level, lynx use a variety of forest types and a broad range of stand ages. Our limited understanding of lynx in the southern part of their range suggests that, as in the North, lynx use habitats with abundant snowshoe hares. However, hare density alone may not be the most crucial factor in lynx hunting success or in habitat selection by lynx. It is unclear how habitat structure affects the vulnerability of hares to capture by lynx. Northern studies suggest that lynx require hare densities of 0.5-1.0 hares/ha to persist, but farther south this relationship may differ. In the North, when hare densities fall below this threshold, lynx expand their home ranges, increase daily travel distances, suffer increased adult mortality, and stop reproducing (Chapter 9). Additional information on this relationship is a critical research need for southern populations.

Limited evidence for the southern part of the range suggests that lynx are associated with mesic forest types, and that dry forest types (e.g., ponderosa pine) are used mostly to move among mesic stands. These mesic forest types are southern extensions of boreal forests, commonly dominated by spruce and fir, Douglas-fir, and lodgepole pine. In the southern part of the range, these types occur as islands and peninsulas within a matrix of drier, montane forest, typically dominated by lower elevation conifers (Chapter 8).

Dense, small-diameter woody vegetation supports high hare densities and, thus, is important for lynx. Such conditions are created by natural disturbances of varying sizes, including gap-phase processes found in late-seral forests (Chapter 14). The successional processes responsible for the creation of the structural features associated with hare habitat are controlled by complex moisture/temperature gradients. Thus, the availability, abundance, and community association of these habitats is spatially variable. However, in the drier portions of lynx range, hare habitat may be increasingly associated with more mesic late-seral forests and riparian areas (Chapter 14). Although areas of regenerating forest created by natural or human-made disturbances can provide important hare habitat, such areas are temporally transient. On the other hand, late-seral forest appears to be moderately productive for hares, very productive for red squirrels, and temporally more stable. The pattern of hare habitat that is optimal for lynx is unknown and represents a critical information need. The negative exponential forest model provides a range of stand ages (Chapter 15) and holds potential as a basis for ensuring persistent populations of hares and lynx.

Limited data for southern areas suggest that lynx den in forested sites with relatively large, complex physical structure near the ground, primarily in the form of coarse woody debris. The optimal size and arrangement of such sites is unknown and constitutes another critical information need.

We conclude that a snowshoe hare density greater than 0.5 hares/ha is likely required for lynx persistence. Hare habitat occurs in a range of stand ages, including regenerating disturbed stands and late-seral forest. Regenerating stands can be highly productive for hares, but such stands are temporally transient. Late-seral forests tend to be moderately productive for hares but also produce red squirrels and are temporally stable. For lynx to persist, a range of stand ages may be necessary to provide adequate habitat for hares and for denning. However, on drier sites where regeneration is sparse, the value of regenerating stands as hare habitat may be diminished relative to the value of late-seral stands. The negative exponential forest model provides a range of stand ages and thus provides a possible template for landscape management. Our generally poor understanding of lynx-habitat relationships at all spatial scales hampers the development of specific habitat-management prescriptions.

4. Food Habits of Lynx

Snowshoe hares are the primary prey of lynx throughout its range; in studies conducted to date, hares comprised 33-100% of lynx diets. However, when hares are scarce, red squirrels are an important alternative prey (Chapters 9 and 13). In addition to hares and red squirrels, lynx diets include ground squirrels, voles, grouse, ungulates, and carrion. However, a predominance of hares in the diet is believed to be an important determinant of reproduction and recruitment in the taiga, where studies have shown that when lynx diets were composed primarily of species other than hares, productivity approached zero (Chapter 9). Very little is known about lynx diets during snow-free periods, yet foraging ecology during these periods may be an important determinant of habitat use and survival during dispersal and of survival through the critical period of food shortage in the spring. Hence, a more comprehensive understanding of seasonal diets represents an important research need.

We conclude that snowshoe hares are the dominant prey of lynx throughout its range, but that red squirrels are an important alternative prey, especially if hares are scarce. However, available evidence suggests that lynx populations are not likely to persist where snowshoe hares do not predominate in the diet. Research is critically needed on lynx food habits in southern boreal forests during both snow and snow-free periods.

5. Habitat Requirements of Key Prey Species

Two key prey species for Canada lynx are snowshoe hares and red squirrels. Snowshoe hares are limited to forested landscapes in snowy climates. Hares are closely associated with low, woody vegetation and are most abundant in stands with high densities of small-diameter stems. Hares are most likely to occur in coniferous stands or mixed coniferous-deciduous stands, but in some areas pure stands of deciduous forest are occupied (Scott and Yahner 1989). The critical habitat element for hares is horizontal structure, which serves as both food and cover (Chapter 7). Given the appropriate environmental conditions, this dense vegetation is associated with early seral conditions (e.g., regenerating young stands). This vegetation structure is also associated with late-seral conditions (e.g., in gaps that are part of the natural heterogeneity of old-growth stands - see discussion under item 3 above). Cover for protection from predation is more important than cover as a food source for hares in northern populations (Chapter 6). Reducing dense horizontal structure through silvicultural thinning will likely reduce an area's carrying capacity for snowshoe hares.

Red squirrels are closely associated with mature, cone-bearing coniferous forest for food and shelter (Klenner and Krebs 1991; Larsen and Boutin 1995). Densities of pine squirrels, including both red squirrels and the closely related Douglas' squirrel, tend to be highest in late-successional forests with relatively high amounts of coarse woody debris (Buchanan et al. 1990; Kemp and Keith 1970; Rusch and Reeder 1978). Red squirrels are generally absent in regenerating forests that lack cone production.

We conclude that to support abundant snowshoe hare and red squirrel populations, landscapes must contain forested areas with low, dense horizontal structure and late-successional areas with cone-bearing trees and coarse woody debris. The optimal amounts and arrangement of these elements relative to lynx persistence is unknown and represents a critical research need (see Chapter 15 for additional discussion).

6. Population Dynamics of Key Prey Species

A key assumption about southern snowshoe hare populations has been that they are relatively stable, in contrast to the dramatic fluctuations seen in northern hare populations (Keith 1990). However, available evidence suggests that southern hare populations may be less stable than previously thought (Chapter 7). Some populations in the Lake States show strong fluctuations over relatively long time intervals, including some evidence of synchrony with northern hare populations. Very limited evidence from hare populations in the western United States is suggestive of fluctuations, but hare populations in the West have been insufficiently studied and their dynamics remain largely unknown. In northern hare populations, predation and food interact to drive changes in numbers (Krebs et al. 1995). The causes of population fluctuations in southern hares are unknown, and we do not know how the fragmentation of hare habitat in the south may influence hare dynamics.

Red squirrel populations throughout their geographic range appear to be food-limited, with conifer cone crops driving their population changes. Predation appears to be relatively unimportant to northern red squirrel populations (Stuart-Smith and Boutin 1995), but the impact of predation on southern red squirrel populations is unknown.

Red squirrel populations fluctuate but they likely do so independently of snowshoe hare populations. Since red squirrels are important alternative prey when and where hares are scarce, a coincidence of low hare and low squirrel numbers would likely be a significant cause of mortality in food-stressed lynx populations.

We conclude that some southern snowshoe hare populations fluctuate strongly and that, in general, southern populations are likely not as stable as previously thought. Depending on the strength and ubiquity of such fluctuations, southern lynx populations may also be less stable than previously believed. Red squirrel populations fluctuate with conifer cone crops in both the North and the South. The fact that populations of these two key prey species exhibit strong population fluctuations has potentially important implications, i.e., such fluctuations could result in local extirpations of lynx if prey populations bottom-out simultaneously.

7. Principal Community Features Affecting Lynx

Various mammals and birds, including coyotes, cougars, bobcats, fishers, great-horned owls, and goshawks may compete with lynx. This competition may reduce available food for lynx and may also result in their displacement or death (Chapter 4). The number of generalist competitors with lynx increases from the northern part of the range to its southern periphery. Moreover, the increased fragmentation of habitats near the southern periphery of the range, and habitat fragmentation in general, may give generalist predators a competitive advantage over lynx. Cougars are locally sympatric with lynx in the western United States during snow-free periods and available evidence suggests they may be an important source of lynx mortality. Coyotes appear to be especially effective competitors with lynx in human-dominated landscapes. Coyotes have expanded their range into the northeastern United States since 1970 and appear to represent an important factor in lynx ecology there. Based on research in the North, humans facilitate coyote access into areas occupied by lynx by compacting snow with snowmobiles, snowshoes, or skis. However, in the southern part of the range few data address competition between coyotes and lynx.

We conclude that, in the contiguous United States, competitors, especially the cougar and coyote, likely influence lynx recruitment and survival. Factors that facilitate movement of generalist predators into areas occupied by lynx should be considered a conservation risk. However, data addressing these relationships are very few, and a better understanding of community interactions, and the ways in which landscape pattern may mediate these interactions, is a key research need.

8. Principal Factors Affecting Lynx Movements and Dispersal

Knowledge of a species' movements and dispersal capabilities is critical to the conservation of fragmented, peripheral populations. In northern populations, lynx movements up to 1,000 km have been recorded (Chapter 9), and limited data from southern lynx populations documents movements in excess of 100 km (Chapter 13). However, even though long-distance movements may be characteristic of lynx populations, we have no empirical basis for tying such movements to successful dispersal (i.e., establishment of a home range and subsequent reproduction). Understanding the basis for successful lynx dispersal is therefore a key research need with important implications for conservation (Chapters 2 and 8).

Lynx readily move across landscapes fragmented by conventional industrial forestry (Chapter 11). Documented lynx movements have involved crossing open valley bottoms and large rivers (Chapter 13); thus, these landscape features are not absolute barriers to dispersal. Although the effect of roads on lynx movements, dispersal, and demographics has not been studied, we have anecdotal accounts of lynx crossing roads of various types. Additionally, we have reliable lynx occurrence records (mostly from trapping) in areas very distant from forested zones (Chapter 8). Assuming these lynx were dispersing from the nearest forested areas, highways were crossed prior to their capture. Although 16 of 83 lynx translocated into New York were killed by vehicles, none of the 89 resident lynx that have been studied with radiotelemetry in southern boreal forests were road-killed (Chapter 13). Although limited, these observations do not support the hypothesis that roads represent a significant mortality factor for lynx.

We conclude that lynx can move long distances, but we do not know if these movements result in successful dispersal or the augmentation of distant populations. Existing data, though sparse, do not indicate that roads are a major mortality factor for lynx. However, the indirect effects of roads on lynx populations, including the effects of urbanization along highway corridors, are unknown.

9. Key Demographic Properties and Dynamics of Lynx Populations

Northern lynx populations cycle with hares and dispersal is highest after hare populations start to decline (Chapter 9); we do not know if southern populations behave similarly (Chapter 13). We know little about lynx densities in the southern part of the range, but evidence suggests that they are comparable to those at cyclic lows in the North. In the North, lynx are highly fecund and can double their population size every year under optimal conditions, but the reproductive potential and factors affecting fecundity in southern populations are unknown.

Theory suggests that the risk of local extinction increases due to spatially and temporally correlated population fluctuations. Lynx populations in the southern part of the range appear to be small (Chapter 8). Small population size, particularly in combination with population fluctuations, predisposes these populations to the risk of local extinction (Chapter 2). The probability that such populations will persist depends on many factors, including the degree to which they interact with other populations within a metapopulation structure. However, metapopulation structure *per se* does little to ensure persistence when colonization rates are low and population sizes are very small.

Occupancy of habitat islands in a metapopulation will be governed by rates of colonization and extinction (Chapter 2). For most of the islands to be occupied most of the time, rates of colonization need to greatly exceed rates of local extinction. Dispersal to distant islands from other islands with small populations is unlikely, and even successful dispersal frequently will not result in successful colonization. Population size, distance, and barriers to dispersal between islands are therefore critically important to the stability of the metapopulation. Reductions in population size on the islands simultaneously increases extinction rates and decreases rates of colonization. The removal of habitat islands through land conversion or through large disturbances increases the distance between the remaining islands, and therefore also decreases colonization rates. To maintain a stable metapopulation, it is therefore critically important to maintain or increase the carrying capacity of all areas capable of supporting lynx.

We conclude southern lynx habitat must provide for local recruitment and survival. Additionally, southern lynx populations may require immigration from larger contiguous habitat areas. In cases where local populations are relatively small, dispersal rates must be sustained and, in some cases, substantial in order to be effective (from a demographic vs. a genetic standpoint). We know virtually nothing about the vital rates of southern lynx populations, thus assessments of population viability via demographic modeling are not possible. Additional information regarding the influence of prey abundance on lynx population dynamics is critically needed.

10. Geographic Variation Among Lynx Populations

All widespread species show some degree of geographic variation among populations. Variation may be primarily inherited or it may be largely based on the responses of individuals to local environments. Regardless of the mechanism, variation among populations can influence fitness and is often adaptive, meaning that populations within species are usually not interchangeable parts (Chapter 5). Knowledge of geographic variation among populations is therefore important for conservation, yet we know little about how much geographic variation exists among lynx populations. Conventional wisdom suggests that highly mobile species may show little geographic variation, but we cannot assume this for lynx without data, especially considering the broad range of environments occupied by lynx (Chapter 14). In general, variation among populations has important ramifications for conservation, including identification of distinct population segments, the consequences of translocations, and the degree to which ecological understandings apply from one population to another.

We conclude that we know little about geographic variation in lynx, and thus the transfer of either knowledge or animals from northern to southern populations entails significant conservation risks. Moreover, this knowledge gap hampers the identification of potentially distinct population segments for conservation purposes. Understanding the range of genetic, ecological, and behavioral variation among lynx populations is a high research priority.

11. Direct Human Influences on Lynx

Direct human influences on lynx include trapping and shooting, vehicle collisions, and behavioral disturbance. Except in Montana, lynx trapping seasons are closed throughout the contiguous United States but lynx may be trapped incidentally or illegally. Evidence from northern areas indicates that when lynx densities are low, human-caused mortality adds to natural mortality (Chapter 9). This means that incidental or illegal killing can significantly affect lynx population dynamics under some circumstances.

The effects of recreational activities on lynx populations have not been studied. However, limited anecdotal observations do not support the hypotheses that snowmobiling, ski touring, or hiking result in significant behavioral disturbance to lynx. Winter trails may impact lynx indirectly by providing increased access to competitors, especially coyotes (Chapter 4). It seems likely that disturbance at den sites could increase the vulnerability of kittens to a variety of threats. Lynx exhibit some indifference or curiosity toward humans, which may predispose them to hunting or trapping deaths. Although there is no empirical basis for concluding that roads represent a major mortality source for lynx (Chapter 13), fenced roads and highways or development along transportation corridors may impede lynx movements (Chapter 12).

We conclude that there is little empirical information on the direct effects of humans on lynx in southern boreal forests. However, trapping for other large furbearers in areas occupied by lynx may pose a risk. Lynx appear to be extremely susceptible to trapping, and where trapping is permitted it can be (and has been) a significant source of mortality. We cannot extrapolate conclusions about the minimal effects of trapping on northern lynx populations to the historical or potential effects of trapping in southern boreal forests.

Conclusions

In this Chapter, we have addressed 11 areas of knowledge that are fundamentally important when planning the management or conservation of any species. In many instances, we were quite tentative in putting forth even "qualified insights" due to a lack of empirical information. When this happened in areas of particular importance, we explicitly included statements of research need as part of our conclusions. In the following chapter we build on these conclusions and present a program of research for closing critical gaps in our knowledge of lynx ecology and natural history.

Literature Cited

Bailey, R. G. 1998. Ecoregions map of North America; explanatory note. USDA Forest Service, Miscellaneous Publication 1548, Washington, DC.

Buchanan, J. B., R. W. Lundquist, and K. B. Aubry. 1990. Winter populations of Douglas' squirrels in different-aged Douglas-fir forests. Journal of Wildlife Management 54:577-581.

Kemp, G. A. and L. B. Keith. 1970. Dynamics and regulation of red squirrel (*Tamiasciurus hudsonicus*) populations. Ecology 51:763-779.

Keith, L. B. 1990. Dynamics of snowshoe hare populations. Pages 119-195 *in* H. H. Genoways, editor. Current mammalogy. Plenum Press, New York.

Klenner, W. and Krebs, C. J. 1991. Red squirrel population dynamics. I. The effect of supplemental food on demography. Journal of Animal Ecology 60:961-978.

Krebs, C. J., Boutin, S., Boonstra, R., Sinclair, A. R. E., Smith, J. N. M., Dale, M. R. T., Martin, K., and Turkington, R. 1995. Estimation of snowshoe hare population density from turd transects. Canadian Journal of Zoology 65:565-567.

Kuchler, A. W. 1964. Potential natural vegetation of the conterminous United States (map and manual). American Geographical Society Special Publication 36. 116 p.

Larsen, K. W. and Boutin, S. 1995. Exploring territory quality in the North American red squirrel through removal experiments. Canadian Journal of Zoology 73:1115-1122.

Litvaitis, J. A., Kingman, D., Lanier, J., and Orff, E. 1991. Status of lynx in New Hampshire. Transactions of the Northeast Section of the Wildlife Society 48:70-75

Rusch, D. A. and W. G. Reeder. 1978. Population ecology of Alberta red squirrels. Ecology 59:400-420.

Scott, D. P. and Yahner, R. H. 1989. Winter habitat and browse use by snowshoe hares, *Lepus americanus*, in a marginal habitat in Pennsylvania. Canadian Field-Naturalist 103:560-563.

Stuart-Smith, A. K. and Boutin, S. 1995. Predation on red squirrels during a snowshoe hare decline. Canadian Journal of Zoology 73:713-1722.

Chapter 17

Conservation of Lynx in the United States: A Systematic Approach to Closing Critical Knowledge Gaps

Keith B. Aubry, USDA Forest Service, Pacific Northwest Research Station, 3625 93rd Ave. SW, Olympia, WA 98512

Leonard F. Ruggiero, USDA Forest Service, Rocky Mountain Research Station, 800 E. Beckwith, Missoula, MT 59807

John R. Squires, Wildlife Biology Program, University of Montana, Missoula, MT 59807

Kevin S. McKelvey, USDA Forest Service, Rocky Mountain Research Station, 800 E. Beckwith, Missoula, MT 59807

Gary M. Koehler, Washington Department of Fish and Wildlife, 600 Capitol Way N, Olympia, WA 98501

Steven W. Buskirk, Department of Physiology and Zoology, University of Wyoming, P.O. Box 3166, Laramie, WY 82071

Charles J. Krebs, University of British Columbia, 6270 University Blvd., Vancouver, BC V6T 1Z4 Canada

Introduction

Large-scale ecological studies and assessments are often implemented only after the focus of study generates substantial social, political, or legal pressure to take action (e.g., Thomas et al. 1990; Ruggiero et al. 1991; FEMAT 1993). In such a funding environment, the coordinated planning of research may suffer as the pressure to produce results escalates. To avoid haphazard research and to maximize the benefits to lynx conservation with limited research funds, a carefully coordinated approach to lynx research is needed. The purpose of this chapter is to provide a systematic framework and rationale for conducting future research in ways that will maximize the applicability and utility of new information.

Research on the ecology of rare and sparsely distributed vertebrates, such as the lynx, is often opportunistic because research must be conducted on populations that are large enough to allow rigorous scientific investigation. Even an intensive, long-term study of a few individuals results in anecdotal information that may or may not represent the population of interest. Consequently, populations are often selected for study simply because their existence and relative abundance is known, and because they are logistically feasible to study. This opportunistic impetus must be tempered, however, with the knowledge that the value of such research will be limited if there is no larger context in which to evaluate study results. Without this context, there will be no scientific basis for applying results beyond the geographic or ecological scope of each study.

To avoid these problems, wildlife scientists must expand the scope of inference by designing research to be representative. To generate reliable inferences about the biology and ecology of lynx in the contiguous United States (U.S.), we must conduct multiple studies that encompass the range of variation in habitats occupied by lynx. The program of research contained in this chapter is predicated upon such an approach. Throughout this book, we have stressed that we know relatively little about lynx biology and ecology in the U.S. (Table 17.1), and we have cautioned against overgeneralization or inappropriate extrapolation of existing information. We believe the lack of representative data on lynx in the U.S. to be a significant impediment to science-based conservation and management.

New research on lynx in the U.S. must address multiple spatial scales and multiple levels of biological organization. In both cases, studies at lower strata are logically nested within higher strata. One of the most useful outcomes of such a hierarchical research approach is that new efforts are facilitated and augmented by results from studies at both lower and higher strata. For example, the results of a survey designed to determine lynx

Table 17.1–Published and unpublished studies on lynx in the contiguous United States by subject. Studies are listed under all appropriate headings but are indicated with an asterisk (*) the first time they are listed in the table.

Topic and author	Location	Method	Duration	Sample size and summary of results
Distribution and relative abundance				
* McKelvey et al. (Chapter 8)	Contiguous United States	Museum and historical records, trapping data, track surveys, questionnaires	N/A	3,865 occurrence records: historical distribution
Habitat relationships				
McKelvey et al. (Chapter 8)	Contiguous United States	Museum and historical records, trapping data, track surveys, questionnaires	N/A	3,865 occurrence records: patterns of association with broad vegetation types and elevation zones
* Brittell et al. (1989, unpublished)	North-central Washington	Radiotelemetry	34 months	23 lynx: patterns of association with forest types
* Koehler (1990)	North-central Washington	Radiotelemetry	25 months	7 lynx: patterns of association with forest types; 4 maternal dens described
McKelvey et al. (Chapter 10)[a]	North-central Washington	Radiotelemetry	76 months	22 lynx: patterns of association with forest types and topographic features
* Koehler et al. (1979)	Western Montana	Radiotelemetry	8 months	2 lynx: patterns of association with forest types
* Smith (1984, unpublished)	Western Montana	Radiotelemetry	23 months	5 lynx: patterns of association with forest types
Squires and Laurion (Chapter 11)[b]	Western Montana and Wyoming	Radiotelemetry	Montana = 22 months, Wyoming = 34 months	Montana = 18 lynx, Wyoming = 2 lynx: 1 maternal den described in Wyoming
Movements and dispersal				
Brittell et al. (1989, unpublished)	North-central Washington	Radiotelemetry	34 months	23 lynx: 2 long-distance movements documented
Squires and Laurion (Chapter 11)	Western Montana and Wyoming	Radiotelemetry	Montana = 22 months, Wyoming = 34 months	Montana = 18 lynx: 4 exploratory movements documented; Wyoming = 2 lynx: 2 exploratory movements documented
Smith (1984, unpublished)	Western Montana	Radiotelemetry	23 months	5 lynx: 1 long-distance movement documented
* Brainerd (1985, unpublished)	Western Montana	Radiotelemetry	25 months	2 lynx: 1 long-distance movement documented
* Mech (1977)	Northern Minnesota	Radiotelemetry	25 months	14 lynx: 1 long-distance movement documented

(con.)

457

Table 17.1.—Con.

Topic and author	Location	Method	Duration	Sample size and summary of results
Demography and population dynamics				
Brittell et al. (1989, unpublished)	North-central Washington	Radiotelemetry and snowtracking	34 months	23 lynx: mean density = 2.0/100 km^2, 4 litters: mean litter size = 2.0; mean annual adult mortality rate = 11%
Koehler (1990)	North-central Washington	Radiotelemetry and snowtracking	25 months	7 lynx: mean density = 2.3/100 km^2, 3 litters: mean litter size = 2.7; mean kitten mortality rate = 88%
Brainerd (1985, unpublished)	Western Montana	Carcasses	N/A	18 females: mean litter size = 3.3
Squires and Laurion (Chapter 11)	Western Montana and Wyoming	Radiotelemetry and snowtracking	Montana = 22 months, Wyoming = 34 months	Montana = 3 litters: mean litter size = 2; Wyoming = 2 litters: mean litter size = 3
Relationships with prey				
Koehler (1990)	North-central Washington	Scat analysis	25 months	29 scats: 79% snowshoe hare, 24% red squirrel, 7% deer, 3% white-footed mouse
Community interactions				
Brittell et al. (1989, unpublished)	North-central Washington	Radiotelemetry	34 months	23 lynx: 1 bobcat or lynx kill
Koehler et al. (1979)	Western Montana	Radiotelemetry	8 months	2 lynx: 1 mountain lion kill
Squires and Laurion (Chapter 11)	Western Montana	Radiotelemetry	Montana = 22 months, Wyoming = 34 months	Montana = 18 lynx, Wyoming = 2 lynx: 2 mountain lion kills in Montana
Human impacts				
McKelvey et al. (Chapter 10)	North-central Washington	Radiotelemetry	76 months	22 lynx: no evidence of road avoidance
Brocke et al. (1991) and K. Gustafson (personal communication)	New York	Radiotelemetry	24 months	83 lynx translocated from Yukon: 16 road-killed

[a]McKelvey et al. (Chapter 10) is a reanalysis of data collected by Brittell et al. (1989, unpublished) and Koehler (1990).
[b]Data presented by Squires and Laurion (Chapter 11) represent preliminary results of ongoing studies.

presence or absence at a broad spatial scale (e.g., the western U.S.) provide the basis for selecting study areas for more intensive research on lynx at smaller spatial scales (e.g., northeastern Washington). Conversely, habitat and topographic use patterns derived from intensive studies can help delineate forest types where lynx surveys should be conducted.

We must know where lynx are before we can identify geographic areas where more intensive research should be conducted. Some research questions, such as determining the potential metapopulation structure of lynx in the U.S., cannot be addressed until we adequately describe broad-scale patterns of habitat occupancy. However, the urgency of ongoing lynx conservation efforts precludes us from waiting until we have a more complete understanding of the current distribution of lynx before initiating new research. We must support and expand lynx research in the U.S. while comprehensively delineating current lynx range and describing patterns of relative abundance to provide a framework for planning future research.

Information Needs

We have identified critical knowledge gaps in many of the previous chapters and emphasized the most important of these in the Qualified Insights (QIs) presented in Chapter 16. Here, we summarize key information needs for the conservation of lynx in the U.S.

Distribution and Relative Abundance

We have documented the historical distribution of lynx to the extent possible with existing information, but we lack a clear understanding of the distribution or relative abundance of extant populations in the U.S. (Chapter 16 - QI 1). This research need must be addressed before new intensive studies are initiated. Knowledge of lynx distribution will also provide a framework for investigating geographic variation among southern lynx populations. This information is essential for assessing the potential impacts of translocating lynx among populations (Chapter 16 - QI 10).

Habitat Relationships

We have a very limited understanding of lynx habitat relationships at any spatial scale (Chapter 16 - QIs 2 and 3). Our current understanding of habitat selection for southern populations comes mostly from research conducted on a single, relatively small population in north-central Washington. However, populations occupying more xeric coniferous forests or mixed coniferous-deciduous forests may have very different habitat relationships. In southern boreal forests, only a few natal dens have been described, but all were in late-successional stands with relatively dense understory cover from large woody debris and other complex structures near the forest floor. However, timber harvesting designed to improve habitat conditions for snowshoe hares by creating dense, young stands may eliminate such structures. Management of forest habitats for lynx will be severely constrained until new information is obtained on their habitat relationships at both small and large spatial scales.

Movements and Dispersal

Dispersal processes will strongly influence conservation planning for lynx, especially for small, isolated populations at the southern extent of their range (Chapter 16 - QI 8). Southern lynx populations may exist in a metapopulation structure maintained by the dispersal of individuals among "islands" of suitable habitat at varying distances from one another. Although long-distance exploratory movements have been documented in several southern populations, successful dispersal (i.e., reproducing in an established home range) has not. Thus, we have no empirical information on success rates for dispersal, dispersal distances, responses to anthropogenic and natural barriers, or the use of corridors.

Demography and Population Dynamics

Assessments of the population viability of southern lynx populations will not be possible without new information on densities, birth rates, adult and kitten survival rates, and population dynamics (Chapter 16 - QI 9). Limited data from north-central Washington suggest that lynx populations in southern boreal forests may not exhibit the strong cyclic fluctuations characteristic of lynx populations in the taiga; however, trapping data from several states suggest otherwise. High-amplitude fluctuations may have a strong influence on dispersal and connectivity among isolated populations. Thus, conservation planning for southern lynx populations will be influenced strongly by the nature of their population dynamics.

Relationships With Prey

Limited data indicate that lynx in southern boreal forests depend on snowshoe hares as their primary prey, with red squirrels as important secondary prey (Chapter 16 - QI 4). Management of habitat for snowshoe hares in southern regions must consider how hare abundances vary along both ecological and successional gradients. However, patterns of hare abundance in southern boreal forests are not well understood. We do not know how differences in habitat structure may influence the vulnerability of snowshoe hares and other prey species to lynx predation.

Community Interactions

Many species potentially compete with lynx for prey (Chapter 16 - QI 7). Exploitation competition may reduce prey availability and result in displacement of lynx, whereas interference competition may affect lynx habitat selection and, in extreme cases, lead to intraguild predation. Mountain lions are absent from the taiga but co-occur with southern lynx populations, and limited data suggest that they may be an important source of lynx mortality. Coyotes are very effective predators of snowshoe hares, are capable of killing lynx, and have recently expanded their range in southern boreal forests. We do not know if predation affects the population dynamics of lynx, nor do we understand the nature and extent of competition with generalist predators or how changes in landscape pattern may mediate these processes.

Human Impacts

Lynx often appear indifferent toward humans, which may predispose them to direct, human-caused mortality. The indirect impacts of human activity may exert a stronger influence on lynx populations but are difficult to quantify (Chapter 16 - QI 11). The effects of outdoor recreation on lynx populations have not been studied. Observations suggest that some carnivores, especially coyotes, use compacted snow from snowmobiling, skiing, or snowshoeing as travel routes. However, we do not know if snow compaction increases predation rates or competition from generalist predators.

Snowshoe Hare Habitat Relationships

In Montana and Washington, limited data suggest that hares may have a bimodal pattern of abundance, whereby they reach highest abundances in young, dense stands and old, gap-phase forests. High stem densities in regenerating forests provide dense horizontal cover that is important for hares (Chapter 16 - QI 5), and old forests have similar cover in gaps formed from the death of one or several trees. However, in drier forest types in the northern Rocky Mountains, where regenerating stands often lack high levels of horizontal cover, hares may be most abundant in older forests. We do not understand how patterns of hare abundance change according to forest type, moisture regime, or successional stage.

Snowshoe Hare Population Dynamics

In the taiga, population dynamics of lynx are closely tied to those of snowshoe hares, and lynx populations fluctuate in lagged synchrony with hare population cycles. We do not know if this model fits southern lynx populations. Limited data suggest that southern hare populations are not as stable as previously believed (Chapter 16 - QI 6), but whether their populations cycle as they do in the taiga, or simply fluctuate stochastically, is unknown.

A Research Framework

Where Do Lynx Occur?

As of 1999, we have only a general idea of the current distribution of lynx in the U.S. (Chapters 8, 11, 13). We have documented at least one verified record of occurrence since 1990 in Washington, Oregon, Idaho, Montana, Wyoming, Utah, Minnesota, Wisconsin, New Hampshire, and Maine. If we include track data collected by knowledgeable individuals as evidence of occurrence, we can add Colorado and Michigan to this list. We also know there is at least one reproductive female lynx in both western Wyoming and northern Maine. However, strong evidence of the presence of established populations is limited to western Montana and north-central Washington. In most areas of historical lynx occurrence, we need to determine if populations of lynx are present before we can select new study locations or assess the representativeness of resident populations occurring in Washington and Montana. This information gap must be addressed initially with broad-scale, presence/absence surveys conducted throughout the historical range of lynx.

Do Lynx Detections Represent a Researchable Population?

Although broad-scale surveys may demonstrate the presence of at least one lynx at a given locality, an intensive radiotelemetry study should not be implemented until surveys conducted at a finer spatial scale have verified the presence of a sufficiently large and established (i.e., "researchable") population. For example, we know that there are at least two lynx (a male and female) in the Wyoming Range in western Wyoming, and that the female had kittens in 1998 and 1999. These lynx occur farther south than any known native population and are therefore of special interest. Before committing research funds to intensive study, however, we must determine if these lynx are an isolated pair or are part of a larger population occupying contiguous portions of the Greater Yellowstone Ecosystem.

How Do We Prioritize the Implementation of Intensive Studies?

Simply locating a researchable population does not mean that knowledge gained from an intensive study would be worth the cost. Additional and more useful benefits to lynx conservation may be realized by using research funds in other ways or at other locations. We prioritize intensive studies in locations where researchable populations are identified according to the following three criteria:

Would an intensive study increase the representativeness of existing information? For lynx, a representative sample of populations to study should be selected from all known populations within the geographic area of interest. At this time, however, such an approach is impractical because we do not know the locations of extant populations. We therefore need to apply simple criteria that are likely to increase the representativeness of current information on lynx, such as maximizing the geographic extent or variability in major climatic and ecological gradients among lynx studies within the geographic area of interest.

What will the value of new information be to lynx management and conservation? New research on lynx in the U.S. must make a significant contribution to lynx management and conservation. Throughout this book, we have identified critical gaps in our knowledge of lynx biology and ecology. Examples include the ecology and population dynamics of principal prey species, competitive interactions with other carnivores, and human impacts. Thus, we would give high priority to potential study areas where assemblages of alternative prey or potential competitors differ markedly from those of previous lynx studies, or where unique opportunities exist to study human impacts on lynx populations, such as adjacent landscapes with and without snowmobile use.

How feasible is the study and what are the costs? The cost of lynx research increases with the difficulty of access. In addition, certain types of studies may be infeasible in particular localities, such as snowtracking in areas with significant avalanche danger. Consequently, logistical constraints on research and resulting unit costs for generating new information must be considered when setting research priorities.

A Research Approach

Broad-Scale Surveys

Broad-scale surveys are intended to provide information about lynx at large spatial scales (e.g., physiographic regions, ecological provinces, or states). These surveys are most useful when the objective is to document the presence of lynx (Fig. 17.1). Such a survey is currently underway nationally and is designed to provide reliable and representative information about lynx presence/absence and genetic variation. The detection device used is a modification of a rubbing-pad technique for collecting hair samples originally developed by J. Weaver (personal communication; see also Weaver and Amato 1999, unpublished). Survey implementation is based on a protocol developed and tested by the USDA Forest Service's Rocky Mountain Research Station (McKelvey et al. 1999, unpublished). Genetic evaluation will be based on analysis of DNA taken from hair samples.

The first year of the survey (1999) represents a pilot study designed to assess the feasibility of meeting survey objectives, which include determining where lynx occur and where they do not, the pattern of lynx detections

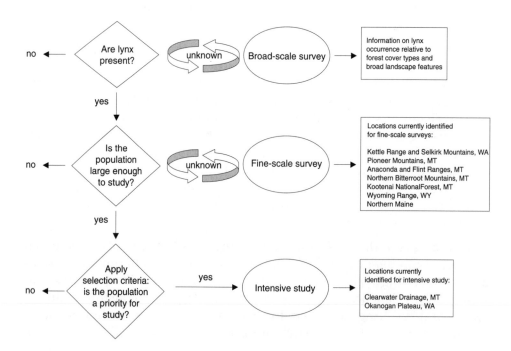

Figure 17.1—A schematic representation of the process for identifying potential study areas and implementing intensive research on lynx in the contiguous United States.

relative to broad-scale environmental features, and the degree of genetic structuring among lynx in different geographic areas.

Fine-Scale Surveys

Fine-scale surveys are conducted in areas where lynx are known to be present. Because these surveys are intended to determine if lynx occur in sufficient numbers to support intensive research (Fig. 17.1), they will most likely employ a combination of detection methods, with snowtracking surveys being the primary means of assessing the relative abundance of lynx. Although most fine-scale surveys will be based on information obtained from broad-scale surveys, there are a number of areas that have already been identified where fine-scale surveys would be appropriate (Fig. 17.1).

Intensive surveys of snowshoe hare distribution and abundance using pellet plots and live-trapping will be used to determine how differences in forest composition and structure (including thinning of young forests) and forest succession along complex moisture/temperature gradients influence patterns of hare abundance.

Intensive Studies

Intensive studies will be necessary to address most of the information needs we have identified (Fig. 17.1). These studies will employ a variety of research techniques, with radiotelemetry being the primary methodology. Radiotelemetry involves intensive monitoring of the activities of individual animals, enabling data to be gathered on a broad range of research questions including habitat relationships, movements, demography, community relationships, and responses to natural and human-caused disturbance. Radiotelemetry also facilitates the study of snowshoe hare habitat relationships, especially with regard to demographic responses and source-sink phenomena. Accordingly, intensive studies address many objectives at multiple spatial scales and are central to our proposed research program.

Currently, there are three radiotelemetry studies of lynx being conducted in the U.S. These include an intensive study in the Clearwater drainage of western Montana involving 18 radio-collared lynx (Chapter 11), radiotelemetry monitoring of two adult lynx in the Wyoming Range of western Wyoming (Chapter 11), and radiotelemetry monitoring of two adult lynx in northern Maine (Chapter 8). We do not know, however, if radio-collared lynx in Wyoming and Maine are part of more extensive populations. Although all three of these studies will contribute to our understanding of lynx biology and ecology in the U.S., only the western Montana study represents an intensive study of a researchable population (Fig. 17.1).

Our current inability to identify all researchable lynx populations in the U.S. is a critical constraint on the establishment of new intensive studies. The failure of broad- and fine-scale surveys to identify additional populations for intensive study would be significant, as it would provide strong evidence that extant lynx populations in the U.S. are severely restricted. However, until ongoing and proposed surveys identify additional populations for study, we must proceed with intensive studies on known populations.

A Program of Intensive Research

At the present time, there are only two places in the U.S. where we can state with confidence that intensive lynx studies should be conducted: the Clearwater drainage in western Montana and the Okanogan Plateau in north-central Washington (Table 17.2; Fig. 17.1). Because virtually all of the research needs identified here are most efficiently addressed through intensive studies, we must increase the number of these studies in regions where lynx conservation and related management activities are at issue. For opportunistic reasons, and because the only intensive study currently ongoing is the Clearwater study in Montana, new intensive research should be implemented on the Okanogan Plateau in north-central Washington. Although lynx were studied recently (1980-1988) in this area (see Chapters 10, 13), a number of important landscape-scale habitat changes have occurred on the Plateau since the earlier study, including a major fire. Furthermore, many of the important information needs identified in Table 17.2 were not adequately addressed in previous studies (Chapter 13).

In addition, ongoing research in Montana must be continued and expanded. The Clearwater study area provides a unique opportunity to study the effects of winter recreation, forest fragmentation, and roads on lynx behavior and on competition with generalist predators. The primary study area is located in a relatively low-elevation, intensively managed landscape. However, radio-collared lynx have been moving in and out of the adjacent Bob Marshall Wilderness, which has very different landscape characteristics. Ongoing studies need to be expanded to understand how adjacent wilderness areas are used by lynx. The inclusion of such areas in the study would also increase the representativeness of this research.

Although expanding the Clearwater study and renewing research activity on the Okanogan Plateau are clearly high priorities, it is important to initiate new studies in areas that are ecologically distinct from previous and ongoing studies. To identify such areas, fine-scale surveys to determine the spatial extent and relative abundance of local populations need to be conducted immediately in areas where we know lynx occur. These include several

Table 17.2–Studies by location indicating information needs to be addressed.

Research approach	Within the historic range of lynx	Pacific Northwest		Rocky Mountains						North-Central U.S.	Northeastern U.S.
		Okanogan Plateau, Washington	Kettle Range and Selkirk Mountains, Washington	Kootenai National Forest, Montana	Clearwater Drainage, Montana	Pioneer Mountains, Montana	Anaconda and Flint Ranges, Montana	Northern Bitterroot Mountains, Montana	Wyoming Range, Wyoming	Unknown	Northern Maine
Broad-scale surveys to determine presence											
Lynx		X									
Fine-scale surveys to assess relative abundance											
Lynx			X	X		X	X	X	X		X
Snowshoe hare	X										
Intensive studies– lynx											
Habitat relationships		X			X				Limited[a]		Limited
Movements and dispersal		X			X				Limited		Limited
Demography and population dynamics		X			X						
Relationships with prey		X			X						
Community interactions		X			X						
Human impacts		X			X						
Intensive studies– snowshoe hares											
Habitat relationships		X			X						
Population dynamics		X			X						

[a] Radiotelemetry monitoring of several individuals dooes not constitute intensive research but will contribute limited information on habitat relatiionships and movements.

locations in western Montana, western Wyoming, northeastern Washington, and northern Maine (Table 17.2; Fig. 17.1). If additional researchable populations are located in the Rocky Mountains, we would give highest priority to studies in cold, dry forest types, such as the Pioneer Mountains in Montana and the Wyoming Range in Wyoming. New studies in these forest types would contribute more to our understanding of lynx ecology in the U.S. than additional studies in mesic forest types.

Recommendations for intensive research in the southern Rocky Mountains and north-central and northeastern U.S. must await the findings of both broad- and fine-scale surveys. Lynx have never been studied intensively in these regions, where habitat conditions vary substantially from those in the Pacific Northwest and northern Rocky Mountains. For these reasons, ongoing radiotelemetry monitoring of several lynx in Maine and Wyoming will contribute useful information. However, fine-scale surveys to determine whether to expand research efforts in these areas should be given the highest priority.

Hare studies are an important component of our proposed research program. Key conservation issues, including reintroduction efforts and the potential natural range expansion by lynx, will be strongly influenced by patterns of hare abundance. To study differences in hare abundance along successional and moisture gradients and to understand the nature of their population fluctuations, we need to quantify hare abundance over time among different forest types and seral stages. A fine-scale survey program involving cooperative efforts with management agencies will be implemented in representative areas within the historical range of lynx. It is essential, however, that these surveys be conducted in a coordinated fashion using sampling protocols that will generate reliable information about hare habitat relationships and patterns of abundance.

Conclusions

This research program will proceed on several fronts simultaneously. Broad-scale lynx surveys are underway and by the spring of 2000, we will know more about the efficacy of the survey protocol and, hopefully, patterns of lynx occurrence in the U.S. Fine-scale surveys and intensive studies of lynx and hares should proceed in Washington, Montana, Wyoming, and Maine. And, if we are able to locate other researchable lynx populations, new intensive studies should be implemented to increase the representativeness of our sample, especially in the southern Rocky Mountains and north-central and northeastern United States. Furthermore, as argued previously by Ruggiero et al. (1994), new lynx studies should be integrated within a broader program of research on forest carnivores and other species of concern so that we can develop the information needed to implement ecosystem management in boreal forest landscapes. We must become more proactive in our research programs if we are to effectively address conservation issues before options for conserving sensitive species have become irrevocably limited.

Literature Cited

Brainerd, S. M. 1985. Reproductive ecology of bobcats and lynx in western Montana. Unpublished M.S. Thesis, University of Montana, Missoula, MT.

Brittell, J. D., R. J. Poelker, S. J. Sweeney, and G.M. Koehler. 1989. Native cats of Washington, Section III: lynx. Unpublished, Washington Department of Wildlife, Olympia, WA.

Brocke, R. H., K. A. Gustafson, and L. B. Fox. 1991. Restoration of large predators: potentials and problems. Pages 303-315 *in* Challenges in the conservation of biological resources. A practitioner's guide. D. J. Decker, M. E. Krasny, G. R. Goff, C. R. Smith, and D. W. Gross, eds. Westview Press, Boulder, CO.

FEMAT. 1993. Forest ecosystem management: an ecological, economic, and social assessment. Report of the Forest Ecosystem Management Assessment Team. USDA Forest Service; USDC National Oceanographic and Atmospheric Administration and National Marine Fisheries Service; USDI Bureau of Land Management, Fish and Wildlife Service, and National Park Service; and U.S. Environmental Protection Agency, Washington, DC.

Koehler, G.M. 1990. Population and habitat characteristics of lynx and snowshoe hares in north central Washington. Canadian Journal of Zoology 68:845-851.

Koehler, G. M., M. G. Hornocker, and H.S. Hash. 1979. Lynx movements and habitat use in Montana. Canadian Field-Naturalist 93:441-442.

McKelvey, K. S., J. J. Claar, G. W. McDaniel, and G. Hanvey. 1999. National lynx detection protocol. Unpublished, USDA Forest Service, Rocky Mountain Research Station, Missoula, MT.

Mech, L. D. 1977. Record movement of a Canadian lynx. Journal of Mammalogy 58:676-677.

Ruggiero, L. F., K. B. Aubry, A. B. Carey, and M. H. Huff, tech. coords. 1991. Wildlife and vegetation of unmanaged Douglas-fir forests. USDA Forest Service, General Technical Report PNW-GTR-285.

Ruggiero, L. F., S. W. Buskirk, K. B. Aubry, L. J. Lyon, and W. J. Zielinski. 1994. Information needs and a research strategy for conserving forest carnivores. Pages 138-152 *in* L.F. Ruggiero, K. B. Aubry, S. W. Buskirk, L. J. Lyon, and W. J. Zielinski, tech. eds. The scientific basis for conserving forest carnivores in the Western United States: American marten, fisher, lynx, and wolverine. USDA Forest Service, General Technical Report RM-254.

Smith, D. S. 1984. Habitat use, home range, and movements of bobcats in western Montana. Unpublished M.S. Thesis, University of Montana, Missoula, MT.

Thomas, J. W., E. D. Forsman, J. B. Lint, E. C. Meslow, B. R. Noon, and J. Verner. 1990. A conservation strategy for the northern spotted owl. Report of the Interagency Scientific Committee to address the conservation of the northern spotted owl. USDA Forest Service, USDI Bureau of Land Management, U.S. Fish and Wildlife Service, and National Park Service, Portland, OR.

U.S. Fish and Wildlife Service. 1998. Proposal to list the contiguous United States distinct population segment of the Canada lynx: proposed rule. Federal Register 63(130): 36994-37013.

Weaver, J. L. and G. Amato. 1999. Lynx surveys in the Cascade Range: Washington and Oregon. Unpublished, Wildlife Conservation Society, Bronx, NY.

Chapter 18

Epilogue
The Scientific Basis for
Lynx Conservation: Can
We Get There From Here?

Leonard F. Ruggiero, USDA Forest Service, Rocky Mountain Research
Station, 800 E. Beckwith, Missoula, MT 59801

Keith B. Aubry, USDA Forest Service, Pacific Northwest Research Station,
3625 93rd Ave. SW, Olympia, WA 98512

Steven W. Buskirk, Department of Zoology and Physiology,
University of Wyoming, P.O. Box 3166, Laramie, WY 82071

Gary M. Koehler, Washington Department of Fish and Wildlife,
600 Capitol Way N., Olympia, WA 98501

Charles J. Krebs, Department of Zoology, University of British Columbia,
6270 University Blvd., Vancouver, BC V6T 1Z4 Canada

Kevin S. McKelvey, USDA Forest Service, Rocky Mountain Research Station,
800 E. Beckwith, Missoula, MT 59801

John R. Squires, University of Montana, Forestry Sciences Laboratory,
800 E. Beckwith, Missoula, MT 59801

As we emphasized in the Preface, this book was written under very unusual circumstances. We began the book shortly after the lynx was proposed for listing as threatened or endangered under the Endangered Species Act (ESA). Our purpose was to elucidate the scientific basis for conserving lynx for use in listing deliberations and in establishing land management policy, including a strategy for lynx conservation. The listing decision was delayed by six months so that our findings could be considered. Authors, editors, and production staff worked overtime and weekends to produce camera-ready copies of each chapter, and these were posted on the Internet for public comment during a specified time period. Draft copies of the chapters were provided to the U.S. Fish and Wildlife Service and land management agencies prior to publication so they could begin to consider our findings in their ongoing assessments and planning processes. We have, therefore, been in the unusual position of seeing some of the sociopolitical implications of our findings even as we wrote them.

The areas of primary lynx occurrence identified in Chapter 8 cover about 100 million acres (40.5 million ha). This number grows much larger if one considers all the land within the putative range of the lynx in the contiguous United States. Thus, land management policy and related decisions influenced by some or all of the information in this book could affect a vast area. Because much of this land is dedicated to multiple uses, a wide range of activities including timber and range management, outdoor recreation, and the production of other goods and services associated with public lands will potentially be affected. Through its affect on listing deliberations and agency conservation planning, the information in this book may have far-reaching implications. The question is, Is this an adequate basis for such deliberations and decisions? In other words, given the state of knowledge embodied in this book, is there a defensible set of answers to lynx conservation questions?

In answering this question, there are several important considerations. This book illustrates the kind of scientific analysis that we believe should form the basis for conservation strategies and listing decisions. We feel that most of what is currently known, and much of what can reasonably be inferred, has been incorporated into the text. The information we have provided is as reliable as it can be, and we believe it is substantive. In short, although our analyses were severely constrained by the scarcity of reliable scientific information, we have provided a measure of new information and scientific insight that surpassed our expectations given the significant knowledge gaps that exist. We believe this was made possible in part by our approach to the problem, as outlined in our introductory chapter. Perhaps the most important aspect of this approach was an interpretation of existing information based on the explicit application of accepted ecological concepts. In this context, it is very important to discriminate between subjective opinions and carefully constructed interpretations of scientific information made in the context of generally accepted conceptual understandings. Although such interpretations may be inconclusive in the sense of lacking proof, their reliability is more easily assessed, and interpretations are open for further review.

Can we get to a defensible set of answers to lynx conservation questions based on these analyses and interpretations? The answer is yes, but only on an *interim* basis. Answers will come in the form of judgments based in part on what we have presented here. Not everyone will agree with those judgments, but our work provides a reasonable basis for developing a rationale for and evaluating the quality of such judgments. However, although we may be able to get to an interim position, we are still a long way from understanding many essential aspects of lynx ecology, and thus from essential understandings necessary to conserve lynx. As emphasized throughout this book and as summarized in Chapter 17, there is a great deal of information that we need to acquire before we can develop precise long-term land management plans that will ensure the persistence of lynx. Our lack of knowledge necessitates a less precise, and thus very conservative, approach to interim conservation measures.

The key point here is that although we believe our effort provides an adequate basis for interim conservation planning, our work must not be viewed as a surrogate for a well-developed body of reliable scientific data. In matters of conservation planning, the interpretation of limited information by even the most qualified scientists is no substitute for the organized acquisition of pertinent data. As a basis for making policy decisions, there is no reliable surrogate for a sustained commitment to scientific research, especially when the effects of human activities on species persistence are at issue. If the decision is made to list the lynx under the ESA, the current state of knowledge, including the information we have presented here, will not provide an adequate basis for a reliable recovery plan. Only with a determined and sustained commitment to a comprehensive program of research (Chapter 17) can we obtain the information needed to effectively manage and conserve lynx populations in the United States.

Plants

Common Name	Scientific Name
Alder	*Alnus* spp.
Alder, speckled	*Alnus rugosa*
Alder, Sitka	*Alnus crispa*
Antelope-brush; bitter-brush	*Purshia tridentata*
Apple, common	*Pyrus malus*
Ash	*Fraxinus* spp.
Ash, mountain	*Sorbus americana*
Ash, white	*Fraxinus americana*
Aspen	*Populus tremuloides*
Aspen, bigtooth	*Populus grandidentata*
Aspen, quaking	*Populus tremuloides*
Basswood	*Tilia* spp.
Bearberry	*Arctostaphylos uva-ursi*
Beech	*Fagus* spp.
Beech, American	*Fagus grandifolia*
Birch	*Betula* spp.
Birch, bog	*Betula glandulosa*
Birch, gray	*Betula populifolia*
Birch, low	*Betula pumila*
Birch, paper	*Betula papyrifera*
Birch, sweet	*Betula lenta*
Birch, white	*Betula alba*
Birch, yellow	*Betula lutea*
Birch, yellow	*Betula alleghaniensis*
Blackberry, Allegheny	*Rubus alleghaniensis*
Blackberry; dewberry; raspberry; bramble	*Rubus* spp.
Blueberry	*Vaccinium* spp.
Blueberry, dwarf	*Vaccinium caespitosum*
Bogmyrtle, sweetgale	*Myrica gale*
Buckthorn, alderleaf	*Rhamnus alnifolia*
Buffaloberry, russet	*Shepherdia canadensis*
Cattail	*Typha latifolia*
Ceanothus	*Ceanothus* spp.
Cedar, northern white	*Thuja occidentalis*
Cedar, western red	*Thuja plicata*
Cedar, white	*Thuja occidentalis*
Cherry, black	*Prunus serotina*
Cherry, pin	*Prunus pensylvanica*
Chokecherry, common	*Prunus virginiana*

Plants

Common Name	Scientific Name
Cottonwood	*Populus* spp.
Cottonwood, black	*Populus trichocarpa*
Cranberry, highbush	*Viburnum edule*
Cranberry, mountain	*Vaccinium vitis-idaea*
Cranberry, southern mountain	*Vaccinium erythrocarpum*
Dewberry, bristly	*Rubus hispidus*
Dogwood	*Cornus* spp.
Elm	*Ulmus* spp.
Elm, American	*Ulmus americana*
Filbert, beaked	*Corylus cornuta*
Fir	*Abies* spp.
Fir, balsam	*Abies balsamifera*
Fir, balsam	*Abies balsamea*
Fir, Douglas-	*Pseudotsuga menziesii*
Fir, grand	*Abies grandis*
Fir, noble	*Abies procera*
Fir, Pacific silver	*Abies amabilis*
Fir, red	*Abies magnifica*
Fir, silver	*Abies amabilis*
Fir, subalpine	*Abies lasiocarpa*
Fir, white	*Abies concolor*
Fireweed	*Epilobium angustifolium*
Grape, Oregon	*Mahonia repens*
Hemlock	*Tsuga* spp.
Hemlock, eastern	*Tsuga canadensis*
Hemlock, mountain	*Tsuga mertensiana*
Hemlock, western	*Tsuga heterophylla*
Honeysuckle	*Lonicera* spp.
Hophornbeam, American	*Ostrya virginiana*
Huckleberry, black	*Gaylussacia baccata*
Huckleberry, blueleaved or Cascade	*Vaccinium deliciosum*
Juniper, common	*Juniperus communis*
Juniper, Rocky Mountain	*Juniperus scopulorum*
Kalmia	*Kalmia* spp.
Kalmia; mountain-laurel	*Kalmia latifolia*
Labrador-tea	*Ledum groenlandicum*
Larch, eastern (tamarack)	*Larix laricina*
Larch, subalpine	*Larix lyallii*
Larch, western	*Larix occidentalis*
Leatherleaf, Cassandra	*Chamaedaphne calyculata*
Ledum, crystal-tea	*Ledum decumbens*
Lupine	*Lupinus* spp.
Maple	*Acer* spp.
Maple, mountain	*Acer spicatum*

Plants

Common Name	Scientific Name
Maple, mountain	*Acer glabrum*
Maple, red	*Acer rubrum*
Maple, striped	*Acer pensylvanicum*
Maple, sugar	*Acer saccharum*
Oak	*Quercus* spp.
Oak, Gambel	*Quercus gambelii*
Oak, northern red	*Quercus rubra*
Pine	*Pinus* spp.
Pine, eastern white	*Pinus strobus*
Pine, gray or jack	*Pinus divaricata*
Pine, jack	*Pinus banksiana*
Pine, limber	*Pinus flexilis*
Pine, lodgepole	*Pinus contorta*
Pine, ponderosa	*Pinus ponderosa*
Pine, red	*Pinus resinosa*
Pine, Scotch	*Pinus sylvestris*
Pine, southern	*Pinus taeda, P. elliottii, P. palustris*
Pine, white	*Pinus strobus*
Pine, whitebark	*Pinus albicaulis*
Poplar, balsam	*Populus balsamifera*
Poplar, necklace	*Populus virginiana*
Poplar, Pensylvanian	*Populus pensylvanica*
Rhododendron, Canadian	*Rhododendron canadense*
Rhododendron, Lapland; rosebay, Lapland	*Rhododendron lapponicum*
Rose	*Rosa* spp.
Sagebrush	*Artemesia* spp.
Serviceberry	*Amelanchier* spp.
Serviceberry, Saskatoon	*Amelanchier alnifolia*
Snowberry, common	*Symphoricarpos albus*
Spruce	*Picea* spp.
Spruce, black	*Picea mariana*
Spruce, Engelmann	*Picea engelmannii*
Spruce, Norway	*Picea abies*
Spruce, red	*Picea rubens*
Spruce, white	*Picea glauca*
Sweetfern, alien	*Comptonia peregrina*
Viburnum	*Viburnum* spp.
Viburnum; arrowwood	*Viburnum dentatum*
Wheatgrass	*Agropyron* spp.
Whortleberry, grouse	*Vaccinium scoparium*
Willow	*Salix* spp.
Willow, scouler	*Salix scouleriana*
Willow, grayleaf	*Salix glauca*
Witchhazel, common	*Hamamelis virginiana*

Animals

Common Name	Scientific Name
Bachman's sparrow	*Aimophila aestivalis*
Badger	*Taxidea taxus*
Bear, black	*Ursus americanus*
Bear, brown	*Ursus arctos*
Bear, grizzly (brown)	*Ursus arctos*
Bear, polar	*Ursus maritimus*
Beaver	*Castor canadensis*
Bison	*Bos bison*
Bison, plains	*Bos bison*
Bison, wood	*Bos bison*
Blackbird, red-winged	*Agelaius phoeniceus*
Bobcat	*Lynx rufus*
Caribou	*Rangifer tarandus*
Caribou, woodland	*Rangifer tarandus*
Cheetah	*Acinonyx jubatus*
Cottontail, dessert	*Sylvilagus audubonii*
Cottontail, mountain	*Sylvilagus nuttallii*
Cougar	*Felis concolor*
Coyote	*Canis latrans*
Deer	*Odocoileus* spp.
Deer, mule	*Odocoileus hemionus*
Deer, white-tailed	*Odocoileus virginianus*
Eagle	*Haliaeetus* spp.
Eagle, golden	*Aquila chrysaetos*
Elk	*Cervus elaphus*
Feral cat	*Felis catus*
Feral dog	*Canis familiaris*
Ferret, black-footed	*Mustela nigripes*
Fisher	*Martes pennanti*
Flicker, northern	*Colaptes aurantus*
Fox, arctic	*Alopex lagopus*
Fox, gray	*Urocyon cinereoargenteus*
Fox, red	*Vulpes vulpes*
Goat, mountain	*Oreamnos americanus*
Goshawk, northern	*Accipiter gentilis*
Grouse	*Dendragapus* spp., *Bonasa* spp.
Grouse, ruffed	*Bonasa umbellus*
Grouse, spruce	*Dendragapus canadensis*
Hare, east Finland	*Lepus timidus, L. europaeus*
Hawk, Harlan's (red-tailed)	*Buteo jamaicensis*
Hawk, red-tailed	*Buteo jamaicensis*
Ibex, Tatra Mountain	*Capra ibex*
Jackrabbit, black-tailed	*Lepus californicus*

Animals

Common Name	Scientific Name
Jackrabbit, white-tailed	*Lepus townsendii*
Kestrel	*Falco sparverius*
Lion, African	*Panthera leo*
Lion, mountain	*Felis concolor*
Lynx	*Lynx canadensis*
Lynx, Canada	*Lynx canadensis*
Lynx, european	*Lynx lynx*
Lynx, Iberian	*Lynx pardinus*
Lynx, Newfoundland	*Lynx canadensis subsolanus*
Macaque, Japanese	*Macaca fuscata*
Marmot, hoary	*Marmota caligata*
Marten, American	*Martes americana*
Mink	*Mustela vison*
Mink, sea	*Mustela macrodon*
Moose	*Alces alces*
Mouse, white-footed	*Peromyscus leucopus*
Mouse, wood	*Apodemus sylvaticus*
Murrelet, marbled	*Brachyramphus marmoratus*
Muskrat	*Ondatra zibethicus*
Owl, boreal	*Aegolius funereus*
Owl, great-horned	*Bubo viginianus*
Owl, hawk	*Surnia ulula*
Owl, Mexican spotted	*Strix occidentalis*
Owl, northern spotted	*Strix occidentalis*
Owl, spotted	*Strix occidentalis*
Pine beetle	*Dendroctonus* spp.
Pine beetle, mountain	*Dendroctonus ponderosae*
Pine beetle (western)	*Dendroctonus brevicomis*
Ptarmigan	*Lagopus* spp.
Raccoon	*Procyon lotor*
Salmon, Chinook	*Oncorhynchus tshawytscha*
Salmon, Pacific	*Onchorhynchus* spp.
Sheep, bighorn	*Ovis canadensis*
Sheep, Dall's	*Ovis dalli*
Sheep, desert bighorn	*Ovis canadensis*
Shrew, masked	*Sorex cinereeus*
Skunk	*Mephitis* spp.
Snowshoe hare	*Lepus americanus*
Spruce beetle	*Dendroctonus rufipennis*
Spruce budworm, western	*Choristoneura fumiferana*
Squirrel, arctic ground	*Spermophilus parryii*
Squirrel, Columbian ground	*Spermophilus columbianus*
Squirrel, eastern gray	*Sciurus carolinensis*

Animals

Common Name	Scientific Name
Squirrel, fox	*Sciurus niger*
Squirrel, ground	*Spermophilus parryii*
Squirrel, northern flying	*Glaucomys sabrinus*
Squirrel, red	*Tamiasciurus hudsonicus*
Timberwolf	*Canus lupus*
Trout, bull	*Salvelinus confluentus*
Trout, cutthroat	*Oncorhynchus clarki*
Turkeys, wild	*Meleagris gallopavo*
Vole	*Microtus* spp.
Vole, bank	*Clethrionomys glareolus*
Vole, southern red-backed	*Clethrionomys gapperi*
Weasel	*Mustela* spp.
Weasel, long-tailed	*Mustela frenata*
Wolf, gray	*Canis lupus*
Wolverine	*Gulo gulo*
Woodrat	*Neotoma* spp.
Woodrat, bushy-tailed	*Neotoma cinerea*
Woodrat, dusky-footed	*Neotoma fuscipes*